AF449161

Encyclopaedia of European Elections

Encyclopaedia of European Elections

Edited by

Yves Déloye
Professor of Politics
University Paris I Panthéon-Sorbonne, France

and

Michael Bruter
Lecturer in European Politics
London School of Economics and
Political Science, UK

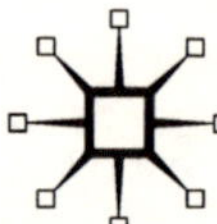

First published 2007 by
PALGRAVE MACMILLAN
Houndmills, Basingstoke, Hampshire RG21 6XS and
175 Fifth Avenue, New York, N.Y. 10010
Companies and representatives throughout the world

PALGRAVE MACMILLAN is the global academic imprint of the Palgrave
Macmillan division of St. Martin's Press, LLC and of Palgrave Macmillan Ltd.
Macmillan® is a registered trademark in the United States, United Kingdom
and other countries. Palgrave is a registered trademark in the European
Union and other countries.

ISBN-13: 978–1–4039–9484–4   hardback

This book is printed on paper suitable for recycling and made from fully
managed and sustained forest sources.

A catalogue record for this book is available from the British Library.

Library of Congress Cataloging-in-Publication Data

Encyclopedia of European elections / edited by Yves Déloye and Michael Bruter.
     p. cm.
   Includes bibliographical references and index.
   ISBN-13: 978–1–4039–9484–4 (cloth)
   ISBN-10: 1–4039–9484–6 (cloth)
     1. European Parliament—Elections. 2. Legislative bodies—Encyclopedias. 3.
   Elections—European Union—Encyclopedias. I. Déloye, Yves. II. Bruter, Michael, 1975–

   JN36.E53 2007
   324.24′055—dc22   2006052769

10   9   8   7   6   5   4   3   2   1
16   15   14   13   12   11   10   09   08   07

Transferred to Digital Printing in 2008

Contents

Conclusion: European Parliament Elections and the Emergence of a European Demos   504
Michael Bruter, Yves Déloye and Sarah Harrison

Foreword and Acknowledgements

This *Encyclopaedia* is the result of close co-operation between a number of academics, friends and colleagues, who wanted to give a new perspective on an exceptional subject in the fields of social sciences and law, namely, European elections. In this respect, the collaboration between the two editors, from the Paris I Panthéon-Sorbonne University* and the London School of Economics and Political Science, and the contributions of academics from almost fifty different universities around the world is symptomatic of the spirit of this volume.

2004 saw 352 million voters from twenty-five member states vote for the 6th European Parliament elections. They elected their 732 representatives at the same time. These elections were thus unprecedented when it comes to their breadth, but also when considering their symbolic value. They were the first European Parliament elections to follow the European Union's largest ever enlargement to the East and South, and they occurred in the midst of the debate on the European Union's first proposed Constitution. This unique moment has therefore put into question some of the most fundamental beliefs and understandings held by a variety of social science and legal specialists, and to tackle the new meaning it confers to European elections as a European democratic act, we need all of their approaches to tell us more about what European Parliament elections represent. As a result, this volume combines contributions that use a variety of disciplinary angles: political science, philosophy, sociology, law, anthropology, history, etc. in order to try and give as 'encyclopaedic'

an understanding of the European elections phenomenon as possible.

The editors would like to thank all of the contributors. We are also indebted to Dominique Bellec, who did some remarkable and patient work on the French part of this project, and Sarah Harrison, who devoted many hours of her time as editorial assistant for this volume. The Conseil Régional d'Alsace, Conseil Général du Bas-Rhin, and Communauté Urbaine de Strasbourg, Ville de Strasbourg, and their presidents should also be thanked for the support they gave to this project from the very start, as should the PRISME-GSPE group from the Institut d'Etudes Politiques de Strasbourg-Université Robert Schuman, and its directors, Didier Georgakakis and Marine Delassalle. With a French-language edition and an English-language edition, this *Encyclopaedia* would not have been possible without a number of gifted and hard-working translators. Our warmest thanks are therefore owed to the translators of the ITI-RI, University Marc Bloch, Chiara Jasson, and particularly Vanessa Pei-Pei Lee, who had to work under extreme time pressure. Finally, we are extremely thankful to Mina Moshkeri for her great help with the maps in the European electoral geography section of this volume, and to Alison Howson and Gemma d'Arcy-Hughes, both from Palgrave Macmillan for their help and advice.

Michael Bruter
Yves Déloye

* And formerly, from the Institut d'Etudes Politiques de Strasbourg, PRISME-GSPE.

Contributors
(in alphabetical order)

ABRIAL Stéphanie, CNRS (PACTE-CIDSP, Grenoble)

BARTHES Jacques-Olivier, CEVIPOF, Strasbourg

BARTOLINI Stefano, European University Institute, Florence

BEAUVALLET Willy, PRISME-GSPE, Strasbourg

BELLEC Dominique, PRISME-GSPE, Strasbourg

BELOT Céline, CNRS (PACTE-CIDSP, Grenoble)

BERTOSSI Christophe, IFRI, Paris

BERTRAND Gilles, Institut d'Etudes Politiques de Bordeaux

BITSCH Marie-Thérèse, IHEE Robert Schuman, Strasbourg

BOISSERIE Etienne, INALCO, Paris

BOUILLAUD Christophe, Institut d'Etudes Politiques de Grenoble

BOZÓKI András, Central European University, Budapest

BRÉCHON Pierre, Institut d'Etudes Politiques de Grenoble

BRUTER Michael, London School of Economics and Political Science

CAUTRÈS Bruno, CNRS (PACTE-CIDSP), Grenoble

COLOME Gabriel, Universidad Autonoma de Barcelona

COSTA Olivier, CNRS (CERVL), Bordeaux

DELASSALLE Marine, Institut d'Etudes Politiques de Strasbourg

DÉLOYE Yves, Université Paris I Panthéon-Sorbonne

DELWIT Pascal, Université Libre de Bruxelles

DEVAUX Sandrine, CNRS (EHESS), Paris

DOMPNIER Nathalie, Université d'Avignon

DULONG Delphine, Université de Versailles Saint-Quentin

FAUCHER-KING Florence, FNSP, Paris

FORET François, Université Libre de Bruxelles

FRANKLIN Mark, European University Institute, Florence

FREIRE André, ISCTE, University of Lisbon

GAXIE Daniel, Université Paris I Panthéon-Sorbonne

GERSTLÉ Jacques, Université Paris I Panthéon-Sorbonne

GILLAND LUTZ Karin, Universitat Bern

GREFFET Fabienne, Université Nancy II

GRUNBERG Gérard, CNRS (CEVIPOF), Paris

HAEGEL Florence, FNSP, Institut d'Etudes Politiques de Paris

HARMSEN Robert, Queens University Belfast

HARRISON Sarah, London School of Economics and Political Science

HASTINGS Michel, Institut d'Etudes Politiques de Lille

HAUSEMER Pierre, London School of Economics and Political Science

HENRY Emmanuel, Institut d'Etudes Politiques de Strasbourg

IHL Olivier, Institut d'Etudes Politiques de Grenoble

JUHEM Philippe, Université Robert Schuman, Strasbourg

KAUPPI Niilo, University of Helsinki

KRAŠOVEC Alenka, University of Ljubljana

LAGO Ignacio, Juan March Institut Madrid

LAJH Damjan, University of Ljubljana

LAURENT Annie, CNRS (CERAPS), Lille

LEGAVRE Jean-Baptiste, Université de Versailles Saint-Quentin

LIPICER Simona Kustec, University of Ljubljana

LOZAC'H Valérie, Institut d'Etudes Politiques de Strasbourg

MAGNETTE Paul, Université Libre de Bruxelles

MARREL Guillaume, Institut d'Etudes Politiques de Grenoble

McELROY Gail, Trinity College Dublin

MICHEL Hélène, Institut d'Etudes Politiques de Strasbourg

MICHON Sébastien, PRISME-GSPE, Strasbourg

MIKKEL Evald, University of Tartu

MOSCHONAS Gerassimos, Panteion University Athens

MUXEL Anne, CNRS (CEVIPOF), Paris
NEVEU Catherine, CNRS-LAIOS, Paris
PAYRE Renaud, Université Lyon II
PEDERSEN Karina, University of
    København
PERRINEAU Pascal, CNRS (CEVIPOF), Paris
PICKER Ruth, Institute for Social Research
    and Analysis (SORA)
PINA Christine, Université de Nice
PUNTSCHER RIEKMANN Sonja, Universitat
    Salzburg
QUERMONNE Jean-Louis, Institut d'Etudes
    Politiques de Grenoble
RAUNIO Tapio, University of Tampere
RAUTU Tudor-Andrei, PRISME-GSPE,
    Strasbourg
SCHMITT Herrmann, Unversitat Mannheim
    (MZES)
SEILER Daniel-Louis, Institut d'Etudes
    Politiques d'Aix en Provence
SERFATY Vivianne, Université de Marne la
    Vallée
SIMON Ágnes, Independent Researcher,
    Budapest

SINEAU Mariette, CNRS (CEVIPOF)
    Paris
STÖVER Philip, Universitat Heidelberg
STRUDEL Sylvie, Université de Tours
SUREL Yves, Institut d' Etudes Politiques de
    Grenoble, France
TEBBAKH Sonia, CNRS (PACTE-CIDSP),
    Grenoble
VAN DER EIJK Cees, University of
    Nottingham
VAN DE WALLE Cédric, Université Libre de
    Bruxelles
VAN WYNSBERGHE Caroline, Université
    Catholique de Louvain
WAELE Jean-Michel de, Université Libre de
    Bruxelles
WARLEIGH Alex, University of Limerick
WINTER Lieven de, Université Catholique de
    Louvain
WÜST Andreas, Universitat Mannheim
    (MZES)
ZALEWSKI Frédéric, LASP
ZILLER Jacques, European University
    Institute, Florence

Introduction: Voting for a European Parliament: a European Civic Act?

Michael Bruter and Yves Déloye

In 1464, George of Podehrady, King of Bohemia, wrote to his various European counterparts to propose the creation of a Union of European states. This early 'Europeanist' explained that the new structure – hastily rejected by his fellow European monarchs – would bring strength, stability and prosperity to Europe and its kings. When Coudenhove-Kalergi and Briand developed their own idealistic European projects in the late nineteenth and early twentieth centuries, they promised a thriving culture and peace for the continent, but again, citizens were only to be the indirect beneficiaries of an improbable integration process. Less than a hundred years later, European unification has ceased to be a grand utopia to become a daily reality in the lives of almost half a billion citizens.

This *Encyclopaedia* deals with what is perhaps the most counter-intuitive *tour de force* of the European project: the desire to invent a trans-European citizenship, the challenge of 'making' European citizens without replacing or destroying their national ties. The election of a European Parliament by all citizens, under universal suffrage, since 1979, is the ultimate laboratory of this emerging European citizenship. This book uses multiple disciplinary angles to better understand the context, rules, outcomes and meanings of these European elec-

tions. Indeed, European elections remain a unique and unparalleled object of study for most legal and social science disciplines. From the point of view of law, they represent a unique transnational – albeit not international – electoral act, which is twice codified at the EU and national levels. For historians, European Parliament elections are a unique step in the history of the European continent. For philosophers, they represent a civic act which questions some of our basic assumptions about the meanings of citizenship and identity. For media and communication specialists, it is still unclear how a pan-European election can survive without trans-European media, campaigns and a true European public sphere. For sociologists and anthropologists, European elections reveal a multitude of holistic patterns of behaviour and mass attitudes, while for social psychologists, they raise original questions about the possible emergence of multiple allegiances and specific systems of European socialisation. For linguists and discourse analysts, European Parliament elections represent a remarkable laboratory to understand how elites, the media and citizens talk about Europe. Finally, for political scientists, they raise an immense array of questions in terms of institutional practice, electoral behaviour and political identities.

Indeed, what do we know about the influence of EU institutions on the development of this new category of suffrage, and about the influence of these elections themselves on the EU political system? Are we dealing with 25 national elections, which happen to take place at the same time, or with a true European civic act? How do voters react to national and European cues in the context of these elections, and what messages do they send (and to whom) via their vote (or, in about 50 per cent of the cases, their abstention)? Finally, to what extent do European Parliament elections measure – and create – a European citizenship and a European identity? Are they a test for the success of this emerging identity, a snapshot of a European 'demos' plagued by apparently low turnout, or, instead, a civic object which has, by its very existence, given an additional face, a momentum, to the political condition of Europeans?

European Parliament elections represent a fascinating object of study. For a quarter of a century, universal suffrage has been used throughout the European Union to elect MEPs. At the time of writing this book, six democratic European Parliament elections have taken place, representing, every five years, the confirmation of an unprecedented transnational European experience. The 2004 elections were the first ones for a newly enlarged European Union. The enlargement was officially completed on 1 May 2004. Fireworks and ceremonies throughout the European Union celebrated an extension of its member states by two-thirds. However, even integrationists feared that this sudden and rapid expansion could impede the deepening of European integration, particularly as many member states seemed to care for the economic aspects of integration more than for its political dimension. Thus, the 6th European Parliament elections were, in a way, unique, because it was nothing less than a completely new

– and, to a large extent, unknown – Europe which voted in June 2004.

The contrast between the aspirations of the old and new member states was particularly well reflected in the question of turnout, which in 2004 seemed to reach an all time low. Yet, if one considers the 15 old member states, turnout actually quite significantly increased between 1999 and 2004 for the first time in European history, notably in the UK and the Netherlands. At the same time, turnout in many new member states was extraordinarily low. So was this turnout a success or a failure? Is a 50 per cent turnout an abysmal result because it is so much lower than national averages in general elections? Or, on the contrary, does it represent an amazingly high level of participation given that whoever wins European Parliament elections was, until 2004, remarkably inconsequential considering the decision-making process of the European Parliament? Indeed, the Strasbourg institution remains in charge of largely non-contentious issues, which, for the most part, tend to lead to consensus votes between the main moderate groups in the Parliament, from centre-left to centre-right. In political science, we have long known that the two main predictors of turnout in any given election are the perceived stakes of the election and the perceived closeness of the race. Fail to convey an impression of urgency and of the race being 'too close to call' and you will irrevocably fail to mobilise the voters. In the context of European Parliament elections, the stakes are by and large perceived to be negligible. Moreover, the 'second order' phenomenon means that there is usually extremely little suspense about the way government will be punished by the voters. In such circumstances, isn't one almost amazed that every other European voter bothered to go to vote in the first place?

Finally, what about the results themselves? Since 1979, European elections have provided an interesting picture of the 'political mood' in Europe, with changing majorities over time. After the socialist victory in 1994 at the European level, the conservative family became the prime group in the European Parliament in 1999. In 2004, with a majority of social-democratic governments in Europe, the centre-right was reinforced as the main party group within the European Parliament. At the same time, European elections are traditionally a platform of choice for extremist parties and the Greens, and with record levels of government unpopularity in a large number of member states, they nourished extremely high expectations in 2004. What was their fate going to be? How would increasingly aggressive Eurosceptic parties perform? Would the liberal family finally manage to emerge as a prime contender on the European political scene?

All these questions are tackled in this volume by some of the world's leading specialists in the field of study of European elections. Each article puts some specific and particularly interesting aspect of European Parliament elections in the spotlight. Whilst the *Encyclopaedia* is organised alphabetically, a certain number of essential perspectives should be borne in mind whilst reading individual articles. Indeed, each of our contributors comes with his or her academic perspective to try and enlighten us on the meaning and significance of European elections. Altogether, these streams of analysis can be divided into four broad perspectives.

Institutional and legal

We first concentrate on the institutional aspects of these elections. McElroy analyses the nature of the European Parliament as an institution, while Raunio looks at its political groups. Quermonne analyses the legal status of its members, and Ziller looks at the proposed European Constitution, which was to be signed just a few days after the vote. Ihl, Costa and Déloye look at various aspects of the institutional conditions of the voters and their representatives, from the rules determining who has the right to vote, to the administration of the elections and their technological variations. Still contributing to our understanding of the institutional and legal context of the election, Seiler analyses the evolution of trans-European political parties, and Strudel discusses the tenets of European citizenship and its relationship to citizens' rights to vote in European elections.

Historical and sociological

From a historical perspective, Bitsch looks at some of the founding treaties and agreements that resulted in European elections being what they are, while Perrineau looks at the evolution of the vote in European Parliament elections since 1979. Similarly, Bartolini looks at the way in which cleavages have come to structure European party systems and remain visible throughout the history of European Parliament elections, while Harmsen answers him by tackling the question of Europeanisation of national politics. Still looking at the sociology of European politics, Gerstlé analyses the slow Europeanisation of the campaigns for European Parliament elections. Answering this perspective, Déloye looks at the symbolic aspects of these European elections and the role played by a European electoral education.

Political

Answering this top-down perspective, the third approach is political. Schmitt redefines our understanding of political cycles in the context of second-order elections and explains how the second-order phenomenon remains characteristic of the 2004 vote, while Franklin looks at the European Elections Study, and Cautrès at Eurobarometer, as two unique tools of electoral and opinion analysis. Harrison points out one of the most counter-intuitive phenomena of the 2004 elections, showing how the successes of the extreme left and of the extreme right in the vote seem to have become mutually exclusive against pre-electoral polls' predictions. Finally, Bruter considers what we understand to be 'European electoral behaviour', and, later, at the role of the elections in the emergence of a mass European identity – and of this identity on citizens' behaviour in European elections.

National and party-specific perspectives

Finally, throughout this *Encyclopaedia*, national experts such as van der Eijk, Puntscher-Riekmann, Delwit and Pedersen, devote specific articles to every single one of the member states. The structure of these articles follows a comparable format, with detailed analyses of the context, campaign and results in each country. Similarly, specialists of various party families, from de Winter to Van de Walle, Moschinos and Grunberg, analyse the specific fortunes of each party family and party group within the European Parliament, providing a comprehensive picture of the relative winners and losers of the 2004 elections. Reading these articles together gives an astonishing picture of the way in which each member state and each party family has, somehow, uniquely illustrated some particularly interesting aspect of the 2004 elections. These country and parties chapters should be considered together with Bruter's separate comparative section on European electoral geography, which brings together these various individualised accounts.

This multitude of perspectives and academic viewpoints allows for almost infinite ways of looking at this unique phenomenon, European elections. It would certainly not be inappropriate to read it as a normal book, from the first to the last page, slowly letting the succession of complex insights make sense, like the pieces of a jigsaw puzzle, which would progressively reveal its image following the random pace of alphabetic order. However, one could also choose to follow any of a multitude of possibly coherent thematic itineraries, guided by the academic background of the contributors, the geography of the European continent, or the ideological lines of fractures of a recently almost-unified Europe. Indeed, each trail may help the reader to bridge the many paradoxes, contrasts and questions related to European Parliament elections, and it is not any less logical to cross the (Schengen) border from Spain to Portugal than it would be to read all the political science contributions together, or move on from European citizenship to European identity, from extreme left to extreme right, or from the legal status of MEPs to the sociology of their function. At the end of each article, we propose a series of indicative – albeit certainly not exclusive – pathways that the reader may want to follow. Most articles also include a list of academic references, which allow the reader to move on to other contributions that are part of what Franklin calls the 'edifice of knowledge' of our disciplines.

A last possible trail that the reader can follow is dynamic. This volume looks at the connection between the 2004 European elections and their historical background, allowing for an exploration of their connection with what has been and will be their future. One year after the elections, the French and Dutch electorates rejected the proposed draft constitutional treaty that was signed by the heads of states and governments only a few days after the European elections, projecting the European Union into a particularly acute crisis. Towards the end of 2005, however, an agreement was reached on the budgetary perspectives of the Union for the next few years, and the progressive replacement of some unpopular governments in some key EU member states led some – particularly Germany, Luxembourg and Belgium – to hope for a revival of the Constitution. At the same time, with the recent accession of Bulgaria and Romania on 1 January 2007, we now know that the 2004 elections were not only the first but the last ones in the history of a 'Europe of the 25'. However, it is also the Parliament itself which has changed. For the first time, after the 2004 elections, it is the majority within the European Parliament – rather than the majority within the Council or some compromise on alternation – which dictated the choice of the new President of the European Commission. Perhaps even more importantly, in the autumn of 2004, the European Parliament reached a new milestone in the affirmation of its independence by signalling that it would veto the proposed Commission team if it was not changed. This was an unprecedented demonstration of strength by the European Parliament, and after trying to ignore the MEPs' message for a few days, the heads of states and governments and the President elect of the Commission had to accept the demands of the European Parliament, withdraw the names of the most controversial Commissioners, change the portfolios of others, and, altogether, present the European Parliament with a Commission it would accept rather than one that pleased the member states. In the space of a few months, it became clear, perhaps for the first time, that the results of the European Parliament elections, who won and who lost, finally mattered and would matter more and more.

In this context, can we doubt that the 2009 elections will be even more interesting than the 2004 edition? Will this institutional breakthrough and the socialisation of the new member states as part of a new enlarged European Union finally lead European Union citizens to appropriate their institutions and make the European Parliament, their primary arena of representation, their own? Will the spiral of lowering turnout levels finally be reversed, and will the role of European Parliament elections be reinforced, as the marker of an increasingly comprehensive European citizenship and of a strengthening European identity? Directly or indirectly, it is rather likely that the 2004 European Parliament elections will be remembered by history as even more of a turning point than we have realised thus far.

Mapping Europe: European Electoral Geography

Michael Bruter

The following eleven electoral maps give a critical overview of what happened in the 2004 European elections throughout the continent. The patterns and equilibria of electoral Europe in 2004 are very different from those of 1979 at the birth of EP elections, and generate some interesting surprises.

Following the May 2004 enlargement, the sixth European elections represented first and foremost a complete revolution in the territory that the newly elected MEPs were to represent. Map 1 shows the stakes of the elections in the various countries and the rules of the game to be used everywhere. The number of seats to be allocated in each country ranged from 5 in Malta to 99 in Germany. The four largest member states (Germany, France, UK, Italy) account for 333 of the 735 seats. When adding Spain and Poland, we find that six countries account for 60 per cent of the Parliament. Electoral systems are predominantly proportional, even though Ireland, Malta and Northern Ireland use single transferable vote systems. Finally, Map 1 shows that only five countries use sub-national constituencies for European elections.

One interesting element has to do with turnout (Map 2). Instead of the overall impression, largely conveyed by the media, that turnout has declined overall, European electoral geography points to a contrasting situation between clearly increasing turnout in the West as compared to 1999, and very low participation in the East. It is no use looking for any signs of a beginners' democratic craze among the new member states, who recently democratised and participated, in 2004, in their first European elections. The map clearly shows, instead, that it is in Central Europe that the lowest turnouts are found, particularly in Poland, Slovakia and the Czech Republic. The abstention phenomenon did not affect the Baltic States as much. Besides, the map shows, albeit slightly less clearly, that many former member states have seen an increase in their turnouts, sometimes even a strong one, as in the United Kingdom. This turnout increase, in many 'old' member states, was rarely reported by the media, rarely commented upon, and hardly accounted for by political scientists and journalists alike. However counter-intuitive it may be in contrast to turnout trends between 1979 and 1999, it is highly interesting and worth noting. More generally, except for Belgium and Luxembourg, where compulsory voting is enforced, it is in the former EU peripheries that the main pool of civic participation lies. Italy, Greece[1] and Ireland are thus today's European voting leaders. Spain and Denmark also voted more than the EU average. The tendency is thus different from what could have been expected in a Europe where the Franco-German pairing has always been seen as the main motor of integration.

The map of the prevailing political

Map 1 Territorial organisation of the vote and number of seats

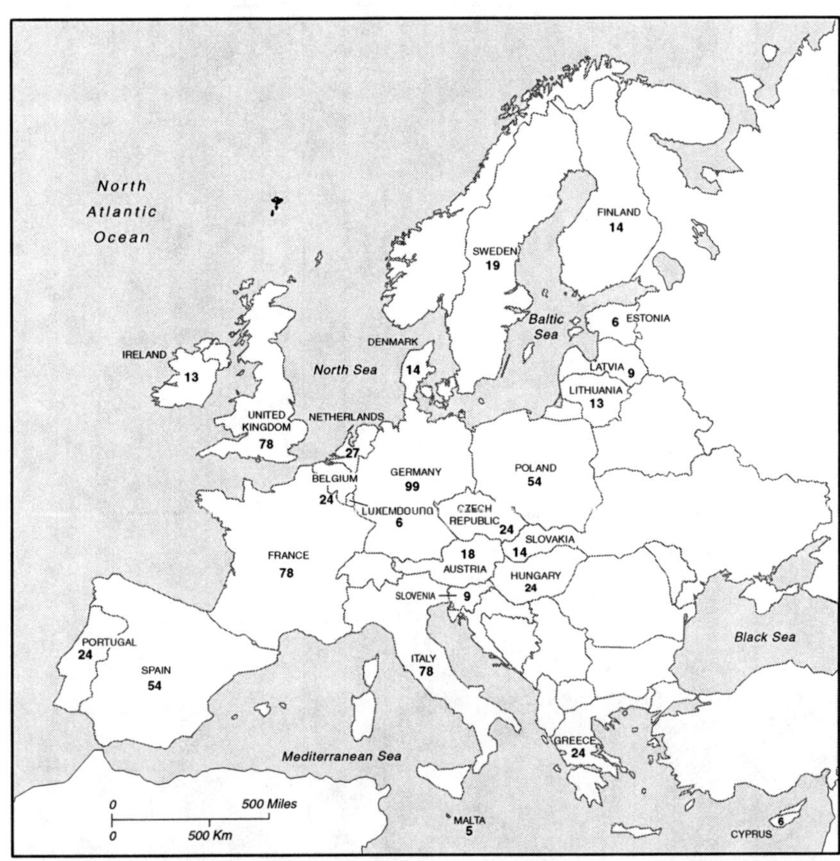

COUNTRY	POPULATION (millions)	SEATS	ELECTORAL SYSTEM	CONSTITUENCIES
Germany	82.5	99	Proportional	1
France	60.0	78	Proportional	8
United Kingdom	59.9	78	Proportional(GB) STV(Northern Irland)	12
Italy	57.8	78	Proportional	5
Spain	40.4	54	Proportional	1
Poland	38.2	54	Proportional	13
Netherlands	6.2	27	Proportional	1
Belgium	10.4	24	Proportional	4
Portugal	10	24	Proportional	1
Greece	10.6	24	Proportional	1
Czech Republic	10.2	24	Proportional	1
Hungary	10.1	24	Proportional	1
Sweden	8.9	19	Proportional	1
Austria	8.1	18	Proportional	1
Finland	5.2	14	Proportional	1
Denmark	5.4	14	Proportional	1
Slovakia	5.4	14	Proportional	1
Ireland	4.0	13	STV	1
Lithuania	3.5	11	Proportional	1
Slovenia	2	9	Proportional	1
Latvia	2.3	9	Proportional	1
Estonia	1.4	6	Proportional	1
Cyprus	0.7	6	Proportional	1
Luxembourg	0.4	6	Proportional	1
Malta	0.4	5	STV	1

Map 2 Turnout in the 2004 European Parliament elections

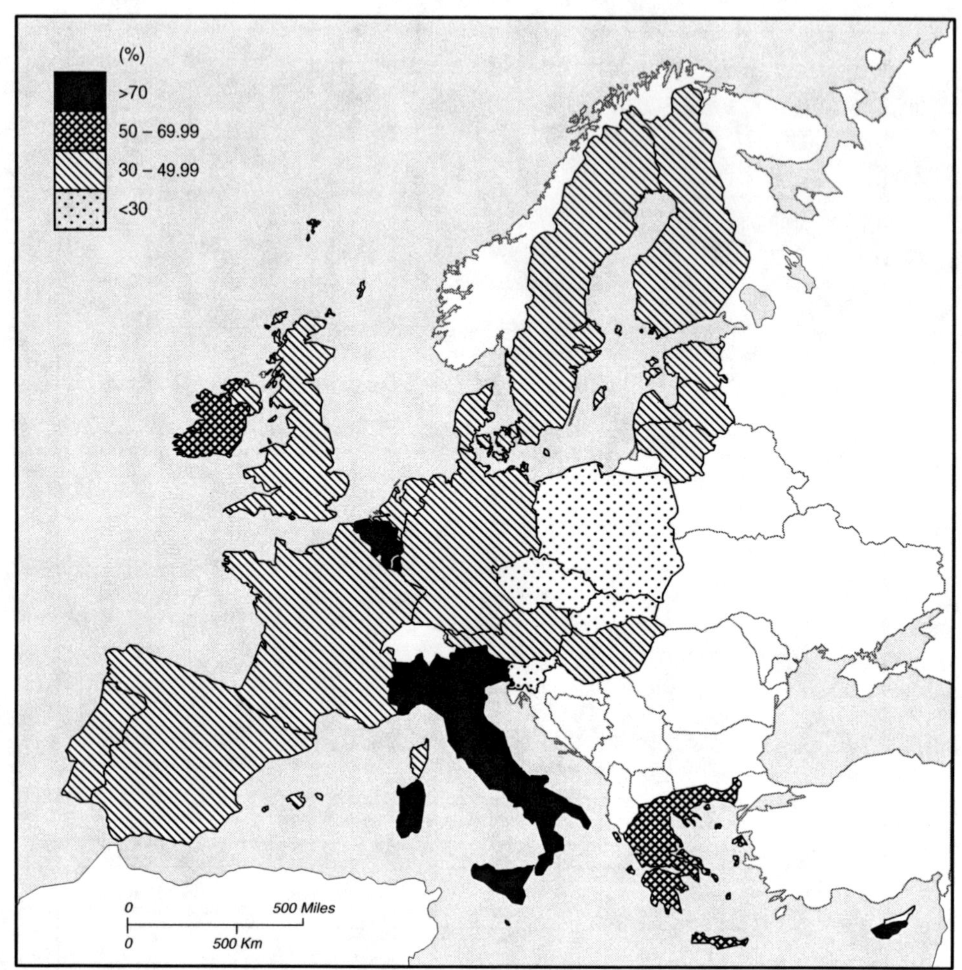

forces in the member states also reveals some fascinating trends (Map 3). The synthetic map highlights in a startling way two symmetric and antagonist stories of the June 2004 elections. Following a north-west/south-east diagonal, the victory indisputably goes to the right along this Central European axis. Of course the victory is sweeter in some countries than in others: in the UK for example, if the Tories remain, as in 1999, the first political force of the country in European elections, they also obtained their worst ever result in any national election. At the heart of Europe, however, from the Netherlands to Hungary, and from Austria to Poland, no state escapes this right-wing wave that will enable more Central European conservatives than ever to recover their global majority in the EP. In the south-west and north-east peripheries of Europe, however, the

Map 3 Dominant political family after the 2004 European Parliament elections

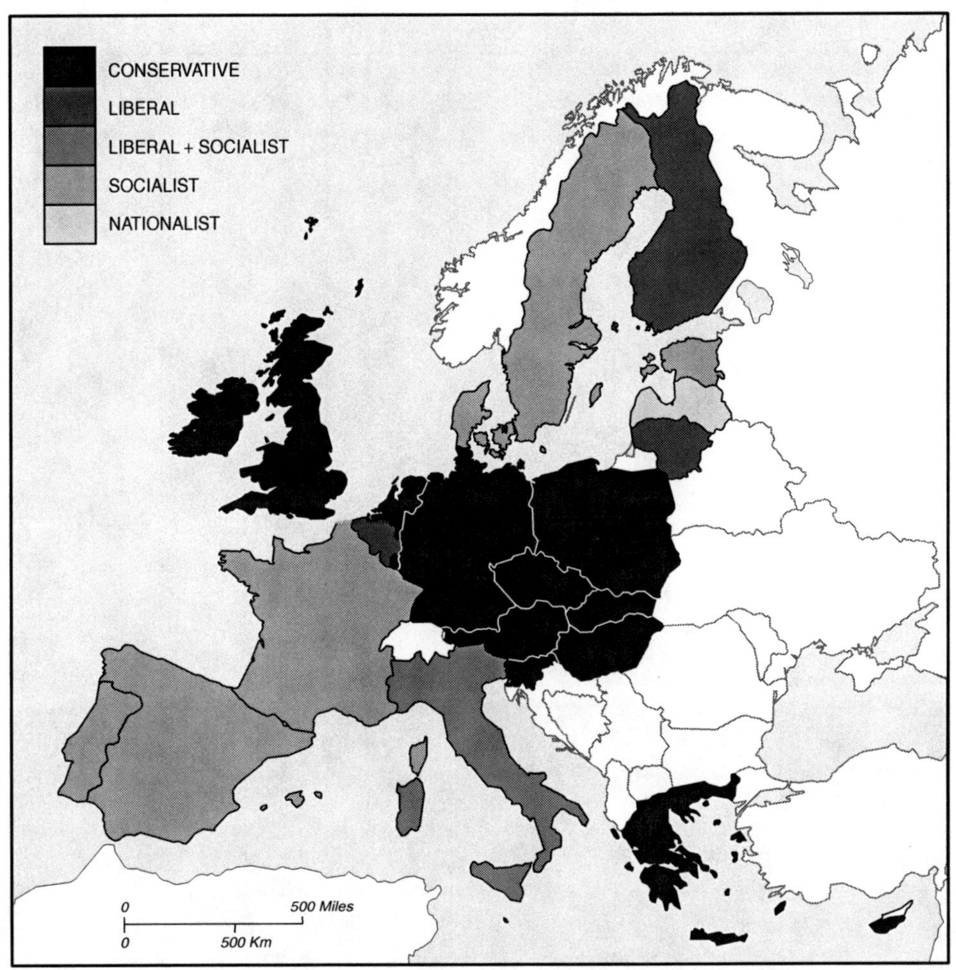

left and liberals dominate and, in several cases, have achieved historical victories, whether these came after an easy fight (France) or a tight race (Italy).

In this other 'two-speed Europe', where losses for the parties in power seem to be a dominating reality, we learn a great deal from the map of majority changes (Map 4). It shows us that if the conservatives have succeeded in remaining the first EU political force, the socialists and the liberals have achieved the most spectacular break-through at the member states' level, whether it is in Spain, Denmark and Sweden (socialists) or in Italy, Finland and Belgium (liberals). By contrast, the conservatives have seen their empire crumble in several of the old member states.

Three maps look in greater detail at the specific fortunes of these three main European party families (Maps 5, 6 and

Map 4 Change in dominant political family between
1999 and 2004

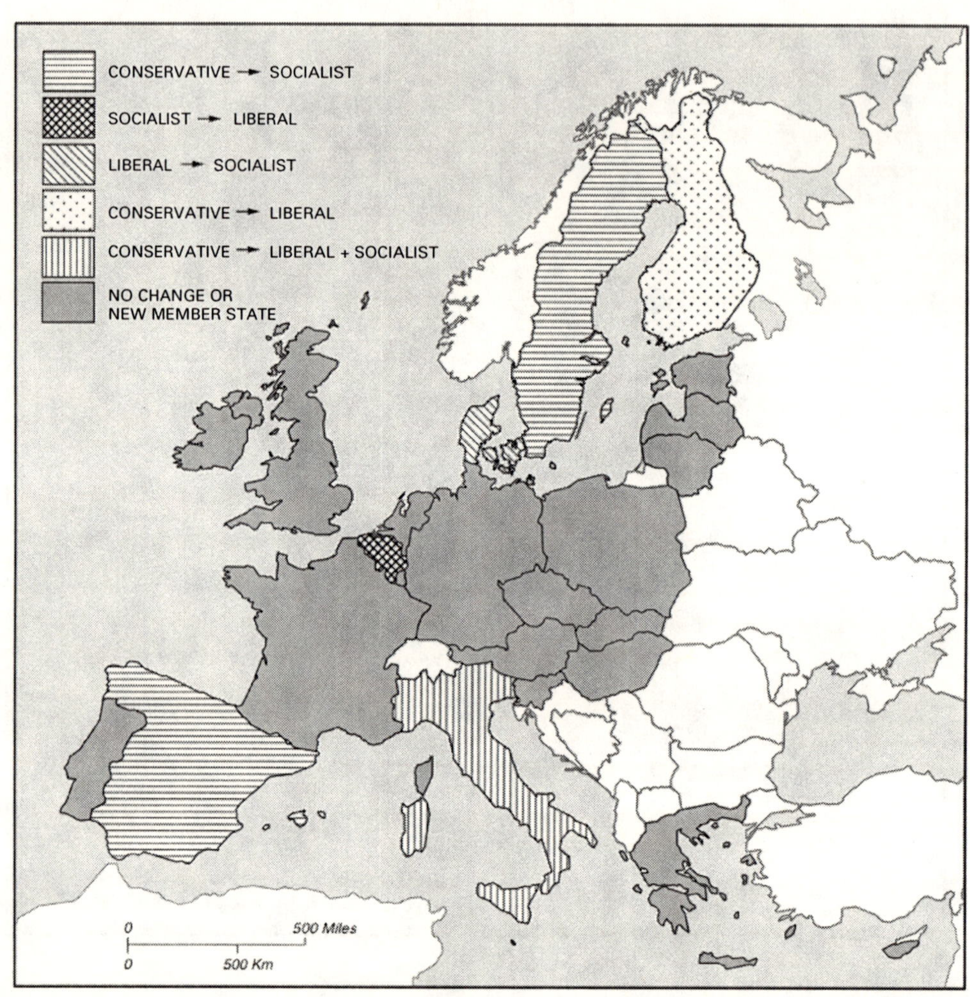

7). They confirm that the conservatives compensated their loss of ground in the West by a strong presence in those same Central European countries that abstained most: the Czech Republic, Slovakia, Hungary, Slovenia and to a lesser extent, Poland. They also resisted well in Greece, Germany and Austria and easily won in Cyprus. By contrast, the socialist and social-democrat left was particularly successful in Spain, while the liberals saw an unprecedented extension of their territorial representation. They gained considerable ground in North-Eastern Europe, particularly in Lithuania, where they are the country's first political force, but also in Estonia, Finland and even Sweden. However,

Map 5 Results of the conservative and Christian-democratic right in the 2004 European Parliament elections

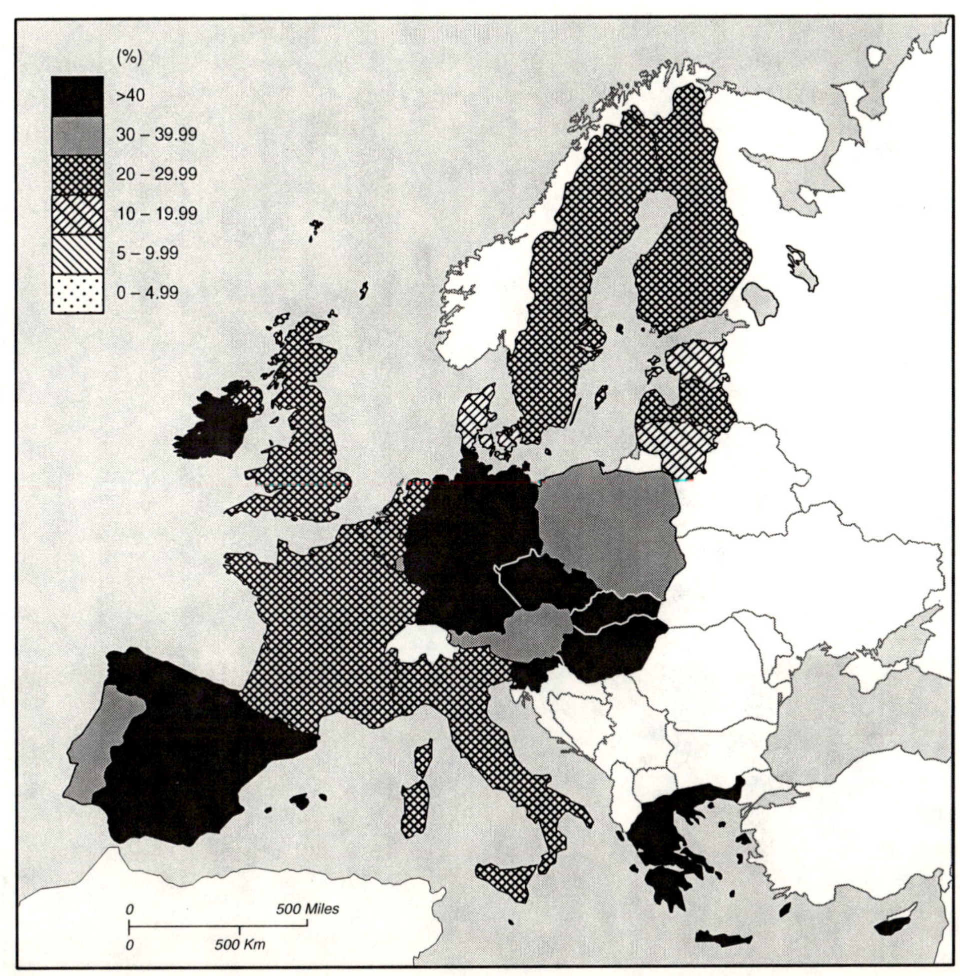

albeit less impressively, they also clearly progressed in the West, particularly in France, Italy, the UK, Denmark, Luxembourg, the Netherlands and Ireland.

However, if we superimpose the three maps, beyond the three 'strongholds' – conservative in the centre, socialist in the south-west, and liberal in the north-east – some states remain the privileged if not almost exclusive hunting ground of two strong traditional movements, conservative and social-democrat (Spain, Portugal, Austria, Greece and Hungary for example), whereas others do not see either of these two party families score anywhere beyond 30 per cent of the

Map 6 Results of the socialist and social-democratic left in 2004 European Parliament elections

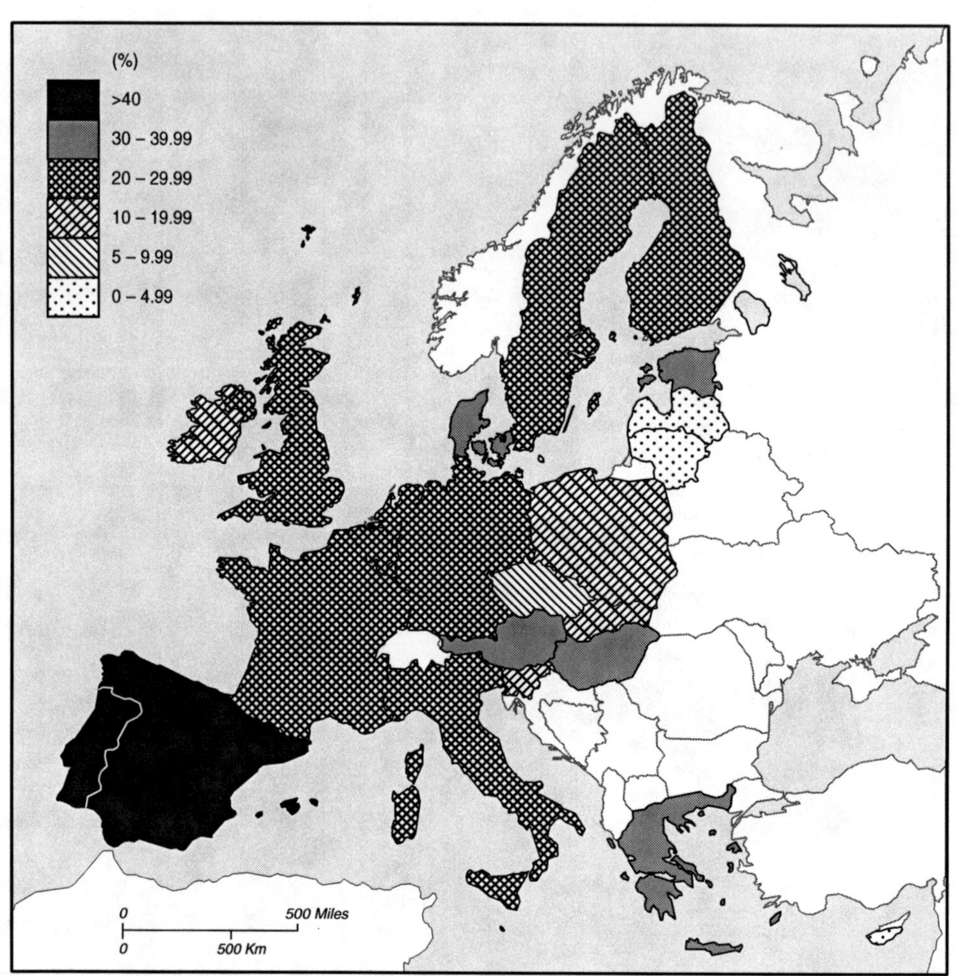

ballots. This is the case for example of France, the UK and Italy, where the crumbling of the traditional 'left' and 'right', that reigned supreme for decades, is confirmed with a certain brutality. Their losses benefit the liberals, whose breakthrough was noted above, but also the small parties that did not exist on the European political scene 25 or 30 years ago.

It is to these 'small political families' that we dedicate the last part of this analysis, looking this time at the four maps specifically dedicated to the fortunes of Greens, Eurosceptics, extreme left and extreme right (Maps 8, 9, 10 and 11).

First, Green parties do not necessarily accomplish the feats they managed a few years ago in some member states

Map 7 Results of the centrists and liberals in the 2004 European
Parliament elections

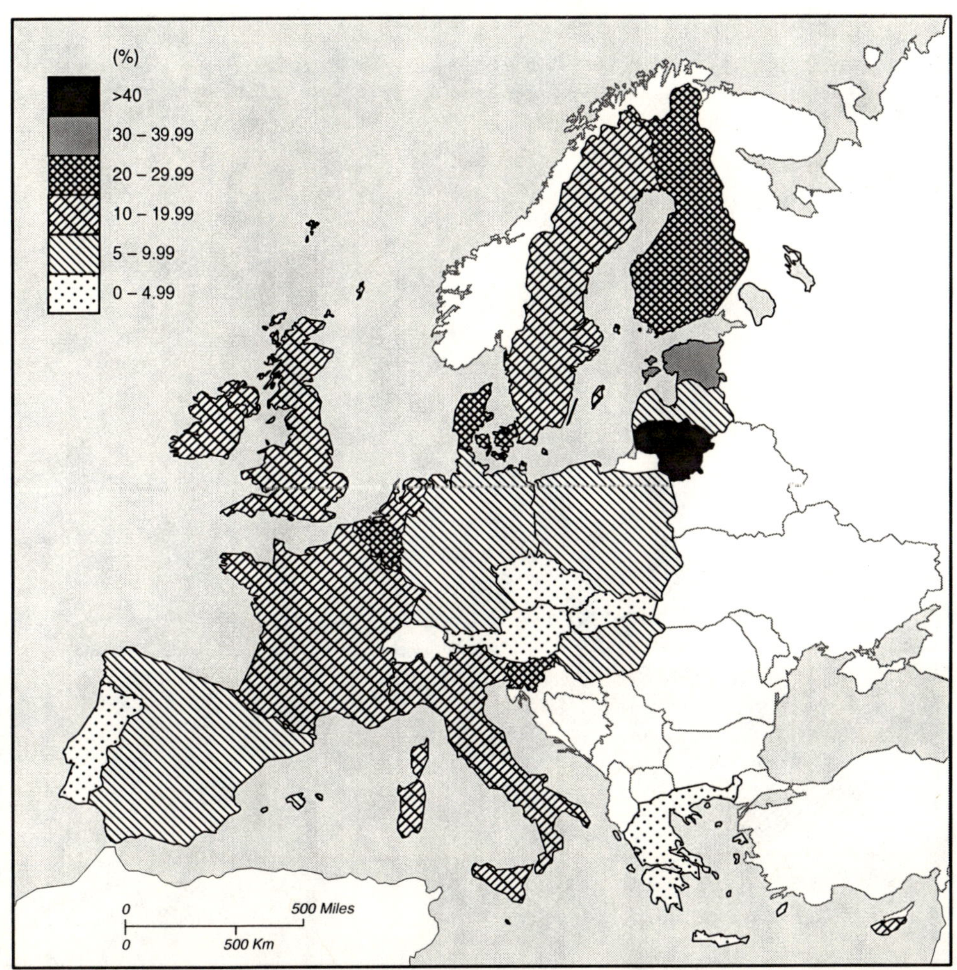

(Map 8). However, they now obtain more than 5 per cent of the ballots in almost all the states of North-Western Europe (except in Ireland) and resist particularly well in countries like Germany, Austria and Finland. Their results are nevertheless quite disappointing in Belgium, France and Italy, and their scores are very low in almost all the new member states.

In some states, one of the most spectacular breakthroughs is to be attributed to Eurosceptic parties, whether or not they have a rhetoric close to the one of the extreme right (Map 11). Britain, which experienced an impressive progression of UKIP in the last election, remains the model of this type of behaviour, but predominantly Eurosceptic parties in Sweden, Denmark, Austria,

Map 8 Results of the Green parties in the 2004 European
Parliament elections

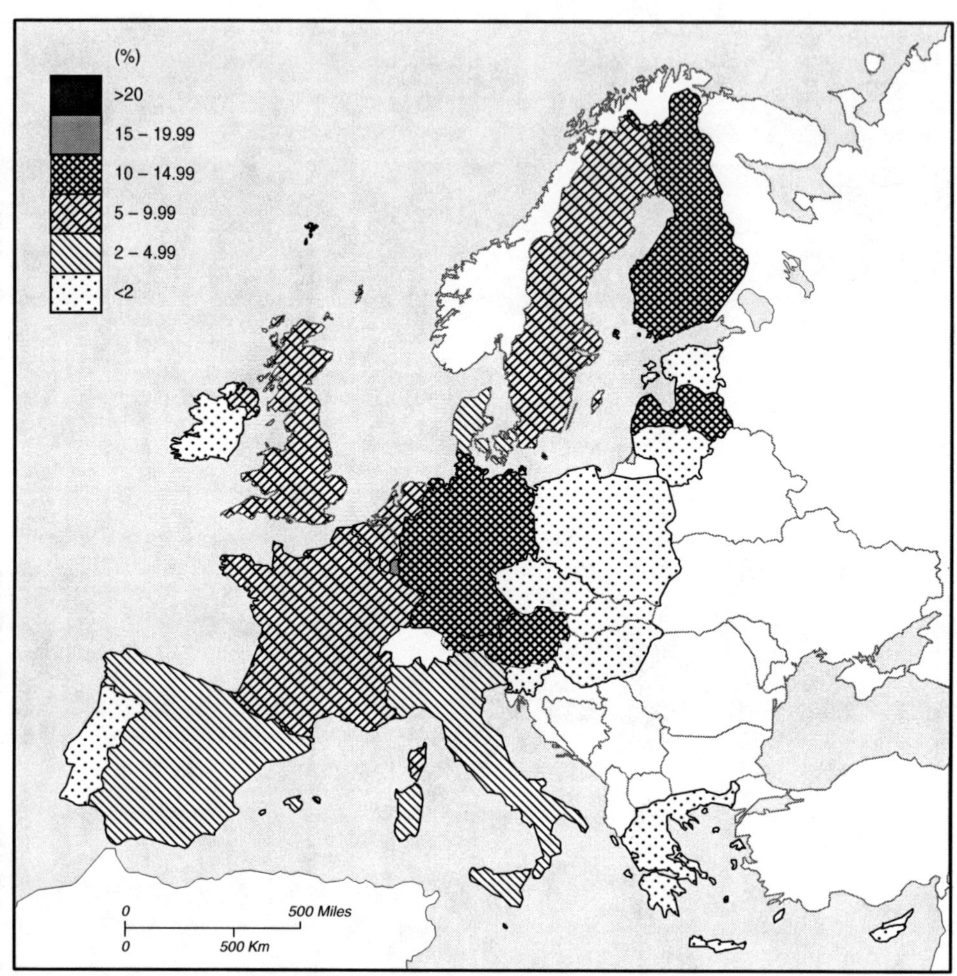

Poland and the Czech Republic also obtained good results. In France, however, the pro-sovereignty parties lost ground as compared to the 1990s.

The last two 'small political families' to disturb the game of the traditional centre-left and centre-right 'elephants' are the extreme right and left, two groups with sometimes controversial boundaries, but which, no matter how they are defined, achieved important victories in the June 2004 elections. Here, it is essential to look at the maps of their respective electoral results together (Maps 10 and 11). Each one of the two families made several spectacular breakthroughs with more than 20 per cent of the votes in the UK (including UKIP due to its clearly extremist rhetoric), in Poland and Latvia for the extreme right,

Map 9 Results of Eurosceptic and populist parties in the 2004 European
Parliament elections

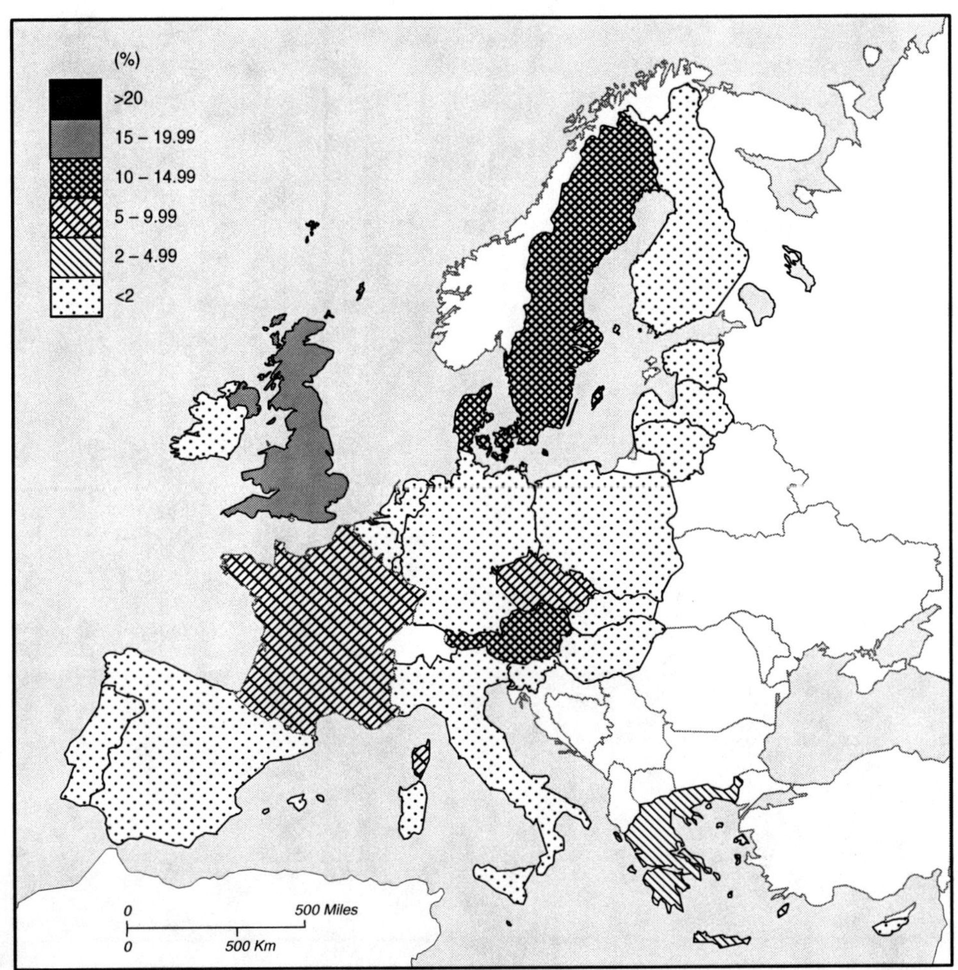

in the Czech Republic and Cyprus for the extreme left. The extreme right also resisted well in Italy, Belgium and to a certain extent (it was hoping for better scores) in France; the extreme left did well in Portugal and Denmark among others. The most striking finding, however, is that the two maps seem first and foremost to be the photographic negative of one another. While good scores for the moderate left and right did not seem mutually exclusive (see the Spanish, Greek and Austrian cases), the extreme left and right successes seem incompatible. Obviously, in many countries, none of these extremist movements managed to break through because of context or party or electoral system specificities; but by contrast, nowhere do they succeed in imposing themselves

Map 10 Results of the extreme left in the 2004 European Parliament elections

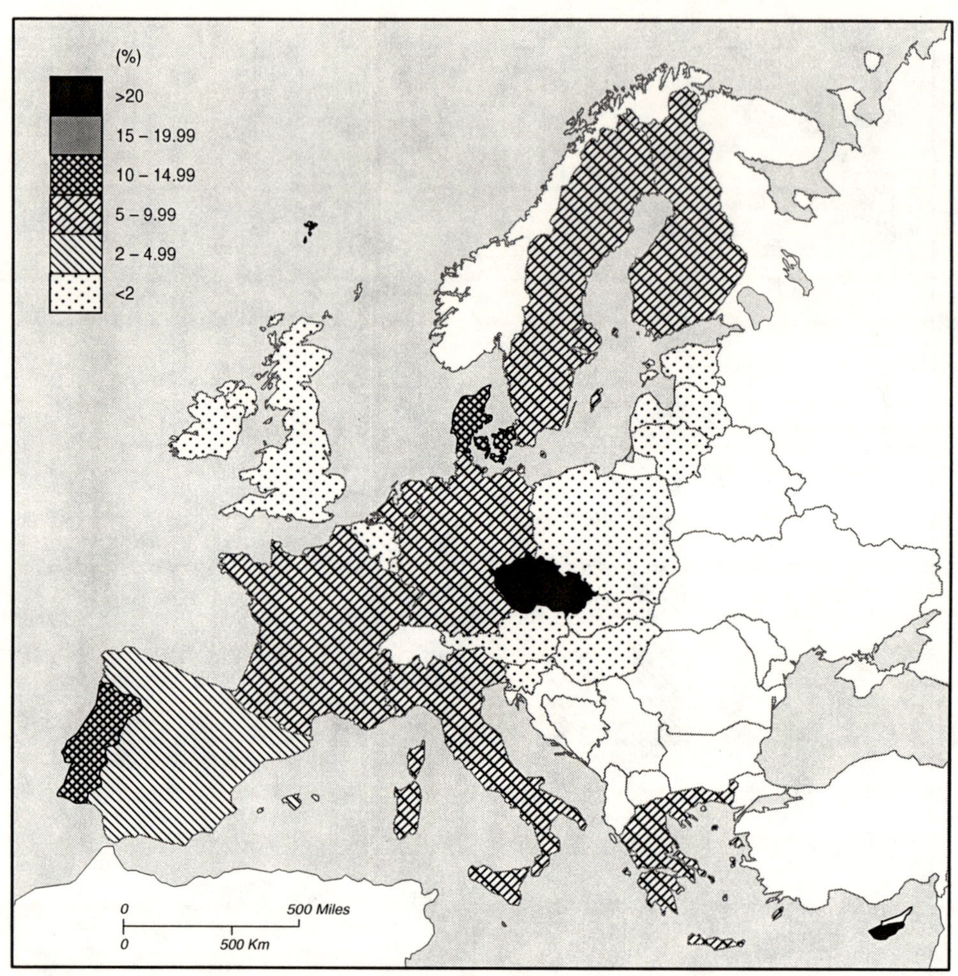

simultaneously. The victory of one thus seems to cut the ground from under the other's feet, although in many cases, pre-electoral polls had announced simultaneous victories.

This phenomenon is explained by Harrison in this volume and will undoubtedly remain one of the most interesting paradoxes of a European electoral geography, which, as we saw, was not short of unexpected tensions and counter-intuitive surprises in 2004. Above all, if these new astonishing trends in the world of voters make their way into the world of parties and politicians, it is not inconceivable that new patterns of competition, alliances and power axes, and also new identity dynamics will result from them across Europe. Despite being in many ways a second-order

Map 11 Results of the extreme right in the 2004 European Parliament elections*

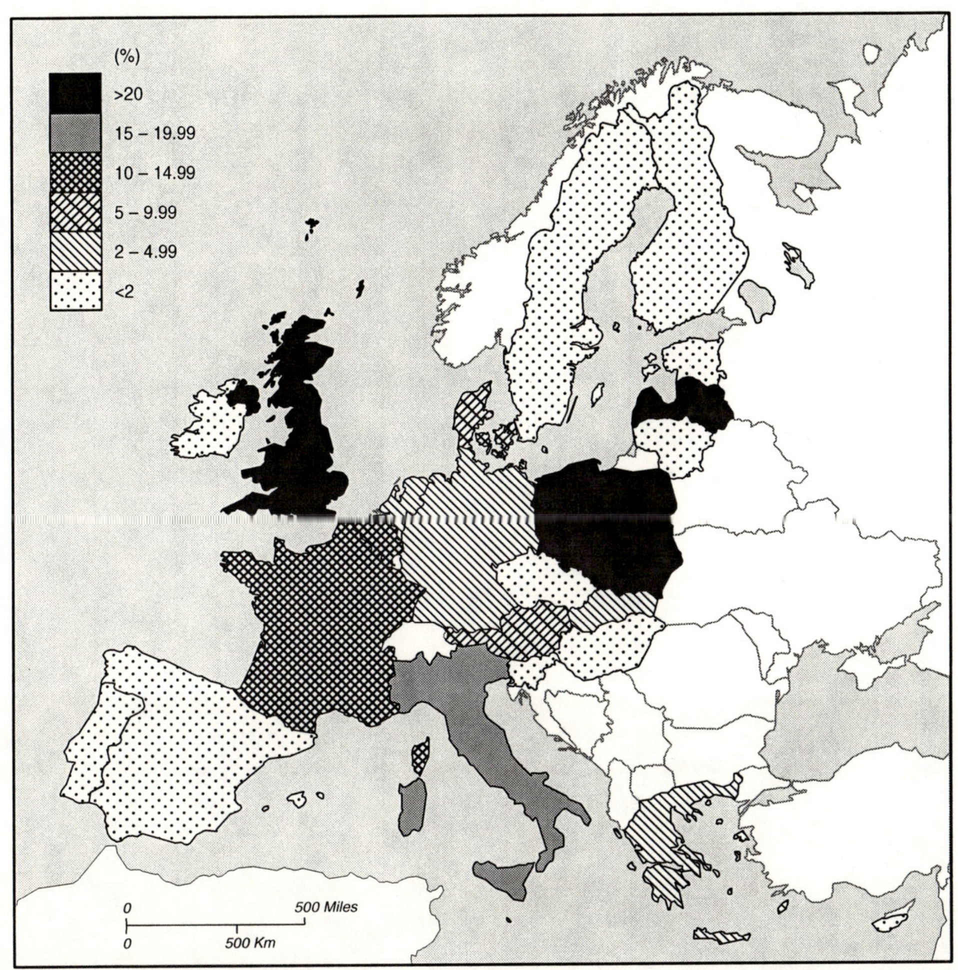

*United Kingdom: UKIP included

contest, European Parliament elections may therefore durably influence some dynamics of electoral competition at the national and European levels, and might finally provide Europe with the democratic diversity it has been lacking for a long time. It may be that in 2009, the European voter will be able to choose between real ideological and policy alternatives within a European democracy that will have reached a new level of maturity.

Note

1. In Greece, turnout is also supposedly compulsory, but the government immediately announced that abstentionists in European Parliament elections would not be punished.

Abstention

Abstention is a form of electoral behaviour that can be defined as the inability or unwillingness to participate in a voting ballot. Within the EU, abstention rates are calculated in each member state by comparing the number of citizens who voted in a given election to the number of registered voters who are eligible to vote. Table 1 shows an increase in abstention levels from 37 per cent in the first European elections of 1979 to an average of 54 per cent in 2004. Since the first European Parliament election, the issue of voter abstention has sparked much debate regarding the nature of the EU and its institutional structure. Today, the phenomenon of abstention continues to grow, and its meaning and significance are still crucial issues in many political debates. Political actors often highlight the issue of abstention as a sign of voter apathy. It is often conceived as a warning 'message' sent by the citizens to their national government to illustrate their disillusionment. Others insist that high levels of abstention mean that the institutions of the EU lack popular legitimacy. It is interesting to note, however, that referendums that are held on EU issues (see the entry on European Referendums) often benefit from a particularly high level of turnout.

Voter abstention is a complex and dynamic phenomenon that varies according to political and historical contexts. In countries such as France, Austria, Sweden, and to a lesser degree Portugal, abstention has increased in a linear or quasi-linear fashion for EP elections. However, the pattern of evolution is different in member states such as Spain, Ireland and the Netherlands, where it varies from election to election. Moreover, some countries are characterised by particularly high abstention levels. In the United Kingdom, levels of abstention have typically been more than 60 per cent. This is also true of a number of the countries that joined the EU in 2004. With the exceptions of Cyprus, Malta and Lithuania, most of the 'new' member states display abstention levels that are higher than the European average. Levels of abstention exceed a very high 70 per cent in the Czech Republic, Slovenia, Estonia, Poland and Slovakia.

European economic and political integration touches the lives of millions of citizens every day. Yet, as we have seen from Table 1, turnout for European elections is disappointingly low. This leads one to wonder why such a high proportion of European citizens are not willing to turn out to vote. Analysts of the abstention phenomenon tend to look for possible explanations in two different directions: (1) the national component of the election, and (2) the European dimension of the election. Scholars adhering to the former seek to explain voter abstention by examining national contexts as well as societal and individual political views. In regard to the second approach, scholars base their analyses on the relationship between citizens' attitudes towards European integration and levels of voter turnout.

Comparative country-based studies tend to focus primarily on institutional regulations that frame European elections.

Table 1   The evolution of voter abstention levels in European Parliament elections, 1979–2004 (%)

	1979	1984		1989	1994		1999	2004
Germany	34.3	43.2		37.7	40		54.8	57
Belgium	8.6	7.8		9.3	9.3		9	9.2
Denmark	52.2	47.6		53.8	47.1		49.5	52.1
France	39.3	43.3		51.3	47.3		53.2	57.2
Ireland	36.4	52.4		31.7	56		49.8	41.2
Italy	15.1	16.6		18.5	25.2		29.2	26.9
Luxembourg	11.1	11.2		12.6	11.5		12.7	11
Netherlands	42.2	49.4		52.8	64.4		70	60.7
UK	67.8	67.4		63.8	63.6		76	61.2
Greece		22.8		20.1	28.8		24.7	36.8
Spain		31.1	(1987)	45.4	40.9		37	54.9
Portugal		27.6	(1987)	48.8	64.5		60	61.4
Sweden					58.4	(1995)	61.2	62.2
Austria					32.2	(1996)	50.6	57.6
Finland					39.7	(1996)	68.6	60.6
Cyprus								28.8
Estonia								73.2
Hungary								61.5
Latvia								58.7
Lithuania								17.6
Malta								79.1
Czech Republic								71.7
Slovakia								83
Slovenia								71.7
EU Average	37	39		41.5	43.2		50.2	54.3

Source: European Parliament

In a study on the 1994 European Parliament elections, Franklin et al. (1996) find that levels of abstention are lower in countries where voting is compulsory and proportional, when voting occurs on a Sunday, and when EP elections occur in conjunction with other ballots. In the few countries where voting is mandatory, levels of voter turnout are indeed significantly higher than elsewhere. In fact, Belgium and Luxembourg (where it is mandatory to vote) report an abstention rate of around 10 per cent. A similar situation is found in Greece and Cyprus, where the legal requirement to vote is not always strictly enforced, but where abstention levels are below 30 per cent nonetheless. Voter abstention in Italy is also lower than 30 per cent despite the fact that compulsory voting was abolished in 1993. Franklin (2001) underlines that compulsory voting was enforced in 3 out of 9 member states in 1979, 3 out of 15 in 1999 and, more recently, 4 out of 25 in 2004. This perhaps helps us to understand that whilst the proportion of member states enforcing compulsory voting has decreased, at the same time European party systems have also experienced lower and lower levels of electoral turnout.

As mentioned earlier, levels of voter turnout tend to be higher when European Parliament elections coincide with other ballots. This observation is useful in shedding light on countries that experience fluctuations in the levels of participation in EP elections. In the case of Ireland, EP elections were held in conjunction with local elections in 1979, with legislative elections in 1989, and a referendum as well as local elections in 1999 and 2004. In Spain, both 1987 and 1999 EP elections coincided with regional and local ballots. Moreover, Lithuania displayed an abstention rate lower than the EU average (51.6 per cent) in 2004, probably due to the fact that presidential and European elections were being held simultaneously. A third institutional explanation lies in the choice of day that is selected for the ballot. Past elections have shown relatively low abstention levels when elections are held on Sundays rather than during the week. While this is generally true in most countries, levels of voter turnout in the 2004 EP elections in Slovakia and Poland were low even though the ballot was held on a Sunday.

Finally, an in-depth analysis of voting systems seems to suggest that proportional representation is more conducive to electoral participation than majoritarian forms such as majority and plurality systems. Nevertheless, the gradual adoption of proportional representation across the 25 member states has not necessarily reduced abstention levels and could even be seen to be increasing the distance between voters and their representatives. In contrast, the introduction of 'remote voting', that is, procedures that allow citizens to register their ballot say, via a postal vote, may prove to be an innovative method of tackling abstention levels across Europe. Analysis of data from the 2004 European Parliament elections shows a decrease in above-average abstention levels across the four regions of the UK where postal voting was the only means of participation.

One must be careful not to overlook the political context of individual countries when trying to understand abstention levels in European elections. Cross-country data on political participation indicate that citizens are more likely to participate in national (legislative) elections than in European elections, and in a local ballot. Nonetheless, the difference tends to be lower if the European ballot is associated with national votes. This is an important aspect of the 'classic' study by Reif and Schmitt (1980) – later elaborated by Marsh (1998) – which defines European elections as 'second-order national elections' characterised among other things, by far lower levels of electoral turnout. Similarly, abstention levels tend to increase when European elections occur at the start of a legislative cycle. In contrast, levels of voter turnout appear to be higher when EP elections occur at or after mid-cycle. This is largely because they are seen by the public as 'mid-term elections' allowing citizens to 'punish' ill-performing governing parties and leaders. The 2004 elections provide evidence to support this thesis. In Greece and Spain, where EP elections were taking place immediately after legislative elections, abstention levels were higher than in 1999. Conversely, in the case of the UK, the Netherlands and Italy, higher levels of voter turnout were seen to represent a 'protest vote' against the governing parties.

In spite of these results, the relationship between turnout levels and protest voting is far from being straightforward. In fact, the 2004 results in countries like Germany, France and Hungary showed high levels of protest voting coupled with low levels of electoral turnout. Generating explanatory hypotheses on phenomena which are as complex as abstention is extremely difficult. Each election needs to be considered in relation to its specific historical context and to the relationship that each individual citizen has with different types of elections. In this respect, it is impossible to identify a clear category of 'non-voters' within a population, given that abstention is an intermittent behaviour that can be alternated with periods of political activity (Blondel et al. 1997). For example, around 60 per cent of individuals who did not vote in June 2004 had not abstained in previous national elections. Despite fluctuations in electoral mobilisation, it is possible to identify general trends. For instance, social categories that do not usually participate in legislative elections are also less likely to vote in European elections. According to a Eurobarometer study, 67 per cent of people between 18 and 24 years old, and 64 per cent of 'working class' citizens reported not taking part in the June 2004 EP elections.

However, these sociological factors appear to be less decisive than the political opinions and attitudes of non-voters. It seems that people who abstain are far more critical and cynical about politics than those who do vote. When asked to identify the main reasons why they did not take part in the 2004 election, the largest answer (22 per cent of respondents) was citizens' general dissatisfaction with the state of political affairs, followed by a lack of interest in politics (14 per cent). Similarly, 68 per cent of interviewed non-voters compared with 32 per cent of voters did not identify with any political party. This study confirms the applicability of the multivariate model of analysis elaborated by Schmitt and Mannheimer (1991) from the post-electoral *European Election Study* (1989) and later confirmed

by Jadot (2002). These models suggested that the main factor in predicting voting behaviour in European elections is 'habitual voting'. The tendency to vote is higher among people who are interested in politics and identify with a specific political party. This suggests that voting behaviour as such is not linked to any particular socio-demographic characteristics. Moreover, only those individuals who have a firmly rooted tendency to vote are likely to participate in low-salience European elections, regardless of their sociological characteristics.

These arguments perhaps lead us to question whether one should abandon the hypothesis of a European dimension of abstention. In other words, should non-voting be dissociated from the public's opinion of the European Parliament and more generally of the European Union in terms of both its institutions and the affective identification it generates? In the early 1980s, two concurrent arguments seemed to decrease the salience of this question. The first thesis stated that voters would eventually 'get used' to the existence of European elections and realise the presumed necessity of legitimising the EP through voting. The opposing argument maintained that abstention levels would increase after the fading of the so-called 'first-time boost'. The 1984 elections were a clear illustration of this, since they showed that levels of voter turnout decrease as the novelty of a new type of election wears off. However, neither argument seems to explain the current situation: the progressive increase in abstention levels for EU elections and the lack of 'first-time boost effect' displayed by new member states in the 2004 elections.

It is also important to understand the profile and characteristics of the population that abstains from voting in European elections. Blondel et al. (1997)

argue that attitudes towards European integration influence one's propensity to vote in European elections. The distinction between 'European-only abstainers' and 'double abstainers' is quite small. The difference between them and the actively voting population is that the non-voters are less familiar with the EU, less informed about it, less interested in EU matters and more sceptical of the EP than those who vote. Therefore, there seems to be an information deficit between the abstainers and the people who vote time and time again. According to Niedermayer (1991), the majority of European citizens overestimate the powers of the European Parliament. As underlined by Irwin (1995), increasing the public's levels of information would involve teaching them about the EP's limited competencies and role, and, consequently, pointing out that there is even 'less at stake' in European elections than they assume. This relationship has also been explored in previous studies that associate low levels of public awareness and information with the likelihood of abstention, while paradoxically also indicating low levels of turnout among the best-informed sections of the population. In any attempt to improve voter turnout in EP elections, the optimum level of EU information among citizens should ideally be neither low nor very high.

Finally, one must not neglect the importance of the affective dimension of the European Union. As remarked by Frognier (2000) in a study conducted across member states, the level of electoral participation in a given country is strongly related to citizens' identification with Europe. In other words, the higher the proportion of voters who see themselves as 'Euro-nationals' or 'European citizens', the higher the levels of electoral participation. Conversely, when a large section of the population identifies exclusively with the nation-state, this indicates a likely low turnout in European elections. The low profile of European electoral campaigns coupled with the inability of political messages to appeal to the wider population (Irwin 1995) raise more questions about European institutions' lack of visibility rather than the issue of their legitimacy. As shown by Jesuit (2003) citizens of European regions benefiting from EU structural funds are more inclined to participate in EP elections, most likely because they perceive the European Union in a more positive manner. This shows that widespread voter abstention in European elections is not only about the European parliamentary arena, but about the visibility of the whole EU political system.

Fabienne Greffet

Bibliography

Blondel, J., Sinnott R. and Svensson P., 'Representation and Voter Participation', *European Journal for Political Research*, 32, 2, 1997, pp. 243–72.

Franklin M. N., 'How Structural Factors Cause Turnout Variations at European Parliament Elections', *European Union Politics*, 2, 3, 2001, pp. 309–28.

Franklin, M. N., Van der Eijk, C. and Oppenhuis E., 'The Institutional Context: Turnout', in C. Van der Eijk and M. N. Franklin (eds), *Choosing Europe? The European Electorate and National Politics in the Face of Union*, Ann Arbor, University of Michigan Press, 1996.

Frognier, A.-P., 'Identité et participation électorale: pour une approche européenne des élections européennes', in G. Grunberg, P. Perrineau and C. Ysmal (eds), *Le vote des Quinze. Les élections européennes du 13 juin 1999*, Paris, Presses de Sciences Po, 2000, pp. 75–94.

Irwin, G., 'Second-order or Third-rate? Issues in the Campaign for the Elections for the European Parliament 1994', *Electoral Studies*, 14, 2, 1995, pp. 183–99.

Jadot, A., '(Ne pas) être un électeur européen: Une analyse multiniveaux des déterminants individuels et contextuels de l'abstention en 1999', *Revue internationale de politique comparée*, 9, 1, 2002, pp. 31–45.

Jesuit, D., 'The Regional Dynamics of European Electoral Politics: Participation in National and European Contests in the 1990s', *European Union Politics*, 4, 2, 2003, pp. 139–64.

Marsh, M., 'Testing the Second-Order Election Model after Four European Elections', *British Journal of Political Science*, 28, 4, 1998, pp. 591–607.

Niedermayer, O., 'Turnout in the European Elections', *Electoral Studies*, 9, 1, 1991, pp. 45–50.

Reif, K. and Schmitt, H., 'Nine Second-Order National Elections: a Conceptual Framework for the Analysis of European Elections Results', *European Journal of Political Research*, 8, 1, 1980, pp. 3–44.

Schmitt, H. and Mannheimer, R., 'About Voting and Non-voting in the European Elections of June 1989', *European Journal of Political Research*, 19, 1, 1991, pp. 31–54.

→ Compulsory Voting; Democratic Deficit; Electoral Cycles; Electoral System; European Elections Studies; European Elections (1979–1999); European Elections (2004); Nationalisation of European Elections; 'Null and Void' (Votes); Postal Voting; Protest Voting; Registration; Second-Order Elections; Young People.

Act of 1976

(Act Concerning the Election of European Parliament Representatives by Direct Universal Suffrage, 20 September 1976)

The Act adopted by the Council on 20 September 1976 marked the end of a long process. Under Articles 21 (ECSC), 138 (EEC) and 108 (Euratom), the European Parliamentary Assembly is accountable for devising proposals for elections by direct universal suffrage in agreement with a standardised procedure in all member states. However, in spite of this right being enshrined in the treaties as well as in Article 2 of the Treaty of 25 March 1957, its application had repeatedly been deferred due to opposition coming from the French government. The process was relaunched in 1974 when, despite British and Danish resistance, the heads of states expressed an interest in reconsidering the Assembly's proposals, which were to be ruled on by the Council in 1976.

At the Paris Summit of 1974, the European Parliament was informed that direct elections should occur in or after 1978, and it was asked by the Council to present new proposals to replace its draft Convention. In fact, after the first enlargement took place in 1973, it had become clear that the original Dehousse project needed to be updated. Consequently, the Parliament designated Dutch socialist Schelto Patijn to produce a report. The report was approved by the political commission in November 1974 and later voted on in the plenary session held in January 1975 by 106 favourable votes and 2 against, including 17 abstentions mainly from the communist and Gaullist members. Contrary to the Dehousse project, the Patijn report provided for the election of all MEPs by direct universal suffrage (Article 1). Representatives were to hold their positions for a fixed five-year term (Article 3). Furthermore, Article 13 stipulated that the first election was to be held at the latest on the first Sunday of May 1978, in accordance with the internal provisions of each member state. However, from the second election onwards, the EP was to devise its 'uniform electoral procedures', to be completed by 1980 at the latest (Article 7).

The Patijn report also stipulated that the 'quality' of European Parliament representatives was to be comparable to that of national MPs. Moreover, it fixed the number of seats at 355, to be allocated based on proportional representation (Article 2). Slightly slowed down by negotiations with the UK, where a referendum was being held on 5 June 1975, the Council decided to wait until the second semester of the year, when it established a working group to examine the changes suggested by the Patijn report. The European Council met in Rome on 1–2 December 1975, confirmed the conclusions reached at the Paris summit of 1974, and finally agreed that the European Parliament would be elected by direct universal suffrage on a common date to be agreed.

The drafting of the Act establishing the election of the EP by direct universal suffrage was not always a smooth process. In fact, member states found it difficult to agree on the distribution of seats. Paris strongly opposed the allocation suggested by the Assembly, mainly because it challenged the status quo, putting an end to the parity (in terms of number of seats) that had existed since the early 1950s between France and Germany. Other governments also appeared to be siding with France, while presenting alternative solutions. London, which had gradually abandoned its initial reservations, argued that 36 MEPs would not be enough to ensure the adequate representation of the UK's different regions. After lengthy negotiations a compromise solution, quite different from the original Patijn report, was finally reached at the July European Council. The Act was eventually signed by foreign ministers on 20 September.

According to Article 1 of the 1976 Act, representatives to the European Parliament of the peoples united under the Community must be elected by direct universal suffrage. The Act adopted the designation of the original treaties, and the Assembly was to be composed of 410 members. The distribution of seats was clearly less favourable to smaller member states than to the four larger ones who, contrary to what had been suggested in the Patijn report, succeeded in maintaining an equal number of seats (Article 2).

Article 3 stipulated that representatives were to be elected for five-year terms and kept their right to vote (Article 4). Moreover, they were allowed to, but not obliged, to be simultaneously members of national parliaments, thus

Table 1

Member state	Population (millions)	Old distribution	Patijn project	1976 Act
Germany	62.0	36	71	81
UK	56.0	36	67	81
Italy	55.3	36	66	81
France	53.8	36	65	81
Netherlands	13.5	14	27	25
Belgium	9.8	14	23	24
Denmark	5.1	10	17	16
Ireland	3.1	10	13	15
Luxembourg	0.4	6	6	6
Total		198	355	410

fulfilling a dual mandate (Article 5). However, Article 6 clarified the conditions under which their responsibility as MEPs conflicted with other functions. The Assembly proposed a uniform election procedure, according to which European Parliament elections were to be held on 'a date falling within the same period starting on a Thursday morning and ending on the following Sunday', so as to account for the different electoral traditions of member states. Moreover, the counting of votes was not allowed to start until after the end of polling in all the member states (Article 9).

The establishment of direct universal suffrage was welcomed with great enthusiasm within European circles, and it was seen as a clear step forward for European integration, bringing it closer to European citizens. The Community's institutions pledged to launch an information campaign to sensitise public opinion to European developments and promote the importance of European elections. Could these initiatives stimulate the polling of political groups under new criteria? How would they promote the formation of a European political sphere? Would these efforts allow the EP, with its improved democratic legitimacy, to increase its relative importance vis-à-vis the Council and strengthen its decision-making, budgetary and legislative powers?

The delay between the signature of the 1976 Act and its enforcement led the year of 1976 to be dissociated from the first direct European elections. As mentioned, the Decision and Act were signed in Brussels on 20 September 1976, but the lengthy ratification process characterised by a fierce debate over the Parliament's powers, meant that they could not be enforced before 1 July 1978. The disputes were mainly due to the position adopted by France and the UK, who argued that direct elections did not

imply the extension of the Parliament's competencies, which would involve a revision of the treaties unanimously accepted by all governments and national parliaments. In addition, the fact that nine of the member states had to establish appropriate electoral procedures led to further delay before the first elections could take place on 7–10 June 1979.

Marie-Thérèse Bitsch

Bibliography

Lodge, J. (ed.), *Institutions and Policies of the EC*, London, Pinter, 1983.

Parlement Européen (Secrétariat – Direction générale de la recherche et de la documentation), *Élections du Parlement européen au suffrage universel direct. Rapport, résolutions et débats du Parlement européen*, Luxembourg, Office des publications officielles des Communautés Européennes, 1977.

→ Dual Mandates; European Elections (1979–1999); European Parliament; Incompatibility; Ineligibility; Members of the European Parliament (Legal and Political Status); Paris Summit; Parliamentary Mandate; Treaty of Rome; Universal Suffrage.

Advertising

Propaganda, electoral advertising and political marketing are all terms that refer to the same reality: a set of rules and techniques aiming at making voters vote for a particular vision of the world embodied by a partisan organisation. Marked by the monopoly of message emission and the use of manipulation techniques, the notion of propaganda stands out by its coercive connotation. Nowadays, most people refer to electoral advertising, even though in France, 'propaganda' remains the term of reference in electoral law.

In general, advertising is about the strategic definition of a party's positioning and its varied communication through messages that will be diffused through different media (commercials, posters, websites). In the reality of European electoral campaigns, advertising is not limited to a mere 'message engineering' concerned with mastering the content and form. It integrates a set of techniques from other areas of expertise: public relations for local and national meetings; press relations for agenda setting; and last but not least, marketing to emphasise individualised contact (door-to-door, distribution of flyers, direct distribution of leaflets in mailboxes, phoning).

Shaped by behaviourism, advertising is defined by three objectives that must follow on from each other in a linear manner. The first objective is cognitive: advertising must enable the party to make people aware. Then, there is an affective objective: advertising must lead to a positive judgement. Finally, a behavioural objective: advertising must generate action and reaction. To achieve such a programme, several techniques are implemented. Firstly, the party will use opinion polls (quantitative surveys and qualitative studies) to determine its image in public opinion. This image can be global or sectional according to the stakes. This allows the party to evaluate its notoriety and credibility and that of its main opponents over a set of issues considered relevant. The next stage is crucial. It corresponds to the evaluation of the image the party wants to have in the public's minds. Equipped with information on its perceived characteristics, the communication experts set benchmarks that will determine the 'ideological parameter' of the campaign, that is, a vision of the world and future made up of a set of

claimed values. This positioning will constitute the thematic axes that will be reflected in simple and strong messages or 'slogans'. Finally, in order to crystallise the image of the party, the campaign tone (aggressive or positive) is set. The third stage of the campaign organisation is the selection of the media that will be used. In the case of television, each channel is a different medium. If the choice of the media (TV, radio, written press) is made according to budget constraints, the type of message and the campaign sequence, and the choice of the ways in which information will be spread are determined by the targeted publics.

In general, considering legal constraints, the strategy of most parties is multimedia-based (press, mailing, and radio and TV commercials). Across European countries, it is generally believed that the best 'cocktail' in terms of efficiency combines a TV commercials campaign with a mailing campaign. However, today, most electoral advertising mainly aims at making the headlines to arouse the journalists' interest and obtain press coverage, rather than relying on more traditional advertising strategies.

Originally largely intuitive, electoral advertising has become clearly more 'scientific' over the past 30 years. Today, during an electoral campaign, the communication services have two options: they either lead the campaign with their own teams, or resort to the services of consulting agencies specialising in advertising. As in any communication project, one of the determining questions is the total budget allocated. We must also differentiate between the institutional campaigns to promote voting, either financed by the European institutions or the member states, and the parties' campaigns.

In the first case, efforts were made to devise homogeneous campaigns (slogans, visuals) at the European level.

In 1979, this was a failure with eleven different slogans, but the next elections were the occasion for the first unified European campaign. The campaign, conceived by Intermarco-Publicis, comprised three thematic commercials (Third World; Freedom; Environment and Unemployment) and a recurrent slogan: 'One democracy unites us: Europe. On 17 June, you will vote'. These institutional campaigns, which benefited from large budgets, legitimately needed the resort to international advertising network agencies providing integrated and global services at the European level.

On the other hand, the main characteristic of partisan electoral communication is its minimalism at the European level. European campaigns hardly go beyond one-third of the amounts incurred for strictly national election campaigns. The resort to an external service provider is limited most of the time to the conception of commercials, the official poster and some newspaper advertisements. As an example, in 1999 in Germany, the SPD allocated 5.5 million euros to its electoral advertising including a 90-second TV commercial, a radio commercial, a cinema commercial, six visuals for posting, and press advertisements. In the 2004 campaign, the French Socialist Party only contracted out TBWA-Corporate to make their campaign's official commercial, the rest being conceived in-house. This state of affairs may be related to the lack of visibility of European elections, and, in turn, their relatively low turnout, and further emphasises the lack of a global campaign strategy and the lack of a shared public sphere.

Jacques-Olivier Barthes

→ Campaign (Sociology of); Communication; Electoral Behaviour; Europeanisation; Issues; Political Market.

Age

While the voting age is fixed at 18 throughout the European Union, the age of eligibility for European Parliament representatives varies from country to country. The minimum age of eligibility is 18 in Finland, Sweden, Denmark, Germany, Spain, the Netherlands, Portugal and, amongst the new member states, Slovenia, Hungary and Malta. However, it is 19 in Austria, 21 in Belgium, Greece, Ireland, Luxembourg, the United Kingdom, Poland, the Czech Republic, Slovakia, Lithuania, Latvia and Estonia, 23 in France and 25 in Italy and Cyprus. Similar variations can be observed with respect to the eligibility age of candidates for national elections.

European Parliament elections have one of the lowest average turnouts of all types of elections, and they are often considered to be second-order elections, where voters largely react to national stimuli. However, in many other respects, electoral behaviour for European elections is largely characterised by the same sociological and political factors as those that affect national elections. The impact of age on European elections is based on principles that are grounded in electoral sociology and apply to other types of elections (Cautrès and Mayer 2004). In fact, among the main explanatory factors of electoral behaviour, age, seemingly one of the most obvious, is among the most complex to analyse. Age not only refers to the process of biological ageing, but also to important societal considerations. Indeed, behind the effects of age lie a number of causal links that involve both an individual's position in life, and those of his socio-cultural and behavioural characteristics that are shaped by generational factors.

The nature and the context of a given election are also to be taken into account, not least because age conceals differences in the composition of age groups. The socio-demographic composition of society can vary across different time-periods, affecting individuals' socio-cultural and economic conditions, and, consequently, influencing their electoral decisions. Studies in political behaviour have shown that this variable does not always influence electoral behaviour in the same way, and calls for some degree of caution in employing it to explain variations in voting behaviour.

In order to assess the effects of age, the political science literature always distinguishes between two types of effects, referred to as 'life-cycle' and 'generational' effects. The position of an individual in his or her 'life-cycle', in other words, where a person stands in the course of his or her individual life, affects political attitudes and behaviour alike. A number of studies show the existence of specific rhythms and regularities in individuals' political agendas, and in their electoral behaviour in particular (Percheron 1993). The behaviour of young voters varies greatly both in terms of turnout and age of registration, making this period of one's life an 'electoral moratorium' (Muxel 2001a, 2001b). It appears that it is not before voters reach their forties that their turnout becomes closer to older age groups. However, significant variations show that even over a relatively short period of time, the effects of age on participation are neither linear nor continuous. The youngest registered voters often participate in greater numbers than their immediate elders. However, higher levels of turnout are observed amongst voters aged 25–34 than among those aged 18–24. Nevertheless, the 2004 European elections presented an occasionally unusual pattern. For example, in France, abstention levels reached 60 per cent for the 18–24-year-olds, almost similar to the national average of 57 per cent, but 71 per cent voters aged 25–34, while at the EU level, 67 per cent of 18–24-year-olds abstained, compared to 54 per cent overall.

Electoral mobilisation appears to be greater for middle-aged categories, especially for voters aged 50 and over. In fact, the likeliness of participation keeps growing through the second half of people's life, and only starts to decrease again after the age of 80. The relationship between turnout and age follows a reversed U-curve. While this is true in all European countries, the amplitude of this curve is proportional to national levels of participation. It therefore looks different in highly mobilised countries such as Belgium, Italy and Greece, and in those with weaker levels of turnout, such as France and Portugal.

While many trends based on voters' stages of life can be observed, age has no 'pure' effect on voting behaviour. Electoral behaviour remains narrowly correlated with individuals' levels of social integration. Such levels account for significant variations in the layout and complexity of the model as their effect is interactive with that of other key variables. For instance, education is an important variable in the analysis of voting behaviour, and is particularly discriminating among young people. Young voters displaying the lowest levels of education appear to be the most distanced from political affairs. Conversely, interest in politics, likeliness of registering on electoral rolls, and turnout appear to be highest amongst individuals with high levels of education. Moreover, they are least supportive of protest parties.

While the relationship between education and electoral behaviour proves to be determining, one cannot speak of it in purely mechanical terms. In all Western democracies, the continuous decline in turnout levels appears paradoxical given the overall increase in education levels, and stresses the relevance of generational effects. When considering the generational impact of age, we therefore need to consider the influence of historical, political and social contexts across age groups. This context includes the combined effects of political socialisation in various time-periods, and the socio-demographic composition of the youngest age groups. For example, Franklin (2004) argues that the first five years of an individual's voting habits influence and determine his future electoral behaviour. This argument implies that the participation deficit of the youngest generations will be with them throughout their future political lives, leading to a further decline in the overall levels of turnout.

In order to shed light on the effects of age in European elections, it is also necessary to disentangle several groups of factors. Most obvious are those resulting from the effects of the crisis of representation that largely affects all Western democracies and age groups. It is characterised by a decrease in levels of confidence towards institutions, and weakening levels of partisan identification. This problem is further reinforced by the difficulty of the general public in delineating a European public sphere. The second group of factors concerns effects more closely associated with the younger generations, particularly those induced by the specific context of their political socialisation. The latter is marked by the greater mobility and fragility of social and political allegiances, as well as the increasing complexity of models enabling them to interpret their surroundings. Interestingly, younger generations display greater levels of European identity (Bruter 2005) and are most likely to embrace the new European project, culture and political space. Paradoxically, however, it is amongst this age group that levels of political expression and participation are traditionally lowest, which has often made young people less involved in the democratic game, and more removed from key electoral decisions. Nevertheless, these high levels of European identity might explain the higher than expected participation of the 18–24-year-olds in some countries in the 2004 elections (see above), and the fact that this category displays very little support for Eurosceptic and Europhobic parties. Instead, young voters express particularly high pro-European feelings.

Similarly, in terms of values, the younger generations are shown to be increasingly more open, more tolerant, more prone to embrace universalism and cultural liberalism, than older generations. The same is true among those whose levels of education and awareness are relatively low (Inglehart 1997; Galland and Roudet 2001).

Altogether, the combination of generational and life-cycle effects of age allow for the understanding of certain tendencies that appeared important in the 2004 European elections, and ranged from occasionally paradoxical levels of participation, to varying levels of electoral volatility, particularly among young people (Muxel 2001a, 2001b).

Anne Muxel

Bibliography

Bruter, M., *Citizens of Europe? The Emergence of a Mass European Identity*, Basingstoke: Palgrave Macmillan, 2005.

Cautrès, B. and Mayer, N. (eds), *Le nouveau désordre électoral*, Paris, Presses de Sciences Po, 2004.

Franklin, M. N., *Voter Turnout and the Dynamics of Electoral Competition in Established Democracies Since 1945*, Cambridge, Cambridge University Press, 2004.

Galland, O. and Roudet, B. (eds), *Les valeurs des jeunes: Tendances en France depuis 20 ans*, Paris, L'Harmattan, 2001.

Inglehart, R., *Modernization and Post-modernization: Cultural, Economic, and Political Change in 43 Societies*, Princeton, Princeton University Press, 1997.

Muxel, A., *L'expérience politique des jeunes*, Paris, Presses de Sciences Po, 2001a.

Muxel, A., 'Les choix politiques des jeunes à l'épreuve du temps: Une enquête longitudinale', *Revue française de science politique*, 51, 3, 2001b, pp. 409–30.

Percheron, A., *La socialisation politique*, Paris, Armand Colin, 1993.

→ Abstention; Citizen (EU); Democratic Deficit, European Electoral Act; European Electoral Sociology; Identity; Registration; Second-Order Elections; Young People.

Austria

Introduction

Austria joined the European Union in 1995. Thus, in 2004, the elections to the European Parliament were held for the third time. Due to enlargement in May 2004, the number of Austrian MEPs fell from 21 to 18. Six parties ran in these elections, five of which gained seats. To a degree, results offered a different picture compared to the elections in 1996 and 1999 with regard to turnout and distribution of votes among parties. The steady decline in turnout from 67.7 per cent in 1996, to 49.4 per cent in 1999 down to 42.4 per cent in 2004 is one interesting phenomenon. Another one can be seen in the dramatic losses of the Eurosceptic Freedom Party (FPÖ)[1] as well as in the emergence of a new party campaigning on the single issue of alleged expense account riding among MEPs. Although in line with the general European trend, the low turnout in European elections is in rather sharp contrast with turnouts in national elections (turnout at

national election, November 2002: 84.3 per cent; turnout at presidential elections, April 2004: 71.6 per cent). Moreover, while utter Euroscepticism was no longer an issue in these elections, abstention and protest voting call for explanations going beyond European trends.

In order to grasp the electorate's behaviour some historical information is needed. Due to neutrality, Austrian membership in the European Union did not become a real option until the mid-1980s when the fall of the Iron Curtain began to lose the aura of utopia. Although two parties, the Freedom Party and the Greens, campaigned against membership, in 1994, 66.6 per cent of the Austrian electorate voted in its favour, turnout being at 80 per cent. The incumbent coalition of Social Democrats (SPÖ) and Conservatives (ÖVP) advocated membership, espousing a discourse focused on the socio-economic gains that would almost automatically result from accession. Problems for the status of neutrality as well as the dangers of new social cleavages were largely denied. Once membership was achieved, as in other member states, explanations of the complex European institutional set-up and decision-making process were never high on the agenda of the political elite. In addition, the national parliament hardly ever made use of its constitutionally granted rights of participation in the government's European policies (Pollak and Slominski 2003). Hence, the electorate's misunderstanding of the role and growing power of the European Parliament persists, and European elections continue to be considered as 'second-order elections'. This perception is reflected in the answers of non-voters when asked why they did not participate in the EP elections in 2004: 40 per cent of the respondents named 'disinterest', 'no relevance' or 'had something better to do' as reasons (Zeglovits and Picker 2004).

Moreover, promises given during the referendum campaign appeared to be false at least to some of the citizens, while the liberalisation of the Austrian economy gradually impinged upon the traditional decision-making process between social partners and the model of consociational democracy. The latter had already started to erode in the late 1980s due to the sudden, yet continuous success story of the Freedom Party, an extreme-right party. The formation of a coalition government between the conservative People's Party and the Freedom Party in 2000 marked the end of an era. The diplomatic measures of the 14 other member states against the Austrian government (called 'the EU sanctions') as well as the delegation of the four 'Wise Men' investigating possible infringements of European values disillusioned considerable numbers of Austrian citizens about the Union. 'The sanctions' were repeatedly exploited for political campaigns (e.g. during the EP election campaign, the FPÖ defamed the candidate of the SPÖ as a 'traitor', referring to his attitudes towards the sanctions). Apart from that, issues like the Union's policy with regard to nuclear energy or transit may have contributed to Euroscepticism.

However, Eurobarometer surveys measuring Austrian attitudes towards EU membership show interesting oscillations. Asked whether they consider membership a good or a bad thing, 39 per cent answered positively in May 1995. After some ups and downs during the following years this value reached 41 per cent in December 1999, declining to 32 per cent in June 2000 ('sanctions' being imposed in February) and climbing up again to 44 per cent in December 2001 ('sanctions' having been abolished in September 2000) and even to 46 per cent in October/

November 2002. After that there was an ever sharper downward trend towards 30 per cent in February/March 2004. However, by the summer of 2006, support had gone back up to 36 per cent versus 23 per cent of negative opinions (Eurobarometer 66).

With regard to the European Parliament the following data are highly intriguing: while in February/March 2004, 93 per cent of Austrians claimed to know of the EP and 74 per cent (ibid., p. 23) considered its role important for life in the Union (ibid., p. 24), only 43 per cent trusted this institution (ibid., p. 25) and not more than 17 per cent believed its impact on citizens to be great. However, 41 per cent thought that the EP has some effect, whereas 28 per cent considered this effect to be non-existent (ibid., p. 48).

Results of the elections 2004

The most striking result of the elections was the breakdown of the FPÖ (from 23 per cent in 1999 to 6 per cent in 2004) together with the surprising success of the 'List Hans-Peter Martin' (Table 1). This list was initiated by a MEP and former main candidate of the SPÖ who dominated large parts of the campaigning period by focusing on the alleged abuse of privileges by MEPs and more generally on the 'wasteful and deficient' EU bureaucracy. He thus convinced 13.98 per cent of the voters – a result that is beyond the success of the Green Party.

Mr Martin attracted the highest share of the FPÖ voters of 1999 (SORA 2004). Although he may have demobilised some voters by his criticism of the EP, his list also offered voters the opportunity to vent their Euroscepticism which may in turn have increased turnout.

Table 1   Results of EP elections in Austria (1999, 2004) (%)

	Result 1999	Result 2004
SPÖ	31.71	33.33
ÖVP	30.67	32.70
FPÖ	23.40	6.31
Die GRÜNEN	9.29	12.89
Liste Hans-Peter Martin	–	13.98
Other parties[2]	4.93	0.78
Turnout	**49.40**	**42.43**

Source: BMI (Austrian Ministry for the Interior).

Analysis of socio-graphic data

Data analysis based on the European Election Studies/Austria[3] shows that there is a linear effect of age on voting turnout (Table 2): the younger a person is, the higher is the likelihood that they did not cast their vote in the EP elections. The highest share of non-voters is found among young women (74 per cent), followed by young men (67 per cent). Turnout increases with age for both genders. Elder women (60 or more years) have the highest turnout.

An equal share (about 10 per cent) of young men (18–29 years) voted for the SPÖ, the Greens and the List Hans-Peter Martin. Young women showed a different voting behaviour: the highest number (9 per cent) voted for the Greens. The men in the two other age groups show similar voting preferences with the highest percentages for the two major Austrian parties (SPÖ and ÖVP). Women older than 30 years display the same trend, except for those in the oldest age group: They show a clear preference for the ÖVP.

Voting turnout in Austria also seems to be linked to education (Table 3). The percentage of non-voters is lower among higher educated people (50 per cent of

Table 2   Electoral behavior by gender × age (% of all respondents)

	Male, 18–29	Male, 30–59	Male, 60 plus	Female, 18–29	Female, 30–59	Female, 60 plus
SPÖ	10	16	18	2	13	17
ÖVP	3	13	14	3	13	26
FPÖ	0	2	9	0	1	6
Die GRÜNEN	10	6	2	9	6	2
Liste Hans-Peter Martin	9	5	6	3	7	5
Die LINKE	0	0.4	0	1	0.4	0
Cast invalid vote	1	1	0	2	2	1
Answer refused	0	3	4	5	2	4
Did not vote	67	55	48	74	56	39

Column = 100 per cent; deviations due to rounding

Table 3   Electoral behaviour by education (% of all respondents; highest completed education)

	Compulsory education (9 years)	Compulsory education plus vocational training	Intermediate education (11 years)	High school diploma (eligible for university)	University
SPÖ	18	16	12	7	7
ÖVP	17	10	13	13	21
FPÖ	1	3	4	3	7
Die GRÜNEN	0	2	5	14	7
List Hans-Peter Martin	6	6	5	7	3
Die LINKE	0	0	1	1	1
Cast invalid vote	0	1	2	3	1
Answer refused	1	4	1	3	5
Did not vote	57	58	60	50	32

Column = 100 per cent; deviations due to rounding. Small sample size for 'university' (n = 75)

Table 4   Electoral behaviour by social class (% of all respondents)

	Working class	Lower middle class	Middle class	Upper middle class	Upper class
SPÖ	24	12	12	7	0
ÖVP	8	15	15	19	18
FPÖ	2	1	3	2	18
Die GRÜNEN	2	5	6	11	0
List Hans-Peter Martin	8	7	5	6	0
Die LINKE	0	1	0.4	0	0
Cast invalid vote	1	3	1	2	0
Answer refused	2	3	3	4	0
Did not vote	55	54	54	50	63

Column = 100 per cent; deviations due to rounding. *Very small sample size for 'upper class' (n = 11); should only be interpreted with caution.

respondents with high school diploma, 32 per cent of respondents who finished university studies). Also, those with a high school diploma were more likely to vote for the ÖVP or the Greens (about 13 per cent each).

Analysed by self-reported social class (Table 4), there are no clear differences with regard to turnout*. Non-voters are almost equally represented in all social strata. However, results show that for the EP elections, the SPÖ still functioned as 'party of the working class' (24 per cent). In contrast, the ÖVP has the highest share among persons considering themselves upper middle class, but it is also strongly represented among the lower middle class and middle class.The Greens have their highest share in the upper middle class.

Conclusions

In Austria, the European Parliament elections 2004 led to a consolidation of the electorate of SPÖ and ÖVP (slight increases of 1.6 and 2 per cent), to considerable gains for the Greens and to the emergence of a new list (List Hans-Peter Martin) reaching almost 14 per cent, while the heavy losses of the FPÖ (–17 per cent) once more confirmed the end of a former success story. Thus, we hold that the protest voters turned from the FPÖ to the List Hans-Peter Martin or to abstention. Moreover, turnout fell even below the EU average which conspicuously contradicts participation in national elections. Abstention is highest among young voters and seems to correlate with the perception of Austrian citizens that their individual vote as well as their country counts for little in the Union (only 26 and 27 per cent answering relevant questions positively), whereas 76 per cent believe large member states to be the really powerful players (Eurobarometer 61, p. 37). The feeling of a hierarchy between big and small members may also be rooted in the experience of having been 'sanctioned'. This – together with controversial issues like the EU transit policies – may have contributed to Austrian Euroscepticism. The perception that the EP elections are 'second-order elections'

furthermore exacerbated declining participation.

Sonja Puntscher Riekmann
(Salzburg/Vienna)
Ruth Picker
(Vienna)

Notes

1. This marginalisation is part of a bigger trend: the FPÖ lost all recent elections, except for the regional elections in Carinthia in March 2004.
2. 'Other' 2004: Linke; 'Other'1999: Liberales Forum, Christlich Soziale Allianz (Liste Karl Habsburg), Kommunistische Partei Österreich.
3. Source: Data collected for the European Election Studies 2004; n = 1000, random sample, Austrians eligible to vote (older than 18 years); telephone survey, conducted: 17–25 June 2004; Weighted data. Fieldwork: Institute for Panel Research/Vienna. Study conducted by: SORA (Institute for Social Research and Analysis); in co-operation with ÖGfE (Österreichische Gesellschaft für Europa-Politik).

Bibliography

Eurobarometer 61, Spring 2004.
Flash Eurobarometer 162, Post-European elections survey (2004). www.europarl.eu.int/press/Eurobarometer/index_en.htm
Pollak, Johannes and Slominski, Peter, 'Influencing EU Politics? The Case of the Austrian Parliament', *Journal of Common Market Studies*, 41, 3, 2003, pp. 707–29.
SORA (Institute for Social Research and Analysis), 'Voter Transition Analysis EP Elections 2004', www.sora.at/wahlen/wsa/EU-Wahl2004.
Zeglovits, Eva and Picker, Ruth, 'European Election Studies 2004: Die NichtwählerInnen bei den Wahlen zum Europa-Parlament in Österreich', unpublished research report, SORA (Institute for Social Research and Analysis).

→ Mapping Europe: European Electoral Geography.

B

Ballot Paper

A unit of expression and a measure of electoral acts, ballot papers have yet to be uniformly codified at the European level. Whether tangible or abstract (with the development of voting machines or electronic voting, designed especially to suit the needs of voters residing outside their country of nationality particularly in Sweden, the Netherlands, etc.), the ballot paper is presented in a variety of shapes and formats. When the EU decided to develop a uniform voting procedure for European Parliament elections, the main and almost sole recommendation concerned the candidates' order of presentation (which had to comply with the lists originally submitted).

Since the generalisation of proportional representation systems for European elections, the type of ballot paper selected has also had to be compatible with proportional or preferential elections as well as to allow for the appreciation of the electorates' varying opinions and choices (Sasse et al. 1981: 300, 309–10). Such broad criteria mean that the definition of the characteristics of European ballot papers is subjected to each member state's preferences and choices, one of the main aims being not to perturb the functioning and structures of other political elections. This preoccupation is partly accountable for the differences in size, colour and textures of ballot papers across the EU.

A number of studies have sought to examine the relationship between the nature and characteristics of ballot papers and the outcome of elections through the use of multiple regressions. Campbell and Miller (1957) have looked at the effects of 'straight ticket' voting. A study by Walker (1966) showed that least-educated voters are more inclined not to consider candidates placed at the bottom of ballot papers, and display signs of 'electoral fatigue'. Moreover, Kelley and MacAllister (1984) examined the effects of ballot paper cues (i.e. the position of the candidate's name on the ballot sheet, the mention of his/her gender or the presence of honorary and academic titles) on voting behaviour in Australia and in the United Kingdom. The results are clear: voters with little information on the candidates or on the issues at stake in elections are more likely to vote in a confused and random manner. Hence the importance of national voting modalities, which express the degree of codification of the electoral competition and are generally better suited to fit individual voting systems. For instance, Article 11 of the Portuguese electoral law of 29 April 1987 stipulates that ballot papers for European elections must be different in colour to those of other elections held at the same time.

Similarly, Lithuania's recent electoral law is even more precise and not only defines the exact format of ballot papers, but also the different mandatory roles they are required to fulfil. Voters are provided with specific instructions explaining the correct way in which ballot papers are to be completed. These procedures also provide for a specific space designed to indicate voters' preferences (Article 56 of the electoral law of 20 November 2003). Furthermore, Articles 57 and 63 also stipulate that, with the exception of postal voting, ballot papers are to be distributed exclusively in polling stations after the voters' identity has been carefully verified. Similar procedures are also found in other member states like Poland, Luxembourg, the Czech Republic and Cyprus.

Aside from format and distribution mode, the drafting of ballot papers is of particular importance. The latter is often complicated by the voting mode applied in European elections. It is probably in Belgium and in the United Kingdom that the attention of electoral administrations has been most pronounced during the 2004 European elections. In the case of Belgium, where electronic voting concerned 42 per cent of the electoral body ('Jites' or 'Digivotes' procedures), authorities have multiplied information as well as online voting simulations in order to familiarise voters with their new 'electronic citizenship'. Voters were also able to prepare themselves prior to election day through a video available on the elections' website.[1] On the screen of this voting machine, voters were able to visualise new ballot papers 'disguised' in traditional format. In contrast with 1999 elections, the experimental 'ticketing' process was not repeated. The process consisted of a printed copy of the electoral choice made by voters on screen automatically falling into the ballot box.

In other countries, the voting ritual has been reinforced. For instance, the United Kingdom has strengthened the value of traditional ballot papers through the implementation of postal voting in four separate instances. Postal ballot papers included a list of competing political parties and independent candidates in alphabetical order influenced by a number ranging from '1 to n', encircled by the twelve European stars. They also included a form necessary to identify the voter and validate papers. Specific stations assisting voters with postal voting procedures were also established. A final innovation consists of the possibility offered to voters by small political parties across Europe to download and print ballot papers from their websites. The use of such technique has been advocated by the French Federalist Party, encouraging the electorate to 'vote differently', thus saving on the elevated costs of electoral propaganda.[2] The process of Europeanisation is slowly advancing also on the electoral equipment market.

Yves Déloye and Oliver Ihl

Notes

1. http://elections2004.belgium.be/fr/automated_voting.html, accessed on 5 August 2004.
2. http://www.jevoteautrement.com/voter.html, accessed on 5 August 2004.

Bibliography

Campbell, A. and Miller, W., 'The Motivational Basis of Straight and Split Ticket Voting', *American Political Science Review*, 51, 3, June 1957, pp. 293–312.

Kelley, J. and MacAllister, I., 'Ballot Paper Cues and the Vote in Australia and Britain: Alphabetic Voting, Sex and Title', *Public Opinion Quarterly*, 48, 2, 1984, pp. 452–66.

Sasse, C. et al., *The European Parliament: Towards a Uniform Procedure for Direct Elections*, Florence, European University Institute, Luxembourg, Office for Official Publications of the European Communities, 1981.

Walker, Jack L., 'Ballot Forms and Voter Fatigue: an Analysis of the Office Block and Party Column Ballot', *Midwest Journal of Political Science*, 10, 4, 1966, pp. 448–63.

→ Ballot Secrecy; Electoral System; Electoral Technology; Postal Voting; Symbols and Practice of Elections.

Ballot Secrecy

Electoral secrecy is one the most widely shared electoral principles in Europe.

The first laws providing for systems to guarantee electoral secrecy in the current EU countries date back to the second half of the nineteenth century and the beginning of the twentieth century. From as early as 1861, Italian law established that voters could make their choices in secret. The United Kingdom started to introduce envelopes and polling booths in 1872, followed by Belgium in 1877. In Luxembourg, an Act was passed in 1884, and amended in 1886 and 1892, enabling voters to use isolated compartments or desks to prepare their ballots. Similarly, in the Netherlands, the Act of 1896 provided for an isolated desk for voting. In Wurtemberg, voters have used separately spaced desks to put their ballots in envelopes since 1899. A similar system was implemented in Denmark in 1901. Envelopes and polling booths were rolled out across Germany in 1903, adopted in Finland in 1907 and in France in 1913.

The Australian ballot, whereby votes are cast in secret in official uniform ballots, thus rapidly became widespread across Europe, entailing a variety of systems: isolated tables or polling booths, folded ballots or envelopes, votes cast in the ballot box by the president of a party or by the voters themselves. The Greek system appeared to be an exception when, in the early twentieth century, voting secrecy became guaranteed by most unusual measures: voters placed a ball in one of the two compartments in a ballot box in order to cast a vote for or against a candidate, with their arms concealed deep in the box to hide their voting choice. The Hungarian case also proved peculiar, whereby public voting was abolished in 1900 but implemented again in 1922, thus temporarily breaching the process of privatisation of political opinions which had expanded across Europe in the twentieth century.

This process has been reinforced, until the present day, by the enforcement of new guarantees in certain countries. Where voting is not compulsory, certain legislations provided for the non-publicity of the list of voters in order to retain the secrecy of the choice of abstention. Moreover, in both Denmark and Ireland, the Acts on the election to the European Parliament state that, in the event of a legal action, voters are not obliged to reveal in which manner they voted. Other procedures facilitate further guarantees of secrecy, not only for the individual, but also for the collective. Thus, in the United Kingdom and in Ireland, all the ballots of a constituency are gathered before they are counted. The issue there is to avoid collective pressures on small communities whose votes could be controlled if counting took place in the polling station.

These mechanisms for secret balloting, which were designed by the legislator to protect electoral expression from pressure by (varying according to the countries), unions, bosses, administration or the Church, now appear as obvious, almost natural, guarantees of the independence of voters. They are matched with the increasing individualisation of social relations and contribute to making voting a strictly personal, almost intimate, act. The Venice Commission, in its guidelines adopted on 5–6 July 2002, classifies electoral secrecy as an essential element of the European electoral heritage and establishes four principles which must preside over its enforcement for democratic elections:

(1) For the voter, voting secrecy is not only a right but also a duty, which must be sanctioned by disqualification of any ballot paper whose content is disclosed.
(2) Voting must be individual. Family voting and any other form of control

by one voter over the vote of another must be prohibited.

(3) The list of persons actually voting should not be published.

(4) The violation of suffrage secrecy should be sanctioned (Commission for Democracy Through Law 2003: 14).

The history of technical provisions for voting secrecy may indeed seem to have come to an end with the adoption of such principles and their enforcement through various systems in the polling stations throughout the European Union. However, the numbering system of ballots in the United Kingdom is regularly criticised for being a means to control votes, although authorities claim they protect the status of secrecy through the precautions given to the use of the bundles. The obligation imposed on voters not to reveal their votes is sometimes breached, but ostentatious bravado more often than not reveals the internalisation of the norm of secrecy. Finally, only minority movements still advocate the reinforcement of public voting. Nevertheless, new challenges have arisen, for instance with the generalisation of postal voting in Great Britain, and above all with the development of computerised and electronic voting. These new electoral techniques, which are meant to enable an increase in turnout, entail problems in terms of securing the right to secrecy and the individual nature of voting.

Even where the use of the polling booth is still maintained, the issue of respect for privacy arises for people who do not know how to use the system or ask for help to vote. Another problem lies with the confidentiality of the collected data: when voters are identified with an electronic chip, it is important to guarantee that no one will be able to detect a link between the data on the card and the expressed vote. Although programming computers in this fashion is possible, voters are usually not able to control voting secrecy for themselves. Rather they have to rely on third parties, public authorities or above all, private companies, for the control of voting operations. Other issues arise from the possibility granted by the internet to vote outside polling stations. Essentially, the question concerns how to ensure that no further pressure is exerted on voters who are no longer protected by the secrecy of polling booths. Problems related to electronic voting underline the extent to which secrecy is far from being obvious but relies on a process of incorporation of electoral normality that the establishment of new voting mechanisms can also call into question.

Nathalie Dompnier

Bibliography

Commission européenne pour la démocratie par le droit (Commission for Democracy Through Law), *Code de bonne conduite en matière électorale*, Strasbourg, Editions du Conseil de l'Europe, 2003.

Ihl, O., *Le vote*, 2nd edition, Paris, Montchrestien, 2000.

Mackie, T., 'Australian ballot' and 'Secrecy ballot', in R. Rose (ed.), *International Encyclopedia of Elections*, Basingstoke Macmillan.

→ Ballot Paper; Electoral System; Electoral Technology; European Electoral Act; Postal Voting; Symbols and Practice of Elections; United Kingdom.

Belgium

On 13 June 2004, Belgians voted for the sixth time in European Parliament elections. In comparison with other EU

Table 1   Turnout in EP elections in Belgium (1979–2004) (%)

	1979	1984	1989	1994	1999	2004
Turnout	91.29	92.09	90.73	90.66	90.96	90.81
Blank and invalid	14.07	10.93	8.37	8.73	6.84	5.22

member states, EP elections in Belgium conceal a peculiarity: voting is compulsory. While abstention is a characteristic of EP elections in most of the member states, turnout – due to the compulsory character of the Belgian vote (as in Luxembourg, Cyprus and Greece) – exceeds more than 90 per cent (Table 1). This low abstention rate particularly contrasts with the extent of the average abstention observed in the EU. In 1999, the gap between the Belgian situation and the European average was already above 40 points. In 2004, it reached 45 points. On the other hand, one element characterises the countries where voting is compulsory: the proportionally increased importance of blank and invalid ballots. Contrary to what was observed about the turnout, the 5.22 per cent of blank and invalid ballots is very high compared to the rates observed in the other states of the EU.

Another element is important in understanding EP elections in Belgium: the absence of cleavage or clear division in the Belgian political scene on European integration. Belgium has a reputation of being a 'Europhile' country or even a 'Euro-enthusiastic' one. If this general idea must be qualified, it remains true that one can observe a kind of consensus on European issues over the last 50 years. The study of European treaty ratifications attests that approval has generally been broader than for the single majority parties (Table 2). As an example, the treaty instituting the Common Market and Euratom or the Single European Act were adopted in an (almost) consensual way in the Belgian House of Representatives.

For 15 years, Belgium's position in relation to European integration has nonetheless become somewhat more complex, due to the birth and development of a more and more powerful extreme-right grouping: the *Vlaams Blok* (now *Vlaams Belang*). The *Vlaams Belang* is the only Belgian parliamentary party

Table 2   Ratification of the European treaties in Belgium

	House of Representatives			Senate		
	For	Against	Abstention	For	Against	Abstention
ECSC	165	13	13	102	4	58
EDC	148	49	3	125	49	3
EC/ Euratom	179	4	2	134	2	2
SEA	180	0	0	148	0	0
Maastricht Treaty	146	33	3	115	26	1
Amsterdam Treaty	105	23	0	49	13	0
Nice Treaty	106	24	7	46	11	2

that, not only is opposed to the construction of a federal Europe but even supports the principle of a Europe which would be confederal by nature. The *Vlaams Belang* parliamentarians discuss any institutional evolution of the European Community towards a political union. The Flemish extreme right considers that the people should be able to choose their fate without being kept in check and asks for a clear sharing of tasks between the EU and the member states. If the *Vlaams Belang* is therefore rather an exception within Belgian political parties, it is important to underline that the European problematic is far from being in the foreground of its electoral propaganda or political communication.

On the other hand, it should be noted that this party is nonetheless favourable to the prospect of the European single market and recognises the pacifying role European construction has played as well as the historical importance of enlargement to include Central and Eastern Europe. Let us add that extreme-left parties hostile to the EU and to the adoption of a European Constitution, have never been very successful including in European elections that generally involve less tactical voting.

One element that makes the relation of social and political actors to European construction increasingly complex is due to the misgivings that some federalist formations occasionally express, either dissatisfied by the institutional path of European construction, or reluctant or hostile to the EU trend considered as neo-conservative. In the first case, we can particularly mention the attitude of Christian Democrats – currently in the opposition – towards the Nice Treaty. Considering the Treaty incomprehensible and insufficient for the EU's development needs, the French-speaking and part of the Flemish-speaking Christian Democrats decided not to support it, a move which was unprecedented for this political group. In the second case, we can mention as an example the Belgian ecologists – *Ecolo* and *Groeni* – who rejected the Maastricht Treaty, both because of its content and the timetabling of Economic and Monetary Union. Since 2002, the Flemish Socialists and part of the French-speaking ones have been particularly critical about the EU's progress and shared the worries of other parties over the effects of the enlargement to CEECs. In addition, in Belgium, since 1999, the European election has been considered as of secondary importance compared to the regional elections to which it is now coupled. The regional elections are of great importance and greatly overshadow their European *alter ego*.

Voting system and constituencies

The electoral regime at work during the Belgian European elections is proportional and organised on the basis of the d'Hondt method. The country is divided into three colleges of a linguistic nature: Flemish, French and German-speaking, but into four electoral districts: Wallonia, German-speaking district, Flanders (except the cantons of Hal-Vilvorde) and Brussels-Hal-Vilvorde. Brussels and Hal-Vilvorde's voters can vote either for a French-speaking list, or a Flemish one. The seats distribution between colleges is realised proportionally to the number of inhabitants revised every ten years according to the results of the decennial census. Due to the enlargement to ten member states, the number of Belgian MEPs is 24: 14 to be elected in the Flemish college, 9 in the French-speaking one and 1 in the German-speaking one. The voters decide in the context of a semi-open list. The citizens have two valid voting patterns. They can choose the list following its presentation order (top box vote). They can also choose to vote for one or several candidates – of the same list (vote of preference). The seats distribution within the list operates then from an electoral coefficient to reach from the first on the list until the last, and the lists must have an equal representation of both sides.

Some key figureheads

The preparation of Belgian European elections is marked by the choice by political parties to place on top of the list some key figures who are not (necessarily) destined to sit in Strasbourg: that was the case of Leo Tindemans, Prime Minister until 1978, in June 1979; of Karel Van Miert, president of the Flemish Socialists, in June 1984 etc. The 2004 election certainly went furthest in this regard. In Flanders, the liberal list was led by Prime Minister Guy Verhofstadt whereas the Christian Democrat one was led by his predecessor Jean-Luc Dehaene. In the French-speaking area, the Socialist Party list was led by its president Elio di Rupo and the liberals list by Minister of Foreign Affairs Louis Michel. The process takes place within a double logic. The first aims at maximising as much as possible the party's results. The second one is connected to the permanent need to estimate its popularity and to highlight its role in Belgian political life.

Analysis of electoral results

In Belgium, European elections tend to conform to the observations that Karl Heinz Reif and Hermann Schmitt (1980) made after the 1979 and 1984 votes, in that they are of a 'second-order' nature. Politicians, the media and the population alike have always shown limited interest in these electoral contests. In particular, the European issue has rarely generated striking and visible conflicts between parties, and no party has yet chosen to distance itself from its competitors in terms of its European preferences. Only the E-non list that was present at the first European poll in 1979 ever chose to campaign on European issues rather than traditional national stakes. Very left-wing, it was hostile to the European project as a whole. It gathered 1 per cent of the votes and was short-lived.

One other list was put forward in European elections: the Debout list. Part of the French-speaking college, it is led by the former leader of the Union Delegation of the FGTB of the Forges de Clabecq, Roberto d'Orozio. Actually, it is broadly led by the Labour Party (the Maoist PTB), which indeed does not put forward a specific list. Incidentally, its line does rest wholly on the theme of Europe.

What about the results? They very much follow the logic of internal political life and the dynamics of sanction towards the current government, that frequently exist in European elections (Table 3). But this dimension has been partially modified since 1999, when the regional elections took place. Beyond the results of linguistic colleges, the observation of the evolution of the political groups' results in European elections confirms the political reality at the national level: there is no longer any dominant political group. Now, the historical groups – liberal, socialist and Christian democrat – record relatively similar results; in the case in point, slightly less than 25 per cent of the votes. In contrast, the combined results of the two extreme-right parties make Belgium one of the nations where the proportion of extreme-right voters is highest.

Pascal Delwit

Table 3 The results of the political groups in Belgium in European elections (1979–2004) (%)

	1979	1984	1989	1994	1999	2004
Liberals	16.26	18.09	17.78	20.58	23.76	24.04
Christian Democrats	37.73	27.42	29.22	24.23	18.78	23.35
Socialists	23.42	30.44	26.91	22.40	18.50	24.66
Extreme right	0.64	1.28	4.09	11.44	10.91	17.55
Greens	3.41	8.17	13.86	11.61	16.00	8.70
Extreme left	4.23	2.73	1.22	1.86	1.51	0.99
Volksunie	5.96	8.47	5.39	4.39	7.57	
FDF-RW	7.62	2.50	1.46	0.00	0.00	

Bibliography

Reif, K. and Schmitt, H., 'Nine Second-Order National Elections: a Conceptual Framework for the Analysis of European Elections Results', *European Journal of Political Research*, 8, 1, 1980, pp. 3–44.

→ Mapping Europe: European Electoral Geography.

Brussels

Along with 18 'communes', Brussels constitutes the federal entity known as the 'Brussels-Capital' region (161 km; 999 899 inhabitants). A bilingual city and region, Brussels serves as the capital of Belgium with its federal entities, as well as the seat of some international organisations (e.g. NATO) and of some of the European Union's key institutions. In journalistic jargon, the term 'Brussels' is now even used perjoratively in reference to the actions of the European Commission. However, this association is only partially correct, given the functioning of EU institutions.

Brussels could have undoubtedly become the headquarters of the ECSC's High Authority since its original creation had the Belgian government not supported Liège's candidature at the time. European heads of states confirmed their choice of Brussels, Luxembourg and Strasbourg as their interim working places in 1956. Brussels was consequently chosen to be the EU's provisional headquarters by the European Parliament on 23 June 1958. It was not until the Edinburgh Summit of 1992 that a declaration confirmed the official appointment of these cities. Member states also agreed at the Treaty of Nice (2001) that all European Council meetings would be held in Brussels.

European Council summits allow heads of states to meet to define Europe's future orientations. The Council shares legislative and budgetary powers with the European Parliament. It is composed of ministers representing all the member states to discuss current issues. As mentioned, this institution's headquarters are located in Brussels' 'Juste Lipse', across the street from the 'Berlaymont' building where the Commission will be moving shortly. The Commission is accountable to the EP, and is responsible for upholding European interests by preparing regulations and directives. Its administration comprises 36 directory general and services. Finally, EP exceptional sessions and committee meetings are also held in Brussels.

The Council and the Commission are

also able to consult with two other institutions based in Brussels: ECOSOC and the Committee of the Regions. The first includes representatives of the economic and social worlds, while the latter comprises delegates representing regional and local authorities.

The presence of European and international institutions has turned Brussels into a particularly attractive city in which diplomatic delegations, journalists and lobbies are based. Moreover, many multinational companies have chosen to open their head offices in Brussels due to the presence of EU decision-making mechanisms.

A resolution of the European Parliamentary Assembly dating from 1958 refers to its members' wish to regroup the institutions of the three communities (ECSC, EEC and Euratom) in one unique location. While lacking specific details, such a resolution even explores the possibility of turning this location into a European district. Probably inspired by the District of Columbia or other federal constituencies, this project was relaunched in the 1990s, although it seemed more concerned with the elimination of the so-called 'Brussels issue' than with the construction of a European capital. Brussels' bilingual status often provokes a rift between the Belgian French and Flemish-speaking sides. Despite early plans to regroup the EU's executive and legislative institutions in one city, the idea of an EU district appears to have been abandoned. MEPs who spend more time in Brussels than Strasbourg are also calling for the transfer of the EP to the Belgian capital, a move that would eliminate the annual expenditure of 200 million euros normally needed to move personnel and paperwork back and forth between the two cities.

The establishment of European institutions in Brussels has important socio-economic consequences. The balance of the 2003 EU budget determined by the Commission presents Belgium as a net contributing member. Nevertheless, when including expenses generated by the presence of EU institutions, Belgium becomes a net beneficiary (743 million euros or 33 per cent of total expenditures remain within Brussels). Of course, these profits should not mask important costs in terms of urban planning as well as the transformations undergone by the city to accommodate EU institutions. Moreover, the 48 buildings occupied by the EU in Brussels in 2001 are all exempt from real estate taxation. These buildings represent 11 per cent of the city's total office surface.

A socio-economic study conducted by the Brussels region in 2001 demonstrates that 60 per cent of the 21 182 'Eurocrats' working in Brussels are also official residents. With their families, they account for 3 per cent of the 19 communes' population. These families are mainly concentrated within five communes, a factor alerting observers to the possibility of a social divide. This fear is reinforced by Eurocrats' complaints, particularly about the lack of social diversity in European schools and nurseries, and the rising real estate prices. Finally, one must not forget the potential effect that 59 384 new European voters could have in local elections given the voting rights given to EU residents by the Maastricht Treaty.

Caroline van Wynsberghe

→ Citizen (EU); European Parliament; European Parliamentary Assembly; Interest Groups; Luxembourg; Strasbourg.

C

Campaign

(Sociology of)

To speak about an 'election campaign' in the singular when referring to European Parliament elections is an audacious choice. In many ways, the 2004 campaign, for example, is more reminiscent of a patchwork than of the fine tapestry of Aubusson. Across the 25 member states, European election campaigns appear to be lacking substance in comparison with national contexts, in which they develop a fuller meaning. It is for this reason that this article endeavours to show that European election campaigns are barely visible, because they are hindered by the 'asynchronism' of the polities involved, as well as by the lack of a common public space or public sphere needed to generate a shared sense of political obligation with the EU.

The untraceable European campaign

The appointment of national representatives to the European Parliament is an event which remains limited in several ways. European election campaigns are still lacking a common electoral system, a list of candidates representing comparable political structures, and even a symbolic common election day. More than 20 years ago, Bon had drawn our attention by asking the question 'what is a vote?' According to him, voting can be considered a form of 'secular ritual'. At election time, the citizen is given the chance to establish direct and temporary contact with those in power, and the election itself allows political language to reach a mythological level. More recently, Déloye has reminded us that the vote constitutes a 'moment of collective effervescence', expressed through the electoral ritual. It is clear that these characteristics hardly apply to European elections.

Expressions like 'a permissive consensus', often employed in the analysis of opinions regarding the European project, are symptomatic of this lack of involvement and thus of the absence of the symbolic dimension essential to the formation and the expression of a common identity through the electoral rite. If one adds to this overall deficiency, the low visibility of the European electoral agenda, the absence of common themes, the apparent predominance of national political stakes at the expense of European ones, the generally dispersed political offer, protest votes, as well as low levels of turnout, one understands why European elections have been called 'second-order elections' by Reif and Schmitt (1980). The question is raised differently by Charlot, who asks if is there such a thing as a European campaign or if we should talk of 25 national ones. In fact, Finchelstein (2004) underlined that virtually nothing gave the impression that the 2004 European Parliament elections were 'transnational': neither the constitution of the lists, nor the development of party programmes, nor the overall organisation of the campaign. The 2004 election even clearly demonstrated a resistance at the national level to candidates coming from another EU country. Consequently, the present article dwells on two points that seem to weigh heavily on the resistible nature of EP elections: the 'asynchronism' of polities, and 'centrifugal purpose' campaigns.

The 'asynchronism' of polities

A polity is a politically organised collective entity. The lack of a consolidated European public sphere is often observed. In the words of Jacques Delors, the EU still remains an 'unidentified political object'. While these observations are certainly relevant, one must not forget the importance of time in the ongoing process of consolidation and integration. More than 30 years ago, Germani (1972), had drawn people's attention to the importance of 'asynchronism' in social change. The enlargement of the EU clearly called for the radical transformation of social orders, which in turn led to a 'loss of integration' characterised by political alienation. It can be said that factors such as 'asychronism', coupled with the alienation of political obligations, played a role in shaping the campaigns for the 2004 election.

This 'asynchronism' has developed at numerous levels. Electoral sociology draws a distinction between 'exchange votes', 'community votes' and 'opinion votes', which perceive transaction, belonging and beliefs as the basis of electoral behaviour. Needless to say, the 25 EU countries have, in this respect, various dominant practices. Electoral campaigns organised in different countries vary in terms of their historical configurations, formed by social and political structures as well as institutional mechanisms. Poland, Spain and the Czech Republic constitute, *inter alia*, good examples of situations where regional differences are felt. Similarly, one could find elements of 'asynchronism' among polities according to the intensity of their 'reflection', 'reflex' and 'reflected' votes. This trilogy distinguishes between electoral behaviours without social and political non-alignments and the individualisation of the vote. In fact, across the 25 member states, the press, television and political parties with consociational structures are still far from presenting the same supervisory powers of information or social organisation. In this respect, it is paradoxical that abstention levels are particularly high in Scandinavia, usually characterised by high degrees of 'awareness' (Milner 2004; Schemeil 2001) and in Central European countries, where the means of information are relatively weak compared to southern European states.

The type of representative government of the different member states is a third crucial cause of 'asynchronism'. The practices of communication and information vary from one national sphere to another. For example, eight of the 25 countries prohibit or limit the publication of pre-electoral surveys. They are Cyprus, Spain, Greece, Hungary, Italy, Luxembourg, the Czech Republic and Slovenia. In addition, access to television for election campaigns varies significantly (Table 1). Many countries have access to a mixed system, while others like France rely exclusively on public television services for the campaign.

It should be specified that certain restrictions on paying for access in certain mixed and digital systems still exist: in Denmark and the Netherlands, paying for advertisements is possible exclusively on local stations (a); in Sweden, satellite television is opened to advertisements prohibited on terrestrial channels, like any official campaign (b); in Spain, Finland and Germany, electoral advertisement is only permitted on private channels (c); in Poland, electoral committees can purchase limited

Table 1   Country division of TV access costs at election time

Free and subscription TV access	Mixed and restrictive system	Only free access to TV
Austria	Germany (c)	Belgium
Greece	Denmark (a)	France
Italy	Spain (c)	Ireland
	Finland (c)	UK
	Hungary (e)	
	Netherlands (a)	
	Poland (d)	
	Sweden (b)	

Source: Gerstlé (2004: 77). For notes a, b, c, d, e, see main text.

commercial time only (d); finally, in Hungary, all political advertising is classified as 'paying electoral advertising' (e). At the same time, in the United Kingdom, free access is guaranteed not only by the BBC but also by private broadcasters. It is clear that the process of harmonisation in this field is far from complete, and still faces very complex issues.

'Centrifugal purpose' campaigns

In many ways, individual national campaigns produce 'centrifugal effects' which slow down the process of integration. However, as underlined by Germani (1972), these changes also allow for a greater legitimisation of this process, while offering concrete possibilities for action to increasingly mobilised groups of participants. In all countries, campaign practices indicate the efforts of the mobilisation to gather votes under the constraint of the legal framework of competition.

Candidate practices are based on social and political preconceptions used to achieve greater levels of political impact and control. Distinguishing between the candidates' tactical interdependence and the effect of their messages' interaction, we define election campaigns as a dynamics characterised by the symbolic composition in which the media and the public take part. In other words, election campaigns can be seen as a process of interaction between strategic interpretations of a political situation intended to influence its collective definition (Gerstlé 2004). With respect to European Parliament elections, the key question revolves around the definition of community. Which community does one refer to? Given the current degree of 'asynchronism', do voters have the same notion of community when casting their ballot?

Given the diverse nature of national political spaces, different cleavages prevail in different member states. For the same reason, electoral offers vary according to the relative degree of participation of actors such as the media, citizens and political entrepreneurs. This relationship is confirmed by the deficit of European electoral agenda, and the diversity of issues focused on by national campaigns. The motto 'unity in diversity' adopted in 2000 is currently far from being achieved. Unity has also not been achieved in terms of a European electoral campaign if one considers criteria such as visibility and legibility, indicating varying degrees of satisfaction in different territories. Discrepancies in campaign size and volume are widespread across EU countries and greatly affect its visibility and importance in the eyes of citizens. It has been shown that the degree of visibility in terms of television coverage given to the 1999 campaign was twice as weak as that of 1994. The visibility of the campaign was slightly higher in 2004. However, the overall airtime devoted by television news programmes to the European election campaign has decreased by 37 per cent over the last decade. In France alone, during the ten weeks preceding regional and EP elections the two major television news programmes devoted more time to the coverage of regional elections (508 minutes) than to the European elections (322). This is an explicit measure of these campaigns' visibility (Table 2).

Over the course of ten weeks, the two major French television stations did not even devote one hour of airtime to exclusive coverage of European affairs. In fact, they both chose to focus on the ongoing electoral competition (Gerstlé et al. 2005). Moreover, the French

legislative election campaign of 1997 received five times more media coverage than the 1999 EP elections. It is worth noting that these figures do not necessarily indicate a progressive deterioration of European communication and information. For a long time, politicians and the media have been using the European elections as a testing ground for the validity of candidates, speeches and campaign resources. Moreover, another reason for the limited coverage of the 1999 European election campaign is perceived to be the war in Kosovo, which overshadowed EP elections until two weeks before the poll. It is therefore clear that an authentic European campaign coverage was eclipsed both by national and international factors. This explains why the emergence of a clear European electoral conscience remains 'in progress'.

National political actors often choose to either discourage electoral mobilisation or to nationalise European elections to further internal political goals such as reprimanding the ruling government. This overshadows the European nature of elections, affecting their legitimacy and importance in the eyes of the people. The situation is unlikely

Table 2   Levels of visibility in TV news

TF1 (private channel)	France 2 (public channel)
5/11 April: 25 seconds	5/11 April: 1 minute 39 seconds
12/18 April: 10 seconds	12/18 April: 16 seconds
19/25 April: 0	19/25 April: 0
26 April/2 May: 6 minutes 19 seconds	26 April/2 May: 4 minutes 24 seconds
3/9 May: 1 minute 8 seconds	3/9 May: 2 minutes 9 seconds
10/16 May: 37 seconds	10/16 May: 3 minutes 36 seconds
17/23 May: 0	17/23 May: 10 seconds
24/30 May: 5 minutes 8 seconds	24/30 May: 40 seconds
31 May/6 June: 8 minutes 33 seconds	31 May/6 June: 55 seconds
7 June/12 June: 15 minutes 36 seconds	7 June/12 June: 3 minutes 36 seconds
Total: 37 minutes 56 seconds	**Total: 17 minutes 25 seconds**

to change for as long as political entrepreneurs continue to perceive the EU as an order with uncertain powers, limits and interests, and keep European elections under national control. The Europeanisation of EP election campaigns will remain impeded until it stops clashing with the internal instrumentalisation of European matters.

Jacques Gerstlé

Bibliography

Germani, G. *Politique, société et modernisation*, Gembloux, Duculot, 1972 (1st edition 1971).

Gerstlé, J., *La communication politique*, Paris, A. Colin, 2004.

Gerstlé, J., Neumayer, L. and Colomé, G., 'Les campagnes électorales européennes ou l'obligation politique relâchée', in P. Perrineau and H. D. Klingemann (eds), *Le vote des Vingt-Cinq*, Paris, Presses de Sciences Po, 2005.

Milner, H., *La compétence civique*, Laval, Presses de l'Université de Laval, 2004.

Reif, K. and Schmitt, H., 'Nine Second-Order National Elections: a Conceptual Framework for the Analysis of European Elections Results', *European Journal of Political Research*, 8, 1, 1980, pp. 3–44.

Schemeil, Y., 'Information et compétence politique: Les bois mystérieux de l'Europe du Nord', in J. Gerstlé (ed.), *Les effets d'information*, Paris, L'Harmattan, 2001, pp. 323–43.

Vreese, Claes H. de and Semetko, Holli A., *Political Campaigning in Referendums: Framing the Referendum Issue*, New York, Routledge, 2004.

→ Abstention; Campaign Accounts; Citizen (EU); Communication; Electoral Operations; European Elections (1979–1999); European Elections (2004); European Electoral Act; European Public Sphere; Euroscepticism; Financing; Identity; Issues; Luxembourg; Nationalisation of European Elections; Protest Voting; Right to Vote; Second-Order Elections; Symbolism; Symbols and Practice of Elections.

Campaign Accounts

The recording of specific accounts undoubtedly comprises one of the most important measures for the financial control of electoral campaigns. But it is also one of the most obscure. Not only because the accounting rules for these largely obscure inventories are predominantly handled behind closed doors at party headquarters, but also because the explicitly technical nature manages to deter any general attention or interest. Yet to scratch beneath this surface reveals a whole new face to party politics. Loan liabilities, real estate, regional and local branch transfers, donation sources, subscriptions and various fees, room hire costs, permanent staff salaries, poster printing, credits, investments: these budgetary lines reveal a particular breed of organisation that can be observed as an economic business specialised in electoral canvassing. There is some truth in Weber's contention that modern parties are the political equivalent of a capitalistic enterprise. Moreover, they are occasionally praised for having a 'transparent system of economic management' (Article 16 of the 1996 Act in Greece). However, what do the 'products' necessarily constitute? State aids, annual membership subscriptions, special contributions (in regards to MPs and also supplementary donations from supporters), profits generated from commercial undertakings, financial proceeds, loans, 'gifts' and interest from fund transfers. With regards to 'overheads', these consist of rents, staff-related expenditure, advertising, and electoral expenses. Income, overheads and profits all become objective in accounting terms, like a firm focused on conquering votes and managing mandates. Recent examples, for example in the UK and France, show that despite the technical nature of the rules on party and campaign financing, how parties obtain and use money becomes an extremely sensitive question, particularly if the media choose to focus their attention on it.

For several years, there has been a generalisation of the use of such accounts. The public financing of political parties has enforced the recording of annual activity accounts almost everywhere. In Belgium, the parties which benefit from parliamentary funding are obliged to submit their accounts to a particular Commission for approval. This body is responsible for the control of electoral expenses and accounting practices of political parties, and is able to draw on the expertise of the Audit Office to check the accuracy and comprehensiveness of the records. The obligations are similar in France for the legislative elections, with the National Commission for Campaign Accounts and Political Financing (CCFP) which acts an 'independent administrative authority'. This particular body is composed of nine members each appointed for five years, who are magistrates recruited from the National Audit Office, the court of cassation and the Council of State. Lacking any investigatory powers, the principal function of the CCFP is to publish simplified versions of the accounts and to present an activity report every other year. Elsewhere (Germany, Italy), a parliamentary committee, composed of MPs from different political parties and presided over by the President of the Chamber, is responsible for auditing the accounts and certifying their compliance with the law. Alternatively, a further possible arrangement is with a specialised court, like the Tribunal of Cuentas in Spain or the Constitutional Court in Portugal. Since campaign expenditure is regulated at the national level, expenditure for European elections is subject to the same checks and balances.

The fear of sanctions related to this public account keeping should not be overstated. Litigation is rare and, excluding a few specific countries, sentences are limited to modest fines. The major risk lies with the loss of grants. The drafting of these financial accounts directly impacts on the maintenance of future public subsidies. In Belgium, in the event of approval being refused, for example if there is an absence or delay in submission, the subsidy will not be granted for the whole duration of the subsequent period (which lasts for at least a month but not exceeding four months). The sanctions induced by the breach of the legal obligations corresponding to these financing arrangements are considerably harsher. In Germany, any party which fails to meet the required deadline for submission of financial accounts will definitively lose the right to access subsidies. If, by 31 December of the following year the party has yet to submit its overdue accounting reports, it also permanently loses its share of the 'votes'. In Portugal, for the same offence, political parties are liable to pay a fine ranging from ten basic national monthly wages to a maximum of 400 basic national monthly wages.

However, the real threat lies with the unwanted publicity that can be attracted from certain fund transfers. Since the administrative party bodies are competing teams, be it internally (promotion scales) or externally (the partisan system), they are reluctant to state the source or the destination of their resources and assets. Nonetheless, this is precisely what they are obliged to do. In Portugal, bank statements, credit card receipts, takings from the collection of funds all have to be appropriated to the parties' accounts. In Greece, every party is required to publish their accounts in two Athens newspapers within the first two months of each year. In addition, a copy of the financial accounts, along with copies of the two newspapers in which they have been published, must be sent to a parliamentary control committee and then to the Home Office. In Italy, a report on the annual financial transactions must be drafted and the accounts published in the *Gazzetta Officiale*. Nevertheless, publication of the list of donors is not required, who can remain anonymous. In Germany, the financial accounts must be regulated by an independent service (auditor, audit firm or, in exceptional terms, chartered accountant). Once certified, the accounts are then transmitted to the President of the Bundestag, who publishes it in the *Bundestags-Drucksache*.

It is therefore necessary to know how to present sensitive information, how to manipulate the rules yet simultaneously have the semblance of adhering to them. The art becomes a form of science when the obligations of publicity begin to mushroom, as is the case in Germany. Exposure then becomes as sophisticated as concealment, always generating an element of risk but with serious repercussions. Falsifying the source or the destination of the resources, taking every measure to disguise the relative indications concerning the receipts and party capital, omitting to include a donation within the shortest of delays are all now punishable by prison sentences of up to three years. In France, where public financing is subject to some of the heaviest duties, the drafting of an exhaustive list of all the donations and fees by officeholders in excess of 10 000 euros per year for example, is a relentless source of unease. Despite being secretive or otherwise prohibited in other countries, transactions from 'big donors' must be publicly declared in France, outlining the names and addresses of the donor, as well as the total sum of donations. This obligation is sanctioned, so if the donor cannot be identified or if the donations

turn out to have been granted in exchange for or prior to a 'favour', the party in question will be asked to forfeit three times the amount of money which was irregularly obtained.

Such an arrangement is still unique within the EU, but useful insofar as it reveals what the partitocratic model of financing encompasses: in order to make political parties, at least relatively, autonomous, there remains a significant level of suspicion surrounding donations from big industrial groups (or 'corporate money'). With the aim of neutralising the threat of plutocratic deviations, party financing in Europe has been brought under state control and thus serves to reinforce the professionalisation of political parties. Notably it has encouraged them to create internal supervisory and controlling bodies: in brief, to expand their accounting and legal teams, who are now professional accounting managers, for an electoral competition that has become as much a financial battle as a political competition.

Olivier Ihl

Bibliography

Lehmann, W. and Coman, R., *Statut et financement des partis politiques européens*, Luxembourg, European Parliament (Direction Générale des Études), Série Affaires constitutionnelles, AFCO 105 FR12 2003, 2003.

Nassmacher, K.-H., 'Parteienfinanzierung in Deutschland', in O. W. Gabriel, O. Niedermayer and R. Stöss (eds), *Parteiendemokratie in Deutschland*, Opladen, Westdeutscher Verlag, 1997, pp. 157–76.

Pujas, V. and Rhodes, M., 'Party Finance and Political Scandal in Italy, Spain and France', *West European Politics*, 22, 3, 1999, pp. 41–63.

Tsatsos, D (ed.), *Parteienfinanzierung im europäischen Vergleich: Die Finanzierung der politischen Parteien in den Staaten der*

Europäischen Gemeinschaft, Baden-Baden, Nomos, 1992.

➜ Campaign (Sociology of); Financing.

Citizen (EU)

The work which went into the revisions of the treaties initiated in Maastricht (1992) and followed by Amsterdam (1997) then Nice (2001), up until the text of the treaty establishing a Constitution for Europe signed on 29 October 2004 in Rome is significant for two reasons. Firstly, it marks the progressive switch from an economic Europe towards a political union. Secondly, it promotes provisions relating to European citizenship, acting as the engine and symbol for both dynamics. The invention of Union citizenship thus inaugurated a new stage in the chronology of the traditional rights of citizenship. In consideration of the original principle of non-discrimination which binds the member states of the EU together, this notion outlines the logic of a 'legal Community' by establishing the status of the individual within the European Union. In so doing, it effectively outlines the contours around the democratic space specific to the European Union through the application of conferred political rights. Indeed, and for this reason, since 1992, any citizen of the Union can vote and stand for both the European and local elections in the member state where he or she is resident, subject to the same conditions as host country nationals (Article 19 TEC).

If Union citizenship was indeed steeped, in the European treaties, in a comprehensive set of democratic virtues, from a factual perspective, it would seem to engender a more problematic mode of functioning, in particular in that it represents a rival tool between the European institutions (Parliament versus Commission), an intolerable objective for certain governments, and an unidentifiable entity for the citizens (Strudel 2003). Its conceptualisation has even been the target of the most severe criticisms as being divided and incomplete on the one hand (Lochak 1991; Balibar 2001), and contradictory on the other hand. This is attributed to the location of a state-centred model of citizenship within the Union, which ultimately denies the state-centric attributes. There has been an early abundance of analysis surrounding European citizenship at both the legal and then the philosophical levels. However, in terms of political science, this field remains relatively untouched by electoral behaviour specialists, which stands in contrast to the theoretical (Leca 1992; Déloye 1998) and institutional approaches (Wihtol de Wenden 1997; Magnette 1999). This imbalance serves to provide a hydrocephalic structure with an academic output which reveals much about the abstract notion of citizenship but ultimately sheds little light on its political reception amongst 'ordinary' citizens. In short, between incantation and incarnation, the principle of realism is dominant. Although imposed 'from above' and constructed by law, if it can also be observed 'from below', does this necessarily signify that European citizenship can command a level of consistency? Is it possible for European citizenship to assume the role of the magical exhilarator of citizens' enthusiasm towards European integration, or is it little more than 'a rather cynical public relations exercise'? More robustly, to what extent can the creation of the category 'voters and eligible Communities' – considered here within the prism of European elections and over ten years following its initial implementation – actually contribute to the process of European integration?

The rights of EU voters: the limits of European convergence

From the first and careful suggestions projected during the Paris Summit in October 1972 until the final texts (treaty and directives), including the letter from the Spanish Prime Minister Felipe Gonzales addressed to the Irish presidency in May 1990, European citizenship has been considered a prospect of considerable institutional reform. In terms of its concrete expression, the political rights component of EU citizens crystallises a level of mistrust and resistance felt amongst a majority of member states, and particularly concerning the points relating to the right of participation in local political life in the country of residence. Indeed, when they have occurred, the constitutional disagreements focused on municipal voting rights which were considered as an open breach notably of the French conception surrounding the indivisible nature of national sovereignty, access to the exercise of public authority, or potential threat towards occasionally fragile electoral balances. Thus, the consequence was the forsaking of the 'second-order' stakes of a rather apathetic election with regard to public opinion and the perception of the European Parliament as being on the outside in relation to national constitutional systems.

Indeed the analysis, being reflective of the conditions of the implementation of the directives laying down the methods of the exercise and eligibility of voting rights (Europe 93/109/EC; local 94/80/EC then 96/30/EC), reveals a striking contrast, with at least one point in common. Indeed, as far as possible, they avoid any interference in the remit of electoral rights of the member states, and systematically refer to the respective national legislations to secure a definition of the criteria of exercise of civic rights. These directives remind us that they 'do not suppose a harmonisation of the electoral systems of member states', thus undermining the objective of European citizenship. In other words, the display of a common electoral procedure and the promotion of a European electorate are compatible with national procedures which organise voting processes. This striking contrast is accounted for by an asymmetrical installation of these political rights. Although what concerns the European Parliament elections has found a rapid and easy implementation, the directive on local elections is careful in its wording (Strudel 2003). It provides for conditions and exemptions, including the exclusion of access to certain elective functions of eligible EU citizens, limits to the EU population (20 per cent of the potential electorate), conditions of minimal residency and clauses of composition of the electoral rolls, etc.

In accordance with Article 17 of Directive 93/109/EC, member states were obliged to adopt the national measures of implementation into national law by 1 February 1994. Contrary to the staggered and sometimes belated implementation of the directive laying down the terms for voting rights and eligibility at local elections, the member states adopted the national measures of transposition for this directive within the given time constraints and urgency of the European elections scheduled in June 1994. In France, it was achieved through national law with the law no. 94–104 of 5 February 1994 (JORF of 8 February 1994) and the application decree no. 94–206 of 10 March 1994 (JORF of 12 March 1994), in preparation for the European elections on 12 June 1994. After the enlargement in 1995, the three new member states were required to adopt the necessary provisions by 1996 at the latest and in response managed to apply them in time for their first European elections (17 September 1995 in Sweden, and 13 October and 20 October 1996 in Austria and Finland, respectively). A transposition case which was difficult to manage arose in 2005. In the run-up to a satisfying conclusion of accession negotiations in December 2002, the European Union honoured its engagement in accordance with granting the ten candidate countries the privilege of participating in the European Parliament elections in 2004. With the date of official accession fixed at 1 May 2004, and the ballot for the European Parliament elections scheduled from 10–13 June 2004, it was thus very tight in terms of timing, implying that the procedural terms in preparation for the elections were actually implemented before the official accession date, as pointed out by the Commission. In practical terms, this assumed that the ten applicant countries would transpose the Directive before accession and for 11 of the 15 member states (the four remaining being Spain, Sweden, Germany and Ireland) would revise the deadlines for electoral registration, so that virtually a million European voters could enjoy their new rights in reality.

In short, electoral procedures, calendars and regulations all fall within the competence of the member states whereby the transpositions are subject to the diversity of the national laws governing the elections. Certain member states grant their nationals residing in another member state the right to participate in the elections in their country of origin, whilst others do not. These votes can be undertaken by proxy, correspondence or in the consulates and the embassies. The minimal age for eligibility ranges from 18, 19, 21 and 23 years; parties, political associations or outgoing MPs are all able to present candidate lists, with or without support from the electorate. Situated at the heart of the political project to recast the foundations of the Union,

European citizenship also bears tensions and reveals inherent contradictions. Certainly by no means does the principle of equal treatment equalise the conditions existing between states, especially given that standardisation 'from above' with common principles enforces specific rules. Each country adopts and adapts its own pace whereby Europeanisation is but limited and remains attached to strong nationalisation impulses.

Voters and eligible EU members: ambiguous practices

If the incantation of European citizenship remains a topic of choice for commenting on the democratic ambitions of the political union, its incarnation by the member states raises, as recently witnessed, a rather provocative and divisive line of questioning. However, what about the other side of the coin, i.e. the opinions held by the citizens themselves? What is actually known about the implementation of voting rights granted to the Union citizens in practice? If the principles are quite detached from the texts, the meaning is just as convoluted from the texts to the practices.

The levels of electoral registration for the European elections in June 1994, June 1999 and June 2004 provide some statistical elements to measure the uptake of new electoral rights as used by the EU migrants and to draw up a first assessment of it, extending beyond the French example to the European level as well. In 2004, there were an estimated 5.7 million non-national EU citizens able to vote in their country of residence, out of a potential 338 million voters across the 25 member states. Of this figure, around 12–15 per cent had registered to vote in their country of residence. Comparatively speaking, this opportunity had only been utilised by

9 per cent of this potential electorate in 1999, that is to say a very marginal increase from the 6 per cent in 1994 (including 1995 and 1996, for the three new member states). Evidently, on the one hand, the aforementioned figures do not include those Union citizens who returned to vote in their country of origin, voted in embassies or consulates or by proxy for their national candidates in their own country. In addition, they relate only to registered voters (and not to actual voters), because except for compulsory voting in Greece, Belgium and Luxembourg, it is impossible at the European level to quantify the level of effective participation: either EU residents are reproduced on the same lists as the nationals without particular mention to draw attention to them (thus making them visible and recordable), or the national rules for the electoral codes prohibit or limit the dissemination of the electoral lists. These more than mitigated results are accompanied by considerable variations in registration rates depending on the countries at hand; for example in Ireland, where non-nationals have been eligible to vote in European elections since 1979, 44 per cent are registered which is in sharp contrast to Greece where less than 2 per cent are registered. Turning to eligibility to stand in elections, in 1994, out of 53 non-national candidates in the Union (including five in France), only one non-national candidate managed to be elected in their country of residence – Mrs Wilmya Zimmermann, a Dutch national who resides in Germany. In 1999, the number of non-national candidates and elected officials on the electoral lists of a member state remained very low with only 62 non-nationals standing as candidates on lists in their country of residence, of which four were successfully elected (two in Belgium, one in France and one in Italy).

France is located in the lower echelon with a registration rate of 3.8 per cent (equivalent to 47 632) registered voters out of 1 250 049 potential voters in 1994. In June 1999, less than 6 per cent of European citizens chose to register for the election in France (equivalent to 72 399 people out of 1 224 492), which marks but a weak progression over a five-year period. In 2004, this changed as the number of registered voters doubled, reaching 147 534 (the total from the 15, including the registered voters from the ten new member states was between 120 and 150 but still subject to contrasting statistics between the Home Office or the INSEE), equivalent to a registration rate of 12.5 per cent, which represents a real progress compared to the preceding election. The nationalities who have the highest level of electoral registration remain, since 1994, the Belgians, the Dutch, the British and the Luxembourgers (all with registration levels over 21 per cent), and in contrast the least registered are the Spanish and Portuguese who consistently have the lowest level (with registration levels below 11 per cent). From the outset, it is notable that the nationals of the two countries – Spain and Portugal – who both have a particularly historic immigration trend to France tend to be have a lower rate of registration, which leaves room for reflection with regard to the implications for political integration. Current qualitative analysis attempts to understand, in greater detail, these national differences at play concerning the levels of registration amongst citizens in the Union.

European nationals are not only voters but are also eligible to stand for elections. Thus, in 1999, out of the eight non-national EU candidates who stood for election, only one succeeded in being elected in France (Franco-German Daniel Cohn-Bendit on the Greens list). This total remained the same in 2004. Ari Vatanen, a former Finnish pilot and outgoing European MEP was the only non-French candidate eligible to stand, and was second on the UMP list in the South-East region. His selection was essentially imposed from above, under the impulse of Michel Barnier and with presidential support, and was highly criticised by the local ranks. Other transnational candidatures failed to generate support from political parties: a Polish candidate in the East and a German standing in the South-West for the Greens, a Portuguese in central Paris and a Spanish in the South-West for the Communist Party, a local representative of British nationality in the Centre and an exchange – albeit unsuccessful – to place the outgoing European MEP Olivier Duhamel from the Spanish PSOE list to the Socialist Party, and finally four non-national candidates for the UDF, including the coach of Nice football club, the Franco-German Gernot Rohr, in the South-West region. In order to circumvent any resistance from political parties, Julian Nundy, a Franco-British journalist, created a non-profit organisation called 'Europeans in France' which aimed to promote non-national candidatures and was eventually combined with the group Africagora which campaigns for the promotion of the ethnic minorities. Their lists, *Diversity for Europe*, will hence be present in two constituencies (the Ile-de-France and the South-East). Certainly the new electoral methods were by no means conducive as for those constituencies in support of partisan logics and the local weighting of electoral lists, these lists became rather problematic, between the supporters of parity, local party executives, immigrant communities, European nationals, and even civil society representatives.

It would indeed seem possible to observe a phenomenon during the time of the local elections in 2001 (Strudel 2004) concerning 'the correct use' of the foreign candidatures on the lists, since they are coupled with possible compliance of rules relating to parity. In explicit terms, if one is going to be the average European, one might as well be the she-average European. However, far from mobilising the electorate as a whole, should the low level of registration amongst European migrants during the European elections not be measured by the yardstick of an election? Over the years, European elections have failed to make a tangible impact on public opinion which is increasingly more indifferent. But why should one be surprised that it is not otherwise? The limited appeal of European elections, bound between others by their obvious national polarity, explicitly plays to the detriment of a European mobilisation and interest in elections which hardly feature in some elections.

In comparison, and whilst remaining overall half-hearted, the mobilisation of EU residents has succeeded in making an initial impact at the local level. During the local elections on 11 and 18 March 2001, the French Home Office had 166 122 non-French Europeans registered as living in France on the complementary electoral lists out of an overall total of over 1 200 000 (equivalent to a registration level of 13.8 per cent), in addition to 991 non-French European candidates out of 255 788 candidates of French nationality. The number of non-French European city councillors who are elected in districts of over 3500 inhabitants amounts to only 204 out of 83 445 (equivalent to 0.24 per cent). Breaking down this group by nationality in order of size, by far the largest nationality comprises the Portuguese (83), followed by the Italians (28), the Spanish (23), the Belgians (21), the Germans (17), the British (16) and further down the scale are the Dutch (8), the Swedish (3), the Irish (2), and finally, one Danish, one Greek and one Finnish. The allocation of these elected officials according to the size of the districts reinforces this weight of local proportionality and of close association. Paradoxically, municipal elections which hold a higher stake and have a direct bearing on daily life (education, transport, taxes, etc.) are more likely to give shape to the construction of a Union citizenship 'from below'. In the same vein, European nationals residing in Belgium constituted only 5 per cent of registered voters on electoral lists during the European elections in 1994 and subsequently 11.5 per cent in 2004, but it contrast rose to 17.6 per cent of the registered electorate during the local council elections in October 2000.

Thus, what is the impact over time in addition to a gradual familiarisation with new rights and/or mobilisations from below? Obviously it is too soon to judge and it is certainly likely that the two factors can complement each other. On the whole, the voting rights of European nationals are only a preliminary sketch of a real-life European citizenship since only those most integrated into the local life will exercise it. However, for some individuals, an element of discriminatory citizenship comes into play. Discriminatory insofar as a selection process is administered amongst foreigners, further excluding access and propensity to political participation for non-EU nationals (in particular foreigners from the former French colonies whose bonds with France and their local areas of residence are often much stronger and more established than with European citizens), a case in point projected by the associated immigrant rights movements and by certain political party policies. Ultimately, this raises a curious and fundamental paradox: those who are refused access to this right of participation are often more mobilised than those who are already granted access. A further helpful insight is that European citizenship plays in its political and electoral constituent a role in magnifying and reflecting the

tensions harboured in national democratic spaces. The use of the voting rights largely puts its impact into perspective, that being beyond the conventional declarations, practical experience is but limited. Between hesitations from citizens and procrastination by member states, the problematic construction of a new form of electoral participation illustrates the recurring discrepancy between theory and practice, remaining firmly rooted in the search for an effective political Union.

If the principle of non-discrimination in accordance with nationality can be regarded as one of the principal bases of the EU legal order, possession of EU nationality is correlatively set up with the opportunity to profit from the rights, and in particular from those relating to European citizenship. Consequently, the evident division between nationality and citizenship is an immediately recognisable smokescreen and which only marginally participates in the 'denationalisation' movement based on subjective rights (Magnette 1999). Rather, European citizenship leans heavily towards the side of the nationality of the member states, which retains the upper hand through retention of national rules attributed over the European aspects. Indeed, the attribution of the eligibility to vote and stand in elections, which is the most symbolic measurement of the rights of Union citizenship, is also subjected to polemic tensions. Considered in a rational frame of light, and in statistical terms, it is possible to qualify a negligible quantity. Notably, given that the population concerned represents less than 2 per cent of the total potential European electoral population and at its core less than 15 per cent of this group are actually registered EU voters. Thus in response to the current topical question which relates to the contribution of EU voters to the process of European integration through the mechanism of European elections, the answer is: 'minimal'. Political rights are conferred to Union citizens with great pomp and ceremony and justifiably credited to the search for European legitimacy in addition to the symbolic status of voting insofar as it affects the basis of our democratic systems, but transform in reality into a rather hushed reception, overlooked by many. Such a compelling concept currently produces only limited fulfilment. A substantial difference is visible between declarations of intent and limited and asymmetrical uses of conferred rights. However, is it true to say that the length of time required to form an observation – an assessment over ten years with only three elections – is sufficient to measure the consequences of an extension of voting rights? One of the fundamental points in political sociology underlines the length of time necessary for socialisation and voting familiarisation: witness the period (almost 30 years) required for French women to adapt to their more recently acquired voting rights and to match their level of electoral participation to equal that of the male electorate.

Sylvie Strudel

Bibliography

Balibar, E., *Nous, Citoyens d'Europe*, Paris, La Découverte, 2001.

Bruter, Michael, *Citizens of Europe? The Emergence of a Mass European Identity*, Basingstoke, Palgrave Macmillan, 2005.

Déloye, Y., 'De la citoyenneté stato-nationale à la citoyenneté européenne: quelques éléments de conceptualisation', *Revue suisse de science politique*, 4, 4, 1998, pp. 169–94.

Leca, J., 'Nationalité et citoyenneté dans l'Europe des immigrations', in Jacqueline Costa-Lascoux and Patrick Weil (eds), *Logiques d'Etats et immigrations*, Paris, Kimé, 1992, pp. 13–57.

Lochak, D., 'La citoyenneté: un concept juridique flou', in Dominique Colas, Claude Emeri and Jacques Zylberberg (eds), *Citoyenneté et nationalité: Perspectives en France et au Québec*, Paris, PUF, 1991, pp. 179–207.

Magnette, P., *La citoyenneté européenne*, Bruxelles, Editions de l'Université de Bruxelles, 1999. *Revue internationale de politique comparée*, dossier coordonné par Sylvie Strudel: 'Pratiques de la citoyenneté européenne', 9, 1, 2002.

Meehan, Elizabeth M., *Citizenship and the European Community*, London, Sage, 1993.

Strudel, S., 'Polyrythmie européenne: le droit de suffrage municipal des étrangers au sein de l'Union, une règle électorale entre détournements et retardements', *Revue française de science politique*, 53, 1, 2003, pp. 3–34.

Strudel, S., 'La participation des Portugais aux élections européennes et municipales en France', in A. Cordeiro (ed.), *Portugais de France, immigrés et citoyens d'Europe*, Paris, Fondation Gulbenkian et Cahiers de l'Urmis, 2004, pp. 69–76.

Wiener, Antje, *'European' Citizenship Practice: Building Institutions of a Non-State*, Boulder, Westview Press, 1998.

Wihtol de Wenden, C., *La citoyenneté européenne*, Paris, Presses de Sciences Po, 1997.

→ Multi-Level Governance.

Civil Society

Less and less put in quotation marks, sometimes followed by a question mark when concerning the transposition to a European level, often accompanied by the 'organised' epithet, the term 'civil society' is now part of the vocabulary of the EU. Observers and commentators of European integration, institutional agents and political and social actors all employ the term to represent, and often to salute, those who, outside of the

European institutions and the national authorities, participate – or should participate – in the European political system. The business world and humanitarian militants alike are thus united within this same group which imperceptibly replaces 'people'. Far from agreeing on its contents and contours, all call upon the civil society as a source of legitimacy for the institutions with which it has a dialogue and for the actors who claim to represent it.

Even if the expression has a long history, from Aristotle to the detractors of the state in the 1970s while passing through the Enlightenment, its use within the European Community dates from the mid-1990s, to the time when questions were raised concerning the legitimacy of Europe and its institutions and also relating to the place of the citizens in the EU. In this context, the concept of civil society enables both consideration of the role and the presence of interest groups in the development of Community policies and also provides for the existence of a European people who, failing to turn out to vote, could be represented through the action of representatives specialised in different economic and social fields. Along academic lines, in particular for those who consider 'European public sphere', the concept quickly finds its conditions of success under the effect of a double investment.

The first comes from the Community administrations. Within the European Commission, since the initiation of a civil debate in 1995 on the model of the European social dialogue with the two social partners in the DG V (responsible for employment and social affairs), attempts have been made to regulate this administrative practice of dialogue and consultation. From this viewpoint, various communications of the Commission (4 June 1997 on the 'promotion of the role of associations and foundations in Europe'; 18 January 2000 on 'the Commission and non-governmental organizations: reinforcement of the partnership'; 5 June 2002 'Towards a reinforced culture of consultation and dialogue') contributed to the institutionalisation of civil society as a 'European governance' actor, as defined in the 21 July 2001 *White Paper*. Similarly the European Economic and Social Committee, since 1996, under the impulse of a new Secretary-General (Patrick Venturini, ex-DG V) and of a new President (Beatrice Rangoni Machiavelli), launched a study on civil society which outlined that the EESC would be, if not the representative, then at least the institution acknowledging the rightful place of civil society in the process of European integration. Although broad, the definition provided in 1999 is still used as a reference for discussions concerning its contours, role and future. The European Parliament is also involved in this process of institutionalisation of civil society. The preparation for the Amsterdam Summit in 1997 provided an opportunity for a large flow of exchanges between the European Parliament's institutional committee and the representatives from civil rights organisations. For all these institutions, civil society is now part of the crucial actors to solicit, listen to and mention in any speech and political project. The Constitutional Treaty proceeds along these lines, specifying that 'the institutions of the Union shall maintain an open, transparent and regular dialogue with representative associations and civil society' (Article I-47-2).

As a counterpoint to this institutional investment and according to similar strategies, militant groups seize the concept in order to acquire and preserve a place in the European political system. They then try to realise – in the strong meaning of the term – a civil society by making it speak and act at the European level. The main example is the mobilisation led by the Permanent Forum of Civil Society. Established at the end of 1995 in order to contribute to the 1996 Intergovernmental Conference, this associative network, connecting over 130 organisations around the project of a 'more democratic and social Europe', is positioned as a spokesperson for European civil society. Its leaders not only establish the contents and the borders of the latter, through various actions intended to be implemented (demonstrations during European summits, organisation of the 'States General of civil society', drafting of texts and meetings with representatives of institutions), they provide visibility to this collective. In addition to these political entrepreneurs, often resulting from European movements pushing for a 'Europe closer to the citizens', other actors have contributed to the diffusion of the concept by integrating it in their vocabulary as being synonymous with interest groups, even as a happy substitute of a still rather fiendish term. Even if certain representatives of economic interests are still astonished to see themselves renamed as members of civil society, the majority readily take on this term associated with a group holding unanimously celebrated values. During the meetings with representatives of the European institutions, they do not hesitate to use this label which is supposed to secure them a favourable reception in accordance with the terms of general interest to which they contribute. As 'market forces', they are aware that some of their interlocutors exclude them from civil society, understood as the prerogative of organisations mobilised around stakes considered to be 'public', in opposition to the private interests which they defend. But they hope above all that 'the true' definition of civil society, constitutive of 'good governance', will gradually emerge.

The recurring invocations to civil society also generate certain paradoxical uses. Many MEPs indeed do not hesitate to claim to represent civil society during election campaigns and, sometimes, during their mandate. Against the 'political professionals' who would be too distant from those whom they claim to represent, this quality would constitute a necessary resource to make politics in the EU. Moreover, in accordance with this principle it is European civil servants, keen to challenge allegations relating to the technocracy of Brussels, who are eager to regularly engage with civil society by consulting with the different interest groups. Even MEPs, although democratically elected in each EU member state, make a point of maintaining regular contact with these representatives of economic and social interests. Certainly, the issue at hand concerns an economic means to obtain information and to take note of possibly related claims, but above all it concerns a means of increasing their legitimacy, always subject to caution. Thus, it can be believed that, from henceforth, it is civil society which is sovereign in Europe.

Hélène Michel

Bibliography

Boual J.-Cl. (ed.), *Vers une société civile européenne?*, La Tour d'Aigues, Editions de l'Aube, 1999.

Conseil économique et social européen, *La société civile organisée au niveau européen*, Actes de la première convention, Bruxelles, 15 and 16 October 1999.

Smismans, S., (ed.), *Civil Society and Legitimate European Governance*, Edward Elgar, 2005.

Vogel, J., 'Le Parlement européen face à l'émergence d'une société civile européenne', in P. Delwit, J.-M. de Waele and P. Magnette (eds), *À quoi sert le Parlement européen?*, Bruxelles, Complexe, 1999, pp. 199–219.

➜ Citizen (EU), Democratic Deficit; European Commission; European Constitution; European Parliament; Interest Groups; Lobbying; Members of the European Parliament (Legal and Political Status); Members of the European Parliament (Sociology of Political Office); Representation.

Cleavages

The term 'European cleavages' is neither simple nor uncontroversial. In this article, the term 'European' identifies those cleavages that directly pertain to the process and institutions of European integration. The term 'cleavage' is used in the general sense of divisions, divides or opposition. It therefore refers to implicit or latent cleavages not necessarily ideologically coherent and politically organised.

Two additional problems complicate dealing with 'European cleavages'. First, in national politics we usually identify cleavages in functional terms as opposing parties and voters, while territorial cleavages opposing sub-national territories independently from the parties are more rare. In the EU, territorial divisions in the form of interstate alliances and oppositions exist and they concern both the member states representatives in the intergovernmental institutions and processes (such as the Council and the Intergovernmental Conferences) as well as the Members of the European Parliament on issues cutting across the European party families.

The second problem concerns the content of those cleavages that we call 'European'. European cleavages can simply be defined in terms of 'pro' or 'against', of positive or negative 'general orientation' towards the EU as a project of territorial integration. Next to these general orientations there are more specific divisions that pertain to

'constitutive' or 'constitutional' features of the new polity: membership issues (who should be 'in', and which are the geographical and cultural boundaries of the Union), competencies issues (what should be done at the EU level as opposed to other levels of government), and decision-making rules issues (how collective decisions should be taken). Finally, European cleavages can also be identified as divisions on clusters of specific policies closely corresponding to the national cleavages (such as economic interventionism versus neo-liberalism, welfare, citizenship rights, immigration policy, law and order issues, etc.), which I therefore propose to label as 'isomorphic' divisions. To sum up, by European cleavage we may mean divisions concerning a general and a-specific orientation to the EU, more specific constitutive divisions concerning the nature of the polity, and even more specific isomorphic issues defining the nature of the policies. In a simplified way we can say that the first concern the legitimacy of the polity; the second concern the nature of the regime; and the third its specific policy output.

Combining the three key actors at the EU level (governments, parties, voters) with the three types of divisions (general orientation, constitutive and isomorphic) yields a complex matrix of possible cleavages and opposition lines concerning the EU as reported in Table 1. Given this complexity, considerable efforts have been made to simplify this picture and to identify the main alignments that underline the complex structure. Four main questions help to organise this debate and are the object of the next sections.

First, are European divisions on general orientations, constitutive issues and isomorphic issues salient enough to be a source of cleavage? Such issues are clearly salient for governmental elites. It

Table 1   European cleavages: actors and type of issues

		Agents		
		Voters	Parties/Groups	Territories/ Governments
Type of divisions	EU general orientations			
	EU constitutive issues			
	EU/National isomorphic issues			

is less clear whether they are salient for parties and particularly for voters.

Second, are the alignments that organise and structure national politics reflected in the divisions over EU general orientation, constitutive and isomorphic issues? This is crucial to understand whether European cleavages can slowly be adjusted to the national historical cleavages or whether they are more likely to cut across them.

Third, and closely related to the second question, how much do national and Euro-parties actually represent the preferences of their voters on EU general orientations, constitutive and isomorphic issues?

Finally, the answers to the previous three question lead to the fourth one: is there evidence and possibility for the politicisation of a new cleavage specifically reflecting orientations to the EU and integration?

Are European issues salient for the mass public?

Are the European integration issues sufficiently important in the mind of the public? In a temporal perspective the answer is unquestionably yes. Through ever more frequent ratification referendums, European direct elections, continuous debates about membership enlargement, wider publicity and media coverage of IGC, unexpected implications of EU legislation for everyday life, and the physical tangibleness of the single currency, the public opinion is now more directly involved in the integration process than was ever the case. This is indirectly witnessed by the fact that over time national political elites have been more and more busy convincing their domestic audience that the benefits of further integration are greater than the costs.

Contrary arguments suggest that, this notwithstanding, the level of information and competence about the EU and the treaties is insufficient to justify the claim of their direct significance for the development of European cleavages. The salience of integration issues is very low as referendums and second-order European elections are contaminated by popular feelings about the incumbent government, parties and leaders, and voters react on EU questions mostly on the basis of domestic issues and depending on the unity of their parties.

Moreover, listing the more widespread recent changes in European party systems one study concludes that none of them can plausibly be traced back to the direct impact of Europeanisation and that anti-EU parties tend to context only European elections and stay outside domestic politics.

However, one feels uncomfortable with this conclusion while charting the extent to which European issues have influenced the electoral politics of the 1990s. Single-issue anti-EU parties are significant only in Denmark, Germany and the UK, but explicit anti-EU positions are present in all member states via a number of parties. Green parties with a considerable anti-EU ideological component can be found in Austria, Finland, France, Ireland, Luxembourg, the Netherlands, Portugal, Sweden and the United Kingdom. Non-communist leftist parties with a similar orientation exist in Finland, Ireland, the Netherlands, and in Sweden. Communist parties with an explicit critical view of the integration process are present in France, Greece, Portugal and Germany, and to a lesser extent in Spain and Italy. Right-wing and nationalist parties expressing anti-EU feelings exist in Austria, Belgium, Denmark, France, Germany, Ireland and in Italy. One should add to this list some Protestant orthodox parties in Finland and the Netherlands. Among the core and established parties clear-cut anti-EU factions are more frequent in Northern Europe and particularly accentuated in Britain, in the Swedish Social Democrats and the Finnish Centre Party, to which one should probably add the Portuguese Centre Social Democrats and the Italian National Alliance. In those cases in which EU adhesion or Treaty ratification has been submitted to referendum (36 such referendums were held between 1972 and 2003) the impact of the EU issue dimension on the voters/parties relations has always been considerable,

with tensions and breaks particularly in France, Norway, Denmark, Finland, Sweden and Austria.

In the European post-war electoral history one can hardly identify any single theme with similar large and standardising effects across the European party system. Even allowing that the ideological bases of Euroscepticism are so widely diverging as to make very difficult any positive coalition or alliance, there remains sufficient evidence of a historical trend towards a growing salience of EU-related divisions.

Do party cleavages at the EU level correspond to or fit with the historical national cleavage alignments?

During the Cold War the EEC was generally supported by moderate and conservative forces and more or less vehemently opposed by the left. This made for a relatively good correspondence between national and European left–right divisions. More recently, many left parties have become supportive of integration, while a growing number of right-wing parties have become increasingly critical of it. Therefore, over time the correspondence between the left–right location and con versus pro EU has eroded. For this reason, recent work on the more or less favourable orientation to the EU of national parties has added to the left–right dimension a second dimension defining an authoritarian–libertarian cleavage, or a GAL (Green, Alternative, Libertarian) versus TAN (Traditional, Authoritarian, Nationalist) opposition. The TAN pole – nationalist, populist right-wing radical parties – identifies well the group of Eurosceptical parties. They champion national sovereignty, and favour at most an intergovernmental EU with retention of the national veto; they want to curb the power of the EP; they reject a centralist and bureaucratic European super-state; they want to restore the supremacy of national law over European law; they consistently forge connections between the threat to national identity, 'foreignisation' (*Uberfremdung*), immigrant criminality, political and social corruption; and they are in general opposed to enlargement to the countries of Eastern Europe. Conservative parties with a 'TAN inclination' present similar features although to a lesser extent.

This approach is less convincing when dealing with party families other than the TAN group. There remain still considerable variations within the social-democratic family. Within the denominational party family, most continental Catholic parties favour further integration, while Protestant parties are more reluctant to see positively what they sometimes see as a 'Roman Church'-hegemonised Europe. In addition, even continental Catholic parties need to be divided in sub-categories, with social Catholics being more supportive and right-wing Christian democrats less supportive. The very heterogeneous orientation of the liberal family is interpreted in reference to the three different historical cleavages generating it: the urban–rural cleavage in the case of the British and German liberals (the most supportive); the state–church cleavage for Italy, France, Spain, the Netherlands and Belgium, and the historical centre–periphery cleavage for the Scandinavian (including Finland), and the Welsh and Scottish liberals (the least supportive). The majority of the Conservative parties are in favour of enhancing economic competition and free trade through the Union, but many are also afraid of too much EU interference and regulation (the British Tories since Mrs Thatcher). Therefore, the Conservative Party family requires a crucial sub-division between neoliberal

and nationalist conservative. Further distinctions are then discussed, adding groups such as 'Scandinavian conservatives, and 'postauthoritarian conservatives' (ND Greece and AP Spain).

In my view, these perceptive analyses show the difficulty of interpreting the alignment on the integration issues via national bases. Parties find it difficult to conceptualise an issue that may be read in different ways from the point of view of historical national political alignments (loss of national control versus supranational recovery of such control; economic options versus cultural roots; neo-liberal orthodoxy versus bureaucratic regulations and rule, etc.).

Do Euro-parties represent the European voters on European divisions?

Even if it proves difficult to chart the location of European parties and party families on a restricted number of cleavage dimensions, do these parties at least represent the orientations of the European mass public towards the Union? From the early studies focusing on cross-countries variations, more recent studies mapping the attitudes of the European citizens have considered their support for unification or for membership, for specific EU institutions, and for specific policy areas. Since the 1990s, growing attention has been devoted to the underlining dimensions unifying and structuring the varieties of single issues/institutions/field/policy preferences.

The debate on the structuring of mass public attitudes concerning the EU has evolved around two closely connected issues: (1) whether national and European parties and elites are in tune with their voters' attitudes on EU issues and institutions; and, in such a case, (2) which are the dimension(s) along which such structuring is taking place.

Observers divide about the extent to which representative elites do represent their voters' opinions. Early studies comparing the attitude of voters towards the EC and the attitude of their preferred national parties concluded that on the whole party-voters show a quite strong similarity of position, even if parties appeared to be in general more in favour of EU integration than voters were. In the late 1990s research has documented that considerable proportions of the European electorate have preferences on European main issues that are not represented by the positioning of their respective parties. They cannot therefore choose a party on the basis of its EU position while at the same time keeping a choice on the basis of the party's left–right position. More precisely, survey research concludes that while on a broad ideological characterisation like left–right the voters' and the representatives' positions are largely similar, when individual issues are made specific (such as border control or common currency for instance) the discrepancies between voters of the same party and party representatives are enormous.

Observers also divide over whether a left–right dimension or a more complex dimensionality – including a pro–against integration or even other dimensions – prevails and on how much these dimensions correlate with one another. Several researchers have concluded that for national parties, Euro-parties and voters the addition of a second dimension to the dominant left–right is necessary to properly chart the political orientation. This is generally labelled nationalist versus supranationalist, or integration versus independence. Moreover, with the reconciliation of some left parties with and the growing opposition of some right-wing parties to the integration process, the two dimensions have become more independent one from the other. Finally, it is confirmed by research that the left–right cleavage and dimension of competition satisfactorily links parties and voters when isomorphic issues are dealt with in the EU context, but this cleavage alignment collapses dramatically when the constitutive dimension of EU politics – membership, competencies, institutional design – come to the fore. In that case the second integration/independence dimension is necessary and it cuts across the classic left/right cleavage.

However, what we know about the attitude of European citizens on the integration process does not fit very well either with the national cleavages (see supra) or with an encompassing European left–right cleavage and not even with the independence/integration dimension. Individual positive orientation towards the EU generally relates to level of political awareness and to political values which are less nationalistic and more committed to individual liberty and equality. Early Eurobarometer studies reveal some significant class polarisation, with manual workers and unemployed less favourable than higher income, higher status occupations, executives and professionals. However, across classes and status groups those who do well attribute it to the EU and those who do poorly do the same. On the cognitive mobilisation dimension, the better educated, informed and active, with less parochial views, feel more comfortable with remote large-scale institutions such as the EU. In general, individuals favour the EU more the higher their social status and human capital position. Europeans with higher educational levels and more marketable occupational skills are better prepared to apply their talents in diverse international settings and to adapt to economic changes in their production sector and region. In contrast, less educated and poorly skilled Europeans have less valuable job experiences, possess less mutable skills and qualifications, are less likely to seek additional job training, and are more expendable in times of economic downturn. National surveys concerning nine EC referendums from 1972 to 1994 show that males vote on average more frequently in favour than women; voters without religious affiliation vote more in favour than voters with strong religious affiliation; single people vote more heavily in favour than married, divorced and widowed people; and members of trade unions vote more against than unaffiliated workers.

In-depth research in France reveals that political dissatisfaction and xenophobia, death penalty and other populist issues become powerful determinants of anti-integration after controlling for social background and party identification. Anti-EU feelings in France since Maastricht have progressively revealed a discourse in which Europe is associated with an open door to immigration; it is linked and made responsible thereafter for high unemployment, insecurity and cultural standardisation and homogenisation (if not globalisation *tout court*). Analysis of party elite and interest groups attitudes towards entry in the four referendums held in Austria and Finland, Sweden and Norway underline that in all cases the opposition was between centre and periphery in cultural economic and political terms, between the 'resourceful establishment against the less-established groups'. In an extensive Italian 1998 survey on the advantages and disadvantages of integration and the single currency, the big distribution networks, the banking system, the multinational firms, the big national firms, the shareholders and the liberal professions were consistently identified

as the winners, while the small dealers, the saving families, the small firms, the house owners and those with a fixed income were the losers. This opposition between the big and the small, the mobile capital and resources and the fixed incomes, property and skills, the resourceful and resourceless, the centrally located and the peripheral in the socio-economic system emerged in all these researches.

It is difficult to recognise in these orientations a resemblance with the historical combination of class and religious alignments typical of the left–right dimension. It is also difficult to relate these orientations to the new value dimensions identified by national electoral studies in the last 20 years and opposing duty, law and order, productive efficiency and achievement values to individualistic orientations towards creativity, spontaneity, self-actualisation and hedonism; and dichotomies like authoritarian versus libertarian, solidarity versus prosperity and security, prosperity versus ecology, participation versus security. If an integration versus independence cleavage exists within the European mass electorate, with almost no exceptions the attitudes tend to polarise along a dimension that stresses the opposition line between the perception of new opportunities and mobility options versus the perception of the costs of these. People characterised by objective new life chances and by elements of strong empathy (such as the capacity to see oneself projected in a different existential situation) tend to manifest higher support for integration. Less potentially mobile people tend to oppose the integration process of their country. The distinction seems to cut across traditional social class as well as productive sector divisions and also the above-mentioned cultural orientations.

The structuring of a new 'European' cleavage?

We should not exclude the possibility that there are some underlying common elements in the strange amalgam of discontent across the traditional political spectrum for which the EU could be a strong unifying catalyst. Do the new right of *heimat*, the concern for national identity and independence, the fear of openness of boundaries to immigration, the insistence on the 'we versus the other', the defence and the pride for national welfare, the orthodox Christian refusal of the mundaneness of the economic and technocratic elite, the peripheral fear of distant bureaucracies, have nothing to do with Europe and have nothing to do one with the other? Protest and anti-establishment stands, however ideologically disparate, might find in the anti-EU position a common denominator given the enormous and growing visibility and the highly institutionalised nature of the Union.

It is possible, therefore, that the integration – as previous historical critical junctures have done – generates a new and additional cleavage line based on a new *social polarisation* line related to the costs and advantages of exit versus those of renewed closure. This new cleavage should be rooted in the life chance and material opportunities perceived by different actors as a differentiation of their interests concerning the territorial integration process. It should also culturally cement values and beliefs about the integration with wider normative visions of the self, of the good life, of justice and equity. It should relate to concrete issues concerning the conflicts generated by boundary transcendence versus boundary control options, like economic openness, immigration, multiculturalism, and national welfare autonomy.

These sets of attitudes towards the EU are not consistent with the left–right dimension of alignment prevalent at the national level (and at the EP level). But even the independence/integration dimension presents some ambiguity because more integration or more national independence may mean very opposite things. More integration may mean more market competition and openness, but also more European-level control of the market itself, of immigration fluxes, of the exit options of globalised capital. More integration may be seen as a way to defend 'European' cultural traditions and diversity from globalising multiculturalism; but more independence can similarly be argued as a way to defend national cultural distinctiveness. More independence may mean more protectionism and less international competition, but it can also mean escaping the growing bureaucratic control from Brussels and its regulatory encroachment on globalised markets. More independence can be advocated to defend the achievements of national welfare and democracy, but more integration can be advocated with similar goals, arguing that European national welfare states can only be defended at the level of the European market. Finally, on both the left–right dimension and the independence/integration dimension there is low coincidence of the cultural and economic orientation fronts. On European issues, economic protectionists are not necessarily also cultural nationalists and vice versa. They may be more positively oriented towards multiculturalism, as many left-wing parties are. Similarly, neo-liberal economic globalists are not necessarily also cultural globalists. They may defend national culture within global markets. The point is that economic orientation (more market freedom versus more market control) and cultural orientation (more cultural openness versus cultural closure) in the integration process may sharply diverge and bedfellows on the economic front are not necessarily bedfellows on the cultural one.

These inconsistencies between left and right, independence and integration can be captured at least in part by the new social polarisation between 'exit/entry controls' versus 'exit/entry options' mentioned before. On both left and right one can support integration in order to control exits and entries or to foster them, and one can be against integration in order to control exits and entries or to foster them. The findings concerning individuals' orientation towards integration mentioned before are compatible with a general interpretation that stresses the opposition between the perception and the positive evaluation of new material and cultural opportunities and mobility options versus the perception of the costs of them. There is some evidence to advance the hypothesis that the integration dimension correlates significantly with other traits of an 'choice-centred' versus 'roots-centred' material interests and value orientation.

To find a label for this latent and potential 'European cleavage' we can use 'nomadic' versus 'standing' cleavage. For neither individuals, nor groups and territories does this opposition impinge exclusively on their physical capacity to move, migrate, delocate and secede. One should speak of the possibility of using competing functional and regulative boundaries to their advantage. The nation-state formation was about the cultural limitation of still available exit options on the territorial (centre–periphery) and functional (church–state) axis. The rural/urban cleavage had strong territorial implications, but it was mainly expressed in functional conflicts between social groups in the production and distribution domains. The industrial revolution produced functional conflicts among groups linked to the division of labour within a consolidated territory. The 'integration' revolution could oppose allegiance to a relatively closed territorial entity versus the internationalisation of chances and opportunities (see Table 2). The European integration may reopen the alternative between exit and voice between nomadic and standing oriented individuals, groups and corporate organisations, as well as accentuate latent conflicts between losing and winning territories in the newly accrued territorial competition within the enlarged European polity.

Table 2   Conflict lines of the main phases of European historical development

	nation-state formation (exit versus voice alternative)	industrial revolution (voice versus loyalty alternatives)	integration 'revolution' (again exit versus voice alternatives)
territorial axis	centre/ periphery		losing/winning territories in international/ EU competition for attracting mobile factors
functional axis	church/state	primary/secondary workers/owners	'nomadic'/standing' individuals, groups, and corporate organisations

Like any previous cleavage, this latent integration cleavage can be read in various ways. It can be articulated as a centre–periphery opposition, pointing to groups and territories whose distinctiveness is threatened by the integration drive. It can be conceptualised as a functional/economic divide between groups whose economic interests are threatened or fostered by integration. It can be conceptualised as a cultural opposition to Brussels' bureaucracy and its standardising practices, administrative procedures and political culture. It is difficult to imagine whether the scattered lines of opposition on the economic, cultural and politico-administrative fronts have a potential for convergence and ideological integration into an encompassing cleavage. The new social polarisation may prove very difficult to structure politically in the wide European space. But even if this social polarisation remains latent, the consequences of the European project of boundary redrawing will not lapse and the material and cultural opportunity of supranational and sub-national transcendence will clearly impact on the historical cleavage structures of the nation-states.

Stefano Bartolini

Bibliography

Detlef, J., 'Der Einfluss von Cleavage Strukturen auf die Standpunkte der skandinavischen Parteien über den Beitritt zur Europäischen Union', *Politische Vierteljahresschrift*, 40, 1999, pp. 565–90.

Eijk, C. van der and Franklin M. (eds), *Choosing Europe? The European Electorate and National Politics in the Face of Union*, Ann Arbor, University of Michigan Press, 1996.

Hug, S., *Voices of Europe. Citizens, Referendums, and European Integration*, Lanham, MD, Rowman & Littlefield Publishers, 2002.

Mair, P., 'The Limited Impact of Europe on National Party Systems', *West European Politics*, 23, 2000, pp. 27–51.

Marks, G. and Steenbergen, M. R. (eds), *European Integration and Political Conflict*, Cambridge, Cambridge University Press, 2004.

Marks, G. and Wilson, C., 'The Past and the Present. A Cleavage Theory of Party Responses to European Integration', *British Journal of Political Science*, 30, 2000, pp. 433–59.

Perrineau, P., 'L'enjeu européen, révélateur de la mutation des clivages politiques dans les années 1990', in F. Arcy and L. Rouban (eds), *De la V République à l'Europe: Hommage à Jean-Louis Quermonne*, Paris, Presses de la Fondation Nationale des Sciences Politiques, 1996, pp. 45–59.

Reif, K. and Inglehart R. (eds), *Eurobarometer: the Dynamic of European Public Opinion*, Basingstoke, Macmillan, 1993.

Schmitt, H. and Thomassen, J. (eds), *Political Representation and Legitimacy in the European Union*, Oxford, Oxford University Press, 1999.

Schmitt, H. and Thomassen, J., 'Représentation politique et intégration européenne', in G. Grunberg, P. Perrineau and C. Ysmal (eds), *Le vote des quinze: Les élections européennes du 13 juin* 1999, Paris, Presses de Sciences Po, 2000, pp. 49–74.

Taggart, P., 'A Touchstone of Dissent: Euroscepticism in Contemporary Western European Party Systems', *European Journal of Political Research*, 33, 1998, pp. 363–88.

→ Electoral Behaviour; European Electoral Sociology; European Political Parties; Extreme Left; Extreme Right; Green Politics; Identity; Left; Partisan Identification; Religion; Right.

Communication

To what extent do the electoral communication strategies used by parties during

European campaigns demonstrate specific features that differentiate them from the communication made at the national or local level, in terms of its contents, political controversies, and modes of expression? Those who most fervently favour the European institutionalisation process regularly criticise the campaign platforms advanced during European elections as being hopelessly devoted to national issues, and for being 'mediocre'. In the same vein, these commentators berate both citizens for their inevitable lack of voting interest and politicians for their inability to provide educational explanations in order to support understanding of the issues and achievements entailed by European integration. Within this approach, it is implicitly acknowledged that European elections should address specifically 'European' themes and thus should not be subject to traditional and often bipolar controversies. It is also argued that the simultaneous election of MEPs should generate a 'Europeanisation' of politics, and so replace national partisan cleavages by new political divisions which are tailored to the demands of the parliamentary work in Strasbourg. However, since the European Parliament has been elected by direct universal suffrage, it is of interest to note that this Europeanisation of politics has been rather limited and that European campaigns are more comparable to regional or local elections, which are treated as secondary elections whereby the political cleavages of the country capital (Paris, Madrid or Berlin) – and the related political references – tend to supersede potential local issues.

The analysis of electoral communication themes in the different countries is pertinent in that it reveals that those political actors who produce a rhetoric purposely adapted to European elections tend to be at the fringes of their political space: either because they radically question the process of European integration itself (sovereigntists, Eurosceptics, extreme right) or challenge some of its methods (extreme left parties); or because in accepting both the principle and methods, they struggle to design a political platform on Europe which goes beyond mere support (e.g. UDF in France in 2004). Since the administrative process of Europeanisation has continuously achieved cross-party support, the principal governmental actors responsible for implementation face the problematical reality of translating respective European policies into an efficient partisan axis for their political campaigns and essentially there remains too little to differentiate their position on Europe from either past or future governments. Finally, since the cost of political work for devising and disseminating new political issues requires potentially significant resources for the political teams – notably drafting internal agreements, launching a new political pitch, familiarising journalists and voters to rafts of new proposals – parties usually end up tailoring general programmes to the particular features of the elections at stake, rather than defining specific platforms. Throughout the campaigns, European elections serve to momentarily mollify internal divergences across the Community institutions within labour or socialist parties for instance, and also between opposing factions concerning competition policies, etc. in order to avoid addressing clarifications which would be likely to ignite new divisions that, following the elections, would lose meaning anyway and so make lasting political convergence more difficult to achieve. Therefore, the electoral communication developed by the main political parties for European elections is unsurprisingly similar to the national election process, since it is grounded on the classic logic of partisan confrontation – in particular, defending governmental expenditure, criticising current policies, supporting a protest vote against the government, etc.

The national reflex in European campaigns can also be explained by the limited decision-making powers exercised by the MEPs and the lack of interest on the part of the journalists concerning the activities of MEPs. Indeed, the specific politicisation of the election can be defined as the process by which voters develop partisan interests as a result of parties establishing new problems that their self-contradictory platforms propose to solve. As such, this politicisation also requires the staging of an implicit 'voting contract' between a specific platform and the enforcement of consistent policies. Despite the subsequently perceived or presented failure of such a contract, for example Jacques Chirac's campaign on the 'social fracture' in 1995, the 'turning point towards tenacity' in 1983, the intensity of electoral competition, the degree of party activist involvement and the strength of electoral enrolment all depend on the parties' ability to stress the importance of the voters' decisions, by demarcating their respective projects and through vigorously challenging political opposition in public debates. Currently, two problematic issues can be identified, notably that no executive or policy has yet to directly emerge from the European Parliament and also the difficulty involved in tracing the policies co-ordinated by Brussels. As such, this begs the question as to who should be held politically responsible for European directives. Furthermore, how can the impact of these directives be precisely assessed? A case in point concerns the privatisation of the major French public services, as required by the successive European treaties and the directives on the generalisation of competition, which is perceived more as the inescapable consequence of necessary economic 'modernity' or 'globalisation', than as the result of joint policies by the European executives since the Delors Commission. European election would thus constitute a vote exclusive of politics whilst European institutions would design policies exempt from electoral accountability. Consequently, it is by no means surprising that partisan actors struggle during European campaigns to set forth a specifically political discourse – or rather to connect the electoral outcomes to immediate governmental actions. In an election where nothing is at stake, the European vote appears more like a consultation to an indiscernible result: not only can a local victory of the representatives of the European People's Party (EPP) or the Party of European Socialist (PES) coexist with a widespread decline, but it is also limited by proportional representation and by electoral divisions at constituency level. Ultimately this all means that there is only minimal impact at the European political level since consensual and stable rules govern the European parliamentary game – distribution of presidencies and vice-presidencies of the commissions, necessary enlarged majorities leading to a habit of reciprocal concessions. The origins of policies which have been supported and initiated by a clearly delineated and articulated majority in the European Parliament have never been recognised by the electorate at large, principally due to the nature of the arena whereby main parties never suffer defeat or savour victory over their political opponents.

Thus, relative apathy in regards to the political communication during European campaigns can then be explained in terms of two interrelated reasons. Firstly there is little real political power at stake which inevitably fails to mobilise the staff of the main governing parties and secondly only limited resources are actually invested in the elections to the extent that they are deemed as being of secondary importance and hence unlikely to mobilise party activists or inspire support from journalists. Consequently, the candidates who represent and visibly champion European elections are seldom high-profile members, with fewer resources invested in the electoral campaign than for the national elections which have an explicit redistributive function of political power. Electoral campaigns are largely ignored by the media, following the example of the main political parties themselves who also lack commitment, material or otherwise. Electoral communication for European elections is the result of these specific constraints: few meetings, few posters, few television reports. Hence, the major partisan actors rarely present a *European* campaign but instead end up, by default and at little expense, using European elections to reach national political ends – notably reassuring their electorate majority, measuring their influence, placing the government in a minority position, providing certain candidates with professional political experience. As a result, in those countries with a traditional majoritarian system, European Parliament elections have so far been dominated by small partisan groups who regard the proportional nature of the electoral system as a means to reinforce their position and to promote their respective electoral brand or appeal (environmental organisations, ethno-regionalist movements, extreme right).

Philippe Juhem

Bibliography

Eijk, C. van der and Franklin M. N. (eds), *Choosing Europe? The European Electorate and National Politics in the Face of Union*, Ann Arbor, University of Michigan Press, 1996.

Gerstlé, J., 'La dynamique nationale d'une campagne européenne', in P. Perrineau and C. Ysmal (eds), *Le vote des Douze: les élections européennes de juin 1994*, Paris, Presses de Sciences Po, 1995, pp. 203–27.

Gerstlé, J., Semetko, H. A., Schoenbach, K. and Villa, M., 'L'européanisation défaillante des campagnes nationales', in G. Grunberg, P. Perrineau and C. Ysmal (eds), *Le vote des Quinze: Les élections européennes du 13 juin 1999*, Paris, Presses de Sciences Po, 2000, pp. 95–118.

→ Advertising; Campaign (Sociology of); Election Manifestos; Electoral Strategy; European Electoral Sociology; European Parliament; European Political Parties; European Public Opinion; European Public Sphere; Internal Elections at the European Parliament; Issues; Journalists; Nationalisation of European Elections; Political Affiliation; Political Market; Second-Order Elections.

Composition of the European Parliament

The study of the composition of the EP aims at knowing better the agents who incarnate this institution every day. For long considered as a peripheral parliament with no power, it has obtained throughout the successive treaties a status of co-legislator on a great number of texts. Besides a few indications on the evolution of the European political personnel, it is possible to understand the transformations of European careers from a small group of MEPs who make or have made the institution by holding leadership positions: presidency, vice-presidencies, questors, political groups or parliamentary committees' presidencies (posts filled at the beginning and the middle of each term of office).

The MEPs' socio-political characteristics and evolutions

The changes in the MEPs' political characteristics invite us to question several views that are often formulated about the European mandate: the decision to end a political career, elected representatives' turnover, the non-existence of European political careers, dependence regarding the national contexts and low institutionalisation of the European parliamentary scene. In the 1980s, the elected representatives were characterised by national political experience. In contrast, in the 1990s, many of them thought that accession to the EP corresponded to a political form of professionalisation. More tightly specialised in European questions, they hold less and less simultaneously the position of elected representatives and MEPs, and remain longer in the EP. Forty-five per cent of the 1979 elected representatives, 35 per cent of the 1984 ones and only 28 per cent in 1999 had already been MPs in their own countries, respectively 17 per cent, 13 per cent and 10 per cent ministers (Scarrow 1997; Corbett et al. 2000). Thirty-one per cent during their first term of office (1979–84) had two mandates (national and European parliaments) against less than 7 per cent during the fifth term (1999–2004). The mandate tends to stabilise: during the fifth term of office, almost one MEP out of two was re-elected (Bryder 1998; Corbett et al. 2000) and less than 15 per cent resign during their mandate (24 per cent during the first one). From the third term of office (1989–94), MEPs joined the EP for longer periods. However, the huge gaps between national delegations testify to the weight of national contexts in this selection. From 1979 to 1994, 58 per cent of the British and 43 per cent of the Germans remained at least 7.5 years in the EP against 25 per cent of the French and 28

per cent of the Italians (Scarrow 1997). In the 2004 elections, more than one German MEP out of three and almost four British out of five were re-elected. From 1979, the British indeed appear as a personnel more specialised in Europe than the average (Westlake 1994). If only 31 per cent of the French MEPs were re-elected in 1999, they were 45 per cent in 2004. For Italy, such a rate, which is even lower, also increased: 22 per cent were re-elected in 1999 and 41 per cent in 2004.

The socio-demographic variables (gender, age and professions) are also modified. Term after term, the population pyramid has been tightening. If in 1979 very old personalities represented a great part of the political personnel, at the end of the 1990s, most of the MEPs (73 per cent) were between 40 and 60 years old, only 13 per cent were more than 60 years old (14 per cent less than 40) (Hix and Lord 1997). The professional backgrounds are relatively similar to those of the national political personnel, with a predominance of jurists (12 per cent of all the Parliament in 1996) and mainly teachers (22 per cent) (Westlake 1994; Franklin and Norris 1997; Hix and Lord 1997). For instance, about 75 per cent of the French of the fifth term of office stem from the upper classes of the social space, 25 per cent of them being secondary school or higher education teachers, 15 per cent high-ranking civil servants, 13 per cent exercising liberal professions (medics, lawyers, etc.) and 9 per cent being executive managers. Finally, the proportion of women, greater than at most of the national parliaments' levels, doubled between the first term of office and the last two: 16 per cent in 1979 and 30 per cent in 1999 and 2004. In the same way for the MPs with no previous political experience or the 'Euro-region' MPs (Kauppi 1999), the important part played by women tends to confirm this Parliament as a political space of professionalisation for agents with a socio-political profile rather unfavourable to winning over national posts (Kauppi 1999; Franklin and Norris 1997).

Specialisation of MEPs to leadership positions

The study of leadership positions in the EP specifies the increasing weight of European experience to achieve them and the emergence of a personnel more specialised in European questions. The conditions of access to power positions in the EP were modified. According to the biographies published by the Parliament of 229 MPs holding leadership positions between 1979 and 1999, nearly half of them demonstrate a national political career, three-quarters stem from upper categories of the social space and 28 per cent are teachers (higher education and secondary school). However, the proportion of national elected representatives decreases appreciably as terms of office go by, going from 82 per cent during the first term to 46 per cent during the fourth. At the same time, the number of teachers in higher education goes from 13 per cent in 1981 to 27 per cent in 1998. These professions indeed give resources that fit well with the European political work which is often complex and technical.

For an increasing number of MEPs, Europe constitutes an alternative to live 'for' and 'on' politics. At the beginning of the 1980s, the Europeanisation of political profiles was perceived in a set of symbolic (references to European history and to World War Two) or institutional (participation in the former Parliament, member of the European parliamentary assemblies) elements. It remained dependent, however, on the holding of national political positions. From the 1990s, the European political game has become more and more complex and the Parliament tends to set up a full assembly. The parliamentary involvement enables access to prestigious positions and the development of a career there. In 1998, 75 per cent had spent at least ten years in the EP, during which they had held intermediary posts within the committees, groups or delegations (co-ordinators, committees or groups' vice-chairpersons). For several terms, a strictly European political experience is a condition of leadership exercise: 55 per cent of them can pride themselves on that in 1981 against 75 per cent in 1998. This is all the more true in that the agents appointed to a leadership position shortly after their membership of the Parliament pride themselves on directly European experiences. For instance, Catherine Lalumière, president of the group of the Radical European Alliance (ARE) between 1994 and 1999, held the post of Secretary General of the Council of Europe until 1989. The limited group of 11 chairpersons of the EP between 1979 and 2004 illustrates with a magnifying effect this Europeanisation of careers. The first five chairpersons (between 1979 and 1992) had quite a characteristic profile: presence in the Parliament following a national political career and a more or less symbolical relation to the 'spirit of Europe'. Simone Veil (France, chairperson from 1979 to 1982) was the former Health Minister of Valéry Giscard d'Estaing (President of the French Republic from 1974 to 1981). Pieter Dankert (the Netherlands, 1982–84) spent 14 years in the Dutch Parliament (Lower Chamber) where he was president of the Foreign Affairs committee. Pierre Pflimlin (France, 1984–7) is a former French MP several times Minister during the 1950s and the 1960s. Enrique Barón Crespo (Spain, 1989–92), member of the EP for only two years when he was elected, was an MP in the Cortés (Spanish Parliament) for nine years and a minister in the Spanish socialist government from

1982 to 1985. These figures can therefore be compared to 'notables' for whom the EP presidency can be considered as an honorary position. The first chairpersons have therefore marked not only their countries' history but also Europe's. The biographical record of Lord Plumb (United Kingdom, 1987–9) is in this sense a list of positions held in professional agricultural organisations, particularly at the Community level, then in the EP (president of the Agriculture Commission from 1981 to 1982 and president of the European Democrats group from 1982 to 1984). P. Dankert is a former member of the pan-European parliaments: Western European Union (WEU), Council of Europe, North Atlantic Treaty Organisation (NATO). Former president of the Council of Europe Parliamentary Assembly, P. Pflimlin is a historical figure of the European federalist movements and, until 1983, mayor of Strasbourg, the 'European capital'. S. Veil, finally, is at the heart of the historical and symbolic European universe by opening her parliamentary biography with an account of her concentration camp experience.

Without the division being necessarily linear, the characteristics of the six next chairpersons (1992–2004) confirm the reinforcing of the EP experience to the detriment of a national political experience. In this context, Egon Klepsch (Germany, 1992–4) represents a type of transition. Member of the Bundestag for 15 years (from 1965 to 1980) then a member of the EP, he held several mandates there whose key post is the one of president of the European Popular Party (EPP), one of the largest groups. Klaus Hänsch (Germany, 1994–7), José-Maria Gil-Robles Gil-Delgado (Spain, 1997–9) and Nicole Fontaine (France, 1999–2002), on the other hand, had no national political experience. Their election to the presidency of the Parliament is mostly linked to their political experience of Europe: K. Hänsch has been a member of the EP since 1979, J.-M. Gil-Roblès Gil-Delgado since 1989, N. Fontaine since 1984, and P. Cox (Ireland, 2002–4) since 1989. Each one of them knew how to acquire a specific credit within the Parliament, after a permanent and continuous involvement within the groups and committees. The determining weight of this experience is particularly explicit in the case of N. Fontaine who was successively vice-chairperson and then first vice-chairperson between 1989 and 1999.

The profile of the holders of hierarchical positions within the Parliament illustrates the redefinition of legitimate personalities of the MEP around those who 'make a career at the European level', and those who live 'on' Europe and ended up living 'for' Europe, finally dedicating almost all of their political time to it. This professionalisation of European agents can be seen at various levels: a group of agents likely to instance competencies adapted to stakes specific to the European parliamentary space; a socialisation specific to Europe and the European parliamentary roles that is particularly based on the long term; and a process of recognition by peers who control the access to the EP's power positions, especially those enabling one to talk on behalf of the institution.

Willy Beauvallet
Sébastien Michon

Bibliography

Bryder, T., 'Party Groups in the European Parliament and the Changing Recruitment Patterns of MEPs', in D. S. Bell and C. Lord (eds), *Transnational Parties in the European Union*, Aldershot, Ashgate, 1998, pp. 189–203.

Corbett, R., Jacobs, F. and Shackleton, M., *The European Parliament*, London, Harper, 2000 (4th edition).

Franklin, N. M. and Norris, P., 'Social Representation', *European Journal of Political Research*, 32, 32, 1997, pp. 185–210.

Hix, S. and Lord, C., *Political Parties in the European Union*, Basingstoke, Palgrave Macmillan, 1997.

Kauppi, N., 'Power or Subjection? French Women Politicians in the European Parliament', *European Journal of Women's Studies*, 6, 3, 1999, pp. 329–40.

Scarrow, S. E., 'Political Career Paths and the European Parliament', *Legislative Studies Quarterly*, 22, 2, 1997, pp. 253–62.

Westlake, M., *Britain's Emerging Euro Elite? The British in the Directly Elected Parliament, 1979–1992*, Dartmouth, Aldershot, 1994.

→ Electoral Behaviour; Electoral System; European Elections (1979–1999); European Elections (2004); European Electoral Sociology; Mulit-Level Governance; Territorial Organisation.

Compulsory Voting

In the preliminary debates before the introduction of direct universal suffrage for European Parliament elections, the principle of compulsory voting was hardly mentioned. Nevertheless, in the course of a collective study undertaken from 1977 to 1981, the interdisciplinary team at the European University Institute in Florence suggested, in vain, abolishing it where it existed in order to ensure uniformity across the different electoral procedures practised in the European elections (Sasse et al., 1981). Therefore, some EU countries, which already enforce compulsory voting in national elections – usually a constitutional provision – differ from the rest with regards to their rules on electoral participation, with some important legal and political consequences. Four countries are concerned: Belgium and Luxembourg extended the principle of compulsory voting to European elections from 1979, followed by Greece in 1984 and finally Cyprus in 2004. A completely different case is that of Italy, where the Constitution of 27 December 1947, Article 48.2, states that 'voting is a civil duty'.

Compulsory voting was often entrenched early in the electoral history of the countries which enforce it. Indeed, the Belgian Constitution paired it with the emergence of universal suffrage for men as early as 1893, while in Luxembourg, the electoral Act of 31 July 1924 imposed it for legislative and municipal elections. When relevant, this principle has also been applied to expatriate European citizens still resident in the EU, because of the non-discrimination principle established by the European Commission (Directive 93/109/CE of the Council of 6 December 1993).

The implementation of compulsory voting entails certain substantial consequences for the practical and symbolic process behind European voting, in addition to turnout. The relevant electoral laws stipulate, in the first place, several grounds for abstention and, under certain conditions, facilitate voting by post, in advance or by proxy, and also officially acknowledge blank votes as legitimate votes. At the same time, in Luxembourg and Greece, electoral laws automatically exempt elderly voters (over 70 in Greece, over 75 in Luxembourg, following the electoral Act of 18 February 2003) and encourage this demographic group to submit a postal vote instead. This provision also applies to Greek voters who are further than 200 kilometres from their registered voting place. In Luxembourg, exemption is also granted to 'voters who, at the time of the election, live in a different town from where they are registered to vote'. Derogations are more limited in Belgium, and only apply in cases such as illness, disability, imprisonment, and

Table 1 Comparative analysis of turnout to European elections in four countries of the Union which apply the principle of compulsory voting (%)

Country	1979	1984	1989	1994	1999	2004	Difference 04-99	Abstention for last national elections	Difference EU 2004 – last national elections
Belgium (*)	91.4	92.2	90.7	90.7	91	90.8	–0.2	91.3	–0.5
Luxembourg (*)	88.9	88.8	87.4	88.5	87.3	90	+2.7	86.5	3.5
Greece	–	77.2	79.9	71.2	75.3	63.4	–11.9	74.8	–11.4
Cyprus	–	–	–	–	–	71.2	–	90.6	–19.4
EU average	63	61	58.5	56.8	49.8	45.6	–4.2	–	–

(*) Countries in which other elections were held on the same day in June 2004.

professional reasons. In that country, it is the responsibility of the justice of the peace to rule on the validity of the excuses put forward by non-voters. In order to facilitate the vote, Belgian electoral law provides for the reimbursement of any travel expenses incurred by the voters who no longer live in the town where they are registered. These electoral laws punish non-voting by imposing a warning or a variable electoral fine (between €25 and €250, depending on the country and the cause of abstention) which increases noticeably in case of reoffending (up to €1,000 in Luxembourg). The effects of compulsory voting on turnout in European elections are obvious from Table 1, and confirm the conclusions of Gratschew (2004).

Undoubtedly, compulsory voting promotes participation in European elections and accounts for the virtuous behaviour of the voters in the four countries concerned more than any other macro-institutional variable (Mattila 2003). On average, turnout for European elections in these particular countries is more than 28 points above the average turnout for EP elections across all the counties in the EU collectively. This comparative advantage even seems to have increased since 1999 (+34.7 points in 1999, +33.2 in 2004) because of lower average turnout in other countries. This said, the principle does not produce similar results across the countries concerned. Notably, the two Benelux countries have the highest turnout, and the closest to turnout levels in national elections, whereas in Greece and Cyprus (where the governments announced they would not sanction abstentionists for the European election on 13 June 2004), the difference between the European and national elections is higher (11.4 points in Greece and 19.4 points in Cyprus compared to the latest national election). It is also in Greece that the decline

in turnout between 1999 and 2004 was the most pronounced.

Yves Déloye

Bibliography

Gratschew, M., 'Compulsory Voting in Western Europe', in IDEA, *Voter Turnout in Western Europe since 1945: a Regional Report*, Stockholm, Publications Office International IDEA, 2004, pp. 25–31.
Mattila, M., 'Why Bother? Determinants of Turnout in the European Election', *Electoral Studies*, 22, 2003, pp. 449–68.
Pantélis, A. M. et al., *Les régimes électoraux des pays de l'Union européenne*, London, Esperia, Brussels, Bruylant, 1998.
Sasse, C. et al., *The European Parliament: Towards a Uniform Procedure for Direct Elections*, Florence, European University Institute, Luxembourg, Office for Official Publications of the European Communities, 1981.

→ Abstention; Belgium; Cyprus; Greece; Luxembourg; Postal Voting.

Cyprus

The first European elections in the Republic of Cyprus took place under unusual circumstances. In fact, the Republic of Cyprus was still divided when it joined the EU on 1 May 2004. A week earlier, on 24 April, two separate referendums were held, aiming at reunifying the country in accordance with a UN proposal known as the 'Annan Plan'. Voters in the northern part of the island, known as the 'Turkish Republic of Northern Cyprus' (TRNC), approved the plan by a 65 per cent majority. By contrast, the Greek-dominated southern part rejected the plan by an overwhelming majority (76 per cent), largely due to strong government recommendations and to the weakness of the 'yes' campaigners.

Political context and public opinion

Greek Cypriots, headed by President Tassos Papadopoulos, bore the responsibility for the perpetuation of partition. Such outcome was all the more surprising given that Cyprus' accession to the EU was supposed to have encouraged reunification. Or so thought the 15 member states which, after beginning negotiations with Greek Cypriots in 1998, repeatedly but unsuccessfully invited (under the initiative of then-Council President Glafcos Clerides) TRNC leader Rauf Denktash to send a joint delegation to Brussels. Until 2002, both the Turkish government and the TRNC considered Cyprus's EU candidacy as illegitimate, arguing that such a state had ceased to exist with the institutional separation of 1964 due to serious clashes between the two communities, and with the 1974 partition. According to Ankara, the Greek Cypriot administration was legally entitled to present exclusively the southern zone for EU candidacy.

From 1998 to 2002, the European Commission only negotiated with the Greek side on the accession of the entire island based on the economic performance of the south, and did not take into consideration the development gap existing between the two zones. The sound economic figures characterising the Greek side of the economy allowed the government to respect the conditions set forth by the Stability Pact, thus giving the false impression that the Cyprus accession dossier was far easier to manage than that of Poland or the Czech Republic. The political aspects of accession were addressed in conjunction with the UN, whose successive secretary

generals had tried to solve the issue posed by partition for decades. Partly because of President Clerides' apparent good will, the Commission and the 15 member states optimistically thought that the Greek side would support a UN plan if the northern side and the Turkish government endorsed it too.

Opinion polls indicating a genuine enthusiasm towards accession in the south, the Commission and member states failed to see that the persistence of Greek nationalism relayed by the media as well as school textbooks, still constituted a real threat to the adoption of the Annan Plan. Moreover, President Denktash's firm opposition clouded the hopes of many Turkish Cypriots to join the EU, which was clearly unprepared to face the changing situation in the winter of 2002–3.

The Turkish legislative elections held in November 2002 saw the rise to power of the Muslim conservative party (AKP) headed by Recep Tayyip Erdogan, who proclaimed himself in favour of the future accession of Turkey to the EU, and who declared himself ready to break the impasse of the situation in Cyprus. This change was mainly due to the fact that it would have been unimaginable for the EU to begin accession negotiations with a country occupying part of another state's territory. Seemingly persuaded by Turkey's sincerity, Kofi Annan revealed his plan for the island's reunification. The plan included a new federal constitution and represented a good compromise between the aims of the Greek side, Turkish Cypriots and the Ankara government.

Had the two separate referendums held on 24 April had a positive outcome, the European elections scheduled for seven weeks later would have marked the date of reunification. After the overwhelming victory of the 'no' campaign in the south, the ability of Turkish Cypriots to participate in such elections was seriously compromised. This was seen as an indicator of the relative power of Greek Cypriots over the Turkish side. The future of the DISY, the party founded by former President Clerides, was also at stake in the referendum, due to the candidacy of contenders from the 'no' camp.

Electoral system

As in the case of elections to the chamber of representatives, this ballot used proportional representation. The six candidates receiving the greatest number of votes were elected, two seats being in principle reserved for the Turkish side. The territory of the Republic of Cyprus (the entire island officially) formed a single district. Voting was compulsory for all citizens aged 18 and above who had been officially residing on the island for at least six months. Cases of abstention were not prosecuted. Citizens of other member states were also expected to vote in EP elections and present potential candidates who, in order to qualify, had to be aged 25 or above, and could not hold other ministerial and/or municipal positions nor be a member of the police or armed forces. The funding of the electoral campaign was provided by the state. Polling stations were open on Sunday 13 June from 7.00 to 17.00, and were closed between 12.00 and 13.00.

Turkish Cypriots deprived of voting rights

As predicted, Turkish Cypriots did not vote in the first European elections held on the Island. Due to a tacit agreement between Greek and Turkish nationalist forces based on a mutual understanding resulting from the time of the Greek Cypriot insurgence against British occupation, the Turkish side was not to be represented in European elections. Papadopoulos' government had set the polls' closing date for 2 April, which meant that Turkish Cypriots would have had to register with southern polling stations before the results of the separate referendum on the Annan Plan, without knowing whether the island would be reunified at the time of EP elections. Moreover, since the establishment of the demarcation line on 23 April 2003, Turkish Cypriots who came to the south to apply for a 'Republic of Cyprus' passport were seriously discriminated against by the administrative authorities. The extent of discrimination was such that the Ministry of Interior had to take action to ensure that these citizens would be allowed to obtain their papers after having waited the same amount of time and after paying the same tax as their Greek neighbours. Great numbers of Turkish Cypriots were also heavily discouraged from registering to vote in the Greek territory due to the adamancy and violence of the 'no' campaign. This was coupled with northern political parties' hopes and fears of the victory of 'no' campaigners, which resulted in their failure to encourage their constituencies to vote. Consequently, the number of Turkish Cypriots registered to vote barely reached 503, out of an electorate of uncertain size. In fact, a large share of Turkish Cypriots residing in the northern part of the island since after partition, hold TRNC passports which, since 1974, have no official value. It is estimated that out of a TRNC electorate of 100 000, between 50 000 and 70 000 are Turkish Cypriots eligible to vote in the Republic of Cyprus. These figures clearly make the total number of 503 registered voters seem derisory. The victory of the 'no' campaign resulted in only 97 Turkish Cypriots voting on 13 June. These numbers are indicative of the

Turkish side's profound distrust of their Greek counterparts and, particularly, of the Republic's political class.

Under these circumstances, the two seats reserved for Turkish Cypriots should not have been provided. Following the institutional separation of 1964, 15 (out of 50) seats reserved for Turkish representatives in the Chamber of Representatives remained empty (in 1995 a reform increased the number of seats in Parliament to 80, 24 of which were meant for Turkish members). Political parties on the Turkish side refused to present any candidates after the referendum's outcome, which meant that this community had a sole independent representative: university professor Mehmet Hasan. The TRNC's Prime Minister Mehmet Ali Talat claimed that the two seats should remain empty, and that Turkish Cypriots should be granted observers' status in the European Parliament. The Greek Cypriot government ignored these claims, and allocated the two Turkish seats to fourth and fifth Greek candidates.

Analysis of electoral results

The outcome of the 13 June election was relatively reassuring for the ruling parties DIKO and AKEL, and particularly for the pro-European DISY party, which won the majority of the votes (Table 1). In fact, its leader Ioannis Cassoulides, former Foreign Minister under Glafcos Clerides and negotiator of the Annan Plan, obtained 67 250 votes, while Marios Matsakis (GTE) won 27 371. Cassoulides was placed in a strong position to run for the presidential elections that will be held in 2008.

Results confirmed the DISY and AKEL parties as the major traditional actors in the Greek Cypriot political scene. DISY lost a mere six points compared to the 2001 legislative elections, and GTE obtained 10.8 per cent of the votes. The AKEL party's losses were slightly higher, reaching seven points and disappointing a share of its electors who voted in favour of the referendum. The DIKO party gained three points, and the EDEK four. In spite of its spectacular progress, EDEK did not gain any seats. Smaller parties such as 'New Horizons' (opposing all federal solutions) and 'United Democrats' (EDI, centre-left party in favour of the Annan Plan, founded by former President Vassiliou) only obtained 2 per cent of the votes, compared with 4 per cent in previous elections.

The largest parties consolidated their positions. However, abstention levels reached a worrying and unusual 29 per cent. European elections were negatively affected by their proximity to the referendum, whose significance for the future of Cyprus was extraordinary. This could be partly due to the fact that supporters of the UN plan turned to abstention after the parties they traditionally supported adopted positions that they did not agree

Table 1 Results of 2004 European elections in Cyprus

Parties	EP groups	%	Number of seats won
DISY	EPP-ED	28.2	2
AKEL	GUE/NGL	27.9	2
DIKO	ADLE (ELDR)	17.1	1
GTE	EPP-ED	10.8	1
EDEK	PES	10.7	0

with. This was most likely the case for many DISY and AKEL supporters. This is rendered all the more unusual by the typically strong partisan identifications which had produced very minimal oscillations in previous elections. The effects of the Annan Plan will certainly be felt in the next legislative elections of 2006. As a result, a future erosion of AKEL support in favour of smaller parties like EDI is not to be ruled out. After the referendum, DISY is not free to clarify its ambiguous position on the reconciliation with the Turkish side, while DIKO's future will depend on the course taken by the delicate political situation on the island. Tassos Papadopoulos and his party could pay the price for the perpetuation of partition in the next elections. Their position prevented the repatriation of 100 000 Greek Cypriot refugees from a territory that the Turkish side would have returned to the south according to the Annan Plan. Finally, no women were elected, while they represented a mere 20 per cent of the total number of candidates, and women are also greatly underrepresented within the Chamber of Representatives, as only two were elected in 1996 (former President Clerides's daughter and former President Vassiliou's wife!), with the former the only woman re-elected in 2001.

Gilles Bertrand

Bibliography

Baier-Allen, S. (ed.), *Looking into the Future of Cyprus–EU Relations*, Baden-Baden, Nomos Verlag, 1999.

Bertrand, G., 'Vingt-cinq ans après, où en est la partition de Chypre?', *Les Etudes du CERI*, 59, 1999.

Bertrand, G., 'L'adhésion de Chypre à l'Union européenne: Un déblocage du conflit par le bas?', *Politique européenne*, 3, 2001, pp. 118–36.

Calotychos, V. (ed.), *Cyprus and its People: Nation, Identity, and Experience in an Unimaginable Community (1955–1997)*, Boulder, Westview Press, 1998.

Diez, T. (ed.), *The European Union and the Cyprus Conflict: Modern Conflict, Postmodern Union*, Manchester, Manchester University Press, 2002.

Hottinger, J. T., 'Chypre (république grecque)', in G. Hermet et al. (eds), *Les partis politiques en Europe de l'Ouest*, Paris, Economica, 1998, pp. 95–106.

→ Abstention; Compulsory Voting; Electoral Behaviour; Enlargement; European Elections (2004); Incompatibility; Ineligibility; Issues; Mapping Europe: European Electoral Geography; Observers; Women.

Czech Republic

The first EP elections in the Czech Republic are an opportunity to wonder about the suggestion of an anti-European radicalisation in Central Europe and to determine whether these elections conform with the type of behaviour observed in old member states. The elections that were held as usual in the Czech Republic from Friday 11 June in the morning to Saturday 12 June 2004 at midday, were characterised by a high abstention rate and a bitter defeat for the parties of the coalition in power, the social-democrats and the centre-right, in favour of the liberal and Eurosceptic party of President Klaus, the Communist Party, which ranked second, and two parties labelled as 'independent' and rather pro-European. The theory of 'second-order elections' is confirmed in the Czech case, mainly due to the consequences of the accession referendum that was organised the year before, but must be qualified since the campaign was partially Europeanised. It is, however, undisputable that this electoral event allows us to see the structuring of the political scene on which partisan positioning stakes are defined and

European results are played out. In particular, these results should not be interpreted as a test of the 'democratisation' of post-communist societies.

A partially Europeanised election

The electoral campaign had similarities with previous national elections but also had its own characteristics. The Czech Republic with its 10.2 million inhabitants, stood out by the 31 lists competing on which no fewer than 808 candidates ran for 24 MEP positions. While minority and even extreme parties ran again in this election, others also emerged for the occasion, particularly focused around certain personalities – from a former pornography actress to the former director of the TV channel Nova, whose star presenter Jana Bobošiková was the candidate to obtain the greatest number of ballots. The electoral system was proportional with preferential vote (that is to say with the possibility for voters to modify the rank of two candidates providing they obtained more than 5 per cent of the ballots at the national level), and organised at the level of the *okres* (equivalent of counties). It favoured the big parties while letting small lists emerge around strong personalities.

The opening of the political field during this election was accompanied by a Europeanisation of the election recognisable in the choice of the heads of lists. The Czech electoral law forbids the concurrent holding of several mandates for MEPs, which has an effect on the constitution of lists. This is particularly the case of the main parties competing, that is to say the Social-Democrat Party (ČSSD), the Civic Democratic Party (ODS), the Christian-Democrat Party (KDU-ČSL), and the Communist Party (KSČM). In all these cases, the party leaders were not the ones to lead the campaign except for the involvement of ODS President Mirek Topolanek. The members of the government mobilised during the campaign but the faces visible on the posters covering the walls of Prague's subway and the billboards by the roadside had a smaller stature. This was the case of Zuzana Roithová for the KDU-ČSL or Libor Rouček for the ČSSD who was overshadowed by the charismatic figure of Senator Richard Falbr, former leader of the main Confederation of Trade Unions, the second candidate on the list. In the cases of the KSČM and ODS, the choice of candidates was even more complex due to the Eurosceptic views of these parties during the accession referendum campaign. While the Communist Party had not explicitly called for voting No, it was the ODS whose voters are clearly more in favour of the EU. This therefore explains why the campaign was led by Europhile Communists (headed by a former vice-president of international relations, Miroslav Ransdorf) and by Jan Zahradil, author of the *Manifesto of Czech Eurorealism*. The ODS circumvented this difficulty by mainly focusing its campaign on criticising the government ' and defending national interests within the EU. Its slogan 'The Blue Chance for Europe' summarised the trend of equity between the EU members Ransdorf defended while showing his disagreement with the way in which the social-democrats had negotiated the integration through the symbol of a single upside-down rose.

As a whole, the campaign that began three weeks before the election only led to low 'cognitive mobilisation'. The only strictly European positioning was the one in favour of the European Constitution, the parties having mainly played the proximity card with the electorate. For the ČSSD, it was about voting for a 'government that thinks about people'; the KSČM put forward the slogan 'With you and for you, at home as well as in Europe', as for the Independents' list (Nezavislí) led by the former TV Nova director, its argument was to lobby in Brussels in favour of the development of Czech towns and regions. The KDU-ČSL's primary constituency in Moravia was confirmed by its commitment to the redefinition of aid to farmers as a priority. As for the Green Party, it missed the opportunity to strengthen its position obtained at the local level despite the support of the European Green Party and Daniel Cohn-Bendit's visits in the Czech Republic.

While the complex nature of the political offer for EP electors is not specific to post-communist societies, the constitution of the lists for the EP elections clarifies the mechanisms for participation in redefining national political scenes.

The part of elections in national stakes

With a 28 per cent turnout, the Czech Republic belongs to the group of countries the press tends to classify as the 'bad pupils' of Europe denouncing a 'democratic setback' and a lack of 'public spirit' in post-communist societies. However, not only do the Czech results not confirm the hypothesis of anti-European radicalisation, but the high abstention can be explained by the focus on European issues during the integration referendum and the use by the political parties of this election for domestic policy ends. The expected ODS and KSČM victory as well as the more surprising results of the two independent parties (thus sending the ČSSD back to the fifth rank with less than 9 per cent of the votes), can be interpreted as a criticism of the coalition in power and confirm the trends of the reconfiguration of the party scene in favour of groups claiming to represent 'civil society' and those led by strong personalities.

These EP elections, coming only one month and a half after the Czech Republic's EU membership and a year after the accession campaign that had mobilised a lot of energy on the part of political parties, the media and European institutions and ended up with a 57 per cent Czech turnout, and 81 per cent voting 'Yes' to accession, suffered from a decrease in interest on the part of the

Table 1   Results of EP elections in the Czech Republic in 2004

Name of the grouping	Percentage of the ballots	Number of MPs in the EP
Civic Democratic Party, ODS	30.04	9
Communist Party of Bohemia and Moravia, KSČM	20.26	6
Association of Independents–European Democrats, SNED	11.02	3
Christian-Democrat Party, KDU-ČSL	9.57	2
Social-Democrat Party, ČSSD	8.78	2
Independents (Nezavislí)	8.18	2

Source: Czech Statistical Office.

population for an issue that seemed already settled. Furthermore, the challenge from independent lists also reflects the willingness of certain personalities to enter politics from outside the traditional structures. People's interest in candidates who are able to revitalise politics after a decade of power-sharing between the ODS and the ČSSD was similarly important as the government coalition was particularly weakened by the debate over public finance reform. This dual movement of personalisation of politics and involvement of 'laymen' had already been seen in the Czech Republic in the last two elections, the March 2002 local elections and the June 2002 legislative elections. The Association of Independents–European Democrats led by Senator and former Minister of Foreign Affairs of the first Klaus government Josef Zieleniec, who plays the party independence card, is part of this process. There is also the prospect of offering an alternative to the ODS which would be equally liberal but also Europhile. As for the list of the Independents of the former director of TV Nova, it expresses the logic of openness to 'civil society', and recognises the important role of the media in Czech society.

More than a 'second-order election', the election results express the values of the current Czech political scene, reflected in particular by the good results of Europhile as well as Eurosceptic candidates. This means that those who went to vote expressed themselves as much according to the European cleavage as to their attitude towards the coalition in power. One can see in these results an attempt to revitalise Czech democracy as it has worked for the last 15 years,

centred as it has been around three or four stable parties whose alliances have led to political stalemate. The lists around personalities and independent candidates express the desire for political renewal. On the other hand, the ODS still appears as the main opposition force while the KSČM has strengthened its hold, becoming, in an unprecedented fashion, a proponent of social-democracy. These EP elections having occurred in a period of tension for the coalition but also of internal crisis for the ČSSD; the bad results of this party have emphasised the weakening of Prime Minister and party leader Vladimír Špidla. Internal party dissent, led by Stanislav Gross, the young Minister of Domestic Affairs and vice-president of the party, led V. Špidla to quit his governmental and party functions. Forced to rely on allied forces, Stanislav Gross, appointed by President Klaus to form a new government, opened negotiations with the communists for the first time, although without inviting them to join the coalition which remained composed of the ČSSD, KDU-ČSL and the Freedom Union (US).

The EP election results should not be interpreted as the failure of the 'democratisation test' by the Czech Republic as a new member of the European Union, but rather as a demonstration of the importance of domestic policies and the low level of 'cognitive mobilisation' of the people during the election campaign despite the overall commitment to the EU on the part of the government in power.

Sandrine Devaux

→ Mapping Europe: European Electoral Geography.

D

Data Archives

How does one replicate, verify or simply access the findings of quantitative studies? How does one carry out, through secondary data analysis, research that does not support the entirety of original data sets? How is it possible to harmonise data files in order to allow for intra-European comparisons? These questions are at the core of the creation of modern infrastructures for empirical research in the social sciences, as well as their main instrument: databases. Probably due to a weaker link with public statistics or demography, political science has had and continues to have a pioneering role at the levels of infra-structures and methodological debate in this field. Two major initiatives helped to develop the Data Archives, the guardians of most political science data-bases. The first one took place in the United States in the 1940s, while the other one consisted of initiatives taken in the 1950s by a group of researchers interested in comparative European and international studies.

The establishment of the Roper Public Opinion Centre in 1945 benefited from the American tradition of private entre-preneurship within universities. Public opinion poll expert Elmo Roper deposited data obtained from ten years of field research in a library (at the time in boxes of IBM papers), with the idea that data were underused and could serve for comparative purposes and the study of the evolution of opinions if made available to the public. Roper encouraged colleagues such as George Gallup to follow his example. In 1957,

this fund became a separate department, thus forming the first real social enquiries database.

The original dynamics of data archiving in the social sciences goes back to great post-war intellectual figures specialising in the field of sociology, who undertook an ambitious intellectual project. Their aim was to develop a comprehensive global database that was to serve as a proper infrastructure for comparative research in the social sciences. The leading figure in this group of intellectuals was undoubtedly Stein Rokkan. Internationally oriented due to his multiple stays in the US, his intellectual ambition was to enable, through the establishment of a solid body of data, the historical analysis of the genesis of Western political systems. The collection of demographic, historical, political and economic data was to be placed in historical context. This intellectual venture encouraged social science to present itself as a form of 'statistical anthropology' (a term coined by Frédéric Bon) to investigate the causes of observable partisan phenomena.

The combination of these issues gave rise to a solid scientific programme, heavily supported by UNESCO which, in the immediate post-war years, strongly encouraged the development of multi-cultural scientific collaborations founded on the analysis of empirical data. The scientific community was also in need of material infrastructures for the realisation of this project. The Data Archives showed that empirical data are indeed part of a scientific patrimony that needs to be preserved on a long-term basis.

The establishment of the first Data Archives occurred in the early 1960s within major universities. In the US alone, the Roper Centre was set up at the University of Connecticut, and the Inter-University Consortium for Political and Social Research (ICPSR) was developed at the University of Michigan. However, while the former mainly archived data produced by global polling institutes, the latter formed a sort of 'club of universities', whose members had access to socio-demographic and historical statistics. For instance, it was the ICPSR that launched the 'informatisation' of General Statistics in France. This movement also extended to other parts of Europe, with the creation of the Zentralarchiv (University of Köln), and the ESRC Data Archive at the University of Essex in the UK. The opening of these new centres halted the ICPSR's initial aim of becoming a global database. The newly established databases began to be used for the immediate consultation of research findings rather than as historical archives for future reference. The role played by Data Archives in the diffusion of information, their usefulness to users and their function in terms of documentation and information for users (with the creation of schools such as those of the ICPSR and the University of Essex) fit within this framework. Data Archives have since played a greater role vis-à-vis the access to databases documented by big European comparative studies such as European Election Studies, the European Social Survey and European Values Studies.

Throughout the following decade, other countries joined the three founding fathers, giving birth to new projects characterised by intra-European co-operation. This in turn led to a new network known as Council of European Social Sciences Data Archives, which presently co-ordinates all European database projects. Southern Europe remained outside of this movement, with only Italy joining in the early 1970s (Portugal, Spain and Greece abstained for obvious political reasons). These centres have specific individual characteristics deriving from each country's historical traditions and data-generating structures.

France had to wait until the early 1980s to witness the creation of the Socio-Political Database of Grenoble (Grenoble Institute of Political Studies and CNRS) as well as the LASMAS in Paris. Such lingering was partly cause, partly consequence of the slight delay of French social sciences vis-à-vis the use of and access to empirical data. The efforts undertaken throughout Europe were not quite matched in France, where the creation of the BDSP and LASMAS resulted from the personal efforts of key figures like Frédéric Bon (BDSP), Raymond Boudon and Jacqueline Frisch (LASMAS). Nonetheless, a stronger national commitment was eventually generated as a result of a report written by Roxane Silberman on the use of databases in the social sciences and eventually led to the creation of the Quetelet network.

Bruno Cautrès

→ Electoral Behaviour; European Elections Studies (EES); European Electoral Sociology; European Public Opinion.

Democratic Deficit

'Democratic deficit' is a concept that was first coined by British political analyst David Marquand at the end of the 1970s. Despite the fact that the term was originally limited to constitutional analysis, the expression is now an integral part of the ongoing debate on the EU and its institutions. The concept was used to describe the tendency of

European integration to strengthen executive branches at the expense of parliaments. It also highlighted the accusation of secrecy levied against the European Union. Whilst negotiating behind the Council's closed doors, critics stated that European ministers could easily evade the European Parliament's scrutiny. This formal diagnosis paved the road to a simple democratisation plan based on the notion that, because the integration process was gradually shifting the decision-making process from the hands of national governments to new ones based in Brussels, EU-level control and accountability mechanisms should be reinforced. In other words, the democratic deficit would cease to exist if the European Parliament was directly elected and granted control of legislative and budgetary powers equal to the ones enjoyed by national parliaments. This rhetoric was echoed with great enthusiasm in national parliaments and dominated debates over the nature of European institutions throughout the 1980s. It was also reflected in the European Court of Justice's jurisprudence.

After the Single European Act of 1986, a number of institutional reforms were inspired by the general willingness to lessen the democratic deficit, so as to reproduce national parliamentary mechanisms at the European level. However, this formalist analysis soon appeared insufficient to solve the issue of democratic legitimacy. Since the first direct European Parliament elections were held in 1979, levels of political participation have not ceased to be of concern. The positive scenarios of the 1960s and 1970s gave way to growing levels of voter abstention. This was irrespective of the EP's gradual but continuous acquisition of powers. In an attempt to overcome this deadlock, other avenues were explored in an attempt to give the EU a more democratic profile. To move forward in this quest, political leaders gave up aspirations to recreate a national-style parliament at the EU level. Still thinking in classical institutional terms and acknowledging the limits of 'European parliamentarism', they tried to re-establish government-based forms of control through national assemblies. Within the framework of the European Convention of 2002–3 a number of national parliamentary representatives claimed that the EU's organisational structure continued to limit their scope for action and called for the adoption of European structures that would allow for closer scrutiny of the EU decision-making process.

Aside from institutional analyses, other reflections were meant to further enhance the EU's original structure and purpose. European Commissioners and academics fiercely defended a conception of the EU based on the notion of democratic governance. This initiative was founded on the idea that the EU does not aim to become a 'super-state', and that the diversity of its citizens is such that envisaging the emergence of a European 'people' would be illusory. Moreover, a number of authors stressed that the nature of the tasks and responsibilities undertaken by the EU was different to that of the nation-states. They argued that the vast majority of European policies are aimed at the field of market regulation, while national public action focuses mainly on distributive policies. Moreover, they held that regulation strategies are fundamentally different from national laws. In fact, by focusing on areas such as the protection of the environment, and public and consumer health, they could benefit from greater fluidity than the existing legislative action. In such policy areas, decisions should not be taken without accounting for geographic diversity, technical complexity, task dispersion as well as rapid and constant technological advances. In order to adapt to such a volatile context, it would be necessary to establish forms of governance that are more complex and adaptable than democratic governance, which rests on mere government initiative and parliamentary deliberation. Decentralising the fabrication of norms towards the areas to which they apply, while bearing in mind the actors for which they are devised, would allow for the assimilation of each party's knowledge, resulting in better-informed decisions.

After much hesitation due to fears of diluting its functions and powers, the European Commission pleaded in favour of these new modes of decision-making in a White Paper on 'European Governance' published in the summer of 2003. Echoing the aforementioned arguments, it supported the notion that a greater involvement of civil society in the decision process could make the EU more democratic. A more flexible, new form of democracy based on the equal representation of all citizens within the legislative organs was to emerge through the direct and open participation of civic associations and organised interest groups. The EU constitutional project illustrates the political aspiration to create channels for the direct expression of popular initiatives. Current research warns against the accentuation of intra-party inequalities (favouring of best-organised or most powerful groups or neglecting groups that may be less visible due to confidentiality reasons or the dispersed nature of their support). The Commission is fully aware of such limitations, and faces difficulties in defining viable criteria to determine the 'representativeness' of various groups as well as an overall balance amongst the parties involved. Moreover, studies fail to demonstrate that the involvement of 'private' actors genuinely does not contribute to the lessening of the EU's democratic deficit. In practice, these forms of participation remain very elitist. The movements and interest groups consulted by institutions are increasingly numerous and diverse, but they only make up a minuscule portion of the varied European society. More generally, what is seen as 'democratic governance' does not help clarify citizens' perceptions of the political issues at stake. Finally, it can be said that this type of governance adds to the complexity of the political game by expanding the range of participants in the decision-making process, blurring the lines between private and public spheres, diluting negotiating areas and making norms more fluid.

Paul Magnette

Bibliography

Magnette, P., *L'Europe, l'Etat et la démocratie: Le souverain apprivoisé*, Bruxelles, Complexe, 2000.
Marquand, David, *Parliament for Europe*, London, Jonathan Cape, 1979.
Moravcsik, A., 'In Defence of the "Democratic Deficit": Reassessing Legitimacy in the European Union', *Journal of Common Market Studies*, 40, 4, 2002, pp. 603–24.

→ Act of 1976; European Parliament; European Referendums; Europeanisation; Interest Groups; Investiture of the Commission; Lobbying; Multi-Level Governance; Representation; Second-Order Elections; Universal Suffrage.

Denmark[1]

The Danish EP election campaign in 2004

Even though some candidates had begun their campaigns some time before, the media coverage of the campaign prior to the election to the European Parliament was delayed by the royal wedding of the Crown Prince taking place on 14 May. The campaign therefore did not really take off until two or three weeks before the election. The campaign was not only shorter than those before national elections; it was also less well covered and intense.

Political TV advertising is not allowed in Denmark, but the parties do get free time on national TV. Two nationwide stations have different degrees of public service obligations. One of them, DR, has a tradition of providing free airtime to each of the parties and lists standing for election. In 2004, in the two-week run-up to the election, each party and movement got a 30-minute slot at 7 p.m. in which to present a five-minute election video and field two representatives to be questioned by a journalist. This closed with a lengthy group discussion among the prime candidates on the Thursday night. Besides that, several stations ran debates with one or two candidates, and some campaigning was reported on the news. Instead of TV commercials parties used smaller posters on lamp posts and ran large commercial billboard posters, newspaper and magazine advertisments. They handed out leaflets on the streets and at stalls, ran election web-pages, happenings, campaign buses and election meetings. Traditional election meetings were poorly attended so some candidates tried other means to get out the vote, including workplace and street meetings, and the internet.

The Danish party system at the European level does not correspond to the party system at the national level. There are eight parties in Folketinget, the national parliament, compared to six parties and two movements in the EP. In 2004 seven of the Folketinget parties and both EP movements contested the elections. The most pro-European parties are the Social-Liberals, the Liberals and the Conservatives. The Social-Democrats favour the EU, whereas the Christian People's Party – which lacks an MEP and had little chance of getting one – and the Socialist People's Party are more sceptical supporters of the EU. Only the (right-wing) Danish People's Party opposes European integration. The People's Movement against EU, created in 1972, opposes EU membership. The June Movement was created after the referendum on the Maastricht Treaty on 2 June 1992 and works to halt further Danish integration into the EU. The main difference between the two movements is that whereas the People's Movement strongly opposes integration, the June Movement accepts European co-operation and tries to limit EU integration. The only Folketinget party not to contest the EP elections was the anti-EU Red–Green Alliance, the most left-wing party in Folketinget. Instead of standing for election as a party, several of its members were candidates on the lists of the two movements.

Whenever there is a Danish referendum on an aspect of the EU or an election to the European Parliament, a major issue is the EU's institutional set-up. Consequently, the issue of MEPs' travelling between Brussels and Strasbourg, fraud, the attendance records of Danish MEPs and to some extent their pay were stressed in the campaign in 2004. But campaigning was also about the substance of EU policies. EU financial support for the agricultural industry was put on the agenda when a national TV station broadcast a list of Danish beneficiaries some ten days before the election, thereby provoking a general debate and allowing all parties to indicate their support for changing the system. Environmental protection was also an issue in the campaign and something generally supported by Danish voters.

The prospect of Turkish EU membership was also an issue in the campaign. The Danish People's Party opposed Turkey's accession whereas the other parties saw it either as only a distant possibility or as something that would increase European security. Other than that, terrorism was not an aspect of the campaign. The European Constitution featured to a limited extent only. The anti-integration movements and parties complained that the pro-integration parties did not want to discuss the European Constitution in the campaign whereas the latter argued that the electorate's view on the European Constitution would be covered in a referendum. In general, the parties did not make any use of the EP transnational party groups in their campaigns although a few references to them were made. Voter ignorance about the candidates and the lack of genuine campaigning were major issues throughout the campaign, and insufficient female representation was briefly discussed. All in all, the campaign contributed only to a limited extent to the electorate's chance of developing a real feeling of identification with the EU.

The EP elections in Denmark were held on Sunday 13 June with no other elections held simultaneously. The most recent elections at national, regional and local levels were held in November 2001. Local and regional elections were due in November 2005 and national elections must be held by then at the latest. The EP elections could therefore have turned out to be some kind of midterm evaluation of the parties at the national level.

Danish MEPs are elected by PR where Denmark forms one electoral district. The rules for nominating candidates are basically the same as for national elections so parties (and movements) elected to the national or European Parliament in the most recent elections, who are still represented, may contest the election and nominate candidates. New parties not represented need to collect a number of signatures equal to $1/175$ of the votes cast at the last national election in order to become eligible for election. Eight of the nine parties and movements contesting the EP election paired up in election pacts to boost their chances of an extra mandate. The two movements joined forces, as did the Socialist People's Party and the Social-Democrats; the Social-Liberals and the Christian People's Party; and the Liberals and Conservatives. These election pacts were primarily of a technical nature.

As usual there were a couple of campaigns aimed specifically at getting out the vote. These were run by the EP, the Democracies of Europe and some youth organisations. The Danish electorate is reminded of the election not only by advertisements but also by the official voting card sent out to all voters. This is not only a reminder but also eases the election administration if brought to the voting booth.

Low turnout, Social-Democratic victory and loss of the Eurosceptics

In Denmark EP election turnout has been much lower than turnout at referendums on EU issues and national elections, and also lower than at local and regional elections. Turnout in national elections and EU referendums has generally been around the mid-80 per cent level, whereas turnout at EP elections has varied from 47.8 per cent in 1979 to 52.4 per cent in 1984, dropping to a low of 46.2 per cent in 1989, a high of 52.9 per cent in 1994 and back to 50.4 per cent in 1999. In view of the turnout in 1999, it was decided to try and boost turnout in 2004 by making Sunday the polling day. The reasoning for this was that by departing from normal polling days and opting for Sunday, people would have more time to vote and would, by voting on the final day of EP elections across the EU, be able to get the result shortly after going to the polls. This, coupled with the relative distance of a national election compared to 1999, was also expected to help motivate voters to turn out and at the very least to give an interim verdict on the government. The EP elections did not compete with any major events except the European soccer championship. Nevertheless, in 2004 the electorate did not turn out to vote to the extent that was expected. Turnout was 47.85 per cent, 2.61 per cent lower than in 1999, and this seems to be due to lack of interest in and information about the EP and the candidates, and the sunny weather. So EP elections are indeed regarded by the Danish electorate as second-order elections.

The major winner in the Danish EP elections was the Social-Democrats led by former Prime Minister and former party chair Poul Nyrup Rasmussen. They doubled their share of the votes and went from three to five MEPs even though the total number of Danish MEPs had been reduced from 16 to 14. It was a major personal victory for Nyrup Rasmussen. He got two-thirds of the votes cast for the Social-Democrats, a number that exceeded the total for the Liberal Party (the second largest party) and beat the personal vote record (250 000) set by former Prime Minister, Poul Schlüter, in 1994. This support for Nyrup Rasmussen was due to many factors, among them that he is well-known by the electorate, that he benefited from an element of voting gratitude for his work as Prime Minister, and that there may be a trace of sympathy or compassion for him because he had had to leave his party chairmanship in 2002 following the 2001 electoral defeat. Exit polls showed that the Social-Democrats managed to retain 85 per cent of the voters that would vote for them at a

national election and attracted 23 per cent of Social-Liberal voters, 17 per cent from the Socialist People's Party and 10 per cent of Liberal voters. This indicates how distinct the EP elections are from national elections. The governing Liberals were among the main losers, losing two of their five MEPs (dropping from 23 to 19 per cent of the vote). This was an unsatisfactory result for the governing party that may partly be explained by the list being dominated by candidates unfamiliar to the public and by the electorate voting against the leading government party. The Liberals lost votes to both the opposition and its coalition partner.

It may be argued that the Danish electorate followed the trend seen in many other places in these EP elections where voters expressed dissatisfaction with the leading governing party, the Liberals. Yet, the Liberals did worse than opinion polls predicted for a national election at the same time, thereby suggesting that a genuine European element was at play in the EP elections and thereby also that at least part of the electorate relate somehow to the EU. The Liberals alone fared worse than polls predicted. When comparing the parties' share of the votes cast (excluding the two movements) the Social-Democrats and Conservatives did better than predicted by the opinion polls for a national election in June whereas the other parties did about the same. Besides that, the campaign was modest but did focus on some European issues. If the campaigning had been mainly on domestic issues – or international ones like the situation in Iraq – one could with some justification argue that the electorate had evaluated the government and opposition. But other issues were covered and could therefore also impact on voting behaviour.

The Danes are well known for their Euroscepticism which surfaces especially during referendums on European issues

Table 1 The Danish elections to the European Parliament 2004

	Votes 2004	Vote share 2004 (%)	MEPs 2004	Change in vote share 1999–2004	Change in MEPs 1999–2004
Social-Democrats	618 409	32.6	5	+16.1	+2
Social-Liberals	120 473	6.4	1	–2.7	0
Conservatives	214 902	11.3	1	+2.8	0
Socialist People's Party	150 518	7.9	1	+0.8	0
June Movement	171 927	9.1	1	–7.0	–2
Christian Democrats	24 284	1.3	0	–0.7	0
People's Movement	97 986	5.2	1	–2.1	0
Danish People's Party	128 789	6.8	1	+1.0	0
Liberals	366 734	19.4	3	–4.0	–2
Total	1 894 022	100	14	18.6*	–2

Note: *The volatility, that is, the sum of changes for each list divided by 2.
Source: Karina Pedersen 'Denmark', in Juliet Lodge (ed.), *The 2004 Elections to the European Parliament*, Basingstoke, Palgrave Macmillan.

for which Denmark has a tradition. Five have been held since the 1972 referendum on EC membership. In 1986 the electorate supported the Single European Act. It voted twice on the Maastricht Treaty, once against it in 1992 and then for it in 1993 following the Edinburgh amendment to meet concerns over citizenship. In 1998, the electorate accepted the Amsterdam Treaty but in 2000 it rejected the euro. The European Constitution will also be put to a referendum.

The movements opposing European integration were the losers in the EP elections in 2004. Whereas the European results overall showed a rise in support for Eurosceptics, the support for Danish EU sceptics fell. The June Movement lost almost half their support and lost two out of three MEPs. The People's Movement lost some electoral support but kept their EP seat via their electoral pact with the June Movement. The two movements' defeat, firstly, shifts the balance between parties promoting European integration and parties and movements that do not. Whereas in the outgoing parliament they had almost one-third of the Danish seats, they now have only one-fifth. Moreover, the Socialist People's Party previously had a Eurosceptic MEP but now has one more favourable to European integration. Secondly, the Euroscepticism has shifted a little to the right and become more bourgeois due to the loss of the two movements opposing integration that belong, though formally not tied to any political wing, mainly to the left on the traditional left–right spectrum and the moderate increase in votes for the Danish People's Party opposing European integration.

Overall, the balance between pro-integrationist parties and parties and movements against European integration shifted to the advantage of the former. The shape of the European party system more closely resembles the national party system. Whether this is a one-off or the beginning of a trend remains to be seen. Important in this respect may be the extent to which the movements opposing European political integration mobilise. Before the 1994 and 1999 EP elections, they had been mobilised at referendums shortly before the elections. In 2004 this was not the case since the last referendum was in 2000.

Karina Pedersen

Note

1. Thanks to Lars Bille and Morten Kelstrup for valuable comments on a previous version. Parts of this article are slightly reworked versions of parts of 'Denmark', in Juliet Lodge (ed.), *The 2004 Elections to the European Parliament*, Basingstoke, Palgrave Macmillan, 2004.

Bibliography

Pedersen, K., 'Denmark', in J. Lodge (ed.), *The 2004 Elections to the European Parliament*, Basingstoke, Palgrave Macmillan, 2004.

→ Mapping Europe: European Electoral Geography.

Deposit

In 2004, the payment of an electoral deposit for the elections to the European Parliament was a formal requirement in eight of the 25 member states of the European Union. Candidates from Estonia, the United Kingdom, Greece, Latvia, Lithuania, Malta, the Netherlands and Slovakia must all abide by this rule. Whilst half of the new member states have had the rule written into respective legislations, the tendency in Western Europe leans rather towards its disappearance, having been abolished in Ireland and France after the 1999 elections. However, in some of the countries where this condition for candidacy is not in place, other provisions are enforced, such as a financial contribution towards printing costs in Austria, and a contribution towards electoral expenses in the Czech Republic, that can have similar effects.

The 1975 Patijn report insisted on the need to establish a dialogue between national parliament representatives and MEPs. From that perspective, it would seem desirable for the same parties to serve in both elected bodies. Specific candidacy conditions – such as the payment of a deposit or the collection of signatures – for political parties or groups to secure parliamentary representation have been adopted across many countries. Thus, in the run-up to the first elections by universal suffrage in 1979, many governing parties created some propitious conditions for themselves to access the European Parliament using electoral laws.

In addition to the need for a clearer articulation between the national and European levels, a further argument put forward in support of the deposit concerns its capacity to limit 'phantom' candidacies, according to the expression used by the Venice Commission, or 'frivolous' candidacies for want of an alternative terminology. The sum to be deposited is considered sufficient to discourage any amateurs who wish to stand and develop a campaign platform as an opportunity to vocalise interests wholly unrelated to the European election. The United Kingdom has also presented the argument that the implementation of this measure can limit access from extreme candidacies to the electoral arena.

Occasionally, the deposit can also be used as an instrument to control and regulate political activities. This can be observed in Lithuania where the deposit is fixed to twenty times the average Lithuanian salary. Moreover, Article 40 of the Act on the Elections to the European Parliament of 20 November 2003 establishes that any change in or addition to candidates on an already pre-registered list will automatically generate an increased deposit amounting to the equivalent of an average salary. Additionally, the total deposit is tripled for lists presented by parties which have failed to submit details of their campaign accounts within the legally stipulated time-frame or are proven guilty of having falsified the accounts for the previous three elections to the European Parliament, the Lithuanian parliament (*Seimas*) or local councils. The deposit is thus a mechanism to induce political parties to conform to a series of legal and political norms.

For small groups, this sum can constitute a heavy form of expenditure. Admittedly this amount is reimbursable in all those countries where it is applied, as soon as the party candidates obtain either a certain share of the expressed votes or the electoral quota, or a seat in the European Parliament. However, for smaller parties the stakes are higher and there always remains the possibility that small parties will be unable to meet this threshold and as such, certain parties may decide not to participate in the electoral competition. Consequently, political freedom will then be limited as voters find themselves deprived of a possible electoral choice. In the United Kingdom such an argument has been circulated amongst opposition parties who oppose payment of a deposit, notably the Green Party in 2004. In Northern Ireland, during the revisions to the 1992 electoral laws which increased the electoral deposit from £100 to £500, several elected representatives alternatively proposed to replace this candidacy condition with the collection of 200 or 500 signatures. From the perspective of small groups, this deposit often appears as a shameful condition for eligibility which has no rightful place in modern democracies.

However, the collection of signatures often introduces a number of problematic issues. It requires a certain level of organisation and support which often only the main parties are privileged enough to enjoy. The European Commission for Democracy through Law (Venice Commission) also considers the deposit as preferable to the collection of signatures because of the technical difficulties surrounding verification. It has nevertheless introduced several points of clarification for the proper use of the deposit. The guidelines adopted on 5–6 July 2002 state that: 'if a deposit is required, it must be refundable should the candidate or party exceed a certain number of votes; the sum and the number required should not be excessive' (Commission for Democracy through Law 2003, p. 9).

However, the question remains as to which authority is able to determine what constitutes an 'excessive' deposit. Obviously, such a threshold varies from one country to another, according to the standard of living and political culture. Several legislations even fix the amount of the deposit in proportion to the average salary, such as in Lithuania, or to the minimum salary, as is the case in Estonia, rather than as a fixed amount. Moreover, any increase in the level of the deposit usually coincides with a reduction in the minimum number of votes required to secure a refund. In Northern Ireland, the £1000 deposit was returned upon obtaining 5 per cent of the votes in 1994. When it was raised to £5000 in 1999, the amount was subsequently refundable with 2.5 per cent of the votes. That said, the elevated amounts that were required from the candidates still remain a means of limiting political competition and raise the issue of the freedom of universal suffrage, especially within the framework of European elections where voters are very likely to vote for the 'small party candidates'.

Nathalie Dompnier

Bibliography

Commission pour la démocratie par le droit (Commission for Democracy through Law), *Code de bonne conduite en matière électorale*, Strasbourg, Editions du Conseil de l'Europe, 2003.
Maley, M., 'Deposit', in R. Rose (ed.), *International Encyclopedia of Elections*, Basingstoke, Macmillan, 2000.

→ Campaign Accounts; Dual Mandates; Electoral Operations; Eligibility; Financing; Members of the European Parliament (Legal and Political Status); Symbols and Practice of Elections.

Dual Mandates

The concept of dual mandates concerns the simultaneous exercise of several compatible representative functions and is thus different from the accumulation of functions over time. The expression may have been used for any type of political, party, union or association functions. But in France, where the phenomenon of 'cumul des mandats' has become a national institution, it imposed itself to qualify and regulate the monopolisation of elective mandates of a political nature. Elsewhere in Europe, this term does not really have a translation. *Dual mandates* or *Ämterkumulation* are not part of the usual political vocabulary in the UK and Germany and dual mandates often appear as a 'French specificity'. At the end of the 1970s, the establishing of an elected supranational institution opened new prospects of vertical holding of mandates at three levels of representation. In a space of 'compulsory dual mandates', as long as

its members were delegated by their national parliaments, the EP continued to receive a minority of MPs and senators after 1979 as well as a significant proportion of local elected representatives.

A French experience?

Originating in France on the political markets based on the poll tax of the July Monarchy, the dual mandate was perpetuated through the universal suffrage in 1848 and under the regime of the official candidacy of the Second Empire. After 1870, it developed as an instrument to increase a party's presence for the republican, radical and then socialist left. Encouraged by the district election, the phenomenon became the rule and favoured an early specialisation of the 'notables' and the professionalisation of political entrepreneurs. The weight of MP-mayors and sometimes presidents of departmental councils, explains the creation of electoral strongholds and hinders the party control of careers (Marrel 2003). The phenomenon became above all a cog in the political and administrative regulation system and a factor of relaxing Jacobinism and supervisions. After the 1982 decentralisation laws, it remains an instrument of clarification of a territorialised public action.

Dual mandates thus enjoy a wide consensus, even if their contestation in the 1970s led to a first regulation voted on 30 December 1985 in the name of decentralisation but in favour of party interests. The restriction to only two important mandates caused a recomposition in favour of the MP-mayors and encouraged circumventing practices through frontmen. By penalising the holding of three concurrent mandates, it legitimated the holding of two concurrent mandates. The regulation was strengthened again in 2000, in the name of local democracy and parliamentarism.

Holding several mandates at the same time by local executives is now forbidden. But it is again about maintaining the influence of local leaders on the legislative power, since the strategic combinations of national offices and local executive functions are maintained. The phenomenon thus persists and law now favours new circumventing practices with falling back on the vice-presidencies of the territorial assemblies and greater city councils, carefully kept away from universal suffrage.

The comparison with the data available for 15 European states underlines the atypical importance of dual mandates in France (French Senate 1995). The fact that this phenomenon is restricted, however, is less the result of special rules than the result of party auto-regulation as in Denmark, the result of a former disqualification as in the United Kingdom, or the result of its low electoral and administrative practicality as in Germany. In the Netherlands, Sweden, Finland and Ireland, law does not forbid dual mandates but a federal or decentralised system discourages such practice. In these states dual mandates are exceptional: in the UK, there were 80 members of local councils out of the 659 elected representatives of the House of Commons in 1997. In the Bundestag, elected representatives who were members of a Landtag or a municipal assembly only accounted for about ten individuals in 1997. In Sweden, the Riksdag usually does not receive any local elected representative.

The restriction of the phenomenon is also due to a specific regulation. Incompatibilities can occur between local dual mandates, such as in Italy where regional mandates are incompatible with the mandate of president or vice-president of a provincial junta and mayor or deputy-mayor of towns of the region. Such regulations also exist in certain German Länder and in Belgium where the concurrent holding of provincial and regional or European mandates is forbidden. However, as a whole, incompatibilities concern the local–national dual mandates. Authorised in Spain, Italy and Belgium, the concurrent holding of municipal and parliamentary mandates is forbidden in Greece and Portugal. Concurrently holding regional or provincial and parliamentary mandates is forbidden in Belgium, Italy and Portugal, whereas it is tolerated in Greece. In Spain, the autonomous communities' representatives cannot be MPs.

Some systems include 'compulsory dual mandates', as in the Spanish senate where the autonomous communities appoint at least one senator among their members. In 1995, 155 out of the 256 senators held a local mandate there, among whom 44 were the representatives of an autonomous community, 24 of a provincial assembly and 87 were mayors and town councillors. In Belgium, 21 out of the 71 senators are legally appointed within the senate by the community councils. When they are tolerated, dual mandates remain rare: in 1998, there were only 52 local elected representatives among the 347 members of the Spanish Chamber of Deputies (8 provincial deputies, 14 mayors and 30 aldermen). In Italy, out of 630 MPs in the Chamber, there were only 12 provincial councillors, 23 mayors and 71 town councillors.

Reducing and prohibiting national/European dual mandates

A minority from the 1979 EP election, the national/European dual mandates have been prohibited since the 2004 election, whereas the local/European mandates are still authorised (Table 1). As research stands, the diversity of

80

Table 1 The national/European dual mandates 1979–2004

	12/1979		07/1988		11/1998		11/1999		01/2004	
	Dual mand.	%	Dual mand.	%	Dual mand.	%	Dual mand.	%	Dual mand.	%
Belgium	19	79.2							*Incompatibility 1989*	
France	24	29.6	5	6.2	3	3.7	5	5.7	*Incomp. 2000*	
Italy	25	30.9	11	13.6	3	3.7	17	19.5	13	14.9
Luxembourg	6	100								
Netherlands	3	12								
FRG/Germany	26	32.1								
Denmark	3	18.8	1	6.3	3	18.8				
Ireland	12	80			2	13.3	2	13.3	2	13.3
UK	9	11.1	12	14.8	2	2.5	4	4.6	4	4.6
Greece			2	8.3	*Partial incompatibility 1981*					
Spain					*Incompatibility 1986*					
Portugal					*Incompatibility 1986*					
Austria					*Incompatibility 1995*					
Finland					1	6.3	1	6.3	1	6.3
Sweden										
Total	**127**	*31*	**31**	6	**14**	*2.4*	**29**	*4.6*	**20**	

Sources: European Parliament 1989: 112; European Parliament. Statute of MEP, *Comptage 1998 and 1999*; *Le Trombinoscope. Union Européenne*, Paris, 2003, 4th edition.

national uses does not enable one to specify the nature of the relations between the national electoral recruitment logics and the evolution of multiposition practices in the EP. As a result of autonomisation of the institution, transformation of the role of the European mandate in electoral careers or intensification of the relations between the local authorities and the European decision-making scenes, etc., the explanation for the transformations of the phenomenon is still to be found. We can, however, underline its main features.

At the Community level, the habit of considering the European institution as the product of the national parliaments explains the consensus made in 1976 on the right to dual mandates within a European Parliament that is now elected. Until 2002, Article 5 of the Act Concerning the Election of the Representatives of the European Parliament by Direct Universal Suffrage of 20 September 1976 specified that 'membership of the European Parliament is compatible with membership of a national parliament' (European Parliament 1977: 25). First, it was about not depriving a mainly consultative assembly of the most prestigious national personalities. In the absence of a common status, it was each country's responsibility to set the incompatibilities applicable to the representatives at the national level. After this text was adopted, Germany, Italy, Belgium and France added this right to dual mandates to their electoral laws, whereas the Netherlands, the UK and Denmark passed it over in silence. In Ireland, the presidents and vice-presidents of the two chambers only were excluded from European representation. Dual mandates were provided, in an implicit manner in Luxembourg, through Article 97 of the electoral law that then granted only one compensation. According to the counting made

from the declarations of the elected representatives in 1979, only 31 per cent of the MEPs were also seated in a national parliament. Dual mandates accounted for four-fifths of the small Belgian, Luxembourg and Irish delegations. It only concerned one-third of the main posts of deputies in France, Italy and Western Germany, and only 11 per cent in Great Britain.

During the 1984 EP election, Greece was the first out of the ten to forbid its MEPs to sit in a national parliament, except the two chief candidates. In July 1988, the country thus had two MPs among its 24 MEPs. But as a whole, the phenomenon had considerably decreased: only 31 out of the 518 EP members were still seated in a national parliament (6 per cent) among which there were 12 in the UK, 11 in Italy, 5 in France and only 1 in Denmark (European Parliament 1989: p. 112). The Greek initiative was followed by Spain and Portugal during their accession in 1986. On 7 July 1988, the marginal character of the phenomenon and the first national regulations made the adoption of a resolution of the EP asking for the prohibition of national and European dual mandates easier (OJ C235 of 12 September 1988: 131).

Belgium followed the regulation experience through a revision of its electoral law of 23 March 1989. Austria did the same as soon as it joined the EU in 1995. The Finnish electoral law did not mention the question but specified that the exercise of a national office was suspended during a European office. In Sweden, the government considered that an 'office in itself is so demanding that this very fact was enough to prevent dual mandates'. In fact, all the Swedish MPs elected in the September 1995 election left their national office on 9 October 1995 (European Parliament 1997). At the end of the fourth term of office, national MEPs accounted for less 2.5 per cent of all the MEPs according to the departments of the EP.

In France, the law passed in April 2000 prohibited senators and MPs from sitting in the EP and suppressed the right of option to the advantage of the latest mandate obtained. This measure made easier the resumption of negotiations at the Community level over the 1976 provisions in the context of the debates on the common procedure. In its decision of 25 June and 23 September 2002, the Council of Europe rescinded Article 5 of the Act of 20 September 1976 and made the office of MEP incompatible with the exercise of MP functions. Due to the presence of Seanad Eireann senators and Lords of the British Upper House, Ireland and the UK benefit since then from an exemption until the expiration of national offices for the first one, and until the 2009 renewal for the second one. The ten new EU members conformed to Community law by including incompatibility in their national provisions, thus obliging a certain number of the 138 new elected representatives to leave their national MP offices.

The national experience concerning dual mandates does not directly determine their use in the EP. For many observers, the scarcity of dual mandates is closely linked the obligation of personal voting and the use of qualified majority voting. In Strasbourg, European incompatibility appears as an important step in the emancipation from national parliaments. It testifies to the affirmation of the institution which is concerned with limiting absenteeism and the electoral and party exploitation of EP elections. But on the other hand, it just confirms the quasi-disappearance of national/European dual mandates regulated in six out of the 15 member states in 2002 and takes into account the disinterestedness in the MEP office of the national political leaders, whose logic should be specified beyond explanations based on virtue and morals.

The maintaining of local/European dual mandates

In parallel, the absence of any Community regulation of local/European dual mandates enables direct relations between the European legislative activities and the management of local authorities (Table 2). No Community text forbids local elected representatives of regions and provinces to sit in the EP. The phenomenon is, however, partly limited in uses or due to national regulations.

Greece thus forbids dual mandates to mayors and deputy-mayors. The Spanish law also prevents the members of the autonomous communities' parliaments from sitting in Strasbourg. In Italy, the regulation only concerns regional functions while it applies to municipal and provincial functions in Portugal. In Belgium, a law has provided since 1989 that the European office is incompatible with the functions of membership of the Flemish Council, French Community Council, or the Council of the Brussels-Capital Region, and also with those of membership of a regional council, Community or regional government, permanent deputation, municipality, as well as the functions of burgomaster or alderman. In France, the 1985 law authorised the exercise of only one local office with the European office. The law of 2000 now forbids MEPs all the local executive functions.

There is no list of the local dual mandates in the EP. According to our counting, realised at the end of the fifth term of office, a little less than $\frac{1}{6}$ of MEPs had a seat in a local parliament. Most of the local elected representatives were town councillors (66 per cent) or regional councillors (21 per cent). The

Table 2 Local/European dual mandates, end of 2003

Partial Incompatibility

Incompatibility

	Germany	Austria	Belgium	Denmark	Spain	Finland	France	Greece	Ireland	Italy	Luxembourg	The Netherlands	Portugal	United Kingdom	Sweden	MEPs	%
Member of a town council	5	1	3			1	12	2		7	1	1	3	2	3	40	6.4
Deputy/alderman			1				12				1					14	2.2
Mayor/burgomaster			1							3			2			6	1
Departmental councillor/member of a provincial parliament							4			1						5	0.8
Vice-president of a departmental council or provincial parliament							3									3	0.5
President of a departmental council or provincial parliament										1						1	0.2
Member of a regional parliament	3						11							1	1	16	2.6
Vice-president of a regional parliament							3									3	0.5
Town and region councillor	1						1								1	3	0.5
All the local elected representatives	9	1	5			1	46	2		12	1	1	5	4	5	91	14.5
%	9.1	4.8	20			6.3	52.9	8		13.8	16.7	3.2	20	4.6	22.7	14.5	

Source: *Le Trombinoscope. Union Européenne*, Paris, 2003, 4th edition.

local executive functions were few: there were only six mayors and one president of a provincial parliament. The concurrent holding of three mandates remained marginal. Contrary to the European/national dual mandates, the geographical distribution of local elected representatives seemed to reflect national practices as France remained the 'dual mandates temple' with 46 local elected representatives, that is to say 53 per cent of its representatives.

In May 2004, four out of the ten new member states defined cases of European/local incompatibilities. The Slovene law thus forbids the exercise of executive functions within local communities. In Cyprus, the members of a community chamber or town council – including the mayor – cannot be MEPs. In Malta and Latvia, the municipal mandates and functions are incompatible with the European mandate. In spite of the absence of reliable data, we must underline the marginal nature of local/European dual mandates among the elected representatives of the ten new member states. A number of polls of phonebooks generated the names of only a few Czech town councillors or Slovene former mayors.

In conclusion, the importance of local and/or national electoral experiences has characterised most of the MEPs since 1979, but the maintaining or the winning over of local mandates by MEPs seems to be limited to a few states. It can contribute to the autonomisation of the profession of MEP, by favouring the institutionalisation of peripheral political careers circumventing the national parliamentary scenes.

Guillaume Marrel

Bibliography

European Parliament (Sécretariat, Direction générale de la recherche et de la documentation), *Elections du Parlement européenne au suffrage universel direct. Rapport, résolutions et débats du Parlement européen*, Luxembourg, Office des publications officielles des Communautés Européennes, 1977.

European Parliament (Direction générale des études), *Une assemblée en pleine évolution. Parlement européen, 1952–1988. 36 ans*, Luxembourg, Office des publications officielles des Communautés Européennes, 3rd edn, 1989.

European Parliament (Direction générale des études), *Dispositions nationales en matière d'inéligibilités et d'incompatibilités concernant le Parlement européen*, Working Paper, 'National Parliaments' series, W-9, 1997 (http://www.europarl.eu.int/workingpapers/pana/w9/default_fr.htm).

French Senate (Division des études de législation comparée du Sénat), *Le cumul des mandats électifs*, Paris, 1995.

Marrel, G., 'L'élu et son double. Cumul des mandats et construction de l'Etat républicain en France du milieu du XIXe au milieu du XXe siècle', Political Science Doctoral Thesis, Grenoble, IEP, 2003.

→ Composition of the European Parliament; Eligibility; European Parliament; Incompatibility; Ineligibility; Members of the European Parliament (Legal and Political Status); Members of the European Parliament (Sociology of Political Office); Multi-Level Governance; Parliamentary Mandate; Tenure.

E

Election Manifestos

The political science literature has been little interested in the use of election programmes. The increase in power of the EP elections might not modify this fact. In the absence of a standard electoral procedure, national legislations continue to determine the techniques of appeals to vote. Manifesto, platform, programmes and profession of faith: practices and terminologies continue to vary considerably within the EU. Even the future MEPs' campaigns have difficulty moving away from these strictly national formats and stakes. However, the setting of multinational lists of candidates or the fact, for the European party federations, of campaigning under the name of the Commission's president they propose to induct in the European Parliament, might be able to change this situation. In a word, it could politicise on a transnational basis the programmes proposed to electors.

The question is very important. The commitment to a programme is a crucial element of the democratic mandate theory. It brings into play two key functions that Rallings (1987), Budge (1994) and Rose's (1980) works have recently emphasised: first, proving that the measures approved by a party's members have the status of a genuine 'policy programme'; then, offering to the electors the guarantee that such measures will be part of the governmental agenda in case of victory; in other words, a dual mechanism (party status and setting of the agenda) thanks to which the majority's preferences will legitimately be able to transform themselves into governmental action. Not all the parties and candidates in Europe go so far as to print the catalogue of actions they propose to implement once elected. Nor do they distribute details of their programmes to people's homes, as in Sweden, or sell their manifestos in bookshops, as in the UK, or use websites to encourage debate as was broadly the case in Germany, Italy and France during the latest 2004 campaign. But there is wide use of solemn speeches, radio and TV statements, inaugural speeches, and a campaign launching 'address', etc. The voters can only entrust their representatives with a mission if a choice is offered to them, a choice between known and recognised action platforms. In a word, the parties must create among themselves enough differences to be perceived as distinct. Budge, in his 1994 study of the German and American election programmes from the 1950s to the 1990s, showed that the themes likely to clearly activate the right–left cleavage (concerning social welfare, customs or military alliances) accounted for between 30 and 50 per cent of the total.

What election programmes favour is a mutual and continuous communication between candidates and voters. Friedrich spoke of a 'law of anticipated responses': the politicians would continuously adjust their decisions according to the electors' past and future vote. This suggests that democratic governments are guided by quite a simple calculation: that of the expected judgement of their electors. In his theory of the 'retrospective vote', Fiorina analyses the electoral mandate according to this utilitarian-inspired reasoning: while paying minimum attention to what happened during the months preceding their choice, the voters express themselves less over 'the direction in which society is going' than over 'the responsibilities' attributed to the candidates. They therefore initiate 'a calculation of sanctions based on past results' (Fiorina 1981: 6). This is the definition of the voters' 'power': an anticipation and retrospective judgement game, which generates sanctions and obligations. The role of election programmes is to make 'electoral influence' possible.

Other political scientists go further: the elections are an indicator of public choices that structure the governmental agenda. The main point is that 'the election is the essential event of the democratic process'. Rose and Rallings think, for example, that almost 70 per cent of the commitments formulated by the biggest British and American parties' programmes, indeed transform into action plans and public expenditure. The electoral emphasis is therefore used to orientate the governmental work. However, even if this is the case, this function remains unequal according to the nature of the elections and also of the coalition system in power or the institutional arrangements that govern the implementation of public decisions. Doesn't the development of a 'participatory democracy' reinforce this dynamic? That is what the defenders of referendums argue, all the more so when it spreads out throughout popular initiative mechanisms. The multiplication of referendums since the 1970s encouraged some scholars to hope that they would reflect more faithfully the popular 'will' by transforming the modes of political participation. Studies have shown that the success of consultations or referendums, although limited, is far from being insignificant: 8 out of 76 in Switzerland between 1891 and 1983; 522 out of 1495 attempts in the US between 1900 and 1990. The success rate is higher for abrogative referendums (aiming at rescinding the laws passed by the parliament): respectively, 52 successes out of 93 attempts between 1874 and 1983; 237 out of 699 between 1900 and 1976. In Italy, out of the 15 proposals presented to the Constitutional Court, two-thirds were maintained and approved by the electoral body (almost all of them against partitocracy, and more particularly *lotizzazione*, a rule of sharing of the financing and public employments between the main party groupings). Still, it is difficult to speak of a 'referendum democracy'. The use of such consultation techniques remains restricted and ambiguous, partly because the uses of referendums do not lend themselves well to defining commitments or reorientations in the conduct of European policies. Whether legitimating a decision already made, reinforcing the political credit of a declining authority or even disposing of a problem difficult to deal with, the use of referendums, restricted as it is to the fringes of electoral democracy, questions niether the division of political work, nor the centrality of the delegation principle. Over the last 30 years, around 40 referendums relating to European integration have been organised at the national level in more than 20 European countries. While almost all of them have been positive, and – apart from rare counter-examples – popular amongst populations, they have not prevented the development of a feeling of 'democratic deficit'.

And what if, more broadly, election programmes have another function? Some forgotten texts of political science suggest that possibility. Election programmes may not so much help to represent collective preferences as decide between competing teams; not so much to set the agenda of public decisions as to distinguish (i.e. to identify and designate) the holders of power. Schumpeter claimed that 'the role of the people is to produce a government', an approach that has been extended by those who made out of election programmes an instrument of power control. Downs (1957) proclaimed this relation to define democracy: voters choosing between competing parties for the control of government apparatus. Lipset (1960) also analysed the democratic order as a political system in which the population's weight is used to exercise the right to 'choose the candidates for political functions'. MacKenzie (1955) concluded his study in the same way: 'it is more realistic to say that the essence of democracy is to make possible a free competition for political leadership'.

Views such as these suggest that the expression of class interests or the programmes endorsed by the voters remain secondary in relation to the competition for political power, a fight subject to rules but where victory over the rival remains the supreme objective. What becomes of the principles asserted by the parties? On this view, their commitments are conceived as derivative: in much the same way in which, for a private company, production remains incidental in the overall pursuit of profit. The electoral competition? Nothing but a regulation process which is both oligopolistic and elitist. Freedom to vote? A 'choice' broadly constrained that boils down – but that is no mean feat – to simply producing a government or dismissing it.

Olivier Ihl

Bibliography

Budge, I., 'A New Spatial Theory of Party Competition', *British Journal of Political Science*, 23, 2, pp. 443–67.

Downs, A., *An Economic Theory of Democracy*, New York, Harper, 1957.

Fiorina, M., *Retrospective Voting in American National Elections*, New Haven, Yale University Press, 1981.

Lipset, S. M., *Political Man*, London, Heinemann, 1960.

MacKenzie, R., *British Political Parties*, London, Heinemann, 1955.

Rallings, C., 'The Influence of Election Programmes: Britain and Canada 1956–1979', in I. Budge, D. Robertson and D. Hearl (eds), *Ideology, Strategy, and Party Change*, Cambridge, Cambridge University Press, 1987.

Rose, R., *Do Parties Make a Difference?* Basingstoke, Macmillan, 1980.

→ Cleavages; Electoral Behaviour; European Electoral Sociology; European Political Parties; Issues; Partisan Identification.

Electoral Administration

The advent of democracy in Europe ensured the progressive autonomy of competing parties during election campaigns. This development led to the gradual transition from political confrontation to a state of well-arbitrated political competition. The role of administration has been a crucial component within this slow process. The neutralisation of political stakes, the provision of logistical support, the establishment of a framework for the conduct of operations, as well as the facilitation of the peaceful settlement of disputes have encouraged the separation of electoral competition from other social quarrels. These changes have allowed a large number of outdated practices to be set aside. They have also reinforced the notion that the only means of raising power in Europe is through the victory of democratic elections carried out in accordance with the rules and regulations that transformed what used to be a fierce battle into healthy competition.

Rules for the financing of election campaigns, systems of incompatibility, principles of regularity for the convocation of assemblies, voting formalities, and the definition of the status of elected candidates have all been developed, making it clear that electoral democracy is now framed by an arsenal of regulations. This situation is explained by the simple fact that elections are taking place virtually everywhere. In this context, three major types of framework or means to structure the conduct of elections can be identified. The first one involves the mobilisation of the executive branch of government. In a number of new EU members such as Hungary, Slovakia and Poland, democratic consolidation occurs through a powerful electoral administration, ensuring the proper conduct of elections in newly democratised countries. Here, the problem lies with the lack of statutory defined independence guaranteeing the bureaucracy's independence from the ruling parties.

A second means used is the establishment of independent commissions based on the models of Canada Elections (established in 1920), of the Election Commission of India (1950) or of the Australian Electoral Commission (1984). In post-Franco Spain, a 13 member commission was established by the parliament and judiciary branch. Known as the Central Electoral Council, this commission was composed of provincial and regional councils, as well as electoral councils from the autonomous communities. What was the role of this authority? Its main duty was to supervise all operations related to the European electoral process. The Council itself is responsible for both the logistical and financial aspects of elections. It ensures that security is maintained; that citizens are able to exercise their voting rights freely; and even establishes the opening and closing times of polling stations. Its instructions are supposed to be adhered to without delay. They are put into practice locally by authorities appointed by each state, who also make sure that the printing and distribution of electoral

material is carried out. The Council is also responsible for audio-visual information campaigns broadcast before elections to inform the public on voting procedures and conditions. It is also in charge of informing the electorate about preliminary election results prior to delivering them to political parties and the media. This type of institution is also commonly found in Central and Latin American countries (e.g. Mexico's Federal Institute of Elections).

A final procedure is the establishment of an autonomous court whose objective is to reinforce the influence of electoral rule. In the case of France, the parliamentary assembly ceased to verify the powers of newly elected candidates by transferring their juridical powers to the State Council, which became the sole guardian of national and European elections. In Britain, the task of supervising elections is assigned to the High Court of Justice. In this case, all appeals result in a definitive ruling presented to the speaker prior to being inserted in the official journals.

As a whole, we are witnessing a real 'administrativisation' of voting procedures and controls. This process codifies the rules of the political game in a clear and coherent manner. A summary breakdown of legislative initiatives indicates that, between 1976 and 1995, some 50 regulations have, in countries like France, framed the conduct of this activity. The range of these initiatives is vast, and includes a variety of activities from career development to the advancement of election campaigns. New regulations aim at making procedures more explicit and at publicising them. They also constrain a range of activities that had been previously governed by the mere competitive structure of political markets. The promotion of democracy in Central and Eastern Europe followed the same pattern. In fact, in order to ensure the application of standard notions of political pluralism and electoral 'honesty', the implementation of a specific definition of the role of regulations is essential. It is vital to define the protagonists with their specific roles and competencies, to increase the predictability of electoral behaviour, and to remind everyone of their roles and obligations. These functions should also encourage the development of electoral codification, especially among Central and Eastern European countries.

Olivier Ihl

Bibliography

Diamond, L., *Promoting Democracy in the 1990s: Actors and Instruments, Issues and Imperatives*, Washington DC, Carnegie Commission on Preventing Deadly Conflict, 1995.

Ihl, O., *Le vote*, Paris, Montchrestien, 2000 (2nd edition).

Goodwin-Gills, G. S., *Free and Fair Elections: International Law and Practice*, Geneva, Inter-Parliamentary Union, 1994.

Lewis, P. (ed.), *Party Structure and Organization in East-Central Europe*, London, Edward Elgar, 1996.

→ Electoral Register; Electoral Technology; Incompatibility; Observation of Elections; Symbols and Practice of Elections; Universal Suffrage.

Electoral Behaviour

Three objects of political science studies

Since its emergence as an independent academic and intellectual discipline at the beginning of the twentieth century, political science has had to face the complex multiplicity of its object of study. At first, political scientists only started to develop an interest in the study of political institutions, which represent the 'location' of power in a political system. Throughout most of the twentieth century, this remained the dominant object of interest of comparative political scientists such as Duverger, Rokkan and Sartori, as the roles, functions, organisations and effects of parliaments, parties, governments and electoral systems across countries were studied in their minute detail.

Soon, however, some academics supported the claim that studying institutions without studying their outputs – namely public policy – would make political science an incomplete discipline. The processes of formulation, decision, implementation, and review of public policy started to attract major attention, and to open new areas of knowledge on the development and quality of public policy-making across political systems.

It is only more recently, however, and particularly since the 1950s, that political science as a discipline started to realise that the study of institutions and policy-making could not be complete without the study of human behaviour within political systems. Whether focusing on the behaviour of the elite, the study of public opinion, voting behaviour or political identities, the study of political behaviour and its interaction with institutional designs and policy outputs became the necessary third pillar of the political science trilogy with, as its main sub-component, the analysis of the electoral behaviour of citizens.

Classic models of electoral behaviour and their critiques

When studying the electoral behaviour of citizens, political science relies on a series of fundamental approaches and models, which try to explain why some members of the polity will make a different electoral choice from others. These basic models and theoretical approaches have been continuously developed and modified since the 1950s. They have also been constantly criticised within our disciplines as none of these models – by nature over-simplifications of empirical reality – have been able to universally explain the political behaviour of European citizens.

Rational choice

One of the first seminal approaches to the electoral behaviour of individuals, the rational choice approach, was originally defined by Downs in 1957. It applies economic assumptions to the study of political behaviour by claiming that individuals are rational players who will adapt their behaviour in elections to the need to maximise a political utility function that includes and weighs their various hopes, priorities and expectations from the vote.

This approach is intuitively pleasing, as it suggests that voters consider the various political offers put forward in an election and choose the one that is most suited to their own preferences. However, several criticisms have been made of the rational choice model. First of all, by claiming that citizens will assess the political offering of the various parties competing in each election, the model seems to ignore the relative consistency one might expect from most voters in their vote over time. Indeed, many citizens keep voting for the same party without evaluating systematically the proposals and manifestos of all other competitors. Moreover, the Downsian model of the vote makes a heavy assumption on the level of information and sophistication of voters. Finally, its reliance on the relative 'proximity' between a citizen's favourite policy line and the ones proposed by the various competitors has often been deemed to be quite abstract and artificial, and even been criticised from within the rational choice community by Rabinowitz and MacDonald (1989) who believe that it ignores the existence of a 'zero point' on most policy continua and the directional nature of partisan evaluations (e.g. there may be more difference between being slightly in favour of European integration and slightly against it than between being slightly in favour of European integration or a little bit more so).

Michigan model

Partly as an answer to the 'non-repetitive' economic model proposed by Downs, Campbell et al. (1960) defined the Michigan model of the vote which centres on a new concept: that of partisan identification – that is a long-term attachment of individual voters to specific political parties – as a short-cut which, when strong, will dictate the regular (usual) electoral choice of the voter. However, this choice can also be influenced by short-term factors, such as the issues discussed in the campaign or the personality of the various candidates competing for the voters' choice. In a way, the Michigan model defines the electoral choice as a given quantity, a smaller or larger part of which is occupied by the recurrent and pre-established partisan identification, and the rest (smaller or larger depending on the strength of partisan identification) free for the evaluation by the voter of short-term factors affecting each specific election (Figure 1).

One of the problems identified with the Michigan model of the vote is that it is very hard to falsify. Indeed, there is no guarantee that voters think of their closeness to political parties any differently from their actual vote, and indeed, some seem to 'change' partisan identification over time, which makes the variable difficult to measure independently. Moreover, to some extent, the strength of partisan identification, traditionally measured on the single basis of self-placement, might in fact be best evaluated ex

Figure 1 Decision-making of a strong/weak party identifier

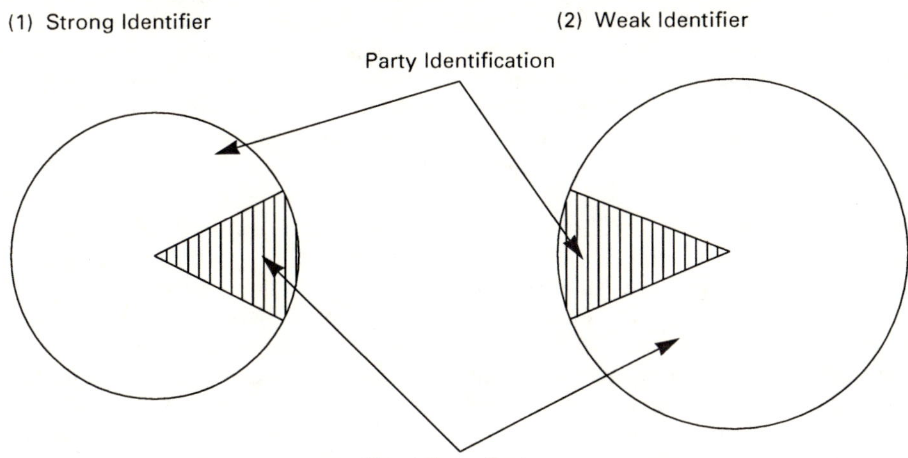

post on the basis of the 'room' left to voters to differ in their actual behaviour from the party they identify with.

Cleavage-based model

For these reasons, some other political scientists tried to go further in explaining the vote of citizens in a way which is less grounded in the ex post rationalisation of voters themselves. Indeed, while intuitively convincing, the Michigan model of the vote is all but speculative about the origins and determinants of partisan identification itself. For this reason, it is only partly contradicting political sociological models (see European Electoral Sociology article, this volume) such as the ones defined by Lipset and Rokkan (1967). Lipset and Rokkan claim that citizens' choices are dictated by their position on the four basic social cleavages which emerged following the Reformation, the national revolution, and the industrial revolution. According to Lipset and Rokkan, these cleavages have structured the party system of particular countries, and may include up to four cleavage dimensions: centre against periphery, religious against secular powers, rural against urban worlds, and owners against workers.

The main incompatibility between this model and the Michigan model is that the former does not allow for the 'short-term factors' identified by Campbell et al., although even for these authors, the impact of these factors is actually expected to be much less significant than that of partisan identification itself. Lipset and Rokkan, however, take the predictability of the vote further. Their model implies a voting behaviour based on who people are rather than what they think, and it implies a great level of social and demographic predictability and stability over time, associated with very minimal effects of electoral campaigns, issues, incumbent records, and the personality of candidates to mention but a few.

Environment and socialisation theory

Furthering the Michigan model in another direction, more grounded in the political psychological tradition, Butler and Stokes (1969) tried to understand how preferences are formed, but also what explains the stability and change of aggregate level electoral results. The authors insist on the impact of both early and continuous socialisation on the preference formation of individuals, marked successively by the voting preferences of their parents, particularly when they are coincident, and by their living environment, when a community is marked by a relatively strong political tradition. They also analyse the difference between the political changes due to long-term conversion ('switching voters', for example because of a realignment), defecting voters (usually because of a response to short-term factors), and replacement (the death or coming to age of a particular voter or of a new generation when franchise laws evolve).

Models of electoral change:
a first theory: realignment

However, it is models of the types of electoral change that have mostly appeared since the 1970s rather than their demographic logic that attracted the attention of scholars after Butler and Stokes's work. The first model of this kind is a model of realignment, which predicts that voters are progressively freeing themselves from the traditional cleavages identified by Lipset and Rokkan, but falling on the two sides of new cleavages that have formed in the second part of the twentieth century.

The main model of realignment that transformed political science perceptions in the 1970s is post-materialist theory. According to post-materialist theory (Inglehart 1971), since the late 1960s, modern democracies have started to be split by a new cleavage between materialists and post-materialists. The latter are mostly the post-war generations who were socialised in conditions of economic prosperity and political security and therefore started to aspire to

more than the economic and political power which structured earlier cleavages. Inspired by Maslow's pyramid of human needs, Inglehart suggests that these new post-materialist voters are indeed predominantly preoccupied by new values such as openness, cosmopolitanism, equality, and the protection of the environment, and are progressively going to represent a greater and greater proportion of European electorates. He also claims that these new post-materialists, often tempted by left-wing radical third parties or dissidence from mainstream political tendencies are mostly members of the wealthy middle classes, which would explain the student riots of 1968 or the profile of Green parties' voters, while having serious implications on the balance between left and right in European party systems. Building on Inglehart's work, several political scientists have tried to understand the impact of post-materialist attitudes (Dalton 2002) and values (Scarbrough and Van Deth 1995) on voters' attitudes.

However, the realignment hypothesis of post-materialist scholars has been largely questioned by the rest of the discipline. Firstly, the data do not always seem to confirm the hypotheses of Inglehart and his followers. Secondly, intuitively, the consequences of the post-materialist model seem to be in conflict with some of the fundamental things we know about contemporary electoral behaviour. The baby-boom generation should still be the main basis of support of Green and post-materialist parties when they are available in a given party system, while this is not clearly the case. Similarly, the generations born in the 1970s and 1980s and socialised in periods of significant economic and social crises should also be less inclined to vote for these parties which is also not clearly the case.

Models of electoral change:
a second theory: dealignment

Instead, authors such as Franklin et al. (1992) suggest that no major realignment has taken place in European politics over the past 30 years but, instead, a dealignment, which has resulted in a weakening of the consistency of the choices of major social and demographic groups, and an increased volatility in the choice of numerous individuals over time. The evidence they provide is overwhelming in a majority of the European Union member states studied, and it explains much better how European Parliament elections can be 'used' by citizens to express more than a simple partisan identification with a given party.

In a way, a dealignment is a necessary pre-condition for the second-order election model (see the article in this volume) to operate. Indeed, it implies a need for voters to distance themselves from a simple expression of partisan identification in an election, however little salient.

Behaviour in European Parliament elections and beyond

In this sense, the dealignment model is not only the most credible for the understanding of electoral behaviour in Europe since the 1970s, but the coincidence of the dealignment phenomenon with the introduction of European Parliament elections under direct universal suffrage makes them, in a sense, 'ideal-typical' dealignment elections in essence. They provide the institutional opportunity for citizens to express their dealigned attitudes in a way that is facilitated by the relatively low salience and expected political impact of the elections.

However, European Parliament elections provide an even more fascinating case study of European citizens' electoral behaviour than the broad confirmation of the dealignment hypothesis suggests, both because of its relevance to some of the other theories outlined above, and because of the peculiarities of an election in which the European question and the question of European identity have, at last, ended up leaving their mark after years of dominant 'national' voting.

We also notice clear 'traces' of other patterns of behaviour when looking at the last few European elections, albeit not in all countries, and not even always in the same countries over time. The analysis of van der Eijk et al. (1996) on the 1994 elections is remarkably telling in this respect.

In terms of the model of cleavage-based politics, in Northern Ireland, in 1994, the results confirm the fundamental differences of choice between Protestants and Catholics. The UUP and DUP were the declared choices of 45.2 per cent of the Protestant voters and 0 per cent of the Catholics, while the SDLP and Sinn Féin attracted the declared vote of 44.7 per cent of the Catholics and 0 per cent of the Protestants. Similarly, the 2004 elections seem to have largely reflected recognisable cleavage lines in Sweden and Spain.

In the case of France, however, in 1994, about 75 per cent of voters still voted for the party they identify with (against about 90 per cent for national elections) which suggests that the findings of the Michigan school were broadly applicable to these particular European Parliament elections albeit with more room provided for short-term factors. Similarly, for the 1989 elections in Greece, compared voting preferences showed a consistency of the vote in European and national elections of 94 per cent for the PASOK (the Greek socialists) and 95 per cent for New Democracy (the right-wing alliance). In a comparable way, partisan identification seemed to remain an important predictor of the vote in the 2004 elections in such countries as Malta, Cyprus, Belgium and Portugal.

Only the post-materialist realignment theory does not seem to be clearly confirmed by electoral behaviour in recent European Parliament elections, although, even then, the progressive consistency of the Green and extreme-right votes for a sub-part of the population suggests that these parties have been able to count on some faithfully aligned voters. In the case of the extreme right, which some might envisage as 'ultra-materialist' parties (a conception controversial in the political science literature) the electorate tends to be even more faithful and disciplined than for any other type of party.

The European dimension

Finally, however, one cannot understand the behaviour of individual European Union citizens in the European Parliament elections without considering the crossroads between 'national' electoral behaviour – in all its complex ambiguity – and the European question.

In Italy, van der Eijk et al. (1996) show that even in 1989, 37.1 per cent of the electorate primarily based their vote upon European questions rather than national ones (which, however, remained dominant for 47 per cent). Similarly, in Denmark, in 1994, the choice of the supporters and opponents of European integration were clearly divided in their electoral preference and differently so than in general elections. Bruter (Identity, this volume) and Bruter and Harrison (United Kingdom, this volume) also note that in the 2004 election, as in 1999, the parties that took a clear stance on European issues got a significant electoral 'bonus' as opposed to political parties which competed primarily on national issues (parties benefiting from this bonus included the UDF and Les Verts in France, UKIP and the Liberal Democrats in the UK, scores of Eurosceptic parties in Central and Northern Europe, pro-European parties of the centre in Italy, etc.).

Moreover, turnout was much lower in the elections for people who were undecided about the question of European integration as compared to supporters and opponents of integration, a finding which seems to mirror Bruter's (2004) findings on the impact of European identity (particularly as a 'squared' term) on participation in European Parliament elections.

While European Parliament elections seem to confirm the complexity of electoral behaviour in Europe and the increasing dominance of dealigned attitudes, it also shows that voters can, within a system of democratised multilevel governance, embrace the ambiguity of multiple party systems of reference. This is probably particularly true of the most sophisticated, young, and educated sub-parts of our societies. However, it is verified a little bit more, European election after European election, by the increased importance of Europeanness, European questions and European identity on the participation and behaviour of a highly cynical but certainly sophisticated and complex European Union citizenry.

Michael Bruter

Bibliography

Bruter, M. 'European Identity and European Parliament Elections', paper presented at the International Colloquium on European Elections, European Parliament, GSPE, AFSP, 17–18 November 2004.

Butler, D. and Stokes, D., *Political Change in Britain*, Basingstoke, Macmillan, 1969.

Campbell, A., Converse, A., Miller, D. and Stokes, D., *The American Voter*, London, University of Chicago Press, 1960.

Dalton, R., *Citizens Politics*, London, Chatham House, 2002.

Downs, A., *An Economic Theory of Democracy*, New York, Harper & Row, 1957.

Eijk, C. van der and Franklin, M. N. (eds), *Choosing Europe? The European Electorate and*

National Politics in the Face of Union, Ann Arbor, University of Michigan Press, 1996.

Franklin, M., Mackie, T., et al., *Electoral Change*, Cambridge, Cambridge University Press, 1992.

Inglehart, R., 'The Silent Revolution in Europe', *American Political Science Review*, 65, 4, 1971, pp. 991–1017.

Lipset, S. and Rokkan, S., *Party Systems and Voters' Alignments*, London, Collier-Macmillan, 1967.

Rabinowitz, G. and MacDonald, S., 'A Directional Theory of Issue Voting', *American Political Science Review*, 83, 1, 1989, pp. 93–121.

Scarbrough, E. and Van Deth, J., *The Impact of Values*, Oxford, Oxford University Press, 1995.

→ Cleavages; European Elections Studies; Identity; Mapping Europe: European Electoral Geography; Partisan Identification; Rational Choice; Second-Order Elections.

See also: all country chapters.

Electoral Cycles

When democracies rest on a stable, consolidated party system, elections are all but independent events. This holds for consecutive elections in the same political arena, where the result of the last contest is usually a more or less close approximation of the outcome of the next. It also holds for elections at different levels of a political system where an election result at the main level tends to affect the outcome of elections at other levels. This is nothing new or extraordinary, as whole libraries of publications demonstrate. The results of US mid-term elections relate in a characteristic way to those of the preceding presidential election. The same goes for German *Landtagswahlen* which are not a unitary mid-term event but scattered all over the federal legislative period. In the early years, their results used to follow the national electoral cycle

rather closely while this connection, perhaps as a result of the complex and complicated process of German reunification, seems to have weakened in the last decade or so. To be sure, it does not take a federal system to establish a link between the results of elections at different levels. By-elections in Britain, or sub-national elections in France and Portugal all seem to follow the same logic.

In earlier work, we have distinguished two interrelated classes, or types, of elections. One of them is generally perceived to be important, sometimes even very important (as when the pre-electoral support of government and opposition is or seems to be almost equally strong, or when stark contrasts about major policy decisions characterise the appeals of the contenders, or both); these are *first-order elections*. First-order elections decide who is in power and (to a lesser extent) what policies are pursued. Every electoral system disposes of a first-order election. But everywhere there are also other kinds of elections. This other and broader class we have called *second-order elections*. They are perceived to be less important, because there is less at stake. Examples are not only the sub-national or partial elections some of which have been mentioned before, but also the supranational election of the members of the European Parliament. For all member countries of the European Union, the supranational European Parliament election is an additional second-order national election (Reif and Schmitt 1980).

Because there is less at stake in second-order elections and in European Parliament elections more in particular, their results have been regarded as different from first-order election results in a number of ways. Probably the most important of them is that government parties may lose: many voters use a second-order election as a low-cost opportunity to voice their dissatisfaction with first-order government parties. Reasons for dissatisfaction are ubiquitous; the likelihood of disappointing voters is much higher for parties in charge of government than for those in opposition. Note that there are two sources of government party losses in European Parliament elections. One is vote switching: some first-order government voters desert and vote for one of the opposition parties. The other is differential mobilisation: first-order government voters abstain in greater numbers than first-order opposition voters. We know from the 1999 European Elections Study that differential mobilisation is the strongest source of government parties' losses: many more first-order government voters (41 per cent on average) than opposition voters (29 per cent on average) abstain.

But there is more to government performance than this. Not only are national government parties expected to lose support in second-order elections compared to their previous first-order result. They are expected to lose in an 'orderly' fashion. The order referred to is known as the (first-order) electoral cycle. According to this, government parties' popularity follows a cyclical pattern: after a short period of post-electoral euphoria in which they enjoy an even higher rate of popular approval, their support more or less drastically declines until after mid-term only to increase again towards the end of the cycle (to some unknown level). There are at least two explanations of this, one economic and one political. The economic variant uses the analogy of the business cycle and proposes that governments tend to deal with unpopular legislation (which tends to harm the interests of many voters) early in the period and come up with all sorts of electoral gifts towards the end of it, when the next election draws close. The political variant emphasises the evolution of electoral mobilisation which reaches a climax at election time only in order to melt away thereafter.

Thus, although the arguments supporting this claim vary from one author to another, government parties are generally expected to lose support in second-order elections. Is this what happened in the European Parliament election of 2004? Broadly speaking, the answer is yes. Of the governments of 25 member countries, 23 lost support compared to their previous first-order (legislative) election result.

It is worth noting at this point that France is the only country for which it is not obvious what the preceding first-order national election actually is. In late spring 2002, the French elected the president of the Republic in two rounds, with Jospin (from the left) defeated in the first round, and Girac (from the right) and Le Pen (extreme right) competing in the second round. Girac was elected with an overwhelming majority stretching from the far left to the (moderate) right. Legislative elections were held shortly thereafter, in which the presidential camp could secure a triumphant victory in a sort of honeymoon period after the presidential result. While this essentially characterises this legislative election as 'second-order' – the power question had been answered before – it is still the most logical election to compare the European result to. For merely technical reasons of the electoral rule applied, it would be odd to compare the distribution of votes between two very uneven candidates in the second round of the presidential election with the European Parliament result. And after all, the result of the legislative election only underscored what the true result of the preceding presidential election was.

National governments were the losers of the 2004 election to the European Parliament. The only true exception to this rule is Slovakia where the government parties gained roughly 10 per cent of the valid vote, but where at the same time participation went down to a record-low figure of 17 per cent. Another exception is

Figure 1 The electoral cycle at work

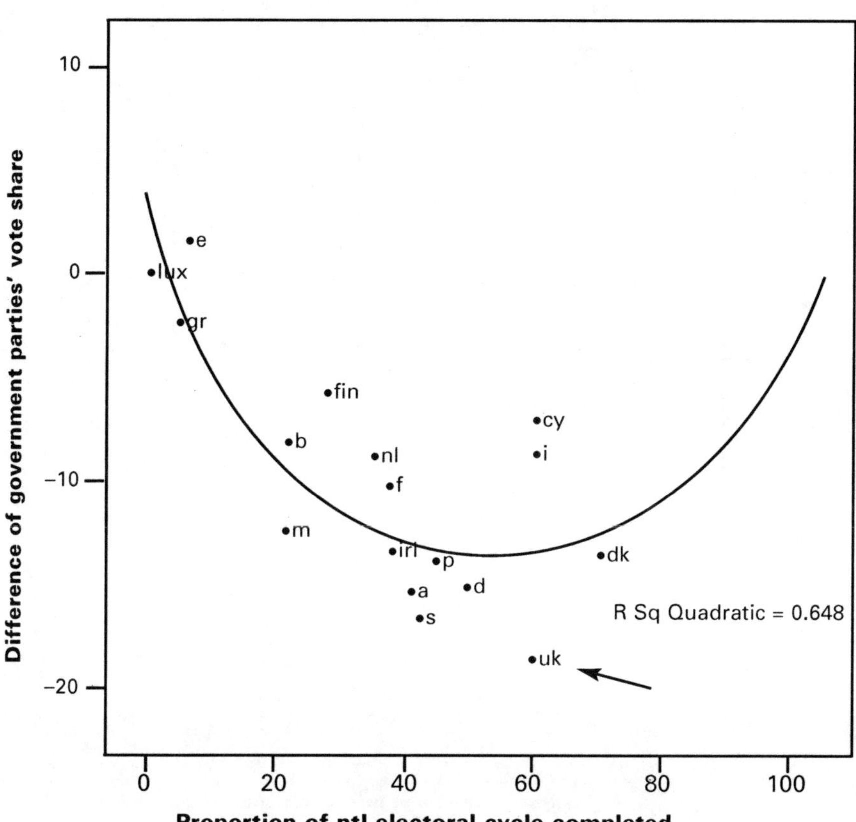

Table 1   The limits of the cycle: the new Central European member states (figures are raw regression coefficients and standard errors below)

Sub-population	Constant	Cycle	Cycle*Cycle	R sq	n
EU 15 + CY+M	1.347	−.522** .144	+.005* .002	.648	17
Post-communist member countries	−14.979	−.064 1.978	+.001	.000 .015	8

Notes: **p = .003 * p = .030. The dependent variable is the difference in the vote share of government parties in comparison to the last first-order election; for example, a '−18,4' means that all government parties together received 18.4 per cent less (of the respective number of valid votes). Cycle is the proportion of the electoral cycle completed at the time when the European Parliament election of 2004 was held; the variable ranges from 0 to 100. Where governments can call early elections at their discretion (as in Britain and Denmark), the latest possible election date is assumed to indicate the end of the cycle.

Figure 2 The volatility discrepancy

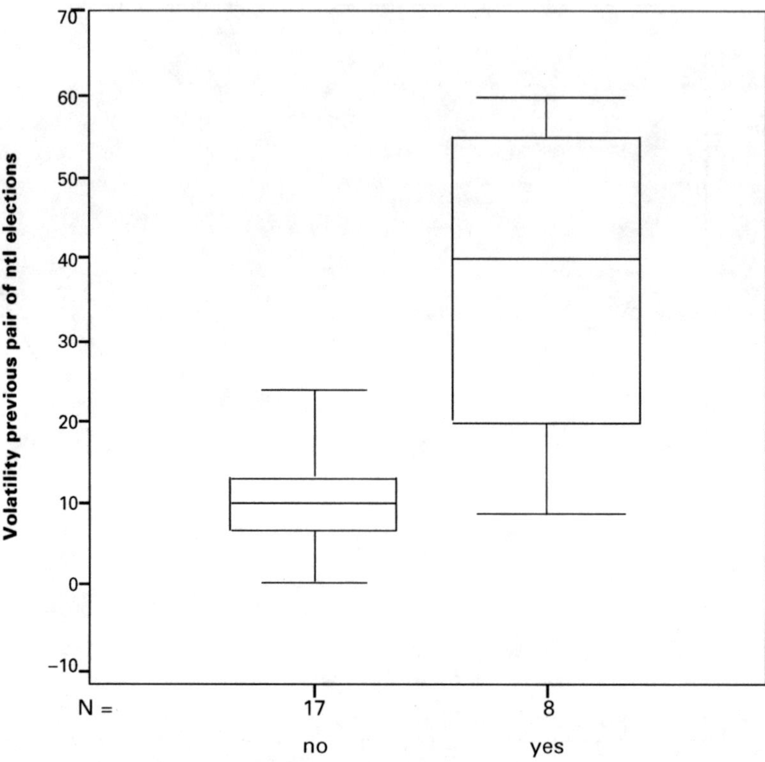

Spain. The new socialist government under Prime Minister Zapatero, which succeeded the conservative Aznar government one month ahead of the European Parliament election, increased its share of the valid vote by about 1 per cent. This, however, is in accordance with the expectation of a post-electoral euphoria shortly after the first-order election and therefore does not really count as an exception to the rule. We conclude that, indeed, governments were the losers of the 2004 European Parliament elections.

Not only are national governments expected to lose support in second-order elections, these losses should follow a pattern known as the first-order electoral cycle. Do we find such a pattern in the results of the parties governing EU member states? The answer is yes and no. There is a clear cyclical pattern in the results of the Western member countries (see Figure 1). But the Eastern results do not fit into it (see Table 1).

If we concentrate our attention for a moment on the results of the European Parliament election in the 17 member countries with consolidated or institutionalised party systems, it appears that the cyclical element is actually stronger in 2004 than it was in most of the previous European Parliament elections. The only serious outlier in 2004 is the UK result: Tony Blair and his Labour Party did considerably worse than the cycle would have predicted. It is of course tempting to attribute this to Blair's Iraq policy and the particularly poor standing of the British government at the time of the election as a result of it. But we must not forget that Britain uses two different electoral systems for the two elections under comparison, which could also explain some of the British particularity. (As is well known, Britain and France are the only two member countries which apply some variant of the single-member majority system for the election of national deputies, while Members of the European Parliament are elected according to a PR system – as everywhere else in the European Union.)

A second-order polynomial regression of the relative performance of government parties on the timing of the election within the first-order electoral cycle is the appropriate statistical model for testing the statistical significance of this cyclical evolution. In the West, it explains 65 per cent of the variance, with both terms being statistically significant. The same regression for the eight new post-communist members produces insignificant results.

The reason for these differences, we propose, is the nature of party alignments in the post-communist democracies. In most of these countries, a stable, consolidated party system has yet to develop. Parties have been changing names and alliances from one election to the next, and in between. As a result, many voters are changing their party preferences as well in between two first-order elections. And even if there were more stable party systems, stable party alignments are known to take some time to develop. It does not therefore really come as a surprise that volatility is still very high in post-communist democracies. How stark the contrasts between consolidated and post-communist electoral systems actually are in this regard is shown in Figure 2.

Median volatility is at 10 per cent (aggregate vote switches) in Western member countries, as compared to 40 per cent in the East. And the range of the distribution is almost three times as large in the East as compared to the West.

Hermann Schmitt

Bibliography

Campbell, A., 'Surge and Decline: a Study of Electoral Change', in A. Campbell, Ph. Converse, W. Miller and D. Stokes (eds), *Elections and the Political Order*, New York, Wiley, 1966, pp. 40–62 (first published in *Public Opinion Quarterly* in 1960).

Reif, K. and Schmitt, H., 'Nine Second-Order National Elections: a Conceptual Framework for the Analysis of European Election Results', *European Journal of Political Research*, 8, 1980, pp. 3–44.

Schmitt, H. 'The European Parliament Election of June 2004: Still Second-order?' *West European Politics*, 28, 3, 2005, pp. 650–79.

Stimson, J. A., 'Public Support for American Presidents: a Cyclical Model', *Public Opinion Quarterly*, 40, 1976, pp. 1–21.

Tufte, E. R., 'Determinants of the Outcomes of Midterm Congressional Elections', *American Political Science Review*, 67, 1975, pp. 540–54.

→ Electoral Behaviour; European Elections (1979–1999); European Elections (2004); European Electoral Sociology; Multi-Level Governance; Second-Order Elections.

Electoral Education

The history of the main European democracies reminds us of the political importance of electoral education as well as the development of a strong sense of civic duty as routine conditions of the principle of electoral delegation present in all types of representative democracy. Is it necessary, in this respect, to recall the famous prophecy of Proudhon, who argued that 'democracy' must in many ways also be a 'demopedy'? When solemnly opening the first session of the new European Parliament after the 1979 poll, a more cautious Louise Weiss spoke of the 'pedagogical hope' that had then been raised by the advent of the first European elections by direct universal suffrage. Deploring the fact that 'the very institutions that have succeeded in producing European beetroots, butter, cheese, wines, calves, and even pigs' had not yet been able to produce 'European men', the senior member of the European Parliament therefore expressed the wish that 'all schools within the Common Market explain that after centuries of conflict and killings a new era had arrived, based in principle on a lower common denominator, consisting of our culture' (*Le Monde*, 18 July 1979). Twenty-five years later, however, the success of this big project of European political and cultural socialisation, remains moderate.

Numerous efforts have been under-taken – under the impulse of the European Council – to reinforce the European dimension of literature curric-ula taught in schools. Such efforts contributed to a greater reflection about teaching methods on European subjects across the educational systems of EU member states (Pingel 2000). Numerous exchange programmes have equally contributed to the increased mobility of students and teachers in the EU, as well as to the improvement of their linguistic skills. Mobility, as one knows, widely favours the development of feelings of European belonging. Similarly, the creation in 1994 of the Youth European Parliament inaugurated a forum for the debate of European and civic questions, further transcending national borders, to encourage the development amongst European citizens of a deeper under-standing of their responsibilities.

The proper electoral and political dimension of this European culture remained largely hidden by this effort of transnational socialisation. Certainly,

associations in favour of communal inte-gration have historically contributed (Weisbein, 2000), here and there, to this socialisation effort, organising demon-strations to promote civic awareness (the European Movement in Latvia filled this role for many years). Political groups have also contributed to this pedagogic effort by publishing, for instance, electoral guides (such as the European election guide by Dominique Prost and Pierre Jacout, published in 1994 with a preface by MEP Henri Chabert) or, more recently, by opening internet sites aimed at raising awareness amongst European electors (this occurred in the United Kingdom in 2004 in constituencies concerned with postal voting, and in Belgium, experi-menting with electronic voting). The European Parliament also conducts campaigns and produces information brochures aimed at legitimising its exis-tence and actions (editing, for instance, comic books for schoolchildren) as well as at encouraging European citizens to vote. There are also numerous declarations call-ing for member states and communal institutions to invest in this democratic training. Since the signature of the Act leading to election of the European Parliament representatives by direct universal suffrage on 20 September 1976, appeals have regularly deplored 'the inex-istence of civic education in Europe' (to quote an official Franco-German brochure published in 1977). Such calls have never ceased recommending the construction of 'European citizenship through education' (in the words of a reflection group on education assembled by the European Commission in 1977). Advocates have continued to underline 'the fundamental role of education in the promotion of the active participation of citizens in democratic life at all levels: local, regional, national, and European' (Declaration of the Council of Ministers committee during the same year, launch-ing a project on Education for Democratic

Citizenship). Moreover, they named the year 2005 as the 'European year of citizenship through education' in order to fight against 'the lack of participation of the youth to democratic life in Europe'. However, scattered initiatives and declarations of principle alone are not enough to provide a concrete answer to the lack of socialisation accompanying the European electoral act. Electoral education does, however, have the virtue of bringing EU voters one step closer to the achievement of post-national citizenship. Due to the lack of adequate means and genuine political will, the latter remains, at the present time, little more than a pedagogic utopia (Ferry and Libois 2003).

Yves Déloye

Bibliography

Ferry, J.-M. and Libois, B. (eds), *Pour une éducation postnationale*, Bruxelles, Editions de l'Université de Bruxelles, 2003.

Pingel F., *La maison européenne: Représentations de l'Europe du XXe siècle dans les manuels d'histoire*, Strasbourg, Editions du Conseil de l'Europe, 2000.

Weisbein, J., 'Construire la citoyenneté européenne? Les contributions associatives à l'Europe politique', *La lettre de la Maison française d'Oxford*, No. 12, 3rd trimester 2000, pp. 57–66.

→ Age; Citizen (EU); Communication; Democratic Deficit; Electoral Operations; Electoral Technology; European Elections (1979–1999); European Elections (2004); European Electoral Act; Identity; Young People.

Electoral Operations

After the single currency, a single way of voting? The need to homogenise the vote's panorama for EP elections has indeed gained supporters. Promised in the Rome Treaty in 1957, this measure would avoid split modes of representation. If the national character of electoral procedures was problematic with 15 member states, it has become an inherent threat to the very existence of a European electoral citizenship in an enlarged Europe. It is not surprising that, despite the facilities offered by European citizenship, most EU citizens continue to vote in their state of origin. The historical sociology of electoral equipment has shown that it is through voting technologies that the citizen's relation to politics is built. From this point of view, the absence of a standard voting format – the strictly 'European' one of a transnational election – might affect durably the autonomy of voting.

From Finland, where a particularly high number of ballots are delivered by mail (sometimes up to 40 per cent of the ballots), with a list election since 1954 but forcing the voters to vote for individual candidates (the voter chooses the number attributed to the candidate and writes it down on his/her ballot paper), to Ireland where a typical system of single transferable vote has prevailed since 1922, according to which voters indicate who is their favourite candidate by writing a '1' next to their name on the ballot paper, then their subsequent choice (second, third, etc.), to the Netherlands, where more than two-thirds of the polling stations are fitted with electronic display, the EU is a mosaic of electoral practices. It is also a mosaic of schedules: the June 2004 EP elections did not take place on the same day, ranging between 10 June for the UK and the Netherlands, 11 June for Ireland, 12 June for Malta and Latvia, and 13 June everywhere else; they were held over only one day for most of the countries (the Czech Republic usually votes from Friday at midday to Saturday at midday) but over two days (12–13 June) for Italy. Note only do electoral schedules vary but there are varying degrees of freedom for voters, for instance to modify the lists of candidates.

In five countries (Germany, Spain, Greece, France and Portugal), voters cannot change the order in which candidates appear on the list. In eight countries (Austria, Belgium, Denmark, Finland, Italy, Luxembourg, the Netherlands and Sweden), this is possible by using the technique of the single transferable vote. In Luxembourg, voters can vote for candidates from different parties instead of for the set list of one party. In Sweden, it is possible to add or withdraw names on the lists.

To accommodate such diversity, the Amsterdam Treaty introduced the idea of 'common principles', hoping in this way to better legitimate the European Parliament and increase the voters' feeling of membership. Since a decision of the Council on 25 June 2002, efforts have been made in this direction: for instance, all the member states must use a proportional representation mode and the lists that cannot reach 5 per cent in Germany and France, 4 per cent in Austria and Sweden, can no longer obtain a seat. The borders of the constituencies have also been modified: until 2003, 11 states used the principle of a single constituency (Germany, Austria, Denmark, Spain, Finland, France, Greece, Luxembourg, the Netherlands, Portugal and Sweden), five of which have now adapted to the principle of multiple constituencies (France, Belgium, Ireland, Italy and the UK). Thus, since 2004, singularities have been diminishing: the Gibraltar territory, whose population had no right to vote in EP elections due to the Anglo-Spanish struggle over its status, has finally been integrated in one of the 12 UK constituencies. In Germany, parties are authorised to put forward lists of candidates at a regional and national level. Finally, the mode of seat attribution also tends to homogenise. Out of the 14 old member states that resort to proportional representation, eight adopted the d'Hondt system to operate the transition from ballot to seat distribution (Austria, Belgium, Denmark, Spain, Finland, France, the Netherlands and Portugal). Germany still uses the Hare-Niemeyer method, and Luxembourg one of its variations; Greece keeps a coefficient method for its proportional representation called 'Eniskhimeni Analogiki', and Sweden the Sainte-Laguë method (attribution by successive common factors).

The assessment of the election results and the rules of campaigning used is possible directly through the European Parliament in Denmark, Germany and Luxembourg, and through the national jurisdictions in Austria, Belgium, Finland, France, Italy, Ireland and Great Britain. In Spain, Portugal and Sweden, it is done through an ad hoc administrative commission. It is still the case that, unlike national elections, no electoral campaign regulation has been initiated at the European level, until the recent attempt of the European Council and European Parliament to set up a party financing system (resolution of 19 June 2003 on European political parties: statute and financing).

The notion of electoral operation thus covers a wide variety of forms of voting in Europe, a situation that, due to an increasing electoral demobilisation since 1979, might be reflected in the curbing of the EP legitimating process. After 25 years of direct universal suffrage, the question of political representation at the European level is still struggling to impose itself. It is true that European elections have always mobilised fewer voters than national elections. In 1999, for the first time, the abstention rate exceeded 50 per cent, an abstention progress of more than 13 points in 20 years. The decrease in the turnout was particularly great in Germany (–20 points), in Austria (–18 points), in Finland (–29 points), in the Netherlands (–28 points) and in Portugal (–32 points). The gaps observed between turnouts in EP elections and those ones of general elections in each country clearly demonstrate that the EU populations may find it hard to approach EP elections directly, that is, without using the frameworks and habits they inherit from national electoral contexts. In 1997, the EP's Institutional Affairs Committee passed a resolution in order to build a standardised electoral procedure. The Council has introduced several aspects of it and refused others, such as the setting up of a European single constituency for the designation of 10 per cent of the seats. There is now an urgent need to codify the notion of electoral operation, in order to give sense and substance to that of 'EU voter'.

Olivier Ihl

→ Electoral Administration; Electoral Technology; Observation of Elections; Observers.

Electoral Register

The registration of voters is a procedure of crucial importance. In fact, it allows for the concrete delimitation of electoral functions, thus establishing those who, within a country's population, can enjoy voting rights. Long associated with property rights, wealth, literacy levels, race or sex, this factor has not lost its political significance. Simply put, the criteria dictating the attribution of the right to vote are the object of a tacit agreement, and are essentially reduced to five main principles: nationality (in the case of EP elections EU nationals residing in another member state are allowed to register on the lists of their country of residence); age (over 18, or civil and political adulthood); individual dignity (as per the exclusion from voting of individuals having committed serious criminal offences); minimal autonomy of judgement (with the exclusion of mentally challenged persons); and finally, residence (determining both the right to vote, and the specific voting district of individuals; it must not be forgotten that close to 300 000 persons are without permanent domicile in a country like France). The existence of flexible yet exhaustive electoral registers is at the core of both the right to vote and of being voted to power. Securing a document that would guarantee the validity of the principle 'one man one vote', preventing multiple registrations and the fraudulent use of identity documents, was amongst the first electoral administration's main objectives.

While Article 137 of the Treaty of Rome stipulates that the European Parliament is composed of 'representatives of the peoples of European Union member states', electoral registers are still drawn up according to each state's individual national regulations and practices. This factor explains the gaps and differences found across the EU. In fact, procedures may vary based on registration systems, but also on the social, economic and demographic characteristics of each member state, as well as on the administrative competencies assigned to 'watchdog' organisations.

There are, within the EU, roughly three ways to elaborate these registration mechanisms: firstly, using civil status registers (abandoning the idea of separate lists compiled for purely electoral purposes as is the case in Sweden and Denmark); secondly, assembling a periodical list (similar to the UK system based on an annual deadline for registration, running the risk of constant delays); thirdly, elaborating a continuous European register or 'permanent list' through the use of data information systems (a potentially effective albeit very costly tool). Such a typology would only be an approximation in practice, since multiple variables play a role in determining the composition and drafting of electoral registers. Amongst the main variables are: conditions under which voters are required to identify themselves at polling stations; the nature of the information contained on voting tickets; whether registration is voluntary or mandatory; and whether identification is left to the initiative of the state or individual citizens.

If a European people is to emerge, should not such criteria be similar – or at least harmonised – across the entire EU territory? This would justify talking about a real political community: a distinct electorate characterised by the aggregation of peoples. Clearly, the work of harmonisation required by such a project is considerable, and its obstacles not exclusively political. The registration of voters at the European level would imply the establishment of a specific bureaucracy; a procedure that, in spite of its financial weight, is at the core of the common administration of elections. In fact, the drafting of electoral registers by the specialised services of single member states represents an average of 50 per cent of their allocated budgets.

While their common administration remains far from being achieved, the definition of European citizenship in Article 8B of the Maastricht Treaty has enabled the elaboration of a certain number of principles largely based on national laws, applied to European and local elections. For instance, part VI of the Spanish electoral law establishes rules and regulations applying to European Parliament elections. People residing in Spain benefit from voting (Article 210) and eligibility (Article 210 bis) rights, even without Spanish nationality by virtue of the fact that they are citizens of the European Union, that they conform to the demands of Spanish electoral law, that of their country of origin, formally declaring that they will not present themselves as candidates or voters in another member state. Such requirements are also found in the majority of member states, and have led to the redefinition during the 1994

European elections of the concept of 'voter': 5.6 per cent in Belgium, 2.5 per cent in France, 2.2 per cent in Germany, 1.8 per cent in the UK. Rather modest figures that, with the enlargement to 25 members are bound to increase, affecting the traditional state-centred concepts of 'national citizens' and electoral body.

Olivier Ihl

Bibliography

Almada, C. R., 'Voters' Identification and Registration Systems', *Trilateral Conference on Electoral System (Mexico, 6–8 April 1994)*, Washington, IFES, 1994, pp. 63–7.

Ihl, O., *Le Vote*, Paris, Montchrestien, 2000 (2nd edition).

Pinto-Duschinsky M., 'Electoral Registration in Britain: Is There a Case for Reform?', in J. C. Courtney (ed.), *Registering Voters: Comparative Perspectives*, Cambridge, MA: Center for International Affairs of Harvard University, 1991, pp. 13–15.

Rose, R., 'Evaluating Election Turnout', in IDEA, *Voter Turnout from 1945 to 1997: a Global Report on Political Participation*, Stockholm, Publications Office International IDEA, 1997, pp. 45–6.

→ Citizen (EU); Registration; Right to Vote; Universal Suffrage.

Electoral Strategy

Political competition impels partisan actors to undertake specific work aimed at mobilising voters through electoral offers tailored to the particular properties of their electoral clientele and the situation at hand. This political work in particular assumes the form of electoral strategies amongst which one can make a distinction between the strategies to establish favourable electoral rules, the strategies to position the party politically in an optimal way (whether to emerge or not as a party, change, join, or quit alliances, to select the list's candidates to widen its appeal, etc.) and the discursive strategies (to modify its discourse in order to adjust to the particular constraints of the European election, its stakes, the perceived concerns of the electorate, etc.). These strategic actions are interdependent since the electoral rules affect relevant alliances, which consequently induce compatible discursive positions.

The fact that the actors who lead these strategies only possess partial information and are entirely unable to control the implications of their actions raises a whole list of questions: Will such a method of election result in a favourable outcome for the government which established it or conversely turn against it? Will a given campaign theme meet a response from the voters? Furthermore, is it preferable for two parties to make a joint list or to run independently? The political actors do not have any means of fully understanding the true consequences of the various options offered to them. The instruments which rationalise their action, notably public opinion polls, remain expensive and often unreliable. The strategies of the actors are thus the product of the difficulties they meet in defining a reasonable action when faced with complex circumstances. The following question thus emerges: To what extent do European elections require the implementation of specific electoral strategies? Although effectively in the process of devolving positions of power in EU institutions, European elections enable political forces to feature in public debates, to secure broadcasting time on television and also to acquire positions as professional spokesmen or to appear to leave a mark in national political competitions. Governments and opposition parties alike cannot consequently ignore these elections and are obliged to adapt their

electoral strategies to the properties of the vote – notably with the configurations of weak political tensions which characterise the elections, the consequent weaker motivations for the voters to participate and their greater propensity to support protest and fringe parties.

Institutional strategies

Electoral strategies begin with the choice of an electoral system. At first, the United Kingdom insisted on preserving single-member districts for EP elections. The crucial issue for the two main established parties in supporting plurality was to prevent the emergence or strengthening of further potential political competitors. The pressure of European institutions in favour of proportional representation led the UK to change its electoral system in 1994 to closer align its electoral practices with those in use on the continent, to the extent that the most recent European elections actually witnessed the decline of the dominant parties to the advantage of the Liberal Democrats and a new party specifically created to criticise European integration (UKIP). In Germany, a nationwide constituency and a 5 per cent threshold have facilitated, since 1979, the emergence of new political forces likely to entrench their electoral brand: Die Republikaner in 1989, Grünen since 1984 and the PDS since 1999. In France the nationwide constituency, which supported any small party likely to exceed a 5 per cent threshold, has now been replaced by eight regional constituencies and a 10 per cent threshold. Initially proposed by Edouard Balladur, followed by the Socialist Pierre Moscovici, before being rejected by Lionel Jospin's 'plural left' partners, the regionalisation of European elections was finally adopted on the initiative of Jean-Pierre Raffarin's government with the unofficial objective of enforcing the marginalisation of secondary parties – notably the UDF and FN. A judgement from the Constitutional Council reduced the mandatory threshold from 10 per cent of the registered voters to 10 per cent of the expressed votes. The consequence of this was that the UDF and FN could avoid the worst effects resulting from the new electoral rules. However, smaller parties, which had previously used European elections as a springboard to nationalise their reputation (LCR-LO, Greens, CPNT, RPF, etc.) suffered from the new system. In certain countries, European elections constitute an important vehicle to transform partisan configurations, undoubtedly less because of their Community dimension than because of the undervaluation, by the dominant political forces, of the opportunities systematically offered to emerging parties by proportional representation, partly contradicting the political games reinforced by majoritarian national electoral systems.

Positioning strategies

Once the institutional framework of the elections has been established, competing parties will seek to determine which tactical alliances and options will offer them the highest gains. In France, until the 1999 European elections, 5 per cent of the vote – threshold of eligibility – was enough to secure the election of four MEPs, and, therefore, to provide a five-year office to as many political personalities as well as their assistants. The European elections thus constituted a particularly advantageous occasion for those parties harmed by the majoritarian electoral system in use for general and presidential elections. They allowed them to appear in public debates, to 'count their supporters' and to make European institutions pay for professional spokespersons whom they could not employ within the context of national institutions. It is thus unsurprising that, until 1999, European elections constituted a propitious occasion on which to launch a new party, to split, to promote a new political brand, etc. The National Front in 1984 and the Greens in 1989 both benefited from European elections to increase their electoral appeal, which used to be rather small; the RPF led by Charles Pasqua and Philippe de Villiers in 1999 used the European elections as an opportunity to develop as a competitive rival to the dominant right-wing parties. In 1989, the Centrists of the CDS presented a list that was independent from their traditional UDF-RPR coalition partners to test the possibility of liberating themselves from the bipolar logic induced by the majoritarian electoral system. Proportional representation in European elections thus encouraged several small parties to compete independently.

The composition of lists in each EU country is also an important occasion to develop electoral strategies. Former prime ministers such as Jean-Luc Dehaene for the Flemish Christian Party in Belgium or Poul Nyrup Rasmussen for the Social-Democrat Party in Denmark, or a former President of the French Republic Valery Giscard d'Estaing in 1989, all tried to benefit from a positive public image on the basis of their European engagement by heading their list. The first fellow candidates can be selected for their supposed capacity to boost the funds for their party or the principal candidates on the list. For example, in 1999, the French communists of the PCF placed Fodé Sylla, president of S.O.S.-Racism, in an eligible position to 'decommunise' the image of the party and open up to 'civil society'. Certain fellow candidates saw themselves selected for their social properties (candidates 'from immigrant backgrounds' in either an eligible or a relegated position, voluntary feminisation of the French socialist list before parity was legally imposed, etc.) or their territorial origins (when voting is not regionalised, the main parties tend to place on their list those personalities with a local reputation who can liven up the campaign in their region and provide a recognised anchoring for their voters). In addition, the electoral effectiveness of the list is not the only strategic objective of the party leaders who might also seek to maintain the political professionalism of an elected official defeated elsewhere, to push aside another candidate on the national political scene, to support a young party hopeful by giving him or her international experience, etc. Moreover, the choices of a party in conceiving its list does not exhaust its strategic possibilities: it is possible for the leaders to create a list which they have reasons to believe will 'steal' voters from another party. Thus in 1994, the French Radical Party list led by Bernard Tapie was reputedly secretly encouraged by President François Mitterrand to divert voters from the PS list led by Michel Rocard, and to force the latter to resign as head of the party. For the same elections, the presence of a second green list, 'Generation Ecologie' led by Brice Lalonde, was partly intended to weaken the leftist official Green party 'Les Verts'. As a result of the split, neither party made the 5 per cent threshold.

Discursive strategies

Finally, political actors are led to select the campaign topics which are best suited to what they consider to be their electoral interest. Campaign themes are particularly dependent on partisan alliances and the structuring of party support. The strategy of association with the Communist Party obliged the PS led

by François Mitterrand to adopt some themes identified with the labour movement to enable argumentative and programmatic agreements to survive. The 'plural left' in France or the governmental agreements SPD-Grünen in Germany have often led those parties engaged in these alliances to adjust their political statements in order to make them more acceptable to their partners and their partners' voters. Since the European elections electoral systems encourage political groups to draw up autonomous lists, the political constraints weighing on the partisan statements are comparatively weaker than for single-member district-based elections. Thus, a diversification of the political offer and a tendency towards a relative radicalisation of ideological lines can be observed since the need for considering the electoral alliances is not presented in the short term.

However, a particular constraint weighs heavily on parties' discourses for European elections. Indeed, parties are obliged, in front of journalists and voters, to state *something* on Europe and its institutions. Of course, this constraint comes short of a need to propose a fully-fledged 'programme of European government' – the absence of a monopoly over decision-making in the European Parliament makes that unnecessary – or even of a duty to harmonise manifestos with the other parties that will sit together in political groups in Strasbourg. Therefore, the development of a specific discourse on Europe does not represent a major difficulty for the candidates who intend to criticise the operational practice of the institutions (notably for the radical parties or Eurosceptics, generally in the opposition). The exercise is, however, more difficult for governing parties who, due to the consensual, cross-partisan and international character of the European project, fail to define an *electoral* speech on Europe. In other words, dividing and dissociating speeches is likely to mobilise voters whilst in most countries, 'supporting' Europe cannot come across as a 'different' offer between moderate left and right.

Moreover, European directives are negotiated by governments of different political orientations and are subjected to a consensus logic which is both cross-sectoral and ceaselessly temporal: partners are led to conclude complex transactions occasionally including later concessions in disjoined sectors of European integration. They must avoid permanently alienating other governments as this might jeopardise and weaken their positions in future negotiations. Consequently, the policies explicitly laid down by European agreements – treaties or directives – are seen as imposing specific constraints to potential government parties: they must not be criticised too vehemently in the partisan language of national politics and should not place any government in an uncomfortable situation with respect to its European partners. Within the EU framework, political actors in the Council and Parliament do not alternate power with ideological adversaries who are potentially electoral rivals but coexist with partners, holding, within their own national space, paradoxical political offers. They are unable to brush aside the proposals from these foreign partners by defeating them in electoral terms – they do not have access to their spheres of political competition – but are constrained by the institutional process of EU negotiation to revise their own position in order to define acceptable agreements which will apply to everyone. There is therefore a hiatus between European policies, less abrupt in their expression, and the specific constraints of another, largely national, institutional dynamic – that of electoral competition. The European discourse of the main parties is therefore largely shaped by frequent references to the 'general interest' of Europe, whereby the Commission acts as guarantor of the principles of fair competition, which ensure that in each EU member state, businesses and their employee-voters will not be disadvantaged. This helps to define a politically 'neutralised' discourse that will facilitate agreement between politically heterogeneous governmental actors. From this point of view, the constraints of expression concerning the discursive strategies of the principal party leaders in government during the European campaigns become understandable. It is impossible for them to claim that European agreements are the policy which they wished to implement, but it is equally impossible for them to withdraw their signature and question their country's participation in policy implementation. Conversely, except in a highly Eurosceptic environment such as Britain, it is equally difficult for the main parties to (1) blame their national political opponents for negatively perceived EU decisions, and (2) to only accuse foreign political actors since it will then be necessary to continue negotiations with them. This results in often awkward or unusual electoral discourses of government parties on the subject of Europe whereby a positive but general discourse on EU policies replaces the sharper populist and Eurosceptic undertones of protest parties.

Altogether, European elections certainly seem to create unique political configurations requiring the implementation of original tailor-made strategies. Proportional representation and the consensus-based inter-partisan foundation of European integration engenders specific constraints which affect both partisan strategies and the contents of political discourse, particularly in the countries which are not used to consensus democracy at the national level.

Philippe Juhem

Bibliography

Blondel, J., Sinnott, R. and Svensson, P., *People and Parliament in the European Union*, Oxford, Clarendon Press, 1998.

Eijk, C. van der and Franklin, M. N. (eds), *Choosing Europe? The European Electorate and National Politics in the Face of Union*, Ann Arbor, University of Michigan Press, 1996.

Gerstlé, J., Semetko, H. A., Schoenbach, K. and Villa, M., 'L'européanisation défaillante des campagnes nationales', in G. Grunberg, P. Perrineau and C. Ysmal (eds), *Le vote des Quinze: Les élections européennes du 13 juin 1999*, Paris, Presses de Sciences Po, 2000, pp. 95–118.

Holbrook, T. M., *Do Campaigns Matter?*, London, Sage, 1996.

→ Advertising; Campaign (Sociology of); Cleavages; Communication; Election Manifestos; Electoral System; Electoral Technology; European Elections (1979–1999); European Elections (2004); European Parliament; European Political Parties; France; Investiture of the Commission; Issues; Nationalisation of European Elections; Parity; Political Affiliation; Political Context; Political Market; Posters; Territorial Organisation.

Electoral System

Main features of electoral systems for EP elections

Even though in 1957, Article 138 of the Treaty of Rome had already instructed the predecessor of the EP, the European Assembly, to '. . . draw up proposals for elections by direct universal suffrage in accordance with a uniform procedure in all member states', EP elections are still not held uniformly. Nevertheless, substantial progress has been made since direct universal suffrage was introduced in 1976. Proportional representation (PR) has always been the key principle most member states of the EC and later of the EU wanted to make mandatory for the electoral systems in all member states. For decades, the first-past-the-post (FPTP) electoral system, applied in Great Britain, was the main obstacle for such a harmonisation, since the Irish and Northern Irish Single Transferable Vote (STV) produces quite proportional results despite the underlying majority principle. Therefore, the shift of Great Britain from FPTP to a PR system in regional constituencies for the 1999 EP elections made it easier for the Council of Ministers in 2002 to prescribe that the electoral system has to be list PR or STV. In addition, the new law allows each country to sub-divide its territory into several constituencies, to permit preferential voting, and to make use of thresholds which are, however, limited to a 5 per cent maximum of the national vote total. The main characteristics of the current electoral systems applied in each member state of the EU are displayed in Table 1. It shows that PR systems are used in 23 member states (in the UK in Great Britain only). STV is applied in Ireland, Northern Ireland, and in Malta.

Electoral system research has shown that the size or number of constituencies (if not only of administrative relevance) has the largest overall effect on the proportionality of a PR system. There are 21 countries in which there is only one (national) constituency. In some of these countries, there are more constituencies technically (Belgium: 4, Germany: 16, Italy: 5, Poland: 13, the Netherlands: 19), but these constituencies either play an administrative (Belgium and the Netherlands) role or serve to determine the distribution of seats within parties (all other cases). In all of these cases, the initial seat distribution is done on the national level. In 21 countries where seat distribution is done on the national level, constituency size only has an effect on proportionality if the overall number

Table 1   Electoral systems for elections to the European Parliament (2004)

Country	In EP since	MEPs	Electoral system	Number of constituencies	Constituency size(s)	Legal threshold (%)[a]
Belgium	1979	24	PR	3	1; 9; 14	–
Denmark	1979	14	PR	1	14	–
France	1979	78	PR	8	3 to 14	5.0 (const. level)
Germany	1979	99	PR	1	99	5.0
Great Britain	1979	75	PR	11	3 to 10	–
Ireland	1979	13	STV	4	4 to 5	–
Italy	1979	78	PR	1	78	–
Luxembourg	1979	6	PR	1	6	–
The Netherlands	1979	27	PR	1	27	-
Northern Ireland	1979	3	STV	1	3	–
Greece	1981	24	PR	1	24	3.0
Portugal	1987	24	PR	1	24	–
Spain	1987	54	PR	1	54	–
Austria	1995	18	PR	1	18	4.0
Finland	1995	14	PR	1	14	–
Sweden	1995	19	PR	1	19	4.0
Cyprus	2004	6	PR	1	6	1.8
Czech Republic	2004	24	PR	1	24	5.0
Estonia	2004	6	PR	1	6	–
Hungary	2004	24	PR	1	24	5.,0
Latvia	2004	9	PR	1	9	–
Lithuania	2004	13	PR	1	13	5.0
Malta	2004	5	STV	1	5	–
Poland	2004	54	PR	1	54	5.0
Slovak Republic	2004	14	PR	1	14	5.0
Slovenia	2004	7	PR	1	7	–

Notes:
PR: Proportional Representation
STV: Single Transferable Vote
(**a**) Except for France, the threshold is applied on the national level.

of MEPs the country elects is very small (especially in Malta, Luxembourg, Estonia, and Cyprus). Given these constraints, an electoral system is hardly able to improve proportionality. The number of constituencies in the four remaining cases ranges from three to twelve (GB plus Northern Ireland). With four constituencies and 13 seats to distribute, the Irish system is expected to produce the strongest 'design effect', followed by Great Britain (11/75), France (8/78), and Belgium (3/24). Another element affecting proportionality is a threshold, especially if the size of the constituency is large (like in Germany, where 99 seats are distributed). There are eleven artificial thresholds, ranging from 1.8 per cent in Cyprus (due to the low number of seats distributed, the threshold is ineffective) to 5 per cent in most (seven) other countries. Only in France and only since the 2004 EP election, a 5 per cent threshold is used on the regional (constituency) level, which makes it easier for regionally strong parties to pass it.

Not as important as the size of the constituencies is the electoral formula. The Hare-Niemeyer formula, which is equivalent to the Hare quota in combination with largest remainders, is closest to mathematical proportionality if the constituency is large, but it is only applied in Germany (since 1989) and in

List type	Votes; pref. votes	Electoral formula	Important changes
closed, non-blocked	1; all	d'Hondt	1994: German minority seat
closed, non-blocked	1; 1	d'Hondt	–
closed, blocked	1; 0	Hare/d'Hondt	2004: threshold; formula
closed, blocked	1; 0	Hare-Niemeyer	–
closed, blocked	1; 0	d'Hondt	1999: PR (& const.)
open (STV)	all; all	STV-Droop	–
closed, non-blocked	1; 3	Hare/largest remainder	–
open	6; 0	Droop/d'Hondt	–
closed, non-blocked	1; 1	Hare/d'Hondt	–
open (STV)	all; all	STV-Droop	–
closed, blocked	1; 0	Droop/largest remainder	1994: threshold
closed, blocked	1; 0	d'Hondt	–
closed, blocked	1; 0	d'Hondt	–
closed, non-blocked	1; 1	d'Hondt	–
closed, non-blocked	1; 1	d'Hondt	–
closed, non-blocked	1; 1	Mod. Sainte-Laguë	–
closed, non-blocked	1; 2	Droop/largest remainder	
closed, non-blocked	1; 2	d'Hondt	
closed, blocked	1; 0	d'Hondt	
closed, blocked	1; 0	d'Hondt	
closed, non-blocked	1; all (+/–)	Sainte-Laguë	not
closed, non-blocked	1; 1	Hare/largest remainder	possible
open (STV)	all; all	STV-Droop	
closed, blocked	1; 0	d'Hondt	
closed, non-blocked	1; 1	Droop/largest remainder	
closed, non-blocked	1; 1	d'Hondt	

Lithuania. The classical d'Hondt formula which is known to work in favour of big parties, is used in most (13) countries. The very similar St Lagüe formula which is considered to be more proportional than Hare-Niemeyer if the constituencies are small, is in use in Latvia while Sweden uses modified St Lagüe which is less proportional than pure St Lagüe, but minimises the disadvantages small parties encounter with d'Hondt. Each of the formulas and combinations (in the case of Hare and Droop) often has situational advantages or disadvantages, yet the effects that constituencies and thresholds usually have should be considered to be much more important.

Another noteworthy feature of electoral systems is the voters' choice among various individual or party candidates, which is essentially determined by the ballot structure. Preferential voting is provided for in 16 out of our 26 cases. In nine countries lists are closed and blocked, i.e. voters cast their votes for lists and only have an indirect influence on the persons representing their constituency. Only in Luxembourg, can voters choose among all candidates of the different party lists, and may cast as many votes as seats to be distributed (six). Where STV is being applied, there are no party lists, and voters can rank all individual candidates according to their preferences. In six countries, lists are closed and non-blocked, so the voter can at least overrule the party ranking of candidates. Choice options range from just one individual preference on a party list to the unique Latvian system in which voters are allowed to vote each candidate on the chosen party list up (+) or down (–). However, the rankings decided on by the parties are rarely affected by this participatory element.

There have been quite a few small changes in many electoral systems, but very few are noteworthy. A modification affecting all EU-15 countries except Luxembourg at least once, is the change in the number of seats per country. This has happened in 1994 (for nine countries, adjustment due to German unification) and in 2004 (for all countries except Germany, due to Eastern enlargement). Four additional changes can be detected affecting seat distribution. As noted before, Great Britain switched from FPTP to a PR system with regional constituencies in 1999. France introduced regional constituencies and regional thresholds in 2004, and gave up the nationwide constituency including the 5 per cent threshold. In 1994, Belgium introduced a (guaranteed) seat for the German minority, and for the same EP election, Greece introduced a 3 per cent threshold. All in all, there is no trend to make electoral systems more or less proportional, yet the most significant 'move' to the electoral systems of the European continent has been made by Great Britain in 1999.

Electoral systems for national and EP elections compared

To what extent do the electoral systems for European elections differ from the electoral systems applied to elect national MPs? France and Great Britain show the greatest deviation. Both countries have introduced PR systems for European elections, while they use an absolute majority (France) and the FPTP system (GB) to elect their national parliaments. In the other cases, differences concern the technical elements of the PR systems. First of all, the assembly size is always larger in the national context, which bears on the electoral outcome, i.e. the proportionality between the shares of votes and seats (see below). Another noticeable deviation consists in the high number of nationwide constituencies for EP elections that many countries – in contrast to their 'national' electoral systems – have chosen. If the above-mentioned development towards PR for European elections is taken into account, these observations can be linked logically: the less a country is sub-divided into territorial constituencies, the higher the number of seats per constituency, and, theoretically, the more proportional the electoral outcome is.

All in all, the electoral systems for European elections are less various and less complex than their national counterparts. This cannot be explained by the trend towards PR, because there exists a large variety of PR systems in 21 member states for national elections (including STV), which generally comply with the EU legislation concerning EP elections. So-called mixed-member systems, combining majoritarian with proportional elements, are not applied for European elections. This also goes for multi-tiered systems (such as the Austrian and Danish), in which the distribution of seats at a second (or third) level compensates the disproportionality at the first (constituency) level.

Apart from the assembly and constituency sizes, the STV systems, which are used both for national and European elections in Ireland, Malta and Northern Ireland (Regional Assembly), are technically equivalent. Due to the fact that Malta sends five MEPs into the EP, this country is the only case where even the constituency size is the same for both types of elections (though it is a nationwide constituency for European elections); yet, such similar electoral systems for both kinds of elections, with a difference limited to the number of seats and the constituency size, also exist in Finland, the Netherlands, Portugal, Sweden and the Czech Republic.

In some cases the real degree of difference is not evident. The German systems, for example, differ with regard to the 'personalisation', i.e. the personal vote for the constituency candidate (mixed-member proportional system), which does not apply for European elections. With regard to the electoral outcomes, however, they are quite similar, because seats are distributed in a large nationwide constituency according to the Hare quota with largest remainder and a 5 per cent threshold.

As to the voter's choice among the candidates of a party list under PR, the possibility of casting a preferential vote is slightly more widespread in the national elections. Italy, with its mixed-member majoritarian system, is the only case where the closed and blocked list type in national elections coexists with a preferential vote in European elections.

Further deviations concern legal thresholds and the electoral formulae. As to the former, which are more common with the PR systems for national elections, it has to be taken into account that in some of these cases they apply for remainder seats to be distributed at an upper tier (Austria, Denmark, Estonia). Such multi-tiered systems do not exist for European elections. The diffusion of a 5 per cent national threshold is not limited to EP elections. For national elections, thresholds have been introduced in all new member states, except for the small ones: Slovenia, Malta (STV) and Cyprus. While for EP elections the d'Hondt method has become widespread, the variety of electoral formulae is bigger for national elections.

Electoral representation

If we move from the predominantly technical aspects of electoral systems to the electoral representation of parties and candidates in the European Parliament, two observations can be made. The first one is: fewer parties are represented in the EP than are represented in the national parliaments. This holds true for eight countries, especially for small EU member states, and it has to do with constituency size. If only six MEPs are to be elected (Cyprus, Estonia, Luxembourg), more than 10 per cent of the national votes were needed to get a seat in 2004. Despite electoral system differences, constituency size had the single largest effect on electoral representation in these countries. Comparatively large electoral groups of small countries are therefore less often represented in the EP while comparatively smaller groups of large countries are. Yet, in five medium- to large-size countries, the opposite effect can be noticed: more parties are represented in the EP than are in the national parliaments. This, however, has nothing to do with constituency size, but primarily with lower participation rates in EP than in national elections, making it easier for small (and anti-EU) parties to get into parliament.

The second observation pertains to proportionality. In countries which apply electoral systems other than PR in their national elections, the vote–seat relation is considerably worse in national elections than in EP elections when they are using PR systems. Based on the last EP and national elections respectively, France (absolute majority), Lithuania (segmented system), and the UK (FPTP) show high disproportions (least square index between 18 and 22). In EP elections, disproportions are significantly lower (7 to 14). The same holds true for Italy (MMM system) and for Hungary (segmented system) where the disproportions between vote and seat shares in national elections are lower than in the countries just named (9 and 7 respectively), but nevertheless lower in EP elections (3 and 5). So all in all, the EP electoral systems produce more proportional results than many electoral systems applied for national elections. This result is remarkable, since all national parliaments have more members than the EP has by country. It is a matter of sheer size that excludes small parties in small countries from gaining a seat. An improvement for small parties could come from multinational party lists which, however, would then require a common European electoral system.

Philip Stöver
Andreas M. Wüst[1]

Note

1. The authors would like to thank David Farrell for his help.

Bibliography

Corbett, R., Jacobs, F. and Shackleton, M., *The European Parliament*, 4th edition, London, Harper, 2000.
Lijphart, A., *Electoral Systems and Party Systems*, Oxford, Oxford University Press, 1994.
Nohlen, D., *Wahlrecht und Parteiensystem*, 4th edition, Opladen, Leske & Budrich, 2004.
Rose, R., *International Encyclopedia of Elections*, Washington, CQ Press, 2000.
Shugart, M. S. and Wattenberg, M., *Mixed-Member Electoral Systems: the Best of Both Worlds?*, Oxford, Oxford University Press, 2001.

➜ European Elections (1979–1999); European Elections (2004).

Electoral Technology

'Cyber-citizenship', 'E-politics', 'Web-democracy', are only some of the expressions which have marked the development of electronic information processing channels that have started to shape our current political environment. Spread by learned editors or disseminated by advertising campaigns, these semantic gimmicks prophesise the birth of a new electoral era: an age of 'interactivity', which some eagerly brandish as a standard-bearer of 'direct democracy'. If distance voting (via the internet) has become the symbol of this electoral fetishism, and one of the many spectres which currently haunt the EU, it can be said to fall under the ideology of managerial positivism, whereby 'technology drives everything'. Within this context, electoral engineering can henceforth be discovered under a double relationship as being both a political source of legitimisation, and a principle of commercial certification. In analysing the impulses at hand, it is important to understand the intricate nature of the interaction between professional strategies, state technologies and scientific (and, sometimes, pseudo-scientific) discourse. Moreover, consideration of the motives behind the action of information technology manufacturers, media specialists and other technological spin-doctors is important in understanding why these individuals have chosen to establish and assert some authority over voting operations. As experienced experts, they can even benefit from being consultants of the electronic era, or even the implicit new judges of democratic modernity.

Thus, within the EU, polling station equipment has become a fully expanding market. Admittedly, electoral technology predominantly remains a bureaucratic activity. Controlled by technical divisions within the Home

Office department, this does not have any bearing on the 'uniform procedure' as stipulated by Article 138, paragraph 3 of the Treaty of Rome (new Article 190 paragraph 4, TEU). Furthermore, the Act introducing universal suffrage to the European elections in 1976 clearly established that until the implementation of this Europeanisation of voting behaviour, 'the electoral procedure [would remain] governed, in each member state, by national provisions' (Article 7, paragraph 2). In fact, rather than stifle this Europeanisation. process, the prospect for consultations at the European level can actually be said to whet and stimulate appetites, including interest surrounding a broad range of experiments. For example the 'Cybervote project' was co-financed by the European Commission and big companies such as Matra and British Telecom. It aims at developing an online voting system specifically designed for the local, national and European polls. Accessible from internet terminals such as PCs, hand-held computers or mobile telephones, it has been tested since 2003 on pilot sites in Germany, France and Sweden (http://www.eucybervote.org). A further example is the E-Poll project. Implemented from 2002 by France Télécom, with the assistance of Siemens, the Aquitaine region, the Italian Home Office, Ancitel (association of Italian mayors) and Polish group, it enables the voter to be identified according to their voting site through a system of finger print recognition sensors. Prior to voting, voters can also access information on national party programmes via a touch-screen. Then upon voting, votes are transmitted to a dedicated server which will enter, break down and centralise the results (http://www.e-poll-project.net).

The clearly visible control over electoral design, which is supported by the expanding use of computer science technologies and the nature of the media market in Europe, constitutes an extremely lucrative sector. Political economists and engineers compete for recognition or simply to receive remuneration. To meet the more technical demand, bar-coded electoral cards, voting chips with holograms, and portable polling station equipment have all been developed. Furthermore, the more recent elections have taken action on 'modernity' which can be taken as further proof that from henceforth technological requirements will empower institutional reformism. In Belgium, half of the electorate vote by using an optical pen on a computer screen. This provides an automated vote which facilitates the counting process at the end of the poll. In the Netherlands, over two-thirds of polling stations use simple touch-screen equipment, where access is controlled by an authorised official. Expertise on voting technologies is certainly very well structured. Driven by financial sectors, new operators often launch innovative action: in Latvia, Sweden, Norway and Denmark, it resulted from a mix of democratic and political science arguments and marketing strategies. Enticed by the promise of saving up to a 'quarter of the voting costs', through 'a simplification of procedures', which 'guarantees an increase in participation', parties and governments are easily tempted by promises of 'rapid results', 'an ease of electoral registration' and yet a 'broad access to candidate information' (for further examples, see the Foundation News Internet Generation 'online voting' section of the French Socialist Party: http://www.fing.org).

Obviously, this commercial prophecy can still run up against unyielding obstacles. Computer access in European households remains relatively low, and from a financial point of view, the level of investment required to install internet access across all 25 member states amounts to several billion euros. Not to mention the several hundred IT servers needed to absorb and manage the traffic data generated by the multitude of offices and electoral populations concerned. The risk of fraudulent activity is also a concern, addressed by Janet Caldow, director of the IBM Institute for Electronic Government, who acknowledges that: 'questions of safety and confidentiality are at present of the utmost importance' and are taken seriously in regard to internet usage. However, it would seem inapproriate to simply apply pure positivist managerial thinking to the world of electoral politics. Indeed, it would probably be misguided to believe that only a 'technological gap' is in question, as it is obviously not only a technical delay which might threaten the reliability of electoral results.

From the point of view of historical sociology, it seems that voting systems and devices illustrate the 'performances' of electoral equipment as being less the result of endogenous properties (despite the proclamations voiced by many experts as well as commercial leaflets) as that of the social reports and partisans who orchestrate them. Admittedly, voting devices keep evolving. Formatted through a process of detailed functional calculation, they come to inflect voting practices. However, the subsequent effect is achieved through re-establishing and organising social relations rather than by a particular constraining relation or standardising power. Thus, the expressions used for the voting systems – equipment and voting regulations – initially influence the conditions under which each technology appears able to mobilise the electorate. During the European elections on 11 June 2004, the deferment of the anticipated widespread experiment to pilot electronic voting (NEDAP technology of the voting machinery) in Ireland attests this 'latency' concerning the traditional procedures of electoral delegation. Despite an investment of 10 million euros in this widely publicised operation, the Commission on Electronic Voting chose to defer implementation to a later date, in particular asserting that more 'time' was necessary for a technology which significantly shakes up accepted electoral routines (http://www.cev.ie/htm/report/view_report.htm).

The question remains as to how it is possible to continue to hold reservations when considering the introduction of new electoral technologies. Performance is by no means defined *in abstracto*. Instead, it depends on the context in which electoral instruments are deployed. Some guidelines are provided by electoral commissions and official committees, that concern the political traditions of participation, the demographic and socio-professional structure of the public who have experienced them, the characteristics of the personnel who will implement them, and of course the campaigns led by the parties and candidates. Essentially, it means that an attempt is made to find electoral techniques that fit the particular social and political uses that will be made of them. The organisation of the material expression of an election does not only define the technical protocol which frames it. It also involves some thinking about the manner in which a voting practice will relate to customary competencies, partisan instrumentalisation and institutional effects. However, only an examination of these practices which socially mould the relationship with voting instruments will open a path to a new horizon of understanding. This is why it is necessary to insist above all on the conditions and the functions of each electoral technology. Each of them will affect the transformations and tensions which shape the political space of electoral contests.

In the same way as the 'Australian ballot' (a written card, printed and distributed by the state) pushed aside the illiterate and the poor, and just as the 'quality democracy' promoted at the end of the nineteenth century in the United States affected the vote, so will electronic voting have its effects. It will modify the system of competencies required to accomplish one's civic duty. This can be achieved within the limits of the uses which will then be defined in order to guarantee equal access for voters or independence of electoral movement. Unless a further requirement is expressly considered: that of preserving the ritual dimension of the electoral institution. It is important to reflect that in Europe more than anywhere, voting is historically connected with political liturgy. With imbued gravity and nourished solemnity, it is a civic act. Moreover, it is perceived as the mark of a social conformism. Lipset (1960: 223) suggested that: 'the feeling of social duty and the influence of their medium can bring voters to vote who do not feel personally interested by the result of the poll.' This is further proof that voting is not only the means to convey an opinion. It also determines the nature of the judgement transmitted. In voting for a candidate, one also votes for the institution. It is thus important to reiterate that technique and politics do not develop separately in electoral terms. For this, there is a simple reason: the control of the range of electoral technologies is always imbued with political stakes. Whereas some already imagine the possibility of voting over the telephone, or using magnetic cards or electronic communication via the World Wide Web, it is worth underlining that the effectiveness of devices of expression and enumeration of 'opinions' depends on a variety of complex relationships. These involve the interaction between payments, which are themselves marked by socially differentiated usages, and the experts engaged in the sacred operation of voting. It is precisely where these forms and practices meet that the importance of voting technologies lies. It is at this crossroads that the true importance of electoral conventions is revealed, that the true democratic meaning and consequences of using a ballot box, a card or a touch-screen button can be understood.

Olivier Ihl

Bibliography

Arterton, F. C., *Teledemocracy: Can Technology Protect Democracy?*, London, Sage, 1987.
Buchstein, H., 'Bittere Bytes: Cyberbürger und Demokratietheorie', *Deutsche Zeitschrift für Philosophie*, 44, 1996, pp. 583–607.
Caldow, J., *The Virtual Ballot Box: a Survey of Digital Democracy in Europe*, Institute of Electronic Government, 1999, manuscript.
Friedland, L. A., 'Electronic Democracy and the New Citizenship', *Media, Culture and Society*, 18, 2, 1996, pp. 185–212.
Grossman, L. K., *The Electronic Republic: Reshaping Democracy in the Information Age*, New York, Viking, 1995.
Ihl, O., 'Un battement d'aile de papillon. Sur les technologies de vote aux Etats-Unis', in J. Lagroye (ed.), *La politisation*, Paris, Belin, 2003, pp. 279–99.
Lipset, S.M. *Political Man*, London, Heinemann, 1960.

→ Act of 1976; Compulsory Voting; Electoral Operations; Identity; Internet; Polling Stations; Symbolism; Symbols and Practice of Elections.

Eligibility

Next to the 450 million citizens (including 352 million voters) in 25 different countries, it is the several thousands of candidates to the 732 seats of the European Parliament who also made the

June 2004 European Parliament election the most impressive since 1979. However, the rules of the games are such that it is sometimes unclear whether one should talk of one single election or of 25 different ones since, alongside the differences in voters' conditions, the rules of eligibility also varied across the member states.

The common condition across all countries is to be a citizen of one of the member states, but apart from the limitation of campaign expenses, the other rules vary from country to country. In 13 countries, official dates are provided for the start of the campaign, while in the other 12, all stems from an agreement between the parties themselves. The minimum age of eligibility is 18 in Germany, Denmark, Spain, Finland, Hungary, the Netherlands, Portugal, Sweden, Slovenia and Malta; 19 in Austria; 21 in Belgium, Ireland, Luxembourg, the United Kingdom, Poland, Slovakia, Lithuania, Latvia, Estonia and the Czech Republic; 23 in France; and 25 in Cyprus and Italy. The candidates must also state that they are not running for election in one of the other member states. The minimum length of residence to be eligible in a given country where one is not citizen also varies significantly. In Luxembourg, it is a minimum of ten of the twelve years before the election, but in Poland, it is only five years, and in France a mere six months of continuous residence. In Slovenia, candidates must simply specify their citizenship and give the address of their permanent residence in Slovenia.

Who can run for elections also follows no common pattern. In six countries (Germany, Denmark, Greece, Netherlands, Sweden and Slovakia), only parties and similar organisations can run. In some other member states, a number of signatures are instead required, whether they are signatures from officials (four MPs in Slovenia), or

from voters supporting the list (10 000 in Poland, 20 000 in Hungary, 30–35 000 in Italy). In Greece, Ireland, the Netherlands, the United Kingdom, Malta and Slovakia, candidates have to pay a deposit, while in Austria, each list must reimburse the state for the cost of printing the ballots (€3,600). Lastly, the final date to declare one's candidacy varies from two to six weeks before the election date.

The heterogeneity of electoral rules remains a prominent characteristic of European Parliament elections. National historical traditions shape eligibility rules in a sort of (albeit less poetic) Prévert-style inventory, despite the Rome Treaty of 1957 already mentioning the need for uniform rules of selection of the then European Assembly, which institutional designers wanted to be a truly autonomous institution representing directly the European people. The Amsterdam Treaty replaces these common rules by 'common principles', based on a number of legislative instruments such as the Council decisions of 25 June 2002 and 23 September 2002, modifying the Act of 20 September 1976. These principles include direct universal suffrage, the right to vote for all EU citizens in their country of origin or residence, uniform five-year mandates, a synchronised election which can be held between the Thursday morning and the Sunday evening, a list-based proportional or single transferable vote electoral system, the possibility of a threshold no higher than 5 per cent of the votes, and a synchronised counting of the votes after the whole of the European Union has finished voting. However, this sketchy harmonisation seems to implicitly renounce the true establishment of a 'common voting procedure' as specified in Article 128, paragraph 3 of the Treaty. Most of the details of the rules of eligibility therefore appear to reflect national traditions, concerns and heritages rather than a truly unified European rule of the game (Strudel 2003).

Sylvie Strudel

Bibliography

Strudel, S., 'Polyrythmie européenne', *Revue Française de Science Politique*, 53, 1, 2003, pp. 3–34.

→ Act of 1976; Citizen (EU); Dual Mandates; European Parliament; Incompatibility; Members of the European Parliament (Legal and Political Status); Parliamentary Mandate.

Enlargement

The potential effects of enlargement on the composition of the European Parliament awoke the interest of numerous scholars and European political leaders. Was the accession of ten new member states and their subsequent participation in the European elections in June 2004 likely to modify the political equilibrium of the European Parliament? Were the elections going to be won in the East? Was the arrival of new member states going to affect the European political debate and agenda? Would the newly elected MEPs succeed in rapidly integrating the practical regulations of such a complex institution? For instance, party groups and the secretariat feared that the technical and linguistic competencies of accession MEPs, as well as their experience of high-responsibility assignments or international organisations, would be inferior to that of their counterparts (Costa 2004). While it is to early to answer these questions, some preliminary lessons can be drawn.

The ten new states are represented by 162 of the 732 MEPs, that is 22 per cent of the European Parliament. This figure attests the importance of these changes, although, with the exception of Poland, the new member states are not very populated so that their delegations tend to be average or small in size. At the same time, the total number of representatives of 'small states', who often react against the power of 'big states', has grown, particularly with the eight new 'Eastern' countries (which only regained their full sovereignty after 1989 and are very sensitive to instructions coming from abroad). Another consequence of the enlargement has been the eastward shift of the European Parliament's centre of gravity. Consequently, certain EU policies (i.e. regional, fishing) could either increase or decrease in importance.

With the 2004 elections, the accession of the new member states has not modified the balance between political groups in the European Parliament, even though the gap between the EPP and the ESP has significantly widened. In fact, the repartition of MEPs among the different groups for the new joiners is as follows: 69 for the EPP, 33 for the PES, 19 for the ELDR, 1 for the Greens; 8 for the far-left GUE, 11 for the Eurosceptic ID, 13 for the far-right UEN, and 8 unaffiliated MEPs.

At this stage, several points must be emphasised. The following results underline the relative support of the newcomers to the Eurosceptic group. The Greens obtained a particularly disappointing score, partly explained by the fact that 'post-materialist' issues have yet to be incorporated into the agenda of ex-communist countries. Good results were secured by the Liberals. Finally, the weak score obtained by the Social-Democrats can be explained by their presence in the governments of several major countries (including the three largest new members: Poland, the Czech Republic and Hungary) and by the protest vote affecting all governments in power. Interestingly, the Social-Democrats scored particularly poorly in Poland and in the Czech Republic, where they also enjoy great electoral potential. Moreover, many wonder about the consequences within the political groups in the European Parliament of the weight and influence of MEPs from the ten new member states. In fact these factors vary greatly from one group to the other. Newcomers represent 25.7 per cent of the EPP group, with strong representations from the Hungarian and Polish delegations. However, their share of seats within the socialist groups is only 16.3 per cent. Their representation within the ELDR reaches 21.5 per cent, 19.5 per cent in the Communist group, 2 per cent only of the Greens, and 28.5 per cent among unaffiliated members. These figures compare to 22 per cent of MEPs from the new member states. By contrast, new states' MEPs also account for 30.5 per cent in the Independence and Democracy group, coming mainly from Poland and 49.5 per cent in the group UEN. Consequently, the weight of new democracies is particularly important among the sovereignist and Eurosceptic camps.

The enlargement of the European Union is also likely to have political, ideological and organisational consequences among different political groups. An increased sensitivity to certain problems might arise. A 'good neighbour' policy towards states east of the new EU border might, for instance, be introduced by new MEPs. From an organisational standpoint, groups in the European Parliament have seen the number of parties they represent grow substantially. For instance, the EPP comprises more than 19 different political parties coming from new member states alone. Its heterogeneity will considerably increase both by the sheer number of parties involved, and by the different visions of Europe, economic policies, and national competition conveyed by them. The ELDR will welcome nine new political parties, a substantial number considering its political and organisational force. The situation is slightly easier within the Social-Democrat family, which includes eight new parties. These variations can be explained by the different practices relating to the addition of new parties from former communist countries since the early 1990s. Socialists and Social-Democrats have tried to unify these different countries, their unity being one of the accession criteria. By contrast, the EPP has always sought to bring together all centre and right-wing forces, at times admitting four or five parties per member state. Therefore, it is clear that the arrival of 162 new MEPs will also affect the cohesion and consistency of different groups in the European Parliament.

Jean-Michel de Waele

Bibliography

Costa, O., 'Le Parlement Européen après les elections de 2004', Fondation Robert Schuman, Synthèse no. 135, 2004 (http://www.robert-schuman.org/synth135.htm).

Hix, S. and Marsh, M. *Predicting the Future: the Next European Parliament*, 2004 (http://www.bmbrussels.be/files/news_4.pdf).

→ Composition of the European Parliament; Cyprus; Czech Republic; Estonia; European Elections (2004); European Federation of Green Parties; European Parliament; European People's Party (EPP); European Political Parties; Euroscepticism; Hungary; Latvia; Lithuania; Malta; Mapping Europe: European Electoral Geography; Members of the European Parliament (Legal and Political Status); Members of the European Parliament (Sociology of Political Office); Observers; Parliamentary Groups; Party of European Socialists (PES); Poland; Slovakia; Slovenia; Sovereignism.

Estonia

(European Parliament Election,
12 June 2004)

Background

Estonian accession to the European Union has been characterised by a high discrepancy between the positions of political elites and ordinary citizens. On the one hand, Estonian elites have been pushing for fast entry to the EU, using all possible means to speed up Estonian membership in tough competition with other potential candidates. Remarkable efforts were introduced to build up a specific image of Estonia as an exemplary and most promising candidate. As an outcome, no mainstream party seriously questioned EU membership, even those parliamentary parties that flirted with Euroscepticism, especially during the period when public opposition to EU membership was growing, but which soon returned to their pro-EU stances. The only media attention on the EU issue focused on the somewhat vague position of the Centre Party that avoided making a clear statement on the EU during the last national elections and EU accession referendum. However, strong support of the 'Yes' vote dominated clearly among the political establishment during the referendum campaign period.[1] On the other hand, the Estonian public was one of the most sceptical among the candidate countries about the European Union project, showing serious doubts in relation to early membership in the light of its negative historical experience as part of Soviet Union and highly valuing its recently regained independence.[2]

The Estonian electoral process shows, in general, similar patterns to the rest of the post-Soviet environment. Massive fission and fusion of parties, domination of leaders and the candidate-centred process, relatively low turnouts, apathetic and disappointed voters, weak party identification, and high volatility are familiar elements of all Eastern European societies. Some recent studies have shown clear signs towards stabilisation in electoral behaviour. However, the most recent elections in all the Baltic States raise serious doubts as to the presumed stabilisation of their party systems. The time proved to be ripe for the emergence and astonishing success of the new party players underlying the immature character of the post-Soviet political process.

However, there are some specific features that still make the Estonian case somewhat divergent in terms of electoral process. In contrast to other Eastern European countries, the Estonian party system differs from the mainstream in two important ways. Firstly, the general weakness of the left-wing parties and specifically the marginal role of the communist successor party. The communist successor Estonian Social-Democratic Labour Party made only a brief appearance in parliament following the 1999 elections, in a joint list together with the United People's Party of Estonia. The moderates, who claimed to have a modern social-democratic ideology, were struggling with identity problems, participating in the previous right-wing governments throughout the 1990s and backing all of their neo-liberal policies. Only a very poor result in the most recent (2002) local elections and bleak prospects for crossing the required 5 per cent threshold for parliamentary representation forced the moderates to make serious efforts to move towards the left, not only in their programmatic statements but also in their real political behaviour. This sudden shift in positions probably did not do much to help save them in the 2003 national elections, leaving voters confused and the party with a meagre 7 per cent in support (compared to 15.2 per cent in 1999).

However, the moderates survived and their continuous gradual move towards the left, and the change of their name to the Social-Democratic Party, sent a strong symbolic value and clear message to the electorate, establishing the basis for the surprising outcomes of the election to the European Parliament.

The second peculiarity of the Estonian party system is related to the heterogeneity of Estonian society inherited from the Soviet past, providing for a potentially strong basis for the emergence of the ethnic divisions between parties. In fact, ethnic Russian parties have found it extremely difficult to cross the 5 per cent threshold in every election since independence. Even in the 1995 and 1999 elections, when those parties were able to secure parliamentary representation, their share of the vote was still far below the size of the Russian-speaking electorate.[3] One important factor which should have increased support for the Russian parties in the European elections was the opposite trends among Estonian- and Russian-speakers in terms of their attitudes towards the EU membership shown in the September 2003 EU accession referendum. It turned out that support for EU membership was gradually increasing among Estonian-speakers and decreasing among Russian-speakers during the run up to the referendum.[4]

Finally, one should not underestimate the question of timing. The distance between the EU accession referendum and elections to the European Parliament was barely nine months. This, combined with the low salience and weak knowledge of European affairs, left voters with serious doubts about the rationality of participation in these elections.[5]

Electoral design

Until 2003 Estonian electoral engineering was characterised by moderate attempts to modify and improve the existing electoral system as a response to complaints about its performance.[6] With the emergence of new significant political players, in particular the populist Res Publica party, Estonia moved into a new stage involving direct institutional manipulation aimed at improving prospective electoral performance and gaining additional popular support on the basis of playing with supposedly 'increasing democratic means' by delivering more power to the people by introducing a direct presidential vote and converting votes into seats according to the personal votes gained by candidates in elections (in contrast to the closed party lists). Res Publica entered the electoral market with simple and catchy slogans of 'new politics' and 'choose order' and, after taking power, found that the easiest way to realise its promises relating to increasing 'people's power' was by introducing those symbolic elements of direct voting. Playing around with the rules for the first elections to the European Parliament provides a good example of Res Publica's intentions to experiment with the institutional framework.

The legal basis for the elections to the European Parliament was established by the European Parliament Election Act passed in parliament as long ago as 18 December 2002. According to the formal logic of the Estonian legislative process, laws require presidential proclamation within 14 days and enter into force on the tenth day after their publication. All this means quite a prolonged process which, in this particular case, ended on 23 January 2003 when the European Parliament Election Act entered into force. This law provided for a PR system where mandates were distributed according to the d'Hondt method in a single constituency. Winning seats were allocated to the parties according to their nominated candidate lists (closed party lists). The specific intentions of the new constitutional designers in Res Publica found support from the Fatherland Union and some other established parties and *Riigikogu* adopted new rules, determining the allocation of seats according to the popularity of candidates (open list vote), smoothly on 11 February 2004. Opposition to the amendments came, surprisingly, from Res Publica's two coalition partners, the Reform Party and People's Union, on the grounds of the apparently too short time period left until the elections, in conditions when some parties had already started their campaigns, hence confusing and destabilising the whole electoral process. On these grounds President Arnold Rüütel refused to proclaim the amended electoral rules and returned the law to the *Riigikogu* for a new debate and decision. Presidential arguments did not convince the fighters for 'a real democracy' and a parliamentary majority passed the law again without any hesitation. To avoid potential complications related to the proper timing of elections the president proclaimed the new electoral law on 12 March 2004, leaving a short, barely three-month, period for the preparation for the elections.

The campaign

Emotional speculations about the pros and cons of joining the EU were a cause for concern at the beginning of May with an increase in the prices of a number of specific sensitive goods like sugar, bananas and petrol. Eurosceptics celebrated their first pyrrhic victory loudly. The symbolic value of the price levels of sugar, bananas and petrol is difficult to underestimate. The starting point of membership on 1 May, just six weeks ahead of the elections to the European Parliament, gave a clear advantage to those attempting to tap into the Eurosceptical mood. On those grounds, it is probably not surprising that even most of the parliamentary parties – who earlier, during the EU referendum, were campaigning on the positive pro-EU stances – suddenly started to flirt with Euroscepticism. The crucial target of membership having been achieved, all the hidden fears relating to joining a new Union came plainly to the fore. Defending national interests, concerns related to pooled sovereignty, preserving the national language and culture and all the main national symbols[7] generated clear opposition to the further deepening and federalisation of the Union by most political actors. On these grounds the Fatherland Union fought strongly for national interests with its main campaign slogan being 'For Estonia'. The People's Union promised to look after the Estonian currency by 'Protecting (the) Estonian Kroon'. Res Publica was ambitious (and desperately naive) about Estonia's special role in the EU with the slogan 'Breaking Through'. The Reform Party was concerned about defending its dominant neo-liberal discourse with its 'Keep Estonian Success' slogan. The Centre Party was intelligent enough to continue with its vague positions, promising something for everyone by combining 'Our Relic is Freedom' with 'We Believe in Estonia in Europe'.

Only the Social-Democrats, with their slogan 'Common Sense Pays Off', were obviously diverging from the mainstream, openly supporting further deepening of the EU and delivering a bigger role to the main institutions of the EU, in particular to the European Commission. The Social-Democrats argued that the current institutional framework allowed Russia to negotiate with bigger EU member states above the heads of the small Baltic States to introduce supposedly discriminatory statements covering Russian minorities in Estonia and Latvia. Average voters were deeply confused and amazed by such a fast and impressive shift in rhetoric by most of the mainstream political actors. Just a few months before, all those politicians were campaigning on the Yes side, using a broad variety of arguments in support of the EU project, and now they were openly competing with each other in attempting to point out all kinds of negative aspects related to the EU, promising to defend national interests whatever the costs and to protect the nation against all the apparent evils coming from the EU.

Most of the peripheral parties, traditionally Eurosceptics, did not even run in the elections at all. From the five unsuccessful parties in the last national elections, only two of the back runners – the Social-Democratic Labour Party and Russian Party in Estonia – decided to participate. In addition, two minor parties – the Democratic Party and the Pensioners' Party – who missed out in the last national elections, decided to use the European election to gain some publicity this time. The elections also attracted some publicly well-known persons who participated as independent candidates, such as the mayor of Maardu, Georgi Bõstrov, backed by the United People's Party of Estonia with its overwhelmingly Russian-speaking electorate. Marek Strandberg gained publicity for his appearances related to environmental and green issues in the media. Martin Helme was one of the leaders of the Eurosceptic camp who emerged during the EU accession referendum debates. Surprisingly enough, two other well-known Eurosceptics, Igor Gräzin and Uno Silberg, decided to run under the party labels of previously pro-EU parties, the Reform Party and People's Union, respectively.

The campaign only really started two weeks before the election day, leaving far too limited a time span for the development of comprehensive discussion and advanced arguments. The main discussion was still centred on abstract issues related to the further unionisation and/or federalisation of the European Union.[8] As election day neared, opinion polls were showing the increasing popularity of the Social-Democrats and its leader Ilves. Despite the smear campaign waged by other parties, in particular the government coalition, to discredit the Social-Democrats and their leader, the clear trend of increasing support for this party continued.

The official campaign spending amounted to about 1.5 million euros, with a huge watershed between the parliamentary parties and the rest. The front-runners, Res Publica and the Reform Party, spent respectively 433 000 and 287 000 euros, and for minor parties the maximum was about 10 000 euros (the Russian Party in Estonia). On this basis, while the parliamentary parties had the capacity to run their massive campaigns in all main media outlets, small parties and individual candidates largely lacked access to the media. Even Estonian national TV continued with its discriminatory tradition, distributing freely granted public time to different parties and individual candidates unequally. Estonian national TV held three general debates, each lasting 90 minutes, where six the parliamentary parties received 180 minutes of total time (30 minutes per party), but all other parties and individual candidates were covered in one 90-minute programme (11.25 minutes per party/individual candidate).

Results

Estonia elected six MEPs: three socialists, two liberals, and one conservative. The results were a surprise to the Estonian political establishment in various ways. Turnout was remarkably low, at 26.8 per cent, far below even the most sceptical predictions[9] (see Table 1) and provided a

Table 1 Turnout in the June 2004 elections to the European Parliament in Estonia

	Total	% of registered voters	% of valid votes
Registered voters	873 809	100	–
Votes cast	234 485	26.83	–
Valid votes	232 230	26.58	100

Source: Estonian National Electoral Committee 2004.

Table 2 Results of the elections to the European Parliament in Estonia,* June 2004

	EU party group affiliation	Votes (%)	Seats (%)	Share
Social-Democratic Party	PES	36.8 (7.0)	50.0 (5.9)	3
Centre Party	ALDE	17.5 (25.4)	16.7 (27.7)	1
Reform Party	ALDE	12.2 (17.7)	16.7 (18.8)	1
Fatherland Union	EPP-ED	10.5 (7.3)	16.7 (6.9)	1
People's Union	(UEN)	8.0 (13.0)	0 (12.9)	0
Res Publica	(EPP-ED)	6.7 (24.6)	0 (27.7)	0
Democratic Party	(IND/DEM)	1.2 (–)	0 (0)	0
Pensioner's Party	–	0.6 (–)	0 (0)	0
Social-Democratic Labour Party	(GUE/NGL)	0.5 (0.4)	0 (0)	0
Russian Party in Estonia	(Greens/EFA)	0.3 (0.2)	0 (0)	0
Independent candidates (4)	–	5.7 (0.4)	0 (0)	0

Source: Estonian National Electoral Committee 2004.
Note: *Results of the last national 2003 elections are presented in parenthesis. Current governmental parties are presented in bold font.

stark contrast with the 2003 national elections (58.2 per cent) and the EU accession referendum (64.1 per cent).

The main factors accounting for this extremely low participation rate were the low salience, interest in and comprehension of EU affairs in general. An important role was certainly played by the confusion relating to the drastic shifts in rhetoric of the mainstream political actors from blatant Euro-optimism to certain elements of Euroscepticism. The negative experience related to the increase in prices for some sensitive/symbolic goods, and new attempts by Russia to question Estonian minority and citizenship poli-

cies, this time already through the EU framework, which was perceived to provide higher safety against Russian claims on specific matters, certainly did not encourage potential voters to participate in the elections. The lack of a tradition of summer voting in combination with the changed priorities related to the beginning of the short-lasting summer season tended to decrease the participatory intentions of the voters. Disappointment in the government, its policies and controversial stands on the EU, also provided strong grounds for a protest vote. Table 2 provides information relating to outcomes of the elections to the June 2004 European Parliament in Estonia.

As a result, the government parties failed desperately, gaining only 26.9 per cent of the votes and 16.7 per cent of the seats (in contrast to 55.4 per cent and 59.4 per cent respectively in the 2003 national elections). Actually, only one out of the three governmental parties, the Reform Party, secured representation in the European Parliament. The collapse of the vote for the rurally based People's Union was largely unexpected, as the party was running on an apparently strong platform of defending national interests, which was perceived to be an important issue for those people living in the countryside. The main reason for its negative outcome was probably related to the increasingly positive attitudes towards the EU and a relatively low turnout in the rural areas. Eager to repeat its earlier success story, Res Publica's tactics did not work at all in 2004. Its massive and bold Soviet-style 'Breaking Through' campaign did not convince voters this time and the party only received 6.7 per cent of the vote, securing no EP representation, and helping the Social-Democrats to become the leading party and to achieve an astonishing 36.8 per cent of the vote. A party which was, just few months ago, desperately concerned with its further marginalisation in Estonian politics, suddenly presented the strongest left-wing winning case among all the post-Soviet EU member states. Finally, it should also be noted that in the 2004 elections, the total 'wasted vote' amounted to a massive 23 per cent in comparison to only 5.3 per cent for the 2003 national elections. Independent candidates collected a noticeable 5.7 per cent of support (in contrast to the miserable 0.4 per cent in the last national elections), while two of them, Georgi Bõstrov and Marek Strandberg achieved remarkable seventh and ninth positions among the

top vote gainers across the country.[10] Due to the specific nature of the electoral campaign, the dividing lines between Euro-optimists and Eurosceptics were much more blurred this time. However, considering the previous longer track records of the 'permanent Eurosceptics', who have shown their anti-EU stance consistently, this group failed to succeed in these elections. The only individual candidate with a strong Eurosceptic position, Martin Helme, received only 0.6 per cent of the votes. Two other well-known Eurosceptics, Igor Gräzin and Uno Silberg, running under the Reform Party and People's Party labels, received respectively 2.1 per cent and 0.2 per cent of the votes. Russian ethnic parties failed once again to co-operate and to present a clear alternative to the mainstream Estonian parties: they fared miserably, receiving only 3 per cent of the popular vote.[11]

Conclusion and future prospects

The founding elections to the European Parliament underlined the already established patterns of electoral change in Estonia. The trend of decreasing electoral turnout produced a new record low of only 26.8 per cent of popular participation. The fragile foundations of party identification were further undermined by the repeated shifts in parties' positions on crucial issues and the overwhelmingly candidate-centred logic of the electoral process. A continuation of the pattern of dissatisfied voters punishing parties in power provided for a strong protest vote against the right-wing government leaving three coalition partners with only 26.9 per cent of the votes and 16.7 per cent of the seats. Does this swing in voters' preferences mean the real emergence of a left in Estonia? The Estonian party system has been long characterised by the absence of relevant left-wing parties. Only the elections to the European Parliament presented the first signs of shifting voters' minds when the refurbished Social-Democratic Party received 36.8 per cent of votes and half of the seats. Terms like 'left' and 'social-democratic' have been part of a taboo vocabulary in Estonian politics since it regained independence. This break-through by the Social-Democratic Party might increase the chances of left-wing parties to provide relevant alternatives to the mainstream right and, hence, to provide the first signs for the applicability of the left–right party cleavage in Estonia.

Elections to the European Parliament and their outcome illuminated once again the problems related to the Russian-speaking minority and its representation. Hopefully Estonian parties elected to the European Parliament have the capacity and will to represent the whole Estonian population in its uniformity and diversity.

Evald Mikkel

Notes

1. For more on this see: E. Mikkel, 'Europe and the Estonian Parliamentary Elections of 2 March 2003', *Opposing Europe Research Network/Royal Institute for International Affairs Election Briefing No. 11* at http://www.sussex.ac.uk/sei/documents/oernestonianbp11.pdf; and E. Mikkel, 'The Estonian EU Accession Referendum, 14 September 2003', *European Parties Elections and Referendums Network Referendum Briefing No. 11* at http://www.sussex.ac.uk/sei/documents/epernbrefest.pdf.

2. See: European Commission, *Candidate Countries Eurobarometer 2003.3*, Brussels, European Commission; European Commission, *Applicant Countries Eurobarometer*, Brussels: European Commission, 2001; and E. Mikkel and A. Kasekamp, 'Emerging Party Realignment? Party-based Euroscepticism in Estonia', paper prepared for the 30th ECPR Joint Session workshop 'Opposing Europe: Euroscepticism and Political Parties', Turin, Italy, 22–27 March 2002.

3. According to the 2000 Population and Housing Census, the share of Russian-speaking citizens was about 15 per cent, while ethnic Russian parties gained 5.9 per cent of the vote in 1995, 8.2 per cent in 1999 and only 2.4 per cent in 2003.

4. See 'The Estonian EU Accession Referendum, 14 September 2003'; and E. Mikkel and G. Pridham, Clinching the "Return to Europe": the Referendums on EU Accession in Estonia and Latvia', *West European Politics*, 27, 4, pp. 716–48.

5. Elections to the European Parliament were actually the fourth in a row during a relatively short period of 20 months.

6. See: E. Mikkel and V. Pettai, 'The Baltics: Independence with Divergent Electoral Systems', in J. M. Colomer (ed.), *The Handbook of Electoral System Design*, New York, Palgrave Macmillan, 2004, p. 339.

7. In particular, the importance of the national currency, the Kroon, and priority for the foundations emphasised in the Estonian constitution were heavily supported.

8. For example, in its pre-election day edition, the main national newspaper *Postimees* asked leaders of the six main parties about the nature of the developments of the European Union towards a union of states or a united states of Europe. See: 'Kas riikide liit või liikumine liitriigi suunas', *Postimees*, 12 May 2004.

9. Data provided by Saar Poll which already in October 2003 estimated for Estonia the lowest participation of 14 per cent among all the candidate countries. See: http://www.saarpoll.ee/europarlamendi_prognoos2004.rtf; and European Commission, *Candidate Countries Eurobarometer 2003.4*, Brussels, European Commission, 2003, Figure 7.7a, p. 197.

10. 2.7 per cent (6182) and 2.3 per cent (5354) of the votes.

11. Georgi Bõstrov, as an independent candidate, received 2.7 per cent, and the Russian Party in Estonia only 0.3 per cent of the votes.

Bibliography

Mikkel, E., 'The Estonian EU Accession Referendum, 14 September 2003', *European Parties Elections and Referendums Network Referendum Briefing*, No. 11, 2003 (http://www.sussex.ac.uk/sei/documents/epernbrefest.pdf).

Mikkel, E. and Kasekamp, A., 'Emerging Party Realignment? Party-based Euroscepticism in Estonia', Communication to the 30th Joint Workshop of the ECPR, 'Opposing Europe: Euroscepticism and Political Parties', Turin, Italy, 22–27 March 2002.

Mikkel, E. and Pettai, V., 'The Baltics: Independence with Divergent Electoral Systems', in J. M. Colomer (ed.), *The Handbook of Electoral System Design*, New York, Palgrave Macmillan, 2004.

Mikkel, E. and Pridham, G., 'Clinching the "Return to Europe": the Referendums on EU Accession in Estonia and Latvia', *West European Politics*, 27, 4, October 2004, pp. 716–48.

➔ Mapping Europe: European Electoral Geography.

Eurobarometer

The Eurobarometer is a particularly substantial database of surveys, regularly carried out on behalf of the European Commission with the aim of measuring in a consistent and comparable way how EU citizens' opinions and attitudes towards integration evolve over time. From its origin to the early 1990s, the project consisted of classic opinion polls. Following the adoption of the Maastricht Treaty and the expression of doubts regarding the future direction of European integration together with a perceived growth in levels of Euroscepticism, the project has been substantially enriched with new topics and questions. Eurobarometer is now made up of four different types of surveys. 'Standard Eurobarometers' started in 1973 and are conducted from twice to five times a year with representative samples of about 1000 people aged 15 and over in each country (except Luxembourg, Malta and Northern Ireland, where the samples are smaller, and unified Germany, where the sample includes almost 2000 respondents). 'Special Eurobarometers' are usually conducted together with the standard survey but are especially ordered by European institutions to answer more specific questions. 'Candidate Countries' Eurobarometers' were started in 2001 in 13 countries (the candidate countries plus Bulgaria, Romania and Turkey), but most are now integrated into the standard Eurobarometer series. Finally, 'Flash Eurobarometers' are conducted using smaller samples (around 500 per country) but on a more regular basis and at certain critical periods they are often conducted on a monthly basis. To this very comprehensive series, a series of qualitative studies conducted by using non-directive focus group interviews are also included, although they are still few and far between at this stage.

Before the word 'Eurobarometer' was even invented, a series of surveys commissioned by the Press and Communication office of the European Commission in 1962 were carried out between 1970 and 1972 in the six member states. The next survey, carried out in 1973, proved significantly more ambitious, not only by the number of countries included (nine instead of six), but also by the sheer length of the questionnaire. This innovative study could have arguably been labelled the first Eurobarometer. From the very start, Eurobarometer provided an unusual and unprecedented cross-over between a public policy tool, directed towards the communication and information of the European Communities, and an instrument allowing for scientific research on public opinion. This unusual combination can be better understood when one considers the background of the 'founding fathers', who include a mixture of practitioners and academics. Jacques-Rene Rabier (director of Eurobarometer from 1973 to 1987), Jean Stoezel, Helene Riffaut and Jean-Baptiste Duroselle all came from a generation that perfectly understood the value of public opinion surveys to measure citizens' adhesion to the various developments that started after 1945, namely the process of European integration. They also closely followed the methodological innovations and developments that made the field so dynamic. The survey companies responsible for carrying out the surveys also played an important role. They attempted to forge a link between the series and the academic community, particularly the IFOP Company, and then the 'Institut Faits et Opinions', which co-ordinated the surveys between 1973 and 1989, whilst under the direction of Stoezel and later by Riffaut. As Eurobarometer developed, these links improved. In 1978, the scientific supervision of the project was entrusted to Karl Heinz Reif, a political science professor from the University of Mannheim, and then, between 1996 and 1999, to Anna Melich from the University of Geneva. However, things were destined to change. Between 1999 and 2004, the conduct of the project was awarded to a company that almost exclusively worked on the series, the INRA, before a call for proposals resulted in the commercial survey company TNS-Sofres being granted the conduct of the surveys for a five-year period that started in 2005. For a long time, Ronald Inglehart contributed a regular set of questions relevant to his research on post-materialist values. Likewise, the 'European Elections Study' (EES), a group directed by Hermann Schmitt, also submitted questions to be included in the survey. In 1984 and 1989, the EES study was appended to standard Eurobarometer surveys. Sinnott, Blondel and Svenson worked on the analysis of the 1994 European elections, resulting in the follow-up 'PartCom Multilevel' and 'Civic Active' projects.

This part-academic, part-operational aspect of Eurobarometer may contribute to the critical and disenchanted comments it often receives from the academic community. The questionnaires used are often long and complicated and follow more operational goals than they would if it was of a purely academic nature. Researchers are often frustrated to see that a profuse battery of indicators is used to measure the way Europeans get informed about the EU or how much they know about European institutions, while other aspects of public attitudes are poorly studied or even completely ignored (e.g. socio-psychological determinants of Euroscepticism, etc.).

However, these frustrating aspects should not hide Eurobarometer's obvious contribution to political sociology and the study of European public opinion. Indeed, some theories, such as that of a 'democratic deficit', and of a 'European voter' would have never emerged without the data provided by Eurobarometer. Apart from the American 'National Election Studies', no other survey series has inspired or generated more political science publications, theses and comparative research projects, than Eurobarometer. This is largely because Eurobarometer allows for some relatively diversified studies that go beyond the core 'public opinion' aspect of the survey.

It should, therefore, be reiterated that despite its faults, Eurobarometer contributes greatly to our understanding of public attitudes towards European integration. A large proportion of questions target specific aspects of public attitudes: diffuse and general support, instrumental support (how citizens perceive the benefits of integration for their country), affective and evaluative aspects. The retrospective and prospective dimensions of support for integration are also targeted by Eurobarometer. Repetition of a selection of questions in every semestrial Eurobarometer enables the analysis of trends and even 'trend-trends' (for the questions posed since the very first surveys) that allows for time-series analysis.

Among this selection of repetitive questions, four have proved particularly useful and should be underlined. The first is focused on the general support for European integration (on the 'Efforts to unify Western Europe') on a four-point scale (from 'very much in favour' to 'very much against') which does not offer any possibility of a neutral answer and tends to get very high levels of support. The second question refers to support for one's country's membership, which is more specific but relies on a more approximative scale ('good thing, 'bad thing', 'neither a good thing nor a bad thing'), allows for a 'middle' answer, which leads to less extreme levels of support. The third question on the perceived benefits of one's country's membership measures retrospective benefits. Finally, the fourth question is prospective and gauges the respondents' reaction of whether the European Union should be scrapped (from relief to regret, via indifference). This last question is often criticised on the grounds of its fictive character, but nevertheless provides a synthetic measure of diffuse support for the European Union.

A comparative and cross-sectional analysis of these four trend variables that have been included in the series from 1973 to 2004 is a fascinating object of study. It allows for a great insight into the relationship between public opinions, economic and political contexts, and historical events such as the mad cow disease crisis, the resignation of the Santer commission, or the Kosovo war.

Other interesting aspects of European public opinion can be analysed such as the knowledge, image or reputation of institutions, and perceptions of the enlargements of various public policies.

It is important to note the public availability of Eurobarometer data. The data are accessible via two means. Firstly, via the Commission's reports that can be obtained on the Europa website, in many libraries, or from the European Commission itself. They offer a number of tables and trend graphs, which deal with the most traditional Eurobarometer variables on European integration. The analyses proposed are often sufficient for non-professional users in search of some basic measures of public attitudes, or cross-tabs by country or major socio-demographic variable. Other reports focusing on specific themes are also available, usually based on 'special' or 'flash' Eurobarometers. These reports also give a good sense of the preoccupations of the European Commission at a given point in time (for example, attitudes towards development aid, the euro, sport or the internet). Secondly, the actual data are also available as data sets from the 'Zentral Archiv' of Cologne, which was chosen by the European Commission to diffuse the data sets and are also available to academic users via the 'Council of European Social Sciences Data Archives' network. These data sets are available in SPSS format and are directly usable by scholars.

Progressively, the example set by Eurobarometer was followed up by a number of scholars, research groups and survey institutes across other continents, who were also interested in the progression of regional (usually economic) integration. Since 1995, a 'Latinobarometer' (17 Latin American countries), an 'Afrobarometer' (18 countries in 2006), and more recently an 'EastAsianbarometer' have been established. The generalisation of mass surveys based on general principles of Eurobarometer (standardised questionnaires, regular series, large national samples, indicators of support for economic or political integration) may lead to comparisons across several continents, which will take the study of attitudes towards regional integration – European integration being one of its most unusual forms – to yet another level.

Bruno Cautrès

➔ Data Archives; Electoral Behaviour; Enlargement; European Elections Studies; European Electoral Sociology; European Public Opinion; Identity; Second-Order Elections.

European Commission

The relationship between the European Commission and the European Parliament has always been at the centre of institutional analyses of the European Union. The special attention devoted to this issue is mainly due to the discriminatory character of executive-legislative relations in most national political regimes. It also stems from the importance attached to the Parliament's powers over the Commission. In fact, concerns about the democratic deficit make the authority of the only democratically elected body of the EU over the bureaucratic Commission particularly significant. The analysis of the relationship between these two bodies, seeks to evaluate the possibility and degree of a phenomenon often referred to as 'parliamentarisation'.

The 'parliamentarisation' of the EU institutional system

While the application of an ideal parliamentary structure for the EU is debatable, it seems to be justified in the eyes of the public. The media, citizens and political leaders spontaneously refer to it when assessing the nature of EU democracy or considering the reform of its institutions. In other words, this analytical approach has the merit of taking the cognitive framework under-lying attitudes, strategies as well as discourse of actors and observers of the EU system into account. Moreover, it acknowledges the intrinsically non-parliamentary nature of the EU's original institutional structure. The institutional architecture of 1957 was completely unprecedented and driven by the pragmatism of its designers, who sought to overcome partisan national cleavages and turn the process of economic integration into a discreet and efficient project based on elite co-operation and expertise. The newly established system also differed from traditional parliamentary regimes in that it disregarded the principles of power distribution as well as parliamentary sovereignty in favour of the distribution of functions amongst the different institutions. Nonetheless, since the early 1980s, the EU's institutional system has significantly evolved under the influence of the parliamentary model, which has strengthened the elements common to member states, while simultaneously respecting the unique nature of its institutional structure (Costa 2004).

The so-called process of 'parliamentarisation' of the EU's political system can be said to have three major features. The first one is the European democratic legislature, which has gradually succeeded in acquiring most of the powers and characteristics of national parliaments. Over the decades, the European Parliament has managed to acquire traditional instruments of parliamentary control (i.e. written and oral questions, examination of petitions, enquiry committees, public hearings, as well as mediating functions), which have allowed it to increase its influence over the Commission. Nowadays, its powers include the rights to appoint and dismiss the Commission itself. This evolution is particularly impressive if one considers that initial relations between these two institutions were limited to the EP's presentation of an annual report and to its restricted censorship functions.

This 'parliamentarisation' resulted from the reform of the EU system of legislative initiatives. The principle of inter-institutional co-operation, absent from the original treaties, emerged as the Parliament gradually gained new powers. After the ratification of the Single European Act, the EP established a constructive form of dialogue with the Commission, and played an active role in shaping the policy networks that formed the internal market's regulatory framework. Moreover, the Commission took on the role of mediator between the Parliament and the Council of Ministers. This 'double dialogue' gave way to a 'trilogue' after the introduction of the co-decision procedure as well as MEPs' repeated requests for more direct contact with the Council.

The third evolution endorsing the 'parliamentarisation' thesis is the confirmation of the Commission's governmental nature. Since its foundation, its character has resembled that of a national government due to its characteristics, its organisational structure, and its accountability to a parliamentary assembly. The treaties of Maastricht, Amsterdam and Nice increased the relevance of this direct comparison by assigning the Parliament the task of appointing the Commission. The latter is chosen through a procedure of double nomination, whose connotation is all the more 'parliamentarist' in that the Treaty of Maastricht coincided with the mandates of the two institutions.

An incomplete 'parliamentarisation'

Although this parliamentary logic has been behind all institutional reforms undertaken since 1957, Commission–Parliament relations differ from those between most national parliaments and governments. Neither the Council of Ministers nor the Commission is in a position to dissolve the European Parliament. In fact, it does not benefit from the EP's support or confidence. Similarly, the Parliament does not have full power to appoint the President and commissioners, who are proposed based on their experience and competencies by national governments and the President of the Commission. However, similar to US Congressmen, MEPs enjoy the right to audition candidate commissioners within the framework of parliamentary committees. Nonetheless, MEPs used to be more likely to exercise this privilege to end potential institutional crises, rather than to demand policy changes. This changed for the first time in the autumn of 2004 when the EP forced the President elect of the Commission to change its proposed team drastically.

Generally speaking, three essential characteristics of the EU political system influence and shape Commission–Parliament relations. The first one is the undeniable importance of the intergovernmental logic assigning the lead in policy-making to the Council. The second crucial characteristic is the absence of a political class with real political parties to support the 'politicisation' of the functioning of the EU institutional triangle. The third and final factor is the importance assigned to the Commission's partisan neutrality, reaffirmed by José Manuel Barroso, coupled with the belief that European policies can be exempt from partisan affiliation. However, since 2004, the new President of the Commission now stems from the majority group in the EP and his appointment directly follows European elections.

The Commission and EP election campaigns

Amongst the consequences of the weak articulation between the EP and the Commission is the latter's lack of involvement in the campaign for European elections. In the name of their institution's neutrality, of the Parliament's independence, and of member state sovereignty with respect to the organisation of elections and the appointment of a new college of commissioners, commissioners abstain from all official intervention in the debates on this matter. However, there have been exceptions to this official stance. For instance, during the 2004 EP elections, the Commission President Romano Prodi played an active part in the campaign, and affirmed himself as Italy's opposition leader. Nonetheless, this kind of involvement has no institutional basis and is not driven by the search for a new mandate. In fact, it merely reflects the duality of Commissioners, who are portrayed as EU level experts but sometimes fail to give up national political ambitions. In contrast, the Commission itself is a crucial stake in EP election campaigns. Leaders of national and European political parties would like to see its President appointed on the basis of election results, as planned for in Article I-27 of the Constitution. We must, however, underline that the selection of a candidate coming from the PPE in 2004 was due to the internal balance of the European Council rather than the need to please the winning party, and recall that in 1999, Romano Prodi was appointed in spite of election results.

Olivier Costa

Bibliography

Costa, O., 'Le parlementarisme au-delà de l'Etat: le cas du Parlement européen', in O. Costa, E. Kerrouche and P. Magnette (eds), *Vers un renouveau du parlementarisme en Europe?*, Bruxelles, Editions d l'Université de Bruxelles, 2004, pp. 271–94.

Westlake, M., *The Commission and the Parliament: Partners and Rivals in the European Policy-Making Process*, London, Butterworth, 1994.

→ Composition of the European Parliament; Democratic Deficit; European Elections (2004); European Parliament; European Parliamentary Assembly; Investiture of the Commission; Treaty of Rome; Universal Suffrage.

European Constitution

The 1957 Treaty of Rome establishing the European Community (TEC) and the 1992 Maastricht Treaty on the European Union (TEU) have long been considered to be the functional equivalent of a constitutional text. The European Convention (2002–3) drew up a 'Draft Treaty establishing a Constitution for Europe', which was submitted to the European Council on 18 July 2003. After nearly a year of negotiations, prevarication and a series of postponements, the European Council of 18 June 2004 agreed on a text that hardly differs from the Convention's project. Signed in Rome on 29 October 2004 by the representatives of the 25 EU member states, the Constitution was to be submitted to ratification according to the national constitutional procedures. It was due to come into force on 1 November 2006 providing that there were no difficulties with the ratification procedures.

The Constitution establishes a 'new' European Union that simultaneously replaces the former European Community and Union. It will replace the former Rome Treaty, the Single European Act, and the Maastricht, Amsterdam and Nice Treaties, as well as the different accession treaties of 19 new member states since 1972. It is accompanied by 36 protocols, two appendices, and 41 declarations that will replace the pre-existing 300 texts of the same type.

From a technical point of view, it is a reorganisation and an actualisation of the content of the former treaties. Moreover, it is the 'primary legislation' of the Community and the Union. The Convention, completed by the experts of the Intergovernmental Conference, was aimed at simplifying the legislation process, improving legibility and protecting half a century of European integration through law. These multiple goals explain the length of the text: 448 Articles that replace the 432 of the TEC and the TEU, while adding a further 100 Articles representing innovations regarding the state of the previous law. The Constitution itself comprises a general preamble and is divided into four parts.

Part I presents the EU's values and principles in a clarified and simplified way. Its objectives, institutions and functioning are developed in more detail in Part III. It contains a certain number of institutional innovations: the permanent presidency of the European Council, a Union Minister of Foreign Affairs, configurations of the Council of Ministers, and qualified majority based on the member states and their populations. It reorganises and simplifies the EU legal instruments to which it gives more comprehensible denominations than the ones of Community law: European laws, framework laws and regulations. It presents the different types of competencies of the EU and a non-exhaustive list that is later detailed in Part III. It specifies the significance of the principles of representative democracy and participatory democracy in the EU. For the first time, it provides the possibility for a member state to leave the EU and a procedure for doing so.

Part II replaces the Charter of Fundamental Rights of the Union, which was drafted by a first Convention in 2000. It is a contemporary formulation of the fundamental rights, which places social and political rights at the same level. Its integration into the Constitution for Europe will enable use before courts against the EU institutions and the institutions of the member states when they apply the EU law and policies.

Part III takes over from TEC and the TEU all the 'legal bases' necessary to EU actions as well as the detailed institutional

---

EP elections in the Treaty establishing a Constitution for Europe (2004)

Part II Title V: Citizens' Rights

Article II-99: Right to vote and to stand as a candidate at elections to the European Parliament

1. Every citizen of the Union has the right to vote and to stand as a candidate at elections to the European Parliament in the Member State in which he or she resides, under the same conditions as nationals of that State.

2. Members of the European Parliament shall be elected by direct universal suffrage in a free and secret ballot.

provisions. These texts are reorganised to give more importance to social issues over economic issues, and to transpose in detail the innovations of Part I that, in principle, establish the EP as the EU legislator on equal footing with the Council. It also contains a certain number of innovations opening new fields of action to the EU, such as defence, civil protection, tourism and administrative co-operation. It also comprises a general clause that obliges the institutions to take the social dimension into account in all their policies.

Part IV contains the general and final provisions. They concern the organisation of the continuity between the new Union and the former European Community and Union, and the procedure for the adoption, and revision of the Constitution that needs unanimity, which has always been the case.

From the technical point of view, it is an international treaty, adopted according to the TEC/TEU amendment procedure. Its content is characteristic of a constitution: the safeguard of rights, separation of powers, and checks and balances between institutions. The intrinsic quality of the Constitution will be duly assessed by every European citizen according to one's hopes and fears as to the European project. Yet, to assess the usefulness of the new text one must compare it with the existing treaties of the TEC and TEU. It is, undoubtedly, a text of compromise. It strengthens European integration, while increasing the recognition and respect for the member states, as well as their institutional, cultural and linguistic diversity. It also consolidates the internal market, while strengthening the social dimension of the EU, particularly the respect of political and fundamental social rights. The Constitution for Europe does not innovate in the field of elections, and does not bring new solutions to the question of a uniform electoral procedure:

Article III-330 takes over the corresponding provisions of the Treaty of Rome. Indeed, it remains possible that a uniform procedure will be adopted on this basis even before the Constitution comes into force.

Jacques Ziller

→ European Commission; European Convention; European Parliament.

European Convention

In December 2001, the European Council meeting in Laeken (Belgium), launched the 'Convention for the Future of Europe', also known as European Convention. This conference set out to prepare the 'draft treaty establishing a Constitution for Europe' a text that, after lengthy negotiations, was adopted by the heads of states of the 25 EU member states on 18 July 2004. The text was signed in Rome on 29 October of the same year, prior to being submitted for ratification.

The European Convention comprised 105 representatives and 102 replacements. Its members included:

- 1 President: Valéry Giscard d'Estaing;
- 2 Vice-Presidents: Giuliano Amato and Jean-Luc Dehaene;
- 56 national parliament representatives; two for each of the 15 member states and for each of the 13 accession countries;
- 28 national government representatives; one for each member state and one for each candidate country;
- 16 European Parliament representatives;
- Two European Commission representatives.

It also included 13 'observers' (and 12 substitutes) representing the Committee of the Regions, the Economic and Social

Table 1   Praesidium of the Convention

Valéry Giscard d'Estaing	President	French
Giuliano Amato	Vice-President	Italian
Jean-Luc Dehaene	Vice-President	Belgian
Michel Barnier	European Commission	French
John Bruton	National Parliaments	Irish
Henning Christophersen	Governments: Danish Presidency	Danish
Klaus Hänsch	European Parliament	German
Giorgos Katiforis until February 2003	Governments: Greek Presidency	Greek
Giorgos Papand from February 2003		
Iñigo Méndez de Vigo	European Parliament	Spanish
Ana Palacio until March 2003	Governments: Spanish Presidency	Spanish
Alfonso Dastis from March 2003		
Alojz Peterle	Guest, Representing Accession Countries	Slovenian
Gisela Stuart	National Parliaments	British
Antonio Vitorino	National Parliaments	Portuguese

Committee (ECOSOC), social partners and a European Mediator. The Convention was presided over by Valéry Giscard d'Estaing, President of the French Republic from 1974 to 1981. It also had two Vice-Presidents: Giuliano d'Amato, President of the Italian Council from 1992–3 and from 2000–1, and Jean-Luc Dehaene, Prime Minister of Belgium from 1992–9. Moreover, the Convention was directed by a 'Praesidium' composed of 13 members representing all of its components (Table 1).

Members of the European Convention were regrouped according to affinity of political views based on groups represented in the European Parliament. Secretary General John Kerr, a former UK representative to the EU, was personally appointed by President Valéry Giscard d'Estaing. The Secretariat was composed of a total of 19 people. The Convention operated in a very different way from parliamentary sessions and diplomatic conferences. In fact, it mixed plenary debates and consensus decision-making without ever needing to vote on any given matter. Its work was carried out over a total of sixteen and a half months (Table 2).

The vast majority of important deci-sions within the Convention were prepared in nine working groups and three 'discussion circles' (Table 3).

The drafting of the Treaty's Articles can be divided into ten phases in which the roles of both the Secretariat and of the Praesidium were fundamental:

1. Preparation of a project draft within the Secretariat
2. Discussion of such draft by the Praesidium and final draft
3. Presentation of the text and President's comments to the plenary session; publication of the draft text on the Convention's website
4. Suggested amendments by members of the Convention
5. Synthesis of amendments by the Secretary General
6. Plenary debate
7. Rewriting of the text to include amendments resulting from the plenary debate
8. New debate if necessary and evaluation of consensus levels by the President
9. 'Tidying-up' and final arrangements of the project
10. General debate and overall evaluation of consensus levels

Table 2   Work schedule of the European Convention

28 February 2002	Inaugural session	Inaugural speech and discussion of internal regulations
March–October 2002	17 plenary sessions lasting half a day	Listening phase and set-up of working groups
October 2002–January 2003	9 plenary sessions lasting half a day	Presentation of group reports and of constitutional 'skeleton'
February–April 2003	12 plenary sessions	Presentation of draft reports, discussions and plenary sessions
May–June 2003	7 plenary sessions	Amendments, discussions and adoption by consensus of the first two sections of the text
20 June 2003	European Council in Tessaloniki	Presentation of the Constitution parts I and II
June–July 2003	7 plenary sessions	Adoption of parts III and IV of the Constitution
	Closing session	Signature by all Convention members
18 July 2003	Official ceremony in Rome	Submission of the text to the President of the European Council

Table 3   Working groups and discussion circles

Working Group or Discussion Circle	Rapporteur
I Subsidiarity	I. Méndez de Vigo
II Charter of Fundamental Human Rights	A. Vitorino
III Juridic personality	G. Amato
IV National parliaments	G. Stuart
V Complementary competencies	H. Christophersen
VI Economic governance	K. Hänsch
VII External action	J.-L. Dehaene
VIII Defence	M. Barnier
IX Simplification	G. Amato
X Freedom, justice and security	J. Bruton
XI Social Europe	G. Katiforis
Circle on the Court of Justice	A. Vitorino
Circle on Budgetary Procedures	H. Christophersen
Circle on Owen Resources	I. Méndez de Vigo

The Convention did not seek to adopt a homogeneous electoral regime, nor did it seek to find new ways to promote its adoption by EU institutions. In contrast, it preserved the pre-established unanimity rule, well aware that the intergovernmental conference that was to follow it would not have accepted an amendment of this point. Nonetheless, it is possible that a homogeneous regime may be accepted on the basis of the Treaty of Rome prior to the entry into force of the future Constitution. The Convention process has been the most transparent ever achieved for a constitutional project.

Jacques Ziller

Bibliography

All documents are available on the Convention's website http://european-convention.eu.int/ (at least until July 2008)

→ Electoral System; European Commission; European Constitution; European Parliament.

European Democratic Union

Established on 24 April 1978 in Klessheim in Austria, the European Democratic Union (EDU), as a political organisation, brought together 45 political parties (initially 18) at the European level resulting from the Conservative, Christian Democrat and Liberal traditions across 31 countries, including Turkey, Albania and Belarus (Table 1). It thus goes beyond the representative framework for EU member states. The EDU's purpose was to defend, beyond borders, the political values of the three political right-wing families in place across various territories. Its activity primarily consisted of promoting theories of liberalism, exchanging arguments concerning electoral agendas in preparation of electoral campaigns, which directly involved party members, and maintaining dialogue between various party leaders. Closely linked and absorbed into the organisational structure of the European People's Party (EPP) until its virtual disappearance in 2002, the EDU was however always perceived as a political organisation primarily designed to privilege the dialogue between the Christian Democrats and Liberals. Consequently, peripheral to any real decision-making, this structure – at present somewhat reduced to a few honorary representatives without portfolios – remains a privileged witness of the difficulties encountered by the European right in its attempts to establish a federal Europe. The study of this political group constitutes an interesting case regarding the need for these various traditions to be adapted to the context of economic and social evolution in a context of rising liberalism. Hence, it is advisable to reconsider at the same time the context of emergence of the EDU, its operating practice, and its links with the EPP.

Generally affiliated with the development of party federations, particularly related to the democratisation process of European institutions since 1979, the EDU appears under the features of a structure promoting co-operation amongst moderate right-wing formations. The European Democratic Union is defined as a 'working association' of Christian Democrat, Conservative and non-collectivist parties. By and large, the CDU-CSU and the British Conservative Party have been its two main pillars (Delwit et al. 2001). Meetings between principal leaders and working groups are arranged on a bi- or tri-annual basis. These meetings focus on economic, political and institutional questions concerning Europe, for which the EDU has consistently established itself since its creation as a democratic barricade against socialism. Described since the early 1980s as a 'proto-party aimed at fighting "Euro-socialism"', it gathers primarily middle-class parties – especially Conservative ones – and a few others (Seiler 1982). The creation of the EDU was achieved in parallel with the existence of the EPP which was founded in 1976 and was the first European partisan structure to bring together right-wing parties. The founding EDU members – in this instance the German Christian Democrats and British Tories – initially set out to inaugurate an arena for meetings and debates, and an opportunity for European leaders to promote their ideas

Table 1   Member parties of the EDU (2002)

Countries	Political parties
Albania	Partia Demokratike e Shqiperise (PDSH)
Germany	Christlich Demokratische Union (CDU)
	Christlich-Soziale Union (CSU)
Austria	Österreichische Volkspartei (ÖVP)
Belarus	United Civil Party (UCP)
Bulgaria	Demokraticheska Partia (DP)
	Obedinen Christiandemokraticheski Zentar (OHDZ)
	Sajuz na Demokratitschnite Sili (SDS)
Cyprus	Dimokratikos Synagermos (DISY)
Denmark	Det Konservative Folkepartie (KF)
Estonia	Isamaaliit – Pro Patria Union (PPU)
Spain	Partido Popular (PP)
France	Union pour un Mouvement Populaire (UMP)
Finland	Kansallinen Kokoomus (KOK)
Greece	Nea Demokratia (ND)
Hungary	Fiatal Demokratak Szövetsege – Magyar Polgari Part (FIDESZ-MPP)
	Független Kisgazda-, Földmunkas- És Polgári Párt (FGKP)
	Magyar Demokrata Forum (MDF)
Iceland	Sjáltstaedistlokkurinn (SF)
Italy	Forza Italia (FI)
Lichtenstein	Fortschrittliche Bürgerpartei in Liechtenstein (FBPL)
	Vaterländische Union (VU)
Lithuania	Tevynes Sajunga (Lietuvos Konsenvatoriai) (TS(LK))
Luxembourg	Parti Chrétien Social (PCS)
Malta	Partit Nazzjonalista (PN)
Norway	Hoyres Hovedorganisasjon (H)
Poland	Unia Wolnosci (UW)
Portugal	Partido Social Democrata (PSD)
Romania	Partidul National Taranesc Crestin Democrat (PNTCD)
	Romäniai Magyar Demokrata Szövetség (RMDSZ)
United Kingdom	Conservative Party (C)
Czech Republic	Obcanska Demokratická Aliance (ODA)
	Obcanska Demokratická Strana (ODS)
Slovakia	Krestanskodemokratické H n uti e Slovenska (KHD)
	Magyar Koalício Pártja (MKP)
Slovenia	SLS SKD Slovenska ljudska stranka
Sweden	Moderata Samlingspartiet (MSP)
Switzerland	Christlich-Demokratische Volkspartei (CVP)
Turkey	Dogru Yol Partisi (DYP)
Former Yugoslavia	VMRO – DPMNE
	Democratic Party of the Albanians

Source: Laurent de Boissieu, http://francepolitique.free.fr/FEEDU.htm

and interests in Europe. In this sense, the EDU seems to have two major constraints. Firstly, the EDU allows Christian Democrats to create a parallel political organisation to the EPP to maintain and facilitate contact between different right-wing forces. Secondly, the EDU creates a structure opened to countries outside of the EU to emphasise 'non-collectivist' theories, particularly in the East. These two aspects have partly shaped the structure of the EDU.

The operational rules of the EDU must also be analysed in relation to its membership of a larger maternal organisation called the International Democratic Union (IDU). The EDU was officially the European component of the IDU despite the ensuing establishment of the latter in 1983 (Figure 1). At the international level, this broader organisation comprises several geographical and thematic units (Women's organisation, Youth organisation) preceding the operation of a full partisan movement. In its 'Declaration of Principles' (http://www.idu.org), the IDU provides a significant outline of its self-determined missions, which are characterised by the following components: 'defending with conviction the possibilities offered to individuals to guarantee the best conditions as regards political freedom, personal freedom, equality in potential economic development of their country'; 'rejecting any form of totalitarianism'; 'having regard to their common views that political democracy and private property are inseparable components of individual liberty (. . .) of tackling social evils such as unemployment and inflation'; 'emphasising the importance of principal institutions such as the family'; 'believing that these principles form the basis of success of any initiative and individual undertaking'. The vocabulary as well as the solemn tone used in this founding charter show the commitment of its members to the right-wing values that the Conservative, Christian and

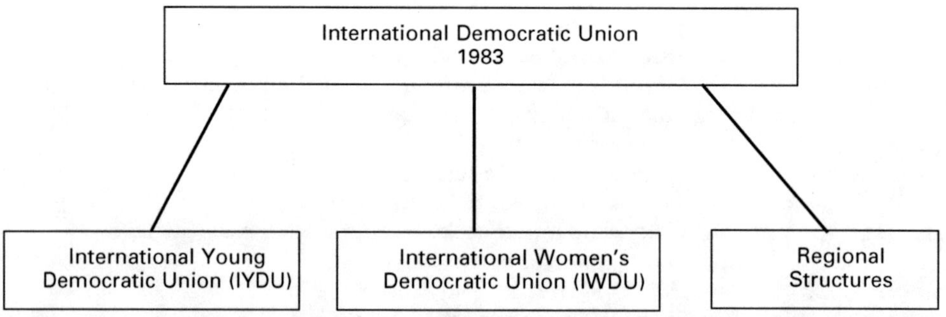

Figure 1 Organisation and components of the IDU

Liberal traditions ultimately seem to have in common.

The IDU executive secretary Richard Normington confirms that the EDU, in its initial form, no longer exists. Since 2002, its activities have been separated from a structure which is more or less emptied of its substance, but nevertheless retained with co-chairmen Kostas Karamanlis (current Greek Prime Minister) and Jan Petersen (Norwegian former Foreign Minister). Currently, the EDU is integrated into the Belgian legislation without any real working committee functioning at the European level. Rather, its existence appears to be merely consolidated by a secretariat based in London, retaining its link to the IDU as well as an annual meeting of its leaders. The working groups which previously met frequently throughout the year to discuss thematic economic issues, high-level foreign and security policy in Europe, no longer function distinctly from the IDU.

The objectives behind the promotion of right-wing values in Europe, delivered through the intervention of such a 'tool' as the EDU, finally seem to have become less crucial. The existence of an intermediary organisation responsible for the co-ordination of the activities of party leaders seems incompatible with the federalist ambitions of the right in Europe. Undoubtedly, the evolution of the EPP since the 1990s (towards a more marked overture towards the Liberals and Conservatives) as well as the recent EU enlargement, have both contributed to undermine the need for a parallel political space. It was also inevitable to organise political supply so that it is more visible to European citizens, which reinforced the dominant structure of the EPP, rendering elite organisations such as the EDU obsolete.

Stéphanie Abrial

Bibliography

Delwit, P., Külahci, E. and Van de Walle, C., *Les fédérations européennes de partis: Organisation et influence*, Bruxelles, Editions de l'Université de Bruxelles, 2001.
Seiler, D.-L., *Les partis politiques en Europe*, Paris, PUF, 1982.

→ Cleavages; European Liberal Democrat and Reform Party (ELDR); European People's Party (EPP); European Political Parties; Right.

European Elections (1979–1999)

The June 2004 European elections were the sixth of their kind. The story of European elections shows constant transformation, which developed alongside successive enlargements of the European Union and frequent changes in the rules of the electoral game and mutations of the different political forces from 1979 to 1999.

Already planned by the Treaty of Rome in 1957, these direct universal suffrage elections of the European Parliament took more than 20 years to become reality. From 1958 to 1979, the European Parliamentary Assembly composed of members of national parliaments did not succeed in agreeing on a 'uniform electoral procedure in all member states' planned by Article 138 of the Treaty of Rome (Charlot 2001). This matter dragged on from summits to the Council of Ministers and it was only in 1976 that the Council of Ministers gave its agreement to the direct universal suffrage election of the European Parliament without endeavouring to find a common procedure. Each country is free to organise the election of MEPs as it wishes. The first elections were held on 17 July 1979 and four others followed in 1984, 1989,

1994 and 1999 without counting the elections of 1987, 1995 and 1996 after the accession of newcomers to the European Union.

The possibility left to member states to adopt their own rules for the election and the constant redefinition of the European Union borders greatly contributed to the diversity of these elections in time and space.

A European Parliament constantly reshaped

The Parliament, which was elected under direct universal suffrage in 1979, comprised 410 members coming from the founding six countries (Germany with 81 MEPs, Belgium with 24, France with 81, Luxembourg with 6, the Netherlands with 25) and three other countries which joined in 1973 (Denmark with 16, Ireland with 15, the United Kingdom with 81). After the adhesion of Greece in 1981, the Parliament comprised 434 seats for the elections in 1984, the Hellenic Peninsula having obtained 24 MEPs. During the 1989 elections, the Parliament gathered 518 MEPs, the newcomers in 1985 – Spain and Portugal – having gained 60 and 24 MEPs respectively. On 11–12 December 1992, the Edinburgh European Council decided to further increase the number of seats taking into account the reunification of Germany and enlargements to come. In the 1994 elections, the Parliament comprised 567 seats, Germany having the largest share with 99 MEPs and Luxembourg the smallest one with six MEPs. After the 1995 and 1996 enlargements, the Parliament enlarged again with 21 more seats for Austria, 16 for Finland, and 22 for Sweden. There were then 626 seats to fill in the 1999 elections.

This constant reshaping of the Parliament and of the limits of the 'European constituency' is such that a comparison over 20 years (1979–99) does not reflect the same territory. In 1979, the European territory included nine countries and 184 million voters; in 1999, it included 15 countries and over 288 million voters. Independently from the demographic dynamic which concerns any electoral body when analysed for a long period, there is above all, in the case of European elections, a dynamic territorial extension which radically renews the voters called every five years to the polls to elect the European Parliament.

Different electoral systems

The difficulty in studying European elections over a 20-year period is reinforced by the diversity of electoral rules used from one country to another and their evolution. The electoral systems used range from plurality (in the British case until 1994) to proportional representation in its diverse forms. Since 1999, when the UK adopted proportional representation, all European Union countries have chosen their MEPs in the Strasbourg Parliament using one form or other of proportional representation.

Some countries adopted a national constituency (Denmark, Spain, France until 1999, Greece, Luxembourg, the Netherlands and Portugal); others organised the elections in infra-national constituencies (Belgium, Ireland, Italy, UK). The vote for lists remained preferential in nine countries while lists were closed in Germany, Spain, France, Greece, Portugal and the UK. The system of seat allocation also varied in terms of thres-hold. Whereas in most countries there was none, five countries established various thresholds during the period studied: 1.25 per cent of the valid vote in Italy, 3 per cent in Greece,

4 per cent in Sweden, 5 per cent in Germany and in France. Methods used were by quota, but the system of partition of the rest also varies from one country to another. In most states the d'Hondt system was used and served the main parties; but in a few states, systems more favourable to small parties were preferred (modified St Laguë in Sweden, Hare-Niemeyer in Germany and Italy, Hagen-Bischoff in Greece).

If the voting age was fixed at 18 in all countries, the vote was only compulsory in three states (Belgium, Greece and Luxembourg) during the 1979–99 period, and the right to vote of EU third country nationals did not follow the same rules everywhere, in particular considering the minimum length of residence (from six months in France to five years in Luxembourg). The day of the poll also varied: Sunday in 11 of the 15 countries, Friday in Ireland, and Thursday in Denmark, the Netherlands and the UK. Finally, eligibility reflected different conditions with a minimum age ranging from 18 to 25. Since 1994, eligibility extended to any EU citizen except in Belgium. The incompatibility rules with other mandates were also heterogeneous. Finally, rules regarding electoral campaigns led to more or less lengthy and expensive campaigns, more or less generous public financing, and a different use of opinion polls.

All these different rules prevented the emergence of a common electoral space. The European arena was fragmented into 15 national spaces, each of which had its own logic. Despite this diversity of rules, the political vote has gradually led to a common political sphere, but European elections remain largely stamped by strong national logics which produce many 'national second-order elections' (Reif and Schmitt 1980).

Despite this strong 'nationalisation' of European elections, they do not wholly function within the logic of domestic elections (Grunberg et al. 2000). Thus, there is a need to understand the shifts in the EU's political centre of gravity. This will involve an analysis of the evolution of electoral participation and the changes which have affected the vote of the electorate, and in particular the balance between the diverse political families that are represented within the political groups of elected MEPs.

Evolution of turnout from 1979 to 1999

Whereas almost two-thirds of the eligible voters participated in the first European elections with direct universal suffrage, the 1999 elections attracted less than one voter out of two. Limited participation in European elections is not new, and they have always attracted less than national polls. For instance, turnout for the 1979 election was 22 points lower in France than for the 1978 legislative election. This apparent European civic apathy continued over the two following decades across countries. Whereas the aggregate turnout reached 63 per cent in the nine European countries in 1979, figures continuously declined thereafter: 61 per cent in 1984, 58.5 per cent in 1989, 56.8 per cent in 1994 and 49.8 per cent in 1999. This represented a 13-point decline over 20 years. This strong fall was particularly noticeable in Germany (–20.5 per cent), and the Netherlands (–27.8 per cent), but also among many 'newcomers': –18.3 per cent in Austria (from 1996 to 1999), –28.9 per cent in Finland (from 1996 to 1999), –32.4 per cent in Portugal (from 1987 to 1996) (see Table 1).

This movement of 'retreat in the polls' is widespread and no country has escaped it, founding countries as well as the most recent newcomers, Northern European countries as well as those of Southern

Table 1   Evolution of turnout in European elections (1979–1999)*

Country	1979	1984	1989	1994	1999	Change from first election to 1999
Denmark	47.8	52.4	46.2	52.9	50.5	+2.7
Belgium**	91.4	92.2	90.7	90.7	91.0	–0.4
Luxembourg**	88.9	88.8	87.4	88.5	87.3	–1.6
Greece****	–	77.2	79.9	71.2	75.3	–1.9
Sweden	–	–	–	41.6°°	38.8	–2.8
Spain	–	68.9°	54.6	59.1	63.0	–5.9
UK	32.2	32.6	36.2	36.4	24.0	–8.2
Ireland	63.7	47.6	68.3	44.0	50.2	–13.5
France	60.7	56.7	48.7	52.7	46.8	–13.9
Italy***	84.9	83.4	81.5	74.8	70.8	–14.1
Austria	–	–	–	67.7°°°	49.4	–18.3
Germany	65.7	56.8	62.3	60.0	45.2	–20.5
Netherlands	57.8	50.6	47.2	35.6	30.0	–27.8
Finland	–	–	–	60.3°°°	31.4	–28.9
Portugal	–	72.4°	51.2	35.5	40.0	–32.4
EU average	63.0	61.0	58.5	56.8	49.8	–13.2

* It is worth comparing this table with Table 1 in the Abstention article, which shows an increase in turnout between 1999 and 2004 in 7 of the 15 member states above. Two further member states reached turnout levels that were higher in 2004 than in their first election (Luxembourg and United Kingdom)
** Vote is compulsory
*** Vote is a 'civic obligation' but there is no enforcement
**** Vote was originally compulsory, but in the last elections, the government announced that it would not penalise abstainers
° Vote took place in 1987 after the countries joined on 1 January 1987
°° Vote took place in 1995 after the countries joined on 1 January 1995
°°° Vote took place in 1995 after the countries joined on 1 January 1995

Europe. It is similar to a general decline of turnout for national elections. In 1999, apart from the three countries with compulsory voting, participation oscillated between 24 per cent in the UK and 63 per cent in Spain. As Muxel noted, 'no obvious reason, neither geographical, nor cultural, nor even political, emerges from this review of electoral participation in Europe. Thus one knows the effects of the political representative crisis which has persistently affected all types of elections and countries for a certain number of years. But the low legibility of the stakes, of the programmes as well as political forces and the complexity of the political institutional workings at the European level, deepen the gap of the democratic deficit associated to the European vote' (Muxel 2004). This movement of 'withdrawal from the polls' finds its origin in the fact that, even if the European Parliament saw a constant increase in its powers, it nevertheless remained far from fields which are at the very heart of the citizen's priorities: employment, social protection, taxes, security, education, housing (see Magnette 2004). In addition, European elections responsible for the composition of the EU's 'lower chamber' did not, until after 1999, have any direct influence on the composition of the EU 'cabinet', that is, on the Commission's political 'colour'.

These elections, which do not lead to the designation of an executive power, clash with the European tradition where all elections, from local to general and presidential, focus on the choice of who will lead the executive. This is particularly true in such countries as France and the UK, but also in Germany, Spain and Italy where left/right rivalries have structured national political life. Instead, in the European Parliament, the dominant coalition combines the views of socialists, liberals and conservatives. This 'centrist compromise', may not surprise the citizens of the small Northern democracies, who are used to seeing parties fighting vigorously before the elaboration of a governmental coalition, but it fails to mobilise citizens of certain nations unfamiliar with the subtle dialectic of European political conflict and compromise.

So, in 20 years, the process of legitimising the European Parliament through the use of universal suffrage has been limited and, for some, has been part of the so-called 'democratic deficit' of Europe. It is also important to understand the changes that have taken place in the 'families' or group of political parties in the European Parliament.

Evolution of party groups from 1979 to 1999

The 'European constituency' is constantly shifting, and the political classification of the lists at each election is complex. These factors, together with the lack of statistical information at the global European level, mean that the evolution of the political forces within the European Parliament can only be understood through the analysis of the political groupings within it.

In the five elections which were held between 1979 and 1999, the right won a majority four times – very clearly in 1979 and 1999, quite clearly in 1984 and narrowly in 1994. In 1989 the left had a clear majority. Because of the duopoly of the Socialists and the EPP, this was not automatically reflected in the political 'colour' of the EP's presidency during the legislature. In fact, from 1979 to 1984, and again from 1989 to 1994 and from 1994 to 1999, the PSE and Christian Democrats took turns for the presidency (Simone Veil, then Piet Dankert, socialist, in 1979–84; Enrique Baron Crespo, socialist, then Egon Klepsch, PPE, in 1989–94; Klaus Hansch, PSE, then Jose Maria Robles, PPE, in 1994–9). Only in the 1984–9 legislature was there a 'pure right' presidency (Pierre Pfimlin, PPE, then Lord Plumb, ED). But, beyond the left–right split, which is not always pertinent in European politics, it is more interesting to look at the evolution of the diverse political families – from extreme right to extreme left – over the 1979–99 period, as a whole (Table 2).

The Communist trend was one of constant decline; it went down from 10.9 per cent to 4.9 per cent of total members in 1994. The fall of the French PCF and the erosion of the Italian PCI and then its social-democratisation were the main vectors of this process of political demise. Communists and their allies only witnessed a slight upturn in 1999 linked to the score of the extreme left and the arrival of the German PDS. Similarly, in 1999, the Unitarian European Left group/Northern Green Left only maintained itself thanks to the uncertain alliance of communist heirs of the purest tradition (PCF, PDS, KKE, PCP, RC), of its Trotskyite (LO, LCR), and Maoist (SP) critics, and of some extreme left radicals and Greens (VP in Sweden). Despite this unusual coalition, communism and its followers were on the way to marginalisation in Europe.

The Socialist family, on the other hand, retained a leading role in European political life. In the long term,

Table 2   Evolution of party groups in the European Parliament from 1979 to 1999 (in % of the number of MEPs)

	1979	1984	1989	1994	1999
Communists and allies (1)	10.6 (44)	9.4 (41)	8.1 (42)	4.9 (28)	6.7 (42)
Socialists (2)	27.6 (113)	30 (130)	34.7 (180)	34.9 (198)	28.8 (180)
Greens, allies, others (3)	2.7 (11)	4.6 (20)	8.3 (43)	7.4 (42)	7.7 (48)
Liberals (4)	9.8 (40)	7.1 (31)	9.5 (49)	7.6 (43)	8.1 (51)
Christian Democrats and Conservatives (5)	41.7 (171)	36.9 (160)	29.9 (155)	32.5 (184)	37.2 (233)
National right and/or sovereigntists (6)	5.4 (22)	6.7 (29)	3.9 (20)	7.9 (45)	7.3 (46)
Extreme right (7)	–	3.7 (16)	3.3 (17)	–	–
Non-registered	2.2 (9)	1.6 (7)	2.3 (12)	4.8 (27)	4.2 (26)
Total members	(410)	(434)	(518)	(567)	(626)

(1) MEPs belonging to the Communist group in 1979 and 1984, to CG and GUE groups in 1989, to GUE group in 1994 and 1999.
(2) MEPs belonging to the Socialist group in 1979, 1984, 1989 then to PSE in 1994 and 1999.
(3) MEPs belonging to the CDI group in 1979, to the ARC group, to the Green group in 1989, 1994 and 1999.
(4) MEPs belonging to the LD group in 1979, to the ELDR group in 1984, 1989, 1994 and 1999.
(5) MEPs belonging to PE and ED groups in 1979, 1984, to PE and DE groups in 1989, to PE and FRE groups in 1994, to PPE-DE groups in 1999.
(6) MEPs belonging to DEP group in 1979, to RDE group in 1984 and 1989, to RDE and EDN groups in 1994, to UEN and EDD groups in 1999.
(7) MEPs belonging to GDE group in 1984, to DR group in 1989.

it always registered between 27 and 35 per cent of the votes and experienced strong positions in 1989 and 1994 (linked in particular to the good results of the Labour Party in Great Britain). For the Socialists, united in the Party of European Socialists (PES) since 1992, 1999 marked an honourable defeat and 'lost illusions' (Grunberg et al. 2000). The Socialists who, at that time, governed 11 of the 15 countries of the European Union, lost the majority which they held in the Parliament in favour of the right. The dream of a 'socialist Europe' collapsed.

Marginal at the end of the 1970s and the beginning of the 1980s, the Green family grew in power and, by the end of the 1980s, represented roughly 8 per cent of MEPs. In the centre-right, the Liberals (assembling parties such as the British Social Democrats, the Liberals and the Dutch VVD) maintained their influence with between 7 and 10 per cent of the seats.

The Christian Democrat and Conservative group faced a strong erosion of its position, in particular in the 1989 elections, after a dominant place in 1979 (41.7 per cent of its members). It then made a come-back in 1994 and, especially, in 1999, a year branded as a return to 'blue Europe'.

Yet, on the right of the Christian Democrat and Conservative Group, a national right and Eurosceptic family emerged (CPNT, RPF and MPF in France, UKIP in the UK, JuniB in Denmark, Alleanza Nazionale in Italy, Fianna Fail in Finland, CDS-PP in Portugal), which progressively won a significant share of seats from 5 per cent in 1979 to 7–8 per cent in the 1990s.

Finally the extreme right experienced

problems in the European Parliament as a party group. It could only create a modest group in 1984 and 1989 and, most of the time, remained divided in several tendencies with many unaffiliated MEPs. This explains the growth in the number of independent and unaffiliated MEPs after 1994. Federation amongst the ultra-nationalist forces at the European level seemed to be a very hard task.

These political trends were largely the effect of combined national situations, which were far from consistent over the period. European elections remain in fact 'national second-order elections', widely structured by national issues and national political parties. Battles for national government control over 'first-order national elections' (general or presidential) remain decisive and the lesson to draw from European elections is that they are more national than European. Real European elections may only be possible when a uniform procedure and transnational parties with transnational and European agendas prevail.

Pascal Perrineau

Bibliography

Charlot, M., 'Élections européennes', in P. Perrineau and D. Reynié (eds), *Dictionnaire du vote*, Paris, PUF, 2001, pp. 365–8.

Eijk, C. van der and Franklin, M. N. (eds), *Choosing Europe? The European Electorate and National Politics in the Face of Union*, Ann Arbor, University of Michigan Press, 1996.

Grunberg, G., Perrineau, P. and Ysmal, C. (eds), *Le vote des quinze: Les élections européennes du 13 juin 1999*, Paris, Presses de Sciences Po, 2000.

Magnette, Paul, 'European: the Stakes of a Missed Election', *Liberation*, 20 July 2004.

Muxel, A., 'L'Europe sans électeurs?' http://fr.news.yahoo.com/europeennes.html, accessed 9 June 2004.

Perrineau, P. and Ysmal, C. (eds), *Le vote des douze: Les élections européennes de juin 1994*, Paris, DEP du Figaro et Presses de Sciences Po, 1995.

Reif, K. and Schmidt, H. 'Nine Second-Order National Elections: a Conceptual Framework for the Analysis of European Elections Results', *European Journal of Political Research*, 8, 1, 1980, pp. 3–44.

→ Citizen (EU); Democratic Deficit; Electoral Behaviour; European Electoral Sociology; European Parliament; European Parliamentary Assembly; Europeanisation (of National Political Life); Incompatibility; Ineligibility; Nationalisation of European Elections; Observations of Elections; Populism; Second-Order Elections; Sovereignism; Universal Suffrage.

European Elections (2004)

Involving 25 states, 350 million voters, 732 MEPs, roughly 450 lists and several thousand candidates, the sixth European elections since 1979 beat all records. Crowning an enlargement process started in the early 1990s, sealed by the 'Spring Referendum' of 2003 and by the official accession of ten new members on 1 May 2004, the June 2004 European poll also represented a historical event of undoubted importance. Besides the 'revolution in numbers', it marked the 'return to Europe' of a part of the continent that had been kidnapped during the Cold War. These European elections were characterised by a blend of hopes and worries, likely to lead to some disappointment. And indeed, this event was widely criticised due to perceived growing abstention levels, protest voting, and the secondary role attributed to the European dimension in most national campaigns; all factors led to increased worries about a growing 'democratic deficit'. Prior to the examination of the lessons to be drawn from this unusual election, we need to remember a few points.

A European election remains, regardless of its outcome, an election on Europe. It must then be analysed from a very unique and idiosyncratic standpoint, rather than compared to elections defined by different logics and objectives. Only a 'European approach' to 'European elections' allows one to avoid the mistake of drawing 'lazy comparisons' (the tyranny of national references) or 'non-cautious comparisons' ('second-order elections'). With this in mind, four main lessons can be drawn from the European vote of June 2004.

The lack of Europeanised voting procedures

Despite the introduction, in the Amsterdam Treaty (1998), of principles common to all member states for European Parliament elections, the persistence of heterogeneous electoral practices has to be recognised. The variable number of MEPs based on each country's population, compulsory voting practices, as well as differences linked to specific electoral limits are amongst the main distinctions to be considered. For instance, while most countries have a 5 per cent threshold, Sweden and Austria have set it at 4 per cent, and Greece at 3 per cent. Similarly, most countries use a single national constituency, while some have opted for more ad hoc divisions: 13 constituencies in Poland, 12 in the United Kingdom, 8 in France, 4 in Belgium and in Ireland. The conjunction of list-based elections, with the constituency effects, structure the transformation of votes into seats, sometimes penalising smaller political constituencies. In certain countries, lists presented by parties or coalitions were grouped (Finland, Denmark, Italy, the Netherlands). When it comes to mechanisms determining the allocation of seats, eight different mechanisms were used. Sixteen countries used the d'Hondt method, designed to favour the strongest parties. However, the St Laguë method was preferred in Latvia and in Sweden, while Slovakia and Luxembourg used a rectified quota method, more favourable to small and medium coalitions. Other technicalities varied across countries. For example, the date and time at which the vote took place ranged from 10 June in Ireland to 13 June for most other member states, and on only one day in principle, with some variations in the Czech Republic where polls are usually held from Friday noon to Saturday noon or, in Italy's case, over two days). Other variations included the candidates' minimum age (18 for half of the countries, but 23 in France and 25 in Italy and Greece). The consequences of such heterogeneity are double. Firstly, the different electoral systems are partly responsible for shaping the results, the repartition of seats and ultimately the composition of political groups and coalitions within the European Parliament. Here we find a classic example of the political instrumentalisation of voting procedures, which leaves them open to circumstantial factors and ultimately limits political competition to a few privileged parties. France constitutes a good example of changed electoral rules that were aimed at correcting the scattering of votes noted during the latest national polls in order to favour the main government coalition. The second effect concerns the difficult emergence of a European electorate and public sphere. With 26 electoral systems in 25 countries, cacophony has, one might think, reached its limits. Only a Europeanisation of voting practices that will at last see Europeans as equal before electoral rules, and within similar constituencies with multinational lists, will allow the present European electoral archipelago to be transformed into a consistent European election.

Elections without voters?

The overall turnout reached 44.03 per cent in 2004, an overall decrease of roughly six points as compared to the 1999 election, despite important cross-national differences and an increase in participation in many countries. With the exception of countries where the vote is fully or partly compulsory and leads to significant levels of turnout (70 per cent in Greece, 71 per cent in Cyprus, 90 per cent in Belgium and 93 per cent in Luxembourg), only three countries surpassed the symbolic 50 per cent yardstick in 2004: Malta (82 per cent), which has a tradition of mass electoral participation, Ireland (61 per cent) and Italy (73.1 per cent), where parallel local and regional polls may stimulate European 'good citizenship'. These weak levels of participation confirm the fact that European elections have a limited mobilising power. In fact, since 1979, overall abstention levels have apparently grown from 37.6 per cent to 56 per cent. Weak participation in the European elections is also part of a general electoral disaffection affecting all European countries and types of elections. However, abstention figures mask important national differences. The 15 'old' member states showed contradictory trends. Eight experienced a lower electoral mobilisation (a two point loss on average, but an 18-point decrease in Spain, and eight points in Denmark), but in contrast, seven countries had sometimes important increases in electoral mobilisation (+14 in Great Britain, +11 in Finland, +10 in the Netherlands). On the whole, the old member states had a global turnout of 45.4 per cent, against 26.3 per cent for the newcomers (with a record low of 17

per cent in Slovakia). Therefore, the overall fall in levels of participation essentially stems from Central and Eastern European countries in which civic life, though very recent, seems already tired and saturated. But beyond the national circumstances, how are we to interpret this apparent disaffection with European polls? Possible explanations often put forward include the absence of clarity of European issues, and their technical, as well as institutional constraints. More fundamentally, European elections suffer from a double handicap. European elections are firstly a legislative poll with no impact on the designation of the executive, contradicting a European tradition of clear choices and alternatives. The lack of enthusiasm may also stem from the fact that the European Parliament, whose powers have considerably increased over the past years, does not enjoy much political visibility. Moreover, it does not benefit from obvious cleavages and polarised fights that generate meaning through the process of conflict. With the exception of Northern countries, compromise is often perceived in many European political cultures as the negation of democracy, the essence of which would reside rightly or wrongly in the expression of a true and free competition.

Punishing governments?

One of the main trends of the June 2004 European election was the frequency and scale of protest votes that hit a number of parties and coalitions in power. In Germany, the Social Democratic Party had its worst result since 1953 with 21.5 per cent of the votes, although the Greens were spared; they gained five points despite being members of the government. In contrast, in Portugal and France, the Socialist opposition surpassed by ten points the ruling Conservative governments. In Italy, Great Britain, Estonia and Slovenia, voters sought to penalise, sometimes severely, government policies relating to the Iraq War, as well as unpopular economic or social measures. Only six countries have escaped the logic of this sanction vote, either because their freshly elected governments were still benefiting from a honeymoon phase (Greece and Spain), or because of the ability of the ruling parties to attract a sort of 'useful vote' often in favour of European integration (Slovakia, Ireland). This phenomenon can be explained by the nationalisation of electoral campaigns by political elites who sought to use such a vote as a sort of mid-term election. On the other hand, this phenomenon was consistent with the broader context of sanction voting. Few Western democracies were spared from this new rationale consisting of saying 'no' as a form of dismissal, as a way to vote against those in power. The electoral setback suffered by the coalitions in power can be interpreted as victory for the democratic reappropriation by citizens of the electoral tool and not only as the sullen expression of a disenchanted and frivolous citizenship.

'Trompe l'oeil' populism

Numerous observers believed that the June 2004 European elections had all the ingredients favourable to a Eurosceptic and populist outburst. Many had already suspected a weakened European integration. The results show that such worries were only partly justified. Firstly, the extreme ideological and socio-cultural heterogeneity of the candidates made their grouping into the same family presumptuous. The divergence of programmes and speeches made it difficult and incautious to combine the votes of the National Front in France (9.8 per cent), those of Samoobrona in Poland (10.1 per cent) with those of the list of June in Sweden (14.4 per cent). The grouping was in fact a mosaic of parties ranging from those supporting the complete withdrawal of their country from the EU (UKIP in the United Kingdom) to pro-Europeans defending the idea of Europe with an ethical and transparent functioning (the Hans-Peter Martin list in Austria). It is clear that the results of these formations were also very diverse. While the Vlams Blok continued to prosper in Flemish Belgium (14.4 per cent), Jorg Haider FPO collapsed, securing only one seat and little more than 6 per cent of the votes. While it is true that 11 per cent of Euro MEPs came from these formations, their dispersion in a plurality of groups of opportunistic character should then limit their political influence. Contrary to what might be feared, pro-European parties have succeeded in extricating themselves from the game, managing to secure a good majority of the votes. As underlined by Le Bras, it was a 'moderate Europe' that emerged from the June 2004 election. With the exception of three countries (Cyprus, Lithuania, the Czech Republic), the Conservatives, the Liberals, the Social-Democrats and the Greens formed majority government blocs. As an echo of Magritte's words, it seems to us that this is not a European election, but the conjunction of 25 simultaneous national elections on Europe.

Can we really speak of the same Europe in Berlin, Vilnius, Helsinki or Bratislava? This phenomenon is not really new. The main lesson to be drawn from the historic June 2004 elections is without doubt that enlargement has not really modified the main lessons that resulted from preceding European polls. The newcomers in Europe have embraced tendencies that had been observed in the past, accentuating them at times, at others showing their democratic 'normality', and condemning the sententious judgements of those who were too hastily accusing them of 'not having made a proper use of their freedom'.

Michel Hastings

Bibliography

Hastings, M. (ed.), 'Ceci n'est pas une élection européenne', *Les Cahiers du CEPEN*, no. 3, 2004.

→ Abstention; Electoral System; Electoral Technology; European Elections (1979–1999); European Electoral Act; Nationalisation of European Elections; Populism; Protest Voting; Second-Order Elections.

European Elections Studies (EES)

Elections to the European Parliament (EP) have been held every five years since 1979. At each of these elections, except for those of 1984, the academic community has held surveys of voters in virtually all the countries that took part. In 1979 a special purpose survey was carried out as part of the regular (November) Eurobarometer, four months after the election, in all of the (then) nine member countries. In 1989 and 1994, a special purpose survey was held as part of a special Eurobarometer, additional to the regular spring/autumn schedule, in June–July of those years in the 12 member countries. In 1999 the 15 member countries were surveyed by means of telephone interviews. In 2004, 24 of the 25 member countries (excluding only Malta) were surveyed by a variety of methods. Additionally, the regular (November) Eurobarometer of 1984 contained enough questions to determine how respondents voted in the 1984 elections of the previous June. For some limited purposes we thus have virtually complete coverage in terms of survey data of all the European Parliament elections ever conducted.

Sample sizes until 1999 were about 1000 per country. In 1999 the samples were about 1000 for each of six countries and about 600 for the remaining countries except for Italy (over 3000). In 2004 the sample sizes were quite varied, but generally above 800 per country.

While each of these voter studies had variables in common (see below), so that from one perspective the series can be regarded as a time series with new readings on various measures at five-year intervals, each of these voter studies formed part of a larger election study with a specific theme. Large parts of each voter study were tailored to focus on that theme, and each theme also involved additional studies to which each voter study was linked.

The 1979 study focused on campaigns, media and elites, with the voters' study being linked to a campaign study (Reif and Schmitt 1980; Schmitt, 1983), a media study (Blumler 1983), and a study of middle-level elites (Blumler and Fox 1982). The most important thing we learned from these studies was the low salience of EP elections to voters, and the fact that the European context made so little impression on voters as to hardly divert them from their normal national political orientations. It was following these studies that Reif and Schmitt (1980) applied to EP elections the term 'second-order elections' to place European Parliament elections in the same category as regional and local elections which, in most countries, also fail to divert voters from national political concerns. However, researchers who used these data also gained the impression that attitudes to Europe did play a role in the electoral behaviour of voters (Reif 1985).

Building on these findings, the 1989 study focused on voter mobilisation, trying to understand why European matters failed to gain prominence at EP elections, and evaluating the role of parties and national political contexts in EP election outcomes. It also focused for the first time on the consequences of EP elections for domestic politics in the member states. This study actually consisted of three linked voter studies, one conducted in November 1988, one in April 1989, and one in June 1989 immediately following the elections. The objective was to provide three points in time at which to track the evolving awareness of voters of a forthcoming or immediately past EP election. This format gave rise to the discovery that if European Parliament elections are studied at any distance from the elections themselves, misleading results arise from the fact that the election appears somewhat hypothetical to voters, and vote intentions or recollections in such a hypothetical situation are coloured by attitudes towards European integration (Schmitt and Mannheimer 1991), whereas actual behaviour even in a second-order election is not.

The 1994 study focused on representation in the European Union, with the voters' study being linked to a candidate study, a study of Members of the European Parliament, and studies of members of national parliaments in the member states. These studies established, first, that there are no very great differences between the attitudes and orientations of national parliamentarians and those who sit in the European Parliament (Katz and Wessels 1999). All are members of a European elite that broadly favours the steps that have been taken and are being taken towards European unity, though members of the EP are somewhat more favourable towards further integration. Secondly, these studies confirmed the fact that representation, as customarily conceived in terms of a responsible party model, does not exist in the institutions of the European Union. The EU is a consensual system, and such a system does not provide clear choices to voters (Schmitt and Thomassen 1999).

The 1989 and 1994 studies taken together also provided the basis for the first extended treatment of voting behaviour in European Parliament elections (Eijk and Franklin 1996). But because European Parliament elections do not provide stimuli that divert voters from national political concerns, this study ends up being a study of party preferences and party choice in cross-national perspective: the first such study to evaluate the impact of country-level institutional and party system differences on turnout and party choice. *Choosing Europe?* essentially viewed EP elections as windows on to national political and electoral processes, taking advantage of the fact that interviews had been conducted in different political contexts to evaluate the consequences of contextual differences for turnout and party choice. Employing an extended series of questions regarding voter behaviour, first fielded in 1989 but included in every subsequent study, the study was able to investigate the preferences of voters for political parties and the way in which those preferences manifested themselves as party choices at the national and European levels. It also focused on the (often unfortunate) consequences for national political processes of conducting EP elections, since they are often viewed as pointless by European voters.

The 1999 EES built on the findings of *Choosing Europe?* by taking further advantage of EP elections as windows on to national political processes. This time the focus was on issue framing and issue evolution, and the voters' study was linked to studies of party manifestos and of media content during the campaign. These linked studies proved so useful (Brug and Eijk, forthcoming, 2007) that they were employed again in 2004 when the recent enlargement of the EU to 25 members, including a number of countries in the course of transition from authoritarian rule, provided the opportunity to use the format of a European election study to investigate processes of EU enlargement and of democratisation in member countries.

With 25 countries now members of the EU, European Parliament elections have gained enormously in importance as indicative of national political processes – promising new insights into the attitudes and behaviour of citizens in the light of economic, social and political circumstances that differ between countries, especially when those countries are as diverse as are the present members of the European Union.

Mark Franklin

Bibliography

Blumler, J. G., *Communicating to Voters: Television in the First European Parliament Elections*, London, Sage, 1983.

Blumler, J. G. and Fox, A. D., *The European Voter: Popular Responses to the First European Community Elections*, London, Policy Studies Institute, 1982.

Brug, W. van der and Eijk, C. van der (eds), *Voting in the European Election of 1999: Lessons From the Past and Perspectives for the Future*, Cambridge, Cambridge University Press, forthcoming, 2007.

Eijk, C. van der and Franklin, M. N. (eds), *Choosing Europe? The European Electorate and National Politics in the Face of Union*, Ann Arbor, University of Michigan Press, 1996.

Katz, R. and Wessels, B. (eds), *European Parliament and European Integration*, Oxford, Oxford University Press, 1999.

Reif, K. (ed.), *Ten European Elections: Campaigns and Results of the 1979/81 First Direct Elections to the European Parliament*, Aldershot, Gower, 1985.

Reif, K. and Schmitt, H., 'Nine Second-Order National Elections: a Conceptual Framework for the Analysis of European Elections Results', *European Journal of Political Research*, 8, 1, 1980, pp. 3–44.

Schmitt, H., 'Party Government in Public Opinion: a European Cross-National Comparison', *European Journal of Political Research*, 11, 4, 1983, pp. 353–76.

Schmitt, H. and Mannheimer, R., 'About Voting and Non-Voting in the European Elections of June 1989', *European Journal of Political Research*, 19, 1, 1991, pp. 31–54.

Schmitt, H. and Thomassen, J. (eds), *Political Representation and Legitimacy in the European Union*, Oxford, Oxford University Press, 1999.

→ Data Archives; Electoral Behaviour; Eurobarometer; Forecast; Identity.

European Electoral Act

In many ways, talking of a 'European Electoral Act' might be excessive, so heterogeneous are the national processes used to select MEPs. With the uniform procedure once promised by the Treaty of Rome never implemented, the various voting rituals faced by the citizens of each member state still largely determine their electoral experience. As a result, we can observe the emergence of highly varied national patterns, which have made the prospect of a standardised format almost inconceivable. Only a hypothetical 'EU format' could have created the necessary unified space and time of a true transnational election, to foster the development of a genuine European civic experience.

As the Act that was to be adopted on 20 September 1976 was being debated, numerous participants mentioned the 'psychological reasons' that should lead the Summit to favour a simultaneous election across member states. Thus, the working group of the European Assembly that prepared the new electoral model concluded that it had 'unanimously recognised' that 'to give some importance to European elections', they should be held on one day and that 'no other election should be organised by any member state on the same day' to avoid the risk that 'the European character of the European elections be overshadowed by local or national [political considerations]'. They concluded that the main objective of the elections, that is, to 'involve the people [in the process of European integration] would undoubtedly be compromised' otherwise (European Parliament 1969). However, because of the rigidity of national 'habits and traditions', the solution adopted was far less ambitious. Article 9 of the Act of 1976 only states that 'elections to the Assembly shall be held on the date fixed by each member state; for all member states, this date shall fall within the same period starting on a Thursday morning and ending on the following Sunday' (European Commission 1976). The same Article states that 'the counting of votes may not begin until after the close of polling in the member state, whose voters are the last to vote within the period referred to in paragraph 1.'

This lack of true simultaneity has undoubtedly impeded the progressive emergence of a consistent feeling of common belonging: the election time does not necessarily allow for an electoral body to invent its own nature in and through its political representation. This is made yet worse by the fact that very often, despite the recommendations of the original committee, other votes are organised at the same time as the European Parliament elections. As a result, European elections find it hard to distinguish themselves from national political agendas.

This nationalisation of the European electoral act is also illustrated by the galaxy of electoral rules and formats to be found across member states. While a few countries enforce compulsory voting (Belgium, Cyprus, Greece, Luxembourg) more or less strictly, the constitutional and social constraints, beliefs and postures associated with the vote remain highly inconsistent across countries. Various member states use different types of voting formats (anticipated, from home, by proxy, postal, etc.), technologies (electronic voting, automated voting, marked or unmarked paper ballots, etc.), times (in June 2004, polling stations opened at 6 a.m. in Luxembourg, and closed at 10 p.m. in Italy where they were opened both Saturday afternoon and Sunday), and locations (hospitals or military institutions were used in some countries, boats and 'mobile ballot boxes' in others). In fact, the context of European elections is often used to experiment with new electoral modes, as in the UK where postal voting was generalised to four constituencies, hence making the average 'Royal Mail' mailbox a fully fledged ballot box. The *Lincolnshire Echo* of 18 June 2004 thus reported the nostalgic reaction of a UKIP voter who complained that the 'heartbeat' of a mailbox was so utterly different from that of traditional polling stations, and had seemingly condemned the traditional excitement of election eve to becoming an old memory. At the same time, 42 per cent of Belgian voters had to get used to new automated polling stations. After arriving and proving one's identity in the station designed by the Digivote company, the voter received a magnetic voting card. He or she then had to enter an 'electronic kiosk', where a dark curtain provided privacy. The voter introduced the card into the machine and used the touchscreen to express his or her preference before collecting the card again and giving it to the president of the ballot station who put it into the electronic ballot box. The machine then processed the digital information contained on all the cards immediately and efficiently.

These experiments should not obscure the more fundamental reality: European elections are largely ruled by national laws, and correspond to 25 different elections with different rules, constituencies, candidacy conditions and processing rules. How could such a heterogeneity contribute to a truly European aspect of European elections? A uniform electoral procedure would not only simplify the election of MEPs, but allow citizens to project themselves in the institution that is designed to represent them. Thus, at the moment, European elections are still all too often perceived as mid-term elections between two general elections, or even as a peripheral vote. This used to be the case even more in countries like Italy, France and the UK, when the law allowed MEPs to also hold a national parliamentary mandate, which is no longer possible. Nonetheless, the great diversity of electoral technologies and procedures helps to explain the large discrepencies in the numbers of EU voters who chose to vote outside of their country of citizenship, despite the possibility offered by the Maastricht Treaty, Article 8.2. This is how an immense majority of expatriated Austrians, Spaniards and Italians still choose to vote in their country of origin (Commission Communication on directive 93/109/EC, annex 7). This proves the extent to which electoral politics are still monopolised by a national logic and deemed to represent the fundamental strength of national links.

Nevertheless, a dynamic of reform is finally emerging. The Amsterdam Treaty installed 'principles which are common to all the member states' (Article 190.4, TEU). In discussing these principles, the European Parliament proposed the generalisation of proportional representation, and of regional constituencies in countries where the population exceeds 20 million inhabitants. They also agreed on the principle of an electoral threshold, the incompatibility of the functions of MP and MEP, and most daringly, proposed the creation of transnational lists for the 2009 European Parliament elections. This unifying project was adopted by the European Parliament on 15 July 1998 (document A4-212/98, JO C292 of 21 September 1998). The text was heavily discussed, then transmitted to the Council, adopted by the constitutional affairs committee of the European Parliament by 21 votes against two (one abstention), and finally adopted on 12 June 2002. In fact, the final text was unusually close to the original proposal of the European Parliament. Not only did it abrogate Article 5 of the Act of 1976 on mandate compatibility, but it imposed a proportional type electoral system (proportional, list, or single transferable vote). The proposals that 10 per cent of the seats be allocated to an EU-wide constituency, and that countries with a large population create constituencies were not included in the final text. However, other elements were added, such as earlier election dates (May instead of June) to improve turnout, and the announcement by the European political parties of their candidates for the presidency of the European Commission should they win the election. As explained by Alain Lamassoure, a former French minister, this was hoped to make EU leaders closer to citizens, giving them a chance to decide who should be 'Mr or Mrs Europe'. So far, the Council has not ratified the new rules of the game, but it is more and more likely that European elections will finally play their part in the creation of a *civis europeus*. A true 'European Electoral Act' will thereby redefine the relationship between citizenship, nationality, and transnational electoral democracy.

Yves Déloye
Olivier Ihl

Bibliography

European Commission, 1976. 76/787/ECSC, EEC, Euratom: 'Decision of the representatives of the Member States meeting in the council relating to the Act concerning the election of the representatives of the Assembly by direct universal suffrage' *Official Journal L 278, 08/10/1976 P. 0001–0004.*

→ Act of 1976; Citizen (EU); Compulsory Voting; Electoral Operations; Electoral Technology; Identity; Nationalisation of European Elections; Polling Stations; Postal Voting; Representation; Second-Order Elections; Symbolism; Symbols and Practice of Elections; Treaty of Rome.

European Electoral Sociology

The origins of European electoral sociology

Since the generalisation of universal suffrage in Europe towards the end of the nineteenth century, political parties and analysts alike realised that the apparent predictability of aggregate level election outcomes had come to an end. However, some of the most eminent members of a recently emerging discipline, sociology, started to understand that some patterns could perhaps be identified in the way various categories of citizens interacted with their political systems and behaved politically.

Historically, sociologists first tried to understand the relationship between the behaviour of individuals and mass phenomena such as religion, social class and geographical groups. The most famous predecessor of European political sociology was undoubtedly Weber who focused, among others, on the role of Protestant and Catholic religions in shaping citizens' attitudes, but electoral sociology *per se* was more significantly represented by the works of Siegfried, who tried to better understand the vote of citizens in a given region, Duverger, for his studies of parties, and Lipset and Rokkan, who tried to provide a generalised theory of the cleavages that had split European polities since the 1920s, and explained the voting behaviour of various groups of people.

By the early 1960s, political scientists tended to quite firmly believe that they had managed to model quite accurately the behaviour of individual voters on the basis of their sociological characteristics, and to understand how the various tensions and splits in most European societies would impact on the fortunes of large political parties election after election.

The traditional conceptions

Amongst the main sociological characteristics they identified were the four main dimensions of politically relevant social cleavages in European societies according to Lipset and Rokkan (1967): the opposition between the Church and secular powers, the tension between workers and owners, the rivalry between centres and peripheries, and the competition between rural and urban areas, all meaningful cleavages in West European liberal democracies. Lipset and Rokkan claimed that these cleavages and the party systems which resulted from them had 'frozen' in the 1920s, although some of them had evolved slightly to match the modernisation of fully mobilised societies to reshape around such tensions as between corporatism and centralism or nationalism and cosmopolitanism.

In the early 1970s, Inglehart (1971), acknowledging that the traditional cleavages identified by Lipset and Rokkan were powerless when it came to trying to explain the revolt of wealthy young students in 1968 in such countries as Germany, France and the USA, claimed that a fifth dimension of cleavage politics, opposing 'materialist' and 'post-materialist' voters, had emerged and would progressively replace the other traditional cleavages, as new generations of voters would emerge who would have been socialised in conditions of economic prosperity and growth and political security, which would make the old cleavages less strong.

However, both the traditional Lipset and Rokkan model and the post-materialist theory have since been challenged by proponents of a dealignment theory, which claims that neither traditional cleavages nor a hypothetical materialist/post-materialist cleavage are very good at explaining contemporary voting behaviour in European societies.

Explanatory power of electoral sociology and the 2004 European elections

By the end of the twentieth century, research showed that the power of electoral sociology to explain the vote of citizens in Europe had diminished globally, but not equally across major West European democracies. The comparative work of Franklin et al. (1992) suggested that while the explanatory power of traditional electoral sociological models of the vote remained very high in countries such as Sweden, and relatively

strong in the United Kingdom, it had significantly decreased in such states as France and Germany, and had never been particularly high in the United States.

The exit polls conducted amongst the various European electorates after the elections of 14 June 2004 confirm this tendency, and suggest the decline of sociological predictability in the voting behaviour of Europeans. Among the dimensions that remain effective predictors of voting behaviour, religion in societies such as Italy and Northern Ireland, and social class in such countries as Sweden and Spain remain relatively meaningful. On the other hand, in a country such as the United Kingdom, the relative power of social class seems to have declined, with working class voters being largely split between the Labour and UKIP votes, and the middle class between the Labour, Conservative, and Liberal Democrat electorate, with a non-negligible UKIP minority again. As for such countries as France and the Netherlands, the power of traditional sociological predictors of voting behaviour has declined for a long time and was confirmed by the result of the June 2004 elections.

These results confirm earlier findings of the political science literature and of the studies of previous European elections. Analysing the 1994 vote, Eijk and Franklin (1996) showed that the correlation between party preference and social class varied from 0.02 in the Netherlands to 0.10 in Wallonia, and the correlation between party preference and religion between 0.02 in Britain and Greece to 0.28 in Northern Ireland, the only political system in which it has a clear impact (Table 1). As for post-materialism, it explained very little variance in party preference in any of the countries studied.

By contrast, the independent variables that correspond to dealignment

Table 1   Correlates of party preference in the 1994 European elections

Country	Traditional sociological variables			Dealignment variables			
	Class	Religion	Post-materialism	Ideology (distance)	Ideology (direction)	Issues	Govt Approval
Denmark	0.08	0.03	0.02	0.31	0.25	0.18	0.14
Flanders	0.06	0.06	0.01	0.09	0.05	0.15	0.08
France	0.04	0.06	0.02	0.32	0.21	0.09	0.10
Germany	0.04	0.06	0.05	0.31	0.14	0.09	0.13
Britain	0.04	0.02	0.05	0.19	0.16	0.10	0.24
Greece	0.04	0.02	0.03	0.34	0.17	0.14	0.25
Ireland	0.05	0.03	0.01	0.17	0.12	0.07	0.08
Italy	0.03	0.08	0.02	0.19	0.12	0.06	0.03
Luxembourg	0.04	0.03	0.05	0.19	0.07	0.18	0.03
N. Ireland	0.05	**0.28**	0.03	0.15	0.14	0.20	0.06
Netherlands	0.02	0.07	0.02	0.21	0.13	0.10	0.12
Portugal	0.03	0.03	0.02	0.22	0.07	0.09	0.10
Spain	0.06	0.06	0.03	0.23	0.15	0.10	0.13
Wallonia	0.10	0.05	0.02	0.19	0.10	0.18	0.04
EU Total	*0.05*	*0.06*	*0.03*	*0.22*	*0.13*	*0.12*	*0.10*

Notes:
- The coefficients represent the variance in party preference explained by the various variables entered.
- Figures in bold represent coefficients superior to 0.10.
- Classification as 'traditional sociological variables' and dealignment compatible variables is the responsibility of the author of this article.

Source: Adapted from Eijk and Franklin 1996.

hypotheses, such as ideology, issue voting and government approval, have a much stronger impact on party preferences across political systems. At the EU level, the main variables used in traditional alignment models and in post-materialist realignment models, combined, barely explain 14 per cent of the total variance in partisan choice, while variables more likely to be used in a dealignment model explain, when combined, 57 per cent of the total variance in the same variable. These results combined seem to confirm the decline of traditional sociological explanations in voting behaviour, a tendency apparently further confirmed with the 2004 elections, not only to the extent that government approval and issues seem to have played a yet increased role in the voters' decisions, but also to the extent that some specific evolutions of electoral behaviour in June 2004 seem to indicate a further weakening of partisan alignment in the few marginal cases in which they had seemed to resist up to then.

Some particularly interesting puzzles for the political sociological approach

Beyond this general decline in traditional political sociological models of voting behaviour, some particular aspects of the election proved just how new models and theories need to be applied if the contemporary European voter is to be understood better in his choices. Extreme-right voting in particular seems to have transcended traditional cleavages and sociological explanations. According to authors like Schain, in the case of France, these parties now seem to appeal almost equally to traditional conservative middle classes and to the blue-collar workers who live in the suburban areas of large French cities. Moreover, while traditionally the

National Front had been mostly strong in the large cities of an area east of a Strasbourg to Perpignan line, the party lost some ground in some of its traditional strongholds such as Provence-Alpes-Côte d'Azur and the Paris region, and, on the other hand, registered higher than ever scores in rural areas of Brittany and Poitou Charentes (see Extreme Left and Extreme Right, this volume).

Similarly, it is clear that the vote in favour of social-democratic and socialist parties – historically, the first to have been tied to sociological variables by electoral sociologists – was, in June 2004, hardly related to the traditional distribution of citizens along social categories. In many ways, the losses of many European social-democratic and socialist parties of their ties with their traditional working class bases in favour of intellectual middle classes is in itself an archetypal example of the decline of traditional cleavage politics analysed by Franklin et al. (1992).

Electoral sociology and European elections in the new member states

Finally, it is important to note that the decline of traditional predictors of the vote in West European political systems stands in contrast to the resilience of some strong remaining cleavages in the new member states in general and in newly democratised ones in particular.

The study of voting behaviour in the Baltic states in June 2004, for example, confirms the remaining impact of national groups on electoral choice. It is very clear that the Russian minority systematically voted differently from 'national' Balts in all three countries. This corresponds to significant national tensions in Latvia, but also holds true in Lithuania and Estonia where national tensions seemed to have been partly appeased since 1990–1. In the same way, the behaviour observed in June 2004 for the European elections in Poland suggests a certain resilience of traditional cleavage politics, be they based around religion or class differences.

In the same way, however, Malta also remains a polity in which the strong ideological polarisation of the two main parties competing for power closely matches some very significant alignments and social predictability. The case of Cyprus is not much different as once again, a very polarised party system seems to favour the resistance of aligned or 'social' politics, even in what is now a relatively established democracy.

Both in the Central European and in the Mediterranean cases that have just been mentioned, it seems that the survival of political sociological patterns of voting is first and foremost explained by unresolved deep social cleavages in these societies. In turn, this allows for a highly polarised party system, in which centrist and extreme parties are equally likely to achieve electoral success to remain in place, with, typically, higher scores for communist or ex-communist parties and for nationalist parties in these regions than in the West, in which the only polarisation of the system is maintained by extreme protest parties. In that sense, it seems that the decline of political sociological trends, which started in North-Western Europe and has now reached most of the 15 pre-2004 member states of the European Union, may partly result from the cleavage resolution brought about by European integration itself. In turn, it may then apply to the new member states, whose strong internal social, political and economic conflicts had prevented their joining the European Union until 2004, and which are counting on European integration to bring about the conditions of internal pacification and economic development

which many believe to be indispensable to internal societal conflict resolution.

Michael Bruter

Bibliography

Eijk, C. van der and Franklin, M. N. (eds), *Choosing Europe? The European Electorate and National Politics in the Face of Union*, Ann Arbor, University of Michigan Press, 1996.

Franklin, M. N., Mackie, T. T. and Valen, H. (eds), *Electoral Change: Responses to Evolving Social and Attitudinal Structures in Western Countries*, Cambridge, Cambridge University Press, 1992.

Inglehart, R., 'The Silent Revolution in Europe', *American Political Science Review*, 65, 4, 1971, pp. 991–1017.

Lipset, S. M. and Rokkan, S., *Party Systems and Voters' Alignments: Cross-national Perspectives*, London, Collier Macmillan, 1967.

→ Cleavages; Data Archives; Electoral Behaviour; Eurobarometer; Extreme Left; Extreme Right; Identity; Left; Religion; Right; Women; Young People.

European Federation of Green Parties

During the June 2004 European elections, 25 European Green parties were able to lead a common European campaign in 22 countries. Twenty years of co-operation amongst Green parties across Europe enabled the creation of the European Green Party, the organisation of meetings, the elaboration of a common electoral manifesto, the establishment of a 'dream team' including heads of lists of diverse national parties, the elaboration of a common visibility strategy, as well as posters, logos and websites.

Before the first European elections by direct universal suffrage in 1979 the scenario was very different. In fact, the Greens did not benefit from the existence of an international body or a political group within the European Parliament. In contrast with other political families, the first forms of co-operation amongst Green parties or movements were established in the extra-parliamentary sphere. With heterogeneous ideological principles, modes of action and degrees of organisation, European environmentalists encountered difficulties in establishing common structures. At the end of the 1970s, they sought to 'lean on' the resources of Italian and Dutch 'radical' parties to co-ordinate their actions. Because of the youth of the 'ecologist family', relations were limited to personal contacts. They were nevertheless formalised by the creation of the ECOROPA (European Ecological Action) association in 1977 and the adoption of a first common political declaration that proved crucial during the European campaign.

In light of the first electoral results, these first instances of co-operation were judged positively. The Greens then created, in July 1979, a network linking their respective organisations: the Platform of Ecopolitical Action for a Peaceful Change of Europe (PEACE). The ECOROPA declaration served as a basis for this programme. The success of these meetings encouraged ecology leaders to develop a free federation based on the principle of unanimity, with a real political programme. As main financial contributors, 'radical' parties refused to establish a common platform, favouring joint actions instead. The European Co-ordination of Green and Radical Parties in Europe was created in February 1982 in the hope of finding a compromise. However, unable to surmount the substantial differences, it was dissolved eight months later.

Encouraged by the first national electoral success, some Green parties considered the creation of a strictly ecologist organisation for partisan co-operation. In 1983, the British, Irish, Swedish, French and Belgian Greens established the European Green Co-ordination (EGC). A common programme basis was founded on the elementary principles of ecologist policy. The party members (independently of the EEC) had to subscribe to it. Two delegates per party met three times a year, reaching all decisions by consensus. The common activities multiplied, and included press communications, common declarations, devising common logos for all European Greens, electoral congress (March 1984), as well as the adhesion of new members (Luxembourg and the Netherlands). In spite of these developments, Green parties still struggled to unify around a common political identity. Internal dissent among the German Greens with their pragmatic and strategic disagreements with respect to other EGC members, affected the image of unity that the young ecologist political party sought to reflect. During the 1984 polls, the EGC was represented in most member states. The Belgian and Dutch Greens both obtained two seats, while the German Greens managed to secure seven. Elected ecologists reunited under the Green Alternative European Link (GRAEL) within the technical Rainbow group formed with other small political formations inside the European Parliament. Due to the predominance of the German Greens in the GRAEL, relations with the EGC only showed signs of improvement at election times.

The EGC essentially organised its activities around the definition of a common identity. New member parties were accepted (Luxembourg, Denmark, Switzerland, Spain, Portugal, Austria, Finland and Italy) among whom were the German Greens, who joined in 1987.

While strategic conflicts between those in favour of radical and reformist strategies subsided, the programme's attitudes towards European integration remained divided, heterogeneous, and split between federalists and confederalists, as well as between environmentalist and liberal tendencies.

Prior to the 1989 European elections, the EGC progressively favoured initiatives based on the multilateral co-operation of Green parties at the pan-European level. In doing so, it became the depository of what was to become a strong ecologist identity. It reinforced its position towards national parties, of the European parliamentary group, and tried to resemble partisan federations of other political families. Nevertheless, its pragmatic developments and its organisational structure remained minimal, essentially because of the absence of consensus regarding its role in the European institutional system.

The fall of the communist regimes in Central Europe and the acceleration of the European integration process towards the end of the 1980s opened new perspectives to the European federations of parties. Coupled with the unprecedented results secured by numerous Green lists both during national and European elections in 1989, partisan co-operation in the EGC experienced a new impulse. Thanks to the establishment of a Green group in the European Parliament comprising 28 elected ecologists, the EGC benefited from new sources of funding. Such funding represented 80 per cent of the Coordination budget (roughly 250 000 euros, excluding 2004 campaign expenses). Changes in the European context forced Green parties to devote themselves more to the formulation of alternative policies and solutions than to organisational issues. While in 1991 the Greens adopted a voluntary affiliation policy towards new related parties of Central and Eastern Europe, they also could not help but notice their evanescence. Progressively, following the increased demands of member parties, the co-operation frame offered by the EGC was no longer an adequate one.

The transformation process ended in June 1993 with the adoption of the statutes of the European Federation of Green Parties (EFGP). While these documents represented more of an evolution than a fully-fledged reform, they set up a politically mandated organ, a majoritarian decision-making process and a means for parties to be represented based on their respective relevance. Delegates met in a Council, and mandated a restricted committee to execute decisions and politically represent the Federation. However, the EFGP did not function on the basis of elite meetings, but applied principles valid in bottom-up democracies, dear to environmentalists.

Differently from other partisan federations, these reforms do not reinforce the need for greater interaction with actors affiliated with European institutions. Rather, they lead to the intensification of relations and dialogue amongst Greens. Moreover, the absence of a common vision towards the EU and the weakness of the Green parties at this level, keep the EFGP in a role essentially oriented towards the ecologist family. Such co-operation has strengthened the power of European Green parties. Through its politics of affiliation, the EFGP granted 'Green' label to formations that needed help. In 2004, it counted 32 member parties and five observers covering the essentials of existing Green parties.

In addition, numerous initiatives led to the formulation of joint political proposals on European as well as international policies. Despite diverging orientations towards the European Union, all agreed to work within the EU's institutional framework. Joint and principally statutory activities (on average two annual meetings of delegates and four of the executive, but also regional ones through informal networks) intensified relations and developed a sense of solidarity. The involvement of certain governmental actors (Greens) has had little effect on the work of the EFGP, while also allowing for a 60 per cent increase in its budget.

European electoral campaigns were at the very heart of such partisan co-operation. Large congresses led to the increased visibility of the weakest Green lists. Whereas in 1984, the Greens had failed to adopt a common manifesto, they succeeded in this task in 1999 thanks to the substantial preparatory work allowing for the development of a unified position. Its relations with Green groups at the European Parliament remained dominated both by antagonism and co-operation. The situation is likely to remain such until the EU fills the gap created by juridical uncertainty relating to the statute and financing of European political parties, and relations between the two are clarified. In order to lead a real transnational campaign, meet the conditions of this new statute and rely on the financing of the parliamentary group, Federation members slightly modified the statute and created, in February 2004, the European Green Party. The latter enables individual affiliation while making meetings among partisan leaders official. Will this suffice for the Greens to preserve their position at the European level? From 1989 to 2004, they represented the fourth strongest power in the European Parliament with about 30 elected members, but their relative weight is constantly decreasing. If they wish to retain their relevance at the European level, it is crucial that they intensify their partisan co-operation to mobilise the necessary resources, strengthen the weakest parties and enhance the visibility of the challenging project of the consolidation of the ecologist political family.

Cédric Van de Walle

→ Campaign (Sociology of); Cleavages; Communication; Election Programmes; Electoral Strategy; European Elections (1979–1999); European Elections (2004); European Political Parties; Europeanisation; Federation of Political Parties; Green Politics; Posters.

European Free Alliance

Pre-history and foundation

Though often autonomist parties are presented by their competitors as anachronistic, isolationist and hostile towards internationalism, European integration stimulated this party family to develop its own transnational federation, a proper group in the European Parliament and finally, a genuine Euro party in March 2004.

While by the 1970s, most of Europe's main political families had established their own transnational federations and political groups, autonomist parties conspicuously lagged behind for several reasons. They differed in the degree of radicalism of their core aim, self-government, ranging from regionalism and federalism to autonomy, separatism and irrendentism. Ideologically they ranged from conservative Christian-democracy to the extreme left, which made several autonomist parties adhere to the EPP or liberal group. Third, these parties often competed among themselves within their own region as well as at the state level. Hence, unlike the other European party families, the constitution of a 'party family' was not evident.

Following the Hague Congress of the European Movement in 1948, the International Congress of European Nations and Regions was formed in order to promote a deeper decentralist impulse to the European integration process (Lynch 1998). The first Congress meeting in Paris 1949 involved delegations from a dozen regions, together with SNP and PC party delegations. The Congress aimed at a united Europe based on regional communities structured along federal lines and at developing common policies, including the drafting of a charter of rights for the European communities and regions promoting autonomy, decentralisation and cultural rights. It institutionalised itself as the Congress of European Communities and Regions. Several congresses were held in the 1950s, continuing policy discussions but failing to develop as a political organisation given the intergovernmentalist turn European integration was taking, and its moderate course advocating regionalism instead of more radical options.

In 1973, new attempts were made at integration, when four autonomist parties combined to form the Bureau of Unrepresented European Nations. While this was a lobby to promote minority nationalist and regionalist parties within the EC (which hitherto had no MEPs) rather than a genuine political organisation, it still provided for the development of some common policy positions, such as the creation of a Europe of the Regions.

The first direct European elections triggered the development of a more explicit political alliance between parties, kicking off with a meeting of nine regionalist parties at Bastia in 1979 agreeing to examine prospects for political co-operation. They formed a loose alliance for the European elections in 1979 through the adoption of a common statement for their election campaign. However, a deeper level of political co-operation only came about in 1981 when the Flemish-nationalist Volksunie (VU, with one MEP) hosted a conference of regionalist parties in Brussels, establishing the European Free Alliance (EFA).

The EFA founders aimed at increasing the number of regionalist parties within the EP, and to include more regionalist parties (especially those that already had MEPs) in order to facilitate the establishment of a genuine regionalist parliamentary group; developing common policy positions for a manifesto for European elections; and developing a wider common programme that would express best the federation's political identity.

Electoral and organisational development

Hence, the direct elections to the European Parliament have been vital in establishing the co-operation between ethno-regionalist parties. Together with fluctuating electoral performances at the European elections, their international co-operation underwent different phases that illustrate well their problems with founding and maintaining a genuine trans-European party (Lynch 1998).

After the 1979 elections, the members of the EFA formed a technical group with some extreme-left parties. In the following term, this group was enlarged with the Greens into the 'Rainbow' group. In the 1989–4 term, the Greens went their own way, but the remains of the 'Rainbow' group now contained a majority (9 out of 15) of ethno-regionalist MEPs. The 1994 elections were a disaster and the three surviving EFA MEPs joined the French and Italian radicals, forming the European Radical Alliance group.[1] In the next term, the EFA counted 10 MEPs who joined the Green group (counting together 47 MEPs on the eve of the 2004 elections). After the 2004 elections they stayed with the Greens, but their number of MEPs dropped to only five, out of a group of 42!

Apart from defection to other groups, the reduction of regionalist MEPs is due to the overall reduction of the number of MEPs per member state, following the enlargement of the EU in 2004. As small parties, the regionalist MEPs often held marginal seats. Hence, they were the first to suffer from the small decrease of seats per member state decided at the Nice Summit.

Thus, the EFA has never been sufficiently strong to constitute a genuine ethno-regionalist parliamentary group. In addition, in most phases, EFA MEPs constituted a small minority within the group they joined. As most member parties of the EFA have not managed to capture regularly a seat in the European Parliament, these parties have therefore been excluded from the party integration opportunities that the European parliamentary arena offers (Hix and Lord 1997). As a European parliamentary formation, the EFA is neither as inclusive as a transnational party, nor predominant in the definition of the political outlook of the parliamentary group to which it belongs. This constitutes a second handicap in comparison with other European party families that are clearly more inclusive and homogeneous, and thus more representative of the ideological tendency they articulate. Third, the striking ups and downs in parliamentary representation jeopardises the consolidation of this group.

Also, while the four other party families have privileged extra-parliamentary access to the EU decision-making bodies (i.e. the European Council and Commission), due to their participation in national executives and their nomination influence on the Commission, such channels of influence and co-ordination are not open at all to ethno-regionalist parties, as currently (apart from the Lega and the SFP) no ethno-regionalist party participates in national government, and very few have done so in the past. Consequently, the EFA does not hold informal Euro party summits on the eve of European Council meetings, and therefore lacks a forum of informal integration of party leaders and of their strategies, as well as an opportunity for gaining visibility as a party family, for voicing its vision on European Union, and for credit claiming.

In addition, before the introduction of the Euro party statute, all parliamentary assistants allotted to EFA MEPs were overloaded with parliamentary assistance work for the handful of EFA MEPs who had to scrutinise an awesome variety of matters, while in the larger Euro parties often one or two dozen parliamentary assistants worked exclusively for the development of their Euro party. The coincidence of the introduction of the Euro party statute with the EFA's setback at the 2004 elections further weakened the organisational competitiveness of the EFA. The new public financing rules allow the EFA to recruit only two full-time collaborators for the EFA party secretariat (which is now situated in the building of the Flemish party SPIRIT). Fortunately, the agreement with the Greens on sharing parliamentary resources by the Green and EFA MEPs allowed the EFA to keep about as many parliamentary collaborators as in the previous legislative term. Still, the novel physical separation of the group from the party secretariat excludes the latter from fully using the informal networking opportunities that abound with EP-building, and thus further weakens the Euro party vis-à-vis its MEPs.

Still, the presence of the EFA in the EP and the Committee of the Regions offers an arena for organising meetings,

Table 1   The European Free Alliance as a representative of a European political family (July 2004) (in brackets the number of MEPs who won at the 2004 elections, and the parliamentary group to which they belong)

EFA

Bloque Nacionalista Galego
Eusko Alkartasuna
Fryske Nasjonale Partij
Mouvement Région Savoie
Esquerra Republicana de Catalunya (1)
Partei Deutchsprachigen Belgier
Partido Sardo d'Azione
Partido Andalucista
Partitu di a Nazione Corsa
Partit Occitan
Plaid Cymru-the Party of Wales (1)
Scottish National Party (2)
Slovenska Skupnost
Spirit
Union Démocratique Bretonne
Union für Südtirol
Union du Peuple Alsacien
Union Valdôtaine
Unione di u Populu Corsu/Scelta Nova
Unitat Catalana
Partido Andalucista
Ligue Savoisienne
Libertà Emiliana-Nazione Emilia

Rainbow – Vinhozito
Chunta Aragonesista
Liga Fronte Veneto
Lithuanian Polish People's Party
Mebbyon Kernow
Silesian Autonomy Movement
Party For Human Rights in a Unified
 Latvia (1)**
Observer parties
Hungarian Federalist Party
Moravian Democratic Party
Partido Nacianalista Vasco
Partit Socialista de Mallorca I
 MenorcEntesa Nacionalista
Transilvanian Party

Non-EFA

Convergencia Democratica di Catalunya
 (1, PLDR)
Partido Nacionalista Vasco (1, PLDR)*
Lega Nord (4, non-attached)
Svenska Folkpartiet (1, PLDR)
Vlaams Blok (3, non-attached)
Magyar Koalíció Pártja (2, EPP)

---

* The PNV abandoned the European People's Party in 1999 and obtained observer status in the EFA. After the 2004 elections it joined the PLDR group while in December 2004 it decided to join the new centre party of former EC President Prodi
** The ethnic Russian FHRUL has one MEP, who has joined the EFA solely as an individual member

co-operation and the elaboration and articulation of a common programme. These cross-national networks provide weaker movements with logistics, programmatic support, political status and prestige, and, last but not least, boost their morale. The EFA also used the EP as an opportunity to build bridges between EFA and other regionalist parties within the framework of the parliamentary intergroup 'Nations Without State'.

Electoral performance in time and space

Over the last 25 years, the electoral performance of autonomist parties, and of EFA parties in particular, has fluctuated widely. The SNP and the VU nearly always managed to capture two seats, some held on to a single 'safe' seat, while many others only occasionally managed to capture a seat.

While the overall results of the autonomist family fluctuated over time (peaking in 1999), they fared particularly badly at the 2004 elections, at a critical moment for European party integration. In most relevant regions, the overall autonomist vote declined dramatically (in Scotland and Wales and in all Spanish autonomous regions). Only the extreme-right separatists (Lega Nord and Vlaams Blok) managed to improve their score.

In the 10 new member states, regionalist parties did not fare well, and often did not even compete (as a single party) in the European elections. In Slovakia the Hungarian Federalist Party ran as a part of the Party of Hungarian Coalition (Magyar Koalíció Pártja) that is basically a Christian conservative party focusing on the Hungarians. The MKP obtained two MEPs who joined the EPP. In Latvia, the ethnic Russian party, For Human Rights in a Unified Latvia (FHRUL), obtained one MEP, and is associated to the EFA by individual membership of its MEP. Hence the new member states do not fit well the Rokkanite centre–periphery cleavage (Rokkan and Urwin 1982). Apart from some problems of protection of cross-border minorities (Hungarians in former territories of the Austro-Hungarian Empire, the Russian minorities in the Baltic States, and the territorially dispersed Roma), all current East and Central European countries are 'Nations With a State'. Hence, of the 112 EP seats allotted to enlargement countries, only three can be considered as having been won by an autonomist party, and of these, only one joined the EFA. Thus enlargement also seriously weakens the relative strength of the EFA vis-à-vis the other Euro parties.

Finally, before 2004, most autonomist parties obtained generally better results at the European elections than at the preceding parliamentary elections, for a variety of reasons: a more proportional electoral system, more opportunities to form electoral coalitions, lower turnout, anti-incumbent governing party vote, and lower campaign costs (De Winter 1998). However, in 2004 this pattern was confirmed for only half of the autonomist parties. Hence, the trend by which European elections tended to systematically advantage regionalist parties may have come to an end.

Europe as a tool of ideological modernisation

The development of a coherent ideology has always been problematic, as EFA member parties have been ideologically disparate and most of their individual platforms have been domestic in focus and unsuitable for transnational politics. Gradually, the EFA managed to adopt a common policy statement at each European election, which initially were brief statements of principles often based on the lowest common denominator between the parties. However, the ongoing European integration process provided an opportunity to overcome large ideological differences, by defining 'traditional' centre–periphery grievances as modern European grievances, by exploiting the good governance principle of 'subsidiarity'.

In fact, viewed from the perspective of a process of transfers of competencies from a lower to a higher level, European integration undoubtedly constitutes an amplification of the 'democratic deficit' defined in terms of widening the distance between decision-makers and the beneficiaries of public policies. Thus, more than for other party families, European integration strikes at the heart of the cleavage on which this party family is built, i.e. the empowerment of a lower level decision-making periphery by devolving powers from the central state/capital. However, for a variety of reasons, as integration progressed, autonomist parties did not turn into Eurosceptics, rather the contrary.

The debates generated by the different IGCs, the Constitutional Convention and the European Constitution have allowed the EFA to develop and fine-tune its ideological corpus. Its electoral manifesto that was published when the EFA transformed itself into a genuine Euro party (Barcelona, 26 March 2004) reflects well these current multilevel federalist stands, pleading for a second chamber composed of representatives of self-governing territorial entities that (with the directly elected European Parliament) would legislate by co-decision. In the meantime EFA advocates full participation for devolved governments in the Council of Ministers and for the regions' direct access to the Court of Justice. It calls for multilevel governance based on constitutional pluralism in which the different levels of government (EU, states, self-governing countries, regions, cities) have different fields of competence and co-operate on an equal basis; and that all languages that have been officially acknowledged by the member states and their internal nations are treated as the current EU languages.

In terms of EU policies, the manifesto combines 'social-democratic' and 'post-materialist' objectives, like a European Social Stability Pact for full employment, social welfare and social equity; sustainability – cultural and linguistic as well as environmental (GM-free regions and zones, fighting climate change, phasing out of nuclear energy etc.); empowering citizens and organised civil society, guaranteeing pluralism in the media, respect for human rights (including self-determination), etc. Finally, it pleads for a common foreign policy that unites security, defence and diplomacy with an emphasis on peacekeeping, on improving the conditions of Third World populations and curtailing the arms trade. Hence, although lip service is paid to the principle of subsidiarity (for instance concerning cohesion policy management), the EFA pleads for the Europeanisation of many policy areas, especially those that belong to the traditional core functions of the state, thus weakening the central obstacle to their own emancipation.

The manifesto's broad policy concerns permit the cohabitation of autonomist parties with a clear socialist or social-democratic profile working side by side with traditional Christian democrats, as well as a close co-operation with the Greens in the European Parliament.

However, even if nearly all ethno-regionalist parties are promoting further integration, large divergences between these parties continue to exist concerning the model of further integration the EU should pursue. Hence, in political practice, the EFA manifesto has been referred to in the member parties' campaigns to very different degrees: for some it constituted the official manifesto for their European campaign, for others it was enlarged with more local concerns, while some hardly referred to it. These differences are due to the parties' size and thus capacity to invest in a genuine European manifesto, and on the other hand the European (pro- or anti-) feelings of their target electorates, which often are less Europhile, as survey analysis indicates (De Winter and Gomez 2002).

Lieven de Winter

Note

1. As a result of provisions in the Maastricht Treaty on political parties, the EFA chose to turn itself into a European political party, following Article 138 of the Treaty on European Union. This change involved the renaming of the EFA as the 'European Free Alliance – Democratic Party of the Peoples of Europe', with a set of statutes which emphasised the democratic nature of the EFA and its commitment to parliamentary democracy, civil and human rights and self-determination for all peoples. Member

parties felt that the EFA label did not express well the party family's specificity, the search for more (full) self-government of nations without a state. The new constitution and organisational set-up was almost entirely similar to the old EFA structure. The DPPE suffix was dropped again when the EFA established itself as a genuine Euro party in 2004, feeling that the double name created confusion.

Bibliography

De Winter, L., 'Conclusion: a Comparative Analysis of the Electoral Office and Policy Success of Ethnoregionalist Parties', in L. De Winter and H. Türsan (eds), *Regionalist Parties in Western Europe*, London, Routledge, 1998, pp. 204–47.

De Winter, L. and Gomez-Reino, M., 'European Integration and Ethnoregionalist Parties', *Party Politics*, 8, 4, 2002, pp. 483–503.

Hix, S. and Lord, C., *Political Parties in the European Union*, Basingstoke, Macmillan, 1997.

Lynch, P., 'Co-operation between Regionalist Parties at the Level of the European Union: the European Free Alliance', in L. De Winter and H. Türsan (eds), *Regionalist Parties in Western Europe*, London, Routledge, 1998, pp. 190–203.

Rokkan, S. and Urwin, D. (eds), *The Politics of Territorial Identity*, London, Sage, 1982.

➔ Mapping Europe: European Electoral Geography.

European Liberal Democrat and Reform Party (ELDR)

Following the example of other political families, the advances of European integration coupled with the prospect of possible direct elections to elect MEPs, European liberal parties decided to develop an organisation for political co-operation amongst them. An initiative was thus launched during the Liberal International Congress in 1972, aimed at establishing an organisational structure to support liberal formations in advance of possible European elections. Partly as an outcome of a debate between Anglo-Saxon and continental conceptions of political liberalism, the term 'democrat' was introduced into the heading of the federation which emerged.

In fact, the organisation, which was established in March 1976, was originally entitled the Federation of Liberal and Democratic Parties in the European Community. The ambition was thus to open the Federation to the greatest number of parties. Paradoxically, however, from the outset, this decision alienated from the Federation a number of parties who were invited to adhere. Five parties refused to join because it was judged to be too right-wing. The accession of the French Republican party in particular stirred some unrest and culminated in the departure of the radical left members from the movement. Similarly, a further controversy emerged between the Dutch libertarian liberal group D66 and the People's Party for Freedom and Democracy (VVD), clearly of a more right-wing orientation, just as it had flared up between the Danish Radicale Venstre (liberal social) and the Venstre, who held very liberal views at the socio-economic level. It was only in 1994 that the former also joined the liberal European organisation.

During the founding electoral congress, a charter of liberal principles, the Stuttgart Declaration, was adopted. Its principal objective was to transform the European Community into a European Union equipped with a liberal and democratic Constitution. The imagined institutional scaffolding was daring indeed. The Federation pleaded 'that the European Parliament profit from increased capacities and legislative competences in all aspects which arise from the European Community, including political co-operation; that the European Parliament is elected according to principles of proportional voting; that the European Commission is held accountable before the European Parliament and the Council of Ministers; that the Council of Ministers endeavours to progressively pass its decisions by majority by voting; that the legitimate interests of the regions and the minorities in the member states are protected in order to preserve the diversity in Europe; that the fullest recourse is made to the activities of the Economic and Social Committee and the Standing Committee on Employment, in particular to carry out at Community level the participation of the workers in the management, control and benefits of companies'.

The enlargement to the south of Europe was not particularly meaningful for the liberals. In 1983, the Federation accommodated the Greek liberal party, although the latter was only a marginal actor in the Greek political system. In 1985, it was the turn of the Spanish democratic reform party to join the Federation but it was very small too. Only Portugal finally brought in a meaningful partner for the Federation: indeed, in April 1986, the social-democrat party, became the principal centre-right group in Portugal, and joined the Federation. At the same time, it imposed the addition of a new priority: reform. The Federation thus became the Federation of the Liberal, Democrat and Reform Parties in the EEC. Then, the size and political weight of the European People's Party (EPP) attracted the PSD early on and it left the FLDRP.

Following the Maastricht Treaty and the official recognition of European political parties in Article 138a, the Federation decided to transform into a 'party' and to rename itself the European Liberal Democrat and Reform Party (ELDR). Faced with the impending accession of Austria, Sweden and Finland, the ELDR initiated contact with the liberal groups within these countries and also with the centre parties, of the old agrarian tradition. Politically, the Swedish and above all Finnish centre parties emerged as being very strong within their respective national political systems but, taking into account their agrarian roots, took a step back to adopt a tentative position towards the EU. In order to numerically strengthen the ELDR, their entry was nonetheless ratified.

The most recent enlargement, to eight Central and Eastern Europe states, in addition to Cyprus and Malta, presented itself as something of a challenge for the liberal family. This was because despite the process of liberalisation in that particular part of Europe, 'liberalism' was clearly conceived differently. In certain cases, such as Slovenia with the liberal democrats and Estonia with the reform party and centre party, political liberalism became an important force and very similar to the Western tradition. However, Western-style liberal values were considered too minimal or even non-existent in Poland, Czech Republic and Hungary to lead to any expansion.

The ELDR and the liberal group in the European Parliament

Because of the relatively small electoral size of liberal parties in Europe, the ELDR group encountered a number of difficulties when compared with the Socialist and Conservative groups. One of the problems was the relative marginality of liberal parties in certain large countries (France, Italy before the Prodi camp joined them in 2004) and also the specific difficulties of the German FDP. Despite being a very important party in the German system, the FDP failed to secure the mandatory 5 per cent threshold in the 1984, 1994 and 1999 European elections, therefore significantly affecting the size and position of the group in the European Parliament, but also, consequently, the status of the party within the group.

Historically, the case was the same for the British Liberal-Democrats, who used to suffer as a result of the uninominal electoral system, until the system was changed in 1999. This system transition heavily changed the electoral picture and gave a new dynamism to the liberal group. However, it was in June 2004 that the most significant reconfiguration and strengthening occurred for the liberal group. The British Liberal-Democrats scored another success and the German FDP succeeded in reaching the 5 per cent threshold and secured seven seats. Beyond that, however, the whole essence of the group changed. The ELDR group was transformed into the Alliance of Liberals and Democrats for Europe group (ALDE), which enabled certain parties to leave their former group and join, notably the Union for French Democracy (UDF) from the EPP, and La Margherita (Italy) from the PES. The new group thus comprised 48 European MEPs (12.02 per cent), whose aspiration is to play a genuine pivotal role in the European Parliament.

Already, during the 1999–2004 legislature, the liberals had concluded an agreement with PPE-DE group regarding a sharing arrangement for the presidency of the European Parliament. Thus, Pat Cox assumed the presidency during the second half of the legislature, after Nicole Fontaine (PPE-DE) had completed the first half. However, the arrangement could not be renewed in July 2004 due to an agreement reached between the Socialist group and the PPE-DE group, which increased the need for a change of strategy.

Political positions and leaders

One of the major problems faced by the ELDR concerns its ideological heterogeneity. Trying to unite the Anglo-Saxon traditions of liberalism on the one hand with continental affiliations on the other has never been a simple undertaking and inevitably generated many internal debates, or even splits. The entry of the Scandinavian centre parties (ex-agrarian) added a further branch to the trunk of European liberalisms. For several years, the ELDR has partially succeeded in overcoming these difficulties by organising a progressively integrated work programme. Whereas for a long time the group appeared less homogeneous in comparison to the EPP, this is no longer true today (although, largely because of the increased heterogeneity of the EPP).

The ELDR has only had four presidents during the 30 years of its existence. From its foundation in 1981, it was led by Gaston Thorn, Luxembourg Prime Minister and leader of the Democratic Party between 1974 and 1979. It was then presided over by the leading Flemish liberal figure, Willy De Clercq, long-standing Belgian Prime Minister until 1985. Colette Flesch, President of the Democratic Party and Luxembourg Foreign Minister succeeded him, before yielding the torch again to him in 1990. Finally, since 1995 the liberal organisation has been chaired by Werner Hoyer, one of the leading characters in the German FDP.

The Benelux liberals have thus occupied the presidency during the bulk of ELDR's existence. Of course, this is not a unique case. In the history of transnational political organisations, the Belgians, who belong to a country crossed with different traditions, and the Luxembourguese, coming from a very small country, have often occupied leading positions, as they have been perceived to be relatively free from strong national duties, preferences and interests. Nevertheless, in the case of the ELDR, the future of leadership will largely depend on the forthcoming strongholds of the liberal family and the way its internal streams organise their power.

Pascal Delwit

Bibliography

Delwit, P., Külahci, E. and Van de Walle, C. (eds), *Les fédérations européennes de partis: Organisation et influence*, Bruxelles, Editions de l'Université de Bruxelles, 2001.

Johansson, K. M. and Zervakis, P. (eds), *European Political Parties between Cooperation and Integration*, Baden Baden, Nomos, 2002.

➔ European People's Party (EPP); European Political Parties; Federations of Political Parties; Parliamentary Groups.

European Parliament

Powers of the European Parliament

The European Parliament (EP) has undergone rapid institutional change over the course of the past five decades, changing from its original role as a mere consultative body to its current position as a fully legislative assembly. Despite the prevailing public perception that it is a weak, powerless and ineffective institution, the EP has in fact considerable authority to change the way the citizens of Europe live, work and travel. The Parliament is far more powerful than most people in the EU realise; Members of the European Parliament (MEPs) possess considerable influence over laws on everything from greenhouse gases to banking regulation. Its creation, endurance and success constitutes one of the major political achievements of modern Europe, with directly elected parliamentarians from 25 nations, working in 20 languages, legislating on behalf of 454 million inhabitants.

The roots of the modern European Parliament may be traced to the Common Assembly of the European Coal and Steel Community (ECSC). This embryonic legislature, by far the weakest of the ECSC's institutions, first met in late 1952 at Strasbourg University. Members of the various political traditions in Europe – liberals, Christian-democrats and socialists – began to collaborate with each other almost from the beginning in the formation of political groups. In June 1953, a new Article was introduced into the Rules of Procedure authorising the formal creation of supranational political groups. The initial alphabetical seating of members was replaced by seating by group affiliation thereafter. Early debates on the Rules of Procedure in the Common Assembly provide evidence of a very conscious effort to encourage the formation of these political groups, underscoring the importance of the institution as a supranational assembly rather than a forum for debating national interests. For instance, the Bureau of the Assembly was intentionally designed to consist of a number of members unequal to the number of member states to prevent it becoming a forum for airing national grievances. Within two years of the establishment of the Common Assembly the groups were not only recognised by the Rules of Procedure but they had gained financial support for administrative costs from the Assembly budget and the office of the President of the Assembly was subject to partisan, rather than national, competition. The Parliament had already begun to take on the appearance of a traditional legislature, though it had no actual legislative powers.

When the Treaty of Rome (ToR) established the European Economic Communities (EEC), the Assemblée Parlementaire Européene increased in size from 78 to 142 members (see Table 1 for further details). However, under the provisions of the ToR the new Assembly had even fewer powers than its ECSC predecessor. The Council's powers were enhanced in an intergovernmental coup; it was to be the final decision-making body in all policy areas. The Assembly (the term Parliament was officially adopted in all languages in 1962) was once more the weakest of the four institutions; it had a strictly advisory role. The European Parliament did not have any significant power until April 1970, when the budgetary procedure was introduced under the Treaty of Luxembourg which gave the EC its own financial resources. Under the budgetary procedure the Parliament has the right to reject the budget as a whole. However, the Parliament cannot vary the amount of compulsory expenditure. If no agreement can be reached between the Council and Parliament the default is the previous year's budget. As such, rejecting the budget is still a negative rather than a positive power for the EP. The directly elected Parliament remained a consultative institution in all other areas until the passage of the Single European Act in 1987. This Act introduced the co-operation procedure. The importance of the co-operation procedure for the Parliament's standing vis-à-vis the Council is a matter of considerable debate (Tsebelis 1994). The Parliament did not become a veto player; the Council can by unanimous vote overrule the Parliament's rejection of the Council's common position under the co-operation procedure. However, the necessity for unanimity to achieve this end undoubtedly constrains the Council's decision-making powers.

Perhaps the greatest increase in the powers of the European Parliament took place in 1992 when the Treaty on European Union (TEU) came into force. Under the terms of the TEU the European Parliament was given co-decision powers in a number of key policy areas, relating largely to the internal market. The co-decision procedure effectively makes the Parliament an equal partner with the Council in the legislative process. If the two institutions cannot agree on a proposed piece of legislation, it does not pass into law. The Amsterdam Treaty (1996) widened the range of activity of the Parliament even further; the co-decision procedure was simplified and applied to several new policy areas and to many policy areas that were previously covered by co-operation or consultation procedures. The EP's assent is now (2004) needed for 70 per cent of legislation that emanates from Brussels and this number will likely increase further in the years to come.

Internal organisation

The increase in formal powers granted to the European Parliament, while of major significance, forms only part of its history. To fully understand the institution one must also examine the evolution of its internal organisation. Under the Treaties of the European Union, the European Parliament is given full power to determine its own internal structure. In the period 1979–2002 there were considerably more than 1000 rule changes proposed by the Rules Committee to the Rules of Procedure (RoP). Some of these changes were inspired by significant revisions of the EU Treaties as discussed above; many more were outwardly technical and some were never adopted (Judge and

Table 1 Membership of the European Parliament

	1952	1957	1973	1979	1981	1986	1994	1995	2004
Belgium	10	14	14	24	24	24	25	25	24
France	18	36	36	81	81	81	87	87	78
Germany	18	36	36	81	81	81	99	99	99
Italy	18	36	36	81	81	81	87	87	78
Luxembourg	4	6	6	6	6	6	6	6	6
Netherlands	10	14	14	25	25	25	31	31	27
Denmark	–	–	10	16	16	16	16	16	14
Ireland	–	–	10	15	15	15	15	15	13
United Kingdom	–	–	36	81	81	81	87	87	78
Greece	–	–	–	–	24	24	25	25	24
Portugal	–	–	–	–	–	24	25	25	24
Spain	–	–	–	–	–	60	64	64	54
Austria	–	–	–	–	–	–	–	21	18
Finland	–	–	–	–	–	–	–	16	14
Sweden	–	–	–	–	–	–	–	22	19
Cyprus	–	–	–	–	–	–	–	–	6
Czech Republic	–	–	–	–	–	–	–	–	24
Estonia	–	–	–	–	–	–	–	–	6
Hungary	–	–	–	–	–	–	–	–	24
Latvia	–	–	–	–	–	–	–	–	9
Lithuania	–	–	–	–	–	–	–	–	13
Malta	–	–	–	–	–	–	–	–	5
Poland	–	–	–	–	–	–	–	–	54
Slovakia	–	–	–	–	–	–	–	–	14
Slovenia	–	–	–	–	–	–	–	–	7
Total	78	142	198	410	434	518	567	626	732

Earnshaw 2003: 197). But the sheer volume of procedural proposals is noteworthy; a great deal of parliamentary time has been dedicated to the structuring of the institution. Matters of procedural choice are 'intelligent means to preconceived ends . . . they are chosen by individuals to accomplish particular purposes' (Gamm and Shepsle 1989: 40). Procedural matters may not be very important in legislatures that possess a large and cohesive majority but where such conditions are absent, as in the EP, legislative rules become important tools for actors who wish to dominate the legislative agenda and build and sustain stable and cohesive parties.

The formal rules of the legislative game in the EP have been highly contested over the course of the past 25 years. The first direct elections to the Parliament took place in June 1979 and with them the membership of the Parliament doubled in size from 198 members to 410 (See Table 1 for full details of enlargement effects of the Parliament). The Rules of Procedure, which contained a mere 54 rules immediately prior to the elections, had more than doubled to 116 by May 1981. The Parliament did not gain any new powers at this time; the reorganisation at this stage was primarily an internally driven process. The debates of Parliament reveal that frequently the two largest parties – European People's Party (EPP) and the Party of the European Socialists (PES) – have acted in concert to shape the rules to their collective benefit. Given that the role of the largest party has alternated between the EPP and the PES, these two parties co-ordinate on rules that favour them but minimise the consequences of being second largest.

The transformation of the European Parliament has been driven by two distinct, but not unrelated, processes: external treaty revisions and internal partisan concerns. It is clear that macro shocks in the form of treaty revisions necessitated internal adjustments. But the evolution of rules and norms were not merely a reflection of this necessity but also reflected issues internal to the Parliament itself. And nowhere is this more notable than when one considers the committee system of the EP. Not only has the committee system expanded to provide 'jobs for the boys', but control over the committee assignment process and committee chairs has been strongly tightened over the years. The committee system provides the political groups with an important source of patronage in addition to acting as a source of policy expertise.

The committee system

As with all legislatures, much of the real deliberation in the EP takes place outside of plenary sessions. Parliaments are large and unwieldy bodies, and increasingly the only way such large chambers can function is to divide into specialised committees. Committees have played a central role in the European Parliament from the outset. The Common Assembly of the European Coal and Steel Community recognised that committees would help alleviate the problems inherent in co-ordinating work in an Assembly which was scheduled to meet in plenary only a handful of times a year. To this end, it created seven committees to conduct Assembly business in January 1953. The establishment of the European Parliament after the entry into force of the Treaty of Rome (1957) brought substantial change to the number, names and prestige of committees, in an effort to reflect the wider areas of responsibility of the European Economic Community. The system was further expanded in the immediate aftermath of the first direct elections in 1979. At this time, the number of standing committees was expanded from 12 to 15. In 1981 two further committees were added and one more was added in 1987, 1992 and 1994. By the end of the fourth parliamentary period (June 1999) there were a total of 20 standing committees in place. This number was briefly reduced in the fifth Parliament but with the expansion of the Parliament from 626 to 732 members in 2004 the number of committees increased to 20 once again (see Table 2 for full details). In addition there are a number of permanent sub-committees and temporary committees of inquiry.

Most of the activity of MEPs is concentrated in parliamentary committees, not in the debating chamber. As is the case with the United States Congress, the European Parliament in committee is the European Parliament at work. The assignment of MEPs to committees in the EP is constrained by the Rules of Procedure. After the number and size of committees is established (during the July session of a newly elected parliament) the appointment of full members is organised by the political groups in such a manner as to reflect the overall balance between the groups in the plenary. 'The composition of the committees shall as far as possible reflect the composition of Parliament' (Rule 154.1). Once the number of members per party on each committee is decided upon, it is the leadership of each political group who decides which actual MEPs should serve on which committees. While members get to rank preferences for particular committees, the party leaders have the final say. The norm is for an MEP to be a member of one committee and a substitute on another, though as is clear from Table 2 there is some flexibility in the application of this norm. Substitute positions are clearly less desirable than full memberships. As a substitute, an MEP can only participate in committee activities in the place of an absent colleague, that is, a member of his or her political group. Furthermore, substitutes are unlikely to receive the much-coveted *rapporteurships*. When a committee receives a piece of draft legislation, it first appoints a *rapporteur*. It is the job of the rapporteur to prepare initial discussion on the draft legislation within the committee, to present a draft text to the committee, and ultimately to present the final report to plenary. Committee prestige is largely dictated by the degree of legislative powers the EP has in the committee's policy jurisdiction and chairs of committees with these powers are highly sought after. Assignments and official positions on 'neutral' committees are far less desirable. This hierarchy of prestige grants the party leaders some power vis-à-vis their members as they lack many of the traditional incentives for fostering party discipline.

Political groups

The challenge of creating cohesive political parties is particularly onerous in the case of the European Parliament. The usual array of mechanisms at the disposal of national parties to punish defectors is absent. The literature on party discipline tends to focus on electoral incentives as a means of inducing party loyalty, but in the European Parliament these inducements are weak, if not missing altogether. The political groups in the EP currently have no control over the nomination process of candidates. National parties in each of the 25 member states control access to the ballot. In fact, elections are not even run on the basis of competition between the political groups within the Parliament. Rather, each election is run along national party lines, making these so-called 'second-order elections'. A second traditional means of imposing party discipline is through control over

Table 2 Committee size in the European Parliament 1979–1999[1]

Committee	Jan. 1979	Dec. 1979	1982	1984	1987	1989	1992	1994	1997	1999
Political/Foreign Affairs	35	41	44	45	50	55	55	53	66	64
Agriculture	35	41	45	44	51	47	45	46	45	38
Budgets	35	34	37	41	44	33	29	34	40	44
Economic and Monetary	35	37	39	42	43	51	48	52	59	44
Energy/Research/Tech	35	36	36	28	32	34	30	28	33	–
Ext. Economic Relations	35	34	34	25	25	28	23	25	23	–
Industry, External Trade, Research and Energy	–	–	–	–	–	–	–	–	–	61
Legal Affairs[2]	35	26	27	25	25	32	30	25	26	34
Employment and Social Affairs	35	27	30	30	30	41	38	43	47	56
Regional Policy & Planning[3]	35	29	30	28	35	38	35	37	44	59
Transport[4]	–	26	25	25	23	31	30	35	40	–
Environment and Public Health	35	27	27	30	36	52	49	45	51	59
Culture, Youth and Education	–	25	22	24	21	32	31	36	40	34
Development	35	26	34	42	51	42	39	36	39	35
Civil Liberties[5]	–	–	–	–	–	–	30	32	33	43
Budgetary Control	–	27	26	30	19	28	23	24	26	21
Institutional Affairs	–	–	37	31	26	37	36	40	37	–
Fisheries[6]	–	–	–	–	–	–	–	23	25	21
Women's Rights	–	–	–	24	31	34	28	35	39	38
Verif. of Credentials	–	–	8	9	–	–	–	–	–	–
Rules of Procedure and Petitions	18	24	27	26	–	–	–	–	–	–
Rules and Verification of Credentials[7]	–	–	–	–	28	27	24	23	25	–
Constitutional Affairs[8]	–	–	–	–	–	–	–	–	–	30
Petitions	–	–	–	–	27	25	23	27	30	30
Total Committee Places	403	460	528	549	597	667	646	699	768	690
# of committees	12	15	17	18	18	18	19	20	20	17
# of MEPs	198	410	434	434	518	518	518	518	626	626
Ave. Assignments	2.04	1.12	1.22	1.26	1.15	1.29	1.25	1.35	1.23	1.1

Notes:
[1] Data compiled by the author from the annual Listes Grises (Grey Lists) of the European Parliament.
[2] Becomes Legal Affairs and the Internal Market 1999 from Legal Affairs and Citizens' Rights.
[3] 1999 amalgamates Transport and Tourism to become Regional Policy, Transport and Tourism.
[4] Transport was part of Regional Planning and Regional Policy until 1979. Becomes Transport and Tourism in 1999.
[5] Becomes Citizens' Freedoms and Rights, Justice and Home Affairs in 1999.
[6] Fisheries was a part of Agriculture from 1982 until 1994.
[7] Verification of Credentials is amalgamated with the Rules Committee in 1986, while Rules and Petitions splits into two.
[8] Amalgamates former Rules and Institutional Affairs committees.

the supply of political goods. If political groups have access to such resources they may sanction rebels by withholding financial support, for instance in election campaigns. However, in the case of the EP these selective incentives are highly constrained. The political groups do not have funds at their disposal to finance members' election campaigns. Election campaigns are funded according to national election laws, though under the Nice Treaty (Article 191) there is the possibility that such funding will be introduced at some stage in the future. More generally, the monetary and administrative resources which the political groups control are quite minimal compared with those of their national counterparts. Finally, while the need to keep a governing party in power normally acts as a powerful incentive for maintaining a majority-voting bloc (Bowler and Farrell 1995), this incentive is absent in the EP. In parliamentary democracies, majority party backbenchers are reluctant to force early elections through voting against the government. The price of ending governments can be high and party typically prevails over principle. However, the institutional imperatives that typically operate in parliamentary democracies are lacking in the political system of the European Union. Within the EP there is no executive resting on the support of a majority party or coalition. The EU Parliament elections are marked by temporal rigidity, held at five-year intervals. There is thus no fear on the part of rebel backbenchers of forcing early elections. The institutional complexity of the EU is such that the executive bodies are largely independent of the Parliament and there is no internal majority resting on a traditional vote of no confidence.

To the extent that electoral incentives shape much of the behaviour of political actors (Mayhew 1974) the political groups in the European Parliament are clearly greatly disadvantaged vis-à-vis their national counterparts in the mechanisms they have at their disposal to enforce unity. They do not control access to the electoral ballot, they do not have valuable resources to finance election campaigns, and MEPs need not fear that their rebellious behaviour will force early elections. The prospects for cohesion appear quite bleak. Scholars of comparative political parties invariably conclude that the political groups in the European Parliament are weak and ineffectual when compared with their national counterparts in the parliaments of Western Europe. However, recent research on voting behaviour in the EP is more optimistic. Levels of voting cohesion have been rising across parliaments, especially for the three largest political groups (Hix and Lord 1997; Hix 2001). The popular perception that they are without any coherence is inaccurate. In fact, cohesion has increased despite increases in parliamentary size and national membership. These rising levels of cohesion are in significant part due to the creation of internal sources of patronage, in the form of committee, parliamentary and party posts, by party leaders. Political groups in the European Parliament may face particularly daunting odds in their bid to build cohesive parties but they are not fundamentally different animals from their national counterparts.

A unique institution?

There is a tendency among scholars to treat the European Parliament as *sui generis*. And while it is undeniably the only directly elected multinational parliament in the world, it is ultimately populated by rational actors who are not motivated uniquely or even primarily by idealism, but like their counterparts the world over are first and foremost ambitious politicians. Treating them as idealistic legislators pursuing some idyllic

European vision is both unhelpful and disingenuous. The European Parliament can be studied in a comparative context, and as its powers continue to grow it will increasingly resemble traditional legislatures in the industrialised democracies of the world. The EP is still in the process of defining itself and unfortunately it suffers from very poor visibility and continues to be widely ignored by the European media. But despite the popular wisdom, it is far from an irrelevancy in Europe, as evidenced by the power the Parliament brought to bear on the Commission hearings in October 2004. In particular, the two largest political groups in the EP are increasingly powerful and cohesive and far from ineffectual. In European countries it is the political party which provides the principal link between citizens and the government. Political parties help to legitimise the state through free elections. It is unlikely that a radically different means of representing citizens will emerge out of the EU system. The political party is integral to European representative democracy and as such it will play a large part in the amelioration of the democratic deficit within the EU.

Gail McElroy

Bibliography

Bowler, S. and Farrell, D., 'The Organizing of the European Parliament: Committees, Specialization and Co-ordination', *British Journal of Political Science*, 25, 2, 1995, pp. 219–43.

Gamm, G. and Shepsle, K., 'Emergence of Legislative Institutions: Standing Committees in the House and Senate 1810–1825', *Legislative Studies Quarterly*, 14, 1, 1989, pp. 39–66.

Hix, S., 'Legislative Behaviour and Party Competition in the European Parliament: An Application of Nominateto the EU', *Journal of Common Market Studies*, 39, 4, 2001, pp. 663–88.

Hix, S. and Lord, C., *Political Parties in the European Union*, Basingstoke, Macmillan, 1997.

Judge, D. and Earnshaw, D., *The European Parliament*, Basingstoke, Palgrave Macmillan, 2003.

Mayhew, D., *Congress: the Electoral Connection*, New Haven, Yale University Press, 1974.

Tsebelis, G., 'The Power of the European Parliament as a Conditional Agenda Setter', *American Political Science Review*, 88, 1, 1994, pp. 128–42.

→ Brussels; Composition of the European Parliament; European Constitution; European Convention; European Parliamentary Assembly; European Political Parties; Internal Elections at the European Parliament; Investiture of the Commission; Members of the European Parliament (Legal and Political Status); Members of the European Parliament (Sociology of Political Office); Parliamentary Groups; Parliamentary Mandate; Political Affiliation; Remuneration; Representation; Strasbourg; Voting Within the European Parliament.

European Parliamentary Assembly (1958–1962)

The European Parliamentary Assembly met for the first time in Strasbourg on 19 March 1958. Strasbourg was originally selected as the Assembly's temporary headquarters, and Robert Schuman, one of Europe's founding fathers, was chosen to be its first president. A former French foreign minister and conceiver – along with Jean Monnet – of the first European Coal and Steel Community (ECSC) Schuman was unanimously appointed to this prestigious position. Robert Schuman was succeeded in March 1960 by Hans Fürler, another Christian-democrat who had presided over the ECSC's Common Assembly from 1956 to 1958. Fürler's presidency lasted until 1962.

The competencies of this unique

assembly extended to all three European Communities: the ECSC, the European Economic Community (EEC) and the European Atomic Energy Community (Euratom). The Assembly comprised 141 members elected via indirect elections in accordance with the provisions of the Treaty of Rome. Fifty of its members had previously belonged to the ECSC's Common Assembly, originally made up of a total of 78 members. A larger Parliamentary Assembly allowed Germany, France and Italy, the EU's three largest member states, to increase their representation from 18 to 36 seats, while allowing Belgium's and the Netherlands' representation to expand from 10 to 14 seats. Slightly less favourable to the Benelux countries, this new set-up was closer to the distribution of seats in the Council (4, 4, 4, 2, 2, 1). The functioning of the new Parliamentary Assembly reflected that of the ECSC Common Assembly. Since 1953, parliamentarians worked in three major transnational groups, rather than sitting in alphabetical order as in the European Council's Consultative Assembly. According to the internal regulations adopted on 23 June 1958, a group had to be constituted by a minimum of 17 members. Therefore, groups were formed with some 60 Christian-democrats, 40 liberals, and a little more than 30 socialists. Moreover, the Parliamentary Assembly had 10 permanent commissions, three of which had been in existence since 1953, and the others were created in 1958 and 1961.

In spite of the modest role conferred on it by the Treaties, the Assembly actively tried to influence the evolution of the European Communities. It deliberated on all sorts of economic and political matters. For instance, it repeatedly but hopelessly called for the transfer of all European institutions to a single headquarters forming a sort of 'European district'. Also, it continuously fought for its place within the EU's decisional 'triangle', strengthening relationships with its counterparts. The representatives of the three executive bodies (the ECSC High Authority, the EEC and Euratom Commissions) on which it exercised some degree of control mainly through censorship, regularly participated in its plenary session as well as in the meetings of the parliamentary commissions. While not obliged to do so by the Treaties, Council representatives submitted their workings and the general budget to its scrutiny. The Assembly also used its agenda-setting freedom to raise the issues it perceived as most important. Among these were the expansion of its powers and competencies, the possibility of its election by direct vote, the fusion of executive bodies, as well as the overall progress of European integration.

Under the influence of the prominent federalist party, the European Parliamentary Assembly set out to execute the task originally assigned to it by the Treaty of Rome: ensuring its election via direct universal suffrage. In October 1958, the Commission for Political Affairs established a working group chaired by Belgian socialist Fernand Dehousse, an expert in constitutional matters, who had been involved in the working group to establish a European political community in 1953. After lengthy political consultations, Dehousse succeeded in launching a convention project accompanied by several explanatory reports. Amongst these were an important general report known as the 'Dehousse Project', as well as an account on the composition of the Assembly by Maurice Faure, the French negotiator of the Treaty of Rome. Their work resulted in the adoption, during the plenary session of 17 May 1960, of a resolution favouring the appointment of Assembly representatives through direct election. The new resolution was not to come into force until after a transitional phase during which one-third of its representatives continued to be appointed by national parliaments. In spite of these significant advances, the Assembly kept pushing for the triplication of its number of seats, the extension of its mandate to a five-year period, as well as the authorisation of dual European and national mandates. The Assembly perceived its direct election and the expansion of its competencies as separate issues. In spite of their moderate nature, the Assembly's requests were supported exclusively by the Italian government, but were firmly opposed both by De Gaulle and by the Council. Nevertheless, the French presidency gave the Assembly the chance to persevere in its quest for reforms and even consulted it on its views on the European political project. The Assembly seized this opportunity and mobilised against the plan put forth by General de Gaulle at a press conference on 5 September 1960; this became known as the 'Fouchet Plan'. Along with Battista, President of the Political Affairs Commission, Fürler and Faure endorsed the vision for a political Europe. Along with Dehousse, they recognised the difficulty of going beyond intergovernmental co-operation, but they refused to let the Assembly be marginalised, and stood up in defence of the *système communautaire*. Only a few 'Gaullists', affiliated to the liberal group, supported the French project. This large body of consensus led to the drafting and adoption of a resolution in the plenary session of 29 June 1961, the day before the meeting of the six heads of states in Bonn. It was followed by a recommendation made on 21 December. The majority of Assembly members along with the Italian and German governments were in favour of endorsing the Fouchet Plan. The Assembly advocated the appointment of a Secretary General for political co-operation whose functions would include the abandonment of unanimous voting in the Council. Moreover, the president was to be appointed on a fixed-term basis by a representative of the people, overseeing the transition of the Assembly into a proper European Parliament selected through direct elections and enjoying both budgetary powers and the right to be consulted in accordance with the Treaties.

These projects, as well as the Fouchet Plan, were abandoned in 1962, but rediscussed a decade later. However, they represented a demonstration of the Assembly's ambition, which later resulted in its transformation into the European Parliament. While the Treaty of Rome originally set out provisions for the establishment of an 'Assembly', the de facto name of this institution varied between 1958 and 1962 based on different languages. French and Italian speakers referred to it as a 'European Parliamentary Assembly', while German and Dutch speakers spoke of a European Parliament. Such variations continued until 30 March 1962, when the Assembly took the matter into its own hands and proclaimed itself a 'European Parliament'. Nonetheless, its new name alone did not suffice to confer upon it a role comparable to that of national parliaments, and it had to wait until the 1980s and 1990s to obtain new competencies and increased political weight.

Marie-Thérèse Bitsch

Bibliography

Bitsch, M.-T., 'Les institutions communautaires face au projet d'union politique, 1960–1962', *Revue d'Allemagne*, 29, 2, 1997, pp. 273–88.

→ Act of 1976; Brussels; Dual Mandates; European Parliament; Incompatibility; Ineligibility; Members of the European Parliament (Legal and

Political Status); Members of the European Parliament (Sociology of Political Office); Parliamentary Mandate; Strasbourg; Treaty of Rome; Universal Suffrage

European People's Party

The European People's Party (EPP) is an amalgamation of the Christian-Democrat, People's and Conservative parties which recognise and have agreed to the articles of association of the EPP. Individual membership has been provided for since the founding statutes of 1976 (as the only European party to have made provisions from this date, being much earlier than the ELDR). Among the most distinguished member parties are the German Christian-Democrats (CDU/CSU), the Spanish People's Party, the British Conservatives, Forza Italia and the French UMP. The EPP-ED group is composed of MEPs elected on the national lists of the EPP part members and the associated MEPs, responsible for representing the EPP in the European Parliament.

On 29 April 1976, the Christian-Democrat group in the European Parliament along with its member parties decided to create the EPP, a federation which became necessary to the co-ordination of national electoral campaigns in view of the first European elections by direct universal suffrage in 1979. It is the first party (or federation of European parties) to have had federalist aspirations, in that it considers itself as a 'federal party' with its consistent support for a federal European political union. Moreover, the EPP acknowledges a series of pan-European political associations (Young EPP, European Democrat Students, EPP Women's Association, SME-Union) as being 'Recognised Associations'. These federal associations

are composed of national partisan associations of EPP member parties. The EPP (Christian-Democrats) and European Democrats (EPP-ED) group is the successor to the original Christian-Democrat group established on 23 June 1953, during the first parliamentary assembly of the ECSC, and was later named the EPP group. The addition of '-DE' included since the 1999 European elections, refers to the parties associated with the group (parties whose MEPs belong to the EPP-ED group but not the EPP party). Since the June 2004 elections, this includes not only the British Conservatives, but also the Czech Conservatives from the ODS, the Portuguese People's party CDS/PP representatives and the Italian Partito Pensionati. The Conservative parties which are members of both the group and party also consider themselves as part of the '-DE'. MEPs from the same national party member of the EPP (or associated to the group) form a national delegation, which is an important decision-making unit of the group (see Table 1).

For the EPP, the 2004 European elections represented a two-fold challenge. On the one hand, the EPP was intent on retaining its majority in the European Parliament, and possibly even increasing it. On the other hand, it needed to maintain its internal cohesion in spite of the problem generated by the Eurosceptic and anti-federalist inclinations of the British Conservatives. Furthermore, the party also had to deal with reinforced pressures in support of protecting the national sovereignty from the Conservatives of the new Central European member states. As such, socialisation within the group of new MEPs resulting from enlargement has sometimes appeared problematic, to such an extent that the founding Christian-Democrat parties of the EPP have feared a weakening of its original federalist identity. Although the EPP-ED accounted for

Table 1 National and partisan composition of the EPP/EPP-ED group between 1979 and 2004

Country	National party	1979–1984	1984–1989	1989–1994	1994–1999	1999–2004	2004–2009
Belgium		11	6	7	7	6/5	6
	CVP (CD&V since 2001)	7	4	5	4	3/2	4
	PSC (CDH since 2002)	3	2	2	2	1	1
	CSP				1	1	1
	MCC (MR)					1	
Germany		42	41	32	47	53	49
	CDU	34	34	25	39	43	40
	CSU	8	7	7	8	10	9
France		7/9	9/7	6/12	13/11	21/20	17
	UDF/La Nouvelle UDF	7/9	9/6	6/8	13/11	9	
	UDF (March 1986)		1				
	UDF (1991)			4			
	RPR-DL					12/11	
	UMP						17
Ireland		4	6	4	4	5	5
	FG	4	6	4	4	4	5
	Independent					1	
Italy		30	27	27	12	34/35	24
	DC	29	26	26			
	PPI				8	4	
	Patto Segni				3	0/1	
	SVP	1	1	1	1	1	1
	FI					22	16
	UDC&DC						5
	UD.EUR (2004: AP-UDEUR)					1	1
	CCD					2	
	CDU					2	
	RI-DINI					1	
	Partido Pensionati					1	1
Luxembourg		3	3	3	2	2	3
	PCS-CVS	3	3	3	2	2	3
Netherlands		10	8	10	10	9	7
	CDA	10	8	10	10	9	7

Table 1 *continued*

Country	National party	1979–1984	1984–1989	1989–1994	1994–1999	1999–2004	2004–2009
Denmark		–	1	2/4	3	1	1
	KD (since 1981)	1	1/2/1	2			
	KF (since 1992)			2*	3	1	1
Greece	1981	–	9/8	10	9	9	11
	ND (since 23.12.1981)	8	9/8	10	9	9	11
Portugal	19/07/86	–	–	3	1/10	9	9
	CDS/PP (before1993; since 2004)		4	3	(PSD)1		2
	PPD/PSD (since 1996)				9	9	7
	Força Portugal PPD/PSD.CDS/PP)						9
Spain	1986	–	–	16	30	28	24
	PP			15	27	26	23
	UPN/PP				1	1	1
	CN-PNV				1		
	CiU-UDC		1	1	1	1	
United Kingdom		–	–	1/33	19	37	28
	CONS (since 1992)			32*	18	34	27
	Scottish CONS&Unionist					2	2
	UUP			1	1	1	1
Sweden	17/09/95	–	–	–	–	7	5
	M				5	6	4
	KD					2	1
Austria	13/10/96	–	–	–	–	7	6
	ÖVP				7	7	6
Finland	20/10/96	–	–	–	–	5	4
	KOK				4	4	4
	Suomen Kristillinen Liitto					1	
Czech Republic		–	–	–	–	–	14
	ODS						9
	KDU-ČSL						2
	SNK						3
Estonia		–	–	–	–	–	1
	PPU						1

Cyprus		–	–	–	–	–	3
	DISY						2
	Gia tin Evropi						1
Latvia		–	–	–	–	–	3
	JL/NE						2
	TP						1
Lithuania		–	–	–	–	–	2
	TS						2
Hungary		–	–	–	–	–	13
	FIDESZ-MPS						12
	MDF						1
Malta		–	–	–	–	–	2
	PN						2
Poland		–	–	–	–	–	19
	PO						15
	PSL						4
Slovenia		–	–	–	–	–	4
	N.Si						2
	SDS						2
Slovakia		–	–	–	–	–	8
	KDH						3
	SKDU						3
	SMK-MKP						2
European Parliament	PPE (PPE-DE since 1999)	107/419	110/434	121/518	157/567	233,232/ 626	268/732
		June 1981: 109/434	109/434	1991: 125	20.09.95: 162		
		1982: 117/434	1986: 118/518 March 1986: 119/518	*1992: 162	13.10.96: 169 20.10.96: 173 11.11.96: 182/626 Oct. 1997: 180		

Sources: Manuel PPE-DE/1997, Brussels: PPE group, 1987; EPP-ED Handbook, 2001, Brussels: EPP-ED Group, 2001; 50 ans d'histoire du groupe du PPE-DE au service de l'Europe Unie, Bruxelles: PPE-DE group, 2003; www.epp-ed.org, www.eppe.org

278 MEPs out of the total 732 MEPs elected in 2004, following the rallying of several member parties to the recently transformed Liberal Party, the group currently only has 268 MEPs with its majority thus decreasing from 38 per cent of the seats to 36.61 per cent. However, the EPP is able to pride itself on having a European Commission which reflects the electoral outcomes and, with its domination in the EU Council, can simultaneously boast both a parliamentary and 'governmental' majority, albeit a relative one, within the European institutions. Thus, the EPP is able to assert its original desire to transform the EU into a federal parliamentary democracy.

In terms of organisation, the EPP has in place hierarchical decision-making structures similar to those of national parties (party congress, political committee, president), with an effective system of internal democracy. In both theory and practice, decisions are taken by the absolute majority of existing members. Votes are held extensively and the outcomes are reflected upon by the internal opposition. Compromise and negotiation are recognised and develop only informally. The latest council when a decision had been set in advance dates back to 1986, following which, discussion of last-minute amendments is now acceptable. Both the party and the group adopt disciplinary measures (such as the Portuguese CDS example in 1993; the use of the whip). For a long time, the inherently supranational organisation for the bodies of the EPP have retained their original features. In fact none of these bodies has ever pursued an intergovernmental form of organisation, excluding the summit, and reunion of heads of governments and parties. The summit co-ordinates the policies and electoral and legislative strategies across all the national parties and of the EPP-ED. Thus, the EPP tries to ensure control over the agenda of the European Council, and formulates

political orientations that conform with its ideology. One of its principal accomplishments has been its level of influence over the main institutional reforms of the Maastricht Treaty. These points include permanent establishment of a time-table for the achievement of monetary union, the co-decision procedure for the European Parliament, independence of the Central Bank, and the creation of the Committee of the Regions. Indeed the only proposal which failed to be adopted related to the compliance of opinion with the European Parliament concerning treaty revisions.

The EPP is the first Euro party to have explicitly called its federation a 'party' and to have institutionally detached it from the group. Although the group is represented within the body of the party, the two organisations are essentially independent. The party often provides political impetus to the group, following decisions formulated on the basis of the findings from the work within the permanent working group (for instance, two-thirds of the proposals behind the draft European constitution of the Convention were originally proposed by the EPP). Over the recent past, the EPP contributed to the recent EU enlargement process, by participating in the decision-making process of the associated parties originating from the candidate countries. However, the effective accession of the 10 new member states into the EU calls into question, albeit on a psychological level, the already difficult cohabitation amongst the Conservative members.

Tudor-Andrei Rautu

Bibliography

Jansen, T., *Die Entstehung einer Europäischen Partei: Vorgeschichte, Gründung und Entwicklung der EVP*, Bonn, Europa Union Verlag GmbH, 1996.

Johansson, K. M., *Transnational Party Alliances: Analysing the Hard-Won Alliance Between Conservatives and Christian Democrats in the European Parliament*, Lund, Lund University Press, 1997.

Rautu, T.-A., 'Organisational Structure and Decision-Making in the European People's Party – Party and Parliamentary Group in the European Parliament', *Studia Politica (Romanian Political Science Review)*, 4, 1, 2004, pp. 39–76.

→ Cleavages; European Democratic Union; European Parliament; European Parliamentary Assembly; European Political Parties; European Public Sphere; Europeanisation; Federations of Political Parties; Members of the European Parliament (Sociology of Political Office); Parliamentary Groups; Partisan Identification; Representation; Right.

European Political Parties

European political parties remain, in many ways, a very complex object of social science study. On the one hand, they are explicitly acknowledged by EU legislation, and are openly mentioned in the Treaties, which even outline their financial status. The Maastricht Treaty in particular stipulates that: 'European political parties are important as a factor of integration within the Union. They contribute to the formation of a European consciousness and to the expression of the political will of Union citizens' (Article 191 TEU). A further Article in the Treaty of Nice additionally specifies that in accordance with the procedure affected by Article 251, the Council establishes the status of political parties at the European level and notably the rules relative to their financing (Article 191 TEU, sub-paragraph 2). The draft EU Constitution Treaty also picks up the momentum by stipulating and providing that, subject to ratification of the Treaty, the President of the European Commission will be selected from the party which will have been successful in European elections. The existence of 'European parties' is thus no longer a wishful or ornamental question tied to a federalist rhetoric, but, instead, reveals two practical issues: one is financial, the other has to do with power. At the same time, beyond this legal situation, it should be noted that the entities referred to as 'European political parties' contribute little 'to the political expression of Union citizens'. Indeed, three tendencies emerge from European elections. Firstly, their tendency to serve as *in vivo* surveys, popularity tests for national parties and, in France, potential presidential candidates, is only matched by their character of systematic exercise of protest voting. Secondly, abstention remains high. Finally, when abstention decreases and a genuine European debate emerges, it is often to the advantage of Eurosceptic candidates who sometimes come across as the only truly 'European' ones. This can be observed in Denmark since the country joined in 1973, and also in Sweden, France and particularly in Great Britain in 1999 and 2004 with the lists of Villiers and UKIP gaining ground in the last two countries respectively.

Thus, after the 2004 European elections, the EPP claimed to have secured electoral victory despite being unable to save the Italian commissioner candidate, accepted by the Council, but challenged de facto by the European Parliament. The Parliament, which does not function according to a Westminster type government/opposition logic, prefers to slowly build large ad hoc majorities. Characterised by protest voting exerted against national governments, European elections do not enable specific European tendencies nor, *a fortiori*, orientations to materialise with regards to the future of the EU or its public policy legibility. Hastings (2004) claimed that the 2004 election was not a European election due to the lack of parties contributing to 'the expression of the political will of Union citizens'; rather, the election is claimed to have meant the elections of 25 national delegations with their respective terms and according to national issues echoed by national parties. Few things have changed, from this point of view, since de la Serre claimed that the first EP election was 'an election with a European pretext'. Thus, EU legislation and treaties refer to legal entities which remain, until this day, largely utopian.

Regarding political parties, while facts usually precede legislation, in the EU, legislation has preceded facts. European parties were indeed included in EU legislation before they existed in reality. Does the wishful thinking of the Council actually aim to respond to the recurring criticisms denouncing the 'democratic deficit' suffered by the EU? Are the manipulations induced by the Socialist and Conservative heads of states intended to siphon off a European financial windfall towards the friendly partisan EPP and PES and, beyond them, affiliated national parties? Perhaps, it is rather the clearly expressed desire to see the birth of European parties following incentives made in terms of power and money as suggested by Magnette (2000).

The principal European parliamentary groups followed the European Christian Democrats who, since 1978, have called themselves the European People's Party. In November 1992, in the aftermath of the ratification of the Maastricht Treaty, the Confederation of the Socialist parties of the European Community was transformed into the Party of European Socialists and, in 1993, the Federation of Liberal Democrat and Reform Parties changed its title and status to become the European Liberal Democrat and Reform Party (ELDR). That same year the European Federation of Green Parties (EFGP) was established. Despite its modest title, it conceals a more integrated organisation than its counterparts. In 1998, the European Free Alliance, bringing together peripheral nationalists, transformed itself into the Democratic Party of the Peoples of Europe. The final stage and impact of the Treaty of Nice resulted in the Communists and other leftist parties from the European United Left (excluding the LCR, Ligue Communiste Revolutionnaire, and the Lutte Ouvrière who were not invited) to create the Party of the European Left. Finally, the EFGP proceeded with the solemn foundation of the European Green Party.

Certainly legal hesitations on the definition of political parties is understandable. In national legislations, which deal with parties (when they do not completely ignore them), an enormous distance separates the German legislation from its French counterpart. This can be explained by the fact that certain legal systems officially regulate the existence of political parties supposed to fulfil a variable range of criteria, whereas others are satisfied with variable registration procedures. However, the situation is quite different for political science for which the focus on political parties constituted a historical moment of distantiation from law. This explains some of the differences between the two disciplines with regards to their analysis of European political parties. If in terms of law 'statements equate with action', the situation is quite different in political science. Therefore, from the point of view of political science, even though European political parties assert themselves as such, they do not 'look' like political parties in a traditional sense of the term. Only the European Green Party seems to match the definition. The other European parties, by contrast, seem to stretch the concept of party far too much. In a way, European political parties may almost come across as a mere convenience of language.

These formations may be said not to constitute parties because they fail to express any European cleavage, their organisations are not traditionally partisan, and they do not directly compete for elections. Since 1978, it has been possible to formulate a hypothesis around European cleavages (Seiler 1998) which have been empirically identified by Hix and Lord (1997) within the European Parliament. According to them, two cleavages cut across each other: a left/right cleavage between supporters of a liberal Europe and those of a social Europe, and a Eurosceptic/federalist cleavage. From the BSE crisis to questions of GM foods, it is also possible to include the possibility of a cleavage between producers and ecologists. However, except for the Greens, who constitute a recent arrival on the EU political scene, and whose ambitions are only achievable at the European level, the other Euro parties largely focus on national cleavages and issues.

Thus, the PES could be identified within the quadrant of social Europe supporters and federalists. However, since the emergence of New Labour, this social Europe connotation is far less clear. A major dividing cleavage in the European Social-Democrats seems to override other variations, separating the British Labour Party from the French Socialist Party on the left, with the SPD somewhere in the middle. The accession of Poland (where the socialist SLD benefits from the support of employers), Hungary and, to a lesser extent, the Czech Republic reinforces a very liberal pole within the PES.

The image of the EPP is still similarly blurred: created by Christian-Democrats, it remains a mainly Conservative pole which has now been abandoned by progressive Christian-democracy parties such as the French UDF and the Italian PPI. It has also been joined by many Eurosceptics (UK Conservatives, Czech ODS) despite its federal foundations. As for the ELDR, it moved from the right to the centre-left, with the support of reforming Christian-Democrats, before focusing on a predominantly European coherence criterion: federalist 'Euro enthusiasm'. This position brings them closer to the European Green Party, whose programme revolves around post-materialist values, corresponding to its recent status within the European political family. The ecological political stances which the Greens use to characterise themselves directly challenge the destruction of natural balances for market purposes and do not acknowledge territorial boundaries thus leading the Green group on to an early European path. As for the European Left Party which revolves around the Confederal Group of the European Left (GUE), its communist and post-communist members largely unite on a Eurosceptic stance.

Ultimately, if EU cleavages exist, the image projected by Euro parties remains resolutely blurred. Only the Greens and the liberals correspond to a true European cleavage, explicitly occupying one of two poles. Consequently, it is unsurprising to note that only the European Green Party corresponds to the 'political party' model, because it is equipped with a federal organisation where only the European level – committee and congress – is qualified to formulate policies with reference to the EU and the European Parliament. Even so, a minority part of the French Greens campaigned against the proposed EU Constitution in 2005.

As for the EPP, the PES, the ALDE, the PDPE and the PGE, they certainly do not look like political parties, focusing instead around a project more representative of an organisation aiming to secure political power through electoral mobilisation. Even the concept of stratarchic party as applied to American parties is not appropriate to understand them. As such, even Delwit et al.'s (2000) concept of 'federations of parties' is not fully convincing. Since the 1970s and the emergence of the first self-proclaimed 'European parties', Claeys and Loeb-Mayer (1979) considered these as confederations of parties, albeit particularly weak ones. Instead, I suggest the most appropriate comparison is that of the old 'Internationales', excluding the Komintern. In other words, European political parties act as quasi-clubs with a predominantly legitimising function, and have a 'travel agency' character.

On the eve of World War Two, in addition to the IC (which went slightly beyond the 'Internationale' model), a range of organisations existed which included: the Socialist Internationale (the model referred to by its competitors), the White Internationale, the liaison bureau of Christian-democrat parties, which later became the New Internationale, and then the UEDC which disappeared into the EPP. There was also the Green Internationale, which brought together agrarian parties, before disappearing in favour of the Liberal Internationale, established in 1947 by the British liberals and various French radical parties. It is thus within these three Internationales (socialist, Christian-democrat and liberal) that European parliamentary groups were born, and where the first three Euro parties emerged. Within the framework defined by the three Internationales, historical 'sister parties' failed to wield the same clout and as early as the time of the ECSC Assembly, the initiative for European inter-partisan co-operation fell to the German parties and radically to their powerful and rich political foundations: Friedrich Ebert Stiftung (Social-Democrat), Konrad Adenauer Stiftung (CDU), Friedrich Naumann Stiftung (Liberal) and Hans Seidel Stiftung (CSU). Their global action was decisive in the context of successive EU enlargements.

Therefore, well before the accession of different countries, the German foundations had been laid. For example, in Spain, the first two election campaigns of Felipe Gonzalez and the PSOE were delivered 'ready-made' by the Friedrich Ebert Stiftung, whilst, still in Spain, the rivalries opposing the Adenauer Foundation to its liberal counterpart contributed to the break-up of Adolfo Suarez's UCD. Ultimately, it benefited the Bavarian Hans Seidel Stiftung which, from the start, supported the extremely conservative Allianza Popular which later became the successful Partido Popular. The process reached its peak with the return of Central European countries to representative democracy. New parties, once created on the basis of specific national issues, proved particularly keen on obtaining the 'European' label conferred by the international level and the Euro parties which go with it. While in Spain, liberal attempts failed – except for Catalan autonomists who joined the Liberal Democrat group in the EP – and as just as the German Conservative foundations encountered some difficulties in imposing the PP on the European Christian-Democrats, the Eastern enlargement largely reinforced the German hegemony on the choice of new members of Euro parties.

Indeed, the Liberal Internationale, the weakest and most divided of the three large alliances, and the European liberals benefited from the support of the Friedrich Naumann Stiftung foundation which proved less hegemonic and demanding (albeit also poorer) than its rival. Since 1979, the liberals found themselves constrained to seek all centre allies (separatists, agrarian and others). They are still consolidating their new

Alliance of Liberals and Democrats, trying to put their weight in the constitutional reform of the EU, and to rally historical Christian-Democrats who feel alienated by the recent changes within the EPP, in order to create a true European centrist and federalist pole. As for the Socialist Internationale and the PES, the Friedrich Ebert Stiftung largely contributed to the victory of the Social-Democrat pole over the more leftist inclinations of the French PS in Southern Europe. The conversion of British socialism to the neo-liberal theses of New Labour as well as the accession of renovated former Communist parties from Central Europe, all reinforced the power of the new entrepreneurial elites. Newly converted former members of the *nomenklatura*, willing to prove their modernist credentials and enthusiastically supporting market economy, reinforced the axial position of the SPD within the PES, a leading position reinforced by the fact that it is the richest Social-Democratic party in Europe, and that it seems to serve as a moderate alternative between old-style French socialism, and quasi-liberal British Blairism. Finally, it is the EPP which has transformed most deeply in recent years. Centrist and federalist from the outset, the EPP and its allies progressively became the rallying point for the Euro right including some Eurosceptics. Conversely, some historical Christian-Democrats (French UDF, Italian Margherita) consequently decided to leave to join the European liberals instead. As, since the late 1950s, the German conservatives had established close contacts with the Anglo-Scandinavian conservatives, these changes may have reasonably suited them.

Ultimately, it is too early to determine what role the reinforcement of the European Parliament's powers will play in the emergence of a true European party system. The European Union is profoundly different from the sum of its member states, and the cumulation of national cleavages does not correspond to European cleavages. However, historically created on an international basis, the old Euro parties largely bring together groups which have diverged across time in occasionally significant ways. Redistributions are thus both needed and foreseeable and the process is already in hand with the establishment of the Alliance of Liberals and Democrats for Europe, which defines a truly European project, if not a fully integrated partisan organisation as the European Green Party is.

Daniel-Louis Seiler

Bibliography

Bardi, L., 'Transnational Party Federations in the European Community', in R. S. Katz and P. Mair (eds), *Party Organizations: a Data Handbook on Party Organizations in Western Democracies, 1960–90*, London, Sage, 1992.

Bardi, L., 'Transnational Trends in Europarties and the Evolutions of the Europarty System', in B. Steunenberg and J. Thomassen (eds), *The European Parliament: Moving Toward Democracy in the European Union*, London, Rowman & Littlefield, 2002.

Bell, D. S. and Lord, C. (eds), *Transnational Parties in the European Union*, Aldershot, Ashgate, 1998.

Claeys, P.-H. and Loeb-Mayer, N., 'Transeuropean Party Groupings: Emergence of New and Alignments of Old Parties in the Light of the Direct Elections to the European Parliament', *Government and Opposition*, 14, 4, 1979, pp. 479–507.

Delwit, P., De Waele, J.-M., Külahci, E. and Van de Walle, C., 'Les fédérations européennes de partis', in P. Magnette and E. Remacle (eds), *Le nouveau modèle européen*, Bruxelles, Editions de l'Université de Bruxelles, 2000, vol. I.

Hastings, M. (ed.), *Les élections européennes de juin 2004*, Lille, IEP-CEPEN, no. 3, October 2004.

Hix, S. and Lord, C., *Political Parties in the European Union*, Basingstoke, Macmillan, 1997.

Magnette, P., *L'Europe, l'Etat, la Démocratie*, Bruxelles, Complexe, 2000.

Seiler, D.-L., *La vie politique des Européens: Introduction aux pratiques démocratiques dans les pays de l'Union européenne*, Paris, Economica, 1998.

→ Cleavages; Composition of the European Parliament; Democratic Deficit; European Constitution; European Democratic Union; European Elections (1979–1999); European Electoral Sociology; European Federation of Green Parties; European Free Alliance (EFA); European Liberal Democrat and Reform Party (ELDR); European Parliament; European Parliamentary Assembly; European People's Party (EPP); European Political Parties; Europeanisation (of National Political Life); Green Politics; Left; Multi-Level Governance; Parliamentary Groups; Partisan Identification; Party of European Socialists (PES), Political Affiliation; Right.

European Public Opinion

Any institutional undertaking which attempts to measure 'opinion' can also be considered as a legitimisation device. In other words, 'European public opinion' is as much the product of a process of assessment as of acknowledgement. Unsurprisingly, it is thus a category of Europhile understanding. Many instruments exist to regularly measure the 'opinions' of Europeans, particularly Eurobarometer, which was created in 1973 by the European Commission. Many other tools exist, quantitative and qualitative, static and dynamic, which have led to a number of analyses of the way the European public relates to European policies, integration, institutions and citizenship (Bruter 2005; Hix 2006).

When discussing 'European public opinion', however, four 'critical' points can be identified. The first has to do with the way 'European public opinion' is often mixed with normative discourses surrounding the defence of or opposition to European integration. On the one hand, it was initially mobilised by integrationists, like the founders of Eurobarometer. From this perspective, its expression is indeed the product of a political setting created by the very European institutions. On the other hand, nobody now comments on 'public opinion' more than the most Eurosceptic parties and media, always keen on claiming that Europe goes against the will of the people(s). 'European public opinion' therefore often sits at the crossroads between strong normative positions and a scientific approach. Thus, like its national counterpart, the articulation of European 'public opinion' holds a certain element of fantasy – originating from a tendency to consider citizens as a single entity, and a principal instrument of measurement (Eurobarometer) which is largely criticised by academics.

The second doubt therefore concerns the mediatised and political abuse of public opinion to present citizens as a completely unified group. While this is a criticism that generally applies to the very concept of public opinion, several critics point out the weakness of a European public sphere, as an aggravating circumstance. Thus, Pierre Giacometti, director of the survey company Ipsos, claimed that 'European public opinion does not exist' (*Le Monde*, 7 March 1996). Similar debates exist between political scientists with some cautiously supportive of the notion (Bruter 2005; Hix 2006) and others altogether sceptical (Dargent 2000).

A third contention point has to do with tensions with regards to the substance and measurement of 'European public opinion'. Should 'European public opinion' be considered as an average of national public opinions within the EU? Should this average be 'simple' or 'weighted' according to the demographic weight of each nation, as recommended by Eurobarometer? Is 'European public opinion' best measured by surveys or by other methods? The origins of the data constitute a permanent source of tension, which relates both to the fact that Eurobarometer is an 'institutional' survey, and the fact that its questions are considered poor by a number of political scientists (Bruter 2005). Many political scientists also stress the (strong) scientific limitations of Eurobarometer and a number of other available surveys such as the European Value Survey, even if many still choose to use them.

The third form of tension concerns a series of conceptual distinctions, such as the suggested differentiation between 'European opinion' and 'European public opinion' (Reynié 2004). The former supposedly represents the 'common' or 'main' opinions of Europeans, in the form of a pre-existing public opinion which is difficult to identify due to the lack of sufficient political union. By contrast, the latter has supposedly grown as a 'spontaneous' European attitudinal specificity since the 2003 anti-Iraq War movements. However, Reynié himself concludes using both expressions as synonyms.

Finally, one could argue that the very concept of 'European public opinion' has failed to take root and flourish to the extent originally anticipated by its promoters. It coexists with other labels: 'European opinion', 'European opinions', 'Community opinion', 'European public opinions', 'European citizens' and above all, 'the Europeans'. These various labels express different types of messages. The plural terms – 'European public opinions' or even 'the Europeans' – indicate the supposed difficulty incurred in constructing

comparative equivalents. The authors who use them claim that one cannot consider a German as 'equal' to a Frenchman, or an Italian to a Swede, etc. Certainly, national social cleavages partly account for some variations in national levels of support for European integration. The authors using these terms claim that only fervent Europhiles firmly believe that European citizens are 'functional equivalents'. This is needed so that numbered units can become, within their models, realities that are sufficiently homogeneous in order to enable the statistics to convey a meaning.

In other words, at the risk of adopting an evolutionist vision of history, European public opinion will only have an opportunity to socially exist when, just like its national counterpart, actors assume an 'interest' in facilitating its existence in order to give it a voice that they could claim to represent. Numerous obstacles impede its widespread diffusion, notably the divide between media and politics, the absence of a unified European political market (in particular national electoral competitions coinciding with European elections, and the absence of a president directly elected by the ordinary social agents). The current enlargement of the EU could render its coherent emergence even more difficult, as the differences of perceptions, histories and experiences of, say, a Pole and a Dutchman, a Brit and a Slovak look extremely different *prima facie*. As a consequence, it is unclear whether one can consider them as various 'parts' constituting a 'whole' endowed with behaviour and will. The analysis of 'European public opinion' is thus pertinent in that it serves as a reminder that all forms of 'public opinion' are based on conceptualised beliefs.

Jean-Baptiste Legavre

Bibliography

Bruter, M., *Citizens of Europe? The Emergence of a Mass European Identity*. Basingstoke: Palgrave Macmillan, 2005.

Dargent, C., 'Citoyenneté européenne: la concurrence des identités territoriales et sociales' in B. Cautrès and D. Reynié (eds), *L'opinion européenne 2000*, Paris, Presses de Sciences Po, 2000, pp. 47–69.

Hix, S., *The Political System of the European Union*, Basingstoke, Palgrave Macmillan, 2006.

Reynié, D., *La fracture occidentale: Naissance d'une opinion européenne*, Paris, La Table-ronde, 2004.

→ Data Archives; Electoral Behaviour; Eurobarometer; European Electoral Sociology; European Public Sphere; Forecast; Identity; Journalists; Political Market.

European Public Sphere

Like European citizenship and European identity to which it is linked, the question of a European public sphere is one of the big question marks of European integration. From the vast literature on this subject, a general consensus seems to emerge on the weakness of this public sphere. As underlined by Quermonne and Smith (1996: 153), the question of the existence of a European public sphere is problematic if it is conceived as a space in which are upheld and practised the rights usually attached to citizenship, an arena in which beyond flows of communications, political deliberation ultimately takes place.

A number of studies point to the imbalance between the weakness of a 'European public sphere' on the one hand, and the rapid development of European public policy on the other hand. This paradox is reinforced by the effects of the lobbying of diverging interest groups operating at the European level. Some would argue that this institutionalised lobbying generates, in certain cases, forms of negotiations that can be seen as the necessary preliminary to a European public sphere. However, lobbying appears as a sector-based, non-democratic public space, as it is not subject to the democratic sanction of citizens. The growing proportion of public policy-making which is generated at the European level can be seen as a 'European referential frame' which imposes a social and political model on citizens, without any prior input on their part. The questioning of fundamental political concepts such as public interest and public services illustrates this lack of pre-emptive democratic decision. In short, the public policy space cannot necessarily be identified as a public sphere, as it does not offer citizens the opportunity to exercise their usual democratic rights and functions (Quermonne and Smith 1996: 154).

The emergence of a European public sphere (or a space for public democratic deliberation) appears to be the *sine qua non* pre-requisite for a true democratisation of 'Europe' as a political system, overriding treaties and other constitutional reforms and giving the notion of European citizenship and identity a new meaning. The emergence of a system of European media modelled on national media structures is frequently mentioned as a crucial factor in the development of such a public sphere. This generalised statement can nevertheless be examined from several viewpoints.

Firstly, apart from regretting the absence of such a European media space, it would probably be useful – and this is starting to be done – to consider the already existing fragmented and partial structures which could be ultimately transformed into the first heart of a European public sphere. A number of examples come to mind, including two

European social forums, held in Florence and Saint Denis, and the so-called 'Euro-demonstrations' (such as the one organised in Vilvorde in 1997). However, one may also think of the multitude of networks (unions, lobbies, civil society groups), which, although sometimes in a less publicised way, are already operating across Europe. The question of their relative influence within European institutions remains open, but the multiplication of such groups can be seen as a clear indicator of the gradual consolidation of European public spaces.

The difference between *a* public sphere and *several* public spaces is far from unimportant, both at the national and European levels. Arguably, it is now indispensable to go beyond the monopolist claim of the national level on such a space, to conceive a multiplication of diversified, 'mosaic' public spheres, which various segments of society might find it easier or harder to use as a channel for deliberation and communication of their preferences. One could then hypothesise that the multiplication and mobilisation of new trans-European networks, far from being a sign of weakness of the European public sphere, may encourage and facilitate its consolidation.

A central element yet to be considered in this brief approach to the European public sphere is language. According to a Habermasian model of the public sphere, the emergence of a European public sphere is treated as an issue of European mass media. They are assumed to be the only means to facilitate the consolidation of common feelings of belonging and European identity. These are related to debates that regularly preoccupy EU institutions and academics on the need (or lack of it) to establish links between citizenship, public European spaces, and European identity. In other words, one may ask whether a European public sphere needs the simultaneous emergence of a homogeneous European culture, or if it can rely on a European demos not defined in ethno-cultural terms but on civic and political ones.

This is why Balibar (2001) puts forward the question of language. He claims that one cannot speak of a public sphere without addressing the question: 'Who is this sphere for?' Balibar goes on to suggest that language in Europe is not a code but a system in permanent transformation and cross-usage. In other words it is a reality of social practices of translation at different levels. (Balibar 2001: 318). Contrary to concerns about the deterioration of linguistic exchanges in a polyglot context, a careful observation of the social uses of translation and linguistic misunderstanding, within the functioning of European networks brings us to the hypothesis that the most abstract concepts can be debated and often clarified by multilingualism.

The diversity of histories and political cultures within the EU means that concepts and representations of any given word can differ deeply. Such notions as 'citizenship', 'public services' or 'community' have meanings that can be quite diverse in each of the languages spoken in Europe, and even across the countries that speak the same language. While this variability can at times lead to the emergence of a European institutional dialect which is hard to relate to for citizens, it also seems to lead to a debate, which is made far richer by the superimposed use of multiple languages. Multilingualism offers citizens the possibility of considering solutions that might appear unthinkable in one language. As underlined by Umberto Eco (1997), the issue with European culture in the future does not lie in the achievement of the total polyglot but in a community of people who can understand the spirit and atmosphere of a different word. In other words, Europe will not rely on people speaking all European languages but, in the best hypothesis, in citizens speaking their own different languages while understanding each other.

If, as shown by Bruter (2005), 'European identity' is not perceived by Europeans as implying the imposition of a homogenised culture, the practice of 'cultural translation' may suffice to encourage the emergence of a European public sphere. This process is not limited to governments' practice or the construction of European media networks. Such emergence at the European level has in any case been singularly slowed down by a series of obstacles, including those pointed out in this volume on the designation of the elected members at the European Parliament (diversity of voting procedures, geographical divisions or electoral calendars, as well as electoral practices themselves). However, the questions of European citizenship, identity and 'demos' are neither self-standing essential debates nor matters of pure legal concern. The complexity and pluralism of cultures in Europe, the variety of social and political practices, and new sets of emerging networks and connections developing at the European level, have in a way questioned the assumed opposition between local spaces and a European public sphere in a unifying continent.

Catherine Neveu

Bibliography

Balibar, E., 'Europe difficile: les chantiers de la démocratie', in E. Balibar, *Nous, citoyens d'Europe? Les frontières, l'Etat, le peuple*, Paris, La Découverte, 2001, pp. 286–319.
Bruter, M. *Citizens of Europe? The Emergence of a Mass European Identity*, Basingstoke: Palgrave Macmillan, 2005.
Eco, E., *The Search for the Perfect Language – the Making of Europe*, London, Blackwell, 1997.
Hix, S., *The Political System of the European Union*, Palgrave Macmillan, 2006.
Quermonne, J-L. and Smith, A., 'Territoire et espace public dans l'Union européenne', *Cultures et Conflits*, 21–22, 1996, pp. 133–58.

→ Electoral Behaviour; European Electoral Act; European Public Opinion; Europeanisation (of National Political Life); Identity; Interest Groups; Lobbying; Mulit-Level Governance; Political Market; Representation.

European Referendums

Referendums originally represented the first form of institutionalised expression for citizens with regard to European integration. Seven years prior to the first election of the European Parliament by direct universal suffrage, referendums were held in four countries (France, Ireland, Norway and Denmark) to address the first European enlargement of the Community. Over 30 years later, there have been no fewer than 42 referendums relating to European integration, organised at the national level in scores of countries (see Table 1). They have also been organised at the infrastate level in Denmark and Finland. In 1972, during the referendum concerning Danish accession, the Faroe Islands, due to their independent status, organised their own referendum, the outcome of which rejected membership of the European Community. After the independence of Greenland in 1979, the Greenlandic citizens voted in 1982 (with a majority of 52 per cent) for a withdrawal of Greenland from the European Community. In Finland, in a 1994 referendum, Åland agreed to become a member of the EU. Referendums consequently constitute a parallel ground with the European Parliament elections to re-examine some of the structuring questionings relating to the field of Community electoral studies, those concerning citizens' attitudes and behaviours with regard to the process of integration and more generally the place reserved for European questions within national political spaces.

Obviously, the more than 40 referendums relating to European integration organised up till now are not all of a comparable nature. Some of them are obligatory, due to constitutional provisions, others optional, some are restrictive, whilst others are only advisory. It is important, for example, to distinguish between the Danish and Irish referendums in 1972, on the one hand, both being obligatory and with a restrictive result, and the French and Norwegian referendums, on the other, which were both optional and advisory. This thus contributes further observational value to the complex analysis that referendums can be constitutionally advisory yet restrictive and constraining in practice. Thus, while the referendum is only advisory in Sweden, the Swedish government announced in 1996, and repeated in 2003, that it would follow the choice of the citizens. Overall, excluding those countries where ratification of European treaties often involves constitutional changes requiring a referendum to be held (Denmark, Ireland), referendums relating to European integration were organised by the governments of various states to meet three types of expectations. A certain number were conceived as plebiscites. The two French referendums, in 1972 and 1992, are examples of this first type. The government's decision to hold a referendum on European integration can also appear as a means of answering a question which expresses strong differences, either within the leading party, or within the governmental coalition, or within the population as a whole. The two Norwegian referendums in 1972 and 1996, and the British one in 1975 constitute examples of this second type. The decision to organise a referendum on European integration could also result more recently from a 'moral obligation'. In the context of strong criticisms pertaining to the term 'democratic deficit' of the EU, the decision to involve citizens in the process of European integration through a referendum became more crucial for political, national and Community elites, as a means among others to demonstrate their will to reduce this deficit. The new accession countries had been strongly requested by the Commission to adopt this direction which consequently led to the organisation of referendums concerning the accession of nine of the ten new entrants. Across these various strategies relating to the use of referendum, the European issue is thus integrated within the national spaces in turn as a foil, a disruptive element or a symptom of the problems which run through them.

Beyond these national strategies, analysis of European referendums enables discussions focused around the analysis of European elections to be developed. The argument which contends that the high level of abstention observed in European elections since 1979 and its subsequent increase results from the notably minimal interest held by citizens concerning European affairs appears to be at least partially called into question. If turnout in the French referendum in 1972 indeed seems to confirm this hypothesis, given that it represents the lowest level observed from all types of election since the war, it is nonetheless important to mention that the Socialist Party and the PSU had then called for abstention within the context of a referendum, which was then very much perceived as a plebiscite for the President of the Republic, George Pompidou. A longitudinal approach to European referendums

Table 1 Level of turnout and results of all the national referendums on European integration

Date	Country	Theme	Turnout	Decision	Majority
1972 (23/4)	France	Accession of new members	60.5*	YES	67.9
1972 (10/5)	Ireland	Accession	70.9	YES	83.1
1972 (25/9)	Norway	Accession	78.9	NO	53.5
1972 (2/10)	Denmark	Accession	90.1	YES	63.3
1972 (3/12)	Switzerland	Treaty on the EC / AELE	52	YES	72.5
1975 (5/6)	UK	EC membership	64.5	YES	67.2
1984 (14/6)	Ireland	Right to vote in European elections for third country citizens	45.8	YES	75.4
1986 (27/2)	Denmark	Single European Act	74.8	YES	56.2
1987 (26/5)	Ireland	Single European Act	43.9	YES	69.9
1989 (18/6)	Italy	Allocation of constituent powers to the European Parliament	81	YES	89.1
1992 (2/6)	Denmark	Maastricht Treaty	83.1	NO	50.7
1992 (18/6)	Ireland	Maastricht Treaty	57.3	YES	64.0
1992 (20/9)	France	Maastricht Treaty	71.1**	YES	50.8**
1992 (6/12)	Switzerland	European Economic Area Treaty	78	NO	50.3
1992 (13/12)	Liechtenstein	European Economic Area Treaty	87	YES	55.8
1993 (18/5)	Denmark	Maastricht Treaty (renegotiated)	86.5	YES	56.7
1994 (12/6)	Austria	Accession	81.3	YES	66.6
1994 (16/10)	Finland	Accession	74.0	YES	56.9
1994 (13/11)	Sweden	Accession	83.3	YES	52.3
1994 (27–28/11)	Norway	Accession	88.6	NO	52.2
1998 (22/5)	Ireland	Amsterdam Treaty	56.3	YES	61.7
1998 (28/5)	Denmark	Amsterdam Treaty	74.8	YES	55.1
2000 (21/5)	Switzerland	Bilateral agreement with EU	48	YES	67.2

Date	Country	Subject	Turnout	Result	%
2000 (28/9)	Denmark	Adoption of the euro	87.8	NO	53.1
2001 (4/5)	Switzerland	Launch of accession negotiations	55	NO	76.8
2001 (7/6)	Ireland	Treaty of Nice	35	NO	53.9
2002 (19/10)	Ireland	Treaty of Nice (renegotiated)	49	YES	62.9
2003 (8/3)	Malta	Accession	91	YES	53.7
2003 (23/3)	Slovenia	Accession	55.4	YES	89.7
2003 (12/4)	Hungary	Accession	45.6	YES	83.8
2003(10–11/5)	Lithuania	Accession	63.3	YES	91
2003 (16–17/5)	Slovakia	Accession	52.2***	YES	92.5
2003 (7–8/6)	Poland	Accession	58.8	YES	77.4
2003 (13–14/6)	Czech Republic	Accession	55.2	YES	77.3
2003 (14/6)	Estonia	Accession	63	YES	67
2003 (14 /9)	Sweden	Adoption of the euro	81.2	NO	56.1
2003 (20/9)	Latvia	Accession	72.5	YES	67
2003 (19/10)	Romania	Constitutional amendment in preparation for EU accession	55.2	YES	89.6
2005 (20/2)	Spain	Treaty establishing a Constitution for Europe	42.3	YES	76.7
2005 (29/5)	France	Treaty establishing a Constitution for Europe	69.4	NO	54.7
2005 (1/6)	Pays-Bas	Treaty establishing a Constitution for Europe	64.8	NO	61.6
2005 (107)	Luxembourg	Treaty establishing a Constitution for Europe	90.4	YES	56.5

* This high level of abstention was accompanied by a significant proportion of blank and null votes (7.1 per cent).
** The results in Metropolitan France. Concerning the whole of France, 69.7 per cent of registered voters voted and 51 per cent voted in favour of the ratification.
*** Since the introduction of the referendum in Slovakia, it is the only referendum where yes prevailed owing to the fact that a minimum of 50 per cent of the voters is required so that the vote is endorsed.

shows on the contrary that the European issues are indeed able to mobilise citizens. Thus the majority of referendums relating to European integration held from the 1980s to the present day in the West European countries mobilised at least seven citizens out of ten – except in four countries: Switzerland, where the turnout levels in referendums are generally low regardless of the topic, Spain, the Netherlands and Ireland. However, it is also of interest to underline that the Irish referendum in 1972 was the most mobilising of all those held in this country to date. Similarly, turnout (64.8 per cent) in the Dutch referendum in spring 2005 was particularly high in comparison with that of the last European elections held in that country (29.9 per cent in 1999 and 39.1 per cent in 2004). Moreover, if the referendums on accession in the new countries have not mobilised the citizens as much overall, except for Malta, this low turnout appears more symbolic of a distanced relationship between citizens in the ex-Eastern countries and voting than of an absence of interest in European issues. Indeed, in four of these countries, Estonia, Lithuania, Poland and the Czech Republic, more citizens went to the ballot boxes during the accession referendums than for the last national legislative elections. The level of citizen turnout in the majority of referendums relating to European integration thus invites a fresh appraisal of the literature which states that high levels of abstention in European elections are symptomatic of the absence of interest in European issues.

Through the highest level of turnout in European referendums, the absence of debate and alternative during the European elections once again appears significant in regards to the pursuit of the process of integration. Referendums appear to mobilise more because they enable citizens to express a true choice regarding the future of integration or at least some aspects of its developments. During the 1970s and 1980s, the favourable results across almost all the referendums were considered by the elites as a confirmation of the existence of a broad 'permissive consensus' amongst the citizens in relation to European integration. Following which, the negative outcome of the Danish referendum in 1992 for the ratification of the Maastricht Treaty, similar to the very lukewarm outcome of the French referendum, appeared as a warning signal of a break in this consensus. A break which subsequently appeared to some extent consummate with the first Irish referendum for the Treaty of Nice, the two Danish and Swedish referendums on the euro, and to which can now be added the French and Dutch referendums on the Constitutional Treaty. It seems but a distant ambition when Europe could be seen as a consensual topic allowing, via a referendum procedure for plebiscitary use, the restoration of the reputation of unpopular governments. In all the EU-15 countries where referendums relating to European integration have been held over the past 15 years, the referendum campaigns succeeded, on the contrary, in stimulating in-depth discussion within the political community. This debate, which largely failed to divide partisan forces according to typical frameworks structuring the national political arenas, contributed to the emergence of new dimensions within national political spaces, or at least the emergence of new forces which exploit over the longer term a considerable part of these spaces. The Movement for France led by Philippe de Villiers in France, or the Danish and Swedish June Movements provide the most striking examples. The argument according to which a 'European' reading of the referendum results is possible, is by no means left unquestioned. According to certain observers, the outcomes of the Danish and Irish referendums (in 1992 and 2001 respectively) are more reflective of a dismissal by the citizens of their governments than a rejection of the Community texts put forward in the referendums. The positive results from a second referendum would thus come to ratify not a change introduced into the text proposed in the ratification but rather a change of government or governmental policy. The attitude of blind conformity amongst the populations compared to the elites regarding European issues described by neo-functionalists in the 1960s would therefore still be a relevant topic. On this point, discussion remains, however, largely open.

The referendums on accession in nine of the ten new incoming countries during 2003 offered some variations and complements of analyses. The high level of abstention in the referendums across the majority of these countries, except for Malta, consequently demonstrates the explicit lack of debate in at least four of the countries: Slovakia, Slovenia, Hungary and Lithuania. More generally, EU accession had been presented in historical and civilisational terms, as a 'return' to Europe, and as such the task of constructing an anti-accession speech was particularly difficult. Accession appeared inextricably linked to the political and ideological references convened by these countries in the early 1990s, and any criticism would seem tantamount to a revaluation of these roots. In this context, certain observers have advanced the argument that the partisans of accession were more likely to have gone to the ballot boxes during the 2003 referendum than its detractors. The important level of abstention should consequently be interpreted as a measurement of the strength of these opponents. This hypothesis reappeared at the time of the 2004 European elections but failed to be

entirely confirmed in practice. More generally, these referendums have provided the opportunity of formulating several types of assumptions (relating to the importance of the relations between the type of discourse developed by the opponents, the intensity of European preferences held by the citizens, and also the force of engagement between civil society actors and the level of abstention, etc.) which facilitate a renewed approach concerning the relationship of citizens to 'European' elections.

Such analyses have recently been further developed following the referendum on the Treaty establishing a Constitution for Europe which will facilitate an emphasis based on a more significant number of cases. During summer 2005, four referendums on the Constitutional Treaty were held in Spain, France, the Netherlands and Luxembourg. Six others were due to follow in Denmark, Portugal, Poland, Ireland, the Czech Republic and the United Kingdom between autumn 2005 and autumn 2006. However, the negative outcomes of the referendums on 29 May and 1 June 2005 in France and the Netherlands led the governments in the other countries to delay the date of their respective referendums. Presently, it appears clear that in three out of the four countries where the referendums on the Constitutional Treaty were held, the referendum campaign provided an opportunity for an unprecedented debate, as much for the political elites as for the citizens as a whole. Moreover, the negative outcome in two of these referendums in countries whose citizens were not hitherto regarded as the most hostile to the integration process has, beyond the institutional upheavals which it implies, highlighted that the European elite can no longer claim to expect citizens to accept a new stage in the process of European integration without preliminary debates. Consequently, it appears probable that these referendums will assume a more significant role in the reorganisation of national political spaces around the European issue.

Céline Belot

Bibliography

Franklin, M. N., Marsh, M. and McLaren, L., 'Uncorking the Bottle: Popular Opposition to European Unification in the Wake of Maastricht', *Journal of Common Market Studies*, 32, 4, 1994, pp. 455–72.
Hug, S., *Voices of Europe: Citizens, Referenda, and European Integration*, Lanham, Rowman and Littlefield, 2002.
Le Duc, L. and Svensson, P. (eds), 'Special Issue – Interests, Information and Voting in the Referenda', *European Journal of Political Research*, 41, 6, 2002.
Szczerbiak, A. and Taggart, P. (eds), Special Issue – Choosing Union: the 2003 EU Accession Referenda', *West European Politics*, 27, 4, 2004.

→ Abstention; Cleavages; Electoral Behaviour; Enlargement; European Constitution; European Elections (1979–1999).

Europeanisation

(of National Political Life)

Definitions and background

The term Europeanisation has been widely adopted by scholars of the European integration process across a range of social science disciplines. As such, the concept has acquired a multiplicity of different, and occasionally contradictory, meanings. 'Europeanisation' has, for example, variously been used to designate: the emergence of European-level structures of governance and policy processes; the export of European models and norms of governance beyond the boundaries of the European Union; and the redefinition of senses of identity and territoriality associated particularly with the emergence of forms of 'everyday Europeanness' through sport, travel or the arts. Nevertheless, the most common definitions of Europeanisation are those concerned with patterns of domestic political adaptation to European integration. Robert Ladrech has put forward one of the most widely cited definitions of Europeanisation in this vein, describing it as 'an incremental process reorienting the direction and shape of politics to the degree that EC political and economic dynamics become part of the organisational logic of national politics and policy-making' (Ladrech 2002: 392).

Most studies of Europeanisation as domestic adaptation have, to date, focused on either governmental institutions or on particular policy sectors. Rather different conclusions have emerged from these two bodies of literature. As regards the patterns of adaptation displayed by governmental institutions, most studies have tended to stress the existence of relatively strong logics of path dependence. Governments in member states have not experienced a fundamental restructuring because of European integration. Rather, the pressures of European integration have generally been dealt with in a manner which is fundamentally preservative of existing national institutional structures and the broader matrices of values in which those structures are embedded. Conversely, a highly variegated picture has emerged from studies concerned with the impact of European integration on specific policy sectors. Here, widely different patterns of adjustment emerge both within and across countries, reflecting both the differential development of European policy itself and the more specific sectoral opportunity structures which exist at the national level.

Relative to these substantial literatures, comparatively little attention has been paid by Europeanisation scholars to political parties or to broader political environments beyond the institutions of the state. Any attempt at generalisation as regards the wider patterns of the Europeanisation of political life must thus necessarily be tentative. Two general trends may nonetheless be discerned. On the one hand, it is clear that there has been a significant Europeanisation of political life, in the sense that European issues have assumed an increasingly higher profile in national political debates. Yet, on the other hand, this development has not been accompanied by a significant Europeanisation of national party systems, whose basic structural properties remain largely impervious to European influences.

The Europeanisation of national political debates

European issues have assumed an increasingly prominent place in national political debates. This heightened profile encompasses two sets of distinct, if necessarily interconnected issues. First, the trajectory of the European integration process itself has increasingly become an object of domestic political contestation. The intensity of this contestation has varied in different national political contexts. Nonetheless, it is clear that the repeated Intergovernmental Conferences on European treaty reform held since the early 1990s have pushed general 'constitutional' issues, concerning the overarching structure and purpose of the European Union, on to the domestic political agenda in virtually every member state. It is rare for a national party manifesto anywhere in Europe not to say 'something' about the broad course of European integration. In this way, a reasonably fine-grained portrait may be drawn of the positions held by virtually all major national parties on the main institutional issues of European integration. National parties may readily be identified in terms of holding positions which tend towards either the supranational or the intergovernmental poles of European political debate, even if these positions only rarely form key elements in the parties' own ideological self-definitions.

Second, a European dimension has also increasingly entered national political debate as a matter of 'normal' politics, concerned with substantive policy choices across an expanding range of sectors. National parties have demonstrated a growing awareness of the impact of European developments on national policy objectives. There has thus been a corresponding engagement with the European level, variously viewed as both an opportunity and a constraint relative to domestic policy choices. This has perhaps been most evident in relation to regulatory and redistributive issues. In this regard, Marks and Wilson (2000) have identified both social-democratic and neo-liberal 'possibility curves' as a means of plotting the responses of national parties to the policy impacts of European integration. Following this logic, social-democratic parties will tend to view Europe as a potential threat in situations where European-level developments risk eroding existing national standards of social protection. Conversely, where Europe is seen as an opportunity for securing policies which are unobtainable at the national level, or where the market liberalisation aspects of European integration are seen to necessitate a countervailing European-level social model, such parties have proven more favourably disposed to the further progress of the integration process. The neo-liberal possibility curve is, in effect, the mirror image of that seen on the social-democratic side. Here, parties will be favourably disposed to European integration where it broadly follows a deregulatory course, while oppositions will arise where it is seen as imposing new or additional regulatory burdens relative to existing national regimes.

The analysis of such general adaptive patterns further gives rise to a consideration of the terms on which national parties have engaged European policy questions. European policies are largely seen through the prism of existing national positions and agendas. As such, although national parties have demonstrated an increasing awareness of the importance of the European dimension, they have done so in essentially strategic terms. Europe is viewed as an alternative or additional policy arena through which domestically defined goals may be or must be pursued by other means. These patterns of strategic adaptation have not, however, been linked to wider changes in partisan identity structures. The participation of national parties in European policy-making processes does not appear to have prompted reformulations of underlying policy objectives; parties have not engaged in forms of 'complex or double-loop learning', whereby core actor interests are themselves redefined.

The Europeanisation of national party systems

European integration has not had a significant impact on the basic structures of national party systems. Neither the format nor the mechanics of any West European party system have been fundamentally reshaped by European integration (Mair 2000). As regards format, no major new parties have emerged, at the national level, which define themselves principally with reference to a pro-/anti-integration cleavage. Relative to mechanics, issues surrounding European integration have similarly not substantially altered the key terms of interparty competition. Existing parties have not redefined themselves with reference to European integration, nor have European issues directly emerged as salient factors in the determination of national electoral outcomes. Divisions concerning European integration show no signs of superseding the existing patterns of predominately class, territorial and confessional cleavages on which European party systems are based.

The impermeability of national party systems to a restructuring on the basis of a possible European integration cleavage finds strong confirmation in the absence of any important 'spill back' from the European Parliament electoral arena to its national counterparts. In contrast to national elections, EP elections have seen occasional inroads made by parties which define themselves principally in terms of a pro-/anti-integration cleavage. More precisely, hard Eurosceptic parties, characterised by their fundamental opposition to (further) European integration, have enjoyed electoral success in a number of member states (most notably, Denmark, France, Sweden and the United Kingdom). Nevertheless, the European successes achieved by these Eurosceptic parties have, to date, not proven translatable into the national political arena. In the Danish case, the principal Eurosceptic movements opted from the outset not to contest national elections, in effect creating a limited dual party system with somewhat different competitive dynamics at the national and the European levels (a pattern perhaps to be reproduced in Sweden). British and French Eurosceptic parties, contesting national elections, have (as yet) failed to make significant breakthroughs at the domestic level. The success of Eurosceptic parties at European elections thus appears to be largely the product of the specific opportunity structures offered by such elections. Combining the protest vote dynamics of an archetypal second-order election with relatively high-profile discussions of European issues, it is perhaps not surprising that European Parliament elections have proven particularly fertile ground for Eurosceptic parties. This cannot, however, be tied to broader mobilisations around European themes which are likely to displace existing political identities.

While European integration has not had a significant impact in terms of interparty dynamics, it has been a source of important intraparty divisions in a number of cases. The emergence of such turbulence is, in itself, explicable with reference to more general dynamics of organisational adaptation. European integration represents a classic form of environmental challenge to political parties as organisations. It introduces new issues into the political arena, or adds new dimensions to existing issues, in ways which often will not correspond to the social and ideological lines of division on which parties were formed. In this way, European issues may create substantial cross-pressures, at variance with existing partisan allegiances. The European dimension may also, perhaps rather more importantly, have the effect of changing organisational power balances and opportunity structures. New challenges to the dominant coalition within a party may arise, as European issues differentially reshape the agendas and strategies of different factions or leadership hopefuls. These intraparty struggles, moreover, may then further lead to changes in the perceptions and prospects of the party within the wider electorate. Intraparty differences over Europe may thus potentially exercise an indirect impact on the terms of interparty competition, though it is intrinsically difficult to gauge the extent of such influence.

The most severe case of intraparty division over European integration in recent years has been that of the British Conservative Party. Tory divisions over Europe lie on a number of wider fault lines within the party. Most notably, attitudes towards European integration tend to correspond to a more general divide between so-called 'wets' (traditional one-nation Conservatives) and 'drys' (Thatcherite adherents of a more vigorously neo-liberal philosophy). The high point of internal dissent came during the years of the Major premiership, from 1990 to 1997. Prime Minister John Major faced a series of important backbench rebellions over the Maastricht Treaty in 1993, as a substantial minority of Conservative MPs refused to vote for ratification. The divisions persisted after Maastricht, prompting Major's staged resignation from the party leadership in June 1995. The resignation was intended as a gambit by the Prime Minister to face down his opponents, whom he had publicly labelled 'the bastards'. Major sought and easily won re-election, but his strategic gamble proved unable to solve the underlying problem. Deep-seated divisions within the Conservative Party over European integration continued to find well-publicised expression, and appeared to be a significant, contributing factor to the party's massive defeat in the 1997 election. These divisions have been more muted since 1997, as the party in opposition has moved in a more resolutely Eurosceptic direction. It remains to be seen, however, if the European issue will remain quiescent as the party seeks to re-establish a broader electoral base, and restore its credibility as an alternative government, within a political landscape redefined by the New Labour project.

British Conservatives have not been alone in facing internal dissension over European integration. At various junctures, divisions over European integration have, for example, marked both the mainstream right and the mainstream left in France. Such divisions have most recently made themselves felt in the French Socialist Party (PS), as regards the ratification of the 2004 Constitutional Treaty. The European Constitution has, within the PS, served to crystallise broader differences concerning the future direction and leadership of the party.

Outside of the United Kingdom, it is nonetheless in Scandinavia that Europe has probably created the highest levels of turbulence within established political parties. The most prominent instances of such divisions concern the Social-Democratic parties in both Denmark and Sweden, as well as the Labour Party in Norway. Here, recurrent patterns of division have led to the deployment of quite distinctive party management strategies. As exemplified by the Swedish Social-Democrats, the trend has been towards the accommodation of differences over European issues, in ways which seek to allow for the cohabitation of both Eurosceptic and pro-integrationist views within an overarching, unified party framework. The issue of European integration is, in effect, compartmentalised or isolated. A broad (if variable) toler-ance of dissent is permitted from the official party line, as a means to prevent European issues from giving rise to a wider destabilisation of party structures or challenges to the party leadership. Such strategies have thus far proved comparatively successful as instruments for maintaining organisational unity and electability, though questions remain as to the implications of this approach for longer-term party cohesive-ness and policy influence.

Patterns and prospects

The Europeanisation of national politi-cal life, understood principally in terms of party politics, conforms to more general trends identified in the Europeanisation literature. The dynam-ics of Europeanisation, as regards the basic structures of political life, may be equated with an overriding logic of domestication. Political parties have largely sought to absorb the increasingly important European dimension of policy processes into existing cleavage structures and patterns of politics. Clearly, in some instances, this strategy of absorption has encountered obstacles. In particular, one may point to instances of serious intra-party divisions, where European integra-tion has had a destabilising impact on internal party structures and balances. Nevertheless, these intraparty tensions, though potentially placing the specific party concerned at a competitive disad-vantage, have not produced wider struc-tural changes in national party systems. Overall, the patterns of organisational adaptation displayed by national parties to European integration have proven successful in maintaining a basic struc-tural continuity and stability.

This pattern of Europeanisation has implications, in turn, for the European electoral arena. The domination of EP elections by domestic concerns and parties – their 'nationalisation' (see *infra*) – stems from the same underlying organ-isational dynamics. The control of the European electoral arena by national parties represents a logical extension of the broad adaptive patterns whereby they have sought to incorporate the European dimension of political life into existing structures and frames of reference. The Europeanisation of political life is princi-pally concerned not with the emergence of autonomous 'European' logics of poli-tics and policy, but rather with the subtle strategies of adaptation whereby national institutions have preserved their own core attributes while accommodating new demands. It is within this framework of domestic adaptive responses that the dynamics of European Parliament elec-tions as second-order national contests find a clear explanation, albeit not perhaps in terms which are apt to endow these elections with a comparably clear sense of purpose.

Robert Harmsen

Bibliography

Harmsen, R., 'L'Europe et les partis politiques nationaux: Les leçons d'un "non-clivage"', *Revue internationale de politique comparée*, 12, 1, 2005.
Ladrech, R., 'Europeanization and Political Parties: Towards a Framework for Analysis', *Party Politics*, 8, 4, 2002, pp. 389–403.
Mair, P., 'The Limited Impact of Europe on National Party Systems', *West European Politics*, 23, 4, 2000, pp. 27–51.
Marks, G. and Wilson, C. J., 'The Past in the Present: a Cleavage Theory of Party Response to European Integration', *British Journal of Political Science*, 30, 3, 2000, pp. 433–59.

➜ Multi-Level Governance.

Euroscepticism

Origins

The term 'Euroscepticism' originated in British political and media discourse in the mid-1980s. Initially, the label 'Eurosceptic' was used interchangeably with the older term 'anti-marketeer', which designated opponents of British membership in the Common Market. A more encompassing use of the word, however, rapidly emerged. The epithet Eurosceptic came to be applied not only to opponents of British EC membership, but also to those who, more generally, expressed strongly critical sentiments as regards the European integration project or who, more particularly, displayed a marked hostility to the further development of that project. Despite this conceptual ambiguity, it is nevertheless clear that the early meanings of the term were deeply embedded in a uniquely British (or English) web of attitudes towards European integration. Euroscepticism was defined in terms of opposition to a continental European project of political and economic integration, deemed to be fundamentally incompatible with the United Kingdom's distinctive institutions and traditions. Euroscepticism of this type might be defined in terms of the insularity of an island nation. Yet, in practice, it tended rather more to oppose the European project on the basis of privileging the primacy of either the trans-Atlantic relationship or the UK's relations with the wider Commonwealth community. While formerly more pronounced in the Labour Party, strong Eurosceptic tendencies have more recently gained greater weight within the Conservative Party. Prime Minister Margaret Thatcher's September 1988 Bruges speech remains a key reference point for much of this Tory Euroscepticism. A strong Eurosceptic discourse also, importantly, finds further support within substantial sections of the British print media, particularly amongst the tabloid press.

Moving beyond its English origins, the term Euroscepticism gradually came to be used more widely in European political discourse from the early 1990s onwards. The label was applied to a progressively broader spectrum of oppositions to or criticisms of the European integration project, as these positions gained support in a growing range of EU member states. The debates surrounding the Maastricht Treaty in the period 1991–3 marked a decisive turning point in this regard. With Maastricht, the 'permissive consensus' which had long surrounded the European integration process in many member states appeared to be called into question. The comparatively high-profile debates which accompanied the Treaty's ratification served to highlight the issue of the

EU's 'democratic deficit', as well as the extent to which key policy competencies had been or were to be transferred beyond national control. 'Europe', though still of persistingly low electoral salience, may nevertheless be seen to have emerged as a more prominent issue in West European political debate from this period onwards. At the same time, one could also detect the growth of Eurosceptic sentiments, on a rather different basis, in the countries of Central and Eastern Europe (CEECs) seeking EU membership. In the CEECs, an initial enthusiasm for a 'return to Europe' quickly gave way, faced with the realities of a markedly long and asymmetrical accession process, to the expression of various forms of disenchantment with the European project.

Forms of party-based Euroscepticism

Building on the existing typologies in the academic literature (Taggart and Szczerbiak 2002; Kopecky and Mudde 2002), one may identify five broadly defined forms of party-based Euroscepticism which have variably emerged in national and European Parliament elections. The first category concerns the adoption of critical stances by mainstream or governmental parties as regards specific EU policies or more general policy orientations. A soft Euroscepticism of this type could, for example, take the form of a socialist or a social-democratic party criticising the EU for the absence of a strong social dimension. Conversely, it might also take the form of a conservative or neo-liberal party criticising European policy for its excessively interventionist character. As these examples make clear, this form of critical engagement with European issues is perhaps best not conceived as a form of Euroscepticism at all. Rather, specific, policy-based criticisms of this type point

to the gradual emergence of a European political debate. Parties are articulating a set of consistently defined policy objectives, together with a strategic framework which recognises the need for measures to be adopted at both the national and the European levels. In this sense, the softer forms of what is commonly termed Euroscepticism are not rooted in an opposition to European integration, but rather reflect the progressive Europeanisation of political life.

The second form of Euroscepticism relates to the adoption by mainstream or governmental parties of a generalised critical posture as regards the overall European integration project. Scepticisms of this sort thus move beyond a discrete concern with particular policies or policy sectors. Rather, they are the reflection of a broader sense of a 'misfit' between the trajectory assumed by European integration and core tenets of a party's political project or its understanding of the 'national interest'. Insofar as this form of Euroscepticism concerns parties which either are or may reasonably aspire to be in government, it necessarily remains limited. Such parties must remain aware of the constraints of office and the consequent need to find practical accommodations with the demands of EU membership. It is still the case, nonetheless, that a Euroscepticism of this type makes the EU itself an object of political contestation, rather than simply viewing it as an arena within which individual policies may be opposed or supported in light of domestically defined objectives. The British Conservative Party is the archetype of this form of Euroscepticism. In this case, an opposition to further European integration in the name of a neo-liberal economic agenda has frequently tipped into the expression of a more general scepticism as regards the EU itself. This attitude was perhaps most memorably encapsulated in the party's 1999

European Parliament campaign, fought under the slogan 'In Europe, but not run by Europe'. Such generalised, mainstream Euroscepticisms may, however, also be seen in other member states. Most prominently, the Czech Civic Democratic Party (ODS) has adopted a similar position to that of the British Tories. This stance was most visibly embodied in the ODS's 2001 *Manifesto of Czech Eurorealism*, which combined a vigorous advocacy of a neo-liberal economic policy with a sharp critique of what it regarded as the EU's excessive and wasteful bureaucratisation.

A third category of Euroscepticism encompasses the expression of fundamental oppositions to the European integration project by parties which have otherwise defined themselves in terms of a radical opposition to the mainstream or governmental parties within a national political system. Euroscepticism in this case forms part of a more general 'protest' agenda, grafted on to a pre-existing ideology or programme which seeks to mark out the party concerned from the 'political class'. Euroscepticisms of this sort may be seen in the case of populist parties, such as the Danish Progress Party (and latterly the Danish People's Party), the Dutch Pim Fortuyn List, or (after an earlier, pro-EU regionalist discourse) the Italian Northern League. For such parties, an opposition to European integration easily forms part of a more general 'anti-establishment' political discourse. Radical Euroscepticisms of this type also characterise parties of the far right, such as the French National Front (FN), the Austrian Freedom Party (FPÖ), or the Flemish Bloc. Such parties may readily adopt a strong anti-EU discourse, usually cast in terms of defending imperilled national interests and identities against the machinations of a 'treasonous' political class (for example, the *Maastricheurs* decried in the rhetoric of the French FN). The Euroscepticisms manifested by parties of the far left also fit into this category.

The radical oppositions to European integration expressed by both the heirs of traditional communist parties and new left or *altermondialiste* movements tend principally to be defined not with reference to the EU itself, but rather in terms of wider oppositions to the international liberal capitalist order of which the EU is taken to be a manifestation. The Eurosceptic stances adopted by many Green parties could also, historically, have been placed within this category. These Euroscepticisms reflected a rejection of the European integration project as an inhospitable terrain for the pursuit of environmental policy goals and inclusive forms of participatory politics. While such strong Eurosceptic stances continue to characterise some Green parties (such as in Sweden), many other Green parties have adopted more reformist positions, often in light of governmental participation (such as in Germany).

The fourth category of Euroscepticism concerns parties which principally define themselves by their fundamental opposition to the European integration project. In contrast to more general protest parties, the advocacy of a strong Eurosceptic position constitutes the *raison d'être* for parties of this type. This strong Euroscepticism will often take the form of campaigning for national withdrawal from the European Union, or for non-accession in the case of candidate states. It may also find expression through demands for a fundamental restructuring of the EU, paring back the Union's range of competencies so as to create looser and more limited forms of co-operation among sovereign states. Eurosceptic parties of this type remain only very marginal forces in national political arenas. The particular opportunity structures offered by European Parliament elections have, however, allowed these parties to make some electoral inroads. Paradoxically, it is in European elections that 'anti-European' parties have enjoyed their only major electoral successes to date.

The most established Euroscepticisms corresponding to this category are found in the Danish case. Here, two parties were created in the aftermath of the first Danish 'No' vote on the Maastricht Treaty in June 1992: the symbolically named June Movement and the People's Movement against the EU. The June Movement campaigns against what it terms the excessive centralisation of EU governance, seeking a restrictive redefinition of the integration project on a more intergovernmental basis with a major repatriation of national legislative powers. The People's Movement against the EU, in contrast, directly advocates Danish withdrawal from the EU. The two parties together were able cumulatively to take a quarter of the vote (25.5 per cent) in the 1994 European Parliament election in Denmark. They have since carved out a distinctive niche for themselves as 'European' parties, which do not contest national elections. Their overall level of support has, nonetheless, declined over time. The two parties together polled only 14.3 per cent of the vote in 2004.

France offers another example of this form of Euroscepticism. The Majorité pour l'Autre Europe list, headed by the dissident UDF (Union pour la Démocratie française) parliamentarian Philippe de Villiers, polled 12.3 per cent of the vote in the 1994 European Parliament elections. This success was repeated in the 1999 EP election, when the Rassemblement pour la France, formed by de Villiers together with the prominent Gaullist politician Charles Pasqua, won 13 per cent of the vote. In the 2004 election, de Villiers, standing alone, saw his support slump to 8.4 per cent of the national vote. De Villiers' position is marked by a deeply traditional conservatism, hostile to the creation of a European 'super-state', as well as more generally to the spread of both 'socialist' and 'free trade' philosophies. The protection of the traditional fabric of the nation-state is held to be of paramount concern. As such, de Villiers has advocated the transformation of the European Union into a 'confederation of sovereign states'.

The United Kingdom Independence Party (UKIP) has similarly enjoyed success in EP elections, campaigning on a platform which calls for British withdrawal from the EU. The party's programme is rooted in a classic British (or English) Euroscepticism. It contends that the UK has been 'trapped' in a progressively expanding project of continental political union, which stands at odds with the country's traditional institutions and underlying interests. Profiting from the use of a proportional representation electoral system in EP elections, UKIP was able to elect three MEPs on 7 per cent of the vote in 1999 and 12 MEPS on 16.2 per cent of the vote in 2004. In the latter election, UKIP moved ahead of the Liberal Democrats to secure third place overall.

The 2004 EP election also saw the breakthrough of a Eurosceptic movement in Sweden. The Swedish June Movement, borrowing its name from its Danish counterpart, won 14 per cent of the vote and secured three of Sweden's 19 seats in the European Parliament. It was able to secure this result despite having been formed only months before the European poll, following the September 2003 referendum in which Swedish voters rejected the adoption of the euro. It is noteworthy, however, that the party's discourse is a relatively moderate one – accepting Swedish EU membership while campaigning against a further expansion of EU competence.

The case of the Swedish June Movement arguably moves towards the borderline of a fifth and final type of

Euroscepticism. This category encompasses movements which principally define themselves in terms of a critical stance as regards the European Union, but which wish to effect relatively modest reforms to the existing institutional structures of the Union, rather than advocating their wholesale refoundation or dismantling. This form of Euroscepticism significantly appeared for the first time only in the 2004 European Parliament election, in the cases of the Austrian 'List Hans-Peter Martin – For Real Control in Brussels' and the Dutch 'Transparent Europe' list led by Paul van Buitenen. The Martin list was led by a dissident MEP and former journalist who had been excluded from the Social-Democrat (SPÖ) list after exposing incidents of fraud and misconduct by his fellow MEPs, controversially through the use of a hidden camera and tape recorder. Martin's campaign thus focused on the need for a reform of the system by which MEPs' salaries and travel expenses are paid. In a similar vein, Paul van Buitenen was a former European Commission official whose 'whistle-blowing', exposing widespread financial improprieties, had significantly contributed to the downfall of the Santer Commission. Van Buitenen centred his campaign on the need for greater transparency and accountability in the European institutions, arguing that fully one-third of the EU budget was not subject to proper controls. Both movements, capturing very similar sentiments, enjoyed surprising success at the polls. The Martin list won 14 per cent of the vote and two seats in Austria, while Transparent Europe took 7 per cent of the vote and two seats in the Netherlands. It remains to be seen, however, whether either these two lists in particular or movements of this type more generally prove able to sustain themselves in the longer term. Dependent on particular personalities,

and likely supported in good part by electorates with more radically sceptical views about the EU than those expressed by the movement itself, there is perhaps an inherent volatility which marks this form of Euroscepticism.

Patterns and prospects

Media coverage of the 2004 European Parliament election tended to highlight a generalised increase in the level of Euroscepticism displayed across the newly enlarged Union. There is significant evidence, in a number of both new and established member states, which supports this analysis. In the Polish case, for example, 'protest' parties of the right (the League of Polish Families, the Law and Justice Party, and the Self-Defence Party) cumulatively won 39.4 per cent of the vote on the basis of platforms which encompassed comparatively strong Eurosceptic elements. Elsewhere, as detailed above, UKIP made major gains in Britain, while other Eurosceptical movements, such as the Swedish June list, successfully appeared on the scene. Yet, at the same time, the support for established Eurosceptical parties in both Denmark and France declined. In effect, it is difficult to speak meaningfully of pan-European trends as emerging from EP elections which remain essentially national contests. The level and form of the Euroscepticisms displayed in different member states is essentially explicable with reference to domestic political factors. It is the complex interaction of such factors as national attitudes towards European integration, the overall dynamics of the party system, the timing of the national electoral cycle, and the specific opportunity structures offered by EP elections which account for the success or failure of Eurosceptic movements and strategies in each individual case.

The influence of those Eurosceptics who have secured election to the Parliament is apt to remain limited. The more radical Eurosceptic tendencies, representing a great diversity of views, will continue to be spread across a number of smaller parliamentary groups. As such, they will, organisationally, carry only limited weight in the Parliament. Moreover, while more reformist agendas may coherently seek expression through the institution, the role which may be played by 'anti-European' MEPs remains singularly unclear – short of the 'wrecking' tactics suggested by the prominent UKIP MEP Robert Kilroy-Silk.

The broader influence of Euroscepticisms should not, however, be discounted. Euroscepticism clearly cannot be equated with only a one-dimensional resistance to European integration. Rather, it encompasses a wide spectrum of critical views and oppositions, which reflect the underlying processes of Europeanisation reshaping politics and governance at both the national and the European levels. In these multiple guises, Euroscepticism appears set to be an enduring feature of the European parliamentary landscape.

Robert Harmsen

Bibliography

Harmsen, R. and Spiering, M. (eds), *Euroscepticism: Party Politics, National Identity and European Integration*, Amsterdam/New York, Editions Rodopi, 2004 (European Studies 20).
Kopecký, P. and Mudde, C., 'The Two Sides of Euroscepticism: Party Positions on European Integration in East Central Europe', *European Union Politics*, 3, 3, 2002, pp. 297–326.
Szczerbiak, A. and Taggart, P. (eds), *Opposing Europe: the Comparative Party Politics of Euroscepticism*, Oxford, Oxford University Press, 2005, 2 vols.
Taggart, P. and Szczerbiak, A., 'The Party Politics of Euroscepticism in EU Member and Candidate States', Sussex European Institute, Working Paper 51, Brighton, Sussex European Institute, 2002 (http://www.sussex.ac.uk/Units/SEI/pdfs/wp51.pdf).

→ Electoral Behaviour; European Public Opinion; European Referendums; Extreme Left; Extreme Right; Identity; Sovereignism.

Extreme Left

The European extreme left: a political octopus?

The origins of left-wing radicalism can be traced back as far as the Ancient Greek realm when Plato described in *The Republic* the foundations of a communist society. However, it was mostly after the French Revolution and throughout the nineteenth century that the various theoretical streams were rejuvenated by contemporary European extreme left-wing parties and formally developed.

Among the best known of these ideologies are Marxism, libertarianism, anarchism, Blanqui-ism, Saint-Simonism, and Fourrierism to name but a few. All these schools of thought stemmed from the historical perception that West European societies of the nineteenth century failed to provide all citizens with equal resources and equal opportunities, or to generate standards of living that reflected the recent rapid progress made within agriculture, industry and the economy.

The anarchic tradition is one of the oldest forms of extreme-left ideologies in Europe. Even Plato and Aristotle themselves described forms of anarchic societies in their critique of democracy, and the liberal thinkers of the seventeenth and eighteenth centuries occasionally adopted elements of anarchism upon social and political grounds. However, it was towards the end of the eighteenth century with Godwin (1793) and the nineteenth century with Proudhon (1840) and Bakounin (1867) that anarchism and libertarianism became entirely theorised ideologies.

The anarchist model is only marginally compatible with the Marxist tradition developed by Marx and Engels (1848) as it tends to defy the materialist stance of Marxism. Marx assessed the evolution of history as based on a perpetual modification of economic tensions between the various social categories. After decades of struggle between the landed aristocracy and the bourgeois, Marx explained that the introduction of the capitalist economy resulted in a new opposition between the owners of capital and those who could only provide labour services. He suggested that while labour had become indispensable to the capitalist economy, the cartelisation of the political superstructure by the bourgeoisie would prevent workers progressing both economically and politically unless they started a revolution.

This perspective highly contrasted the 'idealist' models of Saint-Simon, Fourrier and Blanqui. The Saint-Simonian model of communistic cells inspired generations of extreme left-wing thinkers who were seduced by its reliance on neo-humanism and pure equality, while others were more impressed by the Commune-style organisation suggested by Blanqui who, also similar to Marx, believed in the necessary recourse to violence and revolution to free men from the oppression of the ruling classes.

Beyond these diverging historical roots, however, the extreme-left 'octopus' separated into three main distinct traditions when communist states emerged in 1917 in Russia, and after 1945 in most of East and Central Europe. For the first time, an extreme-left model of governance was given a chance to be implemented and thus became the dominant – if not the only – acceptable form of ideology in approximately half of the European continent.

As a result, three main types of extreme-left wing parties were competing for the 2004 European Parliament elections. Firstly, in most of the new member states, which had belonged to the communist bloc until the late 1980s, radical parts of the former Communist Party regrouped to form new political parties and competed in democratic elections. These parties usually tried to seduce voters who had been left behind by the political and economic transition and modernisation, and campaigned with reactionary and anti-West programmes. Secondly, most countries in Western Europe had strong communist parties throughout the Cold War. After the fall of communism, these parties went through periods of more or less thorough 'renovation'. They still compete in most Western European party systems, but have been marginalised and have tried to react to this by softening their main economic, political and social stances. Some of these parties have kept their traditional name, as in France, while others have preferred to change it, as in the Netherlands. Thirdly, throughout the second half of the twentieth century, but mostly from 1968 and the early 1970s onwards, a number of non-communist extreme left-wing parties emerged and competed in Western European party systems. They range from neo-anarchists to Trotskyites, and have never achieved significant electoral success. They occasionally resorted to violence, as in the German case, but whether they did or not, they have usually survived and remained regular players on their respective national political stage. In France, for instance, leader Arlette Laguiller remains one of the best-known politicians in the country despite never achieving any major electoral success.

The contemporary extreme left in Europe in the twenty-first century

While the extreme left remains a relatively significant political force in many European countries, it is undeniable that it assumes fundamentally different forms on both sides of the former Iron Curtain. To the East, radical minorities derived from the former communist parties tend to attract those who are nostalgic for the former regime, and occasionally present serious contenders to national government. To the West of the former curtain, however, extreme left-wing parties also include former communist parties, but also usually encompass more marginal parties than their Eastern counterparts. The parties that form the latter category are often built upon the foundations of former anarchic groups and of the most radical elements of the 1968 social protest movements.

Most of the communist and former communist parties in Europe belong to the common GUE/NGL group in the European Parliament (Group of the United Left). These parties had 17 seats in the 1999–2004 European Parliament. Other smaller and occasionally more radical parties, however, have tended to remain unaffiliated when they were able to send members to the European Parliament. In the new member states, some of these extreme left-wing parties remain very strong. For example, in Cyprus, the very left-wing AKEL is the first party of the country and obtained more than one-third of the votes in the last Cypriot general elections. In the Czech Republic, the KSČM is currently the third party in the national Parliament and obtained 18.5 per cent of the vote in the last general elections. However, in most other European Union member states, the extreme left regularly attracts anywhere between 0 and 15 per cent of the vote.

Altogether, the extreme left in Europe has survived the fall of communism much better in the South and in Scandinavia than elsewhere. It retains more than a tenth of the electorate in countries such as Greece and Portugal, and almost as many in Italy or France. It also captures about 13 per cent of the voters in Denmark, and about 10 per cent in Sweden and Finland. Since the unification of Germany, the former East German Communist Party, the PDS, also managed to restore a part of its former appeal. On the other hand, there is no sizeable extreme left-wing party in the UK, Belgium, Hungary, Austria or Slovenia.

The extreme left and Europe: positions and programmes

The relationship between the extreme left and European integration has traditionally been rather contentious. Campaigns for the European Parliament elections have predominantly included Eurosceptic themes mostly because the European project is criticised for being 'ultra-liberal' and serving the interests of capitalists and big business rather than those of the workers. In France, the anti-globalisation and 'alter-mondialiste' organisation ATTAC represents an increasingly popular tendency and is associated with the extreme left. It equates Europeanisation with globalisation and free trade and therefore opposes any further European integration. While most extreme-left parties are not as radical as ATTAC, they have capitalised on the widespread protests against the war in Iraq, promoted the use of diplomacy instead of force to install peace and demand the reinforcement of public services against the never-ending path towards greater liberalisation.

Since the 1990s, the parties of the extreme left have joined forces within the European Parliament to create a unified group (GUE/NGL) that represents and echoes their interests in Strasbourg and to propose alternative ways to the present direction of European integration.

The European extreme left in the 2004 European Parliament election

Table 1 illustrates the performance of the European extreme left-wing parties, which obtained representation in Strasbourg. It is very clear from the results that the 2004 European Parliament election was, by and large, a very good showing for the European extreme left, which surfed on the wave of anti-governmental attitudes throughout Europe. It is clear that – as for most other political parties which cannot pretend to have a chance of governing their country – the context of second-order elections makes the European Parliament vote more favourable to the extreme left than general elections. However, it remains significant to note that in most member states, parties of the extreme left have clearly improved their scores since the last general election. This is true in the case of Greece and Portugal, but also in France and Italy, where former communist parties managed to stop what once seemed to be a never-ending freefall. The only clear exception to this pattern is Cyprus, in

Table 1   The European extreme left in the 2004 European Parliament election

Country	Party	Vote (%)	Seats	Change EP/GE	Change E2004/1999
Cyprus	AKEL	27.9	2	–6.8	–
Czech Republic	KSČM	20.3	6	+1.8	–
Denmark	SF	8.0	1	+1.6	+0.9
	FB	5.2	1	–	–2.1
Finland	VAS	9.1	1	–0.8	–1.8
France	PCF	5.3	2	+0.5	–1.5
Germany	PDS	6.1	7	+1.8	+0.3
Greece	KKE	9.5	3	+3.6	+0.8
	SIN	4.2	1	+0.9	–1.0
Italy	RC	6.1	5	+1.1	+1.8
	PCI	2.4	2	+0.7	+0.4
Netherlands	SP	7.0	2	+0.7	+2.0
Portugal	PCP-CDU	9.0	2	+2.0	–1.3
	BE	5.0	1	+2.2	+3.2
Spain	IU	4.2	2	–0.8	–1.7
Sweden	VP	9.8	2	+1.5	–6.0
TOTAL			42 (+25)	+1	–0.4

Notes:
Change EP/GE measures the evolution of the party's share of the vote since the last general election.
All party representatives in the table belong to the GUE/NGL group, apart from the Portuguese BE, which remains unaffiliated.

which the status of the AKEL as the first party of the country and members of the governing coalition, undoubtedly cost them a potential share of the European Parliament vote.

As a whole, the GUE/NGL group, which most of the European extreme-left parties are affiliated to, saw its representation dramatically increase from 17 to 40 members of the European Parliament.

Conclusions

Overall, throughout Europe, while commentators have recently talked about a breakthrough of the extreme right, they usually think of the extreme left as a declining force. Rather, in the past 20 years, traditional communist parties have faced the biggest crisis of their history and have had to fight hard for their survival while many commentators thought that their disappearance was a foregone conclusion. Nevertheless, the 2004 European Parliament election will remain a good vintage for the extreme left more or less throughout Europe. Former communists of the East, former communists of the West, and non-communist parties globally registered better performances than in their last general election races, and most of them also achieved higher scores than in 1999. More significantly yet, the combination of Eastern members with the extreme-left family allowed the GUE/NGL group in the European Parliament to more than double its representation and attain a sizeable weight in Strasbourg. Nevertheless, the European extreme-left family, typically anti-EU, and disagreeing in the various member states on the need to modernise, has found it difficult to find a common ground both prior to and after the European Parliament election. For all these reasons, the European extreme left, which was the first ideology to claim its internationalism in the nineteenth century, remains, ideologically and strategically, one of the most dispersed party families in Europe.

Sarah Harrison

Bibliography

Dunphy, R., *Contesting Capitalism? Left Parties and European Integration*, Manchester, Manchester University Press, 2004.
McClosky, H. and Chong, D., 'Similarities and Differences between Left-Wing and Right-Wing Radicals', *British Journal of Political Science*, 15, 3, 1985, pp. 329–63.
Marks, G., Wilson, C. J. and Ray, L., 'National Political Parties and European Integration', *American Journal of Political Science*, 46, 3, 2002, pp. 585–94.

→ Extreme Right; Mapping Europe: European Electoral Geography.

Extreme Right

The extreme right in Europe: conceptual puzzles

While the extreme right is one of the most discussed party families in Europe at the moment, political scientists have rarely agreed on a common definition or even a common list of the members within this category. Indeed, the plethora of labels used by political scientists to talk about the same party family symbolise these intellectual controversies: 'neo-Fascist' (Cheles et al. 1991), 'radical right-wing' (Betz 1994), 'new populist' (Betz and Immerfall 1998), 'new right' (Minkenberg 2000), 'new radical right' parties (Kitschelt 1995), and 'national populist' (Mudde 2004). Beyond these heterogeneous labels, fundamental disagreements are exposed as scholars fail to agree on the common features and distinctive criteria that allegedly unite the members of the 'extreme right' party family, and often disagree on whether these parties constitute a party family at all.

Among the political scientists that have tried to provide a consensual definition of extreme right-wing parties, Ignazi (2003) claims that 'in order to be a member of the extreme-right family, a party should fulfil three conditions: (1) it should be located at the right-wing pole of the political spectrum such that no other party is further to the right; (2) it should express an ideal-ideological linkage with fascist mythology and principles; and (3) it should express a set of beliefs that undermines the fundamentals of a polity. However, Ignazi's proposal is considered to be highly problematic for a variety of reasons: it does not allow for the emergence of more than one extreme-right party per political system, it is ideologically subjective, and finally, it ties the contemporary extreme right to a narrow historical model, which according to many political scientists it transcends.

By contrast, Bruter and Harrison (2004) suggest that extreme-right parties of several types exist and are defined by varying combinations of four core components: (1) a discourse based on utopia, the demand for a paradoxical revolution, and the rejection of an assumed consensus; (2) an exclusive conception of identity, which usually leads to a rejection of the other, in the form of racism, anti-Semitism, and/or xenophobia; (3) populism: with references to anti-partyism, and anti-systemism; and (4) an implicit link between order and force, with a focus on strong leadership, the fear of crime and insecurity, and a promise to restore law and order in societies deemed to be otherwise chaotic.

The extreme-right party family in Europe

While a theoretical definition of the extreme right has been the focus of many a discussion among political scientists, most will agree on the core members of the party family in Europe – although here again, controversies are not unusual especially concerning the parties on the fringes of the ideological spectrum. In this article, we will include the parties that are identified by most experts as extreme right wing (even though other scholars will disagree with one or another of the members, e.g. the List Pim Fortuyn in the Netherlands is not extreme right for Mudde, the Alleanza Nazionale is not for Ignazi, the Danish and Norwegian nationalist parties are considered to be extreme right depending on the scholars who assess their case, etc) and which usually obtain a relatively sizeable share of the vote in their country, that is, about 1 per cent or more of the vote. In parallel, however, we will not include the UK Independence Party, which is not yet recognised to be an extreme right-wing party by a majority of scholars, even though its style and rhetoric are clearly reminiscent of other members of the party family.

Therefore, our analysis will include: the Freiheitliche Partei Österreichs (FPÖ) in Austria; the Vlaams Blok (VB) in Belgium; the Dansk Folkeparti (DF) in Denmark; Front National (FN) and Mouvement National Republicain (MNR) in France; Die Republikaner (REP), the Nationaldemokratische Partei Deutschlands (NPD) and the Deutsche Volksunion (DVU) in Germany; the Laikos Orthodoxos Synagermos (LAOS) in Greece; the Alleanza Nazionale (AN), the Lega Nord (LN), the Lista Mussolini (AS) and the Movimento Sociale Fiamma Tricolore (FT) in Italy; the Apvienība 'Tēvzemei un Brīvībai'/LNNK

(TB/LNNK) in Latvia; List Pim Fortuyn (LPF) in the Netherlands; the Liga Polskich Rodzin (LPR) and the Prawo i Sprawiedliwość (PiS) in Poland; the Partido Popular (CDS-PP) in Portugal; the Pravá Slovenská Národná Strana (PSNS) and Slovenská Národná Strana (SNS) in Slovakia; and the British National Party (BNP) in the United Kingdom.

The extreme right in the 2004 European Parliament elections – Western Europe

Traditionally, European Parliament elections have been a particularly successful platform for European extreme right-wing parties. The second-order and mid-term election phenomena, combined with the dominant use of proportional representation systems in most countries, including those which do not use it for general elections (France, UK) have enabled extreme-right parties in the past to obtain consistently high scores. Eurosceptic campaign themes have also proved to be quite fruitful for the extreme right over the years. As the 2004 elections were expected to be a particularly caricatural example of second-order elections, in which citizens would take the opportunity to express their widespread discontent with their national governments, extreme right-wing parties were hoping for another major breakthrough.

The results of extreme right-wing parties in each country are summarised in Table 1. In Western Europe, it seems that the election turned out to be particularly successful for the Vlaams Blok, which confirmed its position as the number one party in many Flemish areas. The election results were also deemed to be particularly encouraging by many 'marginal' extreme right-wing parties, such as those of Britain (BNP) and

Germany (Republikaner [REP] and NPD). Finally, in Italy, the Alleanza Nazionale and the Lega Nord resisted much better, on the whole, than their dominant coalition partner, Forza Italia, the efforts of the left to score points two years before the general elections, and the wave of anti-war sentiment in the country.

At the same time, the 2004 election proved to be a bitter disappointment for the French extreme right, with the MNR literally blown out of the water with less than 0.5 per cent of the vote, and the Front National limited to less than 10 per cent of the votes only two years after their much publicised presidential run-off. Similarly, the FPÖ did not manage to halt its progressive downfall as they lost yet further ground after their disappointing performance at the last general elections. As for the List Pim Fortuyn, the European Parliament election confirmed its inability to survive the death of its charismatic leader, and it did not even manage to send a representative to Strasbourg. The score of the Dansk Folkeparti in Denmark was equally disastrous as compared to their last general election performance.

The extreme right in Central Europe

While the West European extreme right did not achieve the spectacular result they had hoped for, the emergence of new extreme-right, nationalist and xenophobic parties in Central and Eastern Europe was dramatically confirmed at the polls. Only a few months after the referendums, which had seemed to show some Euro-enthusiasm amongst the new entrants, extreme-right wing groups used Eurosceptic programmes and took advantage of very high levels of abstention in order to feature amongst the leading political formations of their respective countries (Table 1).

Table 1   The extreme right in the 2004 European Parliament elections: results and trends

Country	Party	Vote (%)	Seats	Change-GE	Change-EP
Austria	FPÖ	6.3	1	–3.7	–17.1
Belgium	VB	14.3	3	+2.6	+5.0
Denmark	DF	6.8	1	–5.2	+1
France	FN	9.8	7	–1.5	+4.1
	MNR	0.4	0	–0.7	–
Germany	REP	1.9	0	+1.3	+0.2
	NPD	0.9	0	+0.5	+0.5
	DVU	–	–	–	–
Greece	LAOS	4.2	1	+1.9	–1.0
Italy	AN	11.5	9	–0.5	+1.2
	LN	5.0	4	+1.1	+0.5
	AS	1.2	1	–	–
	FT	0.7	1	+0.3	–0.9
Latvia	TB/LNNK	29.8	4	+24.4	–
Netherlands	LPF	2.6	0	–3.1	–
Poland	LPR	15.9	10	+8.0	–
	PiS	12.7	7	+3.2	–
Portugal	CDS-PP	*	2	*	*
Slovakia	PSNS+SNS	2.0	0	–5.0	–
UK	BNP	4.9	0	+4.7	+3.9
EUROPE-25			51		+20 seats**

Notes:
Change GE and Change EP represent change in vote share since the last general and European elections respectively.
PSNS and SNS in Slovakia ran a joint list for the European election.
 * The Portuguese CDS-PP ran common lists with the Social Democratic Party (right).
** Total number of seats for the European Parliament increased from 626 to 730 with the last enlargement. Without counting new Central and East European countries, the number of seats of the extreme-right group in the Parliament would have decreased by 1 rather than increased by 20.

In Latvia, the right-wing nationalist TB/LNNK managed to capture the first position in the European Parliament elections. Almost three out of ten voters cast their vote in their favour. Similarly, in Poland, the Christian radical LPR more than doubled its score from the last general election and came second in the national contest, while the right-wing populist PiS made a dramatic entrance onto the European Parliament stage with 12.7 per cent of the votes and seven MEPs.

Conclusions

The 2004 European Parliament elections presented a mixed picture of the fortunes of the European extreme right. Traditionally, European Parliament elections have been the main showcase for

European right-wing extremists. Time after time, they have used the European stage to parade their Eurosceptic and neo-populist programmes, and have benefited from highly mobilised voters, and from helpful electoral systems.

If the 2004 election was a great success for the extreme right in Central and Eastern Europe, and in the countries in which it had traditionally found it difficult to gain a stronghold (such as the United Kingdom and Germany), it proved disappointing for most of Western Europe's relatively large and well-established extreme right-wing parties, except of course in Belgium and Italy. After the results of the election were announced, the extreme-right family was split between a relatively 'moderate' and institutionalised group, which co-operated within the framework of the UEN (Union of European Nations) nationalist group in the European Parliament, and the other parties, which remain unaffiliated. This may serve to illustrate the choice of strategies extreme right-wing parties have faced in recent years, both on the national and European stages. On the one hand, some parties have tried to enter coalitions with mainstream parties in an effort to gain legitimacy and respectability sometimes at the cost of their electoral appeal (FPÖ). Other parties, however, have chosen to reinforce their alleged 'difference' with the political classes of their respective countries, running the risk of remaining on the periphery of their national political system and ultimately seeing prospects of governing their countries progressively fade away (Front National).

It remains to be seen whether the 2004 European Parliament elections will prove to be yet another watermark in the evolution of the European extreme right, and whether the strong progress of the national-xenophobic political discourse in East and Central Europe will durably modify the strategies of the European extreme right, which, recently impressed by the apparent success of the FPÖ in Austria and the Alleanza Nazionale in Italy, might fall for the more radical and aggressive rhetorics of these successful new little brothers from the East.

Sarah Harrison

Bibliography

Betz, H., *La droite populiste en Europe: Extrême et démocratie?*, Paris, CEVIPOF-Autrement, 2004 (1st edition 1994).

Betz, H. and Immerfall, S., *The New Politics of the Right*, London, St. Martin's Press, 1998.

Bruter, M. and Harrison, S., 'Cocktail Politics', paper presented at 'The European and Australian Far Right: Pathology and Prospects', National Europe Centre, Australian National University, Canberra, 6 August 2004.

Cheles, L., Ferguson, R. and Vaughan, M., *Neo-Fascism in Europe*, London, Longman, 1991.

Ignazi, P., 'The Silent Counter-Revolution: Hypotheses on the Emergence of Extreme-Right Parties in Europe', *European Journal of Political Research*, 22, 1, 1992, pp. 3–34.

Ignazi, P., *Extreme Right Parties in Western Europe*, Oxford, Oxford University Press, 2003.

Kitschelt, H., *The Radical Right in Western Europe: a Comparative Analysis*, Ann Arbor, University of Michigan Press, 1995.

Minkenberg, M., 'The Renewal of the Radical Right: Between Modernity and Anti-Modernity', *Government and Opposition*, 35, 2, 2000, pp. 170–88.

Mudde, C., 'Is the "Extreme Right" Really "Extreme Right"?', paper presented at 'The European and Australian Far Right: Pathology and Prospects', National Europe Centre, Australian National University, Canberra, 6 August 2004.

→ Extreme Left; Mapping Europe: European Electoral Geography.

Federations of Political Parties

European federations of political parties have known a significant development in the past 15 years as a new topic of interest for political scientists, in particular since their role was officially enshrined in the Maastricht Treaty. European federations have also benefited from the integrated measures of the Nice Treaty, which aimed at regulating their financing and guaranteeing their legal status. These new measures came into force at the end of 2003. Nevertheless the history of transnational partisan organisations is already old. Considered as essential actors for the good functioning of representative democracy, parties have tried to adapt themselves to the new European environment. At first, they did so by developing original structures in the European assemblies.

History and developments

As soon as the Council of Europe was created, national political parties sent their representatives to that first embryo of a supranational parliamentary arena. In 1953, during the first meeting of the ECSC, the first national and transnational parliamentary groups were created at a European level. Despite strong expectations, these parliamentary groups did not bring about any significant change in the area of transnational democracy. Their ideological diversity, conflicts of partisan and national interests, and the election of the members of the Assembly through national general elections meant that the parties' national identities were reinforced. After several years of hesitation, the first truly European elections took place in 1979. This led to the setting up of the first European federations of political parties: the Party of European Socialists (PES) was born in 1974, the European People's Party (EPP) in 1976, and the Liberal Party Federation of the European Community in 1976. Finally, the European Free Alliance (EFA), which grouped regionalist parties from various member states, was born a few years later, in 1981.

Further European institutional reforms have deeply marked the history of European party federations. The decision to use direct universal suffrage for European Parliament elections implicitly recognised the integrative function of the national parties in society, even at European level. The political sphere in which parties evolve is enriched by a new supplementary power that has to be linked to already existing capabilities. The national partisan elites tried to adapt their partisan structures to this new institutional environment. The Single European Act, the Maastricht Treaty (1992), the Amsterdam Treaty (1997), and the Nice Treaty (2000) all reinforced the European Parliament. They offered European party federations – or rather their constitutive entities – opportunities to influence the European decision-making process. The introduction of Article 138A in the Maastricht Treaty explicitly recognised the role of 'European political parties', claiming that European political parties are important as integrating factors in the

Union and that they contribute to the formation of a 'European consciousness' and to 'the expression of the political will' of EU citizens. This institutional recognition led to a certain crystallisation of European party federations. Symbolically, the socialists transformed the party federation into an actual 'political party', the European Socialist Party (ESP). The liberal federations did the same and created the ELDR party, and so did the regionalists with the creation of the EFA. At the same time, the Green party family made a very important symbolic step by creating a strongly structured Federation of Green Parties.

However, this evolution did not provide European party federations with legal status or strong sources of public funding. The Nice Treaty (2000) did both, confirming the supposed place of European party federations in the European political system. In what became Article 191 of the Amsterdam Treaty an important paragraph was added to explain that the Council, ruling in accordance with the procedure of Article 251, 'establishes the status of European political parties' and, in particular, defined the rules relating to their financing.

After some tough and complex discussions, an agreement was reached on the modes of public funding affecting European parties. The agreement on the new measures generated some new developments. The first one was the constitution of two new European political party federations: the Party of the Democratic Left, which incorporates some communist and post-communist parties, and the European Democratic Union aiming at federating centre parties who had left the EPP. This new group was largely set up on the initiative of François Bayrou, leader of the Union for French Democracy (UDF) and Franco Rutelli, in charge of the Margherita in Italy. Moreover, the Federation of Green Parties changed its name and also became a party, the European Green Party (EGP). No less than seven European parties now work within European institutions and more will undoubtedly emerge.

Functions and organisation

The characteristics of European governance have implications for the functioning of European party federations. Parties have to compete in a system of multilevel governance: regional, national and European. This implies the reinforcement of their functions as links between the different levels of policy-making. By contrast, the important decentralisation of European governance, the complex functional character of the EU, and the subtleties of its institutional system strongly impede the development of the role of European party federations. If the EU is a form of constraint for these new actors, it also provides them, in principle, with a certain margin of manoeuvre. Independently of the institutional context, European party federations are essentially composed of national parties. Until the recent adoption of a public funding system for European parties, it was national parties which concentrated the main source of legitimacy and resources and only indirectly shared it with the party federations. On the political and material levels, the development of the party federations has been intimately linked to the good will of their constitutive entities and of political groups within the European Parliament. For this reason, the main and most obvious arena of action for European parties has been European Parliament elections.

The organisational characteristics of transnational federations are widely conditioned by their character as 'indirect parties' in a Duvergerian sense, and by the specificity of their constitutive elements – the member parties – and of the political systems in which they evolve. The European federations have largely worked as 'meeting places'. Today, to a certain extent, they are also arenas that make it easier to co-ordinate the efforts of national and European partisan elites who feel part of a given political family aiming at influencing European decisions. Each party family tries to create a formal and informal network, linking the different vertical (European, national, regional) as well as horizontal (executive nets, parliamentary, judicial) levels of power around specific themes. European party federations serve an important function as co-ordination centres of partisan networks. As a result, one could say that European party federations are largely confederal in essence. Most of the time, they present a weak centre, whose power is limited by strongly autonomous components, the national parties.

A sort of mimesis, strongly encouraged by the European institutional context, has conditioned the structures of European federations. Most are centred around comparable internal organs. The 'Congress' is by status the prime institution. It assembles the largest number of party delegates and dictates the general political lines of the federation. The Congress often serves national parties in electoral campaigns by attracting the media and promptly conveying the speeches of major European figureheads of each political family. The 'Councils' are assemblies of national delegates who meet several times a year to propose reports and joint declarations on a number of European themes. These are often first debated in working groups composed of a few specialised national delegates and experts. The primary instance in the daily life of the federation is the 'Bureau' or more precisely its General Secretary, which is the only organ of the federation which works with a permanent team.

Councils as well as Congresses are often paralysed by the number of participants, as well as linguistic and financial difficulties. The Bureau is comparatively efficient and assures the federation its political representation. It essentially takes administrative decisions, but it is relatively autonomous regarding national parties in its functioning. Finally, certain federations have a 'Council of Party Leaders', supreme intergovernmental forums which assemble the most influential members of the party family before European Councils. These represent important media-exposed moments, but are also occasions where consensus between national parties may be reached. The decisions taken may concern questions of long- or short-term policy. The meetings organised by the EPP and ESP are the most important ones taking into account the political weight of these two families in the national governments. Considering the member parties of EPP and ESP, which have numerous representatives in national governments and are dominant political forces in most of the 25 countries of the EU, have made these meetings particularly important and largely 'executive oriented'. Although these preparatory meetings have their limits, not to be a member of any can today be a handicap for a party which has national level responsibilities.

Indeed, the relevance of the member parties at the national level is also an important factor. It conditions the structure of the European party federation. Weak parties at the national level have an even greater incentive to try to develop structures at the European level to influence political decisions (European Green Party, regionalist parties, etc.).

With a new chapter of their history opening, European party federations are subject to the same tension as the EU itself, between the contradictory dynamics of enlargement and deepening. The competition between party families and the recent enlargement of the EU has led to an important growth in the number of members of each federation. At the same time, if we take the example of the EPP, it means that an originally consistent Christian Democrat federation has had to open up and diversify to include a number of Conservative and Liberal parties. Thus, on 1 January 2006, it included 41 parties in the federation, 9 associate parties and 11 observers. The other European parties try not to be left behind. The ESP also includes 32 parties, 8 associated parties and 5 observers; as for the ELDR, it includes 47 members, the European Greens, 32, the EFA, 30, and the European left, 15. These figures must be considered with caution. Some parties which are part of the large federations may occasionally have a (very) weak political presence in their regional or national spectrum, particularly outside of the two largest federations. Moreover, this increase in the number of members has sometimes exacerbated internal tensions, either among the parties from the same member state, even more often between parties from different countries but with different ideological affiliations or perceptions.

European party federations are therefore facing important strategic decisions. Official recognition and public funding – however modest – have brought them a new form of autonomy, both from their constitutive entities, the national parties, and from the parliamentary groups within the European Parliament. The new role that they may play within European institutions is still unclear, but the way they manage to impose themselves within the next few years will undoubtedly be a key element of their long-term future influence.

Pascal Delwit

→ European Democratic Union; European Federation of Green Parties; European Free Alliance (EFA); European Liberal Democrat and Reform Party (ELDR); European People's Party (EPP); European Political Parties; Party of European Socialists (PES).

Financing

The procedure of financing political parties in the EU differs greatly from the one in use in the United States. Whilst in the US, one has to deal with a plutocratic process relying on substantial private donations regulated by fierce competition, the financing of political parties in the European Union is characterised by public donations subjected to parliamentary controls. The latter model faces structural difficulties, mainly due to the absence of 'real' European parties, and to the fact that the funding of electoral campaigns remains largely at the expense of the individual member states. Nevertheless, an annual budget of approximately 10 billion euros has been created and managed by the European Parliament, and a codification of funding criteria has been initiated. Regulations lay the ground for what could become, in the words of Weber, 'the material direction of partisan activity' surrounding European elections.

In terms of the European Council and Parliament, the allocation of EU funds is justified by the role played by political parties in the construction of the Union, and 'the education' of the general public in particular. Article 191 TEC, which saw the Council ruling in conformity with Article 251, establishes the status of European political parties and outlines the rules relating to their funding. This act separated the recognition of European political parties on the one hand, and questions relating to their financing on the other hand. Nonetheless, political and judicial friction increased, and a real framework for action only began to emerge after the year 2000. In February 2001, a first proposal for regulations offered a few initial guidelines. Among others, the guidelines stated that parties must avoid transferring funds for national activities of the main European groups such as the EPP and the ESP (principle of subsidiarity). In addition, clarification of relations between these political groups was highlighted.. Finally, initial guidelines also included the reservation of funding benefits to structures represented by European, regional or national representatives elected in at least five member states or obtaining at least 5 per cent of the vote in five member states during the latest European elections. This system was designed to protect the party systems from splits and to avoid the misappropriation of funds. Similarly, the Commission devised a management format to ensure 'financial transparency'. It stipulated that at least 25 per cent of a party's budget had to be autonomous (i.e. coming from donations, membership fees, etc.). In terms of the EU subsidy, 15 per cent of it was shared in equal parts among all parties, while 85 per cent was proportionally allocated to the elected members of 'European parties' represented in the European Parliament. One of the conditions was that parties should publicise their accounts and financing sources (including donations) and submit financial reports to the scrutiny of the EU Audit Office. Several control measures were set up to fulfil this role: external and independent audits, an independent committee in charge of dealing with disputes etc. However, the definition of a 'European party' in practical terms was extremely ambiguous. In fact, the notion was vaguely defined as: 'any mobilising structure which, electing its representatives through democratic suffrage, endorses the respect of the fundamental right of the State established by the Treaty and Charter of Fundamental Rights; it also includes any structure which, dealing with European issues, whether in favour or not of European integration will have secured sufficient votes and agreed to establish a group at the European Parliament.'

Submitted to the European Parliament, this codification of the status and financing of the parties was adopted on 17 May 2001 at the first round with 349 votes in favour, 80 votes against and 17 abstentions (JOCO34E of 7 February 2002). Meanwhile, it must be noted that more than 20 amendments were adopted to reinforce the control mechanisms and to prohibit public enterprises and activities largely controlled by the member state being allowed to make donations or join a 'European political party'. While the vast majority of such amendments were approved by the Commission, the latter point was met with opposition. The issue regarding the status of political parties also caused strong divisions within the Council. The 2002 Spanish and Danish Presidencies were firmly opposed to guidelines. However, the enactment of the Nice Treaty on 1 February 2003, allowed this dynamic to be relaunched: seizing the opportunity of a new European Council, heads of states and governments approved the amendment of Article 191, in accordance with directions given by the European Parliament and Commission. From this point forward, the Council would take its decisions by qualified majority voting. As far as the legislative procedure was concerned, it would become one of co-decision.

A second decision consolidating the model regulating the funding of European political parties was taken on 19 February 2003. Firstly, by accepting a stricter definition of a 'European party', now defined as 'a political party or an alliance of political parties whose status is registered with the European Parliament in conformity with the conditions and procedures defined in the present rules'. As an 'association of citizens', a political party must pursue political objectives, and must be legally recognised by at least one member state. An 'alliance of parties' is defined as structured co-operation established among two or more political parties.

In order to obtain their statute from the European Parliament, the 'party' or 'alliance' has to fulfil a certain number of conditions: (1) it must exist in at least three member states; (2) have participated in elections or have communicated in writing its intention to do so to the European Parliament; (3) designate the organs responsible for its political and financial management; (4) respect the principles of freedom, democracy and human rights, as well as the fundamental rights of states.

With respect to funding benefits allocated from the EU budget, parties require legal status in one of the member states. Moreover, they also need to be represented by elected members of the European Parliament or of national or regional assemblies, in at least one-third of the member states or have gained at least 5 per cent of the votes during European elections in at least one-third of the member states. If EU funding is secured, party leaders must publish an annual list of expenses, as well as a declaration of income. Moreover, all sources of funding including donations over 100 euros have to be made public. Certain sources of funding such as anonymous donations from political groups in the European Parliament, as well as contributions from legal entities in which the state owns more than 50 per cent of the capital, and donations exceeding 5000 euros per year per donor are forbidden. However, it was possible for a European party to receive funding from one of its members.

A new proposal based on Article 7 stipulated that funding deriving from the EU budget could not be used to finance electoral campaigns or national parties. They were also subjected 'to administrative expenses, to information and publications as well as meetings and fees relating to studies'. Adopted by the Parliament on 19 June 2003, by 345 votes in favour, 132 against and 34 abstentions, this resolution was one of the first instances of the co-decision procedure in an institutional matter. The amendments appeared to only marginally modify the main points outlined in the original Commission proposal. In fact, these amendments stipulated that a 'European party' had to be a legal entity in the member state where it has its headquarters. It had to be represented in at least a quarter of the member states through MEPs or national and regional parliamentarians. Alternatively it had to have gained 3 per cent or more votes at EP elections in a minimum of a quarter of member states. In addition, a list of all donations above 500 euros (rather than the 100 originally proposed by the Commission) had to be published. As far as the upper limit of donations by legal and moral entities was concerned, it was fixed at 12 000 euros per year (well over the 5000 euros originally suggested by the European Commission). While the source of membership fees was accepted, they could not exceed 40 per cent of its annual budget. The Commission proposal outlining which EU funds could not be used to finance electoral campaigns was suppressed on 29 September 2003 at the Council, when Denmark, Italy and Austria voted against. All of the aforementioned clauses came into force following the June 2004 European elections.

What lessons can be drawn from the European financing model? Firstly, it is one that is not centred on the candidates unlike the system in the US. Secondly, it limits the potentially fraudulent practices of some industrial and commercial groups in securing favours for donations. The management of funding is controlled at the national level. In

Germany, the so-called Rhineland model is a system of funding combining parliamentary control, the delegation of competencies, and the partisan co-management of resources. The recent Presidents of the three federations of European parties have looked towards Article 21 of the Fundamental Law of the German Federal Republic that recognises a party as an association aiming at informing and promoting civic knowledge. The European Popular Party (EPP) created in April 1976 (taking over the Christian Democrat European Union, established in 1965), the European Socialist Party (ESP), established during The Hague Congress in 1992 (replacing the Socialist Party Union of the European Community created in 1974) and the Federation of Liberal-Democratic Parties created in 1976 have all used this guideline. Their leaders have, since September 1990, organised a number of meetings in order to devise a set of common rules to this complex game. They finally reached an agreement testified by a joint letter addressed on 1 July 1991 to the Presidents of the European Council, Commission and Parliament (signed by Wilfried Martens in the name of the EPP, by Guy Spitaels for the European Socialist Party, and by Willy de Clercq for the reformist Federation of Liberal-Democratic Parties). After this agreement, the EU funding model would neither be a liberal one characterised by external subscriptions, nor a social-democratic one based on members' contributions. In contrast, it would become a party-oriented one, based on public subventions adding a transnational dimension to the resources that have to be mobilised for and by electoral campaigns at the national level. Such specific, albeit still marginal, regulation is surely indicative of the type of democracy characterising electoral politics in the European Union.

Olivier Ihl

Bibliography

Bardi, L., 'Transnational Party Federations, European Parliamentary Groups and the Building of Europarties', in R. S. Katz and P. Mair (eds), *How Parties Organize*, London, Sage, 1994, pp. 357–72.

European Parliament (Constitutional Affairs Commission), Resolution A5-0167/2001, of 17 May 2001 (JO C154E of 29 May 2001).

European Parliament (Constitutional Affairs Commission), Resolution A5-0170/2003, of 19 June 2003 (PV PE333.022).

Johansson, K. M. and Zervakis, P., *European Political Parties between Co-operation and Integration*, Baden-Baden, Nomos, 2002.

→ Campaign (Sociology of); Campaign Accounts; European Political Parties.

Finland

European Parliament elections in Finland have been characterised in the past by demobilisation and a distinct lack of interest of the electorate and the national political elites. Since 1995, the year in which Finland joined the EU, the three leading parties, the centrist (KESK, ELDR), the conservative (KOK, EPP-DE) and the social-democrat (SDP, PSE) have secured between 69 per cent and 81 per cent of the votes in the European elections. The first group of MEPs was selected by the national parliament in 1995. During the first elections of 1996, participation rates were recorded at 57.6 per cent, but levels of turnout have subsequently dropped to a low 30.1 per cent in 1999. The third European Parliament elections in 2004 saw an increase in levels of participation that brought the figure back up to a better 41.1 per cent. Nonetheless, participation rates for the 1999 and 2004 elections were below the EU average (49.8 per cent in 1999, 45.7 per cent in 2004). In contrast, levels of participation recorded during national legislative elections (65.3 per cent in 1999, 69.7 per cent in 2003) are significantly higher than their European counterparts.

Electoral system and campaigns

The voting system is proportional and preferential. Elections are based on a national single-constituency. Parties and electoral associations (*valitsijamiesyhdis-tys*) need a minimum of 2000 voters in order to be officially recognised, and have the right to designate candidates. Each party may present a maximum of 20 candidates. During European elections, the electorate votes for individuals rather than for parties. In this respect, European elections resemble presidential rather than legislative elections. The allocation of the seats takes place in accordance with the d'Hondt method, classifying candidates based on the number of votes they obtain. In order to be considered for the distribution of seats, parties and electoral associations must secure a minimum of 5 per cent of the votes cast. European campaigns are characterised by the absence of traditional political organisations. Since 1996 candidates, media, national newspapers (the most important daily is *Helsingin Sanomat*, which issues 440 000 copies in a country of 5.2 million inhabitants) as well as national TV programmes have contributed to initiating electoral campaigns.

As in most other EU member states, European election campaigns are centred on national policy themes. During the last elections, the issue of structural funding, the future of Finnish agriculture, social security and national defence issues dominated the agendas of 227 candidates from 14 political parties,

ensuring fierce competition. Similar to the 1999 elections, the campaign was characterised by the withdrawal of the leaders of the main political parties. This is partly explained both by the general consensus existing among the executives of the Finnish political elites on the European question, and by the diversity of opinions on Europe within political parties. The preferential voting mode and the high rate of abstention have hindered the creation of an anti-European populist movement opposing the ruling party, as was the case in Denmark and Sweden. Consequently, in 2004, as in 1999 and 1996, European elections in Finland have not been transformed into sanction votes against the government, elites or the EU as a whole (contrary to Reif and Schmitt's analysis, 1980). Nevertheless, this lack of involvement of the key political elites sent a negative message to the electorate: if political leaders do not take European elections seriously, why vote?

In order to encourage citizens to vote, the government allocated a budget of 1.9 million euros dedicated to information campaigns carried out by political parties in 2004 (1 million euros in 1999). This increase was necessary due to the rising costs of an election campaign revolving around the appointment of individuals in a national constituency. The average budget available to Finnish MEPs increased by about 50 per cent, going from 67 000 euros in 1999 to 99 000 euros in 2004. For instance, the official budget available to centrist candidate and MEP Kyosti Virrankoski grew from 150 000 euros in 1999 to 299 000 euros in 2004.

Analysis of electoral results

Finnish European elections are generally characterised by political stability. In fact, the three major parties won

Table 1 Finnish European election results in 2004, 1999 and 1996, and national legislatives (PN, Eduskunta) in 2003

	EP 1995	EP 1996	EP 1999	NP 2003	EP 2004
KOK (PPE-DE)	4	20.2 (4)	25.3 (4)	18.6	23.7 (4)
KESK (ELDR)	5	24.4 (4)	21.3 (4)	24.7	23.4 (4)
SDP (PSE)	4	21.5 (4)	17.9 (3)	24.5	21.2 (3)
VIHR (Greens)	1	7.6 (1)	13.4 (2)	8.0	10.4 (1)
VAS (GUE/NGL)	1	10.5 (2)	9.1 (1)	9.9	9.1 (1)
RKP (ELDR)	1	5.8 (1)	6.8 (1)	4.6	5.7 (1)
SKL (PPE-DE)	–	2.8 (–)	2.4 (1)	5.3	4.3 (–)

Source: Tilastokeskus, http://www.stat.fi/tk/he/vaalit/vaalit2004eur/
Notes: Percentage of votes (number of seats in brackets), for 1995 in number of seats (election by the national parliament).

between 69 per cent (1999) and 81 per cent (1995) of the seats. The three main parties won between three and five seats, while small parties like the Greens, the Swedish People's party, the left and the Christian Democrats, secured between one and two seats (Table 1).

In 1999, the Greens and Conservatives were the undisputed election winners. According to a study by the Finnish Statistics Bureau, these parties gained a maximum number of votes in regions where services constituted the main profession and where the percentage of unemployed and retired was relatively low. Among the losers of the election, the Social-Democrat Party was pushed back mostly in regions dominated by the professions of services and industries, whereas the centrist party acquired new votes in rural regions, whilst losing ground in tertiary areas.

In 2004, participation rates had increased by 11 per cent compared to preceding elections. This meant that 400 000 people had chosen to vote in the 2004 European elections. This increase was clearest in the Southern electoral constituencies. In the Helsinki constituency, more than half of the people (52.3 per cent) voted, whereas the lowest participation rates were recorded in Northern Carelia, near the Russian border (32.6 per cent), a rural region severely affected by unemployment.

The main losers of the 2004 European elections in terms of seats were the Greens (VIHR, Greens), who lost one of their two seats despite a higher number of votes (+ 2.4 per cent) than the one recorded at the 2003 legislative elections. Similarly, the Christian Democrats (SKL, PPE-DE) lost their only seat. In contrast, the main winners were the Conservative Party (KOK, PP-DE) and the Swedish People's Party (SFP, ELDR). These two groups maintained all their seats despite the smaller number of seats allocated to Finland (from 16 to 14) in the European Parliament. This can be mainly attributed to the higher number of votes compared to the 2003 legislative elections (KOK +5.1 per cent and SFP +1.1 per cent). Of the main parties in power, the Social-Democrats (SPD, PSE), managed to preserve three seats, despite their 3.3 per cent loss compared to the 2003 legislative elections.

As a whole, the three main parties, the Conservative opposition, centrist and Social-Democrats, maintained their seats and together won 11 of the 14 seats and more than the two-thirds (68.3 per cent) of the total number of ballot papers cast. As was the case during the 1999 European elections, the Conservative Party came out as the 2004 election winner with 302 771 votes, i.e. 23.7 per cent of the total number of votes. Nevertheless, compared to previous European elections, the Conservative Party lost 1.6 per cent of the votes. In second place, behind the Conservative Party, the centrist party was elected by 387 217 voters, securing 23.4 per cent of all votes, marking a 2.1 per cent increase compared to the 1999 EP elections during which the party shared a list with the Swedish People's Party and Christian Democrats. Maintaining its seats, the Social-Democratic party won 350 525 votes, an increase of 3.3 per cent compared to the preceding European elections. In terms of European parliamentary groups, the 2004 European election results for Finland are as follows: ELDR, 5 seats; PSE, 3 seats; GUE/NGL and Greens, 1 seat each.

A 'professionalisation' of European MEP position can be observed. On the one hand, the share of those who succeed in renewing their mandate has increased from 12.5 per cent ($^2/_{16}$) in 1996 to 50 per cent ($^7/_{14}$) in 2004. On the other hand, the share of political newcomers has decreased from 12.5 per cent ($^2/_{16}$ in 1996) and 18.8 per cent ($^3/_{16}$ in 1999) to 7.1 per cent ($^1/_{14}$) in 2004. Simultaneously, the share of women has fallen from 62.5 per cent in 1995 to 35.7 per cent in 2004. This is partly due to the transformation of the political supply. Several male candidates with experience in European or national politics attracted votes in 2004. Among these were Lasse Lehtinen, who won 47 186 votes. He was a former representative, President Martti Ahtisaari's collaborator and TV presenter. Also, Alexander Stubb (115 224 votes) had been adviser to

Romano Prodi at the European Commission and civil servant at the Finnish Foreign Affairs Ministry. Thanks to substantial financial contributions, Stubb led an intensive campaign in which he came across as an expert on European politics. Despite the successes of these two candidates, one in particular secured the greatest number of votes (149 646): former Prime Minister Anneli Jaatteenmaki of the KESK. Since her resignation as Prime Minister following accusations of having used confidential documents in her 2003 election campaign, Jaatteenmaki had repeatedly appeared on newspaper headlines. The documents implied that the Social-Democrat Prime Minister, in a meeting with US President George W. Bush, had pledged his support to the American intervention in Iraq, without informing the government. While proven innocent, Jaatteenmaki nonetheless paid the price in this affair.

Several Euro MEPs (50 per cent of the elected members) succeeded in renewing their mandates for 2004. Two of these have held their seats at the European Parliament since 1995. In contrast to the 1996 and 1999 European elections where several candidates with a strong media background had been elected, the 2004 electorate chose to give its votes to candidates with substantial European political experience. This has meant that out of seven new elected members, six retained a background in European or national politics. The only elected media-related candidate was Social-Democrat Lasse Lehtinen. It appears that a transformed political supply, favouring candidates combining media presence and/or European political experience has led to the defeat of the media candidates with no political experience who had been elected in 1996 and 1999.

European Parliament elections in Finland did not serve as a protest vote against the EU or the ruling government and elites. However, growing levels of

Euroscepticism may be indicated by high abstention rates. Critical voices towards Europe were channelled within political parties and, contrary to many member states, were not transformed into broader anti-European movements. A combination of preferential voting systems, voters' lack of interest and confidence in the government's European politics partly explain the outcome of the European elections in Finland.

The 2004 European elections in Finland are also indicative of the increasing professionalism of European political representation. The number of Finnish MEPs new to European politics decreased from 25 per cent in 1999 to 7 per cent ($\frac{1}{14}$) in 2004. Meanwhile, studies on the social origin of the MEPs show that 90 per cent of them have a higher education diploma, and that their average income is three times higher than that of the electorate. Out of the 14 MEPs elected in 2004, all are either professional politicians or European experts. In contrast to previous elections, candidates with little political experience have not succeeded in being elected. Eight out of 14 had a solid background in European politics, and five of them have succeeded in renewing their MEP mandate. Out of the newly elected members, five had previously been national parliamentarians, four of whom had served as ministers and prime ministers. On the whole, a change in Finland's political supply is partly responsible for the election to the European Parliament in 2004 of candidates with traditional political backgrounds.

Niilo Kauppi

Bibliography

Kauppi, N., *Democracy, Social Resources and Political Power in the European Union*, Manchester, Manchester University Press, 2005.

Raunio, T. and Tiilikainen, T. *Finland in the European Union*, London, Frank Cass, 2002.
Reif, K. and Schmitt, H., 'Nine Second-Order National Elections: a Conceptual Framework for the Analysis of European Elections Results', *European Journal of Political Research*, 8, 1, 1980, pp. 3–44.

→ Abstention; Campaign (Sociology of); Communication; Composition of the European Parliament; Electoral Strategy; European Elections (1979–1999); European Elections (2004); Euroscepticism; Issues; Mapping Europe: European Electoral Geography; Members of the European Parliament (Sociology of Political Office); Populism; Protest Voting; Representation; Second-Order Elections; Tenure.

Forecast

Background to electoral forecast

It was in the US in the 1920s that the first pre-election poll was 'invented' by a local newspaper who asked their readers to send the name of the candidate they wanted to vote for in the next local election. The number of readers who reacted to the newspaper's demand was much higher than expected, and the success of the operation led other newspapers to launch similar studies before Gallup, in the 1930s, became the first survey institute to officialise electoral forecast and try to make it a more scientific process, which would enable the elite to evaluate the state of public opinion prior to an important election. Today, the reliance of the mass media and the political elite on increasingly numerous pre-election surveys to evaluate the effect of political campaigns and to assess public opinion trends is more developed and more generalised than ever.

In most countries, these surveys no longer rely on the self-selection of respondents willing to volunteer a virtual vote for the benefit of polling companies.

Instead, since the 1970s, most surveys have been based on a random sample of the population targeted, which means that the survey company interviews a relatively large number of respondents, chosen randomly within the voting population, before correcting for any social or demographical bias via a weighting technique. In a few countries, such as France, most survey institutes never use random samples, but, instead, rely on a 'quota' technique, which means that the country's population is characterised along a few lines judged meaningful by the survey company (sex, age groups, region of origin, etc.), which then creates a sample designed to provide a miniature representation of the population studied. According to the vast majority of the scientific community, the quota technique, whilst cheaper than random samples, is also less efficient as it prejudges what characteristics matter in the electoral choice of voters. As a result, this technique has, for example, proved relatively inefficient at predicting the results of extreme right-wing parties. (However, in recent years lower costs associated with an increased demand for surveys by the mass media has resulted in a multiplication of quota samples and phone-based surveys by commercial companies despite the criticisms of the scientific community.)

How are surveys conducted?

Before any election that takes place in a European Union member state, scores of survey institutes try to sell their expertise to political parties, the mass media and non-governmental bodies alike. While these surveys are heavily commented upon by journalists – and occasionally criticised when they do not predict accurately the result of an election – few citizens know much about how they are conducted.

Usually, surveys take place at relatively regular intervals from about a year before the election to the day of the election itself. Surveys will usually be few and far between long before the election, regular from about two to three months before the election and very frequent (more than weekly) in the month preceding the vote. As a matter of course, each survey institute will normally use the same sample for all the surveys that will take place before an election. This allows for analyses of trends, and corresponds to the dominant political science perception that surveys should be analysed as a whole to indicate a trend rather than considered as individual measures of the candidates' or parties' forces (Crespi 1989).

In the case of quota-based samples, a survey institute will design a 'mini-country' of anywhere between 100 and 1500 respondents who represent, at best, in realistic proportion, the basic geographical (regions, size of towns), demographical (sex and age groups), and social (education and social categories) make-up of the country. Similarly, in the case of a random sample, the survey institute will go to great lengths to obtain anywhere between 500 and 2500 respondents whose selection is not biased in any way. In the latter case, when analysing the results the institute will use a weighting system to compensate for any remaining disproportion between the actual sample interviewed and the 'real' make-up of the country's population.

Finally, a third type of election poll has recently emerged using completely different methods. Trying to make use of new technology, institutes such as Yougov in the UK, or AOL-Libération in France, have multiplied the use of internet-based surveys. While these particular polls have the advantage of being particularly cost-efficient, they are criticised by most political scientists for not being random, as the people who choose to answer them are not a simple random sample of the population, but self-selected respondents with particular characteristics such as a relatively high level of internal political efficacy. However, these institutes claim to have gone a long way in understanding how to correct the bias of a self-selected sample. In many ways, they have indeed managed often to provide better estimates than their phone-based counterparts.

Election forecast and the 2004 European election

Today, numerous survey companies compete in each EU member state to provide politicians and the mass media alike with predictions about how citizens will vote in forthcoming elections. Large survey institutes include US-based Gallup, French-based Ipsos and CSA, British-based Mori, NOP and Yougov, and Scandinavian GsK. In each of the member states, several dozens of opinion polls were published in the three months preceding the 2004 election. In France, for example, Ipsos and Louis Harris published five pre-election surveys each in the two months preceding the election, Ifop and Sofres four each two months and one month before the election respectively, and CSA eight in two months. This gives a total of 26 pre-election survey in two months in France, as the country had already experienced two elections in March. In Britain, the number was lower as several elections were yet to take place on 10 June.

Theories of election forecast and prediction

Many political scientists have tried to predict the results of a given election. Traditionally, three main types of tools have been used to try and understand what will be the outcome of a particular vote. The first type of model uses a number of variables measuring the state of the economy or economic perceptions to predict the results. The second type of model uses 'betting odds'. Finally, the third type of model is used when political scientists try to derive the likely result of an election from pre-election surveys.

Amongst the 'economic models', most have used the concept of election cycles and the influence of the economic situation or economic perceptions on the vote. The works of Lewis-Beck (1988), Palmer and Whitten (1999), Erikson (1989) and MacKuen et al. (1992) all point to the clear effect of the economic situation (Lewis-Beck and Palmer and Whitten) or economic perceptions (Erikson, MacKuen et al.) on the chances of the incumbent government to perform well in elections. The theory is that a good economic situation in the first two cases, or positive economic perceptions in the latter ones, will make voters more likely to 'reward' the incumbent government and confirm them in office. Lewis-Beck's work includes several European nations as case studies.

The 'betting odds' model uses 'election markets' to predict the results of a vote on the basis of the assumption that markets are efficient aggregators of information, so that equilibrium evaluations on such markets are close to the most efficient estimate of the actual future vote. The best-known election market was created in the United States in 1988 by the University of Iowa and is called the Iowa Electronic Market. It allows willing gamblers, including political science experts, to purchase 'stocks' of a party or candidate with the promise of being rewarded if the party or candidate in question gains a majority of the popular vote. Research on election betting markets is recent but has often suggested that these models actually perform better than traditional poll-based and economy-based models (Forsythe et al. 1992; Shaw and Roberts 2000), probably because they actually focus primarily on the dynamics of the race rather than static perceptions.

Several authors, however, also try to use pre-election polls themselves to forecast the results of a forthcoming election. The works of Erikson and Wlezien (1999), Althaus (1996), and Jackman and Marks (1994) are all examples of this tradition of scholarly work trying to predict the result of an election on the basis of existing polls. Various authors have reached different conclusions, suggesting that the most efficient poll-based prediction is achieved by aggregating and averaging pre-election polls, using the most recent poll, and using polls published about a month before the election respectively. However, many political scientists are keen to stress the difference between a pre-election poll and an actual election. Polls indicate the state of opinion rather than an actual virtual vote; pollsters target samples representing the country as a whole while only a smaller proportion of the polity participates in elections (although many institutes try to control for the likely participation of respondents); polls can be used to convey messages to politicians rather than to express a straight opinion; some categories are notoriously under-represented in polls as they are hard to communicate with for pollsters, etc. Nevertheless, I will now evaluate the power of these three methods on the basis of the pre-election polls published in France for the 2004 European Parliament election.

How good are polls at predicting the results of an election? The 2004 European Parliament election example

Using the case study of the 2004 European elections in France, it is interesting to look at the extent to which the actual result of the election can be predicted on the basis of the pre-election polls published in the three months that preceded the vote. Table 1 looks at three possible models of

Table 1   Using election polls to predict election results: the example of the 2004 European Parliament election in France

Force	Result	Average	E1	Latest	E2	2 Months	E3
Extreme left	3.3	4.9	1.6	5.3	2.0	4.0	0.7
Left	42.9	41.0	1.9	41.2	1.7	42.5	0.4
Right	37.4	36.5	0.9	35.5	1.9	37.0	0.4
Front National	9.8	11.8	2.0	9.5	0.3	12.5	2.7
MNR	0.3	1.1	0.8	1.0	0.7	1.0	0.7
CNPT	1.7	2.6	0.9	2.8	1.1	2.0	0.3
Other	4.5	2.4	2.1	4.5	0	2.0	2.5
Average error			1.5		1.1		1.1

Notes:
Results based on ten surveys published between April and June 2004 (excluding exit polls) by IPSOS and CSA in France.
'Average' category is the average result of all ten surveys, 'Latest' category is the average of the latest survey published by each institute on 10 June, '2 Months' category is the average of the surveys published by IPSOS on 3 April and by CSA on 14 April.
Error (E) is the total distance between a given prediction and the actual result of the election. It is averaged by the number of forces in the last row.

prediction that respectively rely on the latest poll a few days before the election, the polls published two months before 13 June, and the global average of all the polls published within three months of the European Parliament elections.

It is clear from Table 1 that the pre-election surveys in France gave a relatively good indication of the state of opinion during the election campaign. All three models actually give reasonable approximations of the dominance of the left over the right, the relative decline of the extremes, etc. However, it is interesting to note that of all three models, the 'average' technique, usually most praised by political scientists, is the least efficient.

Nevertheless, the findings also confirm that the fairest insight into the state of the opinion is actually obtained between one and two months before the vote rather than at the last moment. The only exception to this result was that the vote of the extreme right was grossly overestimated a while before the election while other parties – presumably not well known to the voters until late in the campaign – saw their ratings progress consistently to the day of the election.

Contemporary democratic life has seen a multiplication of surveys and other attempts by the mass media, 'experts' and politicians alike to predict the outcome of elections. The progress of social sciences and the use of new technologies, particularly the internet, have made opinion polls more available and potentially cheaper – if not necessarily more scientifically sound – than ever. While political scientists have found increasingly diversified ways to predict electoral outcomes and stress that opinion polls are anything but a replicate of the actual vote, it is clear that for the European Parliament elections 2004, as for most elections, opinion polls conducted about a month before an election give a relatively clear image of the closeness of the race and the balance of powers between the main parties.

Michael Bruter

Bibliography

Althaus, S., 'Opinion Polls, Information Effects and Political Equality: Exploring Ideological Biases in Collective Opinion', *Political Communication*, 13, 1, 1996, pp. 3–21.

Crespi, I., *Public Opinion, Polls, and Democracy*, Boulder, Westview Press, 1989.

Erikson, R. S., 'Economic Conditions and the Presidential Vote', *American Political Science Review*, 83, 2, 1989, pp. 567–73.

Erikson, R. S. and Wlezien, C., 1999, 'Presidential Polls as a Time Series: the Case of 1996', *Public Opinion Quarterly*, 63, 2, 1999, pp. 163–77.

Forsythe, R. and Nelson, F. et al., 'Anatomy of an Experimental Political Stock Market', *American Economic Review*, 82, 5, 1992, pp. 1142–61.

Jackman, S. and Marks, G. N., 'Forecasting Australia Elections: 1993 and All That', *Australian Journal of Political Science*, 29, 2, 1994, pp. 277–91.

Lewis-Beck, M., *Economics and Elections: the Major Western Democracies*, Ann Arbor, University of Michigan Press, 1988.

MacKuen, M. B., Erikson, R. S. and Stimson, J. A., 'Peasants or Bankers? The American Electorate and the US Economy', *American Political Science Review*, 86, 3, 1992, pp. 597–611.

Palmer, H. D. and Whitten, G. D., 'The Electoral Impact of Unexpected Inflation and Economic Growth', *British Journal of Political Science*, 29, 4, 1999, pp. 623–39.

Shaw, D. and Roberts, B., 'Campaign Events, the Media, and the Prospect of Victory: the 1992 and 1996 US Presidential Elections', *British Journal of Political Science*, 30, 2, 2000, pp. 259–89.

→ Data Archives; Electoral Behaviour; Eurobarometer.

France

On 13 June 2004, French voters elected their European Parliament representatives. While the existing proportional electoral system, and threshold of 5 per cent remained unchanged, several elements of the electoral system were modified. In order to make room for the ten new member states in a European Parliament comprising 732 members, the number of seats given to France was reduced from 87 to 78. A second innovation was the enforcement of the 6 June 2000 law, favouring equal access for men and women to electoral mandates and elective functions. From this moment on, every list had to comprise equal numbers of alternated male and female candidates. Moreover, contrary to the 1999 elections, the total number of candidates on a list had to be twice as high as the number of available seats. Furthermore, the mandate of MEP was made incompatible with those of national MP, senator, and any local or regional executive position (law of 5 April 2000). The last important change was due to the law of 11 April 2003, whereby eight interregional constituencies replaced the single constituency that had been used until 1999. The idea of regionalising European polls was not a new one. In fact, it was successively defended by Michel Barnier, member of the Juppé government, and by the Jospin government, before being rejected by the two main coalition partners of the Socialists. The arguments put forward by the Raffarin government to justify the new system included the wish to bring elected MEPs closer to their voters, as well a desire to represent the whole national territory in its geographical diversity. The most virulent opposition to this plan came from the UDF and its president, François Bayrou, who denounced the UMP's intention to denationalise and politicise European elections while excluding national issues from the debate.

Voting system and electoral divisions

Within this new electoral framework, the number of MEPs elected in each region had to vary according to the latest population census. For instance, three MEPs were thus elected by the French Overseas Territories and 14 for the Ile-de-France region (Table 1). Whereas previously, any list securing 5 per cent of the

Table 1   2004 European elections in France: splitting and figures

Constituency	Regions included	Seats
North-West	Basse-Normandie; Haute-Normandie; Nord-Pas-de-Calais; Picardie	12
West	Bretagne; Pays de Loire; Poitou-Charentes	10
East	Alsace; Bourgogne; Champagne-Ardenne; Franche-Comté; Lorraine	10
South-West	Aquitaine; Languedoc-Roussillon; Midi-Pyrénées	10
South-East	Corse; Provence-Alpes-Côte-d'Azur; Rhône-Alpes	13
Massif Central-Centre	Auvergne; Centre; Limousin	6
Ile-de-France	Ile-de-France	14
Overseas Territories	Overseas	3
Total		*78*

votes was certain to have at least one MEP, due to variations in district magnitudes, and the regional strongholds of the various parties, the same share of the national vote occasionally resulted in less positive outcomes for the parties. A new double challenge therefore faced political parties. On the one hand, they needed to obtain more than 5 per cent of the votes in a given constituency to be official contenders to the constituency's seats; on the other hand, the effective threshold was sometimes much higher, particularly in regions with a low district magnitude.

This reform, portrayed by the Raffarin government as a 'technicality', had substantive effects on the French political scene, since it contributed to limit the bulk of the competition for MEPs' positions to the main political forces (PS, UMP, UDF) to the detriment of 'minor' political parties, who either saw their number of MEPs decrease (PC, Greens, Front National), or did not manage to have anyone elected altogether (extreme left, RPF, CPNT). Moreover, the new electoral law spared major political figures the duty of getting directly and personally involved in the electoral campaign as they would not have been eligible unless they abandoned some of their other, more prestigious, mandates.

The electoral results

Europe and opposition to Turkish accession to the EU were amongst the main issues addressed by the Eurosceptic (lists of Charles Pasqua, Philippe de Villiers, the movement for fishing and hunting, nature and traditions) and federalist camps alike. However, many parties seemed to be primarily interested in the state of the competition between the left and right, three months after the March 2004 regional and local elections, which resulted in a landslide vote against the government party. Rather than Europe, most parties seemed already to be thinking about the next presidential and legislative ballots due to take place three years later and assessing their own 'electoral shape' and that of their main competitors. The left, however fragmented, wanted the forthcoming elections to serve as another national test. By contrast, the Raffarin government hastened to announce that the results would have no national character, using the regional constituencies as a pretext. The UDF sought to reinforce its weight within the moderate right by running separate lists in every region. The National Front hoped that Eurosceptic lists would not deprive it of too many votes. Because of their success in the 2002 presidential elections (10 per cent of the votes) and the 5 per cent threshold, the two extreme-left parties (LO-LCR) presented a united front for the 2004 electoral campaigns (regional and European) despite strong internal divergences. However, questions arose relating to their survival at the European level, following the very disappointing results they obtained in the regional and local elections three months earlier. To this already fragmented picture another series of lists with regionalist, categorical and communitarian characters was added. These small parties sought to test their luck in proportional regionalised polls. A total of 168 lists (21 per region on average, that is, far more than in the 1994 and 1999 elections when only 20 lists competed at the national level) representing 41 parties and movements competed for the 78 MEP seats available. It was in the Ile-de-France constituency that competition was fiercest with 28 lists (while the Overseas Territories only had to choose between 15 lists).

In France, as in most EU member states, the turnout seemed to reveal the relatively low salience of the election. Abstention rates reached an unprecedented 57.2 per

Table 2   2004 European election results in France

Registered	41 518 225
Voting	17 764 049
Valid	17 168 995
Invalid	595 054
Abstention	57.21 %

	Votes	% valid votes	Seats
LO-LCR	440 196	2.56	0
Other EXT-G	131 312	0.77	0
PCF	900 396	5.24	2
PS	4 960 245	28.89	31
Other Left	231 028	1.35	0
Greens	1 271 059	7.4	6
Other Greens	166 560	0.97	0
UMP	2 856 186	16.64	17
UDF	2 051 142	11.95	11
Other Right	1 516 506	8.83	3
CPNT	297 303	1.73	0
FN	1 684 868	9.81	7
Other Ext. Right	53 600	0.31	0
Regionalists	15 718	0.09	0
Other	592 876	3.45	1
Total	17 168 995	99.99	78

cent (respectively four and ten points more than in 1999 and in 1994). This figure is slightly worse than the European average (55 per cent for the EU-25, and 53 per cent in the case of EU-15). As shown by Table 2, the specific results of the various parties seem to confirm that the election was used by many voters to protest against their government. When asked for the reasons for their choice, voters primarily insisted on their desire to show their opposition to government politics (52 per cent). This was a dominant factor not only for left-wing voters (64 per cent) but also for right-wing ones (47 per cent). Of those polled 40 per cent claimed to have still been influenced by the consequences of the April 2002 vote, and 38 per cent by the prospective 2007 presidential elections (Louis Harris-AOL-Arte survey of 13 June 2004).

Despite its failure to specify its position vis-à-vis Europe, the Socialist party emerged as the relatively clear winner of these elections. With nearly 29 per cent of the total votes, it gained 31 seats. This was a significant improvement compared to the 22 per cent of votes and 22 seats it secured five years earlier. In fact, it successfully attracted a number of voters opposed to the economic and social reform projects put forward by the Raffarin government. The other traditional left parties did not enjoy the same success. The Communist Party, which won slightly more than 5 per cent of votes, compared to 6.8 per cent in 1999, only obtained two seats (one in the North-West region and one in the Ile-de-France) compared to the six won in 1999. With more than 7 per cent of the votes, the Greens got two points less than they had in 1999, when Daniel Cohen-Bendit led the list. They only managed to keep six of their nine MEPs. These results were partly linked to the effective threshold which was raised by the lowering district magnitude. It is for this reason that the Greens are not represented in the least populated regions such as the Centre and the Overseas Territories despite obtaining more than 5 per cent of the vote: with six and three seats to allocate to all winners, their score proved in fact insufficient.

After its defeat in the March 2004 regional elections, the governing UMP was not expecting such a rapid comeback, but it successfully managed to achieve several objectives: it obtained a better result than in 1999 when Nicolas Sarkozy was leading the party's list (12.8 per cent), and it did better than both the pro-European UDF and the Eurosceptic camp. With more than 16 per cent of total votes and 17 seats (12 in the outgoing EP), the party's first objective was apparently reached. However, comparisons with preceding polls are not really significant, since the UMP now included a number of UDF candidates. Tensions between the different components of the moderate right, which were already obvious during the regional elections, grew steadily. The UDF took an impressive third position in the election with nearly 12 per cent of the votes, improving its result by three points since 1999. It also secured 11 seats. While the UMP was ahead of the UDF in all of the eight main interregional constituencies, the difference between the two lists was of less than two points in the North and South-West constituencies, and barely three points in the Western region. In fact, the UDF was even ahead of the UMP in 10 of the 22 French administrative regions. In 1999, the success of the Eurosceptic right, united behind the Philippe de Villiers and Charles Pasqua list (MPF-RPF), caused a shock: with 13 per cent of the votes and 13 elected members, it was just ahead of the RPR-DL list (12.8 per cent and 12 seats). Instead, in June 2004, the two Eurosceptic lists gained less than 9 per cent of the votes. This time, with 6.7 per cent of the valid votes, the MPF went over the 5 per cent limit in seven regions but only gained three seats, all in large constituencies: Ile-de-France (14 seats to allocate), South-West and West (both 10 seats). In the other regions, the effective limit was too high for the MPF to gain seats, or the party did not perform well enough. Charles Pasqua, who presented himself independently, lost his seat.

Finally, the results of the extreme right and extreme left came short of the overwhelming success expected by their party leaders. Jean-Marie Le Pen was hoping to secure 12–14 seats, but with less than 10 per cent of votes, the FN, which passed the 5 per cent threshold in seven metropolitan constituencies, only managed to gain a total of seven seats in only in five of them. While gaining nearly 10 per cent of the votes in the Centre region, the new electoral system meant that the party got no seat. In comparison with the 1999 poll, this result might appear as an improvement (5.7 per cent and five elected members), but at that time, the creation of the MNR led by Bruno Mégret caused the party a loss of three points. Compared to 1994, the FN lost five seats and more than 360 000 votes. Jean-Marie Le Pen obtained a modest result in the South-East (12.2 per cent) as did his daughter Marine in Ile-de-France (8.6 per cent), whereas with a mere 5.6 per cent his son-in-law failed to be elected in the West. The united extreme left (LO-LCR) only gained 2.6 per cent of the votes (compared to a little more than 5 per cent in 1999). As their results were evenly distributed across constituencies and they had no real stronghold, they failed to have a single MEP elected.

Until 1999, the national character of European elections favoured the emergence of new political forces (the Front National in 1984, the Greens in 1989, Eurosceptics in 1994 and 1999). In 2004, the fragmentation of the electoral map contributed to slowing down – and eventually halting – such an emergence, allowing the system to benefit more 'traditional' political forces. While nine political parties currently have MEPs in Strasbourg, as compared to eight in 1999, three of them concentrate more than 75 per cent of the seats (PS 40 per cent; UMP 22 per cent; UDF 14 per cent), whereas in 1999, the PS, RPR-DL and MPF-RPF lists only gained 54 per cent of the seats. With the new multi-constituency system, the great majority of the lists did not succeed in reaching the 5 per cent threshold. In Ile-de-France, 21 of the 28 lists in competition gained less than 5 per cent. In the North-West, the proportion was 12 out of 19. Similarly, it reached 15 out of 21 in the West, 14 out of 20 in the East, 15 out of 22 in the South-East, and, finally, 9 out of 14 in the Overseas Territories. In several cases, some of the lists that reached the 5 per cent threshold were nonetheless excluded from political representation.

Apart from a higher level of abstention, the June 2004 European election seemed to confirm the verdict of the regional elections that took place three months earlier. Both helped to restructure the bipolarisation of the French political scene, just two years after the 2002 presidential crisis, which was still in citizens' memories. Moreover, both elections were largely marked by the punishment of the governing UMP and, implicitly, attacks on the party's presidential performance and credentials. In both instances, protest voting was obvious and beneficial to the dominating left party, the PS. Finally, both cases were affected by the link between the electoral candidate and the poll's outcome. Closely related in time, the regional and European elections of 2004 appeared as true traditional 'mid-term' elections, and second-order national political tests, rather than votes on the specific issues at stake, or votes that the government would have liked them to be.

Annie Laurent

Bibliography

Taagepera, R. and Shugart, M., *Seats and Votes: the Effects and Determinants of Electoral Systems*, New Haven, Yale University Press, 1989.

Rae, D. W., 'Thresholds of Representation and Thresholds of Exclusion: an Analytic Note on Electoral Systems', *Comparative Political Studies*, 4, 3, 1971, pp. 479–88.

→ Abstention; Dual Mandates; Electoral System; European Elections (1979–1999); European Elections (2004); Extreme Right; Incompatibility; Mapping Europe: European Electoral Geography; Parity; Protest Voting; Second-Order Elections; Sovereignism; Turkey.

Fraud

Within the context of European elections, fraud is defined by national laws. All countries must respect international and European norms, a prerequisite for belonging to the EU. However, in the absence of a common institution and of a uniform judicial system regulating elections to the European Parliament in the 25 member states, each country is free to establish its own set of penalties and legal recourse. Each state entrusts a national body with the responsibility of monitoring electoral irregularities. Since this electoral task is far from uniform, the issue of electoral fraud is one that requires further research, especially on a national rather than European scale.

Fraud detection and evaluation

The level of fraud is obviously an important consideration. Are European polls tainted with irregularities and if so to what extent? Which are the countries concerned? Regardless of the election considered, answering these questions is very complex. One of the conditions for fraud to take place is obviously its secrecy, and a well-planned manoeuvre is hard to detect. Certain contentious actions can be taken openly and may even seek publicity. However, these then become acts of bravado whose objectives are not so much to modify the results of an election, as to express a sense of dissatisfaction with certain candidates or with authorities organising the polls. Any practice aiming at changing the issue at stake during the election is only exposed if it fails or is denounced. Not all allegations correspond to actual manoeuvres. The protest can sometimes be irrelevant, only aiming at discrediting an opponent or trying to nullify election results. Nonetheless certain contentious acts, although known, are not contested. They can benefit candidates who are not elected, who then fail to press charges. They can also be followed by pressure on any eventual witnesses. Sometimes the steps required to contest elections may seem too complex, even if they happen to be known by the electors. Moreover, certain witnesses might not be conscious of the contentious nature of what they have seen. Moreover, the level of public awareness of the legal norms governing the conduct of elections is questionable. Counting fraud allegations does not involve keeping an inventory of the manoeuvres that took place, but rather monitoring the attempts to achieve skewed results or to organise a second poll.

The number of claims varies significantly from one country to another, depending on the number of observed manoeuvres, but also depending on electoral norms, practical modalities, and help for parties or representatives to monitor electoral operations and formulate requests. The influence of these different concomitant elements does not allow for the determination of the countries more affected by electoral frauds both during European Parliament and other types of elections. Nevertheless, certain countries are perceived to be prone towards fraudulent practices. Southern voters often have a reputation for not respecting electoral rules, whereas the polls are seen to take place in a very strict and correct manner in the Northern European countries. These stereotypes are as old as the remarks made by Lefèvre-Pontalis (1902) at the beginning of the twentieth century. For him, England was a model country governed by extremely strict rules and electoral practices. The same was true of Germany, where 'the electorate wants to keep its independence'. The so-called 'good students' of this electoral class were also Austria, Belgium and the Netherlands. Among the bad ones was Hungary, where the use of absent and dead people's votes was regarded as commonplace as were violence, purchasing votes, and exerting pressure on candidates. Lefèvre-Pontalis gave Spain a similar image, suggesting that elections in this country were characterised by the carelessness with which the civil servants and voters alike thought anything was allowed. French polls were seen as no stricter, whilst Italy was known for large amounts of bought votes.

More than the rules and the electoral

dispositions, the author saw 'habits' and current issues as key determinants of different countries' electoral behaviour. In fact, individual characteristics would seem to offer a context more or less favourable to fraud. However, the usual representations of these tendencies towards fraudulent behaviours do not seem well founded. As shown by a survey carried out by the electoral commission of the United Kingdom in 2003, citizens generally acknowledge and recognise the possibility of fraud, but think it does not happen in their country or region. Fraud, a barbarian practice opposed to democratic electoral civilisation, always appears to occur somewhere else, and largely remains the responsibility of others. Negative electoral reputation follows an imaginary geography which conforms to stereotypical views of different national cultures rather than with actual electoral practices.

Explaining fraud and allegations of fraud

If one holds as a criterion for the definition of fraud, the intention to illegally modify the issues at stake in an election, the 'opportunities' for fraud offered by the different types of polls are not equal. Illegal operations, in most European countries, can be carried out at the constituency level. Elements of fraud are found in false electoral lists or in the counting of votes, filling of a polling station, threats and pressure on communities in situations of dependence. In fact, the latter may be dependent on municipal teams, homogeneous voting offices, candidates or supporters in positions of social or economic power. While these practices may sometimes lead to victory in a local election, their efficacy declines in accordance with the importance of the constituency and the number of polling stations.

Similarly, individual and personal requests have little chance of succeeding when polls take place in large constituencies. Different European countries have retained as an essential though contentious electoral principle, that of 'determining irregularity'. When abnormalities are shown to have influenced the outcome of an election, results can be rectified and, in many cases, the election can be deemed invalid. The office in charge of European Parliament elections may decide to validate poll results despite the presence of fraud, in cases when the latter has not been decisive as far as the final result is concerned. The cost of challenging election results, based on irregularities observed in polling stations, can in fact be greater than the expected benefits of invalidating election outcomes. The unlucky candidates may therefore be discouraged from verbalising their objections.

Consequently, either because fraud is becoming less frequent, less effective, or because of the risks of having an election cancelled, the number of objections submitted during European Parliament elections is less high than for local and other polls. Nevertheless, frauds are still regularly denounced and exposed. Most of the time they relate to a number of votes not large enough to modify election outcomes. Since 1979, European Parliament elections have never been cancelled. How does one explain the need for illegal operations that might seem inefficient, and personal requests that seem certain to fail?

Fraud can aim to modify results, not only at the constituency, but also at the national level. Some 26 French accusations were made during the 1989 European elections concerning voting procedures in the constituency of Vitry-sur-Seine. Disorganisation, pressure on candidate delegates, and packs of ballot papers that substituted those already in the ballot box are said to be partly responsible for the Communists' surprising gain of 80 per cent of the votes. If such measures did indeed take place, they clearly did not serve the purpose of modifying national results. They might have simply aimed at reinforcing municipal legitimacy, reaffirming its existence and strength with a positive result at the European elections. Similarly, the formulation of this protest did not aim to cancel the entire election. The objective was, through the publicity later obtained by this claim, to disqualify or discredit a municipal majority and the party to which it belonged. The goal was also to provide an explanation for a local electoral defeat without questioning the quality of competing programmes or candidates.

However, electoral fraud is not always aimed at a candidate, a specific list or party. It can also target the practices of certain actors or social groups who are not directly implicated in the electoral arena. In the United Kingdom, even before the 2004 elections, claims arose to contest manoeuvres allowed by the new legislation replacing, for a third of the electorate, the traditional vote by a postal vote. *The Times* cited the case of a boss threatening to fire his employees who would not vote as he wished. A Labour Party member accused Muslim leaders of depriving their fellow believers of their rights, by voting in their place. Such practices can be carried out by leading citizens, religious authorities, or actors in positions of socio-economic strength, to reaffirm their position of power in a group or in a community. The reasons for contesting results can be of different nature. Again, the aim is not to get the poll cancelled, especially since the fraud allegations often precede the election. Rather, they may seek to cast a negative light on behaviours and social relationships within the groups concerned. They can be part of a 'crusade' against fraud led by moralistic citizens or groups. Such accusations formulated before elections are a way to defend universal suffrage, especially in polls where the issues at stake do not mobilise the electorate.

Fraud allegations can also be seen as attacks against the government, and criticisms directed at legislation passed by the ruling majority. Denouncing instances of fraud resulting from postal voting can, for instance, be a way of highlighting the failures of such a measure, while strengthening the arguments of those who opposed it in the first place. It is a way of reaffirming the regressive character of laws which permit the return of practices one thought were erased for ever. Some do not hesitate in launching direct attacks on the ruling majority whose reforms would aim precisely at modifying the poll results in their favour. Postal voting should favour the Labour Party in the United Kingdom, and the splitting of the French constituencies in France before the 2004 polls would favour the government lists. Unless one holds a very broad definition of fraud, these allegations must be considered not as fraud revelations but as arguments belonging to national political battles.

These different examples lead us to conclude that both fraud and its denunciation are most of the time not associated with European Parliament elections. These polls are scarcely the scene for new contests. They are more of an opportunity to re-examine general aspects of electoral legislations or to reiterate fraud allegations already formulated during other polls (as was the case of the request sent to the State Council asking for the cancellation of European election results in 36 polling stations in Paris's fifth district in 1999). Such claims were essentially based on the absence of a revision of the electoral lists since the 1997 legislative elections marked by numerous illegal registrations. Deemed unacceptable because it did not modify national election results, this claim was made to recall the 1997 fraud and reiterate criticism addressed to the Mayor of Paris. Fraud at the European elections still retains a strong national dimension. The debates it provokes are in line with a new arena of positions and oppositions characterising the national political scene.

Nathalie Dompnier

Bibliography

Leboucq, F., 'Electoral Fraud: Causes, Types and Consequences', *Annual Review of Political Science*, 6, 2003, pp. 233–56

Lefèvre-Pontalis, E., *Elections in Europe at the End of the 19th Century*, Paris, Plon, 1902.

Romanelli, R. (ed.), *How Did They Become Voters? The History of Franchise in Modern European Representation*, The Hague, Kluwer International Law, 1998.

→ Electoral Operations; Observation of Elections; Observers.

G

Germany

'Hast Du einen Opa, schick' ihn nach Europa' (If you have a grandfather, send him to Europe). This saying, which reflected the second-order character of European elections and applied to obscure candidates at the end of their political career, appeared apposite in the 2004 elections, where 24 parties were fighting for the 99 available seats. The composition of the main electoral lists showed that party leaderships favoured representatives with predominantly European backgrounds and expertise. Similarly, the programmes revealed the growing importance of specific European issues nurturing political cleavages. However, the analysis of the electoral campaign appears to contradict these preliminary observations. The debates driven mainly by party leaders continued to be dominated by national agendas. Results such as the low level of participation, and the flagrant defeat of the Social-Democrat Party (SPD), the senior partner of the governing Red–Green coalition, underlined both the weak levels of interest in the election and a domestic context characterised by the contestation of the social reforms undertaken in 2003 by the Schröder government within the framework of its Agenda 2010.

The recruitment of candidates: searching for a 'European profile'

The valorisation of the European experience appears, first and foremost, in the fact that parties already established within the European Parliament favoured incumbents as MEP candidates. Their dominance was equally affirmed within the CDU (Christian Democrat Union), the Bavarian CSU (Christian Social Union) and SPD, where they monopolised the vast majority of eligible positions. This strategy also dictated the choice of the lists' heads, who often occupied positions that portrayed them as European experts (Table 1).

In the case of Hans-Gert Pöttering, his position as head of the list had a high media profile, following the delivery of a letter-bomb to his office at the start of 2004. Martin Schulz also benefited from

Table 1 Mandates and functions of the heads of lists in the European Parliament elections of 2004

	Party	Mandate	Function
H.-G. Pöttering	CDU	since 1979	President of the EPP group (since 1999)
L. Friedrich	CSU	since 1979	Vice-President of the EP (since 1999)
M. Schulz	SPD	since 1994	Chief of the German delegation to the PES (since 1999)
S. Kaufmann	PDS	since 1999	Member of the Convention on the Future of Europe

some media visibility following his conflict with Silvio Berlusconi in July 2003. While Rebecca Harms, head of the Green list (associated with the '90 Alliance', a former East German civic movement) came across as a newcomer, she later succeeded in using the skills she acquired while working as the assistant to a Green MEP between 1984 and 1988. Moreover, her party placed Daniel Cohn-Bendit (who had already represented the German Greens in 1994 as well as their French colleagues in 1999) in second place. Absent from Strasbourg for 10 years, the Liberal Party (FDP) opted for a young team with little parliamentary experience at the European level. Nonetheless, its candidates followed personal and professional trajectories that conferred on them a European stature. This was the case of their head, Silvana Koch-Mehrin, aged 33, whose party incessantly reminded the electorate of her residing and working in Brussels.

The programmes: cleavages and diverging positions on Europe

The different parties agreed, to varying degrees, on the functioning mode of European institutions. For the European political system, partly inspired by the principles of German federalism and by the recommendations of the Commission's White Paper on European Governance, the parties advocated the principle of subsidiarity and of a decentralised structure, attributing an important role to European regions and cities. Transparency, effectiveness and democracy constitute the core principles behind programmes that were sometimes very critical of the European bureaucracy, and conversely favourable to the strengthening of the EP's powers. The European Constitution, which has met with a certain degree of consensus among the major German parties, was only criticised by the neo-communist PDS, which argued that the project had an exceedingly liberal character. Divergences focused essentially on its mode of ratification: contrary to the SPD, favourable to the rapid adoption of the text via the national parliament, the PDS, FDP and the Greens wished to see it adopted through a referendum.

The electoral programmes revealed the existence of different cleavages, the main one being between the supporters of a European liberal model and those who advocated a strong social Europe. The first category was typically represented by the FDP and, to a lesser extent, by the CDU and CSU, who professed to be in favour of a social market economy while simultaneously demanding a relaxation of EC regulations as well as the respect for Stability Pact provisions. In contrast, the PDS's priority remained the establishment and strengthening of a social Europe. Like the Greens, who advocated the importance of its modernisation, the SPD was also broadly committed to the defence of the European social model.

The second major cleavage related to questions of peace and security. The defence of a peaceful Europe (a crucial issue for the German left) was at the heart of the electoral programmes of the PDS, the Greens and the SPD. The latter turned this matter into its primary campaign theme as Chancellor Schröder declared in Dortmund on 3 June: 'We must turn good old Europe into a place of durable peace'. In contrast, the CDU and CSU emphasised the importance of security matters within the European project. These two parties professed to be in favour of the strengthening of the EU's military engagements and of greater co-operation on matters of justice and security, designed to protect Europe from threats such as terrorism, organised crime, ethnic violence and illegal immigration. Such issues were also used by Die Republikaner on the extreme right of the political spectrum.

The affirmation of the EU's Judaeo-Christian values represented an additional source of partisan differentiation. Absent from several programmes (SPD, Greens, PDS, FDP), it was nonetheless underlined by the two Christian coalitions (CDU and CSU), which defined Europe as a community of religious values to be enshrined in the forthcoming constitutional text. Related to this question is the debate about the possibility of Turkey's EU accession. Both the CDU and the CSU occasionally played the cultural and religious card to oppose Turkey's candidacy, supported by parties such as the SPD, PDS, FDP and the Greens. In contrast to its ally, the CSU questioned the whole enlargement of the EU, and portrayed it as a threat both in economic and internal security terms. Such views were also presented, in more radical terms, in the extreme right parties' programmes.

A campaign shaped by internal political stakes

The elections of 13 June 2004 highlight a gap between the contents of European-oriented electoral programmes and national issues-dominated campaigns. Several parties presented themselves as the guarantors of Germany's position in the enlarged Europe. This was one of the main campaign themes of Die Republikaner, and to a lesser extent of the centre-right. The CDU defended its vision of a 'strong Germany', while the CSU insisted on the role of the regions, criticising the enlargement and emphasising its Bavarian heritage. In a very different way, the former Communists defended the continuation of structural fund payments to the Eastern German Länder.

A look at parties' discourses shows that only the Greens privileged truly European themes, while their various opponents preferred national adaptations of European themes. For example, the Conservative opposition to Turkey's membership was arguably part of a larger debate on immigration laws. This rejection, particularly important with regards to Germany's large Turkish minority, was apparently backed by 63 per cent of the population (Politbarometer, 1 March 2004) a few months before the election. Similarly, the SPD exploited the theme of a 'pacific Europe', to try and redefine European themes under a more national light. Indeed, the SPD hoped to benefit from the widespread opposition of the German public to the Iraq War, which helped it win a short victory in the 2002 general elections.

Thus, the European campaign themes betrayed a political market logic dominated by national stakes, and showed that national issues tended to overtake European ones, particularly with the synchronised Länder elections that took place in six Länder (Baden-Wurttenberg, Mecklenburg-Vompomern, Rheinland-Pfalz, Sachsen, Sachsen-Anhalt, and Sarren). This pushed the parties to campaign on several fronts at the same time, encouraging them to focus on their opposition to the reform of the health service, tax policy, pension age reform, and unemployment. This particularly allowed the CDU to refocus the campaign on social and economic issues and feed its campaign on the dissatisfaction of a large proportion of the population with the record of the government. In this respect, the CDU was hoping to continue to profit from a series of electoral defeats of the SPD in local and regional elections and to transform the European vote into yet another occasion for the public to protest against the government's action. As a result, the main campaign slogan of the right was:

'Germany is fed up with the Red–Green coalition'. The SPD tried to counter-attack with its notion of 'Justice for the future' or *Zukunftsgerechtigkeit*, an ambiguous notion referring both to equity and respect of the law and expected to legitimise the governmental reforms by claiming that they are needed by the future generations.

The media contributed to reinforce this national flavour of the campaign. The only 'European' theme that was really covered by the press was the prospect of Turkish accession to the EU, which, again, was largely treated as an internal topic. Moreover, the list leaders, who were largely unknown to the public because of their lack of visibility outside of the EU sphere, found it hard to counter-balance the weight of party leaders. Thus, the short-lived visibility of Martin Schulz or the relatively marginal visibility of Daniel Cohn-Bendit in Germany (he is better known in France) did not suffice to invert the national tendency.

The results

The election took place using proportional representation with closed lists. The parties had two possibilities: either to constitute national lists, or to constitute them in each Länd. Only the CDU-CSU chose the second option because of the regional importance of the CSU, which only runs in Bavaria. The voters could use postal voting, and 43 per cent of the population participated. This is the lowest level of turnout since 1979 after a short improvement in 1989 as shown in Table 2.

The 5 per cent threshold was reached by five parties in 1999 and six in 2004. The CDU-CSU obtained a large victory despite a decline of 4.2 points as compared to 1999. Similarly, the SPD suffered an extremely severe defeat, declining by 9.2 points and getting less than half of the seats of the CDU-CSU. In fact, since 1979, the SPD did less well in each election as compared to the previous one. This could be analysed as a protest vote similar to those observed across most member states, but which does not seem to apply to the Greens who, despite being members of the coalition, managed a real success as shown by their progression of 5.5 points since 1999. This may be due to the fact that Green voters mostly stem from the urban middle classes, who have a strong cultural capital and seem more receptive to the arguments for the necessary modernisation of the socio-economic system as represented by the reforms of the Agenda 2010. Indeed, the Greens

Table 2   Results since 1979

	1979	1984	1989	1994	1999	2004
Turnout	65.7	56.8	62.3	60.0	45.2	43.0
CDU/CSU	49.2	45.9	37.8	38.8	48.7	44.5
SPD	40.8	37.4	37.3	32.2	30.7	21.5
Greens	3.2	8.2	8.4	10.1	6.4	11.9
FDP	6.4	4.8	5.6	4.1	3	6.1
PDS	–	–	–	4.7	5.8	6.1
Republikaner	–	–	7.1	3.9	1.7	1.9
Others	0.8	3.7	3.8	6.3	3.7	7.9

obtained particularly high results in a number of western cities where they become the second party after the CDU. It is likely that this good performance was also partly due to the personal credit of Joschka Fischer, who, as Foreign Affairs Minister appeared to be the voice of the country's opposition to the Iraq War. The elections also proved a success for the FDP which re-entered the European Parliament in 2004, with 6.1 per cent of the vote. The same score was obtained by the PDS which only slightly improved its performance since 1999, but recovered significantly from the 2002 general elections when it did not manage to pass the 5 per cent threshold. The party seems to have capitalised on protest against the social policy of the government, particularly in the eastern Länder where unemployment is rampant. As always, its results are highly contrasted between the East (25.2 per cent) and West (1.7 per cent) of Germany, which reminds the country of its inherent divisions. At the extreme right of the spectrum, Die Republikaner (1.9 per cent) slightly improved since 1999 but confirmed a clear longer-term decline since 1989. The other extreme left, extreme right, and unaffiliated parties with various idiosyncratic programmes (for the defence of the elderly, animals, family, etc.) shared an unprecedented 7.9 per cent of the vote.

Altogether, the low turnout showed a relative lack of interest in an election in which only 22 per cent of the population participated. The campaign proved particularly uninspiring, with European themes only being used as pretexts for national issues and partisan attacks. However, unlike many other member states, Euroscepticism remained largely absent from the German debate. Amongst the main parties, only Die Rebublikaner echo traditional sovereignist stances and reassert their rejection of political integration in favour of a community of sovereign nation-states. Conversely, the good scores of the FDP and particularly the Greens show that the parties which talked about Europe and supported its fuller integration benefited from a clear electoral bonus.

Valérie Lozac'h

Bibliography

Padgett, S., Patterson, W. and Smith, G., *Developments in German Politics*, Basingstoke, Palgrave Macmillan, 2003.

➔ Abstention; Campaign (Sociology of); Electoral Cycles; Electoral Strategy; European Constitution; European Elections (1979–1999); European Elections (2004); Euroscepticism; Issues; Mapping Europe: European Electoral Geography; Political Market; Postal Voting; Protest Voting; Second-Order Elections; Social Europe.

Greece

Greece joined the EEC on 1 January 1981 making it the tenth country to join the Union. A particular feature of EP elections in Greece is the high turnout (78.6 per cent in 1981, 80.4 per cent in 1994). Whilst this phenomenon is certainly related to the fact that compulsory voting is implemented, it also highlights the context of strong political mobilisation since the end of the 1974 military dictatorship, to the extent that governments systematically explain that they will not enforce the compulsory voting law.

A very stable political scene

Greek political life is marked by a strong left/right confrontation. Over the years, this tension has, however, become less salient since historical 'charismatic

Table 1   Results of the EP elections in Greece (1994–2004)

Political parties	2004 Ballots obtained	%	Seats	1999 Ballots obtained	%	Seats	1994 Ballots obtained	%	Seats
ND	2 633 574	43.01	11	2 314 371	36.00	9	2 133 372	32.66	9
PASOK	2 083 327	34.03	8	2 115 844	32.91	9	2 458 619	37.64	10
KKE	580 396	9.48	3	557 365	8.67	3	410 741	6.29	2
SYN	254 447	4.16	1	331 928	5.16	2	408 066	6.25	2
DIKKI				440 191	6.85	2			
LAOS	252 429	4.12	1						
POLA							564 778	8.65	2
Registered	9 938 863			9 555 326					
Voters	6 283 637	63.18		6 712 684	70.20		6 803 884		
Valid	6 122 632			6 428 696			6 532 591		
Blank/ invalid	161 005			283 988			283 988		

Table 2   Results of the EP elections (1981–1989)

Political parties	1989 %	Seats	1984 %	Seats	1981 %	Seats
ND	40.45	10	38.05	9	30.30	8
PASOK	35.94	9	41.58	10	40.10	10
KKE	14.30	4	11.64	3	12.8	3
SYN						
KKE-ES	3.42	1	5.30	1		
EPEN	1.16	–	2.29	1	–	–
Left miscellaneous (several parties)	1.37	1	–	–	5.40	2
Valid ballots	79.88		77.17		78.60	

Abbreviations: EPEN: National Political Union, Extreme right; KKE-ES: Communist Party of Greece-Interior (dissidents of the KKE, close to Italian Communists' political line). This party joined the SYN (Coalition of the Left) for the 1989 election and integrated with it while the KKE left it.

leaders' such as Constantine Karamanlis have passed away. Karamanlis, founder of the new Republic and of the Néa Dimokratia (ND) party in 1974, died in 1998. Andreas Papandreou, son of the centre-left former Prime Minister and himself founder of the Panhellenic Socialist Movement (PASOK), died in 1996. ND and PASOK generally succeed in winning 75 per cent to 85 per cent of the ballots in the elections. As such, they leave very little room for small rival parties to manoeuvre (Tables 1 and 2).

Those that stand to the political right of the ND only occasionally succeed in challenging its supremacy. Antonis Samaras's party, Political Spring (PolAn), managed to succeed in obtaining two seats in the EP elections of 1994. The main challenger today, however, is the

Popular Orthodox Rally (LAOS). Yet, most of the time, dissidents defect back to the ND; for example, Antonis Samaras was elected MEP on the ND's list in 2004.

To the political left of PASOK, dissidents are rare: the Democratic Social Movement (DIKKI), rival of the reformist trend that took over the party after Andreas Papandreou's death, obtained 7 per cent of the ballots (and two seats) in the 1999 EP elections: a performance it could not repeat. The Communist Party (KKE) maintains a hard line that seems to be successful with its electorate as their share of the vote remains stable (between 5 and 10 per cent of the vote). The Coalition of the Left (SYN), an alliance of former Communists, Trotskyists, and ecologists generally manages with difficulty to find its way between PASOK and the KKE. Its electoral results vary according to the issue and the discontent towards PASOK. SYN has had two seats in the EP since 1994.

Political context and electoral situation

The results of the EP elections in Greece were easily predictable. Usually, EP elections take place at the same time as legislative elections or a few months apart (1981, 1984, 1989, 1994, 2004). The winner of the national election is usually confirmed by the EP elections. In other cases, they are intermediary (mid-term) elections that often punish the party in power (1999). This explains the repeated victories of PASOK (in power from 1981 to 1989 then from 1993 to 2004), but also its defeats in 1989 and 2004.

Indeed, the 2004 EP elections occurred three months after a decisive election in Greek political history: the 7 March 2004 legislative elections. As such, they put an end to a period of deep transformation of

PASOK and of the ND in parallel. PASOK is no longer a monolithic party with a low internal democracy led by Andreas Papandreou but a grouping closer to the Western Europe social-democratic parties. Prime Minister and leader of the party since 1996, Costas Simitis did not run for his succession. He was replaced by Yorgos Papandreou, son of Andreas, but retaining a political ideology similar to that of Simitis. This renewal in leadership did not dissuade the voters from sanctioning a party jaded by a decade in power, too liberal in the eyes of part of its electorate, and discredited by a series of corruption scandals. The ND also experienced a change in leadership. Here, it is also an heir who leads the party: Costas Karamanlis, at the head of the party since the 1996 defeat, is Constantine's nephew. The party line moved towards the centre, which repositions the ND slightly to the left within the EPP party group.

Mode of election and voting modalities

Greece constitutes one single constituency and the representation is proportional (blocked lists). The seats are distributed between all the lists that have obtained more than 3 per cent of the valid votes (a rule that also applies to legislative elections). Any national of the EU aged 18 or more and living in Greece can vote. The parties that obtain more than 1.5 per cent of the valid votes receive public financing. With 24 seats in 1981, the Greek representation won an additional seat since the 1989 EP elections.

Analysis of the electoral results

The low turnout reflects the absence of the perceived salience of the election and the Greek voters' disaffection: 63.18 per cent on 13 June, against 70.2 per

Table 3   Results of the EP elections in Greece in 2004

Party	Group in the EP	%	Number of MEPs (including outing)	Number of MEPs in 1999
ND	EPP-ED	43.06	11 (4)	9
PASOK	ESP	34.03	8 (9)	9
KKE	GUE/NGL	9.46	3 (0)	3
SYN	GUE/NGL	4.15	1 (0)	2
LAOS		4.11	1	0

DIKKI (GUE/NGL) lost the two seats it had obtained in 1999

cent in 1999 and 76.5 per cent in the 7 March 2004 legislative elections. Still benefiting from a 'state of grace' and certainly from the stronger abstention of left-wing voters, the ND was clearly victorious in this election. With 11 MEPs, the ND obtained a result unprecedented in Greece and widens the gap (one seat) with PASOK. It also confirms the results of the legislative elections (45.4 per cent of the ballots). The KKE kept the two seats it has had since 1994. SYN did slightly better than in the latest legislative elections (3.24 per cent) but remains below its previous European performances.

Gilles Bertrand

➜ Mapping Europe: European Electoral Geography.

Green Politics

The 1970s were marked by publications that drew attention to the physical limits of economic development, dispelling the myth of infinite growth in a finite world. The interdependence of societies in an era of globalisation has given a new dimension to problems that had previously been viewed as temporary and limited in space and time. Environmental protection has become a central issue, raising questions about the previously unchallenged benefits of technical progress, of economic growth and industrialisation. Although candidates have been running for elections under the label 'ecologist' since 1973 (when 'People', the precursor to the British Green Party was founded), European elections have deeply influenced the development of Green politics. Indeed, they have provided a forum where Green ideas, as well as organisations and their representatives, could gain visibility (Table 1).

Since 1979, in many countries, the election of MEPs by direct universal suffrage has been a catalyst for the creation of lasting, national electoral coalitions, most of which chose the colour green and the sunflower as their emblems. In France for example, the list led by Solange Ferneix in 1979 triggered the co-ordination of regional groups that had previously been reluctant to accept any degree of centralisation and institutionalisation. The Movement of Political Ecology eventually led to the foundation of 'Les Verts' in 1984. In Germany, the provision of public funding for electoral campaigning was used to organise a founding congress as well as to open a registered head office. Membership of 'Die Grünen' rapidly increased. Since 1979, ecologists

Table 1   Electoral results of Green parties in European Parliament elections, 1979 to 2004 (%)

Country	Party	2004	1999	1994	1989	1984	1979
Germany	Grünen	11.9 (13)	6.4	10.1	8.4	8.2	3.2
Austria	Grüne	12.75 (2)	9.3	6.8	/	/	/
Belgium	Groeni	4.94 (2)	12.0	10.7	12.3	7.1	2.3
	Ecolo	3.69 (3)	22.3	12.9	16.5	9.8	5.1
Finland	VIHR	10.4 (1)	13.4	7.6	/	/	/
France	Les Verts	7.4 (6)	9.7	3.0	10.6	3.4	4.4
Ireland	Green Party	4.5 (1)	6.7	7.9	3.7	0,1	/
Italy	Fed. Verdi	2.5 (2)	1.8	3.2	6.2	/	/
Luxembourg	DEI	15.04 (1)	10.7	10.9	10.4	6.1	1
Netherlands	Groen Links	7.4 (2)	11.9	3.7	6.8	5.6	/
Portugal	CDU-PEV	9.1 (2)	10.3	/	/	/	/
United Kingdom	Green Party	6.21 (2)	6.2	3.2	14.9	2.6	0.1
Sweden	Milio partei	5.90 (1)	9.5	17.2	/	/	/
% average			9.9	8.1	9.9	5.3	2.6

have regularly run in European Parliament elections. Through the election of Green MEPs, political ecologists have gained legitimacy, institutional experience and media visibility, all of which have consolidated their base in the European arena and in national political scenes.

The general public tends to see the Greens as mere environmentalists. This apparent single-mindedness explains why they have occasionally been branded as dangerous extremists without a global outlook on political issues. Until the 1990s, ecologists were often mocked for their alarmist camapigns. Ironically, factual events (nuclear and chemical accidents, food-related scares linked to the so-called 'mad cow' disease, natural disasters), world summits and scientific research (on issues like the depletion of environmental resources, global warming and the rapid extinction of plant and animal species) later confirmed the accuracy of their analysis. Though perhaps not the most salient, protecting the environment has become an unavoidable political issue whilst once reduced to environmentalism, Green demands could be selectively integrated into the agendas of traditional political parties.

The focus on environmental protection has been crucial to the electoral successes of Green parties but it has also concealed the diversity of their proposals and crystallised internal conflict between environmental purists and those open to the demands of the new left. Despite their occasional co-operation in national movements, these different approaches became apparent in the 1980s, when French, Swedish, English and Belgian Greens turned out to be more conservative than their German counterparts. Disagreements between environmental purists and other factions have led to the multiplication of small rival groups. In certain cases, ideological or strategic disagreements were genuinely present, especially on the issue of government alliances, but in others, rival organisations were founded for opportunistic reasons in order to divide political opponents and weaken their credentials. Personal ambition also played a crucial role where the leadership of a national movement was at stake. These divisions have often had severe repercussions. In France for instance, Green lists competed for votes in the European elections in 1984 and 1994 and failed to elect any MEP. Thanks to co-operation and co-ordination efforts occurring within the European parliamentary group, these tensions, partly linked to the youth of a movement in search of an autonomous identity, have slowly faded away. While differences in terms of approach to problematic issues remain, they no longer represent a great source of division.

Indeed, political ecology is now perceived as advocating solidarity and technological prudence; reconciling long-term economic development with social justice; human rights and the protection of species. Moreover, European integration has allowed the Greens to present a united front as critics of contemporary representative institutions and governmental practices. They have demanded the democratisation of national governments as well as of over-complicated and bureaucratic European institutions seen as removed from the concerns of the wider electorate. The commitment and work of Green European MEPs have contributed to proving not only that the EU represents an adequate forum and level of action for the elaboration of political solutions to environmental problems, but also that it could and should play a pioneering role at the international level. European public opinion has gradually become aware of the cross-border nature of environmental issues, whilst neo-liberal globalisation has facilitated the conjunction of the demands of political ecology with those of the anti-capitalist movements, especially on issues linked to the precautionary principle, economic and social rights or international solidarity.

European electoral campaigns have favoured the international co-ordination of the Green movement. A common platform was established as early as 1984.

Since then, co-operation at the European level has continued to deepen. In 1999, Green parties campaigned with a pragmatic, 14-point programme. Amongst its main features were: the democratisation of European institutions; proposals regarding unemployment (limitation of working hours); human rights; the management of energy resources (characterised by the opposition to nuclear power programmes); public transport; the acknowledgement that pollution is not confined by national borders and that the fulfilment of social and economic rights implies the co-ordination of economic policies. Finally, concerns were expressed about the state of transport infrastructures; labour costs; and the opening of European markets to genetically modified organisms. All these issues raise questions about our model of economic and social development, to which the Greens articulate responses that are innovative and increasingly integrated in the mainstream. In 2004, co-operation went further. The first European party was established at a congress in Rome by the fusion of 32 Green parties from 29 countries (among them six non-EU members). This new political party then co-ordinated the electoral campaign in June even though its organisation remained limited by European legislation (it cannot present itself as such at the elections, nor may it recruit individual members).

At the European level, the electoral successes of the Greens have been noticeable, increasing from 2.6 per cent in 1979 to 9.9 per cent in 1999. Results are nevertheless heterogeneous, as parties from Southern Europe are generally weaker in organisational and electoral terms. In 1999 the gaps were considerable: the Verdi gained 1.8 per cent of the votes in Italy whilst Ecolo attracted 22.3 per cent of the votes in francophone Belgium. In 2004, Green lists were successful in three countries

(Germany, Austria and Luxembourg) and progressed slightly in Italy but they stagnated in the United Kingdom, and even decreased their share in seven countries. The protection of the environment remains a marginal issue in the ten new member states despite the established presence of small Green parties usually focused on specific environmental concerns (often linked to industrial pollution). The Green group at the European Parliament was established in 1984 with 11 elected representatives. In 2004, the new group Green/ALE counted 34 Greens and seven associate members from small, 'alternative' groups with environmental inclinations. In 2004, the group welcomed for the first time one Latvian and two Spanish Greens.

Two different but nevertheless complementary explanations are put forward to explain the progress of this new political family whose electorates present common characteristics throughout Europe. Green voters tend to be young, university-educated and they work as professionals in the social and the public sectors. Thus, the success of Green politics is linked to the structural transformation of advanced industrial societies, and in particular to the development of wage earnings and services. A second interpretation suggests that Green sympathisers are defined by their adherence to post-materialist values as they declare putting individual fulfilment, quality of life and cultural liberalism, above priorities such as law and order, economic growth and national defence. According to this theory, the emergence of political ecology is the outcome of a 'silent revolution' linked to the coming of age of the post-war generation who grew up in an era of economic growth and stability. However, the electoral results and the political progress of Green politics remain patchy and irregular. This is partly due to the fact that, despite their

interest in politics, post-materialist citizens favour 'à la carte' participation in new social movements over traditional partisan engagement.

The successes of Green parties have also been limited by 'political cartelisation', that is by a collusion amongst established political parties. Such parties take advantage of their institutional positions to limit the entrance of new competitors in the electoral game. Indeed, they control access to resources (the existence and allocation of public funding) and legislate on electoral expenses (such as deposits for national and European elections), on television and radio broadcast campaigning and on electoral rules. The electoral fortunes of the Greens vary greatly from country to country and are affected by the electoral system. Most countries have chosen proportional representation for European elections, but the simple majority system excluded British Greens from being represented until 1999. Thanks to the adoption of a proportional ballot in regional constituencies, they now have two MEPs. In 2004, a similar, regionally based system was introduced in France with negative effects on Les Verts' delegation (compared to the former proportional poll in a single nationwide constituency). Even though their durability on the European political scene is no longer in doubt, the success of Green parties is contingent on a voting system favourable to new parties. Besides, the election of Green MEPs contributes to ensuring that environmental issues are at the heart of the European political and electoral agendas because they serve as stimuli for the institutions and speakers in the media.

European elections are often viewed as 'second-order elections' that have little effect on either national governments or European decision-making bodies. Because of this perception, voters are less inclined to vote 'tactically' and often take the opportunity to vote expressively in a fashion that is less common when the selection of a national government is at stake. Consequently they are often characterised by low turnout as well as the dispersion of votes between small electoral lists. Environmental concerns are not the only motivations for a Green vote in European elections. The Greens also attract voters willing to find a safe way to sanction ruling governments. The excellent score (15 per cent of the votes) obtained in 1989 by the British Green Party can be explained by the frustration of the Conservative electorate with the Thatcher government and their unwillingness to vote in favour of the Labour Party. Finally, criticism of institutionalised parties is not only reflected in the decline in electoral participation but also in the rise of protest votes. In the 1980s and the early 1990s, before the Greens participated in governmental coalitions (in France, Finland and Germany), the Green vote was sometimes a vote rejecting old cleavages and the left–right binary opposition. Nevertheless, environmental parties have affirmed themselves as potential partners for social-democratic parties, confirming the leftist orientation of most Green party members and voters. Finally, the Greens have asserted the originality of their world vision. Green politics cannot be reduced to the science from which it originated, nor to the mere defence of the environment; it has become a major political issue on the European agenda, and is the core impetus of a new partisan family.

Florence Faucher-King

Bibliography

Bomberg, E., *Green Parties and Politics in the European Union*, London and New York, Routledge, 1998.

Delwitt, P. and De Waele, J.-M., *Les partis verts en Europe*, Bruxelles, Editions Complexe, 1999.

Richardson, D. and Rootes, C. (eds), *The Green Challenge: the Development of Green Parties in Europe*, London, Routledge, 1995.

'The Lifespan and the Political Performance of Green Parties in Western Europe', *Environmental Politics*, Special Edition, 11, 1, 2002.

→ Democratic Deficit; Deposit; European Elections (1979–1999); European Elections (2004); European Federation of Green Parties; European Parliament; European Political Parties; European Public Opinion; Europeanisation (of National Political Life); Federations of Political Parties; Financing; Issues; Political Market; Protest Voting; Second-Order Elections; Territorial Organisation.

Hungary

European elections took place in Hungary for the first time in 2004. This offered a unique historical opportunity for the electorate, politicians and political scientists alike. It would demonstrate whether Hungary would conform to European trends and how Europeanisation would affect the domestic political field.

The legal framework

The Hungarian parliament accepted Act 113 on the Election to the European Parliament on 15 December 2003. Pressure of time and a highly divided Hungarian political society meant that this law included only the minimal regulations necessary to hold the elections. The system of European parliamentary elections is significantly different from the two-round, mixed system that is used in national parliamentary elections in Hungary. Therefore, it was necessary to work out the model of a new election system as well as to modify Act 100 of 1997 on the Election Process.

Hungary elects 24 members of the European Parliament. According to the 2003 election law the country is a single electoral district. All political parties are free to participate and they may compete through individual or joint national party lists. Each party list has to receive 20 000 recommendations from the electorate in order to be able to compete. These closed party lists may include up to 72 names. However, only parties that receive at least 5 per cent of all votes cast may win mandates. Mandates are conferred by the d'Hondt method. If a tie occurs in relation to the last mandate, it is the place of the party lists in the ballot that determines the winner. If a mandate is vacated, the next person on the list of the party that won that seat becomes the member of the EP. If the list includes no more candidates, the party that would have won the next mandate at the elections wins the seat. Similarly to national elections, there is a campaign moratorium from the day preceding the voting day until the closing of the ballot boxes.

All Hungarian and EU citizens who reside in Hungary and wish to vote in this country may cast their votes in the Republic of Hungary. A voter may only recommend one party list and vote for only one list. They cast their votes in 10 871 voting districts. However, unlike in national elections, Hungarian citizens abroad on election day are also allowed to vote and they constitute one voting district.

Similarly to national elections it is the National Election Committee (OVB) that is responsible for the organisation of the elections. During the 2004 EP elections the OVB had 13 members: five independent members (with two MEPs) and eight members delegated by the political parties that participated in the elections. The OVB is the organ to which parties had to announce their wish to participate at the elections, that verifies whether they fulfilled the legal requirements of taking part in the elections and draws the order in which party lists appear on the ballot. Through the National Election Bureau (OVI) the OVB is responsible for the organisation and administering of the elections. It pronounces the official result of the elections and investigates any wrongdoings in relations to the election and the campaign. The official election result can be challenged in front of the Supreme Court.

The first modification of the Act on the Election to the EP occurred before the elections, due to an extensive media campaign that argued against a four-member committee consisting of the representatives of the parliamentary parties being sent to each country where Hungarian citizens expressed their wish to vote on the embassy. The committee was to count the votes and report the result to the OVB. On 24 May 2004 this costly solution was abolished. Instead, ballot boxes are closed and sent to the OVB from abroad and a three-member committee elected from the members of the OVB counts the votes (Act 43 of 2004). In addition, the Hungarian parliament regulated the legal standing of the Hungarian Members of the European Parliament only after the elections (Act 57 of 2004). Moreover, there are no specific provisions on the financing of EP election campaigns. Therefore, it is the provisions of the much-disputed finance regulations of national elections that remain in force. However, they are not fully compatible with the EP elections campaign system.

Political parties in the EP elections

Although initially 16 parties intended to compete in the elections, only nine party lists tried to register for the election. Yet, only eight party lists received the required number of recommendations because the joint list of the Green Party and the Hungarian Countryside and Civic Party failed to meet the regulations concerning the process of collecting the recommendations (www.valasztas.hu/04/hu).

The eight participants included the four parliamentary parties: the leftist Hungarian Socialist Party (MSZP), the liberal Alliance of Free Democrats (SZDSZ), the centre-right Fidesz–Hungarian Civic Alliance (Fidesz-MPSZ) and the Hungarian Democratic Forum (MDF). There were also four extra-parliamentary parties taking part in the elections: the Social Democratic Party (SZDP), the Hungarian National Alliance (MNSZ), the extreme-left Worker's Party (MP) and the extreme-right Party of Hungarian Justice and Life (MIÉP).

The present Hungarian political landscape is dominated by the four parliamentary parties. It is determined by the result of the 2002 general elections that ended in a narrow left-liberal/left majority. Thus, the governing coalition is made up of the MSZP and its junior partner, the SZDSZ. The cabinet is headed by Péter Medgyessy, who is not a member of any of the coalition parties. The leading party of the opposition is Fidesz-MPSZ. However, the relatively weak MDF, that used to closely co-operate with Fidesz, has tried to distance itself from the main opposition party and develop an independent profile.

The 2002 general elections were also formative in that they brought an unprecedented sharp rivalry between the MSZP and Fidesz-MPSZ. As a result, Hungarian politics has become increasingly dominated by the deep division between the two camps. Hence, political analysts anticipated a tight race between the two big parties for the most of the 24 seats at the EP elections. They forecasted a clear Fidesz victory. The SZDSZ and the MDF was expected, at best, to win one seat in the EP. None of the extra-parliamentary parties was predicted to pass the 5 per cent threshold.

The election campaign

Although the political elite created a sharp social division between the centre-left and the centre-right, ordinary people preferred the softening of this confrontation. This popular demand made it impossible for the parties to return to a deeply divisive, emotional campaign. Both sides made an effort to arrive at national unity. Prime Minister Péter Medgyessy proposed that all parties unite forces in one joint national list at the EP elections, which would have included politicians of the government and the opposition on an equal basis. This idea, however, was quickly rejected by the junior coalition member (SZDSZ) as well as by the opposition parties (Fidesz, MDF) as being anti-democratic and going against the logic of a multi-party system. On the other hand, Fidesz put forward an initiative containing a nine-point list to defend the 'common interests' of the nation. Meanwhile the smaller opposition party, the MDF, issued a statement, called 'The Monok Manifesto', calling for national discussion and partnership to establish long-term national goals.

The campaign of the leading governing party, the MSZP, was twofold. On the one hand, it emphasised the recovery of the economy and Hungary's accession to the EU as the success of the ruling coalition. Secondly, it employed a negative campaign against Fidesz, which is more than unusual from a party in power. These strategies aimed at reaching out to its usual voting base, but diminished the image that the party achieved in the 2002 election as the peace-seeking side. In addition, domestic issues dominated their campaign: despite treating the EU accession as a Socialist success story, the MSZP spoke very little of the Union and its nine-page campaign flier did not reach the voters. In their campaign they proposed no vision of either Hungary or Europe.

Furthermore, the Socialist Party list included politicians who could not boost the party's campaign. The leaders of the list (Foreign Minister László Kovács and ex-Premier Gyula Horn) were respected figures in Europe, but proved too grey and old to attract attention at home. Moreover, before the elections it was known that upon their election to the EP they would both resign their seats to other Socialist members of the list.

Meanwhile their coalition partner, the Free Democrats, came out with a very strong and fresh campaign. This helped them to make the first move in stepping out of the shadow of the Socialists and overcoming their long-standing image problems. The SZDSZ offered a Liberal alternative in a political arena that has been strongly determined by a Socialist/Conservative division. In their campaign they aimed at educating the electorate about this new three-dimensional political field and the meaning of liberalism. They also tried to exploit the fact that their policies have always been more popular than the party itself and their campaign focused on policy issues. Consequently, they pursued a positive campaign. As a result, the SZDSZ used the EP elections for image building and looked towards the 2006 domestic general elections (Tóth 2004). The rhetoric of the leader of the party list and mayor of Budapest Gábor Demszky linked local governmental issues with the European Union. He spoke of working in the interest of the capital city in the European Parliament in order to win the votes of his supporters in Budapest.

Fidesz-MPSZ used the EP elections as a vote of no confidence against the incumbent social-liberal coalition. Therefore, it used a strategy that would address wide segments of the public. Besides its usual supporters, such as the young or the countryside citizens, Fidesz tried to reach out to the assumed losers of the country's EU accession (pensioners, farmers, small entrepreneurs) or the opponents of Hungary's EU membership (radicals) with whom Fidesz's reservations towards the Union resonated well. Fidesz employed an anti-capitalist rhetoric and questioned the 'social' character of the government so as to win the votes of those who were disappointed with the ruling coalition (urban population, lower middle class people) as well as undecided voters.

Hence, their campaign primarily focused on national political issues. It centred on the 'national petition' that aimed at collecting one million signatures for a programme that stressed security in everyday life. Fidesz also attacked the government's economic performance by claiming that the government would introduce an austerity package after the elections. This was very effectively communicated by negative TV and leaflet commercials with visions of worsening living conditions. The active role of party leader Viktor Orbán was well complemented by the widespread but somewhat dull campaign of Pál Schmitt, the front-runner of the Fidesz party list. The latter helped in communicating a positive party image.

In relation to the European Union Fidesz emphasized the representation of national interest, Christian values, the reunification of the Hungarian nation in the EU, and the importance of a united, one-tier Europe. Interestingly, Fidesz tried to avoid using such words as 'accession' or 'expansion' in relation to the Union; instead, it spoke of a reunification of Europe.

The smaller opposition party, the MDF, used its campaign to build a separate identity from Fidesz. In this effort it tried to open up both towards the right and the left so as to gain votes from both Fidesz and the MSZP. Its strategy was built on a negative moral campaign under the slogan 'For a normal Hungary', which enjoyed the support of two non-contesting parties: the Independent Smallholders' Party (FKGP) and the Hungarian Democratic People's Party (MDNP). The MDF took a very strong position on the question of the Hungarian troops in Iraq and demanded their withdrawal. EU issues, however, was almost completely missing from their EP election campaign. One asset of their campaign was party and EP list leader Ibolya Dávid, who has been the most popular politician in Hungary.

The campaigns of the extra-parliamentary parties were characterised by the media appearance of their leaders as well as local meetings with the electorate. The leaders (István Csurka, Gyula Thürmer) of the extremist and ideologically committed parties (MIÉP and MP) are long-standing actors in Hungarian politics and they only needed to reinforce their earlier images. The appearances of party leaders Mátyás Szürös of SZDP and Gyula Balog of MNSZ were to make their parties and programmes known and thus more popular. Their statements, however, often proved clumsy and unprofessional. At local meetings the SZDP regularly joined forces with Fidesz. Probably due to the OVB's call for equal opportunity in the media, extra-parliamentary parties received considerably more media attention than at the national elections. Yet, proportionately they significantly lagged behind the parliamentary parties. Nevertheless, the MNSZ's attempt to challenge the results of the elections, and thus to force a repeat of the elections because of unequal (= unfair) media attention was beyond the reality of multiparty election competition.

Results

In Hungary, European elections were held on 13 June 2004. Polling stations

Table 1 EP election results in Hungary (13 June 2004)

Parties	Votes		Seats
	In number	In per cent	
Fidesz-MPSZ	1 457 750	47.40	12
MSZP	1 054 921	34.30	9
SZDSZ	237 908	7.74	2
MDF	164 025	5.33	1
MIÉP	72 203	2.35	0
MP	56 221	1.83	0
MNSZ	20 226	0.66	0
SZDP	12 196	0.40	0

Fidesz-MPSZ	Fidesz-Magyar Polgári Szövetség = Fidesz–Hungarian Civic Alliance
FKGP	Független Kisgazdapárt = Independent Smallholders Party
MDF	Magyar Demokrata Fórum = Hungarian Democratic Forum
MDNP	Magyar Demokrata Néppárt = Hungarian Democratic People's Party
MIÉP	Magyar Igazság és Élet Pártja = Hungarian Justice and Life Party
MNSZ	Magyar Nemzeti Szövetség = Hungarian National Alliance
MP	Munkáspárt = Worker's Party
MSZP	Magyar Szocialista Párt = Hungarian Socialist Party
OVB	Országos Választási Bizottság = National Election Committee
OVI	Országos Választási Hivatal = National Election Bureau
SZDP	Szociáldemokrata Párt = Social Democratic Party
SZDSZ	Szabad Demokraták Szövetsége = Alliance of Free Democrats

were open from 6 a.m. to 7 p.m. In general, elections were conducted fairly (the OVB established misconduct only in relation to the media that failed to observe the campaign moratorium in a few cases, but this did not seriously effect the outcome). Voter turnout was lower than the 45 per cent that public opinion agencies predicted. Only 38.5 per cent of the eligible voters (that is 3 097 657 people) decided to cast their votes on election day. Valid votes reached 99.28 per cent (www.valasztas. hu/04/hu/). The results are summarised in Table 1.

The first four parties passed the 5 per cent threshold and thus could send representatives to the European Parliament. Fidesz-MPSZ secured victory as expected by winning 12 seats. However, the MSZP won only nine seats, and hence, it came short of its worst expectations of ten seats in the EP. The

two small parliamentary parties performed better than they had expected: the SZDSZ won two seats and its leaders came to evaluate it as a 'liberal landslide', while MDF leader Ibolya Dávid took the party's winning of one seat as her personal victory. No extra-parliamentary parties came even close to passing the threshold and winning a seat.

Conclusions

Hungary reflected European trends in that the incumbent government lost the European elections similarly to 22 other EU countries and that voter turnout was low. Socialist voters expressed their dissatisfaction with the government by staying away from the elections in great numbers. The MSZP's attempt to play down the importance of the elections also encouraged abstention. On the other hand, it was crucial in Fidesz's victory that it was more successful in mobilising its supporters.

The characteristics of the campaign were also advantageous for Fidesz-MPSZ. It was the leading opposition party that determined the campaign themes and the domestic topics were favourable to them. It was also fortunate that Fidesz tried to emotionally influence its voters and suggested worsening everyday life for citizens in case of a Socialist victory. Against this vision it urged solidarity among voters, a move that had a very positive message. The 'national petition' built on the trinity of 'jobs, family, security', that is, traditional leftist values, helped to attract disappointed or not fully committed Socialist supporters. Its organisational development was also an asset especially in voter mobilisation. Yet Fidesz understood that its victory was ambiguous for it failed to mobilise those segments of the society that would prove crucial in winning national elections. Therefore, its celebrations were modest: no reference was made to the immediate change of government. On the whole, Fidesz and especially its leader Viktor Orbán saved its credits by re-establishing itself as the victorious side.

The small parties of the SZDSZ and the MDF were winners of the elections. The low level of participation was most beneficial for the SZDSZ and the MDF in that they could pass the threshold at ease by mobilising their small but committed circle of supporters. Moreover, it is very likely that the SZDSZ profited from the disappointment of leftist government sympathisers who decided to warn the MSZP by giving their votes to the junior member of the coalition. Both the MDF and the SZDSZ could profit from their EP election performance in the long run and strengthen their positions in the Hungarian political arena.

The big – and the only – loser of the election was the MSZP. Although Socialist/Social-Democratic parties seem to be in crisis throughout Europe, the Hungarian Socialist Party could only blame itself for its defeat because of a misguided election campaign. Its negative campaign proved ineffective: it alienated those who chose the MSZP two years ago because of its less militant rhetoric and failed to mobilise those who were unsatisfied with the government's performance. Inner party considerations outweighed campaign needs. Consequently, there was no politician that could have given a 'face' to the campaign – in this sense, it might have been a liability that the Prime Minister is not a member of the party. The day after the elections the chairman of the MSZP László Kovács announced his resignation and later he changed the position of the foreign minister to the Commissioner of Energy in the new European Commission. During the summer of 2004 the cabinet was also reshuffled. Meanwhile the MSZP faced renewal at its October 2004 party conference, which is essential in order to save its chances for victory at the next general elections.

András Bozóki
Ágnes Simon

Bibliography

Tóth, Csaba, 'Az SZDSZ kampánya és választási szereplése' [The Campaign and the Electoral Results of the SZDSZ], presented at the 10th Conference of the Hungarian Political Science Association, Siófok, 25–26 June 2004.

→ Mapping Europe: European Electoral Geography.

I

Identity

The concept of political identity

The concept of identity has been of interest to philosophers and psychologists long before it started to attract the attention of social scientists. Since ancient times, scholarly attention has been dedicated to how and why an individual defines him/herself in a certain way. However, the emergence of holistic social sciences in the late nineteenth century inspired a new wave of interest in the phenomenon of 'collective identities'. Anthropologists, sociologists and historians in particular started to try and understand hypothetical 'common' identities of groups belonging to a common nation, race or religion. This created a level of scholarly tension between the adherents of an individual perspective of identity and those who focused on broader mass or collective identities instead.

In academic terms, efforts were made to try and unify these two perspectives by defining two possible forms or components of identities usually known in the social psychological literature as 'personal' and 'social' identities. A 'personal' identity is expected to address specifically the individual characteristics of a person, to be inductively derived from his/her perception of him/herself, and to result in more emotional identity reactions. Conversely, a 'social' identity emerges from the ex-ante consciousness of a pre-existing group with which numbers of individuals will 'identify', and which they will together define.

However, in recent years, psychologists such as Breakwell (2004) have questioned the relevance of the distinction between social and personal identities. Moreover, if one believes in such dualism, it can be argued that political identities, far from being a mere component of social identities, transcend this distinction to create a category in its own right (Bruter 2005). Political identities will often lead to the same emotional reactions as personal identities, and may assume such a variety of self-perceptions, definitions and emotions, that the concept of collective political identities can easily be challenged.

Despite a growing interest in ethnic and gender identity studies, political identities are often primarily conceived in reference to territorial politics and citizens' attachment to their town, region, nation, continent, etc. It is usually admitted that these attachments may affect citizens' attitudes and political behaviour. Despite what is usually believed, the primary level of territorial identification of citizens remains small communities such as their town or region rather than their country, as shown in Table 1.

The concept of European identity

'Common knowledge' and the media usually assume that there is no such thing as a European identity. This may be partly because the concept of European identity, as a potential emerging political identity, has only been of interest to scholars of the social sciences in the last few years.

Table 1   Citizens' primary territorial identity in Europe (%)

Country	Nation	Town	Region	Europe/other
Poland	**47.3**	29.7	13.3	9.6
Slovenia	39.3	**44.8**	8.6	7.3
Finland	**39.2**	35.7	12.3	12.7
Czech Republic	**36.0**	28.8	20.2	14.9
Ireland	31.4	**47.4**	13.6	7.5
Britain	31.3	**37.7**	16.6	14.5
Netherlands	31.0	**44.2**	7.7	17.2
Denmark	29.2	**45.7**	16.4	8.7
Spain	29.1	**45.2**	16.1	9.5
France	28.1	**37.7**	15.6	18.5
Austria	27.3	**34.5**	31.4	6.9
Hungary	26.8	**56.8**	5.7	10.7
Latvia	26.2	30.0	**30.7**	13.2
Portugal	25.9	**39.2**	18.5	16.4
Italy	25.5	**41.1**	9.6	23.9
Sweden	24.8	**57.0**	11.7	6.4
Slovakia	23.0	**36.9**	30.7	9.4
Lithuania	22.1	32.5	**36.2**	9.2
West Germany	20.9	**39.7**	20.4	18.9
Belgium	19.9	**52.8**	9.5	17.7
Northern Ireland	19.4	**44.5**	29.1	7.0
East Germany	15.8	**36.6**	24.0	23.6
Estonia	14.8	**36.6**	36.0	12.6
EU AVERAGE	*27.6*	*40.7*	*18.9*	*12.9*

Notes:
Figures are computed from the World Value Surveys 1981–1997.
Countries are ranked by the proportion of respondents quoting the nation as their dominant community of reference.
Europe/Other is the sum of Europe, world, and other communities.
Figures in bold represent the primary community of reference for each country.

Two main approaches have been used by those who have wanted to study or characterise this new European identity. Firstly, a 'top-down' approach – close to the socio-historical collective identity tradition – which has attempted to identify common objective characteristics or a 'shared heritage' (values, history, ethnicity, etc.) between Europeans. Secondly, a 'bottom-up' approach, yet more recent, which, in the political psychology tradition, has been more concerned with which – and how many – individuals actually define themselves as European and what they mean by this.

The top-down approach has been used by a number of scholars. Wintle et al. (1996), who are primarily concerned with the existence of a shared historical heritage between Europeans, point out the existence of shared images and, to an extent, the impact of a common series of historical traditions, including Judaeo-Christendom, the Renaissance, and Greek and Roman antiquity. In contrast, Van Deth and Scarborough (1995) prefer to focus on the existence of shared values, which, according to them, unify Europeans, and distinguish them from the social norms in other parts of the world. Finally, Shore (1993) and Abeles et al. (1993), looked at the existence of collective social images, particularly amongst the European elites.

In contrast, the bottom-up approach to the emergence of a European identity is of primary interest in understanding citizens' behaviour in the context of the 2004 European Parliament elections. Indeed, the bottom-up approach seeks to study the progressive emergence of a mass European identity, differences among Europeans' perceptions of their own Europeanness, and the impact of feeling European on citizens' political behaviour in general – and behaviour in European elections in particular.

Theorising the emergence of a European identity

One of the main questions faced by scholars during the past ten years has concerned the compatibility of European and sub-European (particularly national) identities.

Traditionally, post-materialists, and particularly Inglehart (1977), have conceived support for European integration and European identity as similar concepts, and European identity as a virtual 'non-identity' based on cosmopolitanism and emerging in opposition to national feelings. However, other scholars believe, on the contrary, that European and other identities are both compatible and even positively correlated. Risse (2004) proposes several conceptions of the compatibility and

interaction between various identities, such as the 'marble cake' and the 'Russian doll' models. The 'Russian doll' model suggests multilayered identities, which superimpose and include each other. Any change in one layer will in effect modify the definition of the other. By contrast, the 'marble cake' model of nested identities implies a less straight-forward interaction between multiple intertwined political identities.

In this context, Bruter (2003, 2005) goes even further, and shows that not only are multiple identities compatible for most citizens, but they are also positively correlated. In other words, far from being a 'natural tension' between national and European identities, it is generally true that the more 'Belgian' or 'Italian' a citizen feels, the more (and not the less) likely he is to feel European as well. The same positive correlations exist between European identity and regional and local identities respectively. At the same time, Bruter claims that European identity – like any other political identity – can be divided into two components: a 'civic' identity (identification with one's image of the European Union as a political system), and a 'cultural' identity (identification with one's image of Europe as a human community, perceived, in whatever way, rational or irrational, to share 'something', be it defined by some ethnic, cultural, value-related, human-related or any other feature).

The emergence of a mass European identity 1970–2004

In this context, recent work by Herrmann et al. (2004) and Bruter (2005) suggests that a European identity has largely progressed in the European Union since the early 1970s. The research suggests that the emergence of a mass European identity is what explains the paradox, since the mid-1990s, between a continuing support of citizens for European integration (and indeed demands for faster and faster political integration) on the one hand, and a decreasing sense amongst the European citizenry that integration is actually beneficial to their individual country on the other hand.

While large comparative differences remain between countries, this progression has concerned, at different levels, all 15 pre-2004 member states, including the most Eurosceptic. On a scale from 0–1, the level of European identity in Great Britain was in the low 0.20s in the early 1970s and reached the high 0.40s by the turn of the century. Similarly, European identity scores did not surpass the low 0.50s in the 1970s in France and the Netherlands but were consistently between 0.70 and 0.75 in the late 1990s.

Finally, in Italy, the level of European identity in the country was in the high 0.50s in the mid-1970s and above 0.80 throughout the late 1990s. The only exception to the upwards trend was Germany, where levels of European identity declined in the 1990s, but the country's integration of largely Eurosceptic East Germans certainly largely explains this trend (Bruter, 2005).

Table 2 confirms the same progressive increase of levels of attachment to Europe in the shorter term. It shows that over the past five years, levels of attachment to Europe have increased in 13 of the 15 member states and in the European Union as a whole. It is only in the Netherlands and Luxembourg (in this last case, starting levels were particularly high) that attachment to Europe decreased over the same period of time.

Table 2   Evolution of citizens' attachment to Europe: 1999–2003

Country	1999	2000	2003	Change 2003/ 1999
EU TOTAL	*56*	*58*	*58*	*+2*
Luxembourg	78	82	76	–2
Denmark	71	66	73	+2
Sweden	71	74	72	+1
Italy	65	66	68	+3
Spain	68	72	67	–1
Belgium	63	63	67	+4
Austria	62	64	66	+4
Portugal	61	61	63	+2
Germany	58	58	62	+4
Finland	53	56	62	+9
Ireland	57	52	58	+1
France	53	56	57	+4
Greece	41	43	52	+11
UK	37	41	41	+4
Netherlands	49	53	29	–20

Notes:
Figures are % of citizens claiming to be very or fairly attached to Europe according to Eurobarometer surveys 51, 54 and 60.
Figures in the last column (change 2003/1999) are in bold if attachment to Europe increased during the period, in plain font otherwise.

At the individual level, research has shown that young people, citizens with a relatively high level of education, and those who have had opportunities to live or travel abroad tend to have a higher level of European identity, and that, except in countries such as the United Kingdom, the European identity of citizens tends to be primarily civic rather than cultural (Bruter 2005).

European citizens and European institutions

Does European identity impact citizens' behaviour in the European Parliament elections?

Many journalists have attributed the relatively low turnout in European elections to a lack of European *demos* and absence of a widespread European identity. The state of political science tends to invalidate their point and suggest that decreasing levels of turnout must be explained by other factors than by the level of European identity of citizens, which has increased, on average, over the years whilst turnout was in decline. If anything, it is likely that the increasing level of European identity of citizens may partly explain why turnout for European Parliament elections is not lower given the very limited powers of the European Parliament, the absence of impact of party politics on the behaviour of the MEPs, and the weakness of campaigns, in most member states, on European politics and policy-making.

However, existing research clearly suggests that greater involvement in European integration increases the likelihood of a given voter participating in the European Parliament elections regardless of his/her perceptions of the campaign, the offerings of the various candidates, and the powers of the European Parliament. Similarly, Eijk et al. (1996) show that in Italy, the proportion of citizens deciding on who to vote for on the basis of parties' stances on European rather than national issues had quite significantly increased between 1989 and 1994.

Conclusion: effect of European elections on European identity

Clearer than the effect of European identity on the vote of citizens, is the fact that European elections themselves have not been immune to the progressive emergence of a mass European identity. Bruter (2005) shows that all symbols of European integration – including European Parliament elections held at the same time throughout the European Union – have had a strong impact on citizens' European identity. Researchers on the emergence of a European public sphere, such as Risse (in Hermann et al. 2004 and Neveu in this volume) also point to the lack of emergence, so far, of a European public sphere (see related article) and the fact that, in the long term, European Parliament elections, if they become increasingly important, will be the natural emerging space for such a public sphere. Already, heated debates on the priorities of EU integration and high interest and turnout for the French referendum on an EU Constitution in 2005 show a clear public demand for the emergence of such a public sphere. Indeed, political identities, particularly in their 'civic' component, while individual and subjective, are more likely to grow on the fertile grounds of a pre-existing and significant political system and citizenship, which, in themselves, give reality to the common status and citizenship Europeans may identify with over time.

Michael Bruter

References

Abelès, M., Bellier, I. and McDonald, M., *An Anthropological Approach to the European Commission*, unpublished report, 1993.

Bruter, M., 'Winning Hearts and Minds for Europe: News, Symbols, and European Identity', *Comparative Political Studies*, 36, 10, 2003, pp. 1148–79.

Bruter, M., *Citizens of Europe? The Emergence of a Mass European Identity*, Basingstoke, Palgrave Macmillan, 2005.

Eijk, C. van der, Franklin, M. et al. (eds), *Choosing Europe? The European Electorate and National Politics in the Face of Union*, Ann Arbor, University of Michigan Press, 1996.

Herrmann, R., Risse, R. and Brewer, M., *Transnational Identities: Becoming European in the EU*, New York: Rowmann and Littlefield, 2004.

Inglehart, R., *The Silent Revolution*, Basingstoke, Macmillan, 1977.

Shore, C., 1993. 'Inventing the "People's Europe": Critical Perspectives on European Community Cultural Policy', *Man*, 28, 4, 1993, pp. 779–800.

Van Deth, J. and Scarborough, E., *The Impact of Values*, Oxford, Oxford University Press, 1995.

Wintle, M. et al., *Culture and Identity in Europe*, London, Avebury, 1996.

Primary sources:
Dataset of the 'Understanding Identity Realignments' project (M. Bruter).

Eurobarometer series (available on-line at www.europa.eu.int).

World Values Survey (available on-line at www.worldvaluesurvey.org).

→ Electoral Behaviour; European Electoral Sociology.

Immigrants' Vote

Until the middle of the 1980s, immigrants' political involvement and representation were not relevant issues on the political and scientific agenda in Europe. Immigrants were not considered as potential citizens but as (guest) workers supposed to return to their countries of origin. Their settlement process started when the European states decided to close the borders to labour immigration (1973–4). The immigrant presence has changed in favour of family reunification: it has become a political question. This explains the importance of the nationality theme in the 1980s and the 1990s.

Another factor in the transformation of the immigrants' vote issue was European political integration. While it was traditionally associated with nationality, active citizenship (vote and eligibility) was partly dissociated from nationality by the Maastricht Treaty (1992). This citizenship without nationality project was read by some authors as the kernel of the European project, the non-nationals voting issue becoming symbolic of the debates on the future of citizenship in Europe. But this structuring relation between European citizenship and the immigrants' vote is problematic.

To understand it, one must consider the diversity of the ways of conceiving the 'immigrants' vote' in European countries as well as the teachings relative to the citizenship of populations stemming from immigration or members of ethno-cultural or religious minorities.

Varying situations

The issue of the immigrants' vote covers very diverse questions from the right of nationality to experiences of the local vote by foreigners via debates on integration, mobilisation and ethnic or religious leadership forms, transnational allegiances, and dual nationality. These questions (and the way they are asked) vary quite strongly from one country to another and no situation is static: there is no European conception of 'the immigrants' vote' as such. Three typical groups, however, may be examined in order to discuss the access to political rights of certain groups.

The first group is that of foreigners (non-nationals) coming from a third country (out of the EU). They do not have the right to vote, allowing for some exceptions. Thus, some countries of Northern Europe gave access to political citizenship at the local or even regional level: Sweden (since 1975), Denmark (since 1977 for nationals from Nordic states, and 1981 for the others), Norway (since 1978 and 1982), Finland (1981) and the Netherlands (1985). In Belgium, a constitutional reform in 1998 led to the law – finally voted by the parliament on 20 February 2004 – on immigrants' local franchise, excluding however the right to eligibility. Foreigners will be able to participate in the 2006 local elections provided that they have resided continuously for five years in the town and they commit themselves to honouring the Constitution and the European Convention for the Protection of Human Rights and Fundamental Freedoms. Elsewhere, as in Germany, similar attempts have failed (Hamburg and Schleswig-Holstein Länder). Foreigners' consultation forms had been used before that in Germany, the Netherlands and Belgium (in immigrants' consultative local councils) at the end of the 1960s, whereas they have remained on the verge of illegality in France (particularly Cerizay in 1989, Vandoeuvre-lès-Nancy, les Ullis, Longjumeau in 1990, Portes-lès-Valence in 1992, and more recently, Grenoble in 2000, Paris in 2002, and soon Lyon). Whereas candidate Mitterrand had promised it in the 1981 presidential elections, the foreigners' vote has gone unheeded despite the vote of a bill by the French National Assembly in 2000. The attitudes concerning this right vary: in France, the cons went from 38 to 53 per cent between 2003 and 2004 (during the debates on secularity); the pros are only 34 per cent in Germany but 62 per cent in Spain and 54 per cent in Italy ('new' immigration countries since the 1990s) (*Lettre de la citoyenneté*, May–June 2004).

The second group consists of nationals of foreign origin and their descendants who have obtained the nationality of their country of residence and kept their nationality of origin (or not). Most of them were born in their countries of residence. The rights to nationality in Europe evolved between 1980 and 2000 with the spread of the *jus soli* and the liberalisation of dual nationality legislation. Another aspect of this evolution involves the disappearance of the distinction between 'great' and 'small naturalisation' (particularly in Belgium after 1991). The access to nationality is also often influenced by the colonial heritage. In France, the dual *jus soli* concerns children born in France whose parents were born before 1 January 1963 in Algeria (then a French *département*). Spain plans access conditions to nationality for Latin American nationals provided they reside in Spain and that Spanish nationals do the same in Latin America ('sleeping nationality'). The Portuguese law envisages similar exceptions with Brazil, even if it only concerns local citizenship. Finally, immigrants sometimes have total access to political citizenship as soon as they arrive in a country, such as the Commonwealth nationals who settled in Great Britain after the war (before the return of restrictive immigration policies after 1962). In Germany, opening the right to nationality to the *jus soli* in 2000 concerns populations coming particularly from Turkey (about 2.5 million people). Before the reform, the right to nationality based on parentage had enabled the incorporation of *Aussiedler* into the German nationality, a large number of whom came after the opening of the Eastern borders of Europe after 1989.

The third group are the European citizens (nationals of a EU member state). They have active citizenship in local and European elections in their state of residence (Article 8B of the Maastricht Treaty). This excludes national elections and some executive functions concerning the sovereignty of a state (for instance, the functions of mayor and deputy mayor in France).

We shall also consider the different ways of dealing with the immigrants' vote issue. There are at least two issues, which are sometimes contradictory. For the first one, the immigrants' vote concerns their access to formal citizenship, most of the time through nationality. In France, the political involvement and representation of the immigrant populations are discussed mainly in terms of nationality of origin and place of birth. Created by INSEE (the French National Institute of Economic and Statistical Information) during the 1990 census, the 'immigrant' category adds to the 'foreigners' category and defines people born abroad, living in France and who have kept their nationality of origin (or not). The second issue concerns the ability of the common institutions of political society to represent the real society in its entire diversity. In Great Britain, the census inserted so-called 'ethnic' categories in 1991 ('Whites', 'Caribbean Black', 'Indian', 'Other Asians', etc.) and religious categories in 2001.

An 'ethnic vote'?

The ethnic identity–political involvement relation arouses a suspicion in France that does not exist in Great Britain or the Netherlands. Beyond the political stake (which also concerns the legitimacy of political scientists and sociologists to work on these issues), we must insist on the complex relation between the ethnic belonging criterion and electoral behaviour.

The immigrants' or ethnic minorities' vote is characterised by permanent features: a lower level of registration on the electoral list than the average; a relatively low turnout (in spite of great variations), and a lack of interest in European elections compared to elections considered as more important (local or national). Their vote also poses as a class vote and is reflected in allegiance to left parties (Labour Party in Great Britain, PS in France, SPD and Greens in Germany, etc.). Meindert Fennema and Jean Tillie's work in the Netherlands showed that if ethnicity is a key factor in measuring political involvement, it is no longer important in assessing the political content of this involvement which polarises according to the ideological competition between parties. The groups' elites can nevertheless intervene to 'mobilise' the votes or heighten the young's awareness of registration in electoral lists (e.g. the *Beur* movement associations in France in the 1980s, Operation Black Vote campaigns in Great Britain in the 1990s). In another example, there can be a transnational form of voting that concerns the 'elderly' who sometimes remain active in their country of origin (for instance, 680 000 Algerians were called to vote in the Algerian presidential elections from France in 1999 and 2004).

Involvement varies according to the groups, but these differences fall within the scope of different local and national contexts. For instance, Amsterdam's Turkish people are the best organised and the most active community, followed by the Moroccans, the Surinamese and the West Indians, who are less politically socialised. This involvement is greater in Dutch big cities. Therefore, turnout varied from 5 per cent to 36 per cent for the Turkish and from 18 per cent to 33 per cent for the Moroccans in the 1998 elections. It also evolves with time: it tended to strongly decrease in Amsterdam while it increased in Rotterdam. The strategies can also vary. In Great Britain, unlike the West Indians, the Indo-Pakistani elites have instrumentalised their 'cultural identity' to make the Labour and Tory parties compete for their votes. Despite the ethnic minorities' traditional allegiance towards the former, an investigation carried out on polling day showed that 62 per cent of the Indians and Pakistanis and 92 per cent of the West Indians voted for the Labour Party in London in the 1997 elections. At the same time, an investigation in Bradford (Northern England) showed that 61 per cent of the Pakistanis had voted for the Tories against only 23 per cent of the Indians. The voting strategies cannot be restricted to the groups themselves. Vincent Geisser showed in Marseilles a 'top-down communitarisation' process operated by the local executives of the main political parties, identifying an 'ethnic' electorate and aiming at mobilising the groups thus artificially built around an 'imposed' stake (for instance, the building of a mosque).

Finally, the 2004 EP election was the opportunity in France to see small lists stand separately from the conventional big parties and positioned on the ethnic and cultural diversity issue (the 'Diversité pour l'Europe' list) or echoing the Israeli–Palestinian conflict over intergroup relations (the 'Euro-Palestine' list). This is a French particularity that is explained by the form of national debate over ethnic, cultural and religious diversity, where republicanism crystallises its motives (Islam vs. secularity, citizenship vs. communitarism, etc.). These small lists were sometimes interpreted as a 'voting communitarisation'. Actually, it is not. 'Diversité pour l'Europe' hardly gathered more than 3200 votes, whereas 'Euro-Palestine' recorded a visible vote in Seine-Saint-Denis, but failed to attract an 'ethnic vote' (obtaining less than 10 per cent in cities where 25–40 per cent of the electoral body consisted of electors of North African origin).

The elected representatives stemming from immigration

A permanent reality at the European level concerns the under-representation of the populations stemming from immigration in institutions of representation. This under-representation varies according to the countries and the political levels considered (local, national and European).

At the national level, Great Britain counts 12 elected representatives stemming from minorities (there should be 47 of them to reach a proportional representation of British ethnic minorities). The Netherlands count nine elected representatives stemming from immigration in the parliament. It was only during the 2004 senatorial elections that two representatives of North African origin (PS's Bariza Khiari and the Greens' Alima Boumediene-Thiery) were elected in France, despite the 'integrationist model' claimed. In spite of a right to nationality exclusively based on 'parentage' until the 2000 reform, only two elected representatives in the German Bundestag (out of 605) were born in Turkey: Ekin Deligöz (Greens) and Lale Akgün (SPD).

These variations can be explained not only by the sensitivity of the different contexts to the ethnic issue but also by forms of voting that enable a more or less great change in electoral mandates (for instance, one-ballot uninominal poll or list election), the political parties' local power struggles (candidates' selection) or the position order of candidates on the lists. In 2001, the British political parties put forward 66 candidates stemming from ethnic minorities (against 4 in 1970 and 24 in 1992), that is to say 16 for the Tories, 21 for Labour, and 29 for the Liberals. Twelve were elected to parliament, all of them for the Labour Party (seven Indo-Pakistanis and five West Indians). We must also consider the levels of responsibility obtained by these political professionals and their access to executive mandates.

At the local level, in contrast, we observe an increase in the number of elected representatives stemming from immigration. In the Netherlands, their number rose from 74 in 1994 to 150 in 1998. But they still only account for 1.5 per cent of all the councillors whereas ethnic minorities account for 7 per cent of the Dutch population as a whole. In the same way, an investigation showed in 1992 that 1.6 per cent of the municipal councillors in England and Wales stemmed from ethnic minorities. Fifty-two per cent were elected in London and 85 per cent represented the Labour Party. Five years later, 3.1 per cent of all the municipal councillors come from minorities and 2.4 per cent in 2001.

It is at the European level that under-representation is the most obvious. For the 2004–9 term, only four British members of the European Parliament stem from minorities (two Labour and two Tories). The Netherlands do not have any, while Tokia Saïfi (the UMP top candidate for the North-West constituency) and Abdelkader Arif (PS top candidate for the South-West constituency) represent France. Cem Özdemir (the Greens' top candidate after having been present in the Bundestag between 1994 and 2002) and Feleknas Uca (PDS) represent Germany. Another dimension of these elected representatives is sometimes their transnationality: second on the French Communist Party's list (Ile-de-France), but not elected, Hamida Ben Sadia also had responsibilities in the Algerian Front des Forces Socialistes in 1990, showing a commitment to both sides of the Mediterranean. The plurality of background is reflected for example by Holga Zrihen, a French woman of North African origin representing Belgium in the EP (re-elected PS in 2004).

Europe has difficulties in mobilising populations stemming from immigration as is illustrated by the failure of the European Union Migrants' Forum created under the aegis of the EP in 1992. But the European citizens themselves seem altogether little concerned by the issue of European active citizenship and few MEPs were elected in another state than their own: one French in Italy in 1989 (Maurice Duverger, Communist list); a Belgian in Italy (Olivier Dupuis, 'Emma Bonino' list) in 1994 and 1999; an Italian in Belgium (Monica Frassoni, 'Ecolo' list) in 1999, who became for the 2004 European elections the top candidate of the Federazione dei Verdi in Italy; and a French MEP in Spain (Miguel Mayol i Raynal: Esquerra Republica de Catalunya) in 1999. The 2004 elections saw the election of an Irish in Great Britain (Bairbre de Brun, Sinn Féin), a Dutch in Germany (Willem Schuth, Freie Demokratische Partei-Die Liberalen), a German in the Czech Republic (Franz Stros, Komunisticka strana chech a Moravy) and a Finnish in France (Ari Vatanen, UMP).

It is now the EU enlargement to the East that makes these issues more complex. 'First elected representative of Rom origin', Livia Jaroka (Hungary) wishes to become a 'real representative' of the 8 million Roma of the EU in the European Parliament. Tatjana Zdanoka

(Latvia) wants to represent Russian minorities there. The Hungarian parties' coalition obtained two out of the 14 seats in Slovakia. The issue is no longer restricted to the 'immigrant vote'. The stake is far broader and the minority vote issue has entered the centre stage of new forms of citizenship in Europe. In other words, the question is how can we connect citizenship and common institutions with the substantial involvement and representation of the minorities' members ('migratory', 'cultural', 'ethnic', 'religious', 'national', 'linguistic', etc.)?

Christophe Bertossi

Bibliography

Bertossi, C., *Les frontières de la citoyenneté en Europe: Nationalité, résidence, appartenance*, Paris, L'Harmattan, 2001.
Journal of Ethnic and Migration Studies, special issue on 'Ethnic Mobilisation and Political Participation in Europe', 25, 4, 1999.

→ Abstention; Citizen (EU); Eligibility; European Parliament; Members of the European Parliament (Sociology of Political Office); Representation; Right to Vote.

Incompatibility

Incompatibility originally appeared in European electoral laws as a guarantee of the separation of powers. For instance, in France, the parliamentary mandate establishing the prohibition of office plurality with the civil service became one of the major provisions of the 'parliamentary reform' of 1848, which aimed at putting an end to the corruption of the political civil servants of the July Monarchy. The progressive extension of the practice of incompatibilities was later a response to the drive to protect the independence of elected officials vis-à-vis economic interests, and to guarantee sufficient funds for MPs to fulfil their terms of office. This long-standing demand of the Republican left has contributed overall towards a redefinition of the foundations of electoral legitimacy in a way that favoured those candidates running for elections. Being the result of parliamentary self-regulation, it has become an instrument of autonomisation of the political profession.

Incompatibility is defined as the legal impossibility to accrue certain tasks with an electoral mandate. It is aimed at protecting the effective delivery of the mandate rather than the decision of the electorate (Masclet 1989). Contrary to the principle of ineligibility, incompatible mandates do not prevent elections *a priori*, but impose choices for the elected official *a posteriori*. This limit has thus become an important component of the status of elected officials in European democracies. It was extended to the European Parliament after the adoption of direct universal suffrage, within the definitional framework for the conditions of delivering the mandate. Prior to the realisation of a uniform electoral procedure, the Act of 20 September 1976 on European elections formally established the rule of universal suffrage, and bestowed upon each member state the opportunity to determine the system of incompatibilities to be applicable for their representatives (European Parliament, 1977, Article 6). Nevertheless, in order to clarify institutional issues at the EU level, the Council made a certain number of European offices incompatible. In the absence of a unique status, incompatibilities currently remain addressed by both Community provisions and the respective electoral laws governed in each member state.

Thus, the Act of 1976 initially considered a range of high-level political and judicial posts to be incompatible; notably European Commissioner, judge, Advocate-General and Court of Justice registrar, National Audit Office official, member of the Consultative Committee of the ECSC, the Economic and Social Committee of the EEC, as well as the board of directors and the management committee or employee of the European Investment Bank, and lastly civil servants or active agents of the Community institutions. In accordance with the Dutch, French and Swedish models, yet contrary to the practices in use in Austria, Britain and Ireland, the office of Government Minister in a Member State was made incompatible with the European mandate (European Parliament, 1977, Article 6). However, the Act explicitly authorises the plurality of national and European mandates (European Parliament, 1977, Article 5).

Following the Amsterdam Treaty, the Council revised the original Act of 1976 with its decisions of 25 June and 23 September 2002, initially extending the principle of incompatibility to the offices of the European Court of First Instance, of the board of the European Central Bank and ombudsman of the European Communities. The evolution of these incompatibilities has contributed to the process of differentiation between the political and administrative offices within the European institutional system. Moreover, in enforcing an incompatibility between national and European parliamentary offices, the 2002 decision further serves to reinforce the autonomisation of MEPs. Nonetheless, this process comes up against the broad diversity of parliamentary systems and practices, and the disparity of incompatibility regimes fixed at the national level. Usually, these provisions correspond to those relating to national MPs. Consequently, certain states have extended the application of numerous incompatibilities (France, Germany), whilst others have imposed restrictions and limited incompatibilities to specific proscriptions (Finland, Ireland), or rather more stringently and exclusively to the Community provisions in the absence of national rules (Denmark, Sweden) (DGE, 1997). Upon entering the European elections for the first time in June 2004, the ten new member states chose to apply the Community rule. Where national parliamentary incompatibilities existed, they were generally extended to the MEPs (Poland, Cyprus, Slovenia, Czech Republic). In Hungary, Slovakia and Estonia, the legal status of representatives is currently being adopted.

Not only do incompatibilities concern local and national offices, but above all they also address nominative public offices, which can be classified into the following three categories: (1) the important constitutional offices such as head of state, national ombudsman or member of the State Councils and constitutional or administrative courts; (2) judges, both with a declaration of legal incompetence for members of the supreme courts and high-level judges (Germany, Italy, United Kingdom), and without any declaration (Spain, France); and finally (3) the civil service in general, at the local administrational level or central apparatus, with specific provisions for the police and the army. Some provisions can even limit the professional consequences of such incompatibilities by allowing procedures of leave or secondment (Germany, France and Austria).

Stepping away from the liberal tradition, several national legislations have progressively obstructed the plurality of incompatibilities through certain private economic activities which can lead to many conflicts of interests in the context of a growing mixed economy. The office activities run the risk of infringing the principle of independence of legislative power and have been made incompatible with executive and advisory positions for national public bodies or companies, even private ones, when they benefit from specific state advantages, manage estate business or hold an exclusively financial occupation (banks, insurance companies). Finally, in several member states, MEPs cannot undertake certain advertising activities of a commercial or financial nature in addition to when the elected official holds a professional legal capacity or interest.

The European Parliament and the relevant body in each member state accountable for rulings (parliamentary assembly, supreme court, state council etc.) share the responsibility for controlling and sanctioning incompatibilities. The former assesses the conformity of the situation of each elected official with EU provisions. It takes cognizance of the gaps communicated by the latter and obliged by the enforcement of national rules. When there is an option, the elected official must comply with the law usually within a period of 30 days.

Guillaume Marrel

Bibliography

European Parliament, Act on European Elections by Universal Suffrage, Luxembourg, Office des publications officielles des Communautés Européennes, 1977.

European Parliament (Direction générale des études – DGE), Dispositions nationales en matière d'inéligibilités et d'incompatibilités concernant le Parlement européen, Document de travail, Série 'Parlements nationaux', W-9, 1997.

Masclet, J.C., *Droit Electoral*, Paris, PUF, 1989.

➜ Act of 1976; Dual Mandates; European Parliament; Ineligibility; Members of the European Parliament (Legal and Political Status); Members of the European Parliament (Sociology of Political Office); Parliamentary Mandate; Tenure.

Ineligibility

Ineligibility is the legal impossibility to run for an election. The definition of situations of ineligibility complements the positive conditions required by electoral law to be eligible (age, residence, nationality, etc.) as well as the administrative formalities to be a candidate. By listing specifically the situations limiting the right to candidacy, the law-maker does not seek to check if the candidate is able to exercise his mandate. He only seeks to protect the voters' decision and the principle of free and fair elections. The loss of the right of eligibility results most of the time from a legal decision for civil or criminal offences. It can be related to a physical or mental disability imposing the putting of an adult in care. It then concerns excluding some people from the electoral scene because they cannot fully employ their civic rights. But ineligibility can also derive from the exercise of certain public functions. In this case, it is about guaranteeing free competition between the candidates by keeping away from elections some people who are likely to use the power they are granted, thanks to their function, to influence the course of these elections, influence the votes, or distort the results for their own profit. Ineligibility stems from an individual and objective situation that can only be judged on polling day. Unlike incompatibility, it opposes mandate acquisition or ends it when ineligibility is revealed after the elections.

The Act of 20 September 1976, concerning the election of the Members of the European Parliament by direct universal suffrage, does not mention any ineligibility. Its writers preferred to limit themselves to a series of EU incompatibilities. The ineligibilities applicable to the election of MEPs only comes under the authority of the electoral law of each member state. With the intention of preparing for the 1979 first EP elections, the law-makers of the nine member states most of the time expanded the provisions planned for national MPs. They were imitated in this way by the 16 new members that joined the EU between 1981 and 2004. If today most of the 25 states consider ineligibilities related to a criminal or civil decision, there are few who limit the freedom of candidacy due to a specific activity, reputed to jeopardise the equality of opportunity and the good course of elections. France, Spain, Portugal and Greece list in detail the situations and functions causing MPs' ineligibility whereas in Sweden, there is no provision reducing the right to candidacy for the Reiksdag or the EP (DGR, 1997). Except for Malta, this list is lacking among the ten new member states.

Not enjoying the right to vote is the first ground for ineligibility. Except for Sweden and Italy, psychiatric confinement and putting in care or guardianship are causes of ineligibility in all the states. Furthermore, a European citizen deprived of his or her rights in his or her country of origin generally becomes ineligible in the other EU states. When ineligibility results from a criminal decision, it then stems from a deprivation that is either automatically related to some minimum decisions or certain types of particularly serious offences (rebellion or terrorism in Spain; crime against humanity in Portugal, etc.), or specific offences listed by law (extortion, corruption, trading on one's influence in France and the UK, etc.). Ineligibility can automatically result from the decision incurred or be expressly declared by the judge. The duration of the ineligibility period varies according to the seriousness of the decision, as in Belgium where a decision exceeding four months' imprisonment causes six years of ineligibility and twelve years beyond three years of imprisonment. Declared bankruptcy leads to ineligibility in France, Italy, Ireland and the UK. In Belgium, Spain and Luxembourg, loss of eligibility can also result from decisions for fraudulent or negligent bankruptcy. Let us note that apart from the rare cases of removal of parliamentary immunity, the parliamentary term of office protects the elected representative from ineligibility decisions that he could incur in case of offence during his or her term of office.

Ineligibility related to the exercise of a function only exists in France, Greece, Spain, Portugal, Ireland, the UK and Finland. It can be related to irrevocable properties as in the case of the royal family in Spain. But it concerns most of the time the remunerated civil service, the active list of the army, diplomacy, election bureaux and commissions and decentralised administration (that is to say the prefectoral body in France, civil governor in Portugal) whose members are forced to resign before running in a European election. In Spain, ineligibility also concerns principal private secretaries and the directors of radio and television. The other people who are ineligible are the President of the Republic and the Prime Minister in Portugal, solicitors in Greece, the Attorney General in Ireland, and the Ombudsman in France and Spain. Ineligibility can be applied in all the constituencies or only on the territory in which the function was exercised. Some ineligibilities are sometimes prolonged several years after the resignation. Finally, the ineligible functions are often also declared incompatible.

These ineligibilities finally only concern the candidates for the parliamentary term of office and only rarely hinder re-election. In Community texts, no more than in the national provisions, there are besides no provisions of non re-eligibility. The outgoing MEPs' eligibility remains one of the strongest conventions of Western democracies. However, in the US, such provisions sometimes limit the number of terms that a deputy can successively exercise in the same parliament. That is another use of ineligibility, a use that is based on the principle of rotation of charges and prevents renewing of the political staff or even makes its behaviour more ethical by limiting the participation of the outgoing MEPs in the electoral competition.

Guillaume Marrel
Renaud Payre

→ Eligibility.

Interest Groups

The list of 'accredited lobbyists' gives a good idea of the number and the heterogeneity of interest groups and their representatives dealing with MEPs. Their growing settlement makes us not only wonder about the mobilisation and aggregation conditions of interests at the European level but also the legitimacy of these groups within the European Union.

A difficult count?

Alphabetical ordering of interest groups has the advantage of providing a non-hierarchical list of the organisations that ignores their purpose (profit or not profit-making), their legal status (association, trade union, company, university), the type of interests they defend (economic, social, religious, moral, 'public', territorial), their policy sector, their degree of specialisation or their claim to be universal, the altruistic or selfish dimension of their action, the nature and number of their members (individuals, companies, banks, public services, trade unions, national associations, regions, cities), their size, age, national or transnational features, their coverage (international, EU, national, regional, local) and location (in Brussels and in the Europe of the Six's capitals for 87 per cent of the groups in 2000), to mention the most frequently considered elements in the interest groups' directories only. But putting them all at the same level, this alphabetical (dis)order incites endless scientific or partisan attempts to define, differentiate and classify this broad whole: the regional and local authorities are well distinct; commercial consultancies are isolated; the 20 think- tanks specialising in European questions in Brussels are dealt with separately. We may justly wonder about the 'European' character of the organisations and the interests they defend. Not without difficulty, Balme and Chabanet (2001: 21–120) count almost 890 Euro groups in 2000. Contrasting groups defending interests with those defending causes, they remind us that the private and economic interests greatly dominate (67 per cent of the Euro groups) whereas causes of general interest, which appeared more recently in the 1980s, only represent 23.4 per cent of the Euro groups. Gathering in the same category the liberal and independent workers, employer organisations, the inter-sectorial professional organisations, the small and medium-sized businesses' organisations and the employees' trade unions, they estimate their share to be 9.6 per cent.

As so often, reality resists easy classifications. Should we consider the

European Trade Union Confederation (ETUC), known as a 'European social partner' (1992), as an interest group? Should the European Women's Lobby (EWL) still be classified as an NGO? Does the European Landowners' Organisation represent an economic interest or a basic principle of our liberal societies through the defence of property rights? After arguments relating to the classification of the organisations, follow debates, often in vain, over the relevance of typologies. The counting procedure arouses people's distrust. Should we accept the number made official by the European Commission in 1992 of 3000 organisations that are said to employ 10 000 people? The European Parliament only registers the number of declarations (5108 in 2004) of those who claim to represent a company, a federation, a region, a public service and/or a business consultancy. Considering that each organisation can have a maximum – often reached – of four 'declarations', the number of registered groups is estimated between 850 and 1000. Some question the injustice that gives to great organisations as UNICE (Union of Industrial and Employers' Confederations of Europe) the same representation as a small association; others specify that great structures are represented – and sometimes counted – several times: directly as a national group, indirectly by the federation and confederation to which they belong, and sometimes by paying for consultancy. Furthermore, some groups, that can try to influence the EP by other means (cases of professional associations such as the Society of European Affairs Professionals (SEAP)), or refuse to honour some points of the code of conduct, do not appear on this list. But this absence is largely compensated by the counting of 'paper groups' that only exist thanks to their free registration.

The conditions of a 'lobby boom'

The development of European organisations (many of which are mixed up with those so-called international) is old. Meynaud and Sidjanski (1967) claimed that 1709 groups, among which 1170 still operated, were created between 1875 and 1954. It was in fact after the Second World War that a European interests system was set up, with two key moments in Euro groups' creation: the Rome Treaty (1957) and the Single European Act (1986). However, by the beginning of the 1990s, two-thirds of the groups dated back to before 1980, according to Greenwood (2003). In 2000, half of the existing Euro groups were started after 1974 and concentrated in Brussels where 67 per cent of the groups created after 1992 were located (Balme and Chabanet 2000: 61). How can we explain this mobilisation of mainly economic interests at the European level and the formalisation of the strategy which interest groups use to organise and defend these interests?

The first series of explanations is linked to the development of capitalism and its internationalisation, starting from the end of the nineteenth century, particularly with colonisation and trade intensification between European countries. Indeed, these economic changes were definitely linked to the emergence of groups, on a more or less European basis, aiming at representing certain economic agents (colonials, producers, raw materials exporters, textile manufacturers, etc.) and defending their economic activities within a new trade area (guarantees of manufacturing processes, respect for brands, customs duties). There were many economic conditions favourable to the emergence of 'industrial agreements' at the international level and the emergence of workers' movements that superseded national frameworks. But they were not sufficient to account for the differentiated emergence of groups according to sectors, countries and time, of these collective types of action. However, one has still to restore the different mediations and the mediators that enabled the creation of these interest groups.

Next to this 'spontaneist' vision of the group creation, a second series of explanations insists on the structure of political opportunities constituted, for interest groups, by the setting up of EU institutions and the extension of their field of competencies. Far from suppressing the groups already set up and established in Europe, European integration apparently enabled them to restructure their economic and human resources, and their experiences at the international level, to get involved in this new European political system; such analysis is likely to satisfy the holders of a (neo-) functionalist perspective of European integration. In parallel, the emergence of power centres at the EU level seems to have incited the emergence of Euro groups and the Europeanisation of national groups. Mazey and Richardson (1993) highlighted this logic of interest groups' spreading answering the setting up of policy networks. In a rational perspective, at the risk of personalising these groups, they consider that the groups have the clear and stable will to maximise their influence; consequently, these groups would focus in priority on centres of power such as the European Commission due to its position in the legislative process and its role in policy-making. But many investigations carried out on organisations remind us that their internal coherence as well as action strategies are elaborated in a chaotic way, without any previous objective, and often during interactions with other opposing actors. Then we can insist on the role of these institutions in the structuring of interests and the setting up of groups at the European level. The

European Commission, through its openness and consulting policy towards the interest groups, greatly contributed to their promotion, sometimes encouraging their creation (as for the European Consumers' Organisation, BEUC) and ensuring their existence through financing; it also took part, alongside the Council, in legitimating them by associating them to the political and administrative work of policy-making in several advisory committees. The European Parliament also developed more or less institutionalised relations with interest groups through the hearings of parliamentary committees and political groups, joint committees, and also individual meetings between MEPs and organisations' representatives. Kohler-Koch's investigation (1998) shows how the European Parliament has become more and more important for the various interest groups, in particular for non-economic groups that took advantage of the extension of prerogatives of this institution (co-operation and co-decision procedures), the functioning of a deliberative chamber where the parliamentary groups remain slightly restricting structures, a more 'political' audience more receptive to interests from 'civil society', and MEPs concerned about reinforcing their power and political role within their parliamentary group, towards their electorate, and in the face of the members of the Commission and the Council.

Nevertheless, the European Parliament is not only a source of influence and an access point to try to modify a bill. It also constitutes a forum for the Europeanisation of interests thanks to its EU character and the specificity of its personnel's political work. Investigations based on questionnaires (Kohler-Koch 1998; Wessels 1999) shows that MEPs keep more frequent and steady contacts with national interest groups than with Euro groups. However, these MEPs hardly ever defend them on a national scale, even if they owe their election to the mobilisation of certain sectional groups. Their membership of transnational political groups and their ambition to be real 'Europe professionals' mastering their projects and working for Europe's general interest, encourage them to formalise these interests in a 'European' way, which is allowed by resorting to a technical register and universal viewpoints. EU institutions have thus contributed to shaping and using 'interest groups' as a good way of introducing claims and accessing the power centres by providing expertise and information according to demand.

The states, and more broadly national political arenas, have also contributed to the development of interest groups at the European level: either voluntarily by encouraging some national groups to intervene at the European level (particularly in all the subjects covered by the extension of the vote by qualified majority in the Council after the Single European Act), or by appearing particularly unreceptive to certain interests, adapting themselves badly to the national ways of managing them. For instance, the Women's Rights Movement first developed on the national scale in the 1960s but, in the face of state reluctance, turned to the European Community to defend the cause of women. This is also the case of the Cross-border Workers' Association that used Community law to bypass the states and their legislation, trying to better defend their conditions but also to modify the national laws in force (Hamman 2003). Similarly, the National Housing Organisation tried to conform to EU requirements as a result of the competition between organisations within its sector, in the belief that going through Europe would enable it to improve its position within the sector and modify favourably the power struggle (Michel 2002). These examples

reveal the various ways Europe can be used as an alternative to national arenas, as a lobbying mode on the national level, and as a way to modify the structure of the national game according to the resources available and sector-based constraints. The organisations that can afford to be represented in Brussels (bureau, branch, representative, consultant, etc.) and/or have sufficient and competent personnel at their disposal to act as experts are privileged in the competition to access for European institutions.

Legitimacy stakes

The increasing presence – and maybe the role – of interest groups in the European system arouses different opinions. Some salute their contribution to the good functioning of the system, reminding us that these organisations bring necessary assistance to the political work, in the same way as parliamentary assistants. They offer information, expertise, support and legitimacy, and they save time. They complement the fundamental role of go-between played by political parties in political representation and thus enable the EU decision-making process to be brought closer to citizens. Several observers have highlighted the coalitions that operate between parliamentary groups and interest groups' networks: in the European Parliament, there are various coalitions ideologically and strategically coherent with a 'bourgeois' coalition (Wessels 1999), one comprising the Liberals, Christian Democrats, Conservatives and industrial interests, another comprising Socialists, Communists and labour interests, and a third one, a 'coalition of the weak' (Kohler-Koch 1998), uniting the Greens and the environment and consumer activists. Interest groups and political parties may thus complement one another to establish a link between society and politics.

Others, however, are alarmed by this privatisation of politics in the hands of groups that not only are not elected by 'civil society' which they claim to defend and represent, but that furthermore are not concerned – far from it – about general interest. Interest groups are denounced as democracy troublemakers who, aided by 'technocrats', are in politics without being accountable at all to voters. In addition to this denunciation, it has also been observed that this mode of interest defence and representation favours the haves and those who are better connected in Brussels (Greenwood 1997).

The MEPs questioned about their relationship with interest groups mirror this opposition between those who stand up for a pluralist democracy, as a privilege of North-Western European countries, and those who defend a purely representative democracy where only representatives elected freely should directly represent the people as a whole. Although there is evidence of only a slight tension between the proponents of these two views in the actual practice of European habits, we should recognise that the question of the influence of interest groups is related to that of who is deemed to be a legitimate player in EU governance generally and in the European Parliament in particular. However, placed as they are between the Commission and the elaboration of European standards on the one hand, and the EU's own interest groups on the other (such as the European Council for Voluntary Organisations or the European Citizens' Action Service), MEPs continue to insist on their role as 'real European representtives'. And that is what is at stake in the different uses they make of the presence of interest groups.

Hélène Michel

Bibliography

Balme, R. and Chabanet, D., 'Action collective et gouvernance de l'Union européenne', in R. Balme, D. Chabonet and V. Wright (eds), *L'action collective en Europe*, Paris, Presses de Science Po, 2000, pp. 21–120.

Greenwood, J., *Representing Interests in the European Union*, London, Macmillan, 1997.

Hamman, P., 'Le droit communautaire: une opportunité pour la défense des travailleurs frontaliers', *Sociétés contemporaines*, 52, 2003, pp. 85–104.

Kohler-Koch, B., 'Organised Interests in the EU and the European Parliament', in P. Claeys, C. Gabin, I. Smets and P. Winand (eds), *Lobbyisme, pluralisme et intégration européenne*, Bruxelles, Presses Universitaires Européennes, 1998, pp. 126–58.

Mazey, S. and Richardson, J.J., 'Introduction: Transference of Power, Decision Rules and Rules of the Game', in S. Mazey and J.J. Richardson (eds), *Lobbying in the European Community*, Oxford, Oxford University Press, 1993, pp. 3–26.

Meynaud, J. and Sidjanski, D., *L'Europe des affaires: Rôle et structures des groupes*, Paris, Payot, 1967.

Michel, H., 'Le droit comme registre d'européisation d'un groupe d'intérêt. La défense des propriétaires et la Charte des droits fondamentaux de l'Union européenne', *Politique européenne*, 7 ('Les groupes d'intérêt et l'Union européenne', 2002, pp. 19–42.

Wessels, B., 'European Parliament and Interest Groups', in R. Katz Richard and B. Wessels (eds), *The European Parliament, the National Parliaments and European Integration*, Oxford, Oxford University Press, 1999, pp. 105–28.

→ Civil Society; Democratic Deficit; European Commission; European Parliament; Lobbying; Members of the European Parliament (Legal and Political Status); Members of the European Parliament (Sociology of Political Office); Parliamentary Groups; Parliamentary Mandate; Representation; Voting Within the European Parliament.

Internal Elections at the European Parliament

At first glance, the European Parliament is a particularly democratic assembly, where organisational choices, the attribution of mandates and responsibilities essentially depend on the votes of elected members. Traditions, seniority and experience have little relevance. The election of Josep Borrell as President in July 2004 attests to this. Borrell was a candidate lacking EP experience as well as a 'first-order profile'. The designation of the Assembly's leaders (presidents, vice-presidents, quaestors); of political groups (presidents, vice-presidents); as well as parliamentary commissions and parliamentary delegations, is carried out by MEPs through secret voting. The omnipresence of this electoral logic must, nonetheless, be qualified by taking the partisan and national arrangements underlying most of these elections into account.

Internal elections: democracy, proportionality or convenience?

At the beginning of each mandate and at mid-term, MEPs elect a new assembly bureau. The election of the president occurs first, based on majority voting, on the basis of candidatures presented by a political group or by at least 37 MEPs. If no candidate obtains the required number of votes during the first three rounds, a fourth one establishes the winner between the two best-ranking candidates. The Parliament then proceeds to the election of 14 vice-presidents and five quaestors; elected at the first round if they obtain an absolute majority of expressed votes. If all seats have not yet been allocated, second and third rounds based respectively on absolute and simple majority take place.

Candidate vice-presidents are then selected based on their respective number of votes. In reality, this electoral logic is based on the respect of an essentially consociational proportionality principle, also known as the d'Hondt rule.

This rule applies to all aspects of the functioning of the European Parliament ensuring the equitable coexistence of political parties and of the national delegations within these. It structures the repartition among political groups and national delegations of all parliamentary resources based on proportional representation. This applies to mandates, reports, time allocated to speeches and questions during plenary sessions, as well as to staff and functioning credits (Abelès 1992).

The 'preparation' of elections began informally with the designation of members and presidents of the commissions. However, it has progressively been formalised and generalised. The Parliament's rules of procedure openly refer to it, especially with respect to the composition of the Bureau. In fact, they state that during the election of the president, the 14 vice-presidents and the five quaestors, the equitable representation of all member states and political orientations must be ensured (Article 12.2, 16th edition, July 2004). They also recommend an anticipation of results through the consultation of the heads of political groups. The rules also explicitly foresee such arrangements for the election of the commission members and inter-parliamentary delegations.

At the end of the 1980s, the PES and the EPP decided to move towards the further co-gestion of the assembly, equally preparing the election of its president. The aim was not so much to enforce the rule of d'Hondt, which has no applied meaning in the case of a single mandate to establish turns between the two groups. This is similar to what had already been done for the attribution of essential reports, such as the budget. The PES and the EPP sought to limit the conflicts they had faced during preceding elections, leading to the multiplication of the poll rounds as in 1982 and 1986, which saw the success of candidates who arrived in second position in the first round. From 1989 to 1999, a tacit agreement led to the sharing of the presidency by these two groups. At every election, the group that had 'stepped down' was compensated by the party holding the presidency, by means of an additional vice-presidency. The effects of such agreement were amplified by the successive revisions of the Parliament's rules of procedure, restraining the possibility for non-registered elected members to present a candidate for the presidency. While in 1993, 13 MEPs could act accordingly, the new threshold was progressively changed to 37, exceeding the increase of MEPs' numbers during this period. From 1989 onwards, the election of the president was transformed into a mere validation of the arrangements concluded between the EPP and the PES, passed at the very first round. The announcement by the media of the future president weeks before the elections became standard practice.

The re-examination of the two main groups' 'duopoly'

This process was strongly criticised and it was only the most visible manifestation of the PES and the PPE's 'duopoly'. Today, the perverse effects of the recourse to the rule of d'Hondt and the dominance it granted Socialists and Christian Democrat leaders are still stigmatised by leaders of 'smaller' groups, particularly attached to their independence. In their opinion, the rule of d'Hondt is an unconvincing guarantee

of pluralism, mainly due to the fact that the PES and the EPP comprise more than two-thirds of elected members and have openly co-operated since the 1980s on all issues related to the functioning of the European Parliament.

Agreements preceding the elections have in fact allowed these two main groups to hold a tight control over the Parliament's key posts as well as on deliberation. The repartition of commission presidencies is respectful of the relative political weight of each group, but it postulates that all these mandates represent the same interest. However, the order in which groups are called to make their choice enables the major groups, who are also the first ones to have a say, to secure the most important presidencies. The rule of d'Hondt has enabled the PES and the EPP to share half the posts before others had the possibility to influence the outcome. Numerous MEPs and commentators also denounce the negative impact of systematic arrangements between the two main groups on the image of the European Parliament in the media and public opinion.

The fourth EP legislature (1994–9) was marked by an unprecedented protest against the control of the PES and EPP over nomination and deliberation procedures of the Parliament. The negotiation habits of these two groups, their fear of disturbing each other, their hesitations to take into account the very often firm positions of the 'minor' groups, had repeatedly led them to a series of quasi-systematic agreements, even in cases where decisions were a matter of simple majority. This logic of the compromise was ill-perceived by the public, especially in France, in the United Kingdom and in Germany, where bipolarisation of political life and partisan competition are conceived as the best guarantees of democracy.

The repeated stigmatisation of the 'technical agreement' between the two main groups finally led to its end, at the time of the 1999 elections. During the fifth Parliament's initial session, the EPP (which had become EPP-ED, the group of the European People's Party and European Democrats, after the joining of the British Conservatives) chose not to renew this long-lasting understanding. Instead, it reached a new entente with the liberals to secure the presidency, which was to go to the socialists due to the principle of rotation. A majority in the EPP believed that their group, which had secured a superior number of seats to the PES, should condemn the unpopular 'technical agreement' that could affect their electoral campaign. The EPP-ED and ELDR groups agreed to share the presidency during this legislature. This agreement, seen by some as indicative of a radical change in the Parliament's functioning, only had limited effects on this body's activities because these two groups lacked the number of votes necessary to adopt amendments to legislative and financial texts (Hix and Keppel 2003). Moreover, the rule of d'Hondt continued to apply for the designation of vice-presidents, quaestors and commission presidents, as well as for the composition of the latter and of inter-parliamentary delegations.

The persistence of irresoluteness

Relations between the future Parliament's groups, and possible agreements on its presidency, represented a major question mark in the 2004 European elections. While the identity of the president of the European Parliament remains a relatively secondary piece of information, given the continuous necessity for the EPS and EPP-ED to agree *a minima* on legislative and financial matters so as to obtain the required majority, the symbolic influence of the agreements among political parties must

not be neglected. In fact, they are excellent indicators of the evolution of the EP's partisan structure. From this perspective, the period between the 10–13 June elections and that of the new EP president on 20 July was particularly interesting. For the first time, three options, which shed light on the many facets of the EP's functioning, were clearly presented and defended by MEPs. The first one – the 'consensual' option – was related to the historical agreement between the PES and the EPP-ED. Its advocates underlined the need to be realistic, and to give the European Parliament the means to make itself heard in the inter-institutional game. The second original option consisted of an alliance between the PES, the newly created ALDE group (composed of European liberals and federalists) and the Greens. Its promoters saw it as a means to improve the polarisation of debates at the European Parliament while limiting the power of Eurosceptics (massively present within the EPP-ED). Finally, a great number of MEPs of different political orientations supported the option of 'free' elections. The increase of Eurosceptic MEPs within the EPP-ED as well as the alliance of liberals and federalists blocked the renewal of the existing agreement. Finally, while the members in favour of the renewal of the agreement between PES and EPP-ED won, it has to be stressed that their candidate did not gain all the votes within the two groups.

Internal elections reveal the existence of several modus operandi within the European Parliament. A first and consensual one stems from the nature of the European Union and the history of the European Parliament, and aims at the preservation of the interests of different political groups and national delegations through the systematic use of the d'Hondt rule. A second, partisan tradition opposes and associates political groups along different fracture lines; a left–right cleavage is combined according to variable modalities between federalists and Eurosceptics.

Olivier Costa

Bibliography

Abelès, M., *Daily Life at the European Parliament*, Paris, Hachette, 1992.
Hix, S. and Keppel, A., 'The Party System in the EP: Collusive or Competitive?' *Journal of Common Market Studies*, 41, 2, 2003.

→ European Elections (1979–1999); European Elections (2004); European Federation of Green Parties; European Liberal Democrat and Reform Party (ELDR); European Parliament; European People's Party (EPP); European Political Parties; Investiture of the Commission; Parliamentary Groups; Party of European Socialists (PES).

Internet

The internet has become an important electoral campaign tool since the June 1999 European elections in two ways: through the creation of official sites on the one hand, and through the involvement of news groups on *Usenet* on the other hand. National political parties created websites that took over the key arguments of their programmes and provided very complete archives of parties' manifestos, their leaders' speeches, and campaign schedules. These websites, which contain particularly dense information, are sometimes rarely updated, and do not always leave room for militants' input. Therefore they have seldom used the technical possibilities of interactivity, and were instead used *a minima* around the possibility for everybody to click on a hypertext link and say something on the site via a comment.

Furthermore, on *Usenet*, a great number of news groups are classified by subjects, and numerous 'threads' dedicated to European elections emerged when the 2004 electoral campaign started. Often, numerous messages were sent by small parties' activists, such as the UKIP in Great Britain, and aroused intense debates in which only a few participants could take part. In June 1999, the internet remained marginal as much for the voters as for national political parties and the ones represented in the EP.

Political types and uses of the internet

If the 2004 European elections made use of the internet by the campaign actors fundamentally less marginal, new practices appeared on the official sites, particularly with the emergence of news groups, chat rooms, and 'blogs'. The institutionalisation of political communication on the net also progressed since not only national parties but also the EU itself set up sites entirely dedicated to elections, portals or sub-sites in a general interest site. All of them have clearly identifiable features that, beyond their apparent diversity, testify of the existence of structural improvements.

The EU portal has a hypertext link in the 20 official languages for every group represented in the EP; these links lead in turn to member parties' national sites (http://www.europarl.eu.int/groups/default.htm, accessed in June 2006) in which text, images, audio and video sessions or even interactive geographic maps coexist. The EPP-ED site offers a very complete example of all these elements (http://www.epp-ed.org/home/en/default.asp, accessed in June 2006). The small groups, which, on the contrary, used to offer a more simple showcase, have progressively caught up with their larger competitors. In the pre-election period, the portal also provided information on the elected representatives or links to their sites, the electoral laws of the 25 member states and the polling stations' opening hours in each of these countries. On election day, the portal only displayed an invitation to vote in 20 languages, whereas, at the end of the elections, all the results were put online, with numbers on turnouts (http://www.elections2004.eu.int/, accessed in June 2006).

The great number of hypertext links leading to multiple sub-sites is therefore the distinctive characteristic of the websites' organisation and the feature that has made them closer, in a way, to the organisation of information in the press, where titles are used as catch-phrases. The fragmentation and heterogeneity that result make the process of grasping information rather complex, but also gives the impression of an inexhaustible content. The profusion of information promoted by the accumulation of the data and their heterogeneity, their evolution in time, as well as the minimal interactivity that consists of clicking on a hypertext link, make the portal a tool that at the same time reproduces the highlights of the electoral ceremonial and makes it more difficult to access, due to the navigation and deciphering skills that it presupposes.

While the site set up by the EP for the 2004 elections did not leave any room for the institution itself, the public has found its own place on the national parties' websites, through instantaneous polls, discussion forums where the visitors are encouraged to debate questions suggested by the websites' administrators or chat rooms, which allow for real-time exchange, through a system of instant messaging, with political leaders. The public's interventions contribute to make the site denser and introduce an interactive dimension due to the fact that writing has become 'more oral'. This is reflected in the use of conventional signs, acronyms, and 'smileys', aiming at reducing the dryness of the text by introducing expressions of emotions ('emoticons'). A new e-language, with its own spelling and punctuation, made expressive on purpose by the accumulation of certain signs, such as vowels or punctuation marks, has implicitly been created. Due to the coexistence of two modes of enunciation in the same space, the conventional political communication finds itself both modified and in competition with the new informal mode of communication. The 2004 internet electoral campaign was marked by a common enunciation process or enunciative co-production, insofar as the websites' designers accepted losing control of part of its content.

Other examples of how parties and institutions have innovated in the use of the internet for the 2004 campaign are numerous. The European portal also included a questionnaire presented as a game, whose aim was to test the knowledge of basic European institutions. The French Greens' site included a humorous anti-GMO poster on which a man was threatening another one with a banana mocking a gun. Altogether, the internet proved a remarkable instrument that allowed party politicians to mix together institutional political communication *per se* and playful modules and games. Based on the juxtaposition of disparate elements, the websites play on the perception of strangeness that it provokes and rely on shared laughter and smiles to build up a clearly defined group and maintain its symbolic cohesion. The entertaining approach, characteristic of even the most official sites, contributed to the loosening of political communication's formal rules; this approach has reduced the gap between formal and informal speeches and consequently limited the distance between the elites and the masses by adapting to contemporary popular forms of expressions.

Discussion groups

While the official websites have progressively followed a convergent path, discussion groups or news groups on *Usenet* have experienced a very different evolution. The 2004 elections gave way to prolonged confrontations with militants of extremist parties from all sides who infiltrated the groups. This discursive hijacking led to a declining interest on the part of the oldest groups, which continued to show a great number of messages, but only really gathered a small number of participants. At the same time, the news groups linked to conventional press organs boomed.

'Blogs' finally took advantage of a certain craze during the electoral campaign and clearly became part of the typical internet's political uses in Europe. The word itself is a neologism composed of *web* and *log*, borrowed from the sailing vocabulary. *Weblog* then became *blog*, a word that was very productive from the linguistic point of view, turning among other things into *blogosphere*, referring to all the exchanges made in this manner.

The easy and manageable *blog* technology enables web managers to put text, images or sounds on the internet, without being technologically competent, as it is managed by the companies offering the service. *Blogs* include a commentary form thanks to which the readers themselves can publish their answers whose automatic counting enables the *blog* manager to evaluate the success of an entry. *Blogs* are put on the internet according to a reversed chronological order where the most recent entry comes up first, whereas the archives keep the entries and the comments they generated thanks to a permanent hypertext link. First consisting of lists of links annotated to other sites, *blogs* quickly diversified into three main categories: comments about recent news, personal *blogs*, which are more conventional diaries, and institutional *blogs* set up by militants, individual political actors or parties and used both as mobilisation and agenda-setting tools.

These political *blogs* started to proliferate in Europe after the success of Howard Dean's campaign in 2003. The defeated candidate was not endorsed by the Democrat Party for the 2004 American presidential election, but became a key figure of the electoral campaign on the internet. His website (http://blogforamerica.com/) and campaign team proved highly capable of raising funds and mobilising a young and popular electorate. In turn, his supporters campaigned for him in a great number of *blogs*, where personal and political opinions were running alongside each other, before being relayed by the press and TV at the beginning of summer 2003. Such media coverage gave Dean and his style of political communication a national audience in the United States, then an international one. The political *blogs*, when conforming to what tends to become the enunciation standard on the internet – writing becoming more oral, media cumulation, heterogeneity and a strong entertaining element – proved able to generate answers, and even debates for the EP election as well (for instance, Alain Lipietz's campaign *blog* http://www.lipietz2004.net/). When they only copied the conventional manifesto style, however, they remained unheeded, only generating a few answers (for example, the campaign diary of the Socialist Group's president in the EP, Poul Nyrup Rasmussen: http://www.eurosocialists. org/, or Jo LeGuen's, PRG: http://www. joleguen2004.euro.st).

Blogs nonetheless managed to impose themselves alongside websites and news groups to diversify the types of political communication and interaction with activists and floating voters during the 2004 European election campaign, and confirm the internet as a new key tool of communication. These uses, however marginal at first, have nonetheless been reclaimed, taken over, and adapted by the various EU political actors who then ensured the perpetuation of the use of the internet in politics. However, it is important to note that without the publicity made by the conventional media, the electoral campaigns carried out on the internet would remain available to only a limited audience. The *blogosphere* only thrives insofar as it is incorporated into the pre-existing political tools.

Vivianne Serfaty

Investiture of the Commission

It used to be an established tradition that national executives reserved the power to appoint European Commissioners. Despite the treaty stipulating that they should be appointed 'by common agreement', Commissioners were usually chosen by each government. Cross-governmental negotiation only occurred regarding the selection of the President of the Commission, usually to ensure a certain rotation between member states and party families.

After the introduction of direct universal suffrage in 1979, the European Parliament tried to intervene in this traditionally intergovernmental procedure. Although there was no such provision in the Rome Treaty, the MEPs took the initiative to 'confirm' the Commission presided over by Luxemburger Gaston Thorn in 1981. Anxious to avoid any conflict, the governments granted the European Parliament office the right to express an opinion regarding the appointment of subsequent presidents. However, this proposal was met with a rather luke-warm reception amongst MEPs who considered this to be a limited concession and consequently continued to vote on the 'investiture' of the Commission throughout the 1980s. Eventually, the governments 'constitutionalised' this procedure by incorporating it into the Maastricht Treaty. Following which, upon the request and pressure applied by the European Parliament, the Amsterdam and Nice Treaties further enhanced the power of the Parliament concerning this procedure.

The nomination of the Commission now takes place in four phases: (1) the Council nominates the President by a qualified majority and (2) the Parliament grants its assent. Then, (3) the governments propose 'their' candidate for Commissioner, in consultation with the appointed President, before (4) the European Parliament approves of the college as a whole. Between the main phases, the MEPs have also followed practices utilised in the American Senate and sought to introduce an individual hearing procedure for the future Commissioners, whereby within the specialised EP committees, each candidate is questioned by MEPs, who then communicate their opinion to the President of the Parliament.

This mechanism, which a number of European leaders consider to be a key element of European democratic legitimacy, was debated at length during the European Convention of 2002–3. The procedure was hence set forth in the Draft Constitutional Treaty signed in Rome by the heads of states and governments, inspired by the parliamentary logic in force within most member states, whilst also retaining intergovernmental features. On the one hand, the President of the Commission is elected by the majority of the members of the European Parliament, following the national governmental example. On the other hand, the governments gathered in the European Council still retain the power of initiative, nominating candidates for the presidency through qualified majority voting, despite the Constitutional Treaty obliging them to take the results of the European elections into account.

Under the current system, the 'investiture' of the Commission remains characterised by a blend of intergovernmental tradition and parliamentary logic. It is clear, however, that the parliamentary component gained significant ground following the June 2004 elections. José Manuel Durao Barroso's appointment to the Presidency of the Commission in June 2004 was the result of cross-governmental bargaining, whereby partisan issues were only of relative significance. None of the candidates initially supported by the main political group in the European Parliament (the Conservatives of the EPP-ED) managed to survive the first round of negotiations within the European Council, although the non-EPP candidates suggested by a number of national governments were equally excluded. Similarly, national governments first tried to keep complete control over the selection of Commissioners, all appointing close acquaintances without taking into account the party structure of the European Parliament.

Nevertheless, altogether, as a result of the selection procedure, the Commission encompasses a very broad spectrum of political predispositions. Given that governments take into account respective political affiliations when nominating their candidates, and since governments rarely belong to the same political family, the Commission is perpetually a very broad 'political coalition'. From the mid-1980s onwards, two- thirds of the Commissioners have consistently belonged to the two main European political families: the Socialist parties and the Christian Democrat and Conservative parties. Moreover, the composition of the Commission in partisan terms is very stable, and therefore not predisposed to alternation. As a consequence, the Commission remains very different to a classic parliamentary system. The ability of MEPs, or partisan groups, to influence the choice of the Commissioners ultimately remains very limited. Under the current procedure, they are only able to intervene after the selection of candidates has been agreed by the governments. At best, MEPs can really only express their disagreement. Thus, in 1995, a large number of MEPs voted against Jacques Santer, who had been appointed by the governments, in order to protest against the British veto over the candidature of the Belgian Prime Minister Jean-Luc Dehaene, the latter being supported by the main political groups in the European Parliament. In 1999, the German Conservatives voted against the college as a whole, because Gerhard Schröder had appointed two candidates (a Social-Democrat and a Green) who were close to the governing coalition, although it was the Conservative opposition who had gained electoral ground at the European elections. However, these protests failed to prevent the Commission from being dominated by centre-left candidates, thus reflecting the governmental majorities, whereas the composition of the European Parliament elected in 1999 leaned towards the centre-right.

However, the picture then changed in an unprecedented manner when both the Commission and the Parliament decided that it was time for the procedure of investiture to be both more politicised and more democratic (and less intergovernmental).

Firstly, the investiture vote for the Barroso Commission triggered a stronger polarisation within the European Parliament whereby the majority of Socialist MEP group members refused to support the President of the Commission, because they were keen to draw attention to their disagreement with the presidential options arguing that he had showed favouritism towards Liberal and Conservative Commissioners when distributing portfolios. Consequently, Barroso was approved as President of the European Commission with a majority of only 54 per cent, which constituted. a much narrower majority in comparison with previous investiture votes of the 1980s and 1990s. This was the logical result of a more 'parliamentarian' system of government formation, whereby the European Commission, for the first time, largely reflected the results of the June 2004 election.

In a second ground-breaking evolution, the Parliament decided to change the traditional intergovernmental logic of Commissioners' selection and threatened to veto the Commission, which included a number of proposed Commissioners that were unacceptable to it. As a result, the Parliament managed to force a relatively thorough change of the proposed team, with two highly controversial proposed Commissioners, including the Italian Rocco Buttiglione, simply replaced, and two more were given different portfolios than originally intended, particularly to avoid some potential conflicts of interests for the Dutch Commissioner, Neelie Kroes. Indeed, during the individual hearings of the candidates, the MEPs developed a much more aggressive approach than in the past. The criticisms they voiced

against five of the 25 Commissioner candidates, forced President Barroso to postpone the vote for a month in order to avoid losing support from the vast majority of Socialist and Liberal groups. On this occasion therefore, the pressure exerted by the MEPs had a substantial impact. Although the major political groups of the European Parliament failed to achieve a completely satisfactory outcome, they considered that they had been largely efficient in their pressure and supported the college. As in the past, it was only the former Communists, the Greens, and several Socialists on the left-wing, and the extreme right and the Eurosceptics on the opposite side who rebelled and voted against the college, but still leaving a comfortable majority of 62 per cent support overall. Under such circumstances, the politicisation of the Commission remains only partial: supported by most of the Socialists, Liberals, Christian Democrats and Conservatives, the college is not subject to a stable and ideologically well-defined majority, which enables it to remain the 'impartial' executive as enshrined by the treaty.

Paul Magnette

Bibliography

Hix, S. and Lord, C., 'The Making of a President: the European Parliament and the Confirmation of Jacques Santer as President of the Commission', *Government and Opposition*, 31, 1, winter 1995, pp. 62–76.

Joana, J. and Smith, A., *Les commissaires européens*, Paris, Presses de Sciences Po, 2002.

Magnette, P., 'Appointing and Censuring the Commission: the Adaptation of Parliamentary Institutions to the Community Context', *European Law Journal*, 7, 2, September 2001, pp. 292–310.

→ Democratic Deficit; European Commission; European Parliament; Europeanisation (of National Political Life); Symbols and Practice of Elections

Ireland

Historical and technical aspects

Since Ireland joined the EU in 1973, the Irish electorate has been able to participate in all the direct elections to the European Parliament; consequently, the election on Friday 11 June 2004 was the sixth such occasion. This election took place roughly in the middle of the cycle of Irish general elections (the most recent previous general election having taken place just over two years previously (17 May 2002), and the mandate period extending to a maximum of five years). Furthermore, the Irish government decided to let the European Parliament election coincide with a number of other voting exercises, specifically local government elections as well as a referendum on the question of reforming Irish citizenship laws. Ireland consists of four European election constituencies: Dublin (4 seats, contested by 12 candidates in 2004), East (3 seats, 13 candidates), South (3 seats, 10 candidates), North-West (3 seats, 9 candidates). Sixteen candidates were independents, and 12 were women.

Irish MEPs are elected by the single transferable vote system of proportional representation, using the Droop quota method to calculate which candidates are elected. EU citizens living in Ireland and who are at least 21 years of age can stand for election to the European Parliament in Ireland. The candidate nomination procedure takes place about one month before the election, and candidates can declare themselves as contesting the election for a party or as a non-party candidate. Candidates who receive a political donation of €126.97 or above must open an account in a financial institution (e.g. bank or similar) and comply with specific regulations pertaining to disclosure of funding. Candidates may not receive more than €2539.48 from the same donor in any one year. Anonymous donations exceeding €126.97 are prohibited. There is no public funding of political parties or of non-party candidates.

Every Irish and EU citizen living in Ireland who is 18 years old or over and is listed on the register of electors is entitled to vote. The Minister for the Environment, Heritage and Local Government decides which of the four possible polling days will be used in Ireland, and also decides the hours between which polling stations will be open (at least 12 hours between 7 a.m. and 10.30 p.m.). Most voters vote in person at their local polling station, where the traditional ballot-box method is used. (The government withdrew its plans to switch to electronic voting after widespread public concerns regarding its safety and accuracy.) Postal voting is available to certain categories of voters whose occupations or studies away from the constituency where they are registered may prevent them from voting on polling day, as well as voters with a physical illness or disability. Voters living in hospitals and similar institutions may vote at the institution in question. The local returning officer in each constituency makes arrangements for postal and special voters, and is also responsible for making detailed polling arrangements, and for informing voters about them. Electronic, postal and special votes are counted together, and the local returning officers report the results to the Chief Returning Officer who notifies the European Parliament of the results. There is no recount of votes, but candidates may submit an election petition to the High Court within 14 days of the declaration of election results.

Party approaches to the campaign

2004 witnessed the enlargement of the EU to ten further member states under the aegis of the Irish Presidency. On 1 May, the television and newspapers were saturated with images of and comment on this historic achievement, and the role played in it by both Ireland (which thinks of itself as a model pupil to be emulated by the new member states) and the Irish government of the day (to which the rotating Presidency of the Council happily fell at an opportune time). The European Union agenda was thrillingly full of major issues rather than dreary technical matters; there was consensus across Europe that the Irish Presidency was doing a good job in seeking agreement on a new Constitutional Treaty. In this context it is remarkable, if not perverse, that much of the Irish campaign around elections to the European Parliament was almost entirely free of any reference to European issues.

Astonishingly, one of the parties in the governing coalition of the state holding the Council Presidency at the time of the elections – the Progressive Democrats – failed to nominate any candidates, and ignored the EP elections entirely for the second time in a row. Party campaigns began rather late, typically only three weeks before polling day. The campaign tone was set by the election posters, which appeared very early and were eventually crowded out by those for local elections (held on the same day as those for the EP) and a referendum on changes to Irish citizenship law (also held on 11 June). The posters were universally free of political content or policy statements. Instead, they featured only the faces of the various candidates along with their names and party affiliation (if any), and a request that the voter give each person their number one preference. Some posters deigned to inform the voter whether the candidate was standing for election to the EP or the local council. Some went so far as to ask for voters to give their second, third and fourth preference votes to members of the same party.

Four of the major parties produced a manifesto for the elections, but almost no reference to these was made by the media coverage of the campaign, and distribution of the manifestos to voters was poor. The senior party in the ruling coalition, Fianna Fáil, traded in its manifesto on Ireland's attractiveness as a site for foreign direct investment and on Ireland's holding of the Council Presidency, emphasising also issues of enterprise and market regulation. This was the only major party to include an element of its manifesto in Irish (half a page). Its manifesto spoke principally of party and government achievements rather than what its candidates would do in the EP if they were elected.

Fine Gael, one of the main opposition parties, produced a manifesto which ably mixed declarations of pro-European policy with statements about what Fine Gael members of the EP would do if elected and potentially vote-catching issues such as insurance, where popular unrest in Ireland could hopefully be met with a successful EU policy (Irish insurance premiums are way above the European norm). Fine Gael also used its manifesto to set out clear ideas about Ireland's role in both Europe and the wider world. Focusing on ending Irish neutrality in favour of involvement in the Common Foreign and Security Policy, Fine Gael carved out space for itself as a party with a vision of the kind of EU it wanted and as the occupier of a distinctive position in terms of a key issue in domestic politics.

The Labour Party manifesto emphasised social policy and social justice issues, focusing on what the EU could do to foster social inclusion within its borders and to facilitate fair trade and sustainable development elsewhere. It sought the mainstreaming of measures to fight social exclusion and reform of the Stability and Growth Pact to facilitate both full employment and ecological sustainability. Although brief, the manifesto was clear on key priorities for Labour MEPs were they to be elected.

Sinn Féin (the political wing of the Irish Republican Army) did not produce a manifesto until very late in the campaign. As a result, its stance on EU issues was not always clear to observers, and indeed the eventual manifesto was heavy on matters of 'all-Ireland' propaganda. Nonetheless, the document was a coherent link between the Irish republicanism and nationalism espoused by the party 'at home' with a plan for a reformed EU which would 'return' economic sovereignty to the member states while seeking to set up common standards across the Union for anti-poverty action and a switch towards a more social economy. Sinn Féin also sought an EU which is explicitly demilitarised and in which global social justice and fair trade are seen as key objectives. The party also supported a dramatic extension of EU legislation in anti-discrimination and civil rights issues. The manifesto was thus an interesting mixture of domestic issues and 'constructive engagement' (in the party's words) with the EU which succeeded in carving out a left-wing nationalist perspective on the EU.

The Green Party produced the most colourful and 'European' manifesto, inasmuch as election material was shared between Green parties across the member states. The Greens emphasised the issues of subsidiarity, transparency, citizens' rights, reform of the Common Agricultural Policy, fair global trade, non-militarisation, and environment policy (including the proposal for a Climate Change Stability Pact). This manifesto also had the great advantage of showing citizens how their votes at local and European elections could be joined up, because throughout the manifesto issues were dealt with thematically, with key priorities for elected Greens at both local and European levels clearly set out.

The election campaign for the European Parliament was highly personalised, with the focus squarely placed on individual candidates and, to some extent, national party affiliation. At best very little attention was paid either to EU politics or to candidates' priorities for their hoped-for time as Members of the European Parliament (a two-page spread in the *Irish Times* of 22 May 2004 afforded a small exception to this trend, acting as a forum for both the political parties and the various independent candidates to make statements about their intentions, if elected). Pat Cox, the retiring President of the European Parliament and Member for Munster, had his widely publicised call for the campaign to be a proper debate about European integration ignored nowhere more obviously than in his own country.

The European Parliament's own advertisement urging people to vote in the election was shown on national television, and the broadsheet papers carried regular updates of the campaign process – albeit without focusing much on the issue of Europe itself. Towards the end of the campaign the broadsheets also provided regular analysis and dissection of opinion polls and their likely implications; this reportage was accompanied by very scanty analysis of European issues. Instead, attention was devoted to what the elections might imply about the possibility of a change in the national political complexion, with commentators speculating that Fianna Fáil's hold on power might come under threat at the next general election from a Fine Gael–Labour alliance. The political parties tacitly endorsed this focus, seeking attention for themselves in terms of national popularity rather than as purveyors of good ideas about, and good candidates for, the European Parliament. In this light, it is unsurprising that media coverage of the individual EP election candidates focused on issues of intra-party feuding (e.g. between the Fianna Fáil candidates in the North-West and Dublin constituencies, and between the Fine Gael candidates in the East constituency), mud-slinging between independent candidates (Dana versus Marian Harkin in the North-West), the smart choice of candidates by Fine Gael (looking to recover from a very poor showing in the 2002 general election, the party chose candidates with celebrity status or 'brand identity'), and the ultimately unsuccessful but consistently colourful candidacy of Royston Brady, the Fianna Fáil Mayor of Dublin.

The final week of the campaign saw increased media attention, as it became clear that the winners and losers in each constituency were by no means all obvious in advance. Here again, however, attention was focused on the likely impact of the various possible results on national politics or on the futures of the individual candidates.

Turnout, results and analysis

Turnout in Ireland was high, with the cross-country average for the EP elections reported by the *Irish Times* of 15 June to be 59.2 per cent (1 841 425 votes were cast, of which 60 567 were spoiled (http://www.europarl.ie/ep_elections/index.html, accessed 28 June 2004)), a significant increase on the previous local and European elections. Commentators attributed the high turnout to three factors: the commitment of voters to register their dissatisfaction with the government; the campaigning of Fine Gael and Sinn Féin (which both brought out their core support and extended their appeal impressively); and the fact that there were two elections and a referendum on the same day, which maximised the voters' sense that something significant was at stake.

The elected candidates, in order of first preference votes in each constituency, were as follows:

NORTH-WEST: **Marian Harkin (Independent), Seán Ó Neachtáin (Fianna Fáil), Jim Higgins (Fine Gael).**
EAST: **Mairead McGuiness (Fine Gael), Liam Aylward (Fianna Fáil), Avril Doyle (Fine Gael).**
SOUTH: **Brian Crowley (Fianna Fáil), Simon Coveney (Fine Gael), Kathy Sinnott (Independent).**
DUBLIN: **Gay Mitchell (Fine Gael), Eoin Ryan (Fianna Fáil), Mary Lou McDonald (Sinn Féin), Proinsias de Rossa (Labour).**

The results brought great losses for both the governing party, Fianna Fáil, and the Greens. With the number of Irish MEPs reduced from 15 to 13, the Greens found the competition too stiff and lost both their seats in Brussels/Strasbourg. Fianna Fáil paid the price for widespread discontent with its performance since re-election two years previously. There were impressive gains for Fine Gael, which won a total of five MEPs, and for Sinn Féin, which gained its first MEP in the Irish Republic at the same time as its first MEP in Northern Ireland, and very nearly gained a second. The Labour Party's vote held up well, and it retained its one MEP. Two independents were also elected: Kathy Sinnott, a disability rights campaigner, and Marian Harkin, a regional development specialist and sitting member of the Irish parliament.

Ireland thus conformed to the general (if not uniform) trend across the EU of registering protest votes against the national government. It also returned at least two Eurosceptic MEPs (Mary Lou McDonald and Kathy Sinnott). The number of elected female MEPs – five – is high, but rather less pleasing is the even higher proportion of Irish MEPs for 2004–9 who have little experience of EU politics or little interest in it: of the 13 Irish MEPs, only three have served at least a full term as MEPs, at least two of those elected (Mairead McGuiness and Kathy Sinnott) are beginners as career politicians, and three (Gay Mitchell, Marian Harkin and Simon Coveney) have mandates at both national and EU levels.

It is also clear that in Ireland at least, EP elections remain at best 'second-order' in nature and generate interest rather more as bell-wethers of the political state of the nation than as innovative exercises in democracy beyond the nation-state or as sources of influencing EU politics and policy. One governing party did not trouble itself to field any candidates; independent candidates had a very high success rate, indicating that party discipline is weak; voters were quite prepared to elect candidates with no knowledge of or clear interest in the EU. The 2004 case also indicates that Irish politicians see no gain in advocating European integration as part of a sustained EP election campaign, and that at least some of the issues involved in deepening European integration – e.g. defence and security policy – remain very controversial at political party level. As a result, EP elections are not yet contributing to the development of identification with the EU in Ireland.

Karin Gilland Lutz
Alex Warleigh

Bibliography

Gilland, K., 'The 1999 European Parliament Election in the Republic of Ireland', *Irish Political Studies*, 15, 2000, pp. 127–33.

Holmes, M., 'The 1989 European Parliament Election in the Republic of Ireland', *Irish Political Studies*, 5, 1990, pp. 85–92.

Keating, P. and Marsh, M., 'The European Parliament Election', in M. Gallagher and R. Sinnott (eds), *How Ireland Voted 1989*, Galway, Centre for the Study of Irish Elections, 1990, pp. 131–47.

Marsh, M., 'The 1994 European Parliament Election in the Republic of Ireland', *Irish Political Studies*, 10, 1995, pp. 209–15.

Marsh, M., 'Ireland: An Electorate with its Mind on Lower Things', in C. Van der Eijk and M.N. Franklin (eds), *Choosing Europe? The European Electorate and National Politics in the Face of Union*, Ann Arbor, University of Michigan Press, 1996, pp. 166–85.

→ Mapping Europe: European Electoral Geography.

Issues

Campaigns, agenda and political issues are intertwined concepts in the fields of electoral analysis and political communication. In an article published in *Liberation* on 15 June 2004, Mény stated that 'governments and major parties have failed to debate any of the fundamental European issues, such as the European Constitution, the accession of Turkey, and Euro-Atlantic relations'. Consequently, it is hardly surprising that according to a survey carried out on election day in France by the Louis-Harris Institute, the main issues at stake in the 2004 European elections were perceived to be employment (43 per cent), pensions (37 per cent), public health (32 per cent), economic globalisation (22 per cent), the environment (22 per cent), social exclusion (22 per cent), personal and assets security (21 per cent), income and other taxes (18 per cent), illegal immigration (16 per cent), and EDF-GDF stature changes (9 per cent).

Here, the framing is clearly 'domestic' and this general impression has to be corrected by the BVA survey which focused on other areas marked by the European character of the fight against terrorism in Europe, the defence of public services, or common foreign and security policy. This dichotomy has been persistent since the first direct European elections in 1979 (Blumler 1983; Sweeney 1984; Charlot 1986), although the intensity with which European issues prevail over domestic ones is subject to variations and to a gradual increase. In fact, one should consider the history of European elections in order to understand the balance and evolution between the national and European issues at their heart.

In this article, we shall endeavour to suggest a typology of political 'stakes', or 'issues'. This concept stands for the way in which public opinion focuses on different questions in relation to the producers of such issues, as well as the media who determine their hierarchy and framing to a large extent (Gerstlé 2004). Several macro-categories of content can be identified amongst the campaign issues. A first way to proceed would be to refer to earlier work on political programmes and manifestos of the Budge–Klingemann type (2001), using the issues they identified to follow the evolution of partisan programmes in European elections. A slightly rougher but more useful way consists of separating the *summa divisio* national and European issues, and the principles and opportunities of European integration, from the public policy issues within a legitimate European institutional framework. In this way, sovereignists and Eurosceptics are separated from postnationals, federalists and the defenders of a 'Europe of peoples' described by Chirac and Jospin in 2002. Table 1 will

Table 1   Macro-categories for the analysis of issues

Categories	Nation	Europe
Principle and desirability of European integration	Sovereignist and Eurosceptic issues	Issues promoted by Europhiles
Public policy issues	Examples: priority issues of the Harris Institute study	Examples: priority issues of the Sofres study
European conjuncture (Issues exploited for their relevance/ salience)	Examples: 1999 health crisis; the resigning of the Santer Commission	Example: 'We return to Europe', 2004 PSOE; enlargement to 25
National and international conjuncture	Examples: 2004 government sanctions; decentralisation due to enlargement	Examples: Kosovo War in 1999 Social Europe in 2004

help us analyse the different categories of issues.

European public policy issues are likely to be developed in a preferential manner by parties or lists whose adhesion to European integration is fully assimilated. As far as the two other categories are concerned, they totally depend on the internal European or international scenes and demonstrate the impossibility of presenting a consistent political offer without integrating what is happening outside the national borders. The same is true for mediated issues (Garcia et al., 2003), such as the Kosovo and Iraq Wars, which overshadowed and influenced European election campaigns. A survey conducted in Germany, Belgium and Italy in 1999 considers and compares three different levels: interest in the campaign; importance of national and European levels; issues driving electoral choice (Table 2).

In these three countries, all founding members of the European Communities, the national dimension sometimes proved more important than the European one. So dryly presented, the issues do not tell us much about their exploitation by the media. Does the Kosovo crisis indicate the EU's incapacity to build a Common Foreign and Security Policy, reaffirming the contin-

ued dominance of national autonomy in the military field? Should employment belong to the competencies of a better prepared and determined EU willing and able to increase flexibility? The same questions can be raised with regards to taxes, immigration and the environment. The proper interpretation of the issue cannot occur without the prior knowledge of the preferences of Europeans in these different fields.

Table 3 indicates how the stakes relating to European and national issues are mixed. Based on a Eurobarometer study of candidate countries (CEEB) published in spring 2004, the management of European elections from a 'national' angle matched the wishes of Czech and Polish voters who were far more interested in debating the pressing unemployment issue, than more distant European matters.

In Spain, the electoral battle was centred on Spain-specific issues such as terrorism and the withdrawal of Spanish troops from Iraq, with very few references to the EU and European integration; indicating once more the predominance of national issues in determining election results. Each party either sought to reaffirm the last Socialist victory or cast a doubt on its validity, presenting it as the impact of the 9/3

Table 2 Campaign interest, salience and main issues driving electoral choice in per cent (1999)

Survey 12–22 May BVA	Germany	France	Italy
Interesting campaign	38	25	27
Uninteresting campaign	57	67	55
European politics	43	31	22
National problems	52	58	58
Employment	75	78	60
Kosovo	55	44	47
Taxes	50	33	35
Environment	33	30	18
Immigration	34	21	17

Table 3   Perception of major issues in Poland and the Czech Republic prior to the 2004 polls (%)

Issues*	Czech Republic	Poland
Country-specific issues	50	42
Agriculture	49	57
Environment	42	25
Fight crime	50	35
Employment	70	72
Immigration	31	14
Education	42	35
PESC	27	22
Foreign policy	28	20
EU enlargement	20	15
EU institutional reforms	19	11
European Parliament activities	17	10
Rights of European citizens	50	37

Question asked: 'in your opinion, what issues should the campaign for the next European elections focus on?' (multiple answers)

attacks on Spanish political life (Gerstlé et al., 2005). This predominance is unambiguous, as any electoral offer, since the withdrawal of the troops from Iraq, meant a policy shift for the ruling party towards its European partners in Paris and Berlin. This is clearly expressed in the slogan 'We return to Europe'.

An unquestioned sign of the Europeanisation of electoral campaigns, intended as the infiltration of a European dimension in national issues of electoral campaigns, is the growing importance attributed to European considerations, whether we talk of desirability, forms of 'integration', or policies which have to be undertaken. The aforementioned studies on European elections are indicative of the decline of the debate on simple 'national versus European' dimensions. The growth of Euroscepticism, and the appearance of political parties which have made the defence of identity their trademark since 1984 (in particular the FN which obtained large successes in France), has

slowed down the formulation of European issues in subsequent elections. For instance, in France, opponents to the Maastricht Treaty, such as the RPF and MPF, did not miss the opportunity to make themselves heard both at the 1994 and 1999 elections. However, between 1994 and 1999, these delaying tactics did not succeed in preventing issues put forward by pro-European groups from gaining salience.

Finally, it is European citizens who should have the first say on campaign issues. Their views and perceptions of the current state of European integration and preferences for the future should not be forgotten. The leading political parties in charge of preparing their programmes must choose between two different electoral strategies. The first one consists of satisfying the median voter, leading them to make use of middle-of-the-road measures. The second or 'priming' strategy consists of emphasising in their campaigns issues that resonate with a majority of the

Table 4 Evolution of competencies at the European and national levels (%)

Issues	Reminder, SOFRES TNS Survey December 2001	April 2004
Scientific research		
European level	80	74
National level	17	22
Food security*		
European level	70	74
National level	27	23
Environment		
European level	65	69
National level	32	28
Foreign policy		
European level	67	68
National level	27	24
Immigration		
European level	62	63
National level	33	33
Sending troops abroad		
European level	69	62
National level	25	32
Industrial and economic policies (**)		
European level	57	60
National level	37	34
Security issues		
European level	50	47
National level	46	50
Health issues		
European level	49	46
National level	48	51
Improvement of citizens' quality of life		
European level	44	44
National level	52	52
Taxes		
European level	43	42
National level	50	52
Cultural policy		
European level	–	42
National level	–	53
Employment		
European level	42	40
National level	54	57
Training and education		
European level	39	38
National level	57	59
Social policy		
European level	–	36
National level	–	59
Social protection		
European level	34	30
National level	63	67

Source: Study realised between 28 and 30 April 2004 for the Robert Schuman foundation with 1000 persons representing a panel of the population aged 18 and more questioned in their homes. Quota methods (sex, age, profession PCS), stratification per region and city category
* Question asked: to answer in the most efficient way to all these questions or to each of these problems, would you say it is better to adopt measures at the national or at the European level?
** In December 2001 the proposed item was 'food security'
*** In December 2001, the proposed item was 'economic policy'

Table 5 Interesting issues for the next 2004 European elections in the 15 member states (%)

Employment	59	Agriculture	24
Security	45	Defence	22
Immigration	45	Foreign policy	20
National issues	35	Enlargement	13
Environment	34	Reforms	13
Citizens' rights	33	European Parliament	12
Education	32	No answer/Don't know	2

public, without sacrificing their own policy agendas at the European level. In order to succeed, they must take into account the hierarchy and salience of current issues that citizens wish to see exercised at the EU level. Eurobarometer and national surveys seem to converge to confirm citizens' priorities. Let us take as sole indicator the April 2004 survey by the Robert Schuman Foundation (Table 4).

What is remarkable about these results is the overall stability of preferences expressed by voters. Aside from the progression of a desired European dimension for the environment, foreign policy and a decline of defence issues, the order and scale of responses remains identical. Of course, political leaders and institutions do not want to appear dependent upon surveys based on 'simulated reactivity' shaping the expectations of citizens (Gerstlé 2003). Nevertheless, the May 2004 Eurobarometer sought to establish a hierarchy of issues relevant to the election campaign in all 15 member states. Of course, national variations and ambiguity concerning the interpretation of what constitutes 'national issues' remain apparent. In fact, should they be interpreted as 'doorstep issues', or as management problems that could be addressed by the EU? Table 5 shows that while immigration is perceived as a European affair, security and employment are not. The European Parliament's

low visibility legitimately allows us to reassess the question of European elections as currently organised, as public policy preferences should not be ignored by those in charge of promoting political offers. Moving beyond national borders will allow these actors to benefit from a more homogeneous discourse, all the more so as a European Constitution could facilitate the emergence of common collective perceptions.

Jacques Gerstlé

Bibliography

Blumler, J. G. (ed.), *Communicating to Voters*, London, Sage, 1983.

Budge, I. et al., *Mapping Policy Preferences: Estimates for Parties, Electors and Governments (1945–1998)*, Oxford, Oxford University Press, 2001.

Charlot, M., *The June 1984 European Elections*, Paris, Publications de la Sorbonne, 1986.

Eijk, C. van der and Franklin, M. N. (eds), *Choosing Europe? The European Electorate and National Politics in the Face of Union*, Ann Arbor, University of Michigan Press, 1996.

Garcia, G. and Le Torrec, V. (dir.) *L'Union Européenne et les médias: Regards croisés sur l'information européenne*, Paris, L'Harmattan, 2003.

Gerstlé, J., 'La réactivité aux préférences collectives et l'imputabilité de l'action publique', *Revue française de science politique*, 53, 6, 2003, pp. 859–85.

Gerstlé, J., *La communication politique*, Paris, Armand Colin, 2004.

Gerstlé, J. et al., 'Les campagnes électorales européennes ou l'obligation politique relâchée', in P. Perrineau and H. D. Klingemann (dir.), *Le vote des Vingt-Cinq*, Paris, Presses de Sciences Po, 2005.

Sweeney, J. P., *The First European Elections*, Boulder, Westview Press, 1984.

→ Campaign (Sociology of); Communication; Electoral Strategy; Eurobarometer; European Constitution; European Elections (1979–1999); European Elections (2004); European Electoral Sociology; European Public Sphere; Europeanisation (of National Political Life); Protest Voting; Second-Order Elections; Social Europe; Turkey.

Italy

As one of the founding members of the European Communities, Italy has organised direct universal suffrage elections since 1979 in order to appoint its 'representatives to the European Parliament'. On the one hand, these elections are characterised by a high level of electoral participation compared to other member states; on the other hand, the power tensions between political parties in accordance with a strictly national political agenda which are captured in the elections provide the more significant features. Italian political life post-1945 can be classified into two distinct periods: the 'First Republic' (1946–92) and the 'Second Republic' (1993 onwards). Although there has not been any major constitutional change between these two periods, they can be distinguished by a change in the electoral rules. During the 'First Republic', mass parties, whether small or large, which had emerged from the anti-fascist movement, dominated political life, and the most important of these parties, the Christian Democrats (DC), enjoyed continuous power in government and over the state in general. Moreover, the extreme stability relating to electoral behaviour was reinforced through proportional representation, a system which was key to the political regime, and applied at all levels of representation. However, this was to change as the 'Second Republic' witnessed the electoral collapse of the Christian Democrats and their allies, and in its place observed the subsequent emergence of new political forces exclusively centred around a leading figurehead (similar to the party Forza Italia which dominates the current government coalition and is largely associated with Silvio Berlusconi, its president and founder). Additionally, during this new political era of change, the representation system gradually evolved into a majority electoral system, at (almost) all levels. However, the Council decisions of 25 June 2002 and 23 September 2002, which modified the Act of 20 September 1976 establishing the election of the MEPs by universal suffrage, and which was adopted with the agreement of the current Italian government, ratified the application of proportional representation in all member states. Within this European framework, the enforcement of proportional representation is obligatory, yet the voting rules could have been more closely aligned to the principle of the 'Second Republic' if only to introduce a threshold for the allocation of seats (the Council decision authorises a maximum threshold of 5 per cent at the national level). Nevertheless, the old voting rules remained for the 2004 European elections and thus appear to be the last remnant from the *modus operandi* of the 'First Republic'. This very stability serves to highlight the relatively low importance of these elections in the Italian political game, and of the European Parliament for politicians.

Following the provisions of the Act of

20 September 1976 on the elections of MEPs by direct universal suffrage, the Italian Parliament with the Act 18/1979 of 24 January 1979 introduced a strongly proportional electoral law. Italian citizens over the age of 18 have the right to vote, those over 25 have the right to be elected (in the same way as for the election of the Chamber of Deputies), and those who are official residents of another EU country are entitled to vote in their home consulate (a new provision at the time). Italy, with its mandatory 81 elected MEPs, is divided into five constituencies, which are composed of several administrative regions, whereby seats are distributed according to the size of the resident population. According to the latest census 22 MEPs were allocated to North-West Italy, 15 to North-East Italy, 16 to Central Italy, 19 to Southern Italy and 9 to the Italian Islands. Whilst access to the candidature lists is open to parliamentary parties, other parties are required to gather over 30 000 signatures of support. Competing parties submit full candidate lists for one or more constituencies, but voters are able to express a preference for 1, 2 or 3 candidates according to the constituency, which can change the order of the chosen list. Hence, the electorate is invited to vote for a party (by putting a cross on the party symbol) and if desired, can further express a preference for one (or more) party candidate(s), by writing down the preferred names of the candidates on the ballot paper. This voting process is absolutely identical to the method in force to elect the Chamber of Deputies (or local councils in towns with over 2500 inhabitants, and provincial and regional councils). In terms of the distribution of seats, the Home Secretary is responsible for initially calculating the total number of votes obtained by a party across all the constituencies in a unique national college, before proceeding to determine the number of MEPs for each party based on the 'natural quota' method (total number of expressed votes/number of seats), following which the highest number of remaining votes is then taken into account (including parties unable to reach the 'natural quota'). Even in comparison to the proportional method used for the elections of the Chamber of Deputies and the Senate, this European election method works in favour of small parties' representation (Di Virgilio 1990). At the end of the so-called period of 'historical compromise' (between the Christian Democrats and the Italian Communist Party [PCI]), the Italian legislature attempted to provide the apparently unsettled political regime an opportunity for renewal by clearing all the arising tensions through the channel of voting. The seats obtained by each party are distributed among the constituencies after the election in proportion to the number of votes won in each of them, and the allocation order of the seats is defined by the number of preferences received by the different candidates of the party in the constituency. Thus, a candidate who receives a large number of preferential votes in his or her constituency is very likely to be elected. Given that well-known candidates are able to 'pull in' more votes to boost their respective party's score, and since multiple candidacies are permitted, parties tend to nominate their leader in several constituencies, if not all, in order to maximise the popular appeal of the individual. The Act of 1979 had created a very limited system of incompatibilities, notably allowing national MPs to sit in the European Parliament.

Quite unsurprisingly therefore, the first three European elections (1979, 1984, 1989) held under the 'First Republic' were practically identical to the national elections (Di Virgilio 1990). The first European election took place just a week after the early political elections of 1979 and similar levels of turnout and electoral outcomes were observed in both elections. The European elections secured a turnout of 85.7 per cent, in contrast to a 90.6 per cent level of participation for the national political elections. Moreover, small parties (essentially from the centre majority) made electoral gains in the European elections compared to their outcomes the previous week. In 1984, a year after the national elections, in the context of strong opposition to the centre government, the PCI won more votes and a higher percentage than the DC for the first time in its political history. Such a result can certainly be explained as being attributable to the emotions aroused amongst PCI supporters from the untimely death of their party leader, Enrico Berlinguer. However, this success was short-lived: if it can largely be attributed to the difference made by the mobilisation of the left, it was also brought about, particularly in the south of the country, by the failure of the parties of the centre majority to mobilise the 'exchange votes' (or, more bluntly, the clienteles), but these lost voters could be duly remobilised during national elections, as observed with the centre coalition victory at the 1987 national elections. The ineffective nature of European elections in terms of predicting relative power for subsequent political elections contributed to the reinforcement of the low political relevance of the latter (Di Virgilio 1990; ISTAT 1990). In 1989, elections occurred in the midst of a governmental crisis and helped to assess the relative power of the different parties whereby small parties regained electoral strength, but without significantly modifying the relative powers, since in terms of percentage the variations remained extremely limited. Therefore, the 'second-order election' model functions in a diluted sense in the Italian case (ISTAT 1990). The votes of

the Italian electorate who reside in the European Community had no influence over on the aggregate results (ISTAT 1990), and perhaps only slightly affected the calculation of electoral turnout (Di Virgilio 1990).

The 'Second Republic' did not really modify this pattern. In 1994, the elections took place in the aftermath of electoral victory for the alliances formed around Silvio Berlusconi during the late March 1994 elections. Berlusconi's first government had only been in power for less than a month when the European elections arrived, and his opponents (and allies) were still recovering from the 'blitzkrieg' of television ads that he had forced on them since January. Following the recent election fatigue, turnout decreased dramatically from 86.1 per cent in the national elections of 27 March 1994, to only 75 per cent in the European elections of 12 June 1994. The results merely confirmed the outcomes from the national elections whereby FI obtained 30.1 per cent of the valid votes. Such a result stemmed from an exclusively Italian pattern of political power distribution. However, it had a major consequence for the European Parliament as for the first time the EPP-ED group was no longer dominated by a German–Italian alliance (CDU-CSU and DC), since the main successors to the DC were facing a prolonged continuation of their electoral collapse which was triggered in the autumn of 1992. FI initially faced some years of isolation in the European Parliament, before its enrolment to the EPP-ED group and the EPP in 1998.

As for the 1999 European elections, they took place in the middle of an electoral cycle where the centre-left had been in power since the spring of 1996. For once, European issues featured more prominently in the elections for two distinct reasons. Firstly, Romano Prodi, who had lost his office as head of the government during the autumn of 1998, was attempting, 'in the name of Europe', to resurrect a moderate movement in the centre-left coalition. This movement, then called 'the Democrats', was targeted against the 'Left Democrats' (DS), who had just assumed leadership of the government. Secondly, the radicals in support of Marco Panella and Emma Bonino were dependent on the latter's role as incumbent European commissioner (appointed by Silvio Berlusconi in 1994) and on the financial resources obtained from the sale of their 'family jewel' – *Radio Radicale* – to Silvio Berlusconi, which enabled them to pursue extensive publicity campaigns on television. The electoral results matched the respective advertising expenditure (FI obtained 25 per cent of the votes, the Bonino list 8.5 per cent and the Democrats 7.7 per cent), but the turnout declined further to 70.8 per cent. This significant decrease, compared to the previous European elections as well as to the 1996 national elections (an additional six million voters did not vote (Daniels 2000)), has not really been slowed by the simultaneous setting up of local elections (as repeated in 2004 under the name 'Election Day'). This second European election held under the 'Second Republic' confirmed a tendency towards an amplification of the gaps between the results in the European elections and the results of the immediately preceding (or next) national elections. The radicals had secured 1.9 per cent of the votes in 1996, and received the same outcome in the 2001 elections. In practice, the European elections remain highly beneficial to small parties, who tend to present their own lists to secure at least one seat where they can invest all their efforts. Since 1994, a minimum of 4 per cent of the votes at the national level has been required for representation in the Chamber of Deputies, out of which 25 per cent of seats are reserved (in prin-

ciple) to small parties, who are unable to win a seat by uninominal majority suffrage without participating in a coalition. During the 1999 European elections, with a decreasing turnout, 0.8 per cent of the expressed votes was sufficient to secure a seat. This threshold was the same in 2004, in spite of the reduction in the number of Italian MEPs. Hence, the Italian representation in the European Parliament remains the most divided amongst other large member states. This opportunity for small parties in the essentially majoritarian 'Second Republic', with a proportional electoral system designed for them, is also certainly seen as advantageous given that the salary of an Italian MEP is rather high (currently more than €11 000), to which secretariat costs and expenses can be added. For small parties, such advantages constitute a privileged means to ensure their long-term existence and autonomy, and potentially their future growth (the election of four MEPs of the future Northen League to the European Parliament allowed for its organisational establishment and later electoral growth in 1990–2). An MEP seat also guarantees a desirable parliamentary immunity in a country where political battles often end up in court. S. Berlusconi, U. Bossi and other less famous politicians will therefore enjoy the legal protection granted to them by their European Parliament colleagues.

The 2004 European elections were no different from the previous ones. The Acts of 78/2004 of 27 March 2004 and 90/2004 of 8 April 2004, and the presidential decree of 10 April 2004 merely made do with a few adaptations: the distribution of seats amongst constituencies has been revised according to the latest census; only 78 MEPs can now be elected; all voters have the right to three preferences; a minimum of 30 per cent of women among the candidates is imposed and sanctioned by fines; and the system of incompatibilities has been reinforced and now prohibits sitting both in Rome and Strasbourg. Nonetheless, the overall electoral rules remain unchanged and the rules for the presentation of lists have been made even more flexible for parties represented in Parliament. However, a more significant change occurred during the 2004 European elections: the so-called *par condicio* law, which has regulated electoral campaigns since its enactment in 2000, remains applicable. In particular, it prohibits the use of television adverts, following a vote of the centre-left after the electoral triumph of the 'teleparties' in the 1999 European elections. Moreover, state financing of partisan propaganda, adopted in 1999, through the reimbursement of expenditure, remains extremely generous (up to €250 million can be spent, according to a report by the ANSA dated 4 June 2004). Therefore, when local and European electoral campaigns take place simultaneously, parties receive a double return on their investment. Finally, although television adverts are prohibited, the mobilisation of the electorate via television remains very high. Indeed, according to figures publicised by the Autorità per le Garanzie nelle Comunicazioni (AGC, Authority for the Respect of Rights in Communications: http://www.agcom.it/par_condicio/monitor.htm), politicians frequently appeared on televised news programmes throughout the electoral campaign, and for significant durations. In May 2004, for instance, the overall broadcasted time (amounting to the total of the 'speaking time' – when the audience could actually hear the politician concerned – and the 'news time' which corresponds to the amount of time devoted to talking about a politician or a debate which is of direct concern) for political, partisan and institutional actors in all television news amounted to over 27 hours on the RAI

and more than 14 hours on Mediaset. According to another source – the Canale Tre company, between 10 April and 6 June – the RAI devoted no less than 135 hours to the broadcasting of political and institutional actors, and the Mediaset channels almost 54 hours (Mele 2004). However, the inequalities of access to television news between the different political forces highlighted by these figures cannot be addressed here. In addition, the numerous political shows, broadcasted during prime time on national public and even private channels, and similar programmes aired in the later part of the evening must be included in the figures. Finally, it is important to consider that the AGC figures for May 2004 also show that, as an institutional actor, the European Union represents 0.61 per cent of the broadcasted time of news on RAI (constituting fewer than 10 minutes in a month) and 0.37 per cent of those on Mediaset (representing little more than 3 minutes over the same period). Thus, means and motives for mobilisation were by no means lacking: electoral turnout marginally increased to a level of 73.1 per cent (as opposed to 70.9 per cent in the previous European elections) and amounted to just over 8 points less than that achieved in the 2001 political elections, which had a turnout of 81.4 per cent.

Since these were mid-term elections for the centre-right majority, influential commentators and actors across the board have defined them, from as early as summer 2003, as representing an opportunity for a potential protest vote against the government, and as the time for redefining political forces within party coalitions in view of the imminent national elections scheduled for 2006. These European elections, which the Italian political class consider to have no direct importance in the redistribution of political power, were all the

Table 1 Results of the 2004 European elections in Italy compared to the 2001 national elections and the 1999 European elections

Coalition or political era in % June 2004	Parties	% Eur. June 2004	% Pol. April 2001		% Eur. June 1999		Seats EP 2004 (affiliation to the EP)	Seats EP 1999 (affiliation to the EP)
Neo-fascism (2)	Mov. Idea Sociale Rauti	0.1	0.4		Mov. Soc. Tricolore	1.6	0	1 (NI)
	Fiamma tricolore	0.7	n.c.				1 (NI)	
	Alternativa sociale	1.2	n.c.		n.c.		1 (NI)	0
'Casa delle Libertà' (43.4)	AN	11.5	12.0		AN+Patto Segni	10.3	9 (UEN)	9 (UEN) (including 1
	FI	21.0	29.4			25.2	16 (EPP)	22 (EPP)
	LN	5.0	3.9			4.5	4 (ID)	4 (NI)
			CCD+	3.2	CDU	2.2	5 (EPP)	2 (EPP)
	UDC Partito	5.9	CDU		CCD	2.6		2 (EPP)
	Pensionati Socialisti	1.1	n.c.		0.8		1 (EPP)	1 (EPP)
Non-aligned centre-right (6.6)	Uniti-Nuovo PSI	2.0	1.0		n.c.		2 (NI)	0
	PRI Liberal Sgarbi	0.7	n.c		0.5		0	1 (ELDR)
	Lista Bonino	2.3	2.2		8.5		2 (ALDE)	7 (NI)
	Lista Segni-Sconamiglio	0.5	n.c.		with AN: 10.3)		0	(1) (EPP)

'Uniti nell'	AP-UDEUR	1.3				UDEUR	1.6	1 (EPP)	1 (EPP)
Ulivo'			Margherita	14.5		IPP	4.2		4 (EPP)
(40.0)	Uniti					Democratici	7.7	25 (16	7 (ELDR,
	nell'Ulivo	3.1				Rinnov. It.	1.1	PES, 8	EPP)
	('listone')							ALDE	1 (EPP)
			DS	16.6		DS	17.3	1EPP)	15 (PES)
			Verdi+S			SDI	2.2		2 (PES)
	Verdi	2.5	DI	2.2		Verdi	1.8	2 (Greens)	2 (Greens)
	PCDI	2.4		1.7	2.0			2 (GUE)	2 (GUE)
			Lista Di						
	Lista Di		Pietro-						
	Pietro –	2.1	Italia dei	3.9	n.c.			2 (ALDE)	0
	Occhetto		valori						
	Union								
	valdotaine	0.1		n.c			0.1	0	0
	SVP	0.5		0.5			0.5	0	0
Non-aligned	Rifondazion	6.1		5.0			4.3	5 (GUE)	4 (GUE)
left (6.1)	e communista								
Others	Miscellaneous	1.9		3.5			1.0	0	0
Total		100		100			100	78	87

Note: n.c. not competing in the election.
All % are calculated on the basis of the valid expressed votes. The % for the legislative elections corresponds to the votes in the proportional part of the vote for the Chamber of Deputies.

more contested and taken seriously by the parties which played out at the same time as the local elections directly involving two-thirds of the electorate and symbolic constituencies for each camp: the city of Bologna (to be recaptured by the left) and the province of Milan (to be retained by the right). Despite an extensive and expensive campaign in praise of governmental action, articulated through commercial posters, postal fliers and the use of the six major television channels, FI could not manage to escape a protest vote. However, the governmental coalition as a whole, and moreover the centre-right more broadly defined, retained an electoral majority in the country, thanks to the successful electoral outcomes of all the other parties, still committed to their respective leaders. Despite attempts from the centre-left to gather around R. Prodi in a 'unitary list', otherwise called 'Uniti nell' Ulivo', this federation ultimately suffered from a dispersed electorate, oriented towards small groups essentially located on its left. Indeed, despite 'R. Prodi's return' to Italian politics, the June 2004 European election was yet again determined in Italy by national issues, appearing as a 'general rehearsal' for the national elections scheduled for 2006. Thus, the 2004 European election did not so much reaffirm the legitimacy of the EU in Italy (as Rentato Mannheimer asserted in his article: 'La Grande Europa piace agli italiani. "Ma che non ci costi come l'euro"', *Corriere della Sera*, 30 March 2004) as reinstate an enduring request for partisan pluralism.

Christophe Bouillaud

Bibliography

Daniels, P., 'Le elezioni al Parlamento europeo del 1999', in M. Gilbert and G. Pasquino (eds), *Politica in Italia*, Bologne, Il Mulino, 2000.

Di Virgilio, A., 'A che servono le elezioni europee?', in M. Caciagli and A. Spreafico (eds), *Vent'anni di elezioni in Italia, 1968–1987*, Padoue, Liviana Editrice, 1990.

ISTAT, *45 anni di elezioni in Italia, 1946–1990*, Rome, ISTAT, 1990.

Mele, M., 'Politici in tv, Rai più equilibrata di Mediaset', *Il Sole 24 Ore*, 13 June 2004.

→ Abstention; Electoral Strategy; Electoral System; European Elections (1979–1999); European Elections (2004); European Electoral Sociology; Incompatibility; Mapping Europe: European Electoral Geography; Nationalisation of European Elections; Political Context; Populism; Protest Voting; Second-Order Elections; Territorial Organisation.

J

Journalists

Do journalists covering European issues, and European Parliament elections in particular, manifest convergent editorial orientations reflecting a common professional vision, as well as shared sources? The specialisation and expertise of journalists and foreign correspondents in European affairs appears to be unevenly distributed amongst different newspapers. While such familiarity with EU issues is certainly well established in Belgium (where EU affairs are seen as local news), it is far more recent in France, and still unknown in several EU countries. Coverage of European institutions is highly dependent upon their visibility in the political and partisan debates of each member state. However, it also results from the saliency of current events within the EU. Information coming from Brussels is often seen by news editors as institutional, repetitive and very unspectacular; all factors that make it unsuitable as public 'entertainment'. Not only do crucial EU decisions take place in political arenas that do not publish transcripts of their debates (College of Commissioners, directorate generals, expert committees, EP committees, Council), but the outcome of these negotiations takes the form of technical texts whose effects are only felt after they have been transposed into national legislations. Affected by the distance separating them from their news agencies' headquarters, correspondents based in Strasbourg and Brussels are professionally damaged by the not-so-journalistic nature of the issues they are covering, a factor limiting their share of articles or reportages as well as their chances of being promoted.

Since the role, the policies and the organisation of European institutions are often very little known, a majority of voters only – at best – hears about them through journalistic articles and reports. Consequently, voters' perceptions of the EU and even identities are largely shaped by press or media agendas that determine what is to fall within the brackets of EU current affairs (Bruter 2005). However, different editorial lines can challenge the establishment of a dominant framework capable of significantly shaping the opinion of large segments of the electorate. Nonetheless, can national or EU-wide trends in the way journalists refer to the EU be observed? The empirical analysis of journalists based in Brussels shows that they do not form a unified and competitive professional group. This differs greatly from the national level, where competition among different news agencies and editorial groups leads to their mutual interdependence, forcing them to adjust their editorial line to that of their competitors (Bastin 2002; Baisnée, in Marchetti 2004). Partly for linguistic reasons, a strong national segmentation of spaces of reference of the journalists specialising in EU affairs can be observed. In fact, each of them aims at satisfying their editor and political field in particular. Amongst the consequences of this segmentation is the unusually high level of co-operation observed between Brussels-based correspondents, often manifested in the joint gathering of information. This is further facilitated by the institutional character of the facts and details (the absence of 'scoops' and the existence of one common source, also known as the Commission's daily press point), as well as the segmentation of the markets for the diffusion of news stories (an 'exclusive' story broadcasted by an Italian journalist can be independently exploited by a Spanish editor etc.). Also contributing to this situation are the Commission's efforts to supply select information to journalists, who then present it to the public. European institutional sources also often enjoy a quasi-monopoly over the divulging and interpretation of series of administrative events deriving from their competencies.

'Europhile' journalists are more inclined to accept the frameworks suggested by European institutions. Moreover, they can also be European 'activists', who justify their choice of a post in Brussels through their active support of the European project. Clearly, this is an attitude EU institutions capitalise on and encourage. Nonetheless, journalists' editorial lines are highly dependent on the boundaries established within the framework of national political debates. In fact, the different and contradictory political offers of each country define the margins and agenda journalists adhere to. Predominantly 'Europhile' political elites, such as the ones ruling in Belgium and Italy, will certainly contribute to limiting the appearance in the media and public debate of negative accounts of European institutions and the overall European project. With the absence of dissident commentaries driven by important political actors, journalistic accounts tend to positively reaffirm the information supplied by their political sources and validate notions that are mostly favourable to European integration to the electorate. Similarly, those journalists who are accustomed to the current structure of the EU and have been exposed to a predominantly pro-European discourse, will tend to dissuade colleagues from differentiating themselves on European matters, thus perpetuating the dominance of 'Europhiles'. By contrast, a rather 'Europhobic' political class such as the one ruling in the UK will tend to favour the reporting of Eurosceptic candidates who will contribute to the perpetuation of critical accounts on European integration and encourage candidates to play the 'Eurosceptic card' to attract voters (Anderson and Weymouth 1999). In France, the predominant orientation appears to be more ambiguous, since the referendum campaign for the ratification of the Maastricht Treaty showed the existence of a journalistic hierarchy massively favourable to the principle and modalities of European integration, coexisting with a political class more ambivalent on issues such as monetary sovereignty and economic policies, even though the ruling parties and elites (around Jacques Chirac and François Mitterrand) negotiated and ratified the treaties that followed.

On the whole, careful observation shows that within each country, journalistic elites rarely adopt orientations opposed to the public attitudes of the main parties when covering European affairs. In most continental countries, administrative and political elites support the process of European integration. Such consensus makes the expression of credible political alternatives very difficult, and usually leads to journalists' support of measures adopted on a majority basis in the EU. In contrast, in Britain, a political class with substantial reservations on EU institutions produces a generally Europhobic press (Anderson and Weymouth 1999). It is therefore difficult to establish the influence of the media on political debates. In fact, the process appears to be an interactive one, involving both journalists and parties. In political configurations characterised by relative consensus between the ruling majority and opposition, editorial hierarchies appear to follow the attitudes of the leading political actors. Only the division of partisan elites allows journalists to play a more active role in the definition of the media's agenda.

Philippe Juhem

Bibliography

Anderson, P. J. and Weymouth, T., *Insulting the Public? The British Press and the European Union*, London, Longman, 1999.

Bastin, G., 'Les journalistes accrédités auprès des institutions européennes à Bruxelles', in D. Georgakakis (ed.), *Les métiers de l'Europe politique: Acteurs et professionnalisation de l'Union européenne*, Strasbourg, Presses Universitaires de Strasbourg, 2002.

Bruter, M., *Citizens of Europe? The Emergence of a Mass European Identity*, Basingstoke, Palgrave Macmillan, 2005.

Gavin, N., 'Imagining Europe: Political Identity and British Television Coverage of the European Economy', *British Journal of Politics and International Relations*, 2, 3, 2000, pp. 352–73.

Marchetti, D. (ed.), *En quête d'Europe: Médias européens et médiatisation de l'Europe*, Rennes, Presses Universitaires de Rennes, 2004.

Tumber, H., 'Marketing Maastricht: the EU and News Management', *Media, Culture and Society*, 17, 3, 1995, pp. 550–96.

→ Communication; Issues.

L

Latvia

Introduction

One of the most recent countries to join the European Union on 1 May 2004, Latvia is also one of the smallest of the 25 member states with a population of 2.3 million inhabitants. Similar to the other two Baltic States, Latvia enjoyed a brief period of sovereignty between the two world wars but was shortly after engulfed by the Soviet Union. Latvia proudly reclaimed her independence in 2001. When 67.7 per cent of the population voted in favour of joining the European Union in the referendum of 20 September 2003, it was obvious to all that many Latvians awaited membership with enthusiasm. Nevertheless, while 72.5 per cent of the population turned out to vote in the referendum, a relatively high score amongst the recently admitted member states, the referendum highlighted some of the main cleavages still dividing Latvian society. Indeed, such deep-rooted societal divisions were vibrantly illustrated by the example of Daugavpils, the most 'Russian' city of the Republic (only 12 per cent of its inhabitants are ethnically Latvian) which voted 'No' to European Union membership in the referendum by a majority of 52 per cent. At the same time, it should also be remembered that 22 per cent of the country's population – mostly because they do not speak Latvian – are not entitled to Latvian citizenship and voting rights accordingly.

Public opinion and context

The 2002 general elections witnessed a transformation of the political majority within the national parliament (*Saeima*) and the emergence of a governing coalition constituted by three centre-right parties. The coalition consisted of the Zaļo un Zemnieku Savienība (ZZS), following the mould of the traditional European farmers' parties, the Tautas Partija (TP) 'People's Party', a conservative reformist party, and finally, the Latvijas Pirmā Partija (LLP), 'Latvia's First Party', thus forming a centre-right coalition of relatively small parties. The opposition – primarily consisting of the centrist Jaunais Laiks (JL) and the Par Cilvēka Tiesībam Vienotā Latvijā (PCTVL) – a coalition of left-wing parties including the former communists – hoped to use the 'mid-term effect' of the European Parliament elections to inflict a defeat on the ruling coalition.

In particular, the former communists tried to use the progressive disaffection of the electorate for the European Union in their campaign. Recent Eurobarometer figures show that Latvia was, at the end of 2003, of all Central European member states, a country where the second lowest level of support for European integration was registered. Indeed, only 33 per cent of the population regarded European integration as a good thing, against 22 per cent who regarded it as a bad thing, and 38 per cent who considered it to be neither a good nor a bad thing. More disquieting, however, was the fact that this level of support had decreased by a whole 13 points during the second quarter of

2003. Similarly, while 49 per cent of Latvians still thought that their country would benefit from European integration, this result indicated a drop of 9 points as compared to the previous survey.

While this phenomenon of declining support for European integration between the accession referendum and the June European Parliament election was in no way peculiar to Latvia, the more pressing issue was that of the widespread unpopularity of the incumbent government, which resulted in a campaign largely dominated by populist and Eurosceptic rhetoric.

Similarly, when compared to most of Western Europe, the Latvian public seemed to remain uncertain and doubtful when asked to express their trust in the European Parliament: 40 per cent of the public claimed that they could place their trust in the main democratic EU institution, while 18 per cent tended not to trust it. The low level of confidence in the European Parliament placed Latvia 24th out of the 25 member states, only superseded by the United Kingdom, for the title of 'most Eurosceptic' country in the EU when asked to place their trust in the European Parliament. However, it should also be noted that when the same question was asked of Latvians about their own national parliament, the proportion of citizens trusting their national institution was halved yet again to a meagre 20 per cent. Moreover, the open 'distrust' figure reached a very high 70 per cent in the case of the national parliament but only 18 per cent in the case of the European one.

Electoral system and constituencies

In order to elect its first nine European Parliament representatives, Latvia chose to implement a nationwide constituency-based proportional representation electoral system. The vote – which, unlike most other member states, occurred on Saturday 12 June – was preceded by primary elections, which lasted three days.

Turnout

With a low turnout of 41.3 per cent, the European Parliament elections clearly did not grab the attention of the majority of Latvian voters. In comparison, interestingly, turnout for the October 2002 general elections was 71.5 per cent, and a similar level of participation was recorded in the referendum of 2003 on EU membership. However, the Latvian case is not fundamentally different from the other nine new member states of the European Union. Although 41.3 per cent is an undoubtedly low score for participation, Latvia achieved the second highest level of turnout of the eight Central European member states of the European Union, and the 13th overall out of 25 member states.

Analysis of results

The results of the 2004 European Parliament elections are detailed in Table 1. The first and most significant lesson to be learned from the election was that Latvian voters chose to severely punish the three members of the governing coalition. In particular, the smaller ZZS and the historical 'Latvia's First Party' failed to obtain any representation whatsoever in Strasbourg. At the same time, the senior coalition partner JL dropped to second place in the Latvian party system, while it was largely dominant in the 2002 general elections.

The great beneficiary of this 'mid-term effect' was the nationalist TB/LNNK, which easily obtained the first position and nearly half of the seats in

Table 1   Results of the European Parliament election 2004

Party	Votes (%)	% 2002	Seats
Apvieniba 'Tevzemei un Brivibai'/ TB-LNNK (Nationalist)	29.8	(5.4)	4
'Jaunais Laiks'/JL (Centre Right)	**19.7**	**(23.9)**	**2**
Politisko Organizaciju Apvieniba 'Par Cilvēka Tiesībām Vienotā Latvijā'/PCTVL (Socialist)	10.7	(18.9*)	1
Tautas Partija/TP (Liberal)	6.7	(16.7)	1
Savieniba 'Latvija Cels'/LC (Reformist)	6.6	(4.9)	1
Tautas Saskanas Partija/TSP (Centre-Left)	4.8	(18.9*)	0
Latvijas Socialdemokratiska Stradnieku Partija/LSDSP (Social Democrat)	4.8	(4.0)	0
'Zaļo un Zemnieku Savienība'/ZZS (Centre Right)	**4.3**	**(9.5)**	**0**
'Latvijas Pirmā Partija'/LPP (Centre Right)	**3.2**	**(9.6)**	**0**

Notes:
* PCTVL and TSP had joint lists in the 2002 general election.
* 2002 column indicates the result of the party in the last general elections in Autumn 2002.
* Parties in bold are part of the ruling coalition.

the nationwide contest. Their four MEPs went on to join forces with the national right-wing movements of the European Parliament alongside parties such as the Danish Dansk Folkeparti, the Italian Alleanza Nationale and the UK Independence Party.

In terms of geographical distribution, a few anomalies can be observed from the results. The first concerns the way the coalition in power resisted the sanction of the voters. In the south-western region of Saldus, for example the three parties in government resisted well and achieved a combined score of 35.8 per cent, well above the national average of 27.2 per cent. Contrastingly, in Daugavpils, the second largest city in the country and the heart of the Russian-speaking community, the same three parties barely managed to attract 11.2 per cent of the voters. The same variations also affected the other Latvian parties. In Riga, for example, the coalition of former Socialists and their allies made a much stronger breakthrough than in the rest of the country. Indeed, they obtained 18.5 per cent of the votes in the capital against 10.7 per cent in the country overall. At the same time, again in Daugavpils, their allies in the form of the TSP scored their biggest success with 18.5 per cent of the votes, almost four times their national performance of 4.8 per cent. By contrast, the big winner of the election, the nationalist TB/LNNK, barely obtained 11.2 per cent of the votes in the region of Kraslava (in the south-eastern and largely Russian-speaking part of the country) but 43.9 per cent of the votes in the region surrounding the Baltic port of Liepaja.

Political significance and conclusions

The Latvian case seems to neatly summarise the general character of the

June 2004 European Parliament elections in Central and Eastern Europe. In terms of election turnout, albeit less dramatically so than in most other countries in this part of the continent, the Latvian electorate showed their disaffection with national electoral politics by staying away from the polling stations. At the same time, they highlighted the general attitude of diffidence towards the ruling coalition government by depriving them of their core votes, and prevented two of the three partners from obtaining any representation in Strasbourg. The winner by default of this exercise in 'democratic punishment' was the country's main nationalist party, the TB/LNNK.

Altogether, this made the June 2004 European Parliament election appear to be a prototypical 'mid-term' election, a particular kind of 'second-order' election in which national issues superseded European themes, and in which the polity mostly endeavoured to reprimand the incumbent government and chose instead to favour the main opposition parties.

However – and subject to confirmation by individual level data – the 2004 European Parliament elections emphasised the persistence of profound and deep-rooted cleavages in many Central European societies. In the case of Latvia, the obvious antagonism between the Latvian majority and the Russian minority (usually supported by its Ukrainian and Byelorussian sister-communities) influenced the choices of many voters. This confirms that the European Union enlargement of 1 May 2004 will have undoubtedly provided a drive and impetus towards greater heterogeneity not only in terms of the political and economic spheres but also within society.

Sarah Harrison

→ Mapping Europe: European Electoral Geography.

Left

In the wider sense of the term the European left today includes three groups within the European Parliament: the Party of European Socialists (PES) which itself includes Socialist, Social-Democrat and Labour MEPs; the Green group (Greens – European Free Alliance); and the confederal group of the European United Left-Nordic Green Left (GUE-NGL). The PES was created in 1992 and the Green Party in 2004. These three constituent parts of the European left, the socialists, ecologists and the extreme left (which includes communist parties and others to the political left of the socialists) all have very different positions on Europe. As a whole, the socialist group is favourable to the historical process of the building of Europe. This is also true for the Green group in spite of a certain internal diversity. The extreme left (as the GUE/NGL shall be referred to) has historically been hostile to the way in which the Community and then the European Union was built. This faction includes parties that were opposed to the Maastricht Treaty. It fights against what it sees as European economic 'neo-liberalism' but also affirms its commitment to European integration in its declaration of 14 July 1994. Two of the three constituent parts of the European left are therefore generally favourable to the building of Europe and the third one is more Eurosceptical. Even if it does make some political sense to see these three groups as a whole, a certain amount of caution should be exercised in assimilating them completely. In terms of the functioning of the European Parliament, the left/right division is only one among many. As far as the PES is concerned, it has always privileged the duopoly it forms with the European People's Party.

Table 1   Variations in numbers of MEPs in the three parliamentary groups in the European political left from 1999 to 2004

Left-wing groups in the European Parliament	1999	2004	Gap	% of MEPs in each group in relation to the total number of MEPs elected in 1999 in the 15 older member states	% of MEPs in each group in relation to the total number of MEPs elected in 2004 in the 25 member countries
PES: Party of European Socialists	180	200	+20	28.7	27.3
The Greens – European Free Alliance: the Green Party group	48	42	–6	7.6	5.7
GUE-NGL European United Left-Nordic Green Left	42	41	–1	6.7	5.6
Total European Left	270	283	+13	43	38.6
Total European Parliament	626	732	+106	100	100

Positions of the European political left after the 2004 enlargement

The PES group is the largest on the left. It had 200 members after the 2004 European elections, which represents a total of 27.3 per cent of European Parliament members, thus placing it in second position after the European People's Party (EPP) group which has 268 members. The numbers of elected representatives from the other two groups (which are of equal size) are considerably lower. The PES is therefore in a position to play an important role within the European Parliament. It should be noted that there are a total of 283 left-wing MEPs which represents only 38.6 per cent of European Parliament members. As a result of EU enlargement the number of European Parliament seats increased by 132 between 1999 and 2004 (Grunberg et al. 2000). Even though the PES group increased its number of seats by 20, it nonetheless declined slightly in terms of relative importance as it represented 28.7 per cent of MEPs in 1999. Both of the other groups suffered much heavier losses relatively. As a whole, the European left lost five percentage points between 1999 and 2004.

The decline of the left in Europe is directly linked to the Europe of 15 becoming the Europe of 25 (Table 2). Between 1999 and 2004, the left was stable in the 15 member states with a slight drop from 43 per cent to 42.5 per cent and an increase for the PES group, a very slight decline for the Green group and a slightly bigger drop for the United Left group. However, the position of the left in the ten new member states is decidedly weaker than in the older member countries: 19.1 per cent as against 29.6 per cent for the socialists,

Table 2 The effects of the 2004 enlargement on the parliamentary weight of the European left

European Parliament groups	% of MEPs in each group in relation to the total number of MEPs elected in 1999 in the 15 older member states	% of MEPs in each group in relation to the total number of MEPs elected in 2004 in the 15 older member states	% of MEPs in each group in relation to the total number of MEPs elected in 2004 in the 10 new member states	% of MEPs in each group in relation to the total number of MEPs elected in 2004 in the 25 member states
PES: Party of European Socialists	28.7	29.6	19.1	27.3
Greens – European Free Alliance	7.6	7.2	0.6	5.7
GUE-NGL European United Left-Nordic Green Left	6.7	5.7	4.9	5.6
Total of the three groups	43	42.5	24.6	38.6
Total number of seats	100	100	100	100

0.6 per cent as against 7.2 per cent for the ecologists and 4.9 per cent as against 5.7 per cent for the extreme left. The left therefore represents only 24.6 per cent within the 15 new member states as against 42.5 per cent in the older member states. In this respect, enlargement has clearly been unfavourable to the left.

The country of origin of MEPs from the three left-wing groups also clearly shows the difference in influence of the European left among the older and newer member states (Table 3). The socialist group has at least one member in each of the 15 older member states and in only eight of the ten new member states. The ecologists and the extreme left are represented in 12 of the 15 older member countries but in only one and two new member states respectively. It can be concluded that, for the time being at least, the left/right division is not as important structurally in the new member states as it is in the older ones.

The socialists

For the 2004 European elections, all the socialist candidates, bar three, represented parties belonging to the PES. The three exceptions were Latvia with the TSP, the Czech Republic with the SMER and Poland with the SDLP, a breakaway group from the SLD. MEPs from the latter two of these parties joined the PES. Table 4, which shows the overall results of the socialists since the first elections in 1977, shows that candidates on the socialist ticket obtained 20 per cent of the vote in the 15 older member states with the exception of Ireland where the Labour Party is historically weak.

On the other hand, the situation is a little more uneven in the 10 new member countries. The socialists did well in Estonia, Hungary and Malta but they did rather badly elsewhere. In the 15 older member states, electoral variations since the first European elections show long-term continued progress for the

Table 3   The distribution of European parliamentary groups in the old and new member states in 2004

European Parliament groups	Number of countries among the older member states where the group has at least one MEP	Number of countries among the 10 new member states where the group has at least one MEP	Number of countries among the 25 member states where the group has at least one MEP
PES: Party of European Socialists	15	8	23
Greens – European Free Alliance: the Green Party group	12	1	13
GUE-NGL – European United Left-Nordic Green Left	12	2	14

Portuguese Socialist Party and a strong decline for the German Social-Democrat Party, and more recently New Labour in Britain. Between 1999 and 2004 there were strong electoral variations both positive and negative in several countries. The socialists did markedly better in Denmark, Spain, France and Belgium. They declined strongly in Great Britain and in Germany. Comparisons made with the general elections which preceded the 2004 European elections show that the socialists progressed or declined in the general election depending on whether they were in power or not in their own countries. In Germany, the United Kingdom, Sweden, the Czech Republic, Poland and Lithuania they were in government when the election took place whereas in Greece, where they had just lost the general election, they bore the full brunt of the protest vote. In France, Denmark, Portugal and Estonia where they were in opposition, or in Spain where they had just returned to power, they benefited enormously from their prolonged absence from power.

Table 5 shows that the results obtained by candidates on the socialist list allowed this political grouping to reach first or second place in 18 of the 25 EU countries. In this way, socialist parties are making a significant contribution to the structuring of European party systems and even to European elections. Although the latter are considered to be second-order elections by many specialists, they are not unfavourable on the whole to large government parties which is what the socialist parties are in the majority of European Union countries. However, it is true that if one only takes the 10 new member states into account the socialists only reach first or second place in four of them. The position of the socialist parties in this part of Europe is therefore not ensured in the long term. It should be remembered that the majority of these socialist parties are former communist parties which broke with communism and joined the PES (Bokozi and Ishiyama 2002).

Table 4 Variations in the scores of socialist candidates in European elections

Country	1979	1984	1989	1994	1999	2004
Germany SPD +	40.8	37.4	37.3	32.2	30.7	21.5
Belgium						
SP +	12.8	17.1	12.4	10.9	8.8	11 (a)
PS +	10.6	13.3	14.5	11.5	9.7	13.5
Total	23.4	30.4	26.9	22.4	18.5	24.5
Denmark SD +	21.9	19.4	23.3	15.8	16.5	32.5
France PS +	23.5	20.8	23.6	14.5	22	28.9
Ireland LP+	14.5	8.4	9.5	11	8.8	10.8
Italy						
PSI (PS-AD en 1994)+	11	11.2	14.8	1.8	(b)	
PSDI +	4.3	3.5	2.7	0.7	2.1 (c)	
PDS puis DS +				19.1	17.4	
Total	15.3	14.7	17.5	21.6	19.5	(d)
Luxembourg LSAP +	21.6	24.9	25.4	24.8	23.2	22.1
The Netherlands PvDA +	30.4	33.7	30.7	22.9	20.1	23.6
United Kingdom LP +	31.6	36.5	38.9	42.7	28	22.3
Spain PSOE +		39.1	40.2	31.1	35.3	43.3
Greece PASOK +		41.4	36	37.6	32.8	34
Portugal PS +		23.1	28.5	34.9	43.1	44.5
Austria SPÖ +				29.2	31.7	33.5
Finland SPD +				21.5	17.8	21.1
Sweden SAP +				28.1	26.1	24.7
Cyprus KISOS +						10.8(e)
Estonia SDE +						36.8
Hungary MSZP +						34.3
Latvia						
LSDSP +						4.8
TSP						4.8
Total						9.6
Lithuania LSPD +						14.4
Malta PL +						48
Poland						
SLD +						10.3
SDLP						5.3
Total						14.8
Czech Republic CSSD +						8.8
Slovakia SMER						16.6
Slovenia ZLSD +						14.2

(a) SP-Spirit in 2004
(b) The Italian Socialist Party disappeared after 1994
(c) SDI: Italian Social-Democrats
(d) In 2004, member parties of the PES were included on the Ulivo list and their scores are therefore not countable
(e) EEK-SKK list in 2004
+member of the PES on 28/10/2004

Table 5   Socialist party rankings in relation to results obtained by the different lists in the 25 countries of the European Union in the 2004 European elections (% of votes cast) *

Countries	Socialist list(s)	Rank
Austria	SPÖ	1
Belgium	PS/SP.A	1
Cyprus	EDK-SKK	5
Czech Rep.	ČSSD	4
Denmark	SD	1
Estonia	SDE	1
Europe of 25	PES	2
Finland	SPD	3
France	PS	1
Germany	SPD	2
Greece	PASOK	2
Hungary	MSZP	2
Ireland	LP	4
Italy	DS/SDI/ind	1
Latvia	LSDSP	6
Lithuania	LSPD	2
Luxembourg	POSL/LASP	2
Malta	PL	1
Netherlands	PvdA	2
Poland	SLD/SDPL	4
Portugal	PS	1
Slovakia	SMER	3
Slovenia	ZLSD	4
Spain	PSOE	1
Sweden	SAP	1
United Kingdom	LP	2

* The rankings are relative to the position obtained by each party in its home country, e.g. the SPO took first place in Austria, the SPD came second in Germany, etc.

The power struggle between the three left-wing factions in the 2004 European elections

The first thing to note is that if the socialists were present everywhere in 2004, the same cannot be said for the ecologists or the extreme left (Table 6). Both the ecologists and the extreme left were present in only 14 countries. In countries where socialist and/or ecologist and extreme-left candidates were present the socialists scored much higher than either of the other two factions. The only exceptions to this are Cyprus and the Czech Republic where the communists were clearly the winners on the left. Thus, in almost all countries, the socialists are the dominant power in left- wing politics.

Table 7 shows the number of members of each of the three left-wing parliamentary groups by country. All the MEPs of the PES were elected on the basis of socialist lists. On the other hand, the

Table 6 Percentage of socialist, ecologist and extreme-left lists by country in the 2004 European elections

Countries	% of the socialist lists*		% of the ecologist lists		% of the extreme-left lists	
Austria	SPÖ	33.5	GRÜNE	12.8		
	PS	13.5	ECOLO	3.7		
Belgium	SP.A	11	GROEN	4.9		
Total		24.5		8.6		
Cyprus	EDK-SKK	10.8			AKEL	27.9
Czech Rep.	ČSSD	8.8	SZ	3.2	KSČM	20
Denmark	SD	32.5			Folk B.	5.2
					SF	8
Estonia	SDE	36.8				
Finland	SPD	21.2	VIHR	10.4	VAS	9.1
France	PS	28.9	Verts	7.4	PCF/PCR	5.2
					LO/LCR	3.3
Germany	SPD	21.5	B.90/GRÜNEN	11.9	PDS	6.1
Greece	PASOK	34			KKE	9.5
					SYN	4.2
Hungary	MSZP	34.3				
Ireland	Lab	10.8	Green Party	4.5		
Italy	**		Fed. Verdi	2.5	RC	6.1
					PdIC	2.4
Latvia	LSDSP	4.8	ZZS***	4.3	LSP	1.7
	TSP	4.8				
	Total	9.6				
Lithuania	LSDP	14.4				
Luxembourg	LSAP	22.1	Déi Greng	15		
Malta	PL	48.4	AD	9.3		
Netherlands	PvdA	23.6	Groen Link	7.4	SP	7
Poland	SLD-UP	9.3				
	SdPL	5.3				
Portugal	PS	44.5			CDU-PCP/PEV	9
					BE	5
Slovakia	SMER	16.6			KSS	4.6
Slovenia	ZLSD	14.2				
Spain	PSOE/ICV	43.3			IU	4.2
Sweden	SAP	24.7	Mp	5.9	V	9.8
United Kingdom	LP	22.3	Greens	6.2		

* All of the lists featured in this column were presented either on their own or as part of an alliance, by PES parties with the exception of the TSP in Latvia, the SdPI in Poland and the SMER in Slovakia.

** It is not possible to count the scores obtained by the PES member parties within the Ulivo coalition.

*** ZZS: list presented both by ZALA, the Latvian Green Party which is a member of the European Green Party and by the Latvian Agrarian Party.

Table 7   Numbers and composition of the three left-wing groups by country in the 2004 European elections

Countries	PES group**		Green group		Confederal group of the European United Left	
Germany	SPD	23	B.90/GRÜNEN*	13	PDS	7
Austria	SPÖ	7	GRÜNE*	2		
Belgium	PS	4	ECOLO*	1		
	SP.A	3				
Total		7				
Cyprus					AKEL	2
Denmark	SD	5	SF	1	Folk B.	1
Spain	PSOE	24	Los Verdes*	1	IU	1
			IC-V*	1		
			ERC	1		
Estonia	SDE	3				
Finland	SPD	3	VIHR*	1	VAS	1
France	PS	31	Verts*	6	PCF/PCR	3
Greece	PASOK	8			KKE	3
					SYN	1
Hungary	MSZP	9				
Ireland	Lab	1			SF	1
Italy	DS	12	Fed. Verdi*	2	RC	5
	SDI	2			PdCI	2
	Indep.	2				
Latvia			PCTVL	1		
Lithuania	LSDP	2				
Luxembourg	LSAP	1	Déi Greng*	1		
Malta	PL	3				
Netherlands	PvdA	7	Groen Links*	2	SP	2
			EurTrans	2		
Poland	SLD-UP	5				
	SdPL	3				
Portugal	PS	12			CDU-PCP/PEV	2
					BE	1
Czech Rep.	ČSSD	2			KSČM	6
United	LP	19	Greens*	2	SF	1
Kingdom			SNP	2		
			CYMRU	1		
Slovakia	SMER	3				
Slovenia	ZLSD	1				
Sweden	SAP	5	Mp*	1	V	2
Total		*200*		*42*		*41*

* elected representatives on a party list belonging to the European Green Party.
** All members of the PES group were elected from lists presented by parties belonging to the Party of European Socialists with the exception of two independent Italian candidates, the three SMER candidates in Slovakia, and the three SdPL candidates in Poland. The SMER sent a formal request to join the PES.

Greens and the United Left accepted MEPs from lists other than their own. Thus the Green group accepted the ERC representative, the nationalist radical left-wing party accepted the Latvian pro-Russian elected representative, the two Dutch representatives from the Transparent Europe list (a somewhat Eurosceptical list), the two representatives from the Scottish Nationalist Party (SNP), the Welsh Nationalist Party (CYMRU) and finally the elected member from the Danish Popular Socialist Party (SF). The latter is an extreme-left party whose elected member was enrolled on the United Left group during the previous term. The party has moved from being Eurosceptic in attitude to adopting a pro-Europe attitude. In 2004, the elected representative of this group joined the Green group. The GUE/NGL accepted the two newly elected members from the Irish party, Sinn Féin (SF).

Almost half of the PES group elected representatives were elected in France, Germany, the United Kingdom and Spain. With regard to the Greens, almost half of them were elected in France and in Germany. Finally, almost half of those elected on the United Left list were elected in Germany, Italy and the Czech Republic.

Conclusion

On 20 July 2004, the socialist Josep Borrell was elected on the first round with 388 votes. He obtained the votes of the PES and the majority of those of the PPE. Bronislaw Geremek, supported by the Liberals and the Greens, obtained 208 votes and Francis Wurtz, the extreme-left candidate obtained 52. Prior to that the Greens and the Liberals had proposed an alliance to the PES in an attempt to win the presidency against the right-wing parties. The PES, whose most powerful delegation, the French one, rejected all compromise with the Liberals, preferred to make a 'technical' agreement with the PPE to share the presidency with it. The PES/PPE duopoly offered more reassurance to the socialists than a hypothetical alliance between the left and the centre. The PPE agreed that the socialists would take over the presidency during the first half of the mandate. These are the conditions under which Josep Borrell was elected.

Gérard Grunberg

Bibliography

Bozoky, A. and Ishiyama, J. (eds), *The Communist Successor Parties of Central and Eastern Europe*, New York, Armond, 2002.

Eijk, C. van der and Franklin, M. N. (eds), *Choosing Europe? The European Electorate and National Politics in the Face of Union*, Ann Arbor, University of Michigan Press, 1996.

Grunberg, Gérard, Perrineau, Pascal and Ysmal, Colette, *Le vote des quinze: Les élections européennes du 13 juin 1999*, Paris, Presses de Sciences Po, 2000.

Waller, M., Coppieters, B. and Deschouwer, K., *Social Democracy in a Post-communist Europe*, London, Cass, 1994.

Website:

The 'European Parties, Elections and Referendums', a network led by Par A. Szczerbiak and Paul Taggart, has created a website which published very interesting reports on each country analysing the European elections. (http://www.sussex.ac.uk/sei/1-4-2.html).

→ European Federation of Green Parties; Extreme Left; Green Politics; Party of European Socialists (PES).

Lithuania

Introduction

Lithuania joined the European Union on 1 May 2004, alongside nine other

Central European and Mediterranean new members. With 3.6 million inhabitants, Lithuania is the largest of the three Baltic States to have entered the European Union, but is ranked 18th out of the 25 member states by the size of its population. On 10–11 May 2003, 91.1 per cent of Lithuanian citizens voted yes (from a turnout of 63.4 per cent) to membership of the European Union, thus Lithuania appeared to be one of the most strikingly Euro-enthusiastic new member states of the European Union at the time of its joining. In some districts, such as Alytus, and in most of the west of the country, the 'yes' vote approached or even exceeded 95 per cent of the ballots. Even though, in the east of the country, where a larger proportion of the population is of Russian or Byelorussian origin, the 'yes' vote was markedly lower, it never fell below 78.4 per cent of the electorate, which was recorded in the north-eastern town of Visaginas.

When compared to Latvia or even Estonia, however, Lithuania is a country in which ethnic and linguistic cleavages are relatively well negotiated, and in which no restriction to citizenship has been imposed on any minority – including the Russian minority – on either linguistic or genealogic grounds. Similarly, some political parties specifically represent the interests of the Polish and Russian minorities within the country. For all these reasons, the results of the June 2004 European Parliament elections in Lithuania were awaited with interest albeit within a relatively tense context.

Public opinion and context

The 2000 general elections led to a complete transformation of the Lithuanian parliament (Seimas). The ruling conservatives of the Tevynes Sajunga (TS-LK) collapsed from 29.8 per cent and 33 seats to 8.6 per cent and 9 seats. At the same time, a centre-left coalition, the Barzausko Social-demokratinie Koalicija (ABSK), became the dominant group in parliament, albeit without an absolute majority, with 51 seats and 31.1 per cent of the vote, up 13 points from the 1996 general elections. Other parties, such as the social liberals of the Naujoji Sajunga (NS) and the Lietuvous Liberalu Sajunga (LLS), made a dramatic entrance onto the parliamentary stage. Several smaller parties also achieved representation. However, these results did little to satisfy the Lithuanians' appetite for change. As a result, the 2003 by-elections had to be invalidated because turnout did not reach the specified level stipulated by the national constitution, and the national political crisis reached a new high when the nation's President Rolandas Paksas was impeached by a split parliament. The procedure began in December 2003, and the president's mandate was terminated in April 2004. Different parliamentary factions disagreed on how to handle the accusations of links between the president's office and the mafia, a criticised businessman, and the Russian secret service, thus provoking a crisis within the ruling coalition.

It was in this context that Lithuania prepared to vote on 13 June 2004, not only for its first representatives in the Strasbourg Parliament, but also for its new president. Unsurprisingly, the presidential campaign attracted most of the attention in this semi-presidential system in which support for European integration seemed to have eroded a little after the 2003 referendum, although it remained stronger in Lithuania than in any of the other new member states. Indeed, with 52 per cent of Lithuanians claiming to support European Union membership in 2004, the country was the only one of the new Central European member states that ranked above the EU average on this question (Eurobarometer 61). Similarly, 585 of Lithuanians against 20 per cent believed that their country had benefited from European Union membership (EU average 48 per cent against 44 per cent) and a mere 15 per cent of the population declared holding a negative image of the European Union, seven points lower than the new member state average. Finally, 52 per cent of Lithuanians claimed to trust the European Parliament, which put Lithuania amongst the 25 member states when it came to trusting the main democratic institution of the European Union.

Electoral system and constituencies

While Lithuania is one of the few European countries to use a mixed electoral system (single and multi-member districts) for its general elections, the system used for the European Parliament elections was one of simple nationwide proportional representation with a 5 per cent threshold. The country had 13 MEPs to elect resulting in the effective threshold being raised to 6 per cent of the valid votes, however.

Turnout

For the European Parliament elections in 2004, turnout in Lithuania was recorded at 48.4 per cent, which was the highest participation rate in Central Europe by far and it was the eighth highest figure in Europe as a whole. Despite the obvious effect of the presidential election on the level of turnout, it is not sufficient to explain the relative enthusiasm for European elections of Lithuanian voters compared to the 26.9 per cent who voted in Estonia, 20.4 per cent in Poland or 16.7 per cent in Slovakia. Lithuanian voters appeared to have genuinely kept

more faith and interest in the European project when compared to the other member states.

Analysis of results

Altogether, the parties of the centre-left, which decided to run separate lists following the national political crisis, resisted relatively well when compared to other incumbent parties within the European Union. In the opposition, the conservatives, who ruled the country between 1996 and 2000 before then collapsing, regained a small part of their political strength while the moderate liberals emerged as the main contender in the centre of the political spectrum, in the place of a somewhat panicking social liberal party. The liberal democratic party of former President Rolandas Paksas obtained a mere 6.8 per cent of the vote, underlining the meagre support enjoyed by the man who served as the nation's president until April 2004.

Regional differences remained relatively significant, both in terms of turnout and actual result. Turnout-wise, only 28.8 per cent of citizens voted in the very Russian and most Eurosceptic town in the country, Visaginas (north-east). In contrast, the region of Neringos, on the southern Baltic coast enjoyed a turnout of 58.2 per cent, ten points above the national average.

Similar differences can be observed when it came to the actual electoral choice of the voters. The coalition representing the interests of the Polish and Russian minorities topped the contest in their stronghold of Salcininkai (65.8 per cent) in the extreme south-east, as well as in the region surrounding the capital Vilnius (55.5 per cent), and in the north-eastern district of Visaginas (29.7 per cent). The capital itself, in contrast, was the only part of the country where the traditional conservatives of the TS-LK,

Table 1   Results of the 2004 European Parliament election in Lithuania

Party	%	Seats	Change 2004/2000
Darbo Partija (LDDP), Socialist	30.2	5	*
Lietuvos Socialdemokratu Partija (LSDP), Social-Democrat	14.4	2	*
Tėvynės Sąjunga (Lietuvos konservatoriai) (TS-LK), Conservative	12.6	2	+4.0
Liberalų ir Centro Sąjunga (LCS), Liberal	11.2	2	+8.3
Valstiečių ir Naujosios Demokratijos Partijų Sąjunga (NDP/LVP), Agrarian left	7.4	1	*
Liberalų Demokratų Partija (LDP), Populist	6.8	1	–
Lietuvos Lenky Rinkimu Akcijos ir Lietuvos Rusu Sajungos Koalicija 'Kartu Mes Jega!' (LLRA/LRS), Russian and Polish minorities parties	5.7	0	*
Naujoji Sajunga (NS), Social Liberals	4.9	0	–14.7
Lietuvos Krikscionys Demokratai (LKDP), Christian Democrats	2.8	0	–0.3
Krikscionys Konservatoriu Socialine Sajunga (KKSS), Social Christian	2.6	0	–
Tautos Pazangos Partija (TPP), National Conservative	1.2	0	–

Notes:
*Change could not be calculated for the LDDP, LSDP, NDP/LVP, and the LLRA/LRS as the LDDP, LSDP, NDP and LRA ran joint lists in the 2000 general election.

who led the independence revolution of 1991, came first in the voters' choice, although they obtained even better scores in the second largest city – and other cultural capital – of the country, Kaunas. Finally, the rural region of Silales acclaimed the social-democrats of the LSDP, who generally scored high in the south-west of the country. While the labour party was a firm favourite at the ballot box in every other constituency in the country, their score varied significantly from place to place, to reach a maximum of 58.4 per cent in the central region of Kedainiu. Among the other parties, the farmers' union of the NDP/LVP obtained more than 20 per cent of the votes in Visaginas (north- east) and

Birzu (north), the liberal and centre union obtained 23.4 per cent of the votes in their stronghold of Klaipeda and resisted well in Vilnius with 17.4 per cent of the votes, and finally, the liberal democrats of former President Paksas only saved face in the north-western districts of Lithuania, particularly in the region of Telsiai, where they obtained 16.3 per cent of the vote.

Political significance and conclusions

The European elections in Lithuania went off with an almighty bang. The joint European Parliament and presidential elections, as well as the tremendous internal political crisis the country faced between December 2003 and June 2004 gave the election a particular significance within the Lithuanian context. The fact that the country remains, so far, the least disillusioned with European integration in Central Europe, and a model of ethnic plurality and integration, added a particular edge to the vote in the European context as well.

Unsurprisingly, the European Parliament elections in Lithuania therefore contrasted with the general picture painted across most of the continent in that they did not seem to represent second-order elections, and indeed, they had all the characteristics of a first-order election. It is very difficult to know which part of this Lithuanian phenomenon can be attributed to context, and which part to more fundamental elements. However, it remains clear that it is in Lithuania rather than anywhere else within Central Europe that the new member states have started to embrace European integration wholeheartedly.

Sarah Harrison

→ Mapping Europe: European Electoral Geography.

Lobbying

Lobbying – an important part of the reality of the European political system – represents a way of accessing political institutions, a repertoire of collective action and specific social practices at the same time.

Access to the European institutions

To characterise European lobbying, many observers have paid attention to the specificities of the modes of access to the European institutions. They used to deal with the theoretical frames created in order to describe the national systems of interest intermediation (pluralism vs. neo-corporatism). But little by little, they gave them up for an approach that is less macro-sociological and more careful in the logic of access according to policy sectors, issues, interest groups, institutions and great periods of European integration. So, pluralism, characterised by the plurality of actors and access points to the institutions, would be the dominant system of the first period of European integration until the middle of the 1970s (Ayberk and Schenker 1998) and of the European Commission, known as a real 'marketplace of interests' (Mazey and Richardson 1993). (Neo-) corporatism, characterised by an institutionalisation of the relationship between institutions and some groups having a monopoly on interest defence within negotiation authorities, only concerns the social field with the establishment of the 'European social dialogue' in 1992. All the observers claim there is not one European pattern of interest intermediation (Smets and Winand 2000) as a result of the gathering of national systems but rather several kinds of relationship between interest groups and European institutions.

The fragmentation of the European intermediation system can be partly explained by the various institutional policies developed towards interest groups. While in the Commission an 'open and structured dialogue with interest groups' has been officially advocated since 1992, the European Parliament prefers an accreditation system: the organisations' representatives have to honour a code of conduct (passed in 1997) and to register in order to obtain a one-year pass allowing access to public areas of the EP buildings and public meetings of the standing committees and joint committees. Such an accreditation system looks like a never-ending story. From MEP Alman Metten's written answer in 1989, the Galle's report (PES, Belgium) on lobbying within the EP, to Simpson's proposal (PES, UK) in 1994 on lobbyists' registration and the difficult passing in July 1996 of Ford's (PES, United Kingdom) and Nordmann's (ELDR, France) second reports – respectively on interest groups within the European Parliament and MEPs' transparency and financial interests – the problem has been contested to the present day. Voices are often raised either to complain that such an accreditation system limits the access to the EP of a set of co-opted groups and further deprives MEPs of information and expertise, or on the contrary to denounce a very loose accreditation system that does not allow either the selection of organisations or the punishment of those which fail to respect the code of conduct. An accreditation system does indeed 'reinforce the strongest' and push the weakest more aside (Greenwood 1997). This argument is often used by the European Commission which aims at defending a self-regulation system. Actually, the EP's regulation seems to be poorly selective and does not absolutely prevent interest representatives from meeting MEPs during informal hearings or conferences they attend, or during ad hoc committees.

Thus, EU lobbying (Andersen and Eliassen 1996) reflects the image of this system of multi-level governance in which 'civil society' and the European institutions are in constant interaction. But such a description of relationships does not explain what lobbyists really do when they defend ideas of interests with a member of the Commission or of the EP. It depends on the resources they have and the state of the competition between the different interest groups.

How to deal with European institutions

Considering lobbying as a repertoire of collective action (as per Tilly's phrase) has the double advantage of locating it amongst all the potential modes of action and of highlighting the logics which govern its use or, on the contrary, its removal. At the European level, lobbying and protest are two kinds of repertoires of collective action (Balme and Chabanet 2000). While for the former, discretion and confidentiality are required, for the latter, in contrast, what is sought is visibility, in particular through the resort to numbers (marches, demonstrations, strikes, counter-summits, etc.) and scandal (newspaper campaigns essentially). The two sets are not exclusive of one another and actors can use them in turn or in a complementary manner. At the European level, lobbying appears to be more developed than protest which still broadly remains a national mode of action despite its occasional European flavour.

The preference for lobbying is linked with the resources that are provided to the actors mobilised at the European level, and with the conditions offered by the institutions to defend their interests and have an advantage over their challengers and opponents. The groups which have the financial and human resources to provide expertise, information and competent interlocutors in technical issues in Brussels are all the more favoured than the interests that are unable to mobilise either large groups of supporters or the sympathetic moral support of the press. Corporate and economic interest groups are in a better position to use a repertoire of actions that gives them a serious advantage over others which are less skilled and, in many cases, ill-prepared for this kind of action. A mode of action for the most powerful groups, lobbying is seen as the most efficient way to assert one's interests, or even the standard method one should employ in order to have any chance of being noticed in Europe. Some groups try to take this chance by accumulating the necessary resources (opening of a bureau in Brussels, training and recruiting of law and statistics experts, setting up enquiry and study services, etc.) and/or sub-contracting their interests' defence to lobbying professionals. This adaptation to the rules of the game generates changes in interest defence and the representation practices in force within the states. Sometimes presented as a 'new' form of collective action, sometimes considered as the best way to operate at the European level, lobbying remains, for all those who are not considered as 'politics professionals', the 'modern' way of being in politics.

Defence and representation practices

Lobbying covers a wide range of actions that encompass various fields of communication, marketing and public relations and requires various competencies (law, political science, economics, etc.): monitoring press releases, reading of the daily bulletin of the *Agence Europe*, website visiting, mail reading (e-mail and letters), policy statements, summaries and position paper writing, oral presentation in hearings, attendance at parliamentary groups' meetings, meetings with MEPs and Commission officials, conference organisation and participation, parliamentary joint committees secretarial work, EU programmes management, fund raising, juridical and sometimes legal affairs transmitted to advocates at the Court, not to mention all that concerns networking, from the setting up and updating of address books to meetings and regular contact making – all so important in being able to 'target

the right person at the right time at the right place'. Lobbying thus requires a sometimes bewildering number of tasks, some of them unrewarding, some secretive (be it because of a confidentiality clause or the need to retain an air of mystery) but always difficult to enumerate as soon as they are part of daily routine. Nevertheless, by specifying these heterogeneous practices, one emphasises even more the vagueness that characterises the nature of lobbying and helps to explain why some regard it as a secretive, and even illegitimate activity and why others regard it as a normal aspect of the European political 'game'.

Those who make lobbying their main and well-paid activity do not appreciate their jobs being described in this way. For them, lobbying is a matter for specialists who have specific skills, tools and techniques required for this activity, and who exercise it according to rules set and honoured by other professionals. Some of them attempt to promote a good public image of consultants by preventing the 'bad professionals' from setting up in this growing market, and advocate the setting-up of a professional association that would control the practices and the admission to the profession. Others, the majority, simply honour the code of conduct prepared in 1997 by the European Parliament in relation to representatives of the profession, which remains a flexible and liberal way of organising and managing the practice of lobbying. Apart from this professional code, those who defend interests often use various techniques that are recognised and taught, both in training centres specialised in lobbying, 'economic war' and public affairs, and in handbooks written, published and put online by professionals promoting their profession and their interest. They emphasise that in order to put pressure on the European Parliament, important MEPs should be targeted (president of parliamentary committees, rapporteurs and shadow rapporteurs, joint committee leaders); that it is best to be clear and concise and to propose to MEPs amendments already formulated with an explanatory memorandum that they will be able to use easily; that it is more efficient to work at the parliamentary committee level than in plenary session where the parliamentarian has less opportunities to propose amendments and vote; that MEPs are more open to European federation representatives and cause defenders than to corporate lobbyists or public affairs professionals; and that it is better to speak to the MEPs in their mother tongue if possible, and even to play on national feelings. All this advice is implemented in interest defence (Bouwen 2004; Judge 1992) and contributes to, if not standardised lobbying, at least to transform it into a very important part of the MEPs' political work.

Hélène Michel

Bibliography

Andersen, S. S. and Eliassen, K. A., 'The EU Lobbying: Between Representativity and Effectiveness', in S. S. Andersen and K. A. Eliassen (eds), *The European Union: How Democratic Is It?* London, Sage, 1996.

Ayberk, U. and Schenker, J.-F., 'Des lobbies européens entre pluralisme et clientélisme', *Revue française de science politique*, 48, 6, 1998, pp. 725–55.

Balme, R. and Chabanet, D., 'Action collective et gouvernance de l'Union européenne', in R. Balme, D. Chabanet and V. Wright (eds), *L'action collective en Europe*, Paris, Presses de Science Po, 2000, pp. 21–120.

Bouwen, P., 'The Logic of Access to the European Parliament: Business Lobbying in the Committee on Economic and Monetary Affairs', *Journal of Common Market Studies*, 42, 3, 2004, pp. 473–95.

Dutoit, L., *Les intergroupes au Parlement européen*, Genève, Europa, 2001.

Judge, D., ' "Predestined to Save the Earth": the Environment Committee of the European Parliament', *Environmental Politics*, 1, 4, 1992, pp. 186–212.

Mazey, S. and Richardson, J. J. (eds), *Lobbying in the European Community*, Oxford, Oxford University Press, 1993.

Pedler, R. and Van Schendelen, M. P. C. M. (eds), *Lobbying the European Union: Companies, Trade Associations and Issue Groups*, Aldershot, Dartmouth, 1994.

Schaber, T., 'The Regulation of Lobbying at the European Parliament: the Quest for Transparency', in P. Claeys, C. Gobin, I. Smets and P. Winand (eds), *Lobbyisme, pluralisme et intégration européenne*, Bruxelles, Presses interuniversitaires européennes, 1998, pp. 208–21.

Smets, I. and Winand, P., 'À la recherche d'un modèle de représentation des intérêts', in P. Magnette and E. Remacle (eds), *Le nouveau modèle européen*, Bruxelles, Editions de l'Université de Bruxelles, vol. I, 2000, pp. 139–54.

Van den Hoven, A., *Le Lobbying des entreprises françaises auprès des institutions communautaires*, Clermont-Ferrand, Presses Universitaires de la Faculté de Droit de Clermont-Ferrand, 2002.

→ Civil Society; Democratic Deficit; European Commission; European Parliament; Interest Groups; Members of the European Parliament (Legal and Political Status); Members of the European Parliament (Sociology of Political Office); Multi-Level Governance; Parliamentary Groups; Parliamentary Mandate; Representation; Voting Within the European Parliament.

Luxembourg
(City and Institutions)

As a founding member of the European integration project tucked between France and Germany, the small Grand-Duchy of Luxembourg plays host to a number of European institutions. At present the European Commission's

Statistical Office (EUROSTAT) and the Publications Office, the European Court of Justice, the general Secretariat of the European Parliament, the European Investment Bank, the European Court of Auditors, the Nuclear Safety Administration and the Directorate-General of 'Credits and Investments' are all based in the country. In addition, various other European organisations (including EFTA) have offices in Luxembourg. Moreover, the sessions of the Council of Ministers take place in Luxembourg three months in the year (April, June and October). The history of this institutional situation and its effects on Luxembourg's society and economy form the core of this essay.

Institutional history of the EP

Among all the institutions listed above, the European Court of Justice has arguably played the most important role for European integration as it has gradually escaped the control of member state governments (Alter 1998). However, it is the seat of the European Parliament's General Secretariat that is most contested. Under current arrangements, the EP sits in Strasbourg, Brussels and Luxembourg simultaneously. This split seat is particularly controversial because unlike the ECJ, the EP depends intensively on contacts with other Brussels-based bodies such as the Council of Ministers and the Commission.

Up until the early 1980s, before direct elections and as long as the EP still played a merely consultative role in the EU legislative process, the struggle for its seat primarily involved France and Luxembourg. As a matter of fact, France protested repeatedly in 1971, 1973 and 1978 against what it perceived as a creeping transfer of the plenary from Strasbourg to Luxembourg (Hermann 1982). Indeed, Luxembourg had constructed three buildings for the Parliament including a chamber for plenary sittings in order to lure a maximum of the EPs' business onto its territory. In 1982, it was Luxembourg's turn to protest against an EP resolution to move the Secretariat to Strasbourg. In the ensuing ECJ case, Advocate-General Mancini allowed the resolution to stand as long as it did not involve any transfer of staff from Luxembourg (Case 230/81). The ruling perpetuated the division of the EP and was a victory for Luxembourg which feared the economic impact of a move to Strasbourg. As the *Financial Times* (1982) commented ironically, in the EU 'ce n'est que le provisoire qui dure'.

As the European Parliament gradually assumed greater legislative powers, the conflict over its seat took on a different dimension. For its now directly elected members, more involvement in EU legislative politics meant more confidence and a greater need to be physically located at the heart of EU politics. In response, most MEPs set up personal offices in Brussels, which also holds the seat of the Commission and many other EU institutions. Shortly thereafter, in an effort to streamline their work and cut expenditure, MEPs started calling for a centralisation of EP business in Brussels. This was incentive enough for former rivals France and Luxembourg to unite in opposition to plans that would deprive them both of their share of the EP.

The matter seemed to have come to a final resolution at the Edinburgh Council in 1992 where the governments agreed to codify the three-way split of the EP, with the Secretariat in Luxembourg, at least 12 plenary sessions in Strasbourg and all other business in Brussels. However, as recently as 1997, both France and Luxembourg united in protest against the deletion of one of the part-sessions due to be held in Strasbourg. For the second time, the ECJ intervened in favour of the two countries (Case C-345/95) and against the express wish of MEPs who continue to manifest their discontent to this day.

In Luxembourg, the location of European institutions plays a considerable role in national politics. Indeed, the electoral manifestos of most major parties in the 2004 European and general elections explicitly highlighted the determination to maintain and strengthen the country's role as one of the Union's institutional hubs due to its social and economic benefits.

Social and economic effects

With almost 37 per cent of its total population, Luxembourg boasts the highest percentage of foreigners in the EU, of which 86 per cent come from other EU countries. Many of these EU foreigners work for or with the European institutions. Together, they employ about 8500 permanent and temporary staff, with the General Secretariat the most important employer (3600), followed by the ECJ (1641), the European Investment Bank (1000) and the Court of Auditors (736).

Economically, it comes as little surprise then that fully 69 per cent of Luxembourgians say their country has benefited from the EU compared with only 47 per cent in the Union as a whole. Indeed, as Budget Commissioner Schreyer noted recently, when the administrative spending of European institutions is passed on to the Belgian and Luxembourg contributions, these countries become net beneficiaries (COM 2004 505 final).

Figure 1   Trust and awareness of European institutions

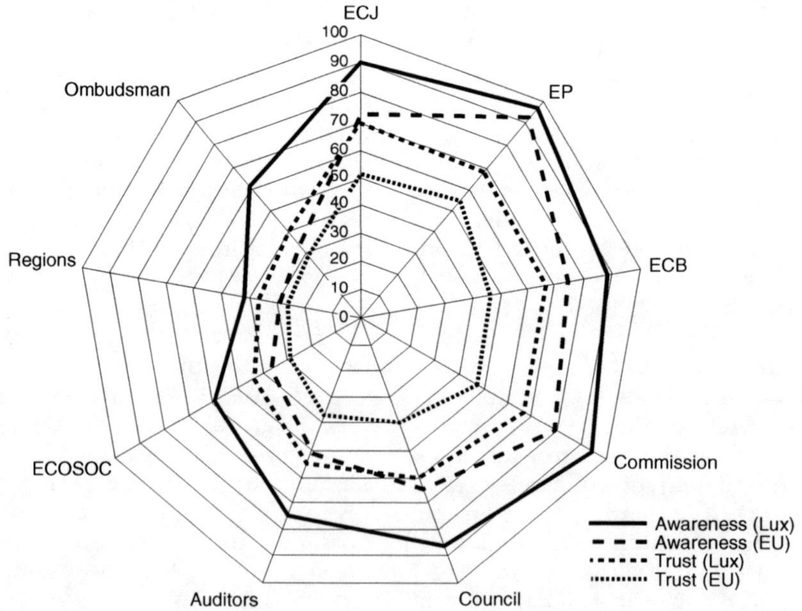

Socially, the most recent Eurobarometer (61.1) poll underlines the impact of European institutions in Luxembourg. Figure 1 plots awareness of, and trust towards, a selection of European institutions. Overall, awareness and trust are much higher than the EU average: 90 per cent of Luxembourgians are aware of the European Court of Justice, compared with a mere 73 per cent across the EU. Also, trust for the ECJ reaches 70 per cent (EU: 52 per cent). A surprising 75 per cent know about the Court of Auditors (EU: 51 per cent). The Council of Ministers also enjoys high levels of awareness (87 per cent). The difference is less marked for the European Parliament which boasts a comparatively high level of awareness (92 per cent) and trust (54 per cent) across the EU.

The seat of European institutions has been an object of controversy ever since the creation of the European Coal and Steel Community. Luxembourg's status as an institutional hub enjoys broad popular support and has an overwhelmingly positive effect on attitudes toward the EU and its institutions. With growing EP independence, however, future conflict among MEPs and member states is likely and might contribute to undermining public support for integration in Luxembourg.

Pierre Hausemer

Bibliography

Alter, K. J., 'Who are the "Masters of the Treaty"? European Governments and the European Court of Justice', *International Organisation*, 52, 1, 1998, pp. 121–47.
Hermann, A. H., 'The Travelling Parliament', *Financial Times*, 10 February 1982, p. 26.

➜ Mapping Europe: European Electoral Geography.

Luxembourg

(Country)

Like most things in the Grand Duchy of Luxembourg, the 2004 elections to the European Parliament were largely marked by continuity. As in previous years, the electoral system and the resulting lack of a true European campaign significantly shaped voting behaviour. A somewhat new phenomenon was the focus on individual candidates in campaigns across the political spectrum. The results confirm the overwhelming dominance of the Christian Socialist Party around Prime Minister Jean-Claude Juncker.

After briefly summarising the results, this article identifies three important technical issues that affect the nature of European elections in Luxembourg: compulsory voting; simultaneous national elections; and the definition of electoral districts. Finally, the article analyses the nature of the 2004 campaigns. The conclusion summarises the shortcomings of European elections in Luxembourg and makes some suggestions for reform.

Results

The results of the European election mirror the concurrently held national elections almost perfectly and largely confirm previous opinion polls. Table 1 summarises percentage votes and seat distribution in the EP for 1999 and 2004. The Christian Socialist CSV wins an additional 6 per cent which translates into a third seat. The Socialist LSAP on the other hand loses 2 per cent and one of its two seats. The Liberals (DP) incur the heaviest losses but manage to keep their seat despite being surpassed by the Greens who achieve 15 per cent of the total vote. The electoral system and

Table 1   Results and seat distribution, European elections, 1999 and 2004

Party	1999	2004	
	Per cent	Per cent	Seats
ADR	8.98	8.03	0 (0)
DP	20.45	14.87	1 (1)
LSAP	23.58	22.09	1 (2)
Déi Gréng*	12.56	15.02	1 (1)
CSV	31.65	37.13	3 (2)
Déi Lénk **	2.78	2.86	0 (0)

Source: www.elections.public.lu
Notes: * Déi Gréng presented a joint list in 2004 but ran on two separate lists in the 1999 elections; ** Déi Lénk ran as one party in 1999 but on two separate lists in 2004.

the ensuing campaigns partly account for these results.

Electoral system

Several technical points significantly marked the 2004 European elections in Luxembourg. Like all previous elections since 1979, the most recent elections were held simultaneously with national elections to the Chambre des Députés and voting was compulsory in both ballots. The country uses List-PR for elections to both the European and national parliaments. Voters can either give all their votes to one party or distribute them among candidates of different parties, the so-called *panachage*. Electoral law further allows candidates to run in both European and national elections at the same time. Candidates who are elected to both assemblies can choose which mandate they prefer to take up. The main difference between the two elections is that the EU contest is held in a single district whereas the national ballot is divided into four electoral districts (North, South, East and Centre) with different candidates.

The peculiarities of the electoral system significantly differentiate European elections in Luxembourg from those in other member states. First, due to compulsory voting, turnout is not an issue. Unlike for the EU as a whole, turnout, at 91.22 per cent of registered voters, was indeed even higher than in 1999 (Table 2). However, the percentage of unexpressed ballots (blank/invalid

Table 2   Participation, European elections 1999 and 2004

	2004	1999	% Difference
Registered Voters	229 550	228 712	–
Ballots Cast	209 402 (91.22%)	199 597 (87.27%)	+2.98
Blank/Invalid	17 516 (8.4%)	18 758 (9.40%)	–1
Valid	191 886 (91.6%)	180 839 (90.60%)	+1
Non-Expressed	*46 664 (20.3%)*	*47 873 (20.9%)*	*–0.6*

Source: Adapted from www.elections.public.lu

plus not cast) was surprisingly high at 20.3 per cent and only marginally lower than in 1999.

In theory, compulsory voting disenfranchises voters because it precludes them from refusing to cast their ballot. The high rate of non-expressed ballots, however, indicates that a requirement to vote does not necessarily encourage high levels of political participation. One in five registered voters in Luxembourg do not express their political preferences in European elections whereas almost one in ten seem willing to run the risk of a €250 fine by abstaining from the ballot. Nevertheless, an overwhelming majority of 81 per cent of the public wants to maintain compulsory voting for both European and general elections (Poirier et al. 2004).

Some reasons for the high abstention rate might lie in the perception of relative powerlessness among the Luxembourg public. Indeed, a recent opinion poll finds that while 35 per cent of foreigners (excluding the Portuguese community) think they have a lot of influence over EU policy, this figure is only 12 per cent among Luxembourg citizens. Poll results and electoral participation paint a very different portrait of Luxembourg than the 'Europhile' picture that the country's politicians like to invoke in national and foreign media.

The unique characteristics of Luxembourg's electoral system not only affect turnout but also the actual voting behaviour of those who do decide to cast their ballot. Dual candidacies and different electoral districts hand enormous powers to national parties for whom it makes sense to select only the most popular candidates for both elections, in the hope that voters will use personal votes to support individuals whom they may not have been able to vote for on the national ballot. Unfortunately, those politicians are also least likely to take up their European mandate. Thus, for instance, Prime Minister Jean-Claude Juncker is the Christian Social Party's top candidate in both European and national elections despite his often affirmed electoral promise to stay in Luxembourg if re-elected. National parties thus speculate on the second-order status of EU elections by encouraging personal votes even though they do not reflect voter preferences on European issues.

As Table 3 shows, 42 per cent of total votes in the 2004 elections were

Table 3   Personal and list votes European elections 1999 and 2004

Party	2004			1999		
	List – votes	Personal votes	% Personal	List – votes	Personal votes	% Personal
1 – ADR	59 856	27 380	31.39	26 267	64 986	71.22
2 – DP	75 684	85 823	53.14	86 339	121 326	58.42
3 – LSAP	139 422	100 545	41.90	104 310	135 192	56.45
4 – Déi Gréng*	107 910	55 294	33.88	47 560	79 764	62.65
5 – CSV	230 286	173 084	42.91	153 213	168 258	52.34
6 – Déi Lénk **	19 602	11 475	36.92	7 688	20 538	72.76
Total	*632 760*	*453 601*	*41.75*	*425 377*	*590 064*	*58.11*

Notes: * Déi Gréng presented a joint list in 2004 but ran on two separate lists in the 1999 elections; ** Déi Lénk ran as one party in 1999 but on two separate lists in 2004.

personal, which indicates that voters still do not consider European elections as stand-alone contests. However, there has been a sharp decline in the use of personal votes from 58 per cent of the total in 1999 to 42 per cent in 2004. Also, with the exception of the liberal DP, none of the parties received more personal than list-votes in 2004. By contrast, in 1999 all parties had received more personal votes. This decline, which is not mirrored in national elections, shows that voters are increasingly dissatisfied with the dual-candidacy system in Luxembourg.

In sum, even though the electoral system allows voters to choose between individual candidates or party lists, the personal vote is firmly rooted in national politics and does not convey a European mandate. The net effect is to disenfranchise the electorate and encourage a perception of the European Parliament as a non-democratic institution over which voters have little power. However, the declining use of personal votes might indicate that the electorate is gradually becoming aware of this problem and adjusting its voting behaviour accordingly.

In order to revalidate the personal vote, two reform proposals were made in the run-up to this year's European elections. First, the liberal DP suggested a decoupling of European and national elections. However, this proposal only constitutes a partial solution because it does not eliminate dual candidacies *per se*. Candidates could still run in national and European contests and decide afterwards which post they want to take up.

Second, opposition parties rejected the ruling Christian Social party's (CSV) proposal to prohibit dual candidatures. As Ben Fayot, Socialist delegate to the European Convention explains, prohibiting the dual candidacy would seriously undermine his party's supply of competent candidates for European elections. Fayot maintains that such a reform favours the ruling CSV because it has a larger number of experienced candidates, including former heads of state, a Commission president, a parliamentary president and a European commissioner (Fayot 2004). This admission by a leading member of the opposition attests to the absolute dominance of the CSV over Luxembourg's political life. Fifty years of nearly uninterrupted participation in government have left their imprint on political competition in the Grand Duchy, to the point where governmental alternation seems undesirable even to politicians from opposition parties. Of course, this overwhelming dominance also affects the shape of electoral campaigning in the country.

Electoral campaign and results

Indeed, in the 2004 elections, the CSV took advantage of the unprecedented popularity of Prime Minister Jean-Claude Juncker to further consolidate its position. Juncker dominated political discussions in the media and is seen as the most competent politician by people across the political spectrum. An opinion poll in the run-up to the election showed a staggering 81 per cent of people wanting him to stay on for another term. One of the most debated electoral issues then was Juncker's promise to stay in Luxembourg if re-elected instead of taking up Romano Prodi's succession at the head of the European Commission.

In the face of these approval ratings, it is not surprising that the CSV centred its election campaign on its top politician both nationally and at the European level. In response, other parties saw no other option but to emphasise candidates over issues as well. Thus, the campaign pitted slogans such as 'If you want Juncker, you must vote CSV' against socialist pamphlets showing Juncker as the powerful and omnipresent (but evil) Mr Smith from the *Matrix* movie trilogy.

European issues only played a very marginal role in campaigns across all parties. As in other member states, the Green Party ran a pan-European campaign. Also, the right-wing ADR, which is a member of the anti-European UEN in the European Parliament, is Luxembourg's first party to run on an electoral platform based on safeguarding national interests and slowing integration. The three most salient European issues were the Constitution, Turkish accession, and tax harmonisation. All parties accept the Constitution except for the extreme left Déi Lénk which deplores the lack of a social dimension and expresses concerns about EU militarisation. The potentially divisive issue of Turkish EU accession is avoided in most electoral programmes except for the ADR which declares itself firmly against. The ADR also assumes a clear position against tax harmonisation within the European Union whereas the electoral manifestos of most other parties avoid the subject or, at best, remain very vague.

The lack of European issues further compounds the importance of individual candidates in EP elections and thereby aggravates the problem of dual candidatures. The trend toward campaigns centred on personalities rather than issues has serious repercussions for the democratic legitimacy of European elections in Luxembourg.

Conclusion

European elections are still very much second-order contests in Luxembourg. Compulsory voting and concurrent national elections, though initially devised to emphasise the importance of the European ballot, help to strengthen their second-order status. The 2004 election was marked by a relatively high abstention rate, a worrying lack of European issues and the overwhelming dominance of Prime Minister Juncker. Ground for optimism, however, lies in the declining trend in the use of personal votes, which might indicate growing voter awareness.

Nevertheless, the current electoral system and the personal nature of political competition undermine voter choice. Reforms must include a decoupling of European from national elections and a prohibition of dual candidacies. It then remains the difficult task of opposition parties to convince voters they have better candidates and electoral platforms than their Christian Socialist rivals.

Pierre Hausemer

Bibliography

Fayot, Ben, 'Immer dasselbe und doch keine Loesung', *Luxemburger Wort*, 24 April 2004.
Poirier, P., Fehlen, F. and Margue C., *La participation politique au Luxembourg*, Luxembourg, Université de Luxembourg, 2004 (http://www.cu.lu/stade/confpresse032004. pdf).

→ Mapping Europe: European Electoral Geography.

M

Malta

On 1 May 2004, Malta became the smallest member state of a newly enlarged European Union. Malta is an archipelago of three islands (Malta, Gozo and Comino), of high strategic importance because of its geographical situation at the heart of the Mediterranean, which makes it a natural intermediary in discussions between the European Union, North Africa and the Middle East. Retrospectively, one can see that the integration of Malta into the EU was not without difficulties. The first official adhesion request was made by the Nationalist Party (PN) on 16 July 1990. However, the victory of the Labour Party (MLP) in the 1996 election resulted in the party's leader and new Prime Minister, Alfred Sant, suspending Malta's application. The Maltese political system is dominated by these two radically opposed political parties, and the debate on Malta's membership in the European Union has been therefore particularly intense. The PN consistently supported EU membership which the MLP equally consistently rejected, encouraging Maltese voters to vote no in the referendum of 8 March 2003. However, 53.65 per cent of citizens voted in favour of membership. Comforted by these results, the PN started its European elections campaign in relatively stable conditions, considering that the vote would represent another plebiscite over its European policy.

A largely national election campaign

As the MLP contested the results of the referendum on membership, Prime Minister Edward Fenech held a general election one month after it. Opposition leader Sant had claimed that the 'yes' vote had not got an absolute majority of voters as 'only' 143 000 citizens had voted yes out of 297 000 registered voters. The new general election was therefore seen by the Conservatives as a way to confirm the victory of the yes vote, focusing their electoral campaign on the likely positive impact of EU membership on economic growth and the unemployment situation while a Labour victory would put the whole process into question. Indeed, the MLP explained that if they won, they would ignore the results of the March referendum and organise a new vote, which, this time, would propose a partnership agreement with the EU rather than membership.

As a result, the European election campaign started with the referendum on membership and the early elections of 2003, the two votes serving as electoral tests before the European elections for both major parties. Nevertheless, a few months before the election, a strange change of context occurred which resulted in the campaign refocusing on primarily national issues. In a country which does not recognise divorce (only marriage cancellations, which are hard to obtain from the courts, or separation), abortion, or the rights of homosexuals, two candidates tried to oppose this social conservatism.

Emma Bezzina of the far left 'Grupp Alpha' scandalously chose as its campaign theme: 'yes to abortion, divorce, and the rights of homosexuals'. As a result, Ms Bezzina was deemed unreliable by the other candidates and more or less ignored by them. The candidate of the Green 'Alternativa Demokratika' (AD), Arnold Cassola, also supported the introduction of a divorce procedure. However, this stance was quickly exploited by his conservative opponents who portrayed him as morally lax and a supporter of abortion, a difficult position in a highly Catholic country. As a result, Mr Cassola had to clarify his position and say that despite his membership of the Green Party family, he remained 'strictly opposed' to abortion. As the third party in Malta, the AD tried to find its place in a traditionally bipartisan party system, campaigning on divorce and on ecological issues. Amongst other issues, the party proposed a restructuring of the agricultural sector and a fight against maritime noise and atmospheric pollution, particularly in the southern part of the country where most industrial activities and ports are concentrated.

By contrast, the PN tried to Europeanise its campaign as much as possible, to avoid a logic of national debate and the possible prospect of protest voting. This was all the more necessary because the economic situation was not outstanding. After a period of high growth in 1999 (4.1 per cent) and 2000 (6.4 per cent), Malta faced a period of economic stagnation (recession first with –2.1 per cent in 2001, then slow growth: 1.2 per cent in 2002 and 0.7 per cent in 2003), with a GDP of 4.2 billion euros that year. The terrorist attacks of 2001 resulted in a slump for tourism, the first economic sector of the island, so that the PN counted on EU membership to dynamise its economy. The party tried to maintain its image as a good negotiator after obtaining 77

derogations in its membership treaty (neutrality, abortion, protection of some agricultural and industrial sectors, etc.). The party also emphasised that it hoped to remain an important player by being part of the EPP group, the largest transnational group in the European Parliament. By contrast, the MLP hoped to focus on the record of the right-wing government, attributing economic difficulties to the adhesion criteria of the EU. The party questioned the privatisation policy of the PN, reasserting its preference for a national control of key sectors such as the aviation and maritime industries. The MLP also accused the government of minimising the levels of unemployment on the island and refusing debate about its economic record. The party even accused the PN of preparing a series of unpopular measures for after the elections, such as tax hikes or a restructuring of some public services. By contrast, the MLP presented itself as the protector of workers' interests, social rights and employment, and the defender of a social Europe. The various opposition parties thus managed to impose national campaign themes against the wishes of the PN.

The European election also re-emphasised the collusion between the mass media and the two main parties. Out of seven parties and five independent candidates, only three (MLP, PN and AD) benefited from regular media exposure. The first two even have their own private media companies. The PN owns 'Radio 101' and the TV channel 'Net TV'. Similarly, the MLP own the largest radio and TV stations 'Super One Radio' and 'Super One TV'. Both parties also have their own newspaper: *In Nazzjon Toghna* (PN) and *L-Orizzont* (MLP). The regulation of TV campaigns, put together by the broadcasting authority, further reinforced the inequality between candidates by favouring the parties presenting more than two candidates (i.e. only the PN and MLP).

The electoral system was that of single transferable voting in one nation-wide constituency. As in many other member states, the election was run alongside local elections in one-third of the local councils. These two elections had similar levels of turnout (82 per cent), making Malta the most electorally mobilised new member state without compulsory voting, even though turnout for European elections remained below that of general elections (97.2 per cent in 1996, 95.4 per cent in 1998, 96.9 per cent in 2003). This very high mobil-isation is partly explained by Malta's status as a recently independent republic (independence in 1964, a fully recog-nised republic in 1974) and by the strong bipartisan system in which the two main parties are radically opposed and their partisans strongly aligned and disciplined.

Analysis of the electoral results

Altogether, the PN seemed to fail to convince Maltese voters of its economic and social reforms and the need to vote on the basis of their attitudes towards European integration. As in 1996, when the government introduced VAT to be in line with European Union standards, leading to a Labour victory, the PN's measures of austerity were perceived as too brutal. The results of the 2004 elec-tion, which correspond to the same logic, are reported in Table 1.

The MLP, main loser of the 2003 general elections and of the referendum, managed to mobilise its forces and led the protest vote against the current government. The party won three of the five seats (and is represented by MEPs Muscat, Attard Montalto and Grelch), while the PN was the main victim of an election which also saw strong support for the Greens.

Altogether, the 2004 European Parliament election in Malta was charac-terised by a strong mobilisation of the electorate (albeit less so than for general elections) and a protest vote against the incumbent government. The political spectrum was more diversified than usual because of the presence of five indepen-dent candidates, but the two main parties continued to share the bulk of the votes,

Table 1   Results of the 2004 European election in Malta

Party	Candidates	Votes (%)	Seats
MLP (Labour)	8	48.4	3
PN (Conservative)	8	39.8	2
AD (Green)	1	9.3	0
Kul Europa (Extreme Right)	2	0.7	0
Grupp Alpha (Extreme left)	1	0.3	0
CDRP (Christian Democrat)	1	0.0	0
Imperium Europa (Right)	1	0.0	0
Independent candidates (Bonnici, Farrugia, Iwueke, C. Zammit, V. Zammit)	5	1.5	0

Notes: 1.63 per cent of the votes were null and void, the threshold for a seat was 40 954 votes and was only achieved by the PN and MLP. The third largest party, AD, only received 22 938 votes in total.

followed by the Greens. The low score of the PN may suggest that some Maltese people were not keen to support European integration. The strong breakthrough of the Greens opens the door to a possible decline of the traditional bipartisan system that has marked Maltese politics since the country's independence and, for the first time, threatens the overwhelming hegemony of the PN and the MLP. The AD indeed progressed by seven points in just eight years and managed to perform better than most other Green parties across Europe (except in Luxembourg where they also progressed significantly). This combination, featuring a protest vote against the governing party, lower turnout than for general elections, and the progress of third parties suggests that in Malta, the 2004 European election largely followed a traditional second-order pattern.

Sonia Tebbakh

→ Campaign (Sociology of); Communication; Electoral System; Enlargement; European Elections (2004); Europeanisation (of National Political Life); Green Politics; Mapping Europe: European Electoral Geography; Protest Voting; Second-Order Elections; Social Europe.

Members of the European Parliament

(Legal and Political Status)

Under the terms of Article 190, paragraph 5, of the TEC, outlined in the Treaty of Nice, 'the European Parliament establishes the status and general conditions regarding the implementation of its functions and of its members, following the decision of the Commission and the approval of the Council, ruling by a qualified majority. Any rule or condition relating to the fiscal arrangements of its members or former members is subject to unanimity within the Council.'

The European Parliament has often developed proposals, following Commission opinions, envisaging that the each MEP be awarded the monthly wage of €9000 (representing half of the salary of a judge in the Court of Justice). However, despite support from the Irish presidency, this proposal was rejected by the Council on 26 January 2004. Indeed, a new compromise suggested by the Parliament on 17 December 2003, relating to the allowances in accordance with the national fiscal law and retirement age, failed to find political consensus. Furthermore, the new legislature introduced from 2004 following the enlargement to ten new member states into the EU, was required to adopt the legal and political status of the MEPs resulting from the combination of several European and national texts, in the quest for a definitive solution.

The complexity of this provisional system is due to the fact that it simultaneously brings together the European level, with the Act of 20 September 1976, establishing elections of the representatives in the European Parliament by universal suffrage and the protocol of 8 April 1965 regarding privileges and allowances, and the national level with its 25 legislations and different regulations. Concerning the MEPs' salaries, their individual monthly wage varies from €761 for a Hungarian MEP, €3000 and €5000 for a Spanish and French MEP respectively to €12 000 for an Italian. These amounts are modelled on arrangements established for national MPs. However, these differences are compensated using a system of allowances whereby travelling expenses are reclaimed from the European Parliament budget, on the condition of the regular attendance of MEPs, similar to a secretariat allowance and contractually fixed overheads.

With regard to electoral behaviour, the measures and terms stipulated in Article 190 TEC, paragraph 4, which state that: 'the European Parliament develops a proposal in order to allow an election by direct universal suffrage according to a uniform procedure in all the member states or [added in the Amsterdam Treaty] in accordance with principles common to all the member states' have still not been adopted. Various electoral methods have emerged in different national legislations and so vary across member states. In general, however, since the replacement of the majoritarian system of European elections in the United Kingdom, those complying with the practice of proportional representation are now widespread at the national and regional level. In France, the law of 11 April 2003 tried to change the foundations and territorial grounds of representation but with limited results, as candidates remain subject to the national political party apparatus. The resulting difficulty for the electorate is thus how to identify their representative in a straightforward manner. Moreover, although under the terms of the Maastricht Treaty national legislations may approve the candidature of nationals from other EU member states, the practice of such overlap is still rather rare, despite the examples of Professor Maurice Duverger in Italy in 1989, Daniel Cohn-Bendit in France in 1999, and more recently Ari Vatanen, the former Finnish pilot, on the UMP list in France in 2004.

Under the system of five-year electoral terms established by the Treaties, the independence of MEPs is recognised by the Act of 20 September 1976. Under the terms of Article 199 in the TEC, the Parliament can freely determine its internal procedures, which specify the methods of the majority of members who constitute it. From this viewpoint, it thus has more freedom than even the French Parliament enjoys. No MEP can be dismissed and any resignations have to be made on a purely voluntary basis by the MEP concerned. Indeed various incompatibilities affect the delivery of parliamentary offices which notably inhibit the accumulation of mandates with involvement in another institution or organ in the Union and also in the government of a member state. Moreover, the internal rules of the European Parliament stipulate that any financial interests of the MEP undertaking a private activity must be declared. On the other hand, the EP's rules do not formally prohibit plurality in parliamentary office with that of a national parliament, except where this is banned in the national legislation, as is the case in Belgium. In France, plurality of offices is regulated by the law of 30 December 1985 which makes 'MEP' one of the functions that can only be cumulated with up to one additional mandate. In fact, since the introduction of elections by universal suffrage, the practice of office plurality of both European and national parliamentary mandates has decreased. In 1979, this proportion accounted for over 31 per cent of MEPs, dropping to 3.8 per cent by 1994.

The Act of 20 September 1976, under Article 4-2 relating to the Protocol of 8 April 1965 outlining the privileges and immunities of the European Communities, reinforces those enjoyed by the MEPs. They comprise a complete freedom of movement to go from their country of origin to their place of work in the European Parliament. In addition, the ruling of 20 March 1995 from the European Court of Justice in Luxembourg interpreted this freedom very widely. Following the case of an obvious offence, the immunity of MEPs concerning possible legal action, which includes responsibility for their respective opinions and votes during the exercise of their functions, is recognised in

Article 9 of the Protocol throughout the duration of their office, and covers the complete calendar year. The applicable system differs according to whether the accusation is made in the original or host member state. In the first case, the national legislation relating to members of parliament applies; in the second, complete immunity from detention remains. Otherwise, the member state concerned must petition the European Parliament if it seeks the suspension of the immunity of one of its MEPs. Its methods are established by the procedural rules of the European Parliament. Thus, under the terms of its Article 6, 'any request addressed to the President by a proper authority in a member state to remove the immunity of an MEP is communicated at a sitting plenary and transferred to the proper committee'. Also, according to a narrowly regulated procedure, the committee recommends a decision to adopt or reject the request. This recommendation will then be discussed but cannot be amended, and it is up to the Parliament to decide the outcome at a plenary sitting.

One can only hope that this practice will progressively reinforce the sense and consistency of this hybrid system. In this respect, except for some modifications in drafting, the draft treaty establishing a Constitution for the European Union fails to bring about any modifications which are sensitive to the *status quo ante* (Articles 1–19 and III-232). Rather it impedes any growth in the political role of the European Parliament as defined by this Constitution, and if it enters into force, it would confer a strengthened authority, which should contribute to the subsequent encouragement of a more liberal Council concerning both the harmonisation of the electoral methods of representatives as well as their financial status.

Jean-Louis Quermonne

Bibliography

Corbett, R., Jacobs, F. and Shackleton, M., *The European Parliament*, London, Harper, 2003.
Delwit, P., De Waele, J.-M. and Magnette, P. (eds), *A quoi sert le Parlement européen?*, Bruxelles, Editions Complexe, 1999.
Judge, D. and Earnshaw, D., *The European Parliament*, Basingstoke, Palgrave Macmillan, 2003.

→ Act of 1976; Composition of the European Parliament; Dual Mandates; Eligibility; European Parliament; Incompatibility; Members of the European Parliament (Sociology of Political Office); Observers; Tenure.

Members of the European Parliament
(Sociology of Political Office)

The paths to office of Members of the European Parliament are numerous and depend to a great extent on their respective backgrounds, careers and ambitions. Nonetheless, this mix of practices, beliefs and expertise tends to become homogenised within the European Parliament. Thus, newcomers are expected to conform to specific roles in order to align with a pattern of the 'job' of Member of the European Parliament.

Diverse modes of involvement

Firstly, parliamentary activity has a clear role in defining the job of Member of the European Parliament (MEP). Involvement in the European Parliament varies between those MEPs who have developed a specialisation in European issues (e.g. Jean-Louis Bourlanges in France, David Martin in the United

Kingdom, and Martin Schulz in Germany), and those with dual mandates – the extreme case being those who are both an MEP and national member of parliament (MP). Since methods of MEP recruitment are closely related to national political environments, approaches to the office of MEP, the roles of political careers, and parliamentary activity vary according to national practices. For instance, British and German MEPs, who are reputedly more involved and active than their French counterparts, seldom cumulate offices and are often successfully re-elected, whereas French MEPs have long been selected on the basis of national criteria which tend to disfavour those who are most committed to the European Parliament. This said, irrespective of nationality, those actors who view the European Parliament as an opportunity for political professionalisation will develop profile specialisation.

The terms of the European political job are also mirrored in the distribution within permanent parliamentary committees. The most well-known MEPs – holding several terms of office in the European Parliament or in former national parliaments and even governments – tend to sit in the committees which oversee the most important issues: foreign affairs, human rights, European security and defence policy, the budget, economic and monetary affairs and even constitutional affairs. Such was the case with Alain Lamassoure and Enrique Barón Crespo for foreign affairs during the fifth legislature. Those who have significant professional expertise – for instance in the field of agriculture or academia – often join committees which are related to their area of competence (Joseph Daul for agriculture and Richard Corbett for institutional affairs). Other MEPs sit in committees which, although less prestigious, may still be at the core of the decision-making process

and so bring strongly symbolic incentives within the assembly (environment, public health, consumer policy, freedom, citizens' rights, justice and home affairs). Finally, actors who have a desire to maintain or develop local issues often express great interest for the regional policy, transport and tourism committees.

MEPs' activities are not limited to committee work. Legislative work offers a number of opportunities for the defence of political interests: proposing amendments, drafting reports, participation in intergroup activity, mobilisation of national delegations and political groups. MEPs work not only on the topics they are familiar with because they have already addressed them in their previous political or professional capacities, but also on issues through which they can acquire further political experience across the European, national, local or partisan levels. Such practices have two advantages. On the one hand, they limit the uncertainties related to the terms of European political representation (who and what do they represent?). On the other hand, they allow for strategies which are likely to place MEPs at the heart of political news or party debates, and which may even strengthen sociopolitical networks. These aspects of the job are intertwined with the process of European integration.

Specific stakes

The European Parliament is one of the main beneficiaries of the successive treaties since the 1980s and onwards. Indeed, the Single European Act (1986), the Treaty on the European Union (1992) and the Amsterdam Treaty (1997) extended its jurisdiction and created new procedures – notably co-decision – which brought about a more complex space of negotiation between the European Parliament, the Commission and the Council of Ministers. From the late 1980s, MEPs have had to deal with complex procedures, face a significant increase in the number of texts submitted for their examination, master the highly technical nature of legislation to support the harmonisation of the internal market, and manage an increasingly pronounced heterogeneity, at both the national level (25 delegations in 2004 versus 9 in 1979) as well as the political (over 20 national parties represented during the 1999–2004 legislature) and the linguistic (20 official languages) levels. The development of MEPs' activities entails a parliamentary rationalisation (Costa 2001), which is illustrated by the reinforcement of the roles of the committees and groups, the redefinition of collective strategies, of stakes specific to the institution, and, hence of competencies which are valued at a given time. For instance, several committees gained importance: legal affairs and internal market – to which the main directives of harmonisation are attributed – environment, public health and consumer policy, and industry, external trade, research and energy – because they are part of the co-decision procedure.

The division of political labour, costs and gratifications of European involvement have increased. The entire parliamentary game has become more complex. The past ten years have witnessed the strengthening of a personnel which has increased its expertise in European issues and the realignment of parliamentary activity along more specific stakes, such as office leadership. Obtaining such jobs requires an endogenous experience and a practical mastering of the assembly's internal game; presidency and vice-presidency of the Parliament, presidencies of the committees and political groups. The case of Martin Schulz, who was elected president of the PES, provides a good example of such a phenomenon. At a further level are the presidencies of delegations and the vice-presidencies of committees, political groups and delegations. In the decision-making process, other offices also appear to be strategic: group co-ordinators within committees, rapporteurs in charge of administering an issue on behalf of their committees and political groups, and eventually the shadow rapporteurs appointed by the opposition groups to follow and scrutinise the issue.

Specificities of the office of MEP

Integration in the parliamentary world requires acquiring the skills which are necessary to master the deliberation process. The first structuring element lies with the absence of integration of the political system. Contrary to what happens in numerous national political systems, such as in France or in the United Kingdom, MEPs are formally independent from the executive power, i.e. from members of the Council and the Commission. Hence, voting on texts with respect to their authors is less relevant. Parliamentary production also occurs following negotiations between the institutions within ad hoc structures (e.g. conciliation committees which gather MEPs and members of the Council).

Deliberation is organised around the creation of compromise which significantly structures parliamentary practices. In consideration of cleavages which are inherent to fragmented European societies (North–South, West–East, old–new member states, big–small member states, etc.), the institutional rules aim at preventing a bipolarisation of the parliamentary arena. The provisions of the internal regulations primarily seek to guarantee each group a representation which is proportional to its numerical weight within the managing bodies of the Parliament (d'Hondt law). Moreover, the voting procedures imposed by the treaties require large majorities (an absolute majority of MEPs, or even a two-thirds majority). In such a framework, an alliance between the two main political groups – the EPP and PES which are the only groups to bring together MEPs from almost all member states – corresponds to an institutional constraint as well as to a kind of political routine allowing for the stabilisation of parliamentary activity. The formation of majorities significantly contrasts with certain national political cultures. For the major groups, and the national delegations of which they are composed, compromise allows each one to take advantage of decision-making (Hix and Lord 1997).

The ability to negotiate is a dominant feature of the MEP office. In order to exert influence, MEPs have to maintain continuous contacts and relations with those who matter, both within and outside the institution: rapporteurs, shadow rapporteurs, co-ordinators, civil servants, commissioners, members of the Council, etc. In order to be able to convince not only one's own group but also members of competing groups and, above all, colleagues from several member states, it is essential to understand how to mobilise arguments that are not merely ideological. Thus, codes of conduct structure exchanges between actors: fair play, necessary open-mindedness and suspicion with respect to any ethnocentric approach. Actors have to comply with some kind of ethics, or they run the risk of excluding themselves from the game and prohibit the formation of compromises. Holding office requires, beyond the knowledge of technical and political aspects surrounding an issue, the mastering of implicit and explicit expectations of a very specific game. In that sense, effective presence in the European Parliament is a determining factor of personal or collective influence.

The relation to foreign languages is a final feature of this European parliamentary culture. Immediate translation implies specific modes of expression. In order to be clearly understood and to avoid misunderstandings in translation – specifically when allocated times are extremely limited and controlled – MEPs must make simple and concise sentences using a precise vocabulary. The rhetorical effects which are valued in many national parliamentary spaces are less central in the European Parliament. The ability to communicate and to make progress in a multilingual environment – notably in English – is then a decisive factor to ensure contact with the whole body of actors. Translation services cannot encompass interpersonal relations and the entirety of meetings. Beyond practical aspects, the ability to express oneself in other languages is considered to be important. By offering language classes, the institution also encourages this multilingualism.

Willy Beauvallet
Sébastien Michon

Bibliography

Costa, O., *Le Parlement européen, assemblée délibérante*, Bruxelles, Editions de l'Université de Bruxelles, 2001.

Hix, S. and Lord, C., *Political Parties in the European Union*, Basingstoke, Macmillan, 1997.

→ Composition of the European Parliament; Dual Mandates; Eligibility; European Parliament; Europeanisation (of National Political Life); Incompatibility; Members of the European Parliament (Legal and Political Status); Parliamentary Groups; Tenure; Voting Within the European Parliament.

Multi-Level Governance

To understand the role of European Parliament elections, one has to consider them in the context of multi-level governance, which has been identified by the political science literature as defining the function of the European Union as another layer of decision-making alongside the national and sub-national levels. The work of authors such as Marks et al. (1996) helps us to define and understand the basic rules of this multi-level governance game, which, like a complex and impressionistic variation on the theme of federalism, allows competing political actors to share initiatives and competencies to make the policies that apply to European Union citizens and their sub-parts.

The concept of multi-level governance is distinct in that it sits at the crossroads between a political science category and a political – and quasi-constitutional – rule. Indeed, the very notion of multi-level governance is also very directly interpreted and operationalised by the reference to the principle of subsidiarity in the Maastricht Treaty of 13 February 1992. This principle states that within the European Union political system, decisions have to be made at the lowest relevant level possible, that is, at the level which is closest to citizens while remaining efficient and equitable. The word subsidiarity was abandoned in further treaties, as it was considered too complex to be intelligible by the mass public, and too abstract not to give rise to a number of legal cases and much exegesis. Nevertheless, it remained, in practice, one of the guiding rules of European governance since the beginning of the 1990s.

Within the context of multi-level governance, policy-making is also based on the existence of democratically elected bodies at each governance level. This means that as the process of Europeanisation generalised the principle of multi-level governance, it also encouraged a clear process of decentralisation in even the most traditionally centralised unitary states. As a result, under the influence of the European Union, the regionalisation of France or the process of devolution in the United Kingdom were clearly encouraged, with, each time, the generalisation of democratically elected assemblies at the regional and local levels. At the same time, however, it is clear that at the supranational level, the principles of multi-level governance implied the progressive democratisation of the European Union political system. This was largely achieved via the strengthening of the powers of the European Parliament, and, since 1979, by the direct democratic election of its members.

In a sense, the fortunes of multi-level governance and European Parliament elections are therefore closely intertwined. The European Parliament remains, for all practical purposes, the lower of the two chambers of the European legislature. It represents the people, while the Council represents the member states. It is noteworthy to see that a number of politicians, who propose to empower national parliaments and suggest giving them a vetting power in EU decision-making, are indirectly suggesting replacing multi-level governance with a rearranged form of renationalised governance, whereby the sovereignty of the people would *not* be foremost anymore in one of the levels of governance which affect them. Instead, it is the member states that would be implicitly represented twice, and would, as a result, replace EU governance by a new form of interstate co-operation.

However, already, it is clear that the focus of the 2004 European election campaign on national issues, and the secondary role of the European Parliament in EU decision-making partly deprive European Parliament elections of their necessary and expected function within a system of multi-level governance. This remains true despite the progress achieved by the introduction of the co-decision 2 procedure in the Treaty of Amsterdam. Indeed, the genuine paradox of these European elections, is that parties, institutional designers and the media have coalesced *not* to make them elections on the European layer of governance, but, instead, secondary national-focused contests.

In conclusion, the system of multi-level governance as defined within the context of the European Union is unique and, in many ways, unprecedented. European Parliament elections are a crucial aspect of this system, because they are part of the need for this new system of democratic governance to rely on the direct democratic election of at least one representative body for each layer of governance. However, the hijacking of European elections, implicitly transformed into yet another platform to discuss national issues by the mass media and political parties, threatens the whole system in that it deprives the public of any democratic arena where it can specifically discuss European-related questions. The case of the 2005 referendum on a European Constitution in France shows a clear demand by the public for such a public arena of discussion. While European Parliament elections have failed to fulfil this role until 2004, it is likely that European elites will be under more and more pressure, election after election, to restore European elections to their core role, if they want to avoid the risk of a growing gap between elite offer and public demand on the democratisation of the European Union.

Sarah Harrison

Bibliography

Marks, G., Hooghe, L. and Blank, K. (1996) 'European Integration from the 1980s: State-Centric versus Multi-Level Governance', *Journal of Common Market Studies*, 34, 3, pp. 342–78.

→ Democratic Deficit; Electoral Behaviour; European Elections (2004); European Electoral Act; European Parliament; European Public Sphere; Identity; Nationalisation of European Elections.

N

Nationalisation of European Elections

Most newspaper and academic comments on European elections borrow the concepts of 'second-order national elections' and 'mid-term elections'. Both expressions refer to elections that would have no effect on the appointment of governmental teams and would therefore be used by voters as an opportunity to reward or punish office-holders. These elections, which would favour 'mood' or 'protest' voting, are also characterised by a low turnout, a fragmentation of the political spectrum, and domination of national political issues, whilst the outcome does not directly affect the balance of national power. Given that the European vote can also be considered as 'second-order' national elections, this situation essentially hinders the Europeanisation of issues and campaigns. This would be understood as the development of specifically European themes, shared across all member states or related to European institutions.

The literature concerning European electoral campaigns may thus, in many ways, seem a boring and routine undertaking. Excluding the times when they represent an important national test, European elections are systematically presented as being of no interest to political actors, citizens and journalists. From one election to another, no European debate seems to emerge. Parties, journalists and European institutions all hold each other responsible for this lack of interest. 'Opaque' and 'undemocratic' institutions, as well as parties still trying to hold on to 'out-dated' national stakes are thus heavily criticised by journalists, who, in turn, are blamed for failing to come up with appealing European perspectives. Obvious technical stakes and a blatant lack of interest, highlighted by the ever-increasing levels of abstention since 1979, are the two favoured approaches for dealing with European elections. Thus, nationalisation of European elections without national effects constitutes the angle preferred by journalists and analysts to tackle them.

The nationalisation of European elections is grounded in a reality: the nationalisation of political life. Indeed, constituencies are national, investitures are controlled by partisan organisations who exist at the domestic level and whose opinions are dominated by national issues, politicians – even where they do not cumulate several offices – are frequently engaged in careers which are organised and have a meaning at the national level, the media are national undertakings, etc. This nationalisation of public life justifies, in all European countries, a national treatment which is specific to each European election. Therefore, the use made by journalists and academics of the term 'second-order elections' appears a rather normative and misplaced criticism, since it is difficult to see how electoral games which are entirely dominated by national political schemes, organised according to largely national legal frameworks, could produce 'Europeanised' stakes. At the same time, this systematic approach which consists of addressing all

European elections through the concept of 'second-order' elections does not account for a number of processes which have been in place since 1979.

For example, contrary to the hypothesis of discontinuity defended by many (European elections could be interesting elections if they were something other than national elections devoid of national stakes), it seems that the appeal of European elections is precisely due to their specific schemes, such as the recent adoption of proportional suffrage in all the EU countries. Thus, for many organisations which are not principally competing for national offices, European elections constitute a forum which could not exist in other types of elections, and represent the opportunity to win votes and possibly offices, while they are usually excluded from electoral coalitions. For instance, in 2004, the UKIP obtained 16.8 per cent of the votes – a score which would be unthinkable in the British bi-partisan set-up – and Sinn Féin, the political wing of the IRA, obtained a seat in the European Parliament, as did the 'June List' in Sweden (14.5 per cent of the votes and three seats), Europa Transparent in the Netherlands (7.3 per cent and two seats) and the list led by Hans-Peter Martin in Austria (14 per cent and two seats).

From this perspective, European elections can be seen to contribute to the reorganisation of national political supply. The Greens, for instance, have often managed to increase their political prominence at the national level on the basis of European electoral victories. European offices are sometimes the only trophies extreme-right and extreme-left parties can win. It seems difficult, at the same time, to deplore the democratic paradoxes of the European Union on the grounds that they are not specifically European and are dominated by Euroscepticism and not to acknowledge the fact that European elections allow for the emergence of new political opportunities. This is more important than gathering political groups under a homogenising and stigmatising 'Eurosceptic' label, which blurs the heterogeneous reality. Indeed, the 'anti-European' projects or 'Euro-criticisms' concerning participation in European elections contribute, in a paradoxical way, to the establishment of Europe as a public sphere for political debates. Since Eurosceptic parties (such as the Polish LPR which campaigned against integration) play a hand in the game of European elections, and occasionally to a greater extent than Europhile parties, European institutions have been somehow strengthened as political arenas. From this perspective, one could observe an increase in 2004, compared to previous elections, in the number of European lists – i.e. which relate their existence and campaign platforms to European integration – be they in favour of more integration (e.g. the Association of Independent European Democrats which obtained three seats in the Czech Republic) or, more frequently, opposed to it.

Moreover, the progressive nature of European integration makes national political competitions seem more and more affected by the emergence of European issues, which in turn impacts on the questions debated during European elections. For instance, in the 1984 European election, numerous analyses stressed the competition between national stakes which were salient during the campaign on the one hand, and European issues on the other, thus producing a competition which obviously favoured the former. 'Berlinguer's death and Negri's trial in Italy, the strike of printers in the Federal Republic of Germany and that of the miners in the United Kingdom, the European football cup, and the international tennis tournament of Roland

Garros in France were competing, quite successfully, for the limelight with the elections to the Strasbourg Parliament' (Charlot 1984). In 2004, the consequences of the single currency were debated in Poland and Italy, enlargement was an issue notably for the Eastern borders of the 'old' EU (Austria, Germany), and the question of strengthened common security (sometimes linked to the intervention in Iraq or to the accession of Turkey) formed part of the campaign platforms in many countries. In Denmark, the issues of EU agricultural aid and the protection of the environment, as well as of the accession of Turkey to the EU were all raised. In Germany, the campaign was characterised by European themes such as the questioning of the Stability Pact, the repatriation of Germans exiled after the Second World War, the principle of subsidiarity, the fight against European bureaucracy, the accession of Turkey to the EU, etc.

Certainly, these debates do not only emerge specifically during European election campaigns and exist because of the 'Europeanisation' of the national context. Indeed, these elections may also and above all represent mock national elections – witness the erosion of Gerhard Schröder's power in Germany, a test for both Tony Blair and Michael Howard, or for the coalition of the Casa della Liberta in Italy. All these issues are undeniably retranslated according to a scale of national perceptions and interests. Nonetheless, the tone of European elections has changed over the past 25 years and cleavages for European elections seem progressively to have become structured around 'European' stakes which contribute to the redesign of the national political game (see the internal referendum in the French Socialist Party). An approach in terms of 'second-order elections' – focused on the national nature of each election – accounts neither for such changes nor for the

differences which are specific to each case (Bartolini 2001). For example, it does not explain why, in rather general terms, the electoral campaign was very national in Italy whereas it was more Europeanised in Germany. The systematic approach in terms of 'second-order elections' hides an incredible diversity of particular situations and national specificities.

Moreover, although there are various forms of 'nationalisation' of European issues, there also exists a 'Europeanisation' of certain national stakes and strategies. Thus, an analysis in terms of 'political market' provides for an alternative to the 'second-order election' model. Revealing that a number of political leaders who benefit from fewer national resources or certain organisations which have a more marginal political role, under certain circumstances, can enforce strategies which are adjusted to the existence of a European 'political market', in turn contributes to its existence. Kauppi demonstrated that, during the 1999 European elections in Finland, European debates arose precisely because the major traditional political parties considered these elections devoid of stakes and because the debates were not exclusively about partisan words (Kauppi 2000). In other words, any investment by major parties and national leaders in European issues opens a window of opportunity for less well-known candidates to enjoy differentiated and strategic uses of the European parliamentary arena. The most famous example is that of the Greens, which, since the early 1980s, have, under the impulse of the Grünen, used these elections to Europeanise their specific brand (reimbursement of campaign expenses of the German and Belgian Greens since the 1984 elections, adoption of the principle of majority in the 1990s, establishment of the European co-ordination of the Green parties prior to the creation of the European Green Party in February 2004). Today, this change does not affect only small parties, as highlighted by the 'duel' between Poul Nyrup Rasmussen and Giuliano Amato for the presidency of the PES. The competition between the two leaders and the fact that the PES voters were delegates rather than national heads of the socialist parties was a major breakthrough for the emergence of a Europeanised campaign. Rasmussen's victory may have been read and publicly presented as the consequence of the attempt by certain members of European socialist parties to transnationalise their partisan labels. The projects for an alliance between François Bayrou and Romano Prodi with a view to creating a new European centre party had a similarly major impact. Therefore, the use by national leaders of the European arena to strengthen their national position paradoxically contributes to the existence of something that can now be perceived as a 'political Europe'. Moreover, it is important to remember that, as asserted by recent studies, certain political actors now build their careers in Europe (MEPs, such as Ingo Friedrich, Danish Jens-Peter Bonde or French Francis Wurtz, former commissioners such as Emma Bonino, etc.), which entails specific resources, expertise and type of political work. These alternative strategies progressively contribute to producing new commonalities which distinguish the European competition from other electoral competitions. Kauppi thus illustrated how the specificity of European elections in Finland in 1999 partially modified the traditional features of electoral competition: the investment by great national leaders favoured a reduced grasp of the political capital *stricto sensu* on the selection of candidates and a new grasp on other types of capital (media, culture) or resources connected to the representation of 'Europeanised' interest groups. We also know that in 2004, in Germany, heads of lists were partially recruited and put forward in accordance with their European expertise.

In light of all this, although European elections undoubtedly remain dominated by the patterns of the national game, it is nonetheless possible to advocate the existence of complex alternative schemes which could enable a reconsideration of the current development of a European political market, both in terms of its conditions of existence and of its effects.

Marine Delassalle

Bibliography

Bartolini, S., 'La structure des clivages nationaux et la question de l'intégration dans l'Union Européenne', *Politique européenne*, 4, 2001, pp. 15–45.

Charlot, M. (ed.), *Comprendre les élections européennes: enseignements de 1979 et problématique de 1984*, Colloque AFSP, Paris, 8 June 1984.

Kauppi, N., 'La construction de l'Europe: le cas des élections européennes finlandaises en 1999', *Cultures et Conflits*, 38–39, 2000, pp. 101–18.

Revue politique et parlementaire, 'Européennes: des élections en mal d'Europe?', 1031, July–September 2004.

→ Abstention; Cleavages; European Elections (1979–1999); European Elections (2004); European Electoral Act; European Federation of Green Parties; European Members of Parliament (Sociology of Political Office); European Political Parties; European Public Sphere; Europeanisation (of National Political Life); Euroscepticism; Extreme Left; Extreme Right; Germany; Green Politics; Issues; Multi-Level Governance; Protest Voting; Second-Order Elections.

The Netherlands

Dutch voters have been called upon to elect MEPs ever since 1979, when the European Parliament was elected for the first time by direct popular vote. Until now, all European elections in the Netherlands clearly were second-order *national* elections: their meaning being overwhelmingly determined by the political dynamics in the domestic political arena (Reif and Schmitt 1980; Brug and Eijk 2005: Ch. 12). Surveys conducted at the time of each of the European elections reveal that orientations and preferences with respect to either the general principles or the actual operation and performance of European integration have so far never been of great significance to voter behaviour and election outcomes (Eijk and Oppenhuis 1990; Oppenhuis 1996; Schmitt and Eijk 2005; Brug et al. 2005; unpublished analyses of 2004 data). For most European election years this is hardly surprising in view of the almost complete absence of contestation between political parties over such matters, and in view of the extremely limited and non-politicised coverage of these elections and their campaigns by the mass media (Vreese 2003; Peter 2003). The campaign in 2004 exhibited, more than on any previous occasion, a semblance of political and public debate on European matters (Harmsen 2004), yet even in that year, the orientations of Dutch voters towards the European Union and European integration hardly affected their behaviour.

Although they are all second-order national elections, European elections differ in terms of their timing. The interval between European elections is fixed at five years, whereas the interval between elections for the second chamber of parliament is at most four years. Unavoidably, European elections vary in terms of their temporal distance to national elections. These differences colour the political meaning and importance of EP elections in the domestic political arena. On four occasions, the European elections were mainly regarded as 'mid-term' updates of popular support for the political parties and for the governing coalition. These occasions were 1979 (two years after previous national elections), 1984 (20 months after), 1999 (13 months after a national election that did not lead to a change in government coalition), and in 2004 (16 months after). In 1989, however, the European elections acquired a different character owing to the fact that the Dutch government coalition had broken up only one month before, which necessitated (early) national elections to be called for September of that year. As a consequence, the European elections were universally regarded as a 'dress rehearsal' for the main event in September. In 1994 a quite different situation existed, when European elections were conducted just one month after elections for the second chamber. In that year, the EP elections were generally regarded as totally irrelevant. Table 1 displays the timing of EP elections in relation to the previous and the subsequent election for the national parliament. These differences in timing generate differences in party and media behaviour and, consequently, in what voters actually do. They effect variations in electoral participation (and thus in turnout) and in the sorts of strategic considerations that influence voters' party choice (Franklin et al. 1996; Oppenhuis et al. 1996). These differences, and the second-order character of EP elections, rule out a direct comparison of turnout levels and of parties' vote-shares.

Electoral system and party system

The electoral system for European Parliament elections is the same as that used for the elections of the national parliament: a list-proportional system in which the entire country effectively

Table 1   Timing of EP elections in relation to national parliament elections

Previous national parliament election	EP election	Subsequent national parliament election
May 1977	June 1979	May 1981
September 1982	June 1984	May 1986
May 1986	June 1989	September 1989
May 1994	June 1994	May 1998
May 1998	June 1999	May 2002
January 2003	June 2004	?? (no later than May 2007)

operates as a single district. In order to win representation, sufficient votes have to be acquired to pass the electoral quotient (number of valid votes divided by number of seats). The application of this familiar system in European Parliament elections had quite novel effects, caused by the difference in the denominator of the electoral quotient: the number of seats at stake.

The number of Dutch MEPs has varied somewhat over time. In 1979, 1984 and 1989, 25 representatives were to be elected; in 1994 and 1999 the number of mandates was 31; and after the 2004 enlargement of the Union this number was reduced again to 27. But these variations are minor in comparison to the discrepancy with the 150 seats to be elected for the national parliament. Whereas 0.67 per cent of the valid vote is sufficient for winning a seat in national parliament, European elections pose a 'hurdle' of 4 per cent (respectively 3.2 per cent and 3.7 per cent) for winning representation. As a consequence, most of the smaller parties that were quite viable at the national level did not have much chance of success in European elections. These parties did not immediately adapt to the new situation. In 1979 no fewer than nine established national parties competed while only four had a reasonable chance of winning at least one seat. In 1984, however, small parties

had learned their lesson, and attempted to pass the 'high' threshold by pooling their support bases. The voters were presented with two 'combination lists'. One of these involved three small orthodox Protestant Christian parties (SGP, GPV and RPF), the other consisted of three left-of-labour parties (CPN, PSP, PPR). Whether this tactic would be successful was strongly contested. But the voters clearly supported these joint ventures. The Protestant Christian combination attracted a larger vote share than could be expected from their separate electoral bases. The left-of-labour group fared less well, but this was largely caused by the appearance of a new party in the same niche of the ideological spectrum, which undermined the aspired pooling of left-wing voters. In 1989 both groups ran again as combinations, and this time they both enjoyed the voters' endorsement for doing so: they acquired demonstrably more votes than the sum of their parts would have done. These positive experiences contributed strongly to formal mergers of erstwhile separate parties. In 1991 the former pacifists (PSP), radicals (PPR) and communists (CPN) merged into the Green left. In 2000 a similar merger occurred between two of the three orthodox Christian parties, the GPV and the RPF, which joined in the new Christian Union (CU). In other words, EP elections contributed to the evolution of the Dutch party system, by forcing small parties to adapt to the higher thresholds for representation (Oppenhuis 1996).

The higher threshold for winning at least a single seat has not deterred new political entrepreneurs from presenting themselves at each of the EP elections so far. Until now, only one of these initiatives has been successful: the 'Transparency Europe' list headed by Paul van Buitenen, which obtained more than 7 per cent of the valid votes in 2004 and two seats in the European Parliament. Yet, in a particular way, EP elections offer also other forms of 'success', owing to which they will remain popular occasions for testing the waters for new parties. News media customarily report the results of EP elections not only in terms of vote-shares and seats in the EP, but they also project these results in terms of a hypothetical party composition of national parliament. This allows them to address the question of whether or not the government would still be supported by a parliamentary majority, had the elections been for the second chamber. And it is here that new entrepreneurs can show themselves as successful even in the absence of having obtained a single seat in the EP: the lower threshold for national representation implies the possibility for a party to be part of this 'hypothetical' second chamber. And such 'success' is more than a vanity-saving device: it serves as a public notification that 'real' success in 'real' elections is not just a figment of the imagination, but that it is within practical reach. And this, in turn, is an important ingredient for motivating a basis of activists and for convincing potential voters that they will not 'waste' their vote by supporting them. Newcomers who do not even succeed in crossing the national threshold while competing in European elections are rarely heard of anymore. But those whose vote-share would have carried them into the second chamber are all the more likely to make new attempts. From this perspective, the 3.2 per cent of the votes that the Animals Rights' Party obtained in 2004 (four to five seats in a 'virtual' national parliament) is likely to boost the determination of its activist support base, in spite of the fact that the second-order character of EP elections makes it much easier for newcomers to acquire votes.

With the exception of 2004, only established national parties have so far been successful in acquiring seats in the European Parliament. Table 2 presents the party distribution of the seats in the various election years. This table serves only an illustrative purpose and it obviously does not lend itself as a basis to study the evolution of parties' electoral support. For that purpose, the consequences of timing differences (see above) would have to be taken into account and these outcomes would also have to be integrated in a wider perspective that includes the results from national elections. Table 2 does, however, reveal that the number of Dutch parties that have succeeded in winning representation in the European Parliament has steadily risen from four parties (1979) to five (1984), to six (1989, 1994), to seven (1999) and finally to eight (2004). On the basis of this evidence from a single country it is impossible to determine to what extent EP elections promote fragmentation of national party systems, but such a link has been suggested elsewhere (Ysmal and Cayrol 1996) and deserves more systematic attention in future research.

The determinants of voters' choices have so far been overwhelmingly of a domestic nature. Many voters chose a different party in EP elections than in elections for the second chamber, but this is mainly caused by the fact that no change in government power is at stake,

Table 2   Distribution of EP seats

	1979 (/25)	1984 (/25)	1989 (/25)	1994 (/31)	1999 (/31)	2004 (/27)
CDA (Christian Democrat)	10	8	10	10	9	7
PvdA (Social-Democrat)	9	9	8	8	6	7
VVD (Liberal-Conservative)	4	5	3	6	6	4
D66 (Liberal-Progressive)	2	-	1	4	2	1
Green Left* (Ecologist – left-of-labour)	–	2	2	1	4	2
Orthodox Protestant Christian**	–	1	1	2	3	2
SP (Socialist – left-of-labour)	–	–	–	–	–	2
Transparency Europe	–	–	–	–	–	2

* in 1984 joint list of CPN, GPN, PPR and PSP, in 1989 Rainbow-list
** in 1984–99: joint list of SGP, GPV and RPF; in 2004 joint list of CU and SGP

and much less by voters' evaluation of parties' positions on matters concerning European integration. But until 2004 the parties offered little real choice in this respect (Eijk and Franklin 2004). The major political parties used to be virtually unanimous in their support for further integration (in terms of policy scope and geographical area). The orthodox Christian parties and the SP have always been most opposed to further integration, but these parties were for other reasons 'beyond the pale' for most voters. The Green left was traditionally in favour of the principle of further integration, but less so of the perceived neo-liberal slant of the integration process. It is only since 2002 that the major parties started to diverge in their stance concerning integration, with the VVD in particular voicing doubts about geographical enlargement and about political (as opposed to economic) integration.

Turnout and political polarisation

Turnout in EP elections has always been low in the Netherlands, not only compared to elections to the second chamber, but also compared to municipal or provincial elections. At the first EP elections turnout was 58.1 per cent, which was then considered to be disappointingly low. In the next four European elections turnout declined to 50.9 per cent (1984), 47.5 per cent (1989), 35.7 per cent (1994) and to an unprecedented low of 29.9 per cent (1999). In 2004 turnout rose somewhat to 39.1 per cent.

The most popular interpretation is that this decline indicates a waning of popular support for European integration. Such an interpretation has, however, repeatedly been shown to be empirically untenable. Attitudes about European integration do not explain whether or not people turn out to vote after controlling for antecedent and more fundamental determinants (Eijk and Oppenhuis 1990; Schmitt and Eijk 2005). Low turnout can be understood from the fact that little seems to be at stake in European elections. But this does not explain the *decline* in turnout, and until now no empirically convincing explanations have been provided for it.

In view of the rise in turnout in 2004 it seems likely that the explanation for these variations has to be found in the political context in which EP elections take place. The extent of political polarisation and contestation is a promising factor to consider. Franklin (2004) demonstrates the importance of this factor for changes in turnout. In the Dutch case, declining turnout occurs in a period of political depolarisation and technocratisation that blurs programmatic and ideological differences between parties (Thomassen 2000). The apex of this development occurred in the period of the 'purple' coalition (1994–2002) when traditional ideological rivals (PvdA and VVD) joined in coalition, and when the main opposition party (CDA) failed to offer rivalling proposals. This lack of real choice promoted apathy and an anti-establishment revolt that was eventually mobilised in 2002 by Pim Fortuyn. The landslides of the 2002 and 2003 parliamentary elections brought an end to the era of 'purple' politics. They were accompanied by a renewed climate of emphasising political differences which stimulated popular political involvement and increased turnout in elections for the second chamber and, arguably, also in the 2004 EP elections.

A second factor that may account for turnout differences is change in media interest for European elections after a first-time boost in 1979. Day-to-day coverage of European politics was (and still is) virtually absent, and European elections and their campaigns since 1984 were increasingly portrayed as irrelevant. The visible lack of attention of Dutch political parties for European affairs and the absence of any kind of public debate reinforced this image. This context only changed after the turn of the century, and the few years since 2001 have generated more debate, more political differences and more media attention then ever before about the desired scope and nature of European integration.

Cees van der Eijk

Bibliography

Brug, W. van der and Eijk, C. van der (eds), *European Elections and Domestic Politics*, Notre Dame, University of Notre Dame Press, 2005.

Brug, W. van der, Eijk, C. van der and Franklin, M., 'EU Support and Party Choice', in W. van der Brug and C. van der Eijk (eds), *European Elections and Domestic Politics*, Notre Dame, University of Notre Dame Press, 2005.

Eijk, C. van der and Franklin, M. 'Potential for Contestation on European Matters at National Elections in Europe', in G. Marks and M. Steenbergen (eds), *European Integration and Political Conflict*, Cambridge, Mass., Harvard University Press. 2004, pp. 32–50.

Eijk, C. van der and Oppenhuis, E., 'Turnout and Second-order Effects in the European Elections of June 1989: Evidence from the Netherlands', *Acta Politica*, 25, 1, 1990, pp. 67–94.

Franklin, M., *Voter Turnout and the Dynamics of Electoral Competition in Established Democracies since 1945*, Cambridge, Cambridge University Press, 2004.

Franklin, M. N., Eijk, C. van der and Oppenhuis, E. V., 'The Institutional Context: Turnout', in C. van der Eijk, M. N. Franklin et al., *Choosing Europe? The European Electorate and National Politics in the Face of Union*, Ann Arbor, University of Michigan Press, 1996, pp. 306–31.

Harmsen, R. 'Euroscepticism in the Netherlands: Stirrings of Dissent', *European Studies: a Journal of European Culture, History and Politics*, 20, 1, 2004, pp. 99–126.

Oppenhuis, E. V., 'The Netherlands: Small Party Evolution', in C. van der Eijk , M. Franklin et al. (eds), *Choosing Europe? The European Electorate and National Politics in the Face of Union*, Ann Arbor, University of Michigan Press, 1996, pp. 209–26.

Oppenhuis, E. V., Eijk, C. van der and Franklin, M., 'The Party Context: Outcome', in C. van der Eijk, M. N. Franklin et al. (eds), *Choosing Europe? The European Electorate and National Politics in the Face of Union*, Ann Arbor, University of Michigan Press, 1996, pp. 287–305.

Peter, J., 'Why European Television News Matters', PhD dissertation, University of Amsterdam, 2003.

Reif, K. and Schmitt, H., 'Nine Second-Order National Elections: a Conceptual Framework for the Analysis of European Elections Results', *European Journal of Political Research*, 8, 1980, pp. 3–44.

Schmitt, H. and Eijk, C. van der, 'There is Not Much Euro-sceptic Non-voting in European Parliament Elections', in P. Taggart and A. Sczcerbiak (eds), *Opposing Europe*, Oxford: Oxford University Press, 2005.

Thomassen, J. 'Politieke Veranderingen en het Functioneren van de Parlementaire Democratie in Nederland', in J. Thomassen, K. Aarts and H. Van der Kolk (eds), *Politieke Veranderingen in Nederland 1971–1998*, Den Haag, Sdu, 2000, pp. 203–28.

Vreese, C. de, *Framing Europe: Television News and European Integration*, Amsterdam, Aksant, 2003.

Ysmal, C. and Cayrol, R., 'France: the Midwife Comes to Call', in C. van der Eijk and M. Franklin et al. (eds), *Choosing Europe? The European Electorate and National Politics in the Face of Union*, Ann Arbor, University of Michigan Press, 1996, pp. 115–36.

→ Mapping Europe: European Electoral Geography.

'Null and Void'

(Votes)

The number of null and void ballots recorded in the June 2004 European election amounted to 2.77 per cent of the total vote. The election concerned 352 million registered voters, but 44 per cent actually voted. Votes were seen as invalid either because they did not comply with the necessary regulations (erroneous ballots), or because they deviated from the polling mode or the electoral offer (protest ballots).

In this election, which was characterised by the success of Eurosceptic and populist parties, the high rate of invalid ballots highlighted the obstacles to a European harmonisation of electoral procedures. The numbers of null and void ballots are so diverse across member states that they cannot be placed into one homogeneous category. Table 1 shows a breakdown of null and void ballots by country.

This table must be interpreted with caution, as the heterogeneity of voting behaviour within the EU makes direct comparisons difficult. While voting is a right in a majority of countries, it is compulsory in Greece, Cyprus, Luxembourg and Belgium. Such obligation makes null ballots all the more likely (they are integrated in the total number of votes). If one calculates the rate of participation based on the number of ballots declared 'valid', rather than on the number of 'cast votes', then levels of participation are weaker in these countries by an average of 2 per cent. Another important variable is the difference in voting methods. Ballots can be cast on touch-screen as in the Netherlands and Belgium, on paper, in envelopes, or by 'ticking' boxes and circles. Varying techniques of voting require different competencies, and allow varying degrees of blank and null voting.

In the United Kingdom's 45 000 polling stations, the ballots are counted by administrators representing the local authorities. Special teams are also recruited for their ability to count votes. Clearly, the quality of such controls will not be the same as that of polling stations employing party employees or voluntary workers. Lastly, member states have different regulations and

Table 1   Null and void ballot by country, 2004 European elections

Country	Turnout	Of which: total valid	Of which: total invalid
Belgium	90.8	85.9	4.9
Czech Republic	28.3	28.2	0.2
Denmark	47.3	47.2	0.2
Germany	43.0	41.8	1.2
Estonia	26.8	26.6	0.1
Greece	63.4	61.8	1.6
Spain	45.1	44.7	0.4
France	42.8	41.3	1.4
Ireland	58.8	56.9	1.9
Cyprus	72.5	69.2	3.3
Latvia	41.3	41.0	0.4
Lithuania	48.4	45.5	2.9
Hungary	38.5	38.2	0.3
Malta	82.4	80.8	1.6
Netherlands	39.3	39.2	0.1
Austria	42.4	41.3	1.1
Poland	20.9	20.3	0.6
Portugal	38.6	37.1	1.5
Slovenia	28.3	26.8	1.6
Slovakia	17.0	16.7	0.3
Finland	39.4	39.4	0.2
Sweden	37.8	36.8	1.1

procedures to reject invalid, null or void ballots. This makes generalisations on the matter virtually impossible to formulate. For instance, in the United Kingdom, a distinction is drawn between 'spoilt ballots' which were inadvertently or voluntarily incorrectly filled, and normal votes. In fact, ballots that are improperly printed, crumpled, dirtied or comprise marks which compromise the secrecy of the vote are not introduced into the ballot box, but placed in an envelope and counted separately. The term 'rejected ballots' is used in reference to votes inserted in the ballot box without being marked, as well as those with unsuitable inscriptions or multiple marks (when only one was necessary). This category can also include ballots marked with a pen other than that provided by the polling station, etc.

The identification of a valid vote is different in countries using envelopes and ballot papers that the voter does not have to mark. In certain countries, in cases where the intention of the voter is clear, a certain tolerance is allowed for possible annotations. By contrast, others regulate the authorised marks in a strict way. In Sweden, votes are counted at the polling stations immediately after closing. The National Tax Commission publishes the results based on the reports it receives from local administrations. Spoilt ballots are counted separately: the null ones on one side, and blank or void ones on another. Ballots which permit the identification of the voter, bear more than one party name, as well as envelopes containing more than one paper are classified as 'spoilt'.

Given the diversity of European electoral systems, the definition of what constitutes a 'good' ballot paper for European elections remains problematic. As for blank votes, their definition is hardly more unified. In certain countries, they are seen as a political expression in their own right. This is the case in Spain, where the law on the 'Escrutinio en las Mesas electoral' specifies that ballot papers not containing any vote, as well as those expressing no preference, are considered blank votes (*voto in blanco*). In countries like France, they are viewed as rejected ballots (*votes nuls*), or even treated as abstentions and deprived of any electoral value. It is clear that a EU-level harmonisation of such classification is essential, in that it will be increasingly difficult to expect EU citizens to elect a common Parliament if no instrument ensures the equality of their vote in Europe. A common EU statute of the blank vote would be a crucial symbol reaffirming the importance of turnout at election time.

Olivier Ihl

Bibliography

Brennan, G. and Pettit, P., 'Unveiling the Vote', *British Journal of Political Science*, 20, 3, 1990, pp. 311–33.

Déloye, Y. and Ihl, O., 'Des voix pas comme les autres: Votes blancs et votes nuls aux élections législatives de 1881', *Revue Française de Science Politique*, 41, 2, 1991, pp. 141–70.

Friedland, Lewis A., 'Electronic Democracy and the New Citizenship', *Media, Culture and Society*, 18, 2, 1996, pp. 185–212.

→ Ballot Paper; Citizen (EU); Compulsory Voting; Electoral Behaviour; Electoral System; European Elections (1979–1999); European Elections (2004); European Electoral Act; Polling Stations; Protest Voting; Symbols and Practice of Elections.

Observation of Elections

In 1857, a commission of delegates from many countries of Europe was in charge of monitoring the legality of the election taking place in Moldavia and Valachia, certainly one of the first missions of observation on the Old World. This isolated experience immediately raised the issue that would haunt similar observations in the twentieth century, particularly after the First World War in Eastern Europe (Boneo 2000), and then more widely after the decolonisation movement or the end of the Cold War: how is it possible to determine whether an election was sincere and legal or not? This can be interpreted as a sign that such expertise does not aim at objectivising an assessment, even less at favouring a mere technical support. It is about a political process of attestation. Each new mission is thus political, not only by its object (collecting, measuring and assessing the violations of the standards that frame the course of elections) but also by its approach: legitimating an election result by referring to a model of democracy that is itself the object and stake of power struggles on the international scene.

The current boom of observation missions comes from the competition waged by the main institutions that are now able to participate in the process of globalisation of election engineering, for example specialised NGOs, international organisations' commissions, etc. Such institutions include of course the Council of Europe and the Community, and the European Union, that occupies a recent but growing position of influence.

Sometimes imposed, sometimes required, its expertise has been intended as one of 'long-term observation' over several years. Observation – despite the 'electoral tourism' criticism – is concerned with promoting a wider geographic and chronological coverage than the polling day itself. This requires special attention to the phases preceding the election – preparation of the electoral lists, declarations of candidacies, access to the media, types of financing – through to the counting of the votes, settling disagreements, and announcing the results. This is in conformity with the recent teachings of neo-institutionalism or the historical sociology of voting which underlines the importance of election engineering in the advent of the 'institutionalised uncertainty' (Przeworski 1988: 63) specific to any real competition, or in the promotion of a type of 'electoral civility' (Ihl 2000: 98). It remains to be seen how the differences of observation traditions among the member states will be standardised. Great Britain, within the Commonwealth, is attached to the standards of a short-term observation preceded by limited visits during the pre-election process and above all accompanied by the training of local observers (indirect rule scheme), while most of the continental European countries prefer a more direct scheme of election running. Elective integrity is then the object of a more and more marked managerial positivism: we might think of a project for an Electoral Integrity Perception Index mentioned by Mozzafar and Schedler (2002: 19) on the model of the international corruption charts published once a year by the NGO Transparency

International and based on opinion polls. The limits of such a managerial conception of voting, however, are due to other factors than the illusion of the technique's neutrality. The interweaving of the political and economic stakes can be observed for instance in the more and more common practice of political conditionality of economic exchange and financial aid. An observation report endorsing the 'good course' of an election is a guarantee for the continuation of the European states' economic activities with the country in question.

Another limitation is the over-dependence of many reports on the diplomatic relations structure specific to the geopolitical situation, as the debates on the democratisation reality in Russia or in the former states of the Eastern bloc underlined. Or, at a different level, the accusations of 'interference', and even 'imperialism', made against several European countries by former colonised countries' leaders. In contrast, there was no observation mission of the EU, the UN and the OSCE to monitor the quality of the Butterfly ballot used in Florida during the October 2000 presidential election. There are few that operate in so-called 'advanced' or 'consolidated' electoral democracies. It is mainly in the name of a democratisation support policy that such assessment and qualification work occurs and that such standardisation operates over the different forms of electoral policies. We have to mention, however, that the EU members have agreed to standardise their legislation and to submit to the monitoring of the Bureau of the Assembly of the Council of Europe an increasing number of their electoral processes (European Commission for Democracy Through Law 2003: 39, 46–7). This should bring about a new voting standardisation, and perhaps give birth to ways of electing and being elected which are more in conformity with the specifically European conception of what a 'democratic election' is.

Nathalie Dompnier
Olivier Ihl

Bibliography

Boneo, H., 'Observation of Elections', in R. Rose (ed.), *International Encyclopaedia of Elections*, Basingstoke, Palgrave Macmillan, 2000.

Commission européenne pour la democratie par le droit (European Commission for Democracy Through Law), *Code de bonne conduite en matière électorale*, Strasbourg, Editions du Conseil de l'Europe, 2003.

Ihl, O., *Le Vote*, Paris, Montchrestien, 2000.

Mozaffar, S. and Schedler A., 'The Comparative Studies of Electoral Governance', *International Political Science Review*, 23, 1, 2002, pp. 5–27.

Przeworski, A., 'Democracy as a Contingent Outcome of Conflicts', in J. Elster, and R. Slagstad (eds), *Constitutionalism and Democracy*, Cambridge, Cambridge University Press, 1988, pp. 59–80.

→ Observers.

Observers

The 1 May 2004 enlargement preparation process was also concerned with preparation for the arrival of the new MEPs from the new member states. In order to ease their understanding of the EP's work and the MEP's function, it was decided after the signing of the accession treaty in Athens on 16 April 2003, that the President of the European Parliament would invite the future member states' parliaments to appoint men and women among the elected representatives of the national chambers as observers in the EP. The number of observers appointed by each parliament would be the same as the number of MEPs attributed to these countries by the accession treaty. The appointment of observers was made by duly taking into account the political composition of the parliament concerned. The 162 observers, whose term of office started as soon as they received their notification of appointment made by the national parliament, and ended with the effective accession, had the right to attend the EP's plenary sessions without taking the floor, voting or standing for elective positions. In the commissions and delegations, observers could be invited by the president to take the floor in accordance with Article 166.2 of the rule of the institution, that provides that 'on special decision of the commission, any other person can be invited to attend a meeting and take the floor'. However, participation in the commissions' work did not give them the right to vote or stand for elective posts. The reading of the document adopted by the Bureau of the EP on 29 January 2003 relating to the welcoming of observers enables us to observe that the role that was given to them in the enlargement preparation period was particularly passive with little incentive or opportunity to participate.

On the other hand, the observers were able to participate in the parliamentary groups' work according to the methods defined by each group. This led to speeding up the relations between the political groups and the elected representatives of the new member states. In the same way, some of them had to take a political stand in certain groups. While the contacts between MEPs and the observers seem to have been reduced, the latter have however been able to observe a series of practices, places, traditions and habits that may have contributed to their future political life within the EP or national parliaments. The interest given to this observation also depended on the likelihood of the observer running for EP elections and

being elected. In that case the observer would be more motivated; if not, he could at least share his observations with his party's leaders. It was more about observing and learning the EP's practices than a progressive involvement in its discussions and work. However, the contacts were reinforced between the various parliamentary delegations, particularly in the case of Central Europe's political groupings that had not yet established relations or were not yet members of European party federations.

An assessment of the procedure aimed at preparing for the arrival of a great number of newly elected representatives can be made by examining how many observers ran for the 2004 elections and how many are now part of the EP. This allows the measurement of the efficiency of the procedure, and also to see if the political parties of the candidate countries have taken into account the status of observer to select their candidates. It is interesting to note that only 79 observers ran for the 2004 EP elections (that is to say less than one in two) but that great differences exist from one country to the other. Fifteen out of 24 observers were candidates in the Czech Republic, 4 out of 6 in Estonia, and 10 out of 13 in Lithuania, while there were 6 out of 14 in Slovakia and 17 out of 54 in Poland. The parties could not risk depriving themselves of too high a number of MPs in national parliaments. Furthermore, to attract the voters in European elections, they favoured candidates from civil society on their lists. Finally, some observers were convinced that their place was not in Brussels or Strasbourg.

The number of elected representatives is even lower. Only 1 observer out of 5 was elected for Malta, 2 out of 6 for Cyprus, 10 out of 54 in Poland, 2 out of 13 in Lithuania, 5 out of 24 in the Czech Republic, 2 out of 5 in Estonia, 8 of 24 in Hungary, 2 out of 9 in Slovenia, 4 out of

14 in Slovakia, and 1 out of 9 in Latvia. That is to say a total of 37 out of 79 observers in contention (finally, less than one observer elected out of four). These results can be explained by the defeat of the parties in power that were the most represented ones in national parliaments. They therefore sent more observers but obtained proportionally fewer elected representatives. Furthermore, not all the candidate observers were in an eligible position. We must also note that a number of parties without seats in their national parliaments obtained seats in the EP. However, they had no observers as they necessarily came from parliaments.

These various elements explain both why few observers found themselves candidates and few candidate-observers were elected in the EP. However, track record results are distorted if we only refer to the figures. Only 79 observers participated in the elections and 37 were elected and are therefore currently MEPs. But we must remember that this proce-dure was only one of the provisions aiming at the preparation for the arrival of the new elected representatives and the objective was not to have the observers elected. As the selection for the observers operated within national parliaments, a distortion concerning the future elected representatives was predictable. Furthermore, we must not only take into account the quantitative effects but also the effects induced by this procedure that allowed a better knowledge and a multiplication of contacts. Finally, we must not underesti-mate the symbolic impact of the arrival of the MEPs from the new member states in the EP several months before the enlargement.

Jean-Michel de Waele

→ Composition of the European Parliament; Enlargement; European Elections (2004); European Parliament; Members of the European Parliament (Legal and Political Status); Members of the European Parliament (Sociology of Political Office).

P

Paris Summit

(9–10 December 1974)

The 9–10 December 1974 Paris Summit was the seventh meeting of the EEC heads of state since the EEC's creation in 1957. Not codified by the Rome Treaty, 'summits' were then organised occasionally and irregularly to answer ad hoc needs. The first two summits were organised in Paris and in Bonn in February and July 1961 respectively, to prepare the political union on the basis of Charles de Gaulle's proposals but were finally unsuccessful. The third summit, in Rome, in 1967, appeared to be mostly a commemorative event, on the occasion of the tenth anniversary of the Treaties. From 1969, the summits, more frequent, became more and more politically significant. They have a direct influence on the EU's development and, importantly, the Commission's president started to participate at least partly in the heads of states' work. The Hague Summit, organised in December 1969 following a French proposal, led the way to the first EU enlargement. The Paris Summit, in October 1972, right after the ratification of the UK, Ireland and Denmark accession treaties, adopted a programme for an enlarged Europe that would ultimately lead to the creation of the European Union (EU). The Copenhagen Summit, in December 1973, soon after the October war in the Near East, could not fully realise its ambitions but came up with the first declaration on European identity.

In 1974, the EEC suffered a crisis, underlined by the Commission (in a declaration on 31 January aimed at governments) and the EP's president (in an intervention on 11 February). Added to the long-lasting monetary turbulence that followed the 1971 American decision to dissociate the dollar from gold, the consequences of the first oil crisis brought to an end the 30-year boom that had continued since the Second World War. Deeply divided over the crisis, the Europeans also had to face the UK's 'renegotiation' demand after Labour returned to power in spring 1974. The enlarged Community seemed to be heading for paralysis: its minimal decision-making capacity did not enable it to implement the 1972 programme that was at a standstill in almost all fields (monetary, regional, employment, energy policies, etc.). An indispensable boost came from the Paris Summit instigated by Valéry Giscard d'Estaing and Helmut Schmidt. Both were brought to power in May after Georges Pompidou's death and Willy Brandt's resignation. The summit resulted in proposals for stronger institutions, as no agreement could be found on how best to boost the economy at that time of crisis.

Ideas for a reform of the decision making process, which had to become more efficient and democratic, had progressed for several years. From 1972 onwards, the Commission was presenting proposals on the functioning of an enlarged Europe. The EP continued to work on the basis of Article 138 of the Rome Treaty and its political commission adopted a second report (after the Dehousse report in the 1960s) in November 1974. Outside European institutions, Jean Monnet prepared a project that linked the institutionalisation of the heads of states and governments' meetings with the election of the European Parliament (EP) by direct universal suffrage. This proposal, which was discussed in 1973 between Paris, Bonn and London but not adopted at the Copenhagen Summit, was also submitted to Valéry Giscard d'Estaing and Helmut Schmidt, who were favourable to these reforms. The novelty in 1974 was that the French authorities agreed not only with the idea of regular summit meetings, but also with the EP's direct election, until then rejected by De Gaulle and Pompidou. The prospect of regular summits with an intergovernmental connotation continued to arouse distrust in Benelux states, however, as they feared a weakening of European institutions. Similarly, direct EP elections met with reservations in the UK and Denmark.

In these conditions, the success of the Paris Summit, which took place on 9–10 December 1974, at the end of the French presidency, was in the balance. One month before the meeting, comments were pessimistic and the tone only began to change at the beginning of December. However, the summit results turned out to be significant. The heads of states and governments adopted a long communiqué containing 37 points. Two-thirds (points 14 to 37) were about rather vague economic proposals, but points 1 to 13 were dedicated to essential institutional aspects.

The communiqué underlines the necessary cohesion between EEC activities and political co-operation (point 2). According to this declaration, it is the heads of states and governments' responsibility to ensure this cohesion. They meet, under the name of the European Council, accompanied by their Ministers of Foreign Affairs, 'at least twice a year and every time it is necessary' as a Community Council and in the name of political co-operation (point 3). The Council has the role of stimulation and arbitration. It implements a common diplomacy in all fields of international life that affect the Community's interests, and associates the European Parliament to its work, in particular through the practice of questions asked to the presidency (point 4). As to the EP, is was to be elected by direct universal suffrage 'as soon as possible'. It had to make proposals on which the Council was able to rule in 1976 aiming at a direct election that 'should take place from 1978 onwards' (point 12). Moreover, the competencies of the Assembly were extended, in particular through the granting of certain law-making powers.

However, a declaration of the British delegation explained that it could not take a stand on this question as the renegotiation process was not over, and the Danish delegation refused to commit to introducing the direct election in 1978 (point 12). Finally, the heads of states and governments asked the Belgian Prime Minister Leo Tindemans to write a summary report on the development towards a European Union (point 13).

The scope of the summit's decisions went beyond what commentators had imagined at that time. The link between EU activities and political co-operation was tremendously improved. The role of the presidency, which became a mouthpiece on the diplomatic scene, also increased in the Community field. The European Council, created in 1974 by a mere declaration and introduced in the Treaty only in 1986, quickly became a key organ that would give much impetus to integration in the 1980s and 1990s. The direct election materialised in 1979 and became a springboard for a great reinforcement of the EP's competencies.

Marie-Thérèse Bitsch

Parity

In a number of European countries, the middle of the 1990s marked the beginning of the definition of a new challenge: to achieve parity between men and women in representative institutions. To this effect, four EU member states introduced new bills, amounting to affirmative action-type electoral mechanisms in favour of women: Belgium (laws of 17 June 2002, 18 July 2002 and 17 April 2003), France (law of 6 June 2000), Italy (law 90-2004) and Slovenia (law of 26 February 2004). The same process was also implemented in Macedonia (law of May 2002). These new electoral laws proved unequally constraining, some nullify the candidacies of non-complying lists (Slovenia, Macedonia, regional elections and municipal elections in cities of over 30 000 inhabitants in France), while others barely impose financial penalties on parties (legislative elections in France, European elections in Italy). They are also unequally drastic, depending on whether they impose strict alternation of female and male candidates (in Slovenia for the first half of lists, except the shortest ones, in France for the first six candidates, and in Belgium the first three) or simply an equal number of candidates from both genders, and whether they try to achieve true parity (France, Belgium), or minimum thresholds of female candidates (40 per cent in Slovenia, 30 per cent in Italy and Macedonia). Finally, while all elections are concerned in Italy, they do not extend to European elections in Slovenia. What is clear is that these new laws, regardless of their specific conditions, all go well beyond the self-imposed quotas of Scandinavian left-wing parties in the 1970s as they concern all parties and partly constrain their ability to choose their electoral lists. Beyond a difference of degree and vocabulary, however, these new laws also convey a specific vision of the way gender should contribute to the social and political spheres.

In this area, the UN initiated an interesting dynamic in 1953, when it officially included women's rights in its political agenda. In the New York convention of 1979, the UN also defined three strategies to fight against all forms sexual discrimination: new education policies, to try and modify socio-cultural stereotypes, temporary laws enforcing affirmative action, and inclusion in national constitutions of the principle of equality between men and women. Ten years later, the Council of Europe also got involved in this debate and played a dominant role in the promotion of equality, ordering a number of studies, recommendations and colloquia on 'paritary democracy'. On 2 December 1996, the Council of Ministers of the EU finally joined the trend. Without talking of 'parity', it adopted a recommendation that promised to look for an 'integrated strategy to promote a balanced system of participation of men and women' for decision-making processes, using, if need be, legislative, regulatory or incentive instruments.

This acknowledgement, at the European level, of the political rights of women, obviously participated in a more general extension of EU competence, as illustrated by Article 141 of the Treaty of Amsterdam, which extends the EU policy realm to the fight against all discrimination. At the same time, since the 1970s the ECJ and the European Commission played a prime role in the promotion of the cause of parity. With the 'Kalanke' decision of 17 October 1995, the European Court endorsed the principle of 'equality of chances' (stipulating that a directive does not guarantee a particular result but an equality of chances). Straight away, this agenda of the EU magistrates was continued by a series of directives on equality between men and women in social and economic arenas. Since 1980, a certain number of measures of positive discrimination were also implemented, particularly under the impulsion of DG V, going far beyond the old border of labour laws as defined in Article 119 of the Treaty of Rome. As in other policy areas, the European Commission rested an extension of its competencies on the legitimacy of a court decision, and with the support of insiders (particularly some women MEPs) as well as outsiders (the Council of Europe, feminists, etc.). Thus, the Commission chose to help finance the European Women's Lobby since its creation in 1990, as well as about 50 other non-governmental organisations and think-tanks with which to organise the 'Women in Power' European meeting in November 1992. Promoting the cause of parity with well-known women politicians from left and right parties alike, and using the third middle-term action programme between men and women (1991–5), the Commission helped to create a network of experts ('Women in decision-making processes'), which tried to denounce as a scandal the under-representation of women in politics in Europe to make it a true public cause (Bereni 2004).

Even though they did not result in constraining European laws, these efforts consolidated a certain number of beliefs and perceptions (Bereni 2004). Indeed, the parity movement paradoxically based its success on the assertion of fundamental differences between men and women, claiming that women inherit specific qualities, such as 'common sense' and 'listening qualities' from their socialisation, which legitimate their right to participate more actively in political life. It also reinforces the need to enforce symbolic representation (Eulau and Karps 1978), stating that representation should represent the various components of any society. These

beliefs constituted strong symbolic arguments for parity once conveyed by Europe and then at the national level. These new 'unquestionable principles' of representation have been largely redefined within national political arenas.

In some countries, however, these discussions gave way to harsh philosophical discussions, as in France where they were perceived to contradict traditional principles of Republican universalism. However, to the extent that these new measures were seen as promoting the end of masculine domination in the political and economic spheres, pro-parity militants tried to take them further and take the battle into the legal arena. In July 1995, the Italian Constitutional Council invalidated the first three parity laws of 1993–5, as its French counterpart had done in 1982 after the French government tried to impose a first law to impose a quota of 25 per cent women in municipal elections in towns of more than 2500 inhabitants. Consequently, France changed its Constitution on 8 July 1999 before adopting a new parity bill. This was soon followed by Belgium (constitutional law of 24 January 2002) and Italy (constitutional law of 20 February 2003), which both imitated Germany, Portugal and Sweden, where constitutions demand that public institutions guarantee effective equality between the sexes. However, these legal advances alone could not guarantee the success of the new measures. In Portugal, the first two bills were aborted in 1999 and 2001 because they lacked sufficient MPs' backing. Similarly, the first Belgian and French experiences in the area of parity were faced with bad will on the electoral scene. In Belgium, where the 1994 laws did not specify the positions women should have on the lists, they were often downgraded to ineligible places, or allowed to run in constituencies that could not be won. The ones that were elected were also rarely included in the executive councils where men remained dominant, even when they were placed lower than them on the electoral lists. Moreover, when the law tried to use positive financial incentives, a number of richer political parties preferred to lose money than to implement parity. In sum, the law guaranteed the legal role of women in politics without making them a legitimate enough resource to access the true positions of power.

More generally, in the European elections of 2004 as in some other elections, the efficiency of pro-parity legislation depended upon a combination of other factors, such as the level of constraint, the electoral system (the proportional representation system used in EP elections proved far better for parity than the plurality and majority systems used in other contexts), and local political contexts, which were more or less propitious to an opening of the lists to new candidates. This is why the new 2002 Belgian laws meant that Belgium elected 35.3 per cent of female MPs (against 30 per cent before) and achieved similar results in the European Parliament elections. This example shows how legislative affirmative action, while not the panacea for female under-representation, was quickly conceived as a necessary step towards equality when parties are lukewarm in their efforts towards equal representation.

Delphine Dulong

Bibliography

Bereni, L., 'Le mouvement français pour la parité en Europe', in S. Jacquot and C. Woll (eds), *Les usages de l'Europe*, Paris: L'Harmattan, 2004, pp. 33–54.

➜ Belgium; Electoral Register; European Parliament; France; Interest Groups; Italy; Representation; Slovenia; Women.

Parliamentary Groups in the European Parliament

The party system of the European Parliament (EP) is dominated by the two main European party families: social-democrats on one hand, and centre-right conservatives and Christian democrats on the other. In the early 1950s, members of the Common Assembly of the European Coal and Steel Community (ECSC), the predecessor of the European Parliament, decided to form ideological groups instead of national blocs to counterbalance the dominance of national interests in the Council. Nevertheless, national parties remain influential within party groups, not least through their control of candidate selection. In comparison with parties in national legislatures, the EP party groups are non-hierarchical, with emphasis on legislative work done in the committees. Without any EU executive office at stake in European elections, the vertical linkage function of the party groups – that of connecting voters to public policy-making – will remain poorly developed in the absence of changes in the balance of power between EU institutions. However, in horizontal terms, the EP party groups and the parties at the European level perform an important function by integrating political interests across the Union.

The development of the EP party system

The core of the EP party system is formed by the main European party families: conservatives and Christian democrats, social-democrats/socialists, and the smaller liberal, Green, and radical left groups. Table 1 shows the distribution of seats in the Parliament between 1979 and 2004. The Party of the European

Table 1   Party groups in the European Parliament, 1979–2004

Groups	1979	1984	1989	1994	1999	2004
PES	113	130	180	198	180	200
EPP	107	110	121	157	233	268
ELDR/ALDE	40	31	49	43	50	88
EDG	64	50	34			
EDA	22	29	20	26		
COM	44	41				
CDI	11					
RB		20	13			
ER		16	17			
Greens/EFA			30	23	48	
EUL			28			
LU			14			
EUL-NGL				28	42	41
EN				19		
FE				27		
ERA				19		
UEN					21	27
TGI					20	
EDD					16	
IND/DEM						37
NA	9	7	12	27	16	29
Total	410	434	518	567	626	732

Abbreviations: PES = Party of European Socialists; EPP = European People's Party, European People's Party and European Democrats (EPP-ED) since the 1999 elections; ELDR = European Liberal Democrat and Reform Party, Alliance of Liberals and Democrats for Europe (ALDE) after the 2004 elections; EDG = European Democratic Group; EDA = European Democratic Alliance, European Progressive Democrats until the 1989 elections; COM = Communist and Allies Group; CDI = Technical Group of Co-ordination and Defence of Independent MEPs; RB = Rainbow Group; ER = European Right; Greens = The Green Group, Greens/European Free Alliance since the 1999 elections; EUL = European United Left; LU = Left Unity; EUL-NGL = Confederal Group of the European United Left, since 1995 the group has included the sub-group Nordic Green Left; EN = Europe of Nations; ERA = European Radical Alliance; FE = Forza Europa; UEN = Union for Europe of the Nations; TGI = Technical Group of Independent Members; EDD = Europe of Democracies and Diversities; IND/DEM = Independence and Democracy; NA = Non-attached. EDA and FE merged in July 1995 to form Union for Europe (55 MEPs). The UPE joined EPP in June 1998.
Date: 1979 = after the European elections (EE); 1984 = after the second EE; 1989 = after the third EE; 1994 = after the fourth EE; 1999 = after the fifth EE; 2004 = seat distribution in August 2004.

Socialists (PES) and European People's Party (EPP) have dominated the chamber throughout this period, controlling more than half of the seats after each election.

For the first time since the introduction of direct elections, the centre-right EPP became in 1999 the largest group. The EPP-ED continues as the largest group, with 268 MEPs (37 per cent) in the Parliament elected in 2004. EPP is also the only group that has members from all 25 member states. The group brings together Christian democratic and conservative parties, and the entry of several powerful conservative parties to the group has caused anxieties among the Christian democrats that have traditionally been strong supporters of European integration. The accommodation of the British Conservatives has been particularly problematic, and the title European Democrats was added to the group name after the 1999 elections so that the Tories could maintain their separate identity in the EPP group.

The formation of the social-democratic PES presents far fewer problems, as almost every member state has a centre-left, social-democratic party. PES was the largest party in the Parliament from 1979 until 1999. Unlike its main rival EPP, the group has become more cohesive over time as the majority of European social-democratic parties have adopted broadly similar views on both socio-economic matters and on the future of integration. The seat share of the European Liberal Democrat and Reform Party (ELDR) remained below 10 per cent until the 2004 elections. The previous enlargement of the Union in 1995, together with the change of electoral system in the UK from single-member plurality districts to proportional representation prior to the 1999 elections, benefited the ELDR. However, as with EPP, this numerical expansion also meant that the group became ideologically more heterogeneous. Particularly the accommodation of Nordic centre parties has proven problematic, especially on integration matters in which the Danish, Finnish and Swedish parties are considerably more Eurosceptical than the group majority. After the 2004 elections the liberal group has 88 MEPs (12 per cent) from 19 member states, the largest seat-share held by the liberals in the Parliament since the first elections held in 1979. The group also changed its name from ELDR to the Alliance of Liberals and Democrats for Europe (ALDE).

The communists, or the radical left, have formed a group under various labels since 1973. The title Nordic Green Left was added to the group name, Confederal Group of the European United Left (EUL-NGL), after the 1995 enlargement. EUL-NGL has 41 MEPs (6 per cent) in the Parliament elected in 2004. The Greens achieved an electoral breakthrough in 1989, and have since then formed a group of their own in the Parliament. They have benefited on average more than most groups from the second-order logic of Euro elections, which favours small parties at the expense of larger mainstream parties. In the fifth Parliament (1999–2004) the Greens formed a group together with representatives from regionalist parties of the European Free Alliance (EFA). The Greens/EFA group has 42 MEPs (6 per cent) in the Parliament elected in 2004.

The conservative party family has been represented by the European Democratic Group (EDG), a group formed around the British Conservatives in 1973 as well as the Gaullist European Democratic Alliance (EDA). The former joined the EPP in 1992 and the latter established the Union for Europe of the Nations (UEN) in 1999. UEN, with 27 MEPs (4 per cent), is the smallest group in the Parliament elected in 2004. It is an alliance of various conservative and Eurosceptic forces, with Alleanza Nazionale from Italy as its leading national party delegation. The extreme-right parties formed a group after the 1984 and 1989 elections. Finally, the anti-EU parties – who have throughout the history of the Parliament been very much in the minority in the chamber – formed the Europe of Nations (EN) group after the 1994 elections and the Europe of Democracies and Diversities (EDD) after the 1999 elections. As a result of the electoral victories gained by

Eurosceptical lists in several countries in the 2004 elections, the former EDD expanded its membership to 37 MEPs (5 per cent) and changed its name to the Independence and Democracy group (IND/DEM). Most non-attached MEPs have been either members of extreme right-wing parties or independents.

The role of party groups in the Parliament

Party groups and committees, and the interaction between them, provide the key to understanding how the EP operates. The party groups have over the decades reformed both their internal rules and the Parliament's rules of procedure, with the explicit goal of strengthening the role of party groups (particularly EPP and PES) in the chamber (Kreppel, 2002).

Group formation is regulated in Rule 29 of the EP's Rules of Procedure:

1. Members may form themselves into groups according to their political affinities. Parliament need not normally evaluate the political affinity of members of a group. In forming a group together under this rule, members concerned accept by definition that they have political affinity. Only when this is denied by the members concerned is it necessary for Parliament to evaluate whether the group has been constituted in conformity with the rules.
2. A political group shall comprise members elected in at least one-fifth of the member states. The minimum number of members required to form a political group shall be nineteen.
3. A member may not belong to more than one political group.
4. The president shall be notified in a statement when a political group is set up. This statement shall specify the name of the group, its members and its bureau.
5. The statement shall be published in the *Official Journal* of the European Union.

The availability of considerable material and procedural benefits acts as a powerful incentive for group formation. It also explains the emergence of technical groups, like the Technical Group of Co-ordination and Defence of Independent MEPs (CDI) in 1979–84, the Rainbow Group in 1984–94, and the short-lived Technical Group of Independent Members (TGI) after the 1999 elections. Material benefits include, for example, office space, staff and money for distributing information. The sum each group receives depends on the number of MEPs and working languages in the group. Turning to procedural rights, appointments to committees and intra-parliamentary leadership positions, and the allocation of reports and plenary speaking time are based on the rule of proportionality between the groups. Certain plenary actions, such as tabling amendments or oral questions, require the backing of a committee, a party group or at least 37 MEPs. Non-attached representatives are thus procedurally marginalised in the chamber.

Appointment of committee seats and chairs and the EP presidency are all controlled by the groups. The President of the EP is elected for two and a half years. The two largest groups, PES and EPP, shared the presidency from 1989 to 1999. This cosy pact was temporarily suspended after the 1999 elections, when a centre-right coalition elected Nicole Fontaine (EPP) as the new president in July 1999. Imitating the deals between EPP and PES, the EPP and ELDR struck an agreement according to which the liberals would support Fontaine and the EPP would in turn back the candidacy of ELDR group leader Pat Cox at mid-term in January 2002. The old alliance between EPP and PES was renewed after the 2004 elections, with the presidency first held by the Spanish socialist Josep Borrell, to be replaced by a member of the EPP at mid-term in January 2007.

Committee assignments are decided in the first session of the newly elected EP held in July. The number and size of the committees are decided first, followed by the appointment of committee members and substitutes. The distribution of committee seats is based on the rule of proportionality, with membership proportional to group size. The majority of members are full members of one committee and substitutes in another one. Committee chairs are highly influential positions. According to the Rules of Procedure committees elect their own chairs, but in practice party groups control the allocation, with the d'Hondt method used for this purpose. Chair allocation is thus roughly proportional to group size, reflecting the procedures found in most European parliaments. Party group co-ordinators are responsible for co-ordinating the work of their groups in the committees. Party groups also have working groups that, to a varying extent, mirror the committee structure.

Committee work revolves around reports. A rapporteur is responsible for drafting a report on the issue handled in the committee. The distribution of rapporteurships is not regulated in the Rules of Procedure. Instead, party groups have developed a system based primarily on the rule of proportionality, with procedures that differ somewhat between the committees. Each group receives a quota of points out of the total point tally based on its share of seats in the committee. Party group co-ordinators and committee chairs decide the value of each report to be produced by the committee, and co-ordinators identify their groups' priority reports and make bids on behalf of their groups in specific co-ordinators' meetings. After a group has won a report, it is distributed to one of its members seated in that committee. The other party groups often nominate a shadow rapporteur to monitor the work of the rapporteur. The rapporteur system means that individual members, and not committee chairs, are the key persons in the passage of individual pieces of legislation. But, when drafting the report, the rapporteur must be prepared to compromise in order to accommodate the views of the committee. Such compromise building is necessary in order to facilitate the smooth passage of the report in the committee and later in the plenary. The draft report, together with amendments, is then voted upon in the committee. Before the plenary stage the groups decide what amendments to propose, and whether to support the report or not. National party delegations, especially the larger ones, often hold their own meetings prior to the group meetings. Finally, the report is introduced in the plenary by the rapporteur and amendments tabled by the committee responsible, a party group or at least 37 members are voted upon.

Embedded in a separation-of-powers system, and with no real EU government to hold accountable, the main function of the Parliament is to influence the EU policy process. That is why the Parliament has delegated the scrutiny of legislation to its committees. Parliament's positions are in most cases decided in the committees before the plenary stage. Both national and party group interests influence committee work. The procedures for allocating committee chairs, seats and reports can be interpreted as mechanisms for the party groups to control the committees in a situation where the former are relatively weak, at least when compared to European national parliaments.

Delegating authority to backbenchers through committee work and reports is also a key way of rewarding group members and tying them into the formation of group positions. However, party group leaders are strongly limited in their ability to direct the actions of their committee members, with national parties possessing – through their right to control candidate selection – at least as much power as party group leaders. With the exception of the assignment process, party group influence within committees is therefore modest, with groups having co-ordinating mechanisms for overseeing committee work instead of hierarchical structures for controlling MEP behaviour in the committees (Mamadouh and Raunio 2003).

Turning next to the organisation of the party groups, they elect their leaders (chairman/president) at the start of the five-year legislative term. The chairs represent their group in the Conference of Presidents, the body responsible for setting the Parliament's agenda and for organisational decisions. The number of vice-chairs varies between the groups. The executive committee of the group is the Bureau, composed of the chair, vice-chairs, heads and possible additional members of national party delegations, and the treasurer. The Bureau is responsible for organisational and administrative issues, and prepares policy decisions for group meetings. Party groups also establish working groups for examining specific policy areas and for co-ordinating group policy on those issues (Raunio 2002).

Lacking the kinds of rewards and sanctions that group leaders normally have at their disposal in national legislatures, the party groups place a lot of emphasis on building consensus in their meetings. Decision-making within groups is often based on protracted negotiations, with group leaders putting much effort into building positions that are acceptable to all or nearly all parties in the group. Unlike national party leaders, EP group chairs do not control or even influence candidate selection, nor can they promise lucrative ministerial portfolios or well-paid civil service jobs. Groups have whips, but they basically just remind MEPs of group positions and indicate which votes are important. The groups convene regularly in Brussels prior to the plenary week as well as during Strasbourg plenaries. The meetings in Brussels constitute a 'Group week', usually lasting two to three days. When MEPs feel they cannot follow the group position, they are expected to make this clear in the group meetings.

National party delegations are the cornerstones upon which the groups are based. Some groups are indeed no more than loose coalitions of national parties, while even in the oldest and most organised groups – EPP and PES – one can occasionally see divisions along national lines. Most national delegations have their own staff, elect their chairpersons, and convene prior to group meetings. However, the impact of national parties is mitigated by three factors. First, national parties are seldom unitary actors themselves. National parties throughout the Union are, to a varying extent, internally divided over integration, and these divisions are reproduced in the Parliament. Second, the EP is a committee-based legislature, with emphasis on building issue-specific majorities in the committees. Third, the majority of bills and resolutions do not produce divisions along national lines. Much of the Parliament's agenda is taken up by internal market legislation, not by constitutional matters or redistributive decisions like the allocation of structural funds.

Roll call analyses indicate that the groups do indeed achieve respectable levels of cohesion, with the cohesion of the larger groups varying between 80 and 90 per cent. The most important reason for this relatively unitary behaviour is policy influence. Cohesive group action is essential for achieving groups' objectives, while co-operative behaviour within groups helps MEPs in pursuing their own policy goals. The voting rules of the legislative procedures also impact on group behaviour and particularly on coalition formation. While the primary decision rule in the Parliament is simple majority (50 per cent + 1 of those voting), for certain issues specified in the Treaty (mainly budget amendments and second reading legislative amendments adopted under the co-decision procedure) the Parliament needs to muster absolute majorities (50 per cent + 1 of its members, 367/732 MEPs after the 2004 elections). Until the 1999 elections the formation of majorities was primarily based on co-operation between PES and EPP. In the fifth Parliament (1999–2004) this co-operation played a lesser role than before, with EPP and PES opposing each other more often regardless of the voting rule. Still, these two large groups voted together on approximately 70 per cent of all votes (Hix et al. 2003). Co-operation between EPP and PES could also be regarded as a sign of 'maturity', as the Parliament needed to moderate its resolutions in order to get its amendments accepted by the Council and the Commission (Kreppel 2002). After all, the overwhelming majority of national ministers represented in the Council and members of the Commission are either social-democrats or Christian democrats/conservatives.

To summarise, the EP party system is dominated by the centre-right EPP and the social-democratic PES. The non-hierarchical group structure, based on institutionalised interaction between the leadership, the committees and the national delegations, facilitates group cohesion. The extensive negotiations taking place both within and between groups, and the need to accommodate national viewpoints, has been argued to lead to lowest common denominator

decisions. However, such policy compromises are a prerequisite for the Parliament to influence EU legislation.

Tapio Raunio

Bibliography

Hix, S., Kreppel, A. and Noury, A., 'The Party System in the European Parliament: Collusive or Competitive?', *Journal of Common Market Studies*, 41, 2, 2003, pp. 309–31.

Kreppel, A., *The European Parliament and Supranational Party System: a Study in Institutional Development*, Cambridge, Cambridge University Press, 2002.

Mamadouh, V. and Raunio, T., 'The Committee System: Powers, Appointments and Report Allocation', *Journal of Common Market Studies*, 41, 2, 2003, pp. 333–51.

Raunio, T., 'Political Interests: the EP's Party Groups', in J. Peterson and M. Shackleton (eds), *The Institutions of the European Union*, Oxford, Oxford University Press, 2002, pp. 257–76.

→ Composition of the European Parliament; European Free Alliance (EFA); European Liberal Democrat and Reform Party (ELDR); European Parliament; European People's Party (EPP); European Political Parties; Internal Elections at the European Parliament; Party of European Socialists (PES); Voting Within the European Parliament.

Parliamentary Mandate

The institutional system established at the origins of the European Communities was fundamentally 'non-parliamentary', and still remains so to some extent. While the European Parliament saw its powers increase spectacularly, it still lacks sovereignty, and remains excluded from some of the EU's crucial decision-making activities. The vast majority of MEPs, who had long hoped that their assembly would, one day, acquire the same powers enjoyed by national parliaments, have abandoned their expectations. They have also given up hopes of being the sole legitimate citizens' representatives within the EU institutional system, acknowledging alternative forms of representation. The persistent 'subsidiary' nature of the electoral logic at EU level also affects the parliamentary mandate.

The paradoxes of parliamentary representation in the European Union

Due to specific institutional characteristics, the weakness of a European public sphere, and the secondary character of European elections, the EU represents an alternative to the traditional state-centred model of representation. While many criticise the weakness of parliamentary representation within the European Union, which they see as generating a 'democratic deficit', alternative models of this political system legitimise it (*Journal of European Public Policy*, 2003). Part of the literature argues that the EU's legitimacy rests above all on a principle of devolution and 'principal/ agent' power control mechanism, rather than on the European Parliament per se (Tallberg 2002).

Within this framework, the Parliament shares legitimisation and representation functions with other institutions (Council, Commission, Economic and Social Council, Committee of the Regions), along with several interest groups and European civil society. The European Union differentiates itself through the pluralism of its modes of representation, and through the absence of a structured hierarchy amongst them. In fact, there is no functional equivalent to parliamentary sovereignty within the EU, whose political system is fundamentally un-hierarchical and multi-polar. The

affirmation of the European Parliament's authority clashes with an internal mechanism based on consensus and expertise that puzzles citizens, in particular in states where a majoritarian logic is perceived as democracy's driving force. Indeed, right–left cleavages are far from salient in the European Parliament, due to majority rule in the legislative and budgetary fields, the converging views of socialist, liberal, and Christian democrat groups on European integration, and the importance of the national dimension on some issues.

The MEP mandate: European or national?

The European Parliament's lack of normalisation, as well as the 'vagueness' of the European mandate, make political representation at the supranational level even more problematic. The EC Treaty, the Act on European Elections of 20 September 1976, and the EP's rules of procedure fail to clarify the nature of the European mandate. Neither doctrine, nor jurisprudence, nor parliamentary practice have specified things. In fact, one must settle for an *a minima* definition of the mandate, focused on two elements: the proscription of the imperative mandate and the affirmation of its 'general' nature.

Article 4 of the 1976 Act and the EP's Rules of Procedure stipulate that MEPs 'cannot be attached to specific instructions, nor receive an imperative mandate' (European Parliament 1977). The EP was confronted at several points with the interpretation of this principle, and has always defended it in its broadest sense, as in the 1980s, when certain parties expected their representatives to resign prior to the expiration of their mandate, asking for this purpose, for blank letters of resignation!

While this point is clear, the nature and existence of state-centred relations between voters and representatives are rather blurred. Article 189 of the TEU stipulates that the European Parliament is composed of representatives of 'the peoples of the member states'. However, the Treaty does not allow for the determination of what 'peoples of the member states' actually means. In fact, it fails to specify whether MEPs are to represent their respective fellow citizens so as to collectively express the sum of general national interests, or whether they should collectively represent the European people as a whole. While apparently purely theoretical, this is a question that arose very concretely when the Maastricht Treaty was first enforced. A number of MEPs had in fact suggested the exclusion of their British and Danish colleagues from votes on policies which their countries choose to stay out of (e.g. the euro). It was on this occasion that MEPs expressed their views on the general nature of their mandate, arguing that they represented a single and un-dividable electoral body. Their choice clashed with the legal doctrine, which confirms the existence of ties between states and their respective delegations in the European Parliament (Constantinesco 1992). Legal experts claim that such ties are not the mere result of past practices, since they were reaffirmed during the Maastricht Treaty's negotiations (Cloos et al. 1993). During the drafting of a new proposal for uniform EP elections in 1998, the Parliament's legal team also questioned the 'integrated' approach to the interpretation of the European mandate. The draft European Constitution refrains from commenting on this debate, stating that 'the European Parliament is composed of representatives of citizens of the European Union' (Article I-20.2), and confirming the national character of seat distribution.

Aside from divergent interpretations, the definition of the mandate clashes with the specificities of the modes of election, organisation and deliberation of the European Parliament. To begin with, representatives are still elected on the basis of national procedures. While proportional representation was applied in all member states in 1999, the diversity of electoral regulations (prerequisites for eligibility, size and number of constituencies, thresholds, distribution of votes, etc.), the focus of electoral campaigns on national political issues, and the uncontested power of national parties over the appointment of candidates, all clash with the theory of the 'generality' of the European mandate. The under-determination of this mandate largely stems from the coexistence within the European Parliament of different parliamentary traditions and diverging perceptions of what constitutes general interests and what representation is about. This can be seen either as a match between the EP and the represented group, as the symbolic expression of feelings of inclusion of the citizens, or as a sign of the quality of representatives (competence and devotion). To some, it also evokes the capacity of judgement of the institution (constructive and independent deliberation), its loyalty to an executive or even to a policy. While all these definitions of representation are equally valid, they command different conceptions of mandate. The empirical definition also clashes with the instability of the organisation and functioning of the European Parliament, deriving from the 'youth' of the institution, the volatility of its composition, the evolution of the European constitutional framework, and the permanent search for power and legitimacy of European representatives. More than 25 years after their first direct elections, MEPs remain trapped in an 'experimental' phase of their practice, and defend their contrasting conceptions of relations with institutions, civil society, citizens and territory.

The contrasting and multiple practices of parliamentary mandates

As is often the case within the EU, these divergences have been largely silenced. With the exception of the aforementioned cases, questions relating to the nature of the European mandate are not debated in the European Parliament. Consequently, MEPs enjoy greater freedom of action and choice of principals (voters, national or European citizens, national parties, political groups, population groups), and even adapt their practices to changing circumstances. The behaviour of each representative can be seen as a response to a complex and moving combination of factors of different nature, such as the voting system, rules of candidate selection, the degree of implication of national parties in the functioning of the European Parliament; the carrying out of other mandates, the worry of re-election or re-appointment; and the organisation of the various political groups, media attention to EP's activities, etc. The sensitivity of MEPs to these variables depends, of course, on personal factors such as nationality, views on European integration, their political beliefs, relationship with territory, as well as their personal 'profile' (retired national politicians, representatives of civil society, newcomers, MEPs carrying out other important mandates). The various factors that affect their conception of representation have been studied by Hausemer (forthcoming).

The doubts (or, to some extent, the advantages) relating to the nature of the European mandate are also linked with the challenges affecting all types of political representation. But the paradoxes of political representation are thus very sensitive within the European Parliament because the mandate of members remains largely unspecified. They are supposed to serve a general interest, but nobody seems to be sure of how to conceive it.

Olivier Costa

Bibliography

Cloos, J., Reinisch, G., Vignes, D. and Weyland, J., *Le Traité de Maastricht: genèse, analyse, commentaires*, Bruxelles, Bruylant, 1993.

Constantinesco V., 'Article 137', in V. Constantinesco, J.-P. Jaqué, R. Kovar and D. Simon (eds), *Traité instituant la CEE: commentaire article par article*, Paris, Economica, 1992, pp. 803–12.

European Parliament (Secrétariat – Direction générale de la recherche et de la documentation), *Elections du Parlement européen au suffrage universel direct. Rapport, résolutions et débats du Parlement européen*, Luxembourg, Office des publications officielles des Communautés européennes, 1977.

Hausemer, P., 'Participation and Political Competition in Committee Report Allocation: Under What Conditions do MEPs Represent Their Constituents?' *EU Politics*, 7, 4, forthcoming.

Journal of European Public Policy, special issue 'The Diffusion of Democracy: Emerging Forms and Norms of Democratic Control in the European Union', 10, 5, 2003.

Pitkin, H., *The Concept of Representation*, Berkeley, University of California Press, 1968.

Tallberg, J., 'Delegation to Supranational Institutions: Why, How, and with What Consequences?', *West European Politics*, 25, 1, 2002, pp. 23–46.

→ Civil Society; Democratic Deficit; Election Manifestos; Electoral System; European Electoral Act; European Parliament; European Public Sphere; Interest Groups; Lobbying; Members of the European Parliament (Legal and Political Status); Members of the European Parliament (Sociology of Political Office); Parliamentary Groups; Representation; Symbols and Practice of Elections; Voting Within the European Parliament.

Partisan Identification

The concept of partisan identification

In 1960, Campbell et al. described in *The American Voter* how the 'Michigan model of the vote' could explain the way voters made their decision. They claimed that voters identify, to varying degrees, with the different parties competing in a given system. This 'partisan identification', consists of (1) a preferred party and (2) the strength of identification with this party. Combined with an individual voter's assessment of short-term factors, it would explain why some citizens vote while others do not, and why the ones who do will cast their vote in a particular way. The strength of an individual's partisan identification will determine the likelihood of his decision being influenced by short-term factors, so that the less strong a citizen's partisan identification, the more influential his perceptions of short-term factors. One can, therefore, conceive the voting decision as the following equation:

$$\text{Vote} = a.\text{PID} + (1\text{-}a)\ \text{STF} \quad [\text{equation 1}]$$

where PID is the party the voter identifies with and STF his assessment of short-term factors. 'a' is the strength of the voter's partisan identification on a scale from 0 to 1, so that '1-a' really expresses the 'room' a voter has to consider short-term factors in his decision. In this sense, 'a' is also a coefficient of stability in the voter's decision over time, while '1-a' will express the voter's flexibility to react to such elements as the contenders' campaigns, programmes, personalities, records, etc.

Short-term factors may include the personality of candidates, the issues at stake in a particular election, the specific temporary circumstances of a given voter, and the campaign of the parties and candidates. Partisan identification, at the same time, is conceived by Campbell et al. as being relatively stable over time, and probably influenced by factors such as early socialisation, citizens' stance on social cleavages, and their environment.

In terms of socialisation, Butler and Stokes (1970) have shown the extent to which partisan identification is inherited by children from their parents. In terms of social origins, however, it is usually the Lipset and Rokkan model (see related articles on social cleavages and political sociology) which is used to describe how political parties emerged along the lines of four main cleavages (centre/periphery, religious/secular, rural/urban, owners/workers), that constrained the identification of a majority of voters with 'their' natural party until the 1960s.

In the American context, it has long seemed that the Michigan model of the vote has been the best existing model when it came to predicting citizens' electoral behaviour. In the European context, this model has long performed well too, but changing party systems as well as claims of realignments and/or dealignments taking place in most major political systems have restricted the explanatory capacity of this model over the past few decades.

In the context of the 2004 European Parliament elections, it is interesting to consider the impact of partisan identification on citizens' attitudes for a variety of reasons. Firstly, because it is important to know whether the erosion of citizens' partisan identification, often associated with the decline in traditional party politics, is continuing. Secondly, within the context of a second-order election, partisan identification should play less of a role than in first-order elections, and dissatisfied voters with weak partisan identification may have a greater incentive to vote for protest parties, than core voters of governing parties have to vote for their own preferred party. Thirdly, the 2004 European Parliament elections provided scholars with an opportunity to test the power of realignment and dealignment theories in Europe in a comparative context and within globally comparable circumstances.

The concepts of realignment and dealignment

While the traditional Michigan model of the vote implies expectations of a relative stability of individual voters' preferences, the increasing instability of voting patterns at the aggregate level in Europe, as well as the multiplying proportion of voters individually claiming to switch their preferences election after election, have resulted in a need for new theories explaining electoral change.

While the concept of realignment was first used in the American case, the changes in voters' behaviour occurring in most European political systems since the 1970s have given it a new meaning in the European context. In particular, the emergence of new parties on the left (Green parties in particular) and on the right (extreme right and new right populist parties) of the ideological spectrum have led several prominent scholars to hypothesise a change in the way citizens' preferences are structured. Post-materialist theories in particular (Inglehart 1977) claim that a new cleavage opposing younger post-materialist voters to 'traditional' materialist voters has transformed the traditional pattern of partisan identification of voters along cleavage lines.

However, many authors question the relevance of the realignment theory, suggesting that the main mass transformation observed in Western Europe over the past 30 years is one of dealignment (Franklin et al. 1992). While a realignment is the evolution of a stable system towards another stable system built around different dimensions, a dealignment is the evolution from a system of stability towards a system of instability and volatility in which large numbers of voters actually lose their attachment to the political parties competing in the system. In other words, while a realignment will consist of a *change* of partisan identification for most voters without its relative impact on the voter's decision being reduced, a dealignment will consist of weakening partisan identification for most voters, whose final decision will be less predictable, and affected more by short-term factors as explained in equation (1).

The state of partisan identification in the European Union in 2004

It is always difficult to compare levels of partisan identification across countries because the type of party system and electoral system varies substantially across countries and undoubtedly affects the way citizens relate to political parties. For example, under the single transferable vote (the electoral system used in Ireland), citizens are to a certain extent encouraged to feel closer to not one but several political parties to varying degrees. However, a reasonably good measure of partisan identification is provided by the European Social Survey, which asked citizens of 22 European countries, including all 15 pre-2004 member states of the European Union and four of the newcomers whether they felt close to any political party more than the others, and how close they felt to this party.

Table 1 reports the levels of party identification in these 19 member-states as of 2003. Across the European Union, approximately as many citizens declared feeling closer to one political party than to any other ones, as those who do not. However, we can see that great variations

Table 1   Partisan identification in 19 member states (2003)

Country	Attached	Not attached	Strong	Moderate	Weak
Sweden	68.5	31.5	9.4	43.6	15.6
Portugal	67.2	32.8	10.5	31.7	24.9
Denmark	66.9	33.1	7.3	36.8	22.7
Hungary	59.8	40.2	13.6	42.2	3.9
Netherlands	58.1	41.9	5.5	46.8	5.8
Greece	57.5	42.5	15.6	36.3	5.5
Austria	55.2	44.8	7.9	37.4	9.9
Finland	55.0	45.0	4.3	35.1	15.5
TOTAL	*52.3*	*47.7*	*6.6*	*33.0*	*12.6*
Spain	50.1	49.9	5.2	27.7	17.3
France	49.9	50.1	5.3	29.3	15.3
UK	48.0	52.0	3.6	28.5	15.9
Germany	47.9	52.1	4.3	30.9	12.8
Belgium	47.8	52.2	5.3	31.9	10.6
Czech Republic	47.4	52.6	5.0	28.7	13.7
Ireland	46.5	53.5	4.9	24.9	16.7
Italy	44.9	55.1	8.1	33.3	3.5
Luxembourg	40.4	59.6	3.0	14.5	22.8
Slovenia	36.1	63.9	3.2	20.8	12.1
Poland	28.7	71.3	2.0	16.2	10.6

Notes:
Countries are entered in decreasing order of citizens expressing some partisan identification.
The first two columns summarise the proportion of citizens declaring to have, and not have, some partisan identification. Their total is always 100.
The last three columns distinguish, within the proportion of respondents declaring some partisan identification, the figures for strong, moderate and weak identifiers. Their total is always equal to the 'Yes' column (except for rounding effect).
Figures are calculated using the raw data of the 2003 European Social Survey.
The 'total' row includes respondents from all 19 member states in the table, as well as Switzerland, Norway and Israel. The inclusion of these three countries has little effect. It only slightly increases the proportion of identifiers.

exist across countries. In Sweden, Portugal and Denmark, more than two-thirds of the respondents declared some attachment to a political party, while in Poland, this proportion approaches a quarter, and in Slovenia, a third. Overall, startlingly, at the beginning of the twenty-first century, the European electorate seems to be split into two more or equal parts which do and do not attach to a given political party. It also means that half of the European political electorate is quite likely to vote more or less systematically for 'their' party while the other half will have to be 'won', election after election, by the parties in competition.

In general, partisan identification on the eve of the 2004 European Parliament elections seemed to be strongest in Scandinavia and most of Southern Europe, as well as in Hungary. On the other hand, it was particularly weak in Central European countries (except for Hungary), and also in the traditional 'heart' of the European Union, including five of the six founding members (the exception being the Netherlands), as well as Spain and the United Kingdom.

Looking at countries in which a high proportion of citizens remain *strongly* attached to a political party, however, it is clear that the highly polarised party systems and perhaps more deeply rooted cleavages of Southern and Northern Europe are more conducive to strong partisan identification than the West and East European political systems.

Altogether, these figures confirm that partisan identification is resisting relatively less well in Europe than in the United States, where about two-thirds of the voters still tend to hold some party identification and call themselves Democrat or Republican. This erosion is particularly emphasised in the secular centre-west of the European continent, and in the disillusioned newly democratic countries of Central Europe. The figures show that about half of the voters of an average European country would make up their mind for a general election on the sole basis of their assessment of 'short-term factors' such as the campaign, programmes, media coverage and personality of the candidates or else chose to abstain. In the context of the European Parliament elections themselves, the relatively low salience of the election in the mass media explains why a large proportion of the voters, without any partisan identification, will have probably chosen to abstain rather than to face the particularly high cost of getting informed about candidates and their programmes.

A natural consequence of this decreasing trend of partisan identification, combined with the relative lack of information about the European election was the high proportion of European voters who claimed not to be sure about who they would vote for a relatively short time before the election. In early June, in France, this proportion was about 30 per cent of the respondents. In the United Kingdom, at the same time, about 35 per cent of the people surveyed still said that they were unsure about their choice and could still change their minds.

Conclusions

Over the past 30 years, most European countries have experienced a sharp decrease in voters' levels of partisan identification, symptomatic of a serious partisan dealignment. In some countries – particularly in Scandinavia and Southern Europe – traditional identification of voters with the existing parties remains relatively strong, while in most secular Western European countries, such as France, the UK, Italy and Ireland, a majority of voters do not identify with any political party at all.

While the citizens who claim to be strong identifiers will have also tended to be faithful to the parties they identify with, this proportion has become so low in some political systems that the final difference in the 2004 European Parliament elections was clearly made by the more volatile voters who do not feel attached to any particular party. For this reason, while partisan identification remains a particularly good predictor of a voter's choice at the individual level in a low salience election such as the European Parliament one, the state of party identification in European countries has become, at the aggregate level, highly disconnected with the final results of the election. Up to half of the voters who participated in June will have made up their mind on the basis of short-term assessment of parties, campaigns, national and European issues, and candidates, and, more than anything else, will have primarily wanted to express discontent with their national governments as in any second-order election, rather than wanted to express some particular attachment to one party or other. In

June 2004, and probably in all the elections that will follow, political parties had no choice but to win the hearts and minds of voters to achieve a face-saving score.

Michael Bruter

Bibliography

Butler, D. and Stokes, D., *Political Change in Britain: Forces Shaping Electoral Choice*, Basingstoke, Macmillan, 1970.

Campbell, A., Converse, A., Miller, D. and Stokes, D., *The American Voter*, New York, Wiley, 1960.

European Social Survey (available on-line at http://ess.nsd.uib.no/nesstarlight/index.jsp).

Franklin, M. N., Mackie, T. and Valen, H. (eds), *Electoral Change: Responses to Evolving Social and Attitudinal Structures in Western Countries*, Cambridge, Cambridge University Press, 1992.

Inglehart, R., *The Silent Revolution: Changing Values and Political Styles Among Western Publics*, Princeton, Princeton University Press, 1977.

Lipset, S. M. and Rokkan, S., *Party Systems and Voters Alignments: Cross-national Perspectives*, London, Collier Macmillan, 1967.

→ Electoral Behaviour; European Electoral Sociology; Identity.

Party of European Socialists (PES)

Following the initiative of the Dutch PvdA, the Liaison Bureau of the Socialist Parties of the European Community was created in January 1957, in Luxembourg, thus giving life to the first European socialist structure with transnational aspirations. The initiative consisted in promoting an interparty co-operation which, up until that point, only occurred between socialist parliamentary members of the ECSC Common Assembly.

The objectives of the Liaison Bureau, formulated during the various congresses of the six founding parties, were clear and vast: to build a common programme concerning the political integration of Europe (Fourth Conference of the Socialist Parties of the EEC, Strasbourg, May 1960), to affirm as a long-term political goal the creation of the 'United States of Europe' (federal option), to work towards the geographical enlargement of the Community, and to influence the construction of Europe towards a more left-wing direction (Fifth Congress, Paris, November 1962). These ambitious political objectives were reconfirmed throughout all the later resolutions (see for example the document entitled *Towards a Social Europe*, Ninth Congress, Bonn, April 1973) and they provided the key elements of a common political agenda progressively established by the socialists. To advance towards a more regular and better constructed interpartisan co-operation constituted the other agenda, the *internal* agenda, of the Liaison Bureau.

The PES before the PES: from the Liaison Bureau to the Confederation

The European project at that period encountered difficulties which, having been amplified during the 1960s by the politics of General de Gaulle, did not support the advancement of the objectives of the European socialists, nor the establishment of a true transnational partisan pillar. The organisational structure for socialist co-operation was rudimentary, being based on two bodies, the Liaison Bureau itself and the plenary body, the Conference (since 1962: the Congress) of the socialist parties of the EEC. In terms of organisational integration, the Liaison Bureau, as indicated by its title, had a structure which was neither compact nor very complex or constraining, partly simulating the model of the Socialist Internationale. The Bureau never became a true transnational organisation: its role was minimal, without any real impact on the life of the national parties. However, it should be stressed that the Bureau showed a relatively high degree of programmatic cohesion (notably following the turning point of Bad Godesberg of the SPD and the determined commitment, since then, of the German Social-Democrats to support European integration). Being ideologically rather cohesive, the Bureau soon managed to develop a political project for Europe at that time. This European project – and plea – was the keystone of socialist co-operation until the early 1970s. Admittedly, the division of European socialists into two groups, those who defended Community integration (six) and those who were rather 'free-traders' (notably the British, Scandinavians and Austrians), largely reduced the representative credentials of the Bureau. The programme of the Bureau, however, even though it was not consistently concrete nor firmly framed and not in a position to suggest the necessary means and transitions for its realisation, went far beyond the Community status quo. In launching a rather straightforward attack on particular problems, and by not concealing its choices behind a smokescreen of rhetoric, the Liaison Bureau (renamed in 1971 the Office of the Social Democratic Parties of the European Community) produced a real programmatic guide for the Community socialists in the 'small Europe' of six.

The Confederation of the Socialist Parties of the European Community (CSPEC) was founded in April 1974, succeeding the Office of the Social Democratic Parties of the European Community. It was an ambitious organisational response to the relaunch of Community dynamics of the time, notably to the European enlargement of the Community (effective in 1973), and to the prospect of the first European elections by direct universal suffrage. However, in spite of its transnational goals, the Confederation failed to revive the political coherence of the Community socialism of the 1960s. The arrival of new, rather Eurosceptical, members (British Labour, Irish Labour Party, Danish Social-Democrats) resulted in a loss of cohesion which, of course, was balanced by a gain in representativeness. Moreover, during the 1970s, the move of certain parties towards the left (and their critical attitude towards the EEC) released centrifugal tendencies, rather adverse to transnational European strategies or to the very construction of a partisan organisation. The impossibility of formulating a common programme for the 1979 European elections (member parties issued a mere 'Appeal to the Electorate'), the revision of the Confederation's statutes in 1980 (towards supporting consensus and autonomy of the national parties), and the four-year delay of the first CSPEC congress (1979) perfectly illustrate the difficulties faced by the CSPEC. In fact, concerning the federal option, the Confederation was far from the Community Social-Democrats of the 1960s, and also from the European People's Party (EPP), which, right from the start, declared its determination, confirmed in the statutes, for the federalisation of Europe. Not only were the socialists unable to direct the process of European Community construction but they gave of themselves, notably during the 1970s, the image of a divided political family with an uncertain 'European' commitment.

Does the Confederation period signal a dramatic 'correction' of the socialist policy towards unification? Does it signal a weakening of the collaboration towards the construction of a transnational partisan pillar? Positive answers to both questions should be supplied with important reservations. The national party leaders' summit was institutionalised during this period (it was decided in 1987 that the summit conferences would be held bi-annually and would precede the Council meetings). A mechanism was hence established in order to bind, albeit in a mediate way, the objectives of the socialist parties to the European Council agenda (Hix and Lesse 2002: 29 and 42–3). The method of forming working groups to develop certain aspects of CSPEC policy, which would be extended and reinforced in the 1990s, also dates to this period. Moreover, notably after the mid-1980s, the ideological and programmatic divergences eventually weakened and a certain 'intimate atmosphere' started to settle, often at the higher level, within the Confederation. Taking into account this tendency towards improved co-ordination and an intensification of exchanges, the creation of the PES in 1992 fitted neatly into the final period of the CSPEC's development.

The difficulties encountered by the CSPEC – at times also its impotence and paralysis – emanate from the real situation of socialism in Europe, whose impossible cohesion they reflect. They also emanate from the fact that the parties' members, as stated by Guy Spitaels, the last Confederation's chairman, 'do not take seriously' the CSPEC (cited by Kulahci 2003: 80). Deep down, the CSPEC's difficulties signify the end of optimistic, political or scientific expectations relating to the dynamics of European federation parties. The convergence of the various approaches and ideas within the latter could only happen slowly, more slowly than originally envisaged, by a gradual process and only by methods which would not run up against national interests. The events of the CSPEC, the great difficulties and stagnation of the first period, and the slow progression over the latter part of the 1980s, demonstrated the virtues of a more pragmatic approach.

The PES: a balanced assessment

The creation of the Party of European Socialists (PES), in November 1992, constitutes a new stage in the co-operation of Community's socialists. The objective clearly asserted by the promoters of this internal reform was to create 'a political instrument to enable socialists to exert a decisive influence in the European Community' whilst orienting itself towards the creation of a 'true party' (Guy Spitaels, *Activity Report of the Confederation*, 1990–1992). And this took place within the framework of an accelerated process of integration, following the adoption of the Single European Act (1987) and the Maastricht Treaty (1992), but also within a framework of increased politicisation of the process in question. Moreover, the internationalisation of markets and economic constraints, which deprived the left of 'the control of the solutions' at the national level, led the Social-Democrat elites to turn more towards Europe. The intellectual and ideological perception of the supranational level as politically 'important' by the Social-Democrat elites and also by an increasing proportion of the *peuple de gauche*, is a decisive development in this direction. The construction of the PES attests to these developments. National parties are gradually beginning 'to take seriously' the Euro parties.

Faced with the contradictions of the preceding phase, the PES clearly contributed to the resourcing, reorganisation and deepening of co-operation within European socialism. The PES was gradually recognised as the undisputed organisational centre of the co-ordination of socialists at the EU level, imparting a new dynamic to social-democratic regional 'integration'.

More homogeneous than the Confederation, the PES appears, nowadays, more unified and better armed than the EPP (whose strategy to encompass the maximum number of Conservative parties has hence called its 'federalist' capacity into question) to lead 'coherent' actions within the European institutions. The party has come a long way since the period of the 1970s, or the early 1980s, when adoption of the electoral manifesto proved to be a perilous exercise: rather, this adoption has now become, according to the phrase used by Urs Lesse (Hix and Lesse 2002: 83), 'a routine'. Much time has also elapsed since the British Labour Party, the traditional 'troublemaker' within the Confederation, first demonstrated a Eurosceptic mood, systematically emphasising thereafter Labour's unique characteristics. In this respect, it is not unimportant that a British member, Robin Cook, was elected president of the party in 2001. Today, all the member parties of the PES are more or less supportive of European integration (despite their important differences). The convergence of opinions over significant issues and political choices (such as the economy) has also grown significantly. The socialists are no longer as divided as they seemed to be and certainly they no longer 'lag behind integration'.

In addition to the tendency towards programmatic convergence, the party now enjoys a greater operational capacity in its transactions with the other actors on the European scene. It exercises a certain influence – and pressure – on the Community's decision-making bodies, notably through summit meetings and through the socialist group in the European Parliament. In this respect, meetings of the national socialist leaders, held under the guise of the Leaders' Conference (recognised in the statutes, since 1992, as an organ of the PES), or the pre-Council meetings, although irregular in the 1970s and 1980s, became increasingly regular and were held at very constant intervals during the 1990s.

The first PES president, the Flemish Willy Claes (1992–4) and his successor, the German Rudolf Scharping (1995–2001) significantly contributed to the uninterrupted operation of the summits as well as to their internal reform, aiming at the increase of participants. Such meetings have given occasion for real dialogue, and they contributed to the creation of a 'true ethos' of co-operation at the highest level; they also contributed to a certain 'Europeanisation' of the left–right cleavage. However, the most important contribution – beyond the integrative effect – of these meetings, is that they exert a certain influence on the Council agenda and, consequently, on the decision-making within the EU. Admittedly, the PES programmatic initiatives, undertaken by the working groups (whose importance is clearly reinforced in the PES), and adopted by the party, are rather rarely adopted by the European Council (Kulahci 2003). It is nonetheless important to highlight that the summit meetings became a driving force for the revitalisation of the PES, whilst also representing, in some aspects, the reintroduction and the reinforcement of an intergovernmental logic in the internal workings of the party (Moschonas 2002: 272–4).

It should also be underlined that the PES assumes, more now than in the past, the role of 'focal organisation' (Ladrech 2000), co-ordinating better the national parties with the parliamentary group. In fact, the PES currently seems more fit to influence the activity of the socialist members of the Parliament (who traditionally have a strong political and logistical autonomy), notably through the reinforcement of links of contact and collaboration between the president of the group and the leading party authorities. Moreover, the 'spirit of party' – the feeling of belonging to a transnational organisation which stretches beyond the walls of the Parliament auditorium – is felt more acutely amongst the socialist members of the Parliament.

The path travelled in comparison to the CSPEC is by no means negligible. However, there are significant weaknesses in this process, which are largely indicative of the limits encountered by a Europe of nations struggling to become a Europe of parties. Firstly, the PES acts largely as a closed vessel: it lacks direct organisational contact with European societies and fails to exert a *direct* political influence on the national party elites. Moreover, the threshold of public visibility has not yet been crossed, or even approached. Admittedly, particularly after 1997 – when the PES Congress, held immediately after the victories of Tony Blair and Lionel Jospin, largely attracted the attention of the media – congresses and summit meetings continue to be given coverage, albeit a small one, in both the electronic media and the newspapers. The PES does not yet have the image and recognition of a *real and influential* actor amongst public opinions in Europe, as confirmed by the 'failing Europeanisation' of the European campaigns in 2004. Also, the PES's programmatic discourse is habitually formulated in an equivocal and irresolute manner, thus blurring the clarity of the message. The often merely declaratory character of this discourse is indicative of an immature transnational construction. The PES – just like the other Euro parties – remains essentially a weak structure, hardly likely to function as a true political force. This fact led the Danish Poul Nyrup Rasmussen, who, with a very short majority, was elected in April 2004 as the new president of the PES, to resume the founding objectives of 1992 and to affirm its will 'to make the PES a true European party'. The task will undoubtedly be difficult.

All in all, the PES as a structure for the co-ordination of socialist action in Europe has been successful: this is demonstrated through the reinforcement of its influence, the renovation of its organisation and also the inclusion of the maximum number of national parties in its ranks. As the narrow historical circle of 'Community Socialists' tends now to be identified with the broad circle of 'European Socialists', the PES represents the entire social-democratic family in Europe. The desire to join the party, fully confirmed during the 2004 enlargement, makes the PES an important and inevitable point of reference for the national socialist parties and their leaders. The PES has become a tool for member parties: it creates a bond between the individual parties so that any attempt 'to act European' must be collective (Ladrech 2005: 56). Admittedly, the PES will have to manage, *inter alia*, the enlargement of 2004 and its contradictions. However, in addition to the fact that enlargement towards Central and Eastern Europe will lead to more problematic consequences for the EPP-ED and its parliamentary group than for the PES, the probability of a new cleavage within the PES between the 15 and the new joining countries is very low. The PES has many weaknesses, but it constitutes an important constraint (and a 'system of engagement') for the member parties. It has demonstrated its capacity to build coherence amongst its own elites. Certainly, the distance to be covered towards real cohesion within socialism in Europe remains considerable. But for the co-ordination of socialist action in Europe, the PES is a structure 'that cannot be ignored'. However, it remains a 'party of parties' and, even in its strengthened form, a weak institution. It is not developed enough as a transnational structure to forcefully influence the strategy of national parties and fill the most important gap of socialist action in Europe: the absence of a social-democratic project for the EU. The socialist parties have yet to implement, according to the expression used by Robert Ladrech, a kind of transnational 'Bad Godesberg' on Europe (Ladrech 2005: 54).

Gerassimos Moschonas

Bibliography

Devin, G., 'L'Union des Partis Socialistes de la Communauté européenne: Le socialisme communautaire en quête d'identité', in Coll. (ed.), *I Socialisti e l'Europa*, Milan, Franco Angeli, 1989, pp. 265–90.

Hix, S. and Lesse, U., *Shaping a Vision: a History of the Party of European Socialists, 1957–2002*, Brussels, Party of European Socialists, 2002.

Kulahci, E., 'Le Parti des socialistes européens et le défi de légitimité socio-économique de l'UE', PhD dissertation, Université Libre de Bruxelles, 2003.

Ladrech, R., *Social Democracy and the Challenge of European Union*, Boulder, Lynne Rienner, 2000.

Ladrech, R., 'Programmatic Change in the Party of European Socialists', in P. Delwit (ed.), *Social Democracy in Europe*, Brussels, Editions de l'Université Libre de Bruxelles, 2005, pp. 49–57.

Moschonas, G., *In the Name of Social Democracy: The Great Transformation: 1945 to the Present*, New York, Verso, 2002.

➜ Cleavages; Election Manifestos; European Parliament; European Political Parties; European Public Sphere; Europeanisation (of National Political Life); Federations of Political Parties; Left; Members of the European Parliament (Sociology of Political Office); Parliamentary Groups; Partisan Identification; Representation.

Poland

The first Polish European elections were marked by a high level of abstention (79.1 per cent) that it would be tempting to attribute to the 'weakness' of democracy supposedly inherent to post-communist countries. However, this level of abstention, like other characteristics of the elections, seems on the contrary to follow an accentuated version of the 'sociological laws' that govern EP elections in the former Europe of the 15. The observations that follow therefore look at the Polish EP elections as representative of electoral practice in Central and Eastern Europe in general.

Classifications and reclassifications in the political game

First of all, the Polish case seems to reflect the 'second-order elections' model, according to which EP elections are marked by national stakes and reorganisations in the domestic political game. Thus, the competition for the 54 MEP seats allocated to Poland, which were clearly disconnected from the system of national political life that give access to public honours, has been the object of only a moderate commitment given the lower chances it offered to take over a key position in politics. On the other hand, the electoral law passed for this election, from certain points of view encouraged a regression towards stakes of national 'electoral policy' by introducing a threshold of 5 per cent of the ballots on the national scale (the country, however, being divided into 13 regional constituencies), with the consequence of making more visible the classification and reclassification of stakes between parties as between leaders or teams within parties almost one year before the legislative elections. The election system offered to voters the possibility of ticking the names of candidates of their own choosing and it planned to recalculate the seats allocated according to the turnout.

Due to the predicted defeat of the social-democrat group the ex-communist SLD (Sojuz Lewicy Demockratycznej, Democratic Left Alliance), in power since 2001, caused by the governmental crisis and the subsequent collapse of the coalition, the main issue of the election was the opposition's accession to leadership. At the head of the major opposition parliamentary group, the pro-European and social-liberal PO (Platforma Obywatelska, Citizens' Platform), was neck and neck in the polls with the Samoobrona (Self-Defence) movement. This organisation, composed of both mainstay unionist and partisan forces, often described as populist, proclaimed itself the mouth-piece of the peasantry and more broadly of the 'losers' of social and economic transformation of the 1990s and does not hesitate to obstruct democratic procedures or to break the law. During the campaign, this party came into conflict with the national electoral commission (PKW), in charge of monitoring the elections, because Samoobrona wished its representatives in polling stations to wear the striped white and red tie (using the colours of the Polish flag) that had become the rallying sign of this party, which the PKW considered as a violation of the ban on campaigning on polling day.

The outsider position was openly claimed by the Polish clerical ultra-traditionalist party, the LPR (Liga Polskich Rodzin, Polish Family League), whose leader declared for instance in April 2004 that 'only the LPR could defeat the PO and Samoobrona' (*Gazeta Wyborcza*, 4 April 2004). Some polls gave the third position to the PiS grouping (Prawo i Sprawiedliwosc, Law and Justice). This party had focused its campaign on security and moralisation of public life in the 2001 legislative elections. Given the power struggle such positioning had entailed, the order at the start of the lists

was not the one expected, with the PO leading very clearly (24.1 per cent) followed by the PLPR (15.9 per cent), then the PiS (12.7 per cent) and the Samoobrona relegated to fourth position (Table 1).

Another source of surprise was the crossing of the threshold of 5 per cent of the votes by two groupings that were considered to be 'dead', the Peasants Party, PSL (Polskie Stronnictwo Ludowe) and the Social-Liberal Party UW (Unia Wolnosci, Freedom Union). Concerning the PSL (6.3 per cent), its predicted electoral downward trend can be interpreted as a slight failure compared to its 1997 results but also its breakthrough in the 1993 legislative elections (15.4 per cent, which means 2.2 million ballots), often used as a point of reference but much beyond the million ballots it seems likely to win from one election to another. Furthermore, these EP elections confirmed its presence in its traditional strongholds (in particular Lublin and Mazovia). In the case of the UW (7.3 per cent), its good results can be related to the political credit stature of some of its leaders, such as Bronislaw Geremek (former Minister of Foreign Affairs) or Jan Kulakowski (former Polish negotiator in the pre-accession negotiations), who were seen as legitimate spokesmen on European issues and valuable representatives of Poland in the EU.

On the other hand, the SLD in power, which had made a list with governmental coalition partner UP (Unia Pracy, Labour Union), achieved only 9.4 per cent of the ballots due to SdPl's competition (Socjaldemokracja Polska, Social-Democracy of Poland) (5.3 per cent), created after its scission. One curious sign of the Polish disappointment towards the post-1989 democratic regime, is the fact that among the MEPs sent by the SLD to the EP was Adam Gierek, son of Edward Gierek, first secretary of the Communist Party between

Table 1   Results of the EP elections in Poland in 2004

Registered	29 986 109
Voters	6 258 550
Abstention	79.13%
Invalid	197 019 (2.67%)

Lists*	Ballots (%)	Seats
Citizens' Platform (PO)	1 467 775 (24.10)	15
Polish Family League (LPR)	969 689 (15.92)	10
Law and Justice (PiS)	771 858 (12.67)	9
Self-Defence (Samoobrona)	656 782 (10.78)	6
Democratic Left Alliance (SLD-UP)	569 311 (9.35)	5
Freedom Union (UW)	446 549 (7.33)	4
Polish Peasants Party (PSL)	386 340 (6.34)	4
Social-Democracy of Poland (SdPl)	324 707 (5.33)	3

Source: Panstwowa Komisja Wyborcza (www.pkw.gov.pl).
* The lists that appear in this table are only those which have crossed the threshold of 5% of votes on the national scale. The total number of lists was 21 (13 being present at the national level, 8 in one to five constituencies).

Table 2   Relation to Poland's membership of the European Union according to electoral preferences (in %)

Electorates	Favourable	Opponents	Don't know
Democratic Left Alliance (SLD)	94	3	3
Citizens' Platform (PO)	94	4	2
Law and Justice (PiS)	85	15	0
Polish Peasants Party (PSL)	77	16	7
Self-Defence (Samoobrona)	64	30	6
Polish Family League (LPR)	45	38	17

Source: Stosunek do czlonkostwa w Unii Europjskiej i pozycja Polski w zjednoczonej Europie [Relation to Poland's membership of the European Union and position in united Europe], CBOS Institute, July 2004 (www.cbos.pl).

1970 and 1980. Finally, it should be noted that the stage when the lists had to be finalised might have resulted in some charismatic but marginalised politicians investing their individual prestige into party resources in exchange for a good position on the party list. For instance one list associated the National Party of Pensioners and Retired Persons (KPEiR) and the small Peasants Party (PLD) (0.8 per cent) headed by a former PSL leader excluded from the PSL in the 1990s, Roman Jagielinski, and also the NKWW list (Narodowy Komitet Wyborczy Wyborcow, National Electoral Committee of Electors) (0.6 per cent) led by a former President of the Lower House of the Polish Parliament (*Sejm*),

Maciej Plazynski. Insofar as this logic of 'partisanisation' of individual political resources occurs mainly in national elections and reorients the structure of the political game, it is interesting that it occurred, with nonetheless lower intensity, during these EP elections.

EP elections have also offered the opportunity to some actors to harden cleavages and identities claimed or attributed. Such is the case of the LPR which posed itself as defender and champion of Polish identity in the face of the EU, adhering strongly to a set of political representations that have had great resonance since the beginning of the 1990s, based on the rejection of the society's westernisation and secularisation. It is also the case of Samoobrona, the object of a denunciation campaign by some actors, including the major daily newspaper *Gazeta Wyborcza* run by former dissident Adam Michnik. Usually close to the UW, this newspaper embarked on a press campaign for a few years against the Samoobrona as representing a 'populist' danger. The newspaper and some of the campaign members were taken to court after *Gazeta Wyborcza* revealed that some candidates had obtained an eligible position on the lists by agreeing to finance part of the campaign themselves.

'It is not enough to govern in my name'

Another characteristic that links these first Polish EP elections to those taking place in the former Europe of the 15 is what it is convenient to call a 'representation crisis'. As in the Czech Republic, but in a less successful manner, there were attempts to create 'socially aware' lists in Poland, a movement that reflects a certain rejection of professionalised political actors' appropriation of the European stake. In addition, 'proud to be' abstainers appeared in the public arena, obviously politicised with a high level of political competence. In particular the Polish press reported the creation of a committee of (secondary school) student protesters in Opole (south-west of Poland), in which one of the leaders declared: 'Our abstention in elections does not mean that we are not interested in politics. It is even the contrary, but we want politicians to have a certain background. The legitimating by a party or posing on a picture with a powerful politician is not enough to govern in my name' (*Rzeczpospolita*, 15 June 2004). Moving away from the authorised commentaries to focus on the opinion of 'ordinary' members of society allows us to realise that individuals can politicise their relations to the European arena without conforming to the work of cognitive guidelines operated by political elites. Even better than the abstention level, two figures reflect the Polish relation to Europe: if 69 per cent of Poles approved Poland's EU membership, only 1 per cent thought that Poland had any influence within the EU (against 44 per cent who thought that it was one of the less influential countries, and 47 per cent thinking that it had an average position).

Frédéric Zalewski

➔ Mapping Europe: European Electoral Geography.

Political Affiliation

The question of political affiliation or electoral label does not pose a real problem in national elections since, in most cases, candidates run for the political party that they will represent. When a candidate is selected he/she is supported during and beyond the campaign process and is automatically affiliated to his/her political party. Political affiliation to a given party provides the candidate with guidance throughout the electoral process and, in the event of victory, during the mandate he/she will exercise. This strong integration of the candidate to the partisan structure has a certain number of effects in terms of the politician's allegiance to the organisation he/she belongs to. Political affiliation thus constitutes an element governing relations between political actors and organisers. Without drastically changing this model, the European elections bring out a certain number of nuances, due, on the one hand to the double origin (European and national) of the candidates or future European parliamentarians and, on the other hand, to the specificities of each member state's electoral rules.

The first specificity introduced by European elections is due to the candidates' national and European origins. The weak institutionalisation of European partisan organisations (Hix and Lord 1997) leads national parties to play a central role in electoral campaigns, contributing to the nationalisation of electoral stakes. Nevertheless, if electoral campaigns are conducted under the banner of a national party, election to the European Parliament will occur primarily under the name of a European parliamentary group, followed by a transnational one. It is then necessary to distinguish, in the words of Leca (1996), between 'electoral politics' and the 'politics of problems'. In the first case, when the election or re-election of an MEP is at stake, relations with his/her national partisan organisation are essential. In the second case, when the question relates to the handling of European Parliament briefs and voting in favour or against a text, belonging to a European parliamentary group – a transnational organisation – is essential (Bell and Lord

1998). At times, issues may arise between these two 'places of origin'. In fact, such a scenario arose during the 2004 election campaign, with the creation of the Alliance group composed of Democrats and Liberals for Europe (ALDE) (following the European Liberal Democrat and Reform Party, ELDR) in France and in Italy. In France for instance, the announcement made by François Bayrou to leave the PPE for the ALDE constituted a driving force for his campaign.

To this general characteristic of the European elections, one must add that the importance of political affiliation varies according to election rules in each member state. When the vote for a non-modifiable list is in use, the importance of the partisan belonging is central in order to gain votes. However, the matter is different in countries where rules place less importance on the selection of candidates by parties, as is the case in Ireland or Malta where the single transferable vote system is in use, or in countries with preferential voting systems. (16 countries allow voters to interfere with the composition of lists; among these are Austria, Belgium, Finland, Latvia and the Czech Republic. Luxembourg even allows the mixing of lists.) When the electorate votes for a given candidate or is allowed to select candidates from a list, the partisan political affiliation becomes less important as the candidate's personality plays a more crucial role. In such cases, the role of the information society during electoral campaigns is fundamental, as the election outcome is often dependent on the candidate's personality rather than on the party's programme. This process, analysed for instance in the case of Finland during the 1999 elections, also brings to light a movement characteristic to smaller EU member states, whereby the role of representation at the European

Parliament is both partisan and national. Thus emerges a new political figure: that of the 'popular diplomat' far less dependent on his political affiliation because he claims to represent the entire nation at the EU (Kauppi 2000).

The question of political affiliation underlines the weak Europeanisation of European elections, as national partisan origins and the modalities of organisation remain centralised and subject to the wishes and practices of individual member states. The preconditions of evolution are linked to the homogenisation of voting procedures across the 25 – as well as to the institutionalisation of truly transnational political parties able to structure national political parties around European cleavages recognised by the electorate.

Emmanuel Henry

Bibliography

Bell, D. S. and Lord, C. (eds), *Transnational Parties in the European Union*, Aldershot, Brookfield, Ashgate, 1998.

Hix, S. and Lord, C. (eds), *Political Parties in the European Union*, New York, St. Martin's Press, 1997.

Kauppi, N., 'La construction de l'Europe: le cas des élections européennes finlandaises en 1999', *Cultures et conflits*, 38–39, 2000, pp. 101–18.

Leca, J., 'La "gouvernance" de la France sous la cinquième République. Une perspective de sociologie comparative', in F. D'Arcy and L. Rouban (eds), *De la Ve République à l'Europe. Hommage à Jean-Louis Quermonne*, Paris, Presses de Sciences Po, 1996, pp. 329–65.

→ Electoral Strategy; Electoral System; European Elections (2004); European Parliament; European Political Parties; Parliamentary Groups at the European Parliament; Second-Order Elections.

Political Context

The concept of political context encompasses all the short-term factors that affect partisan actors, framing their strategies and behaviour, particularly during electoral periods when they seek to channel votes. Notable aspects concern the distribution of power, the state of electoral alliances, perceptions surrounding the economic situation, the level of political tension, the stakes produced by partisan proposals and the journalistic coverage of political affairs. A context-based explanation of voting behaviour can be perceived as either opposing or complementing the dispositional psephological interpretations – notably that electoral choice is informed by family socialisation, rational calculation and partisan identification. Thus electoral logic and analysis tend to consider the social and professional positions of the voter or alternatively emphasise the dynamic of strategic choice. As such, the influence of the context or situation can be used to explain both electoral stabilities as well as a series of political alternations or unexpected electoral victories (Garrigou 1989), as observed in the result of the Spanish legislative elections several days after the attacks in Atocha station which effectively reversed the forecasts as predicted by think-tanks and institutes. However, the explanatory power of the notion of political context remains a problematic feature in light of the persistently partially contradictory nature of the influential factors at stake and the difficulty in operationalising context in a way which would be deductive and falsifiable. This is emphasised in that assessments of the normative impact of context often stem from retrospective comments ascribing electoral victory or defeat to explicit favourable or unfavourable circumstances whilst disregarding the others.

Nevertheless, the difficulty faced by incumbent governments in numerous countries in securing a successive majority can be viewed as constituting evidence of the somewhat situational dimension of the vote. Indeed, on the occasion where there is but limited evolution within the electorate during the period between two consecutive elections, then any differences in terms of electoral outcomes must be attributed to an additional factor – determined by the situation – perceived by the same potential voters as arising from the issues at stake and the respective credibility of both the opposition and the majority party. The impact of political context can hence be seen in terms of parallel evolutions within each electoral constituency. Even though from one election to another, political contests continue to bestow a majority to one of the partisan alliances, a common pattern of regression or progression for the governing party or the opposition can still be observed across all the polling stations. Such a phenomenon is thus an indication that each group of voters within the political space is subject to similar influences and that at least a proportion of the electorate, as a result of their own previous inclinations, sense the influence of identical political circumstances. Notably, this is defined not as the objective assessment of the government's economic performance – which would inevitably involve territorial divergences – but rather as the electoral aggregation stemming from the effects of differential mobilisation or demobilisation of voters' categories through the immersion in a similar political performance. Thus, in accounting for the resulting electoral alternations, as frequently observed in majoritarian systems, it is thus possible to discern three converging processes: the impact of demobilisation generated by the disappointment expressed by the

electoral supporters towards the incumbent majority's political programme; the automatic emergence of new grievances generated from even the most moderate ministerial activity; and finally the mobilisation of voters at a higher level, who identify with opposition parties in reaction to the most controversial governmental proposals.

There is a potentially converging public perception acquired through common and more accessible references, such as Community news coverage, transmitted by European policy journalists. From this viewpoint, one must consider the question: to what extent is the overall aggregate result of the European elections attributable to such perceptions of a specific European situation that would harmonise general electoral behaviour in the different countries? Furthermore, is it possible to simultaneously observe and align both transnational electoral stakes and political debates in the European electoral campaigns in each member state? In other words, how far do potential European circumstances and situations account for the changes in political forces represented in the European Parliament? The most elementary observations show that this is not the case.

Indeed, no clear transnational pattern ever appears in European elections. The 2004 elections witnessed the progression of EPP representatives in Germany and the United Kingdom, and those of the ESP in Spain, France and Italy. Eventually, the EPP made slight progress as a result of the MEPs from the new member states. The European parliamentary groups result from the accumulation of autonomous victories and defeats won and lost by their national representatives. Indeed, since 1979, no single group has ever simultaneously increased its hold in any of the European elections across all the major member states of the European Union. Thus, which are the obstacles that impede the rise of a European political context, as perceived by voters and so likely to homogenise voting behaviour? First, the likelihood of establishing a common and simultaneous European perception of stakes and controversies during electoral campaigns is made more difficult by the national segmentation of political spaces and the linguistic fragmentation of the related debates. Each national political space tends to have not only its own pace but also to retain its own specific controversies, usually differing substantially from those accepted by other neighbouring political classes, in spite of their seemingly similar political history. Indeed there are a range of features which have thus far contributed to differentiating the political languages and practices used in the European countries. These include the national nature behind the processes of partisan cleavage formation during the period of electoral regime establishment between 1870 and 1945, the diversity of historical experiences which has shaped the ideological reference systems and the distribution of political forces (Vichy and the Liberation, May 68 in France, the defeat and then political violence in the 1970s in Germany and Italy, Francoism and democratisation in Spain, communism and the swift return to a market economy and to parliamentarianism in Central Europe), as well as the transformation process of labour movements into parties holding political power. The end result is thus an explicit obstruction to the convergence of political discourse and offers which are required for the emergence of harmonised European context.

However, the weakness of the European institutions is also a compelling factor which equally impedes the emergence of a Community political context which would Europeanise voting behaviour. Indeed, it is more difficult for voters to identify European policies than national ones. In spite of the critical efforts by certain partisan actors, notably the 'Eurosceptics', Community policies fail to be clearly attributable to either a parliamentary majority in Strasbourg or a partisan orientation of the Commission or to a political majority in the Council. From this perspective, the strong divergences between the French Conservatives and the British Labour in relation to the appropriateness of defining European social policies suppress any opportunity to effectively clarify ideological cleavages within the Council (Gerstlé 1996). The Commission directives lack visibility and their origin is neither mainly nor exclusively attributed to the European institutions in order to rouse opposition. The European Parliament and its majority are not identified as being either supporters or partners of the Commission and its policies (Delli Carpini and Keeter 1996). Vocal parliamentary debates may take place for the enforcement of the directives, but they are of a predominantly 'nationalised' nature since the governments usually adopt political responsibility for necessary enforcement and the adaptations, assuming the project to be a product of their own initiative. Thus, voters are rarely aware of the 'Euro-product' nature behind a law.

Where governmental activity creates, at the national level, political passion, involvement and politicisation, i.e. establishes the political context which will periodically realign electoral behaviour, by simultaneously producing electoral supporters and dissenters, this reorientation is blocked by the limited transparency of the Commission's governance. In the absence of the ability to attribute political impact to European decisions, disagreements amongst the European executives come into view. In other words, opposition to

Europe does not lead to a 'politicisation' in the sense that, in order to block a government, it becomes necessary to vote for the opposition. Therefore, European political events, European partisan and state performances – all originating from the Commission, the Council or sometimes the European Parliament – are not sufficient to align electoral behaviour throughout the EU. As a consequence, it is simply not possible to observe a convergence or Europeanisation of political situations across the different European countries. Instead there remains relative fragmentation into as many situations as there are autonomous political spaces, even during European electoral campaigns. Such a phenomenon is not without consequence: in each country, since the European elections occur between decisive elections which redistribute governmental positions, voters more frequently sanction their respective government than reaffirm their confidence in it. During the 2004 European elections, the opposition won electoral ground in France, Italy, Germany and the United Kingdom, and only lost in Spain – such a result merely confirming the legislative elections which had taken place a few weeks earlier. Hence, European elections lead to structurally counter-cyclical voting. The political composition of the European Parliament therefore tends systematically to come up against the Council of Ministers, creating a situation which could constitute a source of institutional tension, particularly when the simultaneous increase of both EP and Council powers (expansion of qualified majority voting) will have led to dismissing the so far dominant intergovernmental or intergroup consensual negotiation rules.

Philippe Juhem

Bibliography

Delli Carpini, M. and Keeter, S., *What Americans Know About Politics and Why It Matters*, New Haven, Yale University Press, 1996.

Garrigou, A., 'Conjoncture politique et vote', in D. Gaxie (ed.), *Explication du vote*, Paris, Presses de Sciences Po, 1989, pp. 357–84.

Gerstlé, J., 'L'information et la sensibilité des électeurs à la conjoncture', *RFSP*, 46, 5, 1996, pp. 731–52.

Jadot, A., 'Mobilité, Rationalité? Une exploration des itinéraires électoraux, 1973–1997', in P. Bréchon, A. Laurent and P. Perrineau (eds), *Les cultures politiques des Français*, Paris, Presses de Sciences Po, 2000, pp. 377–400.

Martin, P., *Comprendre les évolutions électorales*, Paris, Presses de Sciences Po, 2000.

→ Campaign (Sociology of); Electoral Behaviour; Electoral Cycles; European Commission; European Elections (2004); European Electoral Sociology; European Parliament; European Public Sphere; Europeanisation (of National Political Life); Issues; Journalists; Nationalisation of European Elections; Political Market; Protest Voting.

Political Market

The staging of European elections is paradoxical. On the one hand, few dimensions of the daily existence of EU nationals escape decisions from its political institutions. On the other hand, European parliamentary elections are held amongst broad indifference and are met with high levels of abstention from the electorate. There are few issues, and even fewer 'European' issues in these elections. This situation is simultaneously well established and likely to develop. It will develop if a European political market emerges and if European elections cease to be structured around segmented national political markets, as has been the case until now.

'European' elections without European stakes

In a representative democracy, governmental issues and stakes and the orientation of public policies are associated with the election of representatives. An exchange is thus established between voters willing to grant their confidence to collective and individual political actors in 'return' for various goods and political services (among others, visions of the future of the polity, governmental programmes, reforms, decisions and public policies). Elections mobilise voters insofar as they are held within the framework of such spaces of transaction (Gaxie 2003). Because these conditions – which depend more on political factors than on an institutional setting – are not currently met, there is no European sphere of political transactions. Furthermore, it is because 'European' elections are not staged within such a European sphere of transactions (i.e. within the framework of a European political market), that they are hardly 'European' and only weakly mobilising.

Elections of MEPs used to hardly influence (until now) the formation of European 'executives' and, consequently, their guidelines and political decisions. Few immediate European institutional issues were at stake in their outcome. Some specialists simplified this situation by claiming that these elections had no effect on European institutional power and were thus 'second-order' (Reif and Schmitt 1980).

This classification probably gives too much importance to institutional factors. One may observe that these factors are evolving (for the first time in 2004 a link – albeit thin – has been established between the political make-up of the European Parliament and the composition of the Commission) and that, until now, the relative significance of European elections has not been enhanced accordingly. Political factors, and crucially, the absence of true European political parties, are of greater importance for our understanding of the way European elections are structured, and of their weak mobilising power. Although there are many political groups within the European Parliament, their respective compositions are unstable, their activity restricted to the parliamentary arena and they are unknown by most voters. There are also confederations of national parties supposed to belong to the same party 'family', but, until now, these confederations have been miles away from true political parties, i.e. like organisations capable of developing a vision and a programme for the EU and willing and able to enforce discipline amongst their components.

National frameworks thus structure European elections. National political parties nominate candidates to the European Parliament, and they are above all concerned by national stakes. Admittedly, the officially 'European' character of these elections leads candidates to develop European policies more than they usually do. However, European issues are far from being their main concern, and also those of the media and voters. Instead, despite minor inflections, European elections largely reproduce established domestic electoral cleavages.

For a number of reasons, candidates and parties are not urged to stress European issues. They know that most voters are poorly informed of European matters and are easily discouraged by the complexity of European issues. Similarly, because European elections ignore a core public demand for a European debate and are only dimly focused on European issues, they contribute to the persistently low level of interest, information and expectations of the public. It is thus mostly in a few new member states or from the point of view of extremist and

Eurosceptic parties that EU issues are made particularly salient.

European elections thus provide an occasion to continue the games of national politics. It is the same 'play' which is reproduced, but with minor 'actors'. The composition of the lists of candidates, the number of electoral meetings and the cost of campaign expenditures, all show that European elections are only secondary contests in the eyes of party leaders and the media alike. They are often used as a 'giant survey', gauging the popularity of the government, political parties and leaders.

Intermediate national elections with predictable results

As a result, a fundamental recurring outcome of most European elections is a more or less pronounced defeat of the majority party or of the main party in the governing coalition. Like most mid-term elections, the parliamentary opposition is one of the beneficiaries of the electoral losses suffered by the majority. The generalisation of sceptical, critical, even hostile attitudes towards politics has complicated this rather simple 'model'. European governance institutions are too trusted, too remote, and too unfamiliar to most citizens to be the target of protest reactions for a significant proportion of the electorate. Rather, it is the mistrust of national politics that has contributed to increases in abstention – particularly striking in the case of European elections – and to a greater instability of electoral preferences amongst citizens. This volatility is particularly strong during European elections. Voters who are dissatisfied, yet sufficiently involved in politics, and who wish to send a message to political elites, are proportionately more numerous. The absence of immediate stakes in institutional power frees them from any concern of 'effective voting' for those who are likely to win or for the main party of their own political camp. It also frees them from possible concerns regarding the political risks that their choice could induce.

A stronger volatility of electoral behaviour has given momentum to the traditional seesaw between the main established parties of the majority and the 'official' parliamentary opposition. However, European elections also provide a propitious opportunity to express distrust in all large political parties. The consequence is that dissatisfied voters are more likely to vote for parties which express more radical positions (notably nationalist, extreme-left and Eurosceptic stances) as they are perceived as different, because of their populist claims of a 'non-partisan' character, or because they are presented as a new party, or a party excluded from governmental games.

European elections as secondary national elections can, for this very reason, affect power relations within national political fields. Their outcome may occasionally be construed as a warning and may thus encourage established parties to change their positions. Power equilibria between allies within coalitions can be modified. But, as products of volatility, the relative successes obtained by *outsiders* are often transitory. However, in some cases (Green parties in various countries, some far-right movements), they have been an inaugural stage in a process of consolidation.

Electoral showings by movements opposed to European integration must also be analysed along the same standpoint. Their presence is sometimes the only 'European' specificity of European elections. This characteristic is a product of more general national cleavages in a configuration that encourages an emphasis on European components. Thus, in various countries, left- and right-wing factions and groups that remain opposed to various aspects of European integration use them as an opportunity to express or reveal divergences that are not met by any true pro-European alternative. The existence of these Eurosceptic movements may be discontinuous and fragile, but they may also importantly affect the discourse of these parties which cannot afford to lose voters to them.

Few elements thus contribute so far to the construction of a European political market. Few political actors organise themselves on a European scale to propose political visions of Europe to voters interested in such proposals in order to secure positions of power in the EU and to implement their proposals. European elections are the only elections where a few positions of power in the EU are minimally at stake. But they have been structured until now along the cleavages of national political markets. Europe is rarely discussed during the campaigns of these European elections, and when it is, it is more for national than European reasons.

Daniel Gaxie

Bibliography

Eijk, C. van der and Franklin, M. (eds), *Choosing Europe? The European Electorate and National Politics in the Face of Union*, Ann Arbor, University of Michigan Press, 1996.

Gaxie, D., *La démocratie représentative*, Paris, Montchrestien, 2003 (4th edition).

Reif, K. and Schmitt, H., 'Nine National Second-Order Elections: a Conceptual Framework for the Analysis of European Elections Results', *European Journal of Political Research*, 8, 1, 1980, pp. 3–44.

→ Abstention; Campaign (Sociology of); Cleavages; Electoral Cycles; Electoral Manifestos; Electoral Strategy; European Commission; European Elections (2004); European Electoral Sociology; European Parliament; European Political Parties; Europeanisation (of National Political Life); Euroscepticism; Identity; Issues; Parliamentary Groups; Protest Voting; Representation; Second-Order Elections.

Polling Stations

The organisation and institutionalisation of voting practices in the EU are tied to the individual social and political history of member states (Romanelli 1998). Consequently, the spatial organisation of such practices, as well as that of polling stations, appears to be a technical aspect determined by national and historical considerations in each country. The present situation also applies to European elections, where the effects of Europeanisation on national practices are not very pronounced. This phenomenon has nonetheless progressively affected the judicial regulations governing European elections, allowing voters living outside their country of origin to vote in their country of residence. In spite of these developments, all practical aspects governing elections remain shaped by national considerations and traditions, even if European Parliament elections can at times serve as precursors to innovative voting procedures.

The voting procedures progressively consolidated throughout Europe underline that voting is a private and secret action performed by citizens considered able to express political opinions. The structuring of the vote through the establishment of polling stations allows this customary action to be carried out in an organised manner. In spite of this common base, polling stations differ in their opening dates and times. The location of polling centres also varies, and can range from buildings belonging to local authorities and schools to buildings that are not typically associated with public institutions, such as cafés in

Greece. In the latter, the 2004 European elections marked the first time men and women voted in one, mixed, polling station. As mentioned, polling stations across the EU vary considerably in terms of their opening dates and times. In fact, they can be opened over a two-day period as in Italy or in the Czech Republic, half-a-day as in Luxembourg and Belgium, or one day everywhere else. They can also be open during the week in Ireland, the UK, the Netherlands and to some extent the Czech Republic; on Saturdays in Lithuania, Malta and to some extent Italy; or on Sundays in most member states.

The handling of exceptional voting procedures is also indicative of different electoral traditions. Such habits underline the fine balance between the facilitation of polling procedures and the preservation of order and organisation ensuring that a ballot's crucial characteristics are preserved. These guarantee that citizens are protected from fraud and pressures that could interfere with their voting behaviour. For instance, it is for this reason that in Greece, Estonia and Latvia, citizens are allowed to cast their vote on ships bearing national flags. Moreover, Hungary, the Czech Republic, Slovakia, Poland and Latvia have devised mobile polling stations allowing disabled, ill or hospitalised persons to participate in elections. Poland, the Czech Republic and Lithuania have also established polling centres in prisons. Sweden enables its citizens to vote at local post offices.

Postal voting is also subject to different national arrangements and regulations. In fact, while abolished in France in 1975 following numerous instances of fraud, this type of voting is still practised in nearly half of the member states (including Germany, Belgium, Spain and Portugal). This voting mechanism was also permitted in the United Kingdom in an effort to reduce abstention levels, and resulted in the increase of levels of participation from 24 per cent in 1999 to 38.5 per cent in 2004 (the number of individuals voting exclusively by correspondence increased from 20.2 to 42 per cent).

The expansion of voting options is also reflected in the development of electronic voting. Countries like Belgium and the Netherlands have established a form of electronic voting within polling stations, whereby citizens arriving at the centres cast their ballot through an electronic screen rather than on paper. These procedures have yet to be nationally implemented in France, where about 20 communes experimented with them during the 2004 EP elections. Sweden and the Netherlands are currently experimenting with long-distance electronic voting, and are even considering the possibility of telephone voting. Aside from their strong roots within national contexts, European elections offer a good testing ground for new voting procedures by progressively redefining the traditional frontiers of polling stations.

Emmanuel Henry

Bibliography

Ihl, O., *Le vote*, Paris, Montchrestien, 2000 (2nd edition).
Romanelli, R. (ed.), *How Did They Become Voters? The History of Franchise in Modern European Representation*, The Hague, Kluwer Law International, 1998.

→ Ballot; Citizen (EU); Electoral Administration; Electoral Education; Electoral Technology; European Electoral Act; Nationalisation of European Elections; Postal Voting; Symbolism; Symbols and Practice of Elections; Voters.

Populism

Populism unites a type of political movement that shares a notion of opposition but at the same time a high degree of ambiguity. As a political science concept, populism is simultaneously considered to be, amongst others, a 'soft' ideology, a type of regime – particularly in the South American context – and more recently, a new political stream characterised by its opposition to representative democracy throughout contemporary Europe (Betz 1994; Kitschelt 1995). It is striking in its multi-dimensionality and its ability to transform into new-populism, national-populism or video-populism (Taguieff 1997). One of the first comprehensive discussions of populism was provided by Gellner and Ionescu (1969). They discussed a series of differentiated perspectives and interesting case-studies without deriving a unified operational concept of populism. Canovan (1981) went so far as to claim that populism included such an extreme variety of recognised forms that it made any defin-itive analysis impossible.

However, Meny and Surel (2002) suggest that particularly in the European context, the ambiguity of the term populism and the matching reality is unlikely to disappear. In contemporary discourse, populism is often perceived as a rhetorical instrument based on dema-gogy. It provides a somewhat negative label for a number of parties and politi-cians from Bossi to Le Pen via Berlusconi, all accused of using simplistic slogans to threaten traditional representative democracy and the legitimacy of politi-cal institutions. Similarly, the label of populism has often been used to charac-terise the parties of the 'new radical right'. The French Front National, the Belgian Vlaams Blok/Vlams Gelang, the Austrian FPO, and the Italian Northern League have often been used as examples of populist dynamics mainly because they appear to be largely based upon reactionary and authoritarian values.

In an attempt to go beyond these traditional limits and contradictions, it may be useful to change one's angle of analysis and think of populism not as a homogeneous concept or a historical phenomenon, but, instead, as an essen-tial dimension of classic democracy, which emphasises popular sovereignty (Leca 1994). In a way, democracy is defined by a tension between populism (defined as the access of the masses to politics, as a sphere where the allocation of resources, the control of coercion, and the legitimation of political communi-ties is determined) and constitutionalism (understood as a legal state whereby specific rights are protected against discretionary power). Populist rhetoric may, therefore, be conceived as a will to privilege the former over the latter.

In parallel with this normative iden-tity related to the values of democracy, populism relies on some specific discur-sive realities. It is usually made of simple argumentations traditionally based upon three interrelated propositions. The sovereignty of the people is often cham-pioned with a denunciation of the elites, who are accused of egoism, betrayal or even corruption. Economic elites are traditionally the victim of such accusa-tions. This enables the populist politi-cians to propose that the only solution to the common problems is to remove the treacherous politicians who have allegedly betrayed popular sovereignty in the face of power.

The three main discursive arguments detailed above are broad enough to be mobilised by a number of different polit-ical groups, who formulate them in a simplified way to gain popular trust. The difficulty – both empirically and analyti-cally – is that there is no definitive spec-ification of the term populism. The broad discourse of its proponents makes it indeed susceptible to being manipu-lated systematically by almost any polit-ical leader or party. By presenting themselves as the only 'true' defenders of democracy, those who use populist discourse try to differentiate themselves from traditional elected representatives to legitimate their claims vis-à-vis their competitors. However, while this type of discourse can be occasion-specific within the context of a given electoral campaign, it can also be more durable and define the very ideological identity of a party. Chirac in 1995 or Berlusconi in 2001 probably illustrate the first scenario, while a number of reactionary nationalist parties such as the Austrian FPO or the French FN are characterised by the second.

This leads to the questions of what makes the use of such discourse more or less likely and more or less durable in a given context, and what determines its efficiency in a given European party system. Why would a leader use this type of discourse? And to what extent can this rhetoric importantly define the programme and identity of a given politician or political party?

The dynamics of comparative party systems gives us part of an answer to this question. Two mutually exclusive lines of polarisation are usually used, one based on the left–right continuum and another based usually on a cross-cutting dimension. The first line of polarisation remains dominant and rests on traditional ideological cleavages, responsible for the identification mechanisms of many parties and citizens in contemporary societies, as explained by Lipset and Rokkan (1967). The work of Inglehart (1977) suggests that new post-materialist values have emerged to lead a dealignment based on the more traditional cleavages, while other socio-political lines have become relevant (such as the opposition between authoritarianism and libertarianism for Kitschelt (1995)). In this sense, the traditional left–right spectrum may well have been tipped off-balance.

Consequently, the other line of polarisation, based on the main functions performed by political parties, may help to explain the recent transformation of European party systems and the reactivation of populist rhetoric by a large number of parties. The functional analysis based on the tripartisation of the electoral space according to Sartori (1976), distinguishes between three types of parties, each with a different function within electoral competition: government parties (which define public policies and legitimise the system as a whole); opposition parties (which provide a policy and elite alternative); and anti-system parties, which oppose the whole functioning of the system. In this sense, Schedler (1996) suggests that populist parties portray themselves as both parts of and outside of the party system. They do not seek to achieve power but to find a 'niche' to attract the votes and support of those who feel marginalised by the system, without trying to destroy it.

The conception of a populist 'function' can be performed by left- or right-wing parties. Hassenteufel (1991) showed that in Austria this function was performed by both the FPÖ and the Greens. Similarly, the contemporary crisis of the FPÖ and the BRD may be related to the normalisation of the party after agreeing to participate in government, thereby losing its legitimacy as an anti-system party. This leads us to question another observation about the role of populism in European party systems. The crisis of several such parties (declining FPÖ, the divisive FN, the weakening Lega Nord) must not be confused with the permanence of a discourse and positions defined earlier. The appeal of populism to popular sovereignty is attached to a fundamental dimension of democracy; therefore, populist rhetoric is unlikely to disappear. Its legitimising power, its ability to make power contenders claim to be distinct from the elites in power and its combinability with other ideological postures render it compatible within the context of electoral competition. Populism has now established a place of its own in most European party systems, which have been marked by the slow fading of traditional cleavages and alignments. The 2004 European elections have proved that populist parties have the ability to flourish within this contemporary European context, and to capitalise on anti-European stances, illustrating the distinct capabilities of the populist rhetoric and the permanence of its function in contemporary party systems.

Yves Surel

Bibliography

Betz, H.-G., *Radical Right-Wing Populism in Western Europe*, New York, St. Martin's Press, 1994.

Betz, H.-G., *La droite populiste en Europe: extrême et démocrate?*, Paris, Autrement, 2004.

Canovan, M., *Populism*, New York and London, Harcourt Brace Jovanovich, 1981.

Chêne, J., Ihl, O., Vial, E. and Waterlot, G. (eds), *La tentation populiste au cœur de l'Europe*, Paris, La Découverte, 2003.

Gellner, E., and Ionescu, G. (eds), *Populism*, London, Weidenfeld and Nicolson, 1969.

Hassenteufel, P., 'Structures de représentation et "appel au peuple". Le populisme en Autriche', *Politix*, 14, 1991.

Ignazi, P., 'The Silent Counter-Revolution: Hypotheses on the Emergence of Extreme Right-Wing Parties', *European Journal of Political Research*, 22, 3–34, 1992.

Inglehart, R., *The Silent Revolution*, Princeton, Princeton University Press, 1977.

Kitschelt, H. with McGann, A., *The Radical Right in Western Europe*, Ann Arbor, University of Michigan Press, 1995.

Leca, J., 'Types de pluralisme et la viabilité de la démocratie', Communication au XVIe de l'AISP, Berlin, 1994.

Leca, J. (1996), 'La démocratie à l'épreuve du pluralisme', *Revue française de science politique*, 46, 2, 1996, pp. 225–79.

Lipset, S. and Rokkan, S., 'Cleavage Structures, Party Systems, and Voter Alignments: an Introduction', in S. Lipset and S. Rokkan (eds), *Party Systems and Voters' Alignments*, London, Collier Macmillan, 1967, pp. 1–64.

Mény, Y. and Surel, Y., *Par le peuple, pour le peuple*, Paris, Fayard, 2000.

Mény, Y. and Surel, Y. (eds), *Democracies and the Populist Challenge*, Basingstoke, Palgrave Macmillan, 2002.

Sartori, G., *Parties and Party Systems*, Cambridge, Cambridge University Press, 1976.

Schedler, A., 'Anti-Political-Establishment Parties', *Party Politics*, 2, 3, 1996, pp. 291–312.

Taguieff, P.-A., 'Le populisme et la science politique: Du mirage conceptuel aux vrais problèmes', *XXe siècle*, 56, 1997, pp. 4–33.

➜ Euroscepticism; Extreme Left; Extreme Right; Sovereignism; United Kingdom.

Portugal

Historical background

After the Second World War Portugal's relation vis-à-vis the process of European integration was marked by pragmatic approaches: increasing emigration to and trade with Western Europe; membership in EFTA (European Free Trade Association), 1959; and an association agreement with the EEC (European Economic Community), 1972. However, the authoritarian nature of the political regime (New State, 1933–74) did not allow a closer relationship, namely with the EEC (Pinto and Teixeira 2002: 3–25).

Following the April 1974 coup, the transition to democracy in Portugal was a very polarised process. The Communists (PCP: Partido Comunista Português) and other left-wing forces were proposing socialist and Third World alternatives. That is one of the major reasons why for the pro-liberal democracy parties (PS: Partido Socialista, centre-left; PSD: Partido Social Democrata, centre-right; CDS: Centro Democrático Social, conservative Christian democrats), which gathered about 72 per cent of the vote in the 1975 constituent elections, the European option was the major reference for Portugal's future. It allowed a break with the authoritarian, isolationist and colonialist past and, simultaneously, was a strong weapon against the revolutionary projects (Pinto and Teixeira 2002: 32).

In May 1977, Portugal's formal membership application to the EEC was submitted. In January 1986, the country became a full member of the EEC. The aims of this article are to analyse, first, the context of EP (European Parliament) elections in Portugal (1987–2004), and, second, citizens' electoral behaviour and parties' performance in those contests vis-à-vis first-order elections (i.e. for parliament's single chamber).

European elections' institutional framework

People entitled to vote in EP elections are, first, adult Portuguese citizens on the national electoral rolls, even if they have their permanent address in a different member state (but opt to vote in Portugal through postal voting); second, following a 1993 European Legal Directive, all adult EU citizens that are inscribed in the Portuguese electoral census.[1] The right to be elected is reserved for all those that have the right to vote in EP elections, independent of their address, except for 'ineligibilities' and 'incompatibilities'. Candidates must be presented in party lists.

The responsibility for citizens' civic information concerning EP elections is mainly concentrated in the Official Electoral Authorities (CNE: National Electoral Commission; STAPE: Technical Secretariat for the Electoral Process), which have publicised the right of foreigners to vote in those contests.

Except for the presidential contests, all other elections are fought under the d'Hondt system of proportional representation, and voters are not permitted to express preferences for particular candidates (closed lists). That is why the Portuguese case is said to be specially suited to test the second-order elections model (Freire and Baum 2002; Freire 2004). EP elections are fought in a nationwide single constituency (24 seats: 1987–9 and 2004; 25 seats: 1994–9). On the one hand, the difference between EP and legislative electoral systems in terms of benefits/punishments for small (8 per cent of the vote or less) and medium-sized parties (9–20 per cent of the vote) is contradictory: if we consider only the two largest districts (with a magnitude of around 48 and 38), the legislative electoral system can be said to be more fair; if we consider an average district magnitude (1975–87: 11.4; 1991–2004: 10.5), the reverse is true. On the other hand, it clearly can be said that the EP electoral system benefits small and medium-sized parties the most because fewer resources are needed for electoral campaigns in a single district (for details, see Freire 2004).

Political parties have daily free access to radio and TV broadcasting, both public and private, during the official electoral campaign for the EP: 12 days immediately before the election. Free access to media broadcasting is equally distributed among all the parties that present at least 25 per cent of the total number of candidates in dispute. Electoral campaign financing is made through state, party and individual contributions (with strict limits). State assistance is allocated in the following way: 20 per cent equally distributed for all parties in competition; the remaining 80 per cent proportionally distributed according to the electoral outcome.

Electoral campaigns, party mobilisation and turnout

Political parties' orientations vis-à-vis European integration represent a distinctive political cleavage that usually cuts across the traditional left–right divide (see Lobo 2003: 207–11). From the 1970s until 1992 the opposition was mainly between the bourgeois parties (PS, PSD and CDS) and the PCP, although the latter moderated significantly its critical stance since 1988, namely by ending calls for Portugal's withdrawal from the EEC. Between 1992 and around 1997–2002, the CDS-PP joined the PCP in its critical stance towards European integration.[2] Since then, the pre-1992 division between the political parties has been revived. A new party emerged in the 1999 legislative elections, Bloco de Esquerda (BE: left-wing bloc), which was able to elect an MEP in 2004. Although it defends European integration, this party adopts a marked critical stance towards the process, namely in terms of the democratic deficit and Europe's low priority regarding social policy.

So, there is a very low political differentiation between the two major parties (PS and PSD) in European issues, which is a crucial factor in explaining two major traits of EP elections in Portugal. Firstly, the EP's electoral campaigns have been substantially centred in national issues, especially those related to the evaluation of the incumbent governments' performance (Lobo 2003: 207–11). The 2004 campaign was no exception in this respect. Although there was some (new!) opposition between left (BE, PCP and PS) and right (PSD and PP), in terms of criticism towards the EU Stability Pact, espoused by the former and rejected by the latter, the major issues were centred on the evaluation of the incumbent government's performance (economic decline, unemployment growth, tax increases, etc., vis-à-vis the EU averages).

Secondly, the negligible difference between the two major parties is a strong factor in explaining the low turnout rates that we found in EP elections (Table 1). If we exclude the exceptional 1987 elections, which were concurrent with the legislative elections, the average turnout for the period 1989–99 was 41.3 per cent. Considering only the countries without compulsory voting (11), the average European turnout rate (1979–99) was much higher than the Portuguese: 50.2 per cent (Sobrinho et al. 2004: 130). For 2004, the European turnout average for the 23 non-compulsory voting countries was 44.99 per cent; the corresponding figure for Portugal was 38.6 (*Expresso*, 19 June 2004). So, except for 1987, Portugal always exhibited a comparatively low turnout. Of course, there are also reasons for abstention in the EP elections that are common with other EU countries, namely their second-order nature[3] and the absence of a clear connection between the vote for the EP and executive power's formation in the EU.

Turnout in EP elections has been declining between 1989 and 1994 (Table 1). The increase in turnout that occurred between 1994 and 1999 can partly be explained by electoral rolls updates in 1998 (Freire and Baum, 2002). However, this is only part of the explanation because the absolute number of voters did increase significantly. Between 1999 and 2004 there was a slight decrease in turnout, but the 2004 figures were a bit higher when compared with 1994. Again, the difference between 1994 and 2004 can only be partly explained by electoral census updates because there was a significant increase in the number of voters. Diminishing party mobilisation should be ruled out as an explanation for EP elections' declining turnout (1989–04): if we take campaign expenses as a good indicator of party mobilisation, we can see that

Table 1   Turnout in EP elections, 1987–2004

	1987	1989	1994	1999	2004
Registered voters	7 787 603	8 121 564	8 565 822	8 681 854	8 821 456
Actual voters	5 639 650	4 149 756	3 044 001	3 467 085	3 404 782
Turnout (%)	72.41	51.10	35.54	39.93	38.6
Abstention (%)	27.59	48.90	64.46	60.07	61.4

Sources: Sobrinho et al. 2004: 117–20; for 2004: www.cne.pt

Table 2   Parties' campaign expenses in EP elections, 1987–2004

	Total amount (euros)	Between elections variation	Limits for campaign expenses (1)
1987	85 479	–	15
1989	219 309	+157	15
1994	1 360 009	+520	200
1999	2 845 681	+109	180
2004	4 014 913	+41	144

Sources: Sobrinho et al. 2004: 112; for 2004: data furnished by CNE.
Note (1): in terms of national minimum wages by candidate.

they have been growing significantly (Table 2).

Due to the death of the PS's top candidate, António Sousa Franco, four days before the 2004 EP election and during the campaign, participation might have risen and benefited the socialists. Prior to the election, some opinion polls pointed to a huge rate of abstention: around 70 per cent. Additionally, according to the data from EES 04 – 'timing of the electoral decision' and 'acknowledged effects in the decision to participate' – Franco's death probably led to a slight increase in turnout.

European elections, electoral cycles and parties' performance

The results of the 2004 EP elections are the following, respectively for vote percentages and number of seats: PS, 46.4 per cent, 12; Força Portugal (PSD and CDS-PP), 34.6 per cent, 9; PCP-PEV (Greens), 9.5 per cent, 2; BE, 5.1 per cent, 1; others, 4.4 per cent, 0. These outcomes are quite exceptional. First, it was the best result ever for the PS, both in EP and legislative elections. Second, considering the joint vote of PSD and CDS, their outcome was the worst ever both in EP and legislative elections. Third, it was the strongest result ever for the joint forces of the left (PS, PCP, and others) both in EP and legislative elections. Fourth, for the second time since 1987, when PRD (Partido Renovador Democrático, centre-left) got one seat, a fifth party (now BE) was able to achieve representation in the EP.

We believe that only a very small part of the PS's victory in 2004 might be due to the death of its top candidate, mainly for two reasons. First, many opinion polls published in the mass media between the beginning of May and 10 June (all fielded before Franco's death) predicted a very similar result for the PS. Second, both the PS's absolute number of votes (1 493 146 and 1 516 001) and the respective percentages (43.07 per cent and 46.4 per cent) were very similar in the 1999 and 2004 EP elections, in that order. Of course, as already mentioned, a slight increase in turnout that might have benefited the PS cannot be ruled out.

The 2004 EP elections' outcome can perhaps be best understood as a very strong punishment of the incumbent government. The PSD and PP cabinet was in the middle of its term and, due to a huge effort to comply with the budget deficit criteria imposed by the EU Stability Pact, which had been exceeded in 2001 by the socialist government, the performance of the executive was marked by severe reductions in public investments, current expenses and employment admissions, and tax increases (contrary to the 2002 legislative campaign's promises). These measures resulted in a strong recession marked by successive decreases in gross domestic product, significant increases in unemployment, and successive income losses for the average citizen, especially for the civil servants. So, it is no surprise that the 2004 EP elections were used by electors to punish the incumbent government. Actually, prior Portuguese studies have clearly demonstrated that electors do use EP elections to punish incumbent national governments, especially if the European elections take place in the mid-term of the national legislature (Table 3). Moreover, it has been shown that the extent of that punishment also varies significantly with the executive's popularity and macroeconomic performance (Freire 2004).

Although sometimes the differences are not very impressive, from Table 4 we can say that the Portuguese data clearly confirms theoretical predictions derived from the second-order elections model. Probably due to tactical considerations related to government's formation, large parties (PS and PSD) always perform better in legislative (first-order) than in EP (second-order) elections; for symmetrical reasons, electors can 'vote more with their heart', and so medium-sized and small-sized parties have always performed better in European than in legislative elections. What is extraordinary about the 2004 EP elections is the

Table 3   Change in national government vote support in EP elections, 1987–2004

| EP elections | Change in vote percentages of the party(ies) controlling national government: EP elections compared with the prior (or concurrent) legislative election | | |
	Honeymoon: 1–12 months from start of legislative term	Mid-term: 13–36 months from start of legislative term	Later term: 37–48 months from start of legislative term
1987	–12.8		
1989		–17.5	
1994		–16.2	
1999			–0.6
2004		–14.3	

Sources: Freire 2004, updated for the 2004 EP elections with data from www.cne.pt

Table 4   Political parties' average vote percentages by decade in legislative and EP elections, 1980–2004

Political parties	Type of elections	1980s	1990s	2000s	1980s–2000s
PS+PSD	Legislative	61.1	77.9	78.0	72.3
	EP	60.1	71.7	73.8	68.5
PCP+CDS	Legislative	26.5	16.1	15.6	19.4
	EP	27.7	21.1	16.7	21.8
PRD	Legislative	11.5	0.6	–	6.1
	EP	4.4	0.2	–	2.3
Others:	Legislative	4.1	3.6	4.3	4.0
left and right	EP	6.6	4.0	9.2	6.6

Sources: Freire 2004, updated for the 2004 EP elections with data from www.cne.pt
Note: for procedures used to disaggregate coalitions, see Freire, 2004.

extent to which small-sized parties did perform better, largely due to BE's excellent outcome. BE has been showing a very attentive and efficacious opposition in national politics, and that performance seems to have been rewarded in 2004.

Since the 1987 legislative elections, a concentration of the vote in the two major parties has taken place. It has been shown that this bipolarisation trend is also present in the EP elections. That is why, at least in Portugal, relations between second- and first-order elections reflect both short- and long-term effects (Freire 2004).

André Freire

Notes

1. For the relevant legislation concerning EP elections, see Sobrinho et al. 2004: 41–79.
2. After a change of label, to CDS-PP (CDS-Partido Popular), leadership and ideological profile, following the 1991 defeat in the legislative elections, the PP adopted a more critical stance vis-à-vis the EU, namely rejecting the single currency. However, after 1997, following a new change in leadership, the PP began accepting the euro as an unchangeable reality. Additionally, since its participation in national government with the PSD (2002–5), the critical stance vis-à-vis the EU was muted. This process culminated in the coalition between PSD and PP (Força Portugal) for the 2004 EP elections, and on the PP's return to the European Popular Party (July 2004), from which it had been expelled in 1992.
3. As elsewhere, Portugal's turnout rates in different types of elections reflect their relative importance for the functioning of the national political system. That is why, excluding 1987, the lowest turnout rates occur in EP elections vis-à-vis all other Portuguese elections (Freire and Baum 2002). Moreover, individual level data (1987–99) reveals that the same socio-political factors are active in explaining turnout in EP and legislative elections, and that attitudes towards European integration have no independent effect (Freire and Baum 2002; Lobo 2003: 215–20; data from the Portuguese European Election Study 2004 – EES 04 – reveals a similar pattern).

Bibliography

Freire, A., 'Second Order Elections and Electoral Cycles in Democratic Portugal',

South European Society & Politics, 9, 3, 2004, pp. 54–79.

Freire, A. and Baum, M., 'Election Order and Electoral Cycles in Democratic Portugal, 1975–2002', paper presented at the 98th annual congress of the American Political Science Association (APSA), Boston, USA, 2002 (http://apsaproceedings.cup.org/Site/abstracts/014/014004BaumMichae.htm).

Lobo, M. C., 'Legitimizing the EU? Elections to the European Parliament in Portugal, 1987–1999', in A. C. Pinto (ed.), *Contemporary Portugal: Politics, Society and Culture*, New York, Columbia University Press, 2003, pp. 203–26.

Pinto, A. C. and Teixeira, N. S., 'From Africa to Europe: Portugal and European Integration', in A. C. Pinto and N. S. Teixeira (eds), *Southern Europe and the Making of the European Union*, New York, Columbia University Press, 2002, pp. 3–40.

Sobrinho, A. et al., *Um Parlamento Diferente dos Outros*, Lisboa, Gabinete em Portugal do Parlamento Europeu e Comissão Nacional de Eleições, 2004.

➔ Mapping Europe: European Electoral Geography.

Postal Voting

The postal voting system is the most common form of remote voting. It enables voters to participate in elections when absent from their electoral residence on polling day. Most of the time, on the voter's demand, the electoral organisation sends voting documents to him by post. He must then mark his ballot and send it back to an office of the electoral organisation. The control aiming at ensuring the integrity and sincerity of the ballot usually consists in requiring that the voter's proof of identity and authorisation to vote accompanies the ballot sent back. The efficiency of the postal voting system is closely linked to that of the mobilised mail delivery service. For the June 2004 EP elections, this voting mode has been authorised in a great number of countries – sometimes for a long time (it has been used in the UK since 1918) – in the context of their own political elections. In most of them, this remote voting mode is however reserved for expatriate citizens. It is particularly the case in Austria, Belgium, Denmark, Spain, Latvia, the Netherlands, and in Sweden, where electronic remote voting was established for the first time for Swedish expatriate voters. In other countries, the principle of postal voting is authorised in a less restrictive way (Germany, Lithuania, Luxembourg, UK). In Luxembourg, where voting is compulsory, the electoral law of 18 February 2003 authorises it for voters aged more than 75 and for all the voters who, 'for duly justified professional or personal reasons, [are] unable to appear in person before the polling station to which they belong'. In Germany, paragraph 14 of the federal law relating to elections considers postal voting as equivalent to a conventional voting mode. It is, however, in the UK – where a first use of an all-postal ballot was made in several constituencies in the May 2003 local elections – where it has been most widespread and innovative. For the first time in EP elections, an all-postal ballot was organised in four out of the twelve British constituencies (North-West, North-East, Yorkshire and Humberside, and East Midlands constituencies) representing one in ten British voters. In these four electoral constituencies, no polling station was opened, obliging the British and European voters to vote in advance and by post. This electoral experiment was, however, affected by numerous dysfunctions: errors in printing of the ballots and forms; late delivery of the electoral equipment by Royal Mail (three days before the election, one in seven

Table 1   Turnout of the constituencies experimenting with an all-postal ballot in the 2004 EP elections in the UK (%)

Constituencies	Turnout
East Midlands	43.7
Yorkshire and Humberside	42.3
North-East	41.4
North-West	41.0
National average	38.5

Source: United Kingdom Parliament, *European Parliament Elections 2004, Research Paper,* 04/50, 23 June 2004, 12 (available at: www.parliament.uk/commons/ lib/research/rp2004/rp04-050.pdf).

voters on average had still not received their voting material); complexity of the control procedure adopted: voters had to draw a cross on the white ballot aimed at EP elections (a grey ballot was planned, if need be, for local elections organised simultaneously in some constituencies), then fill in an identification form countersigned by a witness, and send it all to the electoral organisation by putting the envelope provided in a mailbox; extension of the duration of the count; allegations of electoral fraud (which was particularly the case for voters who were strongly rooted in community networks favourable to 'ballots capture') that led to several arrests and favoured the development of post-election litigations, etc. In spite of severe criticisms formulated against a reform which the British Labour Party hoped would limit the sanction vote against them, this experience contributes to explain the appreciable increase of the turnout in the latest EP election in the UK (38.5 per cent in 2004 against 24 per cent in 1999; in other words, a record turnout since 1979). Table 1 summarises the electoral performances of the four constituencies that were concerned by the pilot experience.

On average, turnout was 5 points higher in these constituencies as compared to constituencies where local voting was maintained. Furthermore, these four constituencies saw their European turnout double between 1999 (20.2 per cent on average) and 2004 (42 per cent on average). In the rest of the country, the progress in turnout was only 11 points (36.9 per cent in 2004 against 25.8 per cent in 1999). This result is partly linked to the strong mobilisation of the British government in favour of this unprecedented experience in the European electoral history. This mobilisation was backed up by the local administrative authorities and certain British political parties (particularly the Labour Party or the UKIP that made its strongest electoral progression in the East Midlands county with a record result of 26.1 per cent of the valid ballots). These political organisations recovered on this occasion the founding role of 'electoral entrepreneur' capable of 'organising' (in the sense Ostrogorski used to understand it) the meeting between the voters and the candidates in an electoral space in the process of deterritorialisation.

Yves Déloye

→ Ballot Paper; Electoral Operations; Electoral Technology; Polling Stations; Symbols and Practice of Elections; United Kingdom.

Posters

Associated from the beginning with the emergence and development of democratic competition in Western states, the electoral poster has become a natural symbolic and technical device, such as the ballot box or the flyer. From its semantic expression in the different European languages, we can agree on a common definition for the concept of electoral poster: a printed paper sheet, stuck on a fixed support, aimed at bringing to the knowledge of the public a political message at the time of an election. In contemporary communication, a distinction is made between two types of media, according to the main or secondary role played by advertising exposure.

The first group consists of 'information consumption' media (cinema, press, radio and television). Exposure here is a mere consequence of the consumption of informative content. As the only actual advertising exposure medium, the poster forms the second group. It is the pre-eminent mass medium, since it exposes – or even imposes – the message to the eyes of the public, without distinction, through its physical presence. This coverage capacity has made the poster the main medium of electoral campaigns. Since about 15 years ago, the rivalry of television has made the poster's role less central. Within the operational campaign apparatus, the electoral poster has been progressively confined to a subordinate role, devoted to proximity communication as well as militant mobilisation. Then the poster plays the role of a territory marker, whose presence determines the state of the local political forces. For this reason, the poster announces and states a message, but is also a message in itself. The electoral poster is therefore a symbolic device. It works as an arrangement of linguistic and iconic signs (images), combining the means (the sign itself) and what is meant (the signification), the expressive and impressive dimensions. This ensemble is built in order to guide and orientate the glance. A poster is firstly a prevailing colour, which makes up the background and gives the tone of the poster.

The reasons determining the choice of the colour are multiple. It might be the traditional colour of the political tendency (for instance, red for progressive forces or blue for conservative parties); it might also be the current advertising trend or a strategy of rupture with previous campaigns, in order to create a surprise effect. It can also be an ad hoc choice, imposed by the constraints of the picture setting, especially when the poster is focused on one or several faces. It is then an eye-catching visual element, which can be made of a photograph or an illustration. At the 2004 European elections, combinations were multiple: a close-up of Jaime Mayor Oreja's face for the Spanish Popular Party, a stylised rose for the French Socialist Party, or a picture taken from the world of sports for the German CDU or the governmental coalition in Portugal. These creative choices find their pertinence in the goals set up through the elaboration of the global communication strategy. This diversity is also present in the institutional campaigns for incitement to voting. In 1979, for example, no consensus could be reached about the picture of these civic campaigns (the birdlike man of drawer Folon in France, a ballot in Denmark and United Kingdom, a dove in Belgium . . .). The slogan, with its own typography, will deliver the political message. A slogan is a short sentence, which can be easily memorised and identified: it summarises and cuts down the political stance of the one who states the message. Here again, diversity prevails, even for institutional campaigns. In 1979 again, the electorate was canvassed in Belgium by a stimulating 'Europe takes a new impulse', by a very pragmatic 'Cast someone you know to take care of your business' in the Irish campaign, or by a sober 'Vote for the European Parliament' in Germany. The choice of typography is driven by imperatives of legibility, but also by imperatives of differentiation towards competitors. An original and harmonious typography reinforces the impact of the composition. Finally, the signature ends the symbolic arrangement. It is usually made of the political formation's logotype and name, the heart of the party's visual identity.

The electoral poster is in keeping with the print culture that imposed itself in Europe between the sixteenth and nineteenth centuries. Its format is variable. It sometimes depends on national traditions, but above all on the campaign budget. Member states' legislations do not specify a prescribed size for electoral posters. The format ranges from 148×210 millimetres to commercial hoardings of 12 square metres, hired for the occasion. On the other hand, the size of the official posters cannot exceed the surface of the supports made available near the polling stations. Generally, the dimensions of an official poster are about 620×860 millimetres.

Three types of electoral posters can be distinguished. The official poster is the poster that will be placed in various locations during the official campaign. The unauthorised poster, of the usual format are reserved for so-called 'unauthorised billposting'. Taking advantage of electoral campaign allowances, these posters are stuck massively – and sometimes compulsively – at night, in order to occupy space and form some 'controlled ideological micro-territories'. Finally, the electoral poster of commercial format is used in countries where the authorised allowance of electoral expenditure is relatively high, or indeed may not even exist (Finland, Italy, United Kingdom, Slovakia or Sweden), where political parties can hire advertising companies. In order to increase the impact as well as the coverage rate of the campaign, they use electoral posters of commercial format (2×8×12 metres), placed in national and international networks of urban and suburban billposting (e.g. Decaux, Clearchannel-Dauphin or Viacom-Giraudy).

Jacques-Olivier Barthes

→ Advertising; Communication.

Protest Voting

Since 1979, European elections seem to have fulfilled a particular electoral model, notably that of 'second-order elections' (Reif and Schmitt 1980). Amongst the characteristics of this model, it is still rather common to include abstention within the concept of 'protest voting' or 'sanction voting'. Incidentally, 'protest' in English and 'sanction' in French are similarly polysemic: it can simultaneously mean an approval, a ratification, a reprimand, or even a condemnation. In the case of 'protest voting', the second meaning is probably most relevant: through the process of voting, the electorate chooses to issue a warning, using an election for something else than what is traditionally their main purpose: the election of representatives. As such, voters may use European elections, otherwise described by the media as inconsequential, to send a warning at no expense to the governing party or parties in their respective countries. Protest voting exploits this feature of European elections, whereby electoral choice is not based on a party's agenda or projects on Europe, any more than it is an opportunity to select European leaders, but rather on opposing ruling or large national parties. Behind a European exercise, voters are encouraged by state-centric media and opposition parties to react to national stakes. Thus, since 1980, Reif and Schmitt have conceived European elections as so many 'national second-order elections'.

The idea that voters will use election day 'to punish' a governing team, depriving European elections of their fundamental function, which is the selection of MEPs, is often taken for granted by the political science literature. This 'hijacking' is helped by the electoral context: constituencies are national or infra-national, candidates remain national and (generally) non-European candidates, and the debates are organised within each country around typical political confrontations relating to their respective political cleavages and cultures.

At the same time, the protest voting analysis is very dependent on a quantitative reading of European elections. On the occasions where the governing party or parties fail to match their last national electoral performance, protest voting will consider to have occurred. This means that mid-term effects are automatically read as a 'drop' for the parties in power, rather than their national election performance as 'boosted' by campaign momentum. This also forces European elections to be read from a diachronic viewpoint, so that in order to identify protest voting, it is important to compare the results of the same political party over two successive elections (for example, general elections and European election) or to observe this same party over a period of five years and monitor the rise or fall of its results between two European electoral competitions.

Finally, the concept of protest voting induces a 'variability' of the public vote from one election to the other (volatility or electoral rationality) and a differential mobilisation of the electorate, according to the identified stakes of the election itself. Protest voting thus implies a diminishing attachment of voters to the party which they feel closest to and their capacity 'to contravene' this partisan loyalty according to the type of election. Even when we can trace the evolution of dissatisfaction using surveys or qualitative evidence, it is hard to understand how this dissatisfaction is translated in the ballot boxes. It is also interesting to note that conceiving European elections as an arena of protest voting poses two problems. Firstly, a methodological difficulty arises: indeed, to compare results between two elections implies having the resources to put them in perspective, but because of context and electoral rules, European elections are often different because of the presence of single-issue parties or ad hoc parties which do not always stand the test of time. Moreover, electoral constituencies for European elections are not always identical to those used in other elections. As electoral methods vary, simultaneously, the electoral supply is often diversified and broader for European elections due to the generalisation of proportional representation. Thus, protest voting can be partly explained by a greater variety of parties in the race, and abstention made more likely by apathetic campaigns. A further difficulty arises when speaking of protest voting in that it implies a comparative reading: European elections must be analysed in reference to other elections, which implicitly tends to reinforce their 'incidental' character.

Therefore, once these structural problems are taken into account, it seems that protest voting is by no means automatic and, indeed, is not unequivocal. After six European elections, we can develop a more refined analysis which identifies several types of protest voting, depending principally on partisan systems and the political supply present at the time of these elections.

With regards to the non-automaticity of protest voting, one should note that since 1979, European elections have occasionally allowed governing parties to confirm their political positions. In this sense, where the European election falls in electoral cycles constitutes a solid explanatory variable. In other words, when European elections are held shortly after general elections, they will provide governing parties with an opportunity to secure significant electoral gains. In this case, European elections provide an opportunity to confirm domestic political choices, to ratify the general elections by a second or third European 'ballot' in a context of 'honeymoon' or post-election 'euphoria' (Kaase 1973). By contrast, the further away from national elections the European election, the more likely it is to turn into a protest exercise. Typically, European elections held halfway through the legislative mandate regularly provide a platform for protest parties. Having already contributed to the victory of the governing party or parties, voters feel demobilised with a growing social discontent following unpopular reforms, and the will to influence domestic policy decisions is one of the many explanations which can be advanced to explain this phenomenon. As an election warning, European elections therefore assume an obvious

significance for the parties in power, which results from and in political parties often constructing their campaigns around national stakes rather than European questions.

Moreover, protest voting is not unequivocal, in that it can take on several directions and distinct meanings. The most fundamental type of protest voting results in all governing parties being sanctioned, especially in multiparty systems. Often, however, a dominant coalition party or, in the case of a bi-partisan system, the single ruling party, may be most harshly sanctioned. A second variation concerns the beneficiaries of protest. In some cases, it can benefit the main opposition parties, as was the case in Germany in 2004. Then, European elections function as a typical mid-term pendulum, allowing the opposition to make their voices heard and to position themselves in preparation for the next general elections. However, protest voting may also assume another dimension when beneficial to extreme or anti-system parties, which symbolise a more general sanction addressed to national partisan systems and thrive on the disrepute from which the traditional parties suffer. In 2004, a typical example was that of the UK where the Conservatives, the main opposition party, suffered their worst ever result in a national election in the European election, whilst registering a vibrant success in the local elections that were held at the same time.

Protest voting is undoubtedly a useful concept to bear in mind whilst analysing European elections. Nonetheless, it hides a great variety of situations, motives, victors and political implications which certainly should not be overlooked.

Christine Pina

Bibliography

Kaase, M., 'Die Budenstagwahl 1972: Probleme und Analysen', *Politische Vierteljahresschrift*, 14, 2, 1973, pp. 145–90.

Reif, K. and Schmitt, H., 'Nine Second-Order National Elections: a Conceptual Framework for the Analysis of European Elections Results', *European Journal of Political Research*, 8, 1, 1980, pp. 3–44.

→ Electoral Behaviour; Electoral Cycles; European Elections (1979–1989); European Elections (2004); European Electoral Act; European Electoral Sociology; Europeanisation (of National Political Life); Forecast; Germany; Nationalisation of European Elections; Second-Order Elections; United Kingdom.

R

Rational Choice

The origins of rational choice theory can be traced back to the renowned work of Anthony Downs (1957) which laid down the oft-cited classic notions of the functioning of democracy in relation to the principle of instrumental rationality. According to rational choice theory, preferences for possible behaviours or actions are determined by the anticipated values of different outcomes. This can be explained as individuals favour the outcomes which deliver them the greatest benefits and as such will pursue the particular course of actions to enable them to attain such results. Thus, actions are the means to achieve the desired goals, which have a merely ascribed instrumental value.

The actors within rational choice theory can be characterised by certain qualities, which make them behave as shrewd and ubiquitous consumers in a market environment: notably (1) they have fixed and transitive preferences (if A is better than B, and B better than C, then A is better than C) with regards to the anticipated choices. Consequently, there exists a utility function which links each alternative to the net benefit and, moreover, the actors are able to identify the trade-offs between the selection of alternatives; (2) they are also capable of calculating the costs in terms of lost opportunities; (3) they are able to undertake a comparison between present and future benefits; and (4) the utility function encompasses all the aspects behind the decision-making process. In applying the maximal use of neo-classical economics, a decision is only rational when it is grounded within the best motives, and achieves the best results with regards to all the objectives. Of course, instrumental rationality is linked to the principle of methodological individualism, meaning the doctrine which states that social phenomena should only be understood as aggregate results of individual actions.

In an ideal world, any explanation based on rational choice theory should meet three requirements. First, the actor should select a course of action that most suitably meets the individual's requirements and in accordance with the individual's beliefs; these beliefs are developed to the highest level on the basis of the information held by the actor; access to information is as such paramount with regards to the actor's wishes. Second, beliefs and wishes must not have internal contradictions. For instance, the actor cannot act consistently in realising a wish that the individual believes to be less important than others. Third, the action must not only be rationalised by wishes and beliefs, but also generated by them to a certain extent. These causal conditions also apply to the relationship between belief and information (Elster 1986). Rational actors are able to determine an extensive hierarchy of all possible outcomes and decisions, which does not contradict the 'wishes', and also capable of selecting the mode of action which actually or potentially produces the best possible outcome.

Thus, according to rational choice theory, instrumental rationality is the causal mechanism which transforms 'inputs' into 'outputs'. Furthermore, rational choice theory consists of simple but theoretically efficient explanations, since rational action constitutes in itself its own explanation. From this perspective, such a full conception of action warrants no further explanation: all behaviours are explained by messages and signals stemming from the context.

The progressive development of rational choice theory in the field of political science, and in particular in electoral studies since the 1960s, has been particularly intense on two levels: research on electoral behaviour and the political consequences of electoral systems.

Research on electoral behaviour

The classical research and conventional wisdom on electoral behaviour, conducted since the beginning of the 1940s, is heavily based on sociology and social psychology, and considers voters to be bound by either individual social position or limitations surrounding cognitive awareness. Sociologists from the Columbian school of thought argue that electoral behaviour can be explained through the study of collective groups, whereby votes are determined by social position. In contrast, the social psychologists from the Michigan school of thought contend that the relationship between individual characteristics and electoral behaviour is rather shaped in the long-term by psychological predispositions, and in particular by partisan identification which influences individual decisions. Nevertheless, the significance behind these early studies is the contrast between the classic image of citizens in a democracy and the nature of citizens in reality, whereby voters are subject to overwhelming cognitive limitations which inhibit them from organising and developing an effective grasp of their political environment, thus rendering them dependent on a more educated and more politicised elite.

Rational choice theory puts forward a completely opposite conception of voters. Voters act in an instrumental manner: they are able to simultaneously acknowledge their own interests, evaluate the different parties or candidates based on personal interests, and vote for the option which they consider to be the best. Consequently, as underlined by Downs (1957: 40), the most important point in the decision-making process for the voter lies with the difference between the benefits received in the period T and those advantages which would have been acquired had the opposition been in power. Voters and parties can be viewed as points in a space or dimension. The self-placement of a voter corresponds to the ideal position, whereas the location of the party or the candidate represents the anticipated results of respective policies once elected. Voters choose the party or candidate most aligned to their ideal position.

However, contrary to previous reservations concerning voter apathy or demands, rational choice theory considers the lack of information held by the voter as an explicit part of their rationality. Given there is only a very remote chance that citizens can individually influence the outcome of an election – and in regards to the European elections, the decisions taken by the European Parliament – voters are unlikely to benefit directly from their actions, and therefore have less incentive to seek information. Taking into account the fact that each individual holds at least a basic level of information, and that such access is costly (for example, all European citizens are aware that their country elects a certain number of MEPs, but few actually know exactly how many), it is thus considered rational to only gather more information when the anticipated advantages of an additional unit outweighs the costs (of access). Finally, it is perfectly rational for individuals to trust the (scarce) information transmitted by parties regarding their candidates and their proposed policies. In this respect, citizens rely on compelling incentives in order to use shortcuts that enable them to make decisions and to form their own preferences without being fully informed as to the contents and particular details of the political issues at hand. Voters are not limited in terms of cognitive awareness, but instead are ignorant in regards to rational elements.

Research on the political consequences of electoral systems

In regards to the analysis of the political consequences of electoral systems, rational choice theory readdresses the concept of parties and voters as being instrumentally rational actors. Indeed, such an interpretation was implicitly referred to in Duverger's studies which demonstrated gravity as being only an upper limit to fragmentation: the maximum number of viable parties (notably with ambitions to win parliamentary seats) in the relative majority, two-turn and proportional representation electoral systems is equal to the size of the district (M) plus 1, also known as the M+1 rule (Cox 1997).

The behaviour of parties and voters thus exclusively depends on their perceived impact on the final electoral outcome, and so lacks any intrinsic or expressive value. On the one hand, parties and candidates decide to take part in elections only according to their willingness to win seats; on the other hand, the electorate are only prepared to support those parties and candidates which may win seats. Therefore, the effects of electoral systems have been analysed as a series of dilemmas concerning co-ordination, notably as the processes by which groups of voters and politicians co-ordinate respective electoral behaviours in order to win more seats or executive portfolios.

The sequence of elite and voter electoral co-ordination, which, according to Duverger accounts for gravity, occurs in two steps. First, since parties will only enter into competition when it is possible they might win seats, if there are reliable electoral expectations, the number of candidates or parties in a constituency cannot exceed M+1. Second, when this co-ordination of elites has not been completely successful, so that more than M+1 candidates or parties are competing for elections in the constituency, an opportunity for strategic voting to influence the distribution of seats arises. According to the M+1 rule, under certain conditions strategic voting reduces the number of candidates competing for seats to a maximum of M+1. More precisely, the logic behind the M+1 rule is a direct generalisation of the instrumental rationality argument in the context of parties and voters where there is robust information pertaining to the different candidates' possibilities. If the expectations concerning the party rankings in the ballot boxes are already clear, then the first M-1 seats are already secured. The only uncertainty, and thus the effective competition, relates to the last available seat. A maximum of two viable candidates can possibly win the seat: the last candidate to win a seat and first one to lose. For instance, in a uninominal constituency, there should be two viable parties or candidates which may win the last (and unique) seat (a potential third candidate knows the implausibility of electoral success and will therefore have to withdraw). Consequently, a maximum of (M-1) + 2 = M+1 viable parties or candidates must be expected to compete. For example, in

Luxembourg each canton elects 6 MEPs, and the maximum number of viable parties or candidates is 6 + 1 = 7.

Although rational choice theory has allowed significant progress in political science, notably in the field of electoral studies, by no means does it constitute a perfect model. In broad terms, two particular categories of criticisms can be identified: one relates to the contents and underlines the unrealistic assumptions regarding the preferences and cognitive abilities of individuals, and the other addresses the methodology and emphasises the limited value of rational choice theory in explaining how politics functions in reality and the weaknesses in the provision of empirical evidence to support the models.

Referring to the first criticism, neither the contention that political actors behave according to an all-knowing and shrewd persona nor the model of maximisation of anticipated values can be supported by empirical evidence. On the one hand, knowledge and shrewd capacities do not enable actors to achieve an optimal adaptation of means and ends, as set forth by rational choice theory. Since the definition of models is drawn from the concept of limited rationality, the adaptable nature underlining human behaviour can be acknowledged, not only in regards to objective circumstances, but also concerning the emotional and cognitive characteristics which are focused at certain objectives. Moreover, due to the biological limits within cognitive capacities, humans fail to process information proportionately. In other words, reaction to information varies according to the context in which it arises: since different people will instinctively concentrate their attention on selected parts of a whole, and since this attention varies, different responses emerge in situations that are identical except for the interpretation made by the decision-makers.

On the other hand, analyses of human behaviour based on rational choice theory are grounded in a simplification of the *explanandum*: the different available modes of action can always be defined in terms of costs and benefits, whereby the maximisation of the net benefit is regarded as the initial behavioural trigger. However, numerous actions are intrinsically reliant on normative or cognitive beliefs which undermines the explanatory value of such a limited approach to rationality. The reasons which influence an actor can be strong without being instrumental, and cannot be reduced to differences in benefits. Moreover, as is widely known, although assumptions cannot be proved to design a model and its consequences, they must rather be empirically tested: the development, the hypotheses and the models do not solve the problem of empirical assessment of theories.

Addressing the second criticism, rational choice theory is particularly criticised for the virtual absence of empirical research which is necessary to confirm theoretical propositions. As such, increasingly sophisticated models make it more and more difficult to draw conclusions that can be observed empirically. However, according to Green and Schapiro (1994), the occasional empirical occurrences which are relied upon are often pervaded by major conceptual and methodological problems whereby empirical evidence is construed in a biased manner, undermined by a lack of interest in rejecting the alternative hypotheses and a tendency towards ex post explanation.

Regarding the former case, biased observations which allow confirmation of the theoretical predictions are thus sought out, and empirical anomalies are not addressed. Moreover, there is a tendency to avoid the null hypotheses or not to specify them clearly (e.g. the level of strategic voting in elections which allows for the acceptance of instrumental explanations for such electoral behaviour). In the latter case, ad hoc developments increase rapidly (e.g. sociological or expressive benefits in the decision to vote in mass elections).

Ignacio Lago

Bibliography

Cox, G. W., *Making Votes Count: Strategic Coordination in the World's Electoral Systems*, Cambridge, Cambridge University Press, 1997.
Downs, A., *An Economic Theory of Democracy*, New York, Harper and Row, 1957.
Elster, J., 'Introduction', in J. Elster (ed.), *Rational Choice*, Oxford, Blackwell, 1986.
Green, D. P. and Shapiro, I., *Pathologies of Rational Choice Theory: a Critique of Applications in Political Science*, New Haven, Yale University Press, 1994.

➡ Electoral Behaviour; European Electoral Sociology.

Registration

The rules dictating the registration of voters are, like the vast majority of laws pertaining to European elections, dependent on the national regulations of individual member states. In fact, they differ greatly from country to country, ranging from voluntary listing to the automatic selection of candidates for each election based on population records. The only point common to all 25 member states is the minimum voting age, fixed at 18. Consequently, the European Parliament elections of 1979, 1984 and 1989 did not add any interesting or original factors to national modalities for the registration of candidates on electoral lists.

The adoption of the Maastricht Treaty in 1992 slightly modified this situation, stipulating that: 'every citizen of the Union residing in a member state of which he is not a national shall have the right to vote and to stand as a candidate in elections to the European Parliament in the member state in which he resides, under the same conditions as nationals of that state' (Article 19 (8B) TEU). European Council directive 93/109/EU of 6 December 1993 (first applied in all member states at the June 1994 European elections) further specified this right in Article 4 by stating that: 'community voters shall exercise their right to vote either in the member state of residence, or in their home member state. No person may vote more than once at the same election. No person may stand as a candidate in more than one member state at the same election.'

This directive provided European voters the choice of voting in their member state of origin or residence. The only exceptions to this rule are cases where countries of origin prohibit their citizens residing abroad from doing so (France, Ireland, Malta, Poland). The exercise of this right remains highly subjective. For instance, Belgian citizens residing abroad have a tendency to vote almost exclusively in their host countries, while Italians and Spanish rarely make use of such right, and tend to vote mainly in their country of origin (either by postal voting or via diplomatic missions). This directive equally indicates that voters need to consent in order to be registered as candidates in their country of residence. In cases where it applies, the principle of mandatory voting concerns all registered voters depending on their place of residence.

The possibility of registering in countries of residence leads to the establishment of complementary lists for European elections designed to keep track of foreign voters or, in cases where lists are published prior to elections, of all EU voters residing in the given state. These usually differ greatly among states, whose conditions for registration may also vary significantly. For instance, due to the high proportion of non-national EU residents (33 per cent), Luxembourg requires a minimum of five years of official residence. Other countries like Austria, the United Kingdom, Denmark, Lithuania or the Netherlands demand the prior registration of potential voters on population registries. Such electoral lists must be elaborated to prevent any given citizen from voting more than once in the same election (directive 93/109/EU). Article 13 of this directive also stipulates that it is the responsibility of the home member state to take the necessary measures to prevent its nationals abroad from casting more than one vote in the same election. Such obligation leads to the establishment of minimal mechanisms for the co-ordination of national administrations. Despite their gradual improvement, these still leave much to be desired as instances of poor communication and misreporting are still seen at every election. Amongst these, the most problematic ones concern the exclusion of voters from their country of origin even after they no longer reside in the state expressing such a request.

As indicated by the Commission's report on the application of such directive to the 1999 elections (COM (2000) 843), the level of EU citizens registered in countries of residence remain low, though it has increased from 6 to 9 per cent from 1994 to 1999. While 44 per cent of non-national voters are registered in Irish electoral lists, the countries with the lowest rates of registration in 1999 are Greece (1.8 per cent), Germany (2.1 per cent) and France (4.9 per cent). Paradoxically, 63 per cent of the 5 million European citizens residing in another member state are mostly concentrated in these last two countries. It is nonetheless likely that the exercise of

this right will be strengthened over time, as indicated by the progress observed in France, whose level of registered voters reached 12.5 per cent in 2004 (based on a preliminary study by Strudel 2002).

Emmanuel Henry

Bibliography

Strudel, S., 'Les citoyens européens aux urnes: les usages ambigus de l'article 8B du traité de Maastricht', *Revue internationale de politique comparée*, 9, 1, 2002, pp. 47–63.

→ Citizen (EU); Voters; Voting Within the European Parliament.

Religion

To what extent do the religious attitudes held by individuals influence their electoral behaviour? The importance of religion has often been highlighted in France where, in each election, it is observed that the more devout Catholics are most likely to vote right-wing (Dargent 2004). Similarly, atheists are more likely to favour the left. This phenomenon has often been less visible at the European level (Bréchon 2002; Broughton and Napel 2000). However, leading international surveys show that religious practice has an important impact on ethical and political attitudes. In almost all European countries, a high level of Christian religious practice is linked to more traditional, conformist or right-wing attitudes. The differential impact of the various Christian confessions is conversely unclear. Given the individual historical make-up of each country, important comparative differences remain. Significant factors of differentiation include the relationship between church and state, the emergence

Table 1 Membership and religious practices in the former EU-15 countries (European Values Survey, 1999)

	Finland		Denmark		Sweden		France		Netherlands		Great Britain	
	18–29	60+	18–29	60+	18–29	60+	18–29	60+	18–29	60+	18–29	60+
Feel religious	44	78	53	82	25	51	34	61	55	75	24	55
Feel non-religious	41	14	27	8	60	41	44	27	36	18	57	36
Atheist	4	2	9	3	11	3	17	9	7	5	9	2
Catholic	–	–	1	1	3	0	41	69	16	31	11	11
Protestant or Anglican	90	85	86	90	69	74	1	2	10	26	46	63
Other	1	2	2	2	4	3	5	1	5	7	17	16
Agnostic	8	11	12	7	24	23	53	29	70	37	26	10
Attend service once a month	7	25	5	24	7	17	5	23	13	51	12	26
Less often	36	45	35	37	39	53	23	23	28	14	18	13
Never or rarely	57	30	60	39	55	30	72	55	58	36	70	62

Interpretation: Out of 100 young Finnish people aged from 18 to 29 years, 44 feel religious, 41 do not feel religious and 4 are atheists.

of confessional parties and the salience of debates centred around particular problems (the status of schools, legislation on divorce, abortion, homo-parenting, etc.). Moreover, the same religion can develop, in the name of the faith, a plurality of political values.

Religion traditionally constitutes a significant variable in terms of electoral behaviour, alongside social categories (Lipset and Rokkan 1967) and is often more meaningful than age, education or gender. However, the role of religion has clearly changed following a process of secularisation amongst European societies. Religion has been left with a reduced impact on societies, and fewer people identify themselves with religion or claim to practise it. The aim of this article is initially to demonstrate this process of secularisation as being certainly quite real but with a disproportionate and unequal impact in various European countries, before portraying the relationship between religious integration and individual political orientations.

Table 1 shows the current religious setting in the former EU-15 member states in terms of subjective religious identity, denominational membership and levels of church attendance. Overall, 61 per cent consider themselves religious, 46 per cent declare themselves Catholic and 22 per cent claim to belong to a Protestant Church or the Church of England; however, almost half of the population never or hardly ever attends church. A large proportion can be said to hold some form of affinity with the religious universe (for example, religion as morals or an attachment to traditional culture, or a vague belief in life after death) but few people display a structured religious identity. Two extremes remain either side of them: the faithful supporters of the Christian belief system and convinced atheists. However, this panorama differs enormously across different generations.

In all countries, the relationship between young people and religion definitely becomes weakened. Only 1 in 5 attends a religious service at least once a month, and in certain countries this proportion is lower than 10 per cent (e.g. France, Denmark, Sweden, Finland). Other significant disparities remain

	Germany		Belgium		Spain		Austria		Ireland		Italy		Portugal		Greece		Total	
	18–29	60+	18–29	60+	18–29	60+	18–29	60+	18–29	60+	18–29	60+	18–29	60+	18–29	60+	18–29	60+
	40	67	52	75	39	72	66	80	63	84	79	88	73	93	54	89	46	70
	46	24	37	15	44	22	24	13	30	14	15	9	16	6	37	11	40	22
	8	4	8	7	10	3	3	2	1	0	2	1	5	0	4	0	9	4
	32	34	40	70	70	89	81	80	82	93	79	88	78	91	1	0	45	54
	34	48	4	2	0	2	6	6	4	1	0	0	1	1	0	0	16	24
	6	2	11	3	0	0	1	0	0	4	0	0	2	2	96	99	9	7
	27	16	46	26	30	9	11	14	14	3	21	12	20	7	3	1	30	16
	20	46	17	46	13	58	25	57	44	93	40	66	38	64	14	58	19	44
	47	32	29	14	25	20	40	12	35	2	42	19	19	11	82	33	30	20
	33	22	54	41	61	22	35	30	22	6	18	15	43	26	4	9	51	35

across countries, with some particularly advanced in the process of secularisation whilst others remain more rooted in religious values (in traditional Catholic countries such as Ireland, Italy, Portugal, approximately 4 out of 10 young people still attend a monthly service). But even in these countries, the process of secularisation is still present and important differences in religiosity separate the younger and older generations.

Table 2 presents the same indicators for nine of the ten countries which joined the EU in 2004. The diversity of their national circumstances is even stronger than in Western Europe. Poland, Malta and Slovakia are all countries where Catholicism continues to be central. Conversely, the Czech Republic and Estonia are very strongly secularised (at least 80 per cent of 18–29-year-olds declare themselves agnostic). Moreover, the argument that religion is making its comeback after almost 50 years of communism has yet to be confirmed for younger generations, systematically less religious than older cohorts. Communism, however, seems to have failed in eradicating religion (Zrinscak 2004), and the proportion of atheists is no higher than in West Europe.

In spite of the strong secularisation, which affects the whole of Europe, the influence of religious attitudes on electoral behaviour remains important, particularly in the west. A simple comparison of left–right placement and religious practice shows that across the EU-15, the level of right-wing identification ranges from 22 per cent for those who never (or hardly ever) attend a religious service, to 41 per cent who attend at least once a month (Table 3). This relationship is generally confirmed across countries. The situation is slightly different in Central Europe (Table 4). At the aggregate level, the relationship between religion and ideology is ambiguous but nonetheless confirmed in six out of nine countries. However, there seems to be no clear link in Latvia, a weak one in Hungary and a reversed one in Estonia. Certain features of Central European countries can contribute to explain why the link between religion and politics appears more blurred than in Western Europe. The structure of political life around a

Table 2 Membership and religious practices in nine new member states (European Values Survey, 1999)

	Malta		Poland		Hungary		Slovenia		Czech Republic		Slovakia		Latvia		Estonia		Lithuania		Ensemble	
	18	60+	18	60+	18	60+	18	60+	18	60+	18	60+	18	60+	18	60+	18	60+	18	60+
Feel religious	65	91	94	97	47	78	66	80	34	62	74	93	71	83	34	58	77	95	74	87
Feel non-religious	35	9	5	2	47	19	27	14	58	28	20	5	26	15	58	38	22	4	23	10
Avowed atheist	–	–	1	0	6	3	7	7	8	10	5	3	4	3	8	4	2	0	4	3
Catholic	97	97	91	95	33	51	61	81	14	49	55	74	18	23	–	–	68	85	64	75
Protestant	0	1	3	1	8	24	1	2	4	7	9	17	12	30	7	25	2	2	4	8
Other	–	–	0	1	0	2	3	1	2	1	2	1	14	21	7	13	1	8	1	3
Agnostic	3	1	6	3	58	24	35	17	80	43	34	8	56	26	86	61	29	5	31	14
Attend a service once a month	80	92	74	84	10	30	24	44	10	24	41	67	11	22	5	22	17	65	46	61
Less often	11	3	17	9	34	23	40	19	23	22	19	11	36	42	40	39	50	26	24	16
Never or rarely	9	6	9	7	56	48	36	36	67	54	41	22	53	36	55	40	33	10	30	24

Interpretation: Out of 100 Polish people aged 60 years and over, 95 declared themselves as Catholic, 1 as Protestant, 1 of another religion and 3 as being without denominational membership.

Table 3   Religious attendance of right-wing people (6–10) (West Europe, 1999)

	Finland	Denmark	Sweden	France	Netherlands	Great Britain	Germany	Belgium	Spain	Austria	Ireland	Italy	Portugal	Greece	Total
Once a month	64	50	50	44	46	35	44	38	37	43	40	41	38	44	41
Less often	52	45	48	33	38	28	37	30	21	32	24	34	31	30	34
Never or rarely	40	35	37	18	34	20	28	21	10	27	20	23	25	9	22
Average	48	40	43	24	38	24	37	28	22	35	34	36	32	35	31

Table 4   Religious attendance of right-wing people (6–10) (new European member states, 1999)

	Malta	Poland	Hungary	Slovenia	Czech Republic	Slovakia	Latvia	Estonia	Lithuania	Total
Once a month	58	31	24	26	58	33	26	25	36	32
Less often	47	18	24	14	60	27	29	38	23	28
Never or rarely	44	17	16	13	47	21	28	36	15	28
Average	56	28	19	18	51	28	28	36	25	30

Table 5   Age and religious attendance for right-wing voters (6–10) (EU-15)

	Once a month	Less often	Never/rarely	Total
18–29 yrs	35	26	17	23
30–44 yrs	38	36	21	29
45–59 yrs	39	33	27	32
60+ yrs	46	42	25	38
Total	41	34	22	31

Interpretation: Out of 100 people aged 60 years or above who attend religious services at least once a month, 46 are right-wing, whereas out of 100 people aged 18–29 years who never participate, only 17 are right-wing.

Table 6   Age and religious attendance for right-wing voters (6–10) (EU-15) (6–10) (new EU countries)

	Once a month	Less often	Never/rarely	Total
18–29 yrs	27	26	31	28
30–44 yrs	30	25	29	29
45–59 yrs	33	32	27	31
60+ yrs	36	30	23	32
Total	32	28	28	30

Interpretation: same principle as for Table 5.

left–right ideological cleavage seems less apparent than in the West. Recently created political parties are still relatively unstable in terms of their orientations. As such, the system of religious beliefs, which usually leads to the adoption of traditional family values, negative attitudes towards liberal morals, and the condemnation of abortion, as well as traditional political orientations, has a weaker impact.

Therefore, the impact of religion, particularly in the West, largely works as a cohort effect. Secularisation is particularly prevalent amongst younger people. It may therefore not fully explain why, in Western Europe, right-wing identification is significantly more developed amongst older generations (Table 5). However, within generation, the effect of religious practice is particularly manifest, including for young people. With regards to the new member states (Table 6), political orientation is rather insensitive to generational and religious effects. However, on closer inspection, the effect of religious practice remains important amongst old generations, whereas it is minimal for young people. This leaves one thinking that after the fall of communism, the young did not identify the left with secularism but with the Old Regime.

Pierre Bréchon

Bibliography

Bréchon, P., 'Influence de l'intégration religieuse sur les attitudes', *Revue française de sociologie*, 43, 3, 2002, pp. 461–83 (translated as 'Influence of Religious Integration on Attitudes: a Comparative Analysis of European Countries', *Revue française de sociologie*, 45, supplement, 2004, pp. 27–49.

Broughton, D. and Napel, H.-M., *Religion and Mass Electoral Behaviour*, London, Routledge, 2000.

Dargent, C., 'La religion, encore et toujours', in B. Cautrès and N. Mayer (eds), *Le nouveau désordre électoral. Les leçons du 21 avril 2002*, Paris, Presses de Sciences Po, 2004, pp. 161–83.

Lipset, S. and Rokkan, S. (eds), *Party Systems and Voters' Alignments*, London, Collier Macmillan, 1967.

Zrinscak, S., 'Generations and Atheism: Patterns of Response to Communist Rule among Different Generations and Countries', *Social Compass*, 51, 2, 2004, pp. 221–34.

→ Electoral System; European Electoral Sociology; European People's Party (EPP); Young People.

Remuneration

Nowadays, more than ever before, the issue of the indemnity or remuneration offered to MEPs is associated with questions relating to their status. Since the Amsterdam Treaty supplied a legal basis to this demand ('the European Parliament fixes the status, general conditions of exercise and functions of its members after consultation with the Commission and the Council's unanimous approval', Article 190, paragraph 5), the equal treatment of all MEPs has become a sort of emblem. In fact, it covers the 'transparency of regulations', political financing, and 'discriminations on the basis of nationality'. Legal requisites also need to be addressed from a sociological perspective. According to political science, the adoption of systems of remuneration affects the nature of the work of MEPs, by specialising their function based on a truly transnational basis. In fact, such a measure would result in a weakening of the ties between the candidates and their country of origin or residence, heading towards a single European constituency. Moreover, it would contribute to giving greater autonomy to the political role of MEPs, which has, up to this point, remained attached to the role of national MP.

Often targeted by populist movements within the EU, current practice sees MEPs enjoying the same indemnity as national MPs. This system is financed by individual member states (in the case of the Netherlands, however, the indemnity of MEPs is inferior to that of MPs). This lack of harmonisation leads to severe inequalities pertaining to the treatment of MEPs depending on their country of origin or residence (the gap being of 1 to 4 in the 1999–2004 legislature). With the enlargement, this disparity further increased between 1 and 15. In fact, a Hungarian MEP receives €800 monthly (i.e. less than the average salary of an administrative secretary in the EP), while his Italian counterpart earns over €11 000 to fulfil the same political function. To a certain extent, such disparities are compensated by a generous ad hoc system. In fact, the Parliament reimburses its representatives all travel expenses, calculated on the basis of air kilometres, irrespective of the means of transportation actually used, as well as accommodation expenses (€262 per day in May 2004), those incurred during electoral campaigning, and those resulting from trips abroad (within the EU and limited to €3500 per MEP). The Parliament also grants its representatives a 'secretariat indemnity', a 'set telephone indemnity', as well as funds for the hiring of a parliamentary assistant, and a going-away allowance. In 2004 alone, these expenditures amounted to more than €92 million (amounts allotted in

2004 according to the draft EU budget, Article 100, paragraphs 1004–6) complementing basic charges and expenses already included in the budgets of individual member states.

Several parliamentary initiatives have sought, since 1979, to put an end to this situation, a source of frustration and, at times, of fraud. Based on two reports presented by German MEP Willy Rothley (PES) in December 1998 and May 1999, the European Parliament adopted (prior to the entry into force of the Amsterdam Treaty) a resolution on the matter (JOC 279 of 1 October 1999: 171). During the 2000 IGC, the European Commission and Parliament re-emphasised the importance of such a statute, especially with the prospect of constituting transnational lists for the forthcoming EP elections.

The Nice Treaty transformed the rules of the game. The adoption of a common statute of MEPs is no longer subject to a unanimous approval of the Council but to qualified majority instead. By contrast, all decisions concerning the tax regime of current or former MEPs continue to be based on the principle of unanimity. Based on this procedural change, Willy Rothley put forward new suggestions on 21 May 2003 in his 'Report on the Adoption of a Statute on MEPs' (2003/2004; INI). Article 16 stipulates that the indemnity or salary of MEPs must be equal to the basic salary of a judge of the European Court of Justice, €8500 (gross) per calendar month. Moreover, Article 17 seeks to moralise cumulative indemnity or salaries by specifying that all remuneration received from another parliament will be deducted from the representative's EP one. Another technique suggested to make the Parliament's personnel more autonomous consists of financing the benefits of MEPs solely by means of the EU budget, and subsequently subjecting their salaries to standard EU taxation. Finally, this report appears to be in favour of reforming other benefits and expenses claimed by MEPs on the basis of 'expenses actually incurred within their mandate's framework'. Such proposals based on the status of MEPs were adopted by the Parliament with a large majority on 4 June 2003, but subsequently rejected by the European Council of 26 January, due to the explicit demands of four countries (Germany, Austria, France and Sweden). The official reason for this rejection was that the level of remuneration envisaged by such a proposal would have been too high. The European Parliament thus remains, so far, a transnational institution, in which members are compensated and taxed based on the sovereign decisions of individual member states. This situation is indicative of the actual nature of the obstacles preventing the 'autonomisation' of this electoral arena characterised by truly European political parties leading to large mobilising structures that could counterbalance the influence of states on the composition of electoral lists at the European Parliament, on the determination of national boundaries and on the progress of the European legislative arena.

Yves Déloye
Olivier Ihl

Bibliography

Bardi, L., 'Transnational Party Federations, European Parliamentary Groups and the Building of Europarties', in R. S. Katz and P. Mair (eds), *How Parties Organize*, London, Sage, 1994, pp. 357–72.

Pöhle, K., 'Europäische Parteien. Für wen und für was eigentlich? Kritik und Perspektive', *Zeitschrift für Parlamentsfragen*, 31, 3, 2000, pp. 599–619.

Silvestro, M., 'Des groupes politiques du Parlement européen aux partis européens', *Revue du Marché Commun*, 327, 1989, pp. 309–11.

→ European Parliament; Members of the European Parliament (Legal and Political Status).

Representation

During the 2004–9 term of office, the 732 members of the European Parliament 'represent' over 350 million voters. The basic foundation of 'representative democracy' is the representation of the masses by a small minority. This type of link produces the expected effects of legitimacy for a legal and political order, as approved by the representatives of the people, only if a community based on political interests already exists (Costa and Navarro 2003). However, that the European Parliament intends to be located *before* the unique body of the electorate is felt to be obvious by the latter. In contrast to the banal impression which prevails today, the election of such a 'supranational' Parliament, which, through the elected representation of the 'European people', aimed in the long term to create it in the very spirit of those who constitute it through their vote, is by no means apparent (Pasquinucci and Verzichelli 2004).

The Act of 20 September 1976 on the election of representatives in the European Parliament by universal suffrage contemplated the adoption of a uniform electoral procedure, and, failing this, 'common principles'. In 2002, an agreement was reached with both the European Council and the European Parliament on the lesser evil, whereby the proposal of the European Parliament to elect 10 per cent of the MEPs on pan-European lists (contained in the Anastassopoulos report of July 1998) indeed failed to be adopted by the Council, and it was reaffirmed that the organisation of European voting shall only take place in the electoral frame-work chosen by each state. The 'Treaty establishing a Constitution for Europe' does not change anything as to the national character of electoral procedures. However, neither does it obstruct legitimate representation by the European Parliament of the electorate, since, in other federations, the same diversity of electoral systems to choose representatives exists on an exclusively territorial basis.

If the European Parliament is perceived as being awarded the eminent role of representing the citizens, it operates within a multiplicity of possible modes of representation of EU nationals (Costa and Navarro 2003): national governments and parliaments, consultative committees at the European level such as the Economic and Social Council, and European procedures like the 'social dialogue'. The 'Treaty establishing a Constitution for Europe' reinforces this tendency by giving status to an additional form of representation of the 'citizens of the Union'. Indeed, it is now possible to identify a 'participative democracy' emerging (Article I-47), defined as 'an opened, transparent and constructive dialogue with representative associations and civil society'. Therefore it acknowledges, even at the highest possible legal level, the privileged bonds between the European Commission and the interest groups, which constitute the other face of representation within the EU (Kohler-Koch et al. 2004).

The European Parliament remains seemingly based on the simple principle 'one person, one vote', whereby the latter determines the number of elected officials for each member state. Moreover, whilst affirming that an individual possessing any member state nationality can stand as a candidate and possibly be elected in any other member state, this reinforces the idea of a representation of a European people in general. In practice, this opportunity is very seldom used, and, in spite of the mediatisation which surrounds them (as was the example for the Franco-German Green MEP Daniel Cohn-Bendit in 1999), European MEPs who stand and are elected in another country to where they hold nationality are extremely rare (less than five out of 2140 elected officials between 1979 and 1999, according to Pasquinucci and Verzichelli 2004). This absence of mobility of elected officials between member states perfectly reflects one of the essential elements of the EU: that citizen mobility (in terms of residence) between different states is generally speaking extremely weak. The European Parliament thus effectively represents the reality according to which the EU produces law for a cluster of diversified populations whose members, over their lifetime, are registered in only one member state and most of the time have a single nationality.

This representation of the electorate of each European state remains, however, very imperfect since it denies the very principle of equality of suffrage as assumed in the European voting tradition: due to the extreme variation in the sizes of the electorates within member states (from 1 to 288), the voters in (all) the small countries are awarded a disproportionate weight compared to those in the larger countries (Delwit 2003) (Table 1).

The choices of the 'Nice Treaty' and of the 'Treaty establishing a Constitution for Europe' do not introduce any further changes in this respect. The latter stipulates that 'the representation of citizens is ensured in a proportionally graduated way, with a minimum threshold of six members per member state' (Article I-20, paragraph 2). This inequality of representation will maintain itself since the maximum number of members of the European Parliament must be limited to 750 MEPs, even with further enlarge-

ments on the horizon. Neither do the treaties envisage a revision of the number of European MEPs for each member state according to the evolution of its population.

The obligation contained in the 'common principles' to adopt proportional voting (either list or 'transferable single vote') and to not establish a minimum threshold of access to representation of over 5 per cent of the votes, indicates that no significant opinion trend in an EU state should be deprived of representation within the European Parliament. However, small parties in the smaller countries are often excluded from the latter, since, for instance, for only 14 elected officials, slightly over 5 per cent of the votes are required to secure at least one elected official (see recent reflections on 'lost votes' during the European elections from the International Institute for Democracy and Electoral Assistance, www.idea.int). In spite of this aforementioned distortion, the level of reality which the European Parliament represents best at this stage of its evolution is the tremendous variety of parties present in the EU. Indeed, from this point of view, the weak turnout of voters in some states to appoint their representatives in the European Parliament in no way hinders the capacity of the European Parliament to represent this partisan diversity, providing a place of political confrontation (and also of socialisation to the EU) for (almost) all the political parties present in the EU.

In addition, if the European Parliament is evaluated by the yardstick of comparison between the socio-economic structure of the group of elected officials and that of the voters as a whole (and moreover that of the populations which these elected officials are supposed to represent), all the socio-graphic data indicate a considerable

Table 1 Numerical representation across member states

Country	Number of registered voters (a)	Number of MEPs (b)	Number of registered voters per MEP (a/b)=(c)	Average % (C/M%)	Effective theoretical members of Parliament (a/36000)
Spain	34 706 000	54	643 000	134	964
Italy	49 854 000	78	640 000	133	1385
Germany	61 682 000	99	623 000	130	1713
UK	44 157 000	78	566 000	*117*	*1226*
Poland	29 986 000	54	555 000	115	832
France	41 519 000	78	532 000	110	1153
Average (A)	*352 000 000*	*732*	*481 000*	*100*	*9777*
Holland	12 169 000	27	451 000	94	338
Greece	9 910 000	24	422 000	86	275
Portugal	8 821 000	24	368 000	76	245
Sweden	6 828 000	19	359 000	75	189
Czech Rep.	8 283 000	24	345 000	72	230
Austria	6 049 000	18	336 000	70	168
Hungary	8 046 000	24	335 000	70	223
Belgium	7 552 000	24	315 000	65	210
Finland	4 228 000	14	302 000	63	117
Slovakia	4 210 000	14	301 000	63	117
Demark	4 013 000	14	287 000	60	111
Ireland	3 132 000	13	241 000	50	87
Slovenia	1 629 000	7	233 000	48	45
Lithuania	2 654 000	13	204 000	42	73
Latvia	1 398 000	9	155 000	32	38
Estonia	874 000	6	146 000	30	24
Cyprus	483 000	6	81 000	17	13
Malta	304 000	5	61 000	13	8
Luxembourg	214 000	6	36 000	7	6

Source: calculations derived from European Parliament data.

skew between what would be the socio-logical representation of each country and the actual representation of this country in the European Parliament. Certainly, all the parliaments of our time suffer from such representative biases, but, as available studies demonstrate, there are some good reasons for the electorate to prefer a representation which mirrors more their own socio-economic composition (Norris and Franklin 1997). Mather calculated that, of the MEPs elected in 1994 and 1999, around 7–8 per cent had corporate business experience, around 2–3 per cent had agricultural experience, around 4–5 per cent had experience of blue-collar work, and around 1–3 per cent of manual work. All the other elected officials consisted of 18–19 per cent of professional politicians and around 57–64 per cent of 'professionals' (white-collar workers), with the highest number of them being in fact university professors (Mather 2001). This domination of the 'symbol manipulators', drawing on the terminology of Reich, seems to reproduce itself in the current European Parliament. Mather hence concludes that, aside from proportional representation, 'the European Parliament rather resembles the British Parliament before 1832 in the sense that it exclusively represents an economic interest group'. Addressing this socio-economic bias, it is also pertinent to note that 'the average European deputy is white, male, middle-aged, and not disabled. The average European voter has all the likelihood of being a woman or a young or elderly person.' Norris and Franklin (1997) arrived at a similar conclusion concerning the MEPs elected in 1994: if women constituted over 28 per cent of the MEPs, no less than 76 per cent of them held an advanced level of university education ('graduate') and 59 per cent worked for the public sector.

Thus the European Parliament seems to have some degree of representativeness in regards to national and partisan membership (and would like to be so concerning the gender balance), in so far as it considers that the defence of national and partisan (and also gender) interests cannot be transferred to a person with different characteristics (selected, inherited or biological), whereas the defence of any other interest, which arises from other social characteristics of the electorate, can validly be handled by another person who does not possess this characteristic. In other words, a Maltese is needed to defend Maltese interests, a member of the Labour Party socialist interests and a woman female interests, but a university professor is also well able to represent a blue-collar worker.

This social (or socio-economic) discrepancy in representation is so huge and evident that it seems preferable to approach it only from the viewpoint of the capacity of the European elected officials to accurately represent the political interests of their constituents, to make the most of their delegate role. It is inspiring, then, to consider the rich tradition of study inaugurated in the United States by Miller and Stokes (1963). This comparison, notably regarding opinions on European integration (Thomassen and Schmitt 2000), owes its existence to the establishment of the Eurobarometer by the European Communities since the early 1970s. Thus, by confronting the declarations of the elected officials and of the voters to the same set of questions (for instance, since the standard Eurobarometer 41, Spring 1994), it is possible to observe that members of the European Parliament (similar to their national counterparts) are clearly more Europhile than their own constituents, especially when considering the detail of the political questions at stake. Overall a certain inefficiency of political representation at the European level appears to emerge. However, from the point of view of political theory, if one is not averse to the old-fashioned visions of Sieyès or Burke, such a gap does not shed any light on the quality of the latter, since the preference for integration of the elected officials (at all levels) can be conceived as favourable to the 'true' interests of their voters.

Christophe Bouillaud

Bibliography

Costa, O. and Navarro, J., 'La représentation au Parlement européen. Qui représentent les parlementaires européens?', in S. Saurugger (ed.), *Les modes de représentation dans l'Union européenne*, Paris, L'Harmattan, 2003, pp. 123–52.

Delwit, P., 'Les fédérations européennes et les groupes politiques au Parlement européen: vecteurs de la représentation dans l'Union européenne?', in S. Saurugger (ed.), *Les modes de représentation dans l'Union européenne*, Paris, L'Harmattan, 2003, pp. 97–122.

Kohler-Koch, B., Conzelmann, T. and Knodt M., *Europäische Integration, Europäisches Regieren*, Wiesbaden, VS Verlag für Sozialwissenschaften, 2004.

Mather, J., 'The European Parliament: a Model of Representative Democracy?', *West European Politics*, 24, 1, 2001, pp. 181–201.

Miller, Warren E. and Stokes, Donald E., 'Constituency Influence in Congress', *American Political Science Review*, 57, 1963, pp. 45–56.

Norris, P. and Franklin, M. N., 'Social Representation', *European Journal of Political Research*, 32, 6, 1997, pp. 185–210.

Pasquinucci, D. and Verzichelli, L., *Elezioni europee e classe politica sovranazionale 1979–2004*, Bologne, Il Mulino, 2004.

Thomassen, J. and Schmitt, H., 'Représentation politique et intégration européenne', in G. Grunberg, P. Perrineau and C. Ysmal (eds), *Le vote des Quinze: Les élections européennes du 13 juin 1999*, Paris, Presses de Sciences Po, 2000, pp. 49–74.

→ Act of 1976; Citizen (EU); Civil Society; Composition of the European Parliament; Electoral System; Eligibility; Eurobarometer; European Parliament; European Political Parties; Interest Groups; Lobbying; Members of the European Parliament (Legal and Political Status); Members of the European Parliament (Sociology of Political Office); Multi-Level Governance; Nationalisation of European Elections; Territorial Organisation; Voters; Women.

Right

At the beginning of the sixth term of office, the European right maintained its position of prevalence within the EP since it gathered, in its widest definition, 420 out of the 732 MEPs. It is characterised by a great historical, ideological and organisational diversity that is only imperfectly reflected by its institutional structuring. Sometimes reduced by convergence movements, this diversity, however, generates tensions.

Ideological diversity

The classifications based on ideological criteria and the work on the 'political families' usually determine three 'rights' in Europe. The liberal right was born in the nineteenth century around a burgeoning bourgeoisie mobilised against landowners. Stemming from industrialisation, it is historically marked by the defence of economic freedoms, trade and manufacture interests, and political freedoms against absolutism. Rationalist in spirit, it is characterised by a certain distance from religion. The conservative right was born in opposition to the liberal movement since it stood against the affirmation of political freedoms and the extension of universal suffrage, and stood for the defence of landowners and the rural world. Attached to tradition, it favoured respect for social hierarchies. The Christian democrat right was also born in the nineteenth century but only became a genuine political force at the European level after the Second World War. It then participated in the establishment of the welfare state and European integration. It actually mixed together conservative Catholic defence movements and parties attached to the promotion of a third way between capitalism and collectivism. It now displays a will to deconfessionalisation. The existence and weight of each of these branches and the alliances they made among themselves vary according to the national historical paths. Hence, the steps and shapes taken by industrialisation, urbanisation and national unification, but also the various religious configurations (existence of a prevailing religion, minority religions, church–state relations) are decisive variables to understand the different national cases.

Organisations' diversity

Other types of criteria based on the political parties' creation and organisation modes can be identified. We cannot totally agree with the idea that the European right is essentially composed of executives' parties (in Duverger's meaning) created from parliamentary circles and giving prestige to the elected representatives, among whom the notables are those with social resources. Indeed, if this definition usually applies to liberal parties, it does not take into account a certain number of European right parties that can be assimilated to mass parties. Differences relative to the degree of institutionalisation can also be seen. On the one hand, there are highly institutionalised organisations created around a parliamentary circle and marked by the control of the centre (for instance, the Spanish Popular Party); on the other hand, less institutionalised organisations created from local religious associations (for instance, the Italian former Christian Democracy). Between them, there is usually a party such as the German CDU that, while being marked by its decentralised creation, was not created from a network of religious associations and does not have all the characteristics of Christian Democrat organisations.

Institutional structuring

The parliamentary structuring of these European 'rights' only imperfectly reflects today the above-mentioned classifications. The most powerful wing is made of the 268 MEPs of the European Popular Party (EPP-ED) that gathers the biggest parties (by order of numbers: German CDU-CSU, Spanish PP, French UMP and British Conservative Party). It thus incarnates the heart of the European right. A new group, the Alliance of Liberals and Democrats for Europe (ALDE), which gathers 88 MEPs and claims a centrist and integrationist stand, was created by the joining of the EPP-ED renegades to the liberal wing. It pools MEPs who come as much from the centre-left as from the centre-right and has authority to hold a position of mainspring in the European Parliament. Its highest numbers are provided by the Italians from small radical and liberal parties, the French from the UDF and the British Liberal Democrats, but it also welcomes a wide range of liberal and pro-European parties from Northern Europe. The Independence and Democracy group (37 MEPs), which is clearly Eurosceptic by nature, is essentially composed of MEPs from the British UKIP, the Polish Family League and the Italian Lombard League. Finally, one last group, the Union for a Europe of Nations (27 MEPs) is mainly composed of nationalist MEPs, mainly Italians from the National Alliance, Polish from Law and Justice, and Irish from Fianna Fáil.

Another form of institutional structuring is managed by the transnational and extra-parliamentary federations. They try to co-ordinate the right-wing parties adhering to the EPP and the ALDE. However, such co-ordination between national parties remains modest. Indeed, movements of organisational schemes' importation are more and more frequent (for instance, the new

French UMP has explicitly taken the PP or the CDU as examples). But the homogenisation of national campaigns is very low; it has essentially been seen in 2004 through some exchanges between speakers in the electoral meetings of the European right groups.

Convergences

The basic movement since the 1980s has been the European right's acceptance of neo-liberal ideas. This evolution has reduced the differences between liberal and conservative right-wing factions, but also with parties of Christian Democrat origin (such as the Austrian ÖVP and the Dutch CDA) and of Gaullist origin (such as the former French RPR). This pooling has indeed blurred the EPP's original Christian Democrat identity. Its strategy of absorption of a wide range of right-wing parties (Forza Italia, Spanish PP, British Conservative Party, and former French RPR) ensured its hegemony but weakened its specificity.

On social matters, the European right usually share a form of resistance towards the evolution of customs (abortion, homosexuals' rights, etc.). Thus, the EPP, in its declaration of principles entitled 'A Union of Values' adopted in January 2001, reaffirmed its reservations regarding abortion. However, distinctions exist between the parties classified as Christian Democrat, less permissive, and others; and, even more precisely, between the parties of the multiconfessional countries such as the German CDU and the Dutch CDA, and the exclusively Protestant parties of the Scandinavian countries that are even more conservative on moral questions. Furthermore, when talking about big European conservative parties, such as the UK Conservative Party, the CDU and the UMP, the divergences between traditionalists and progressives on moral matters most of the time emerge within these very organisations themselves.

Tensions

Tensions within the European right are greater concerning its relations with extreme-right or populist movements, such as the controversies in the face of the Austrian ÖVP's choice of governing with the FPÖ. This question of course is not asked in the same terms and with the same acuity according to the national circumstances. The differences are due at the same time to the diverse shapes these movements take, their electoral weight and of course the institutional framework of the countries concerned. Various solutions have been implemented: the inclusion of populist or extreme-right movements has thus been made in Austria, Italy and Portugal (the Portuguese CDS-PP, which was excluded from the EPP-ED due to its anti-integrationist stand in 1993, returned to this group in 2004); the inclusion in a parliamentary coalition without any governmental participation characterises the Danish situation; the refusal of any alliance with noticeable local exceptions is the rule in Belgium and France. Beyond the strict question of alliances, we can also consider the role of other forms of integration of these populist movements in the Conservative right. Integration can thus take the shape of a promotion in the right's programme of themes put forward by these movements, or a setting of trends representing these points of view within the parties themselves (for instance, the Greek New Democracy).

The European question is the second point of dissension within the European right. On the right, the most clearly pro-European stands come either from organisations that are clearly part of the weakened Christian Democrat movement, or from the liberal movement, or from a certain number of conservative parties created in the context of democratic transitions of Southern Europe, countries marked by dictatorships (e.g the EPP). In the latter case, the adoption of very favourable stands towards European integration is part of a wider process of relegitimating these national right groupings. For the rest, the European question usually causes cleavages within the right-wing parties and most of the time generates a gap and tensions between leaders and members, the former being more favourable to European integration than the latter. The European issue is, for example, an object of controversy within the British and French rights; it caused the creation of factions, contributed to the organisation of the internal competition within these parties and even generated scissions. The resistance to European integration is not only reflected within the right groups of the former European nations, which are suspicious of the logic of multi-level governance introduced by European integration; it is also seen in federalist countries such as Germany. Hence, the German CDU, under the influence of the Bavarian CSU, is also critical of the European logic and institutions. This right-wing anti-Europeanism mainly uses the ideas of a nationalism sometimes called 'pro-sovereignty', but can also be nourished, as in the cases of the Scandinavian right groups, by an attachment to the virtues of rural life and an opposition to central authority.

The issue for the European 'right' is thus their capacity to frame this plurality and organise themselves institutionally. The progressive integration of parties that are clearly reserved about European integration and particularly of Central and Eastern Europe countries' right-wing organisations will inevitably stir up tensions.

Florence Haegel

→ European Democratic Union; European Liberal Democrat and Reform Party (ELDR); European People's Party (EPP); Extreme Right.

Right to Vote

One sign of European unification's initial hesitations is the fact that the Act of 20 September 1976 concerning the election of representatives of the assembly by direct universal suffrage remained very vague about the legislation on the right to vote in European elections. Though it strongly affirms the principle of universal suffrage (Article 1), the Act leaves to member states' electoral laws the responsibility of precisely defining the outline of the electorate to choose 'in a direct manner' the Members of the European Parliament. This situation continues, awaiting the implementation of a 'uniform electoral procedure', which is not yet complete, despite some progress brought about by the Council decisions of 25 June 2002 and 23 September 2002, amending the aforementioned Act.

One can therefore see that, at the first European elections in June 1979, the criteria used to define the people entitled to vote were different from one country to another. Only the age criteria were harmonised, when Denmark accepted, following the referendum held on 20 September 1978, setting the voting age at 18 (this age was then 20 for the *Folketing* elections), as it was in the eight other EEC countries. Residence conditions required for registration on the electoral rolls varied significantly from one country to another (six months in Belgium and France, three months in the United Kingdom). Likewise, electoral disqualifications were still set by rules reflecting 'electoral customs' inherited from each country's democratic history. In another symbolic fashion, the exercise of the right to vote by citizens residing abroad showed strong disparities, resulting eventually in the drawing of a 'blurred figure' (Sasse et al. 1981). Some electoral laws have nevertheless granted the right to vote to EU nationals residing on their territory: this is the case in the United Kingdom (though this measure is applicable to Irish citizens only), in Ireland and in the Netherlands, where this right is granted to nationals whose member state of origin does not allow them to vote at European elections (Burban 1979: 100–3).

Since the early days, a trend of harmonisation of rules governing registration on electoral rolls, as well as the exercise of the right to vote in European elections, gives some sense to the notion of an 'EU voter'. From now on, the right to vote in European elections is, in all states of the enlarged EU, granted to all 'EU citizens' aged 18 and over, and fulfilling penal and civil conditions for registration on electoral rolls, in their country of origin as well as in their country of residence. This political right was listed among the rights granted by the Treaty of Maastricht, and then the treaties of Amsterdam and Nice, as part of the EU citizenship granted to 'any national from a member state' (Article 17 of EC Treaty). In pursuance of the principle of non-discrimination (Article 19 of EC Treaty, aimed essentially at withdrawing the condition of nationality, on which the exercise of the right to vote was dependent in most member states), EU citizens must henceforth benefit from electoral rights in the same conditions as the nationals of the member state they reside in (Council directive 93/109/EC of 6 December 1993). They must then be able to access the same appeal procedures regarding omissions and errors in the setting up of electoral rolls, be able to fully participate in the political life of the member state in which they exercise their electoral citizenship, without any discrimination with nationals of this member state, and benefit from advance and precise information about the condition of exercise of their European electoral citizenship. Likewise, if the principle of compulsory voting is applied in the country of residence, then it will be automatically extended to the EU citizens having expressed their wish to vote in this country. Let us also add that provisions aimed at implementing the right to vote in European elections leave the choice to European citizens to exercise this right in their member state of origin (in accordance with the electoral rules set up by this state) or in their member state of residence. It is nevertheless forbidden to anybody to vote in more than one member state at the same European Parliament election (Article 8 of the 20 September 1976 Act). Article 14 of the Council directive of 6 December 1993 allows, however, the possibility of implementing derogatory measures when this is justified by problems specific to a member state.

Legal basis of the right to vote in European elections

- Article 39 of the Charter of Fundamental Rights of the European Union (2000)
- Articles 19 (8B) and 189–191 (137–138A) of EC Treaty
- Directive 93/109/EC on the European Parliament election
- Act of 20 September 1976 concerning the election of representatives of the Assembly by direct universal suffrage, amended by Council decisions of 25 June 2002 and 23 September 2002
- Member states' electoral laws

Among these measures, the main one concerns the minimal residence conditions that can be imposed on non-nationals by member states, if the proportion of EU citizens of age to vote and residing in the country is over 20 per cent of the electorate. Since drafting this directive, only the Grand Duchy of Luxembourg has benefited from this derogation, and has been allowed by the Commission to impose a condition of five years of residence for granting the right to vote to EU citizens who were not Luxembourg nationals (Article 3 of electoral law of 18 February 2003).

This partial 'denationalisation' of the right to vote remains, however, largely theoretical, given the reluctance of EU citizens to register on electoral rolls (they were less than 6 per cent in 1994; barely 9 per cent in 1999; Strudel 2000). Furthermore, this denationalisation is reserved to EU nationals only. Non-EU citizens are excluded on the simple ground that they do not hold the nationality of one of the EU member states. In some ways, European citizenship has created a new category of 'second-class citizens' (the expression is borrowed to Sorensen 1996). In the nineteenth century, the codification of electoral citizenship was reinforced by the emphasised threat of the 'foreigner'. European citizenship, through the exclusivity of the political rights granted to EU nationals only, contributes to building a new figure of 'the other': the non-EU national living in Europe, at the margins of its political citizenship and electoral rights.

From this point of view, the 2004 European elections have witnessed several significant events. In Estonia and Latvia, a significant part of the population, belonging to the important Russian-speaking minority, were not authorised to take part in the election, on the respective grounds of the 'unde-termined character of their citizenship' and of their belonging to the category of 'non-citizens' (when Latvia became independent in 1990, only 'genuine' Latvian citizens automatically obtained the citizenship of the new state, condemning more than 21 per cent of the population to join the category of 'non-citizens', waiting for a difficult naturalisation). In Cyprus, though all citizens theoretically benefit from the right to vote, the partition of the island creates a *de facto* partition of the electorate: only a small minority of Turkish Cypriots have effectively participated in the election, which was not organised in the northern part of the island (503 voters – less than 2 per cent of the north's population – took advantage of the possibility offered to Turkish Cypriots to register on the electoral rolls in the south). These elections also led to an interesting quarrel of sovereignty between the United Kingdom and Spain, about the right to vote granted by British electoral legislation – after an explicit demand of the European Court of Human Rights (the case of *Matthews versus the United Kingdom* of 18 February 1999) – to some 20 000 Gibraltar voters, in accordance with its policy towards Commonwealth citizens (since the Law on British citizenship of 1981, the citizens of Gibraltar are British Dependent Territories Citizens (BDTC), but they can claim British citizenship when they wish to do so). The Spanish government contested this extension of the right to vote in European elections, since it benefits, according to its argument, people who are not British nationals, and therefore not EU nationals either. Beyond its legal dimension, still unclear in the absence of a ruling by the European Court of Justice, this conflict stresses that, whilst the granting of the right to vote in European elections remains a national matter, there is no general principle of EU law opposed to the future opening of the European electorate to all foreign residents.

Yves Déloye

Bibliography

Burban, J.-L., *Le Parlement européen et son election*, Brussels, Bruylant, 1979.

Sasse, C. et al., *The European Parliament: Towards a Uniform Procedure for Direct Elections*, Florence, European University Institute; Luxembourg, Office for Official Publications of the European Communities, 1981.

Sorensen, J.-M., *The Exclusive Citizenship: the Case for Refugees and Immigrants in the European Union*, Aldershot, Avebury, 1996.

Strudel, S., 'Les citoyens européens aux urnes: les usages ambigus de l'article 8B du Traité de Maastricht', *Revue Internationale de Politique Comparée* 9, 1, 2000, pp. 31–63.

➜ Citizen (EU); Compulsory Voting; Cyprus; Electoral System; Estonia; European Constitution; Immigrants' Vote; Latvia; Voters.

Second-Order Elections

The model of 'second-order elections' is probably the most famous theoretical formalisation of electoral sociology applied to European elections. Formulated only a few months after the first European elections by direct universal suffrage in June 1979, this 'conceptual framework' was originally presented by two German political scientists, Reif and Schmitt (1980), this article became an indispensable reference for all specialists of European affairs.

The basic idea behind this model is very simple: European Parliament elections are not strictly speaking 'European' in nature, but are in fact the sum of a series of national elections. This Europeanisation deficit condemning European elections to be perceived merely as 'second-order national elections' has a number of characteristics enabling the distinction between the latter and first-order elections (presidential or national legislative).

The first crucial characteristic is the low level of turnout in European elections (63 per cent in 1979; 61 per cent in 1984; 59 per cent in 1989; 57 per cent in 1994; a little less than 50 per cent in 1999; and a mere 46 per cent in 2004). Considered by politicians, journalists and voters alike as rather important ('less-at-stake'), European elections experience great difficulty in interesting and mobilising voters. A second trait is the broadening of the political spectrum observed during these polls. European elections generally favour the emergence and development of new and particularly small political parties. Thanks to the dominating proportional representation system, European elections are synonymous with the diffusion of the votes; a phenomenon that generally benefits partisan forces that are normally poorly represented at the national level (witness the unprecedented success of the Belgian, German and Dutch ecologist lists in 1984; and the consecration of Vlaams Blok as a reference party for the Flemish autonomists in 1994). A third feature is the supremacy of national issues over European ones. This is as much due to the proposed political programmes as to the media's very limited coverage of electoral campaigns, augmenting the challenge of Europeanisation. In spite of growing hopes regarding the rapid emergence of a European public sphere, the continuing nationalisation of electoral campaigns and political stakes attests to the difficulty of organising a trans-national electoral debate transcending national borders and political attitudes. The last characteristic concerns the emergence of sanction voting against political parties in power at the time of European elections. For instance, it is noted that during the first four European elections, the average difference between the number of points secured by such parties in national and EP elections was 5.5. However, during the 2004 elections, numerous government parties were sanctioned nationally as well (only six countries out of 25 have escaped the sanction vote, each time for different specific reasons). The importance of the sanction vote was particularly strong in Germany, where the SPD experienced a historic defeat, winning a mere 21.5 per cent of votes, its lowest score since 1953.

These four traits, susceptible to each member state's institutional and political system as well as to the timing of European elections within each country's electoral cycle, converge to minimise the European dimension of EP elections. They also attest to the weakness of the European parliamentary arena, which fails to persuade the public of its political importance. The success of this conceptual framework, largely validated since its formalisation, is such that the notion of 'second-order elections' is now widely used outside the specific context of the European elections. In fact, it has recently been used to account for the relative strength of the Scottish and Welsh parliamentary arenas in the context of the devolution policy implemented at the end of the 1990s in the United Kingdom.

Some authors do not hesitate in decreeing the obsolescence of this model (Frognier 2000; Studlar et al. 2003). For instance, Frognier (2000) offered an alternative explanation with regard to the 1999 elections. Taking into account the spatial transformations of political representation in Europe as well as the gradual emergence of a European identity able to modify internal political cleavages, the author establishes the increasing autonomy of European stakes in relation to the logic of the functioning of national political markets. Through the cautious use of empirical evidence Frognier argues that nowadays, European electoral participation is based on levels of identification with Europe, rather than on voters' mere participation in previous EP elections (2000: 82–5). This would allow EP elections today to be defined by genuine 'Europeanness', ending their long-term subordination to national contexts.

Yves Déloye

Bibliography

Frognier, A.-P., 'Identité et participation: pour une approche européenne des élections européennes', in G. Grunberg, P. Perrineau and C. Ysmal (eds), *Le vote des Quinze: Les élections européennes du 13 juin 1999*, Paris, Presses de Sciences Po, 2000, pp. 75–94.

Norris, P., 'Second-order Elections Revisited', *European Journal of Political Research*, 31, 1–2, 1997, pp. 109–14.

Reif, K. and Schmitt, H., 'Nine Second-Order National Elections: a Conceptual Framework for the Analysis of European Elections Results', *European Journal of Political Research*, 8, 1, 1980, pp. 3–44.

Studlar, D., Flickinger, R. S. and Bennett, S., 'Turnout in European Elections: Towards a European-Centred Model', *British Elections & Parties Review*, 13, 2003, pp. 195–225.

→ Abstention; Campaign (Sociology of); Cleavages; Election Manifestos; Electoral Behaviour; Electoral Cycles; European Elections Studies; European Elections (1979–1999); European Elections (2004); European Electoral Sociology; European Parliament; European Public Sphere; Identity; Issues; Multi-Level Governance; Nationalisation of European Elections; Political Market; Symbols and Practice of Elections.

Slovakia

Like a caricature of what happened in other European countries, the first European elections for the Slovak people were marked by a remarkably low turnout of 17 per cent. Despite this apparent similarity, the Slovak case was unique in many ways. Indeed, Slovakia is the most recently founded of the current member states; it was excluded from the 'Luxembourg group' in December 1997 for political reasons, and is, of all the new member states, the one which approved membership by referendum with the highest proportion of yes votes,

92 per cent. Thus, the question to be asked is how to interpret this abstention rate of 83.04 per cent. Was it due to defiance towards EU integration of a people disillusioned by the difficult absorption of the *acquis communautaire*? Or was it due to a lack of domestic and European stakes? Exceptionally and surprisingly, in Slovakia, the ruling coalition was not torpedoed in the election. Three of the four parties in the coalition (Prime Minister Mikulas Dzurinda's SDKU, the Magyar SMK, and the Christian-Democratic KDH) obtained MEPs, and all four parties together obtained an absolute majority (51.2 per cent) of the seats. At the same time, some claimed that the vote was a failure for the government, because, as soon as the first estimations were given, the prime minister accused the media of being responsible for the very low turnout. Yet, some more profound reasons account for this lack of participation, which was ascribed to a very worrying electoral dynamic of sanction for ambiguous positions and petty manoeuvres by the main parties. Nationally, there was almost no campaign, and little to motivate the voters.

Political context and public opinion

In the spring of 2004, the country faced a rather negative political context, with internal tensions within the ruling coalition, and a vote prior to the European elections, which contributed to destabilise the Slovak electorate. The leading SDKU had been prey to internal fights since the autumn of 2003. For a variety of rather obscure reasons, pertaining to the party's finances and the control of some key economic posts, the prime minister dismissed Defence Minister Simko in September 2003. As a result, seven MPs left the SDKU, so that the government was only left with a small majority in parliament. There followed days of crisis, in which the government tried to win the support of opposition or unaffiliated MPs on an ad hoc basis. The indirect result of this was the elimination of the foreign minister and main collaborator of the prime minister, Eduard Kukan, in the first round of the presidential elections. Things got worse when the four parties could not agree on a common strategy for the second ballot, with two parties, including the SDKU, supporting abstention at the risk of facilitating the election of Vladimir Meciar. Together with the first ballot, a popular initiative referendum was organised, calling for anticipated general elections. All the members of the coalition called for a boycott of the referendum, hoping that the 50 per cent turnout needed for the results to be taken into account would not be met. As a result, however, the government thus contributed to discrediting the electoral process in general and referendums in particular. The only successful referendum (on EU accession) could not even be considered an exception to this because of the extremely unique context in which it took place. Needless to say, between calling for the boycott of the referendum and abstention in the second ballot of the presidential elections, the prime minister and his supporters did everything to limit the electoral enthusiasm of the Slovak people and reinforce their scepticism.

The electoral campaign

Before talking about the electoral campaign for the 2004 European Parliament elections, it is important to remember that the May 2003 accession referendum was marked by weak turnout, the 50 per cent threshold only being surpassed at the last minute. For the first and last time so far, the campaign had united all main Slovak parties (including the Communists and the National Slovak Party) in a Europhile direction, with no major Eurosceptic opposition. This unbalanced campaign did not help to convince or inform the population, and this had consequences for the 2004 campaign, which was again very minimal and rather uninteresting. Public and private media held no debate, and most journalists, including the most serious ones, focused on the material advantages of MEPs rather than deeper electoral issues. Moreover, the absence of top political figures definitely impacted the campaign. Of course, as in every election, the SDKU used ice hockey star Peter Stastny as one of their candidates, but his bad command of the Slovak language after 15 years spent in the United States did not help. Otherwise, the only visible candidate was Monika Benova (Smer), president of the Foreign Affairs committee in parliament. All other candidates were low-ranking politicians, be they from the very Europhile SMK, or the others. As a result, no party, with the exception of the KDH and to a lesser extent the SMK managed to mobilise their electorates.

The results

The high level of abstention was directly predictable from a more general tendency of electoral disaffection, with abstention levels of 70.1 per cent in the general elections of 2002 already, the highest since the change of regime. Similarly, between 1999 and 2004, turnout in the presidential elections collapsed from 75.5 per cent to 43.5 per cent, while the accession referendum only had a relative success with the voters. In the context of the European Parliament election, turnout was probably made worse by the fact that to many

the important moment had been accession and that the EP election came as a sort of anti-climax in comparison, with the capacity to influence EU politics very much doubted amongst a population which was more generally disillusioned about its ability to influence internal politics in the first place, in what Kubin describes as a 'moral crisis' of the country. This being said, government parties were better on the whole at mobilising their electorates than the opposition, perhaps because of their greater and more consistent pro-European stance which the public wanted to support. Prime Minister Dzurinda's first reaction was to underline the victory of his party: 'foreign reactions were highly human and beautiful: my friends and partners were congratulated over this outstanding victory!' (*Sme*, 15 June 2004). This declaration deserves little comment as the party only gathered 2.84 per cent of the registered electorate, but coalition parties did resist abstention better than the opposition. Indeed, the SDKU remains the first party of the country, the KDH gathered half as many votes as for the general elections (not bad given the much lower turnout), and the SMK recorded a flattering 13.24 per cent of the vote, its best result since 1990. Indeed, the Magyar electorate was on the whole more mobilised than their Slovak counterpart. In fact, Smer and the HZDS tried to play the 'Hungarian threat card' by claiming that 'who does not vote votes Magyar' in the run-up to the election, showing that after six years of Magyar participation in government, the opposition is still ready to use the old rhetoric of the 'enemy from within'. At the same time, this clearly was not echoed by the population in terms of participation. Moreover, the Smer, whose electorate, quite young and highly educated, is not very prone to participate in elections, was penalised for its ambiguous position towards Europe

Table 1 Results of the European
Parliament election, June 2004

Party	Votes (%)	Seats
SDKU*	17.1	3
HZDS	17.0	3
Smer	16.9	3
KDH*	16.2	3
SMK*	13.2	2
ANO	4.7	–
KSS	4.5	–
Slobodne Forum	3.3	–
SNS-PSNS	2.0	–

* Member of the ruling coalition
Source: Statistical Office of Slovakia.

(more pro-EU than pro-US, but rather
unclear in its appraisal of EU institutions), and its history of inconsistent
electoral results. At the same time, the
HZDS of Meciar continued to lose some
ground. Despite its reputation for a
highly stable and compliant electoral
base, it failed to benefit from the low
turnout, unlike what happened a month
earlier in presidential elections where
the personal factor turned out to be very
prominent. In fact, Meciar remained
very shocked by his defeat in the presidential election, and the late support of
the party for EU membership was both
surprising to many voters, and not
necessarily followed by the traditional
electoral base of the party, more reserved
about membership. The results are
summarised in Table 1.

As in many other EU member states,
the national context turned out to be
essential in understanding the election.
No party really presented a programme for
the election, and arguably, none even
really campaigned. This does not mean
that a consensus exists on European issues
in Slovakia, but it is not easy to understand what specifically makes the difference between the main Slovak parties in

this area. Few themes were really likely to
see a major opposition between the main
parties apart perhaps from the desired
proximity to NATO and, beyond, the USA.
Otherwise, the national political debate in
Slovakia was primarily marked by the
obsession about the 'delay' or 'catching
up' that seem to have marked all the
former communist states in their path to
modernisation and Europeanisation.
Focused on issues of visibility and blinded
by its competition with its neighbours on
a number of 'open' and 'closed' areas of
negotiation with the European Union, the
Slovak political class simply forgot to
discuss the more fundamental role of
Slovakia within the European Union. Few
asked or explained 'why' Slovakia should
join the EU, implicitly portraying Europe
under the sole distorting prism of its
wealth and of an accession process
described in absurdly technical terms.
Once this 'technical' accession was
achieved, the Slovak electorate probably
thought it had little reason to show any
further interest in the function of its new
European institutions.

Etienne Boisserie

→ Abstention; Enlargement; European Elections
(2004); European Referendums; Euroscepticism;
Mapping Europe: European Electoral Geography;
Protest Voting.

Slovenia

National legislation on EP elections

Candidacy

The Slovenian legislation on EP elections offers the possibility of voting and
being a candidate to all citizens qualify-
ing as voters or candidates at national

parliamentary elections (citizenship of Slovenia and being aged at least 18). In addition, it allows EU citizens to vote or be a candidate if they have permanent residence in Slovenia and fulfil other conditions to become a voter or candidate at national parliamentary elections. In the same way as for national parliamentary elections, candidates for EP elections can also be proposed by parties (the candidate list must be supported by four MPs or 1000 voters) or voters (where the candidate list must be supported by 3000 voters). There is a maximum of seven candidates on an individual list.

The national legislation on EP elections interferes somewhat in the procedure of selecting candidates within parties. Namely, the legislation provides that a list of candidates cannot comprise less than 40 per cent of representatives of each gender and at least one representative of each gender must be placed in the top half of the list (since Slovenia has seven MEPs this means in the top three positions). If a certain list of candidates does not meet these conditions it is considered invalid. Consequently, all (13) lists of candidates had at least three women among their candidates, but only two parties had four women candidates which was, in terms of the said legal provision, the highest number possible. Women topped the list of candidates in three parties.

Since the law establishes the incompatibility of the position of an MEP with the position of an MP, member of the government or member of local representative bodies, we could have expected that top-ranking politicians, especially those from parliamentary parties, would not have been candidates at the EP elections. These expectations were met in part in the Slovenian case since arguably the only top-ranking politicians from parliamentary parties were Mr Peterle, Mr Kacin, Mr Brejc, Mr But, and Mr Jelinčič, who also topped the candidate lists of their parties. However, in the last few years the first four of these politicians have also heavily reoriented themselves from internal to EU affairs. Consequently, their candidacy for MEP was expected, even their leading position on the candidate list. Three leaders of parliamentary parties (top-ranking politicians) were also among candidates for MEPs. Mr Pahor, President of the United List of Social Democrats – the ULSD (also Speaker of the parliament and the most popular politician in Slovenia in the last year, and who has been always very active and interested in foreign and especially EU affairs), Mr J. Podobnik, President of the Slovenian People's Party – the SPP, and Mr Černjak, President of the Youth Party of Slovenia – the YPS, were candidates at the EP elections albeit they held the last positions on their parties' lists.

Electoral system

The law on EP elections establishes a proportional electoral system (d'Hondt) with a single constituency. In the case of national parliamentary elections Slovenia has 88 constituencies and a nationally defined threshold of 4 per cent and, for the distribution of seats in the national parliament, the d'Hondt and Hare electoral formulae are applied. In addition, at the June 2004 EP elections there was the possibility of a preference vote which does not have an absolute influence.

Finances of the electoral campaign

Financial aspects of election campaigns for EP elections are determined by the Election Campaign Law (passed in 1994 and amended in 1997) which regulates campaigns for elections to national representative bodies. Consequently, each candidate list can spend no more than 60 Slovenian tolars (SIT) per voter on a related electoral campaign. For the EP elections, this meant each candidate list could spend a total of SIT 97 735 08.00 (€407,569).[1] In contrast to the prohibition on financing the list and candidates from abroad at national parliament elections, such financing is allowed with EP elections.

Parties or candidates who have entered parliament or received at least 2 per cent of all votes at the national level are entitled to a reimbursement of their expenditure on election campaigns. Parties or candidates which receive enough votes to enter parliament are entitled to SIT 60 per vote received, while those parties or candidates that did not succeed in entering parliament but received at least 2 per cent of the votes are entitled to SIT 30 per vote received. However, the total levels of reimbursement cannot exceed actual party expenditure. Organisers of election campaigns are obliged to send a financial report on revenues and expenditures to the national parliament and Court of Auditors.

As we can see from Table 1, the Liberal Democracy of Slovenia (LDS) spent the highest amount of money on its election campaign and no parliamentary party spent more on the 2004 EP elections than on the 2000 national parliament elections. This could also indicate the fact that EP elections are second-order elections. The only exception is the YPS

Table 1 Spending on campaigns for the 2004 EP elections

	Financial resources spent on EP election campaign (SIT)	Expected reimbursement (SIT)	Financial resources spent on national parliament election campaign (SIT) – parliamentary parties only
New Slovenia	23 041 852.06	6 165 180.00	52 770 685.00
Liberal Democracy of			94 798 395.00
Slovenia and Democratic	76 994 494.59	5 729 340.00	
Party of Retired Persons			42 336 000.00
of Slovenia			
Slovenian Democratic Party	54 070 420.25	4 616 700.00	74 192 895.00
United List of Social Democrats	43 673 765.32	3 700 320.00	81 860 021.00
Slovenian People's Party	34 230 952.19	1 099 860.00	93 285 299.00
Slovenian National Party	695 079.00	656 490.00	10 340 466.00
Slovenia is Ours	21 178 423.31	537 900.00	
Youth Party of Slovenia and	19 635 132.23	300 810.00	12 029 255.00
Greens of Slovenia			non-parliamentary
Voice of Women of Slovenia	1 275 951.00		non-parliamentary
Party of Ecological Movements	0.00		
National Party of Labour	382 642.00		
Party of the Slovene Nation	39 360.00		
Democratic Party of Slovenia,	n.a.		non-parliamentary
Democrats of Slovenia			

Sources: reports of political parties on financial aspects of election campaigns for 2004 EP election and 2000 national parliament election.

which spent SIT 19 635 132.28 on the EP election campaign and just SIT 12 029 255.00 on its national parliament election campaign.

The election campaign

The campaign for the EP elections started one month before polling day, even though some earlier non-direct forms of campaigning could be detected. We can identify the campaign for EP elections through the three different kinds of sources that were most often used by parties to present their candidates and the key points of their programmes.

Party manifestos

The first form was the presentation of *party manifestos via different kinds of printed documents, brochures or leaflets*. Most parties competing at the elections officially presented their manifestos or other documents that may be interpreted as programme documents. It turns out that the majority of parties presented their programmes soon after the official start of the campaign. The SPP, LDS+DPRS (Democratic Party of Retired Persons of Slovenia) and ULSD were the quickest. It is quite interesting that the winning party New Slovenia (NSi) only officially presented its programme document in the week before the elections. The only exception to this rule was the Slovenian National Party (SNP) whose programme was not officially available, but its standpoints were interesting because at the 2000 national parliamentary elections the party became known as the only parliamentary party to adopt a Eurosceptic position. Its programme standpoints presented in the media on this topic were softened for the EP elections and

only stressed the importance of Slovenian interests before party interests and EU interests in its campaign.

The analysis of the formal programme documents reveals there were generally no huge differences between parties in their decisions on which issues should be stressed. At the same time, we can also talk about similarities in the proposed solutions for they were all very general and principally without any concrete vision or idea of how to resolve the given problems.

Despite these conclusions, we can divide and simultaneously synthesise the key programme topics generally common to all competing parties into:

(1) topics concerning *national issues*: the economy, social policies, agriculture, the environment, Slovenian values, culture, and language;
(2) topics on *EU issues*: the EU Constitution, human rights, distribution of funds, co-operation with neighbours, relations between Slovenia and the EU.

In addition to the common issues, some more isolated aspects can be found such as: the status of retired persons and women, sports issues, equal opportunities and solidarity, security, Eurorealism, transportation and anti-Americanism.

It is also very obvious that non-parliamentary parties largely stressed only national issues. This might be indirectly connected with a party's interest or propaganda relative to the upcoming national parliamentary elections, due to be held on 3 October 2004.

The media

Our analysis of the *electronic media methods of the campaign* focuses on the radio and television participation of parties and their candidates. Presentations made by the parties themselves on the public radio station showed quite similar issue orientations to those seen in the formal party programme documents, but the solutions to problems were somewhat more specific and consequently (ideologically) revealed very general differences between the parties. Another important aspect arising in the radio presentations and widely presented in the programmes was the personal status of candidates, mainly their past experience, references, prestige, positions and contacts within the EU. This coincides with public opinion research (the so-called Slovenian Public Opinion Polls), where respondents in November 2003 declared that the most important qualities MEPs should have are: education (38 per cent), cosmopolitanism (29 per cent), reputation in Slovenia (21 per cent), and political party membership (5 per cent).

The analysis of television confrontations shows that the campaign and presentation of programme standpoints depended greatly on the issues selected by the media. The content analysis of the confrontations reveals that parties did not have the opportunity to stress their programme orientations too much while the journalists selected some key topics on which they expected the party representatives to have comments and therefore indirectly have the chance to express their party's programme positions. It also seems that the selection of such key issues focused on problematic and sensitive internal areas like regionalisation, unemployment, the national economy, minority groups, and interpretations of Slovenian history from the Second World War on. The result of the confrontations over these issues was reflected in the emergence of conflict between the parties as soon as these internal problems were aired.

Finally, we should emphasise that the printed media did not pay much attention to the campaign as such, but looked more at the descriptions and interpretations of the role and responsibilities of the EP and the voting system for EP elections in other EU members.

Other forms of campaign

At the same time, half of the competing parties also decided to animate the campaign with other methods. The most visible non-personal campaign method involved billboards or large posters. They were used by all parliamentary parties (except the SNP) and the newly established non-parliamentary Slovenia is Ours (SIO). The majority of billboards contained European symbols, mostly yellow stars on a blue background, while some parties also used the logo and/or symbol of their sibling European parties. The key messages were relatively dry and non-innovative. Parties expressed the importance of Slovenia on the one hand with slogans like: '100% Slovenia' (SPP), 'In Europe for the Good of Slovenia' (ULSD), 'For new Slovenian victories' (LDS+DPRS), 'Slovenia, My Country. Also in Europe' (Slovenian Democratic Party – SDP), 'In Slovenia is Power' (SIO). On the other hand, the EU aspect was also exposed in the following slogans: 'Europe in the Right Hands' (SPP), 'We are European Social Democrats' (ULSD) and 'You Decide: With Us Europe Will Be Better' (YPS+Greens of Slovenia – GS). The billboards were generally not very innovative, although two of them particularly caught voters' attention. The first one, regarded by some of the public and the media as controversial, was the billboard of the SPP on which there were two young ladies wearing boxer gloves and holding a flower in their mouths, saying 'Come out from your left corner'. The other one was a poster of the non-parliamentary SIO, caricaturing the party president and leader of the party list as Popeye and Olive Oil from the famous

Popeye cartoon, saying: 'Your Voice is Our Spinach'.

We should also mention that some parties decided on more personal contact methods, travelling around Slovenian cities and villages on special buses during the campaign. It turned out this approach was very effective, especially for the winning NSi.

Given the upcoming national parliamentary election in October 2004 it was mainly the non-parliamentary parties (National Party of Labour – NPL, Democratic Party of Slovenia – DPS) and the parliamentary SNP which quite openly connected their interests in competing at the EP elections with the national elections. This merely confirms the generally accepted thesis of the close link between EP and national elections where national elections are held near to EP elections.

In addition, the campaign was also marked by a lack of any 'real' Eurosceptic parties. There were just two self-defined Eurorealist parties (SNP and DPS) and together they received 5.3 per cent of the votes.

The election results

The big (negative) surprise was the very low turnout. As seen in Table 2, the low level of 28.3 per cent turnout is record-breaking (1 628 918 voters had the right to vote, yet just 461 879 voters exercised it); 25 938 voters or 5.62 per cent cast invalid votes. In the last ten years, 13 nationwide referendums have been held, mainly involving specific policy questions. A common characteristic of all of them is the low turnout (the only exceptions were the EU and NATO referendum with a turnout of 60.4 per cent). Only at two referendums were the voter turnout figures somewhat lower than at the first EP election in Slovenia (namely 27.3 per cent and 27.5 per cent). This came as a great surprise since public opinion polls had indicated a turnout of between 55 and 70 per cent.

Table 3 shows that the biggest share of votes (23.6 per cent) was received by the NSi, a party which at the 2000 elections only received 8.7 per cent (the party was established in August 2000, just a few months before those elections). The LDS received a 21.9 per cent share of votes. This result is, in fact, the second big surprise of the EP elections since public opinion polls had forecast it would win.

Data on the election results reveal that the national regulation on gender quotas for the EP elections had some effect on the number of women MEPs, yet, in contrast to the male candidates

Table 2 Turnout figures for parliamentary, presidential and European elections from 1990 to 2004 (%)

	1990	1992	1996	1997	2000	2002	2004
Parliamentary	83.3	85.8	73.7	/	70.3	/	/
Presidential	83.5	85.4	/	68.6	/	72.1	/
	(first round)					(first round)	
	76.9					65.4	/
	(second round)					(second round)	
European	/	/	/	/	/	/	28.3

Source: http://www.rvk.si

Table 3   Results of the 2004 EP elections and 2000 national parliament elections

	2004 European Parliament Elections		2000 National Parliament Elections	
	% of votes	seats	% of votes	seats
New Slovenia	23.6	2 (EPP-ED)	8.7	8
Liberal Democracy of Slovenia and Democratic Party of Retired Persons of Slovenia	*21.9*	*2 (ALDE)*	*36.2*	*34*
			5.2	*4*
Slovenian Democratic Party	17.6	2 (EPP-ED)	15.8*	14*
United List of Social Democrats	*14.1*	*1 (PES)*	*12.1*	*11*
*Slovenian People's Party***	*8.4*	*0*	*9.5*	*9*
Slovenian National Party	5.0	0	4.9	4
Slovenia is Ours	4.1	0	/	/
Youth Party of Slovenia and Greens of Slovenia	2.3	0	4.3	4
			0.9	0
Voice of Women of Slovenia	1.2	0	0.4	0
Party of Ecological Movements	0.6	0	/	/
National Party of Labour	0.5	0	/	/
Party of the Slovenian Nation	0.3	0	/	/
Democratic Party of Slovenia, Democrats of Slovenia	0.3	0	0.7	0

Source: http://www.rvk.si
Governmental parties are marked in italics.
* At the national elections the party competed under the old name Social Democratic Party of Slovenia
** The SPP was a governmental party up until the beginning of April 2004.

who were elected by preference votes, all three women MEPs were elected by virtue of their (high, more precisely second) positions on their parties' candidate lists.

Data on preference votes reveal that 76.8 per cent of voters who cast a vote also cast a preference vote. Many commentators saw this as unexpected but it is apparently a strong signal that voters want to have a decisive role in the election of M(E)Ps. The highest shares of preference votes were cast by the voters of SIO (82.5 per cent), the SNP (82.2 per cent) and the NSi (81.0 per cent), while the lowest share of preference votes was cast by voters of the Voice of Women of Slovenia – VWS (56.3 per cent).

It was also significant that the first names appearing on an individual candidate list received the biggest share of preference votes gained by an individual party. The only exception here was Mr Pahor who, as a candidate in seventh position on the ULSD list, received the lion's share of preference votes on that list.

Alenka Krašovec
Simona Kustec Lipicer
Damjan Lajh

Note

1. On 11 September 2004 EUR 1 = SIT 239.8.

→ Mapping Europe: European Electoral Geography.

Social Europe

(Issue of)

Nowadays, the political use of expressions such as 'economic' or 'monetary' Europe is more and more commonplace. The expression 'social Europe' constitutes, at worst a staged slogan, and at best, the awareness of a shortcoming requiring a remedy. While European integration is based on notions such as free trade and economic development, its social character is almost never taken into account by the constitutive treaties. One had to wait until the mid-1970s to see the adoption of the first programmes for social action as well as the first dispositions and provisions on a 'social Europe'. Thirty years later, while the successive treaties show a real political will to enlarge the European Union, a relatively modest production of legislation pertaining to the 'social field' suggests that it largely remains the domain of individual member states.

Since the mid-1980s, global economic changes, as well as issues like the diverging definitions of the welfare state co-existing within the EU (Esping-Andersen 1999) have gradually brought 'social' issues to the centre of European debates. In order to ensure the durable and sustained convergence of its national economies, whilst facing the double imperative of macro-economic competitiveness and growth, the EU has engaged, since the Amsterdam Council of 1997, in a more controlled management of member states' finances. This decision has hastened a general movement for the reform of the existing systems of social protection; an issue made all the more urgent by the continent's ageing population. This new budgetary rigour affects most areas of state intervention (health-insurance, retirement pensions, unemployment, etc.), concerns wide sections of the population, and affects popular beliefs about the redistributive functions of the state. These concerns have become all the more important now that sluggish international growth rates have accentuated the tensions in the European job market. Increased labour force flexibility, frantic working rhythms, and the precariousness of 'social plans' so familiar to the workers of large companies, add to the threat of 'delocalisation' by the accession of countries with less restrictive fiscal policies and cheaper access to skilled manpower.

The present situation of East German workers is amongst the most typical. The region is marked by persisting high levels of unemployment (9–10 per cent of the population), plans for relaxing working rights, challenging market logics, and the progressive revision of social protection networks. All these factors contribute to a growing debate about social issues within the European public. Indeed, in the spring of 2004, in 11 of the 15 old EU member states, unemployment was cited as the top problem to be urgently addressed by the country (Standard Eurobarometer 61, spring 2004).

Meanwhile, signs indicate that, since the 1990s, the EU and its institutions have progressively tended to be perceived as a full partner in the social field. When asked whether the fight against poverty and social exclusion should depend on national or EU policies, European citizens appear to favour the second option (more than 60 per cent since 1984). There is also a less-strong demand for a common and united European fight against unemployment. This is also confirmed by the first Euro demonstrations in 1997, related to the case of the Renault factory in Vilvorde. On the eve of the June 2004 European elections, the proportion of European citizens wishing to see the problem of unemployment at the centre of the electoral agenda grew from 53 to 59 per cent in one year (Standard Eurobarometers 59–61 spring 2003, spring 2004). It is precisely for this reason that the social issues' position within the European electoral campaign deserves closer examination.

A concealed issue

A first important element is the very low visibility of social issues in the electoral campaign. This is not because candidates chose to avoid social questions, but because when they were raised, several factors certainly contributed to their 'concealment'. As was the case for the preceding European elections (Gerstlé et al. 2000), the electoral campaign turned out to be of little interest to the media. In May–June 2004, the international news agenda was dominated by the situation in Iraq, as well as other nationally idiosyncratic issues, such as the preparation of the Euro 2004 football games in Portugal or, in France, the 60th anniversary of the World War Two Normandy landings. This was made worse by the overwhelming predominance of national issues in the campaign. For instance, in Spain, EP elections were seen as a confirmation test of the March legislative elections; in Cyprus, the poll was held less than two months after the failure of the referendum on the reunification of the island; in Germany, the government's reforms met an increasingly active opposition; and in Lithuania, the presidential election came just after the indictment of Roland Parkas for corruption, thus setting a rather bleak tone for European elections.

Other elements may have contributed, at the European level this time, to marginalise the question of a social Europe in political debates. The existence of controversial issues such as the European Constitution, Turkey's accession, and enlargement, which received relatively little attention, further stressed the secondary role of the social questions debated in the European Parliament. For all these reasons, the social question turned out not to be a polarising one in the campaign. Nevertheless, it was placed at the heart of a large number of programmes provoking the embarrassment of those wishing to see it as a core European issue, and fuelling political debates about European integration.

The troubles of the pro-European left

While part of the liberal group (ELDR) claimed that social questions could be solved by increased growth and market deregulation, the EU was invited to make recommendations and suggestions to the member states by the EPP. By contrast, social issues largely structured the programmes of the pro-European left, which argued in favour of the amendment of the common economic sphere by offering social guarantees (ESP), or the development of a European welfare state tradition (EFGP). Within the new member states, such aspirations are not entirely new. Increased growth and internal market competitiveness remain the undisputed priority. In fact, as underlined by the centre-right Czech Minister for Social Affairs, Miroslav Beblavy, membership of the EU was perceived in itself as a promise of higher living standards (*Le Monde*, 8 June 2004). Even for the Czech Social-Democrats of the SSD, the harmonisation of social policies constitutes, in the best cases, a distant objective (SSD 2004 election programme). By contrast, in Western Europe, a few left-wing parties tried to focus on the social nature of European integration, but without success. In Sweden, where the population recently voted against the adoption of the single currency, the public's fear regarding the dilution of the 'Swedish model' in the EU was cleverly manipulated by Euro-sceptics (Junilistan or June list) rather than a campaign theme for the ruling Social-Democrats. In France, the socialists preferred to focus on national issues and anti-government dynamics. The example of Germany was equally prominent. The economic situation and reforms undertaken by the government led to growing discontent in the eastern part of the country, leaving the PDS to exploit social themes in its campaign. Criticisms resulted in Chancellor Schröder declining a leading role in the SPD campaign, while the party's position on social issues remained elusive. The SPD campaign theme of *Zukunftgerichtkeit* ('Justice for the Future') remained ambiguous and limited and fell well short of a plan for a 'European social state'.

Generally, concrete proposals formulated for the promotion of a 'social Europe' were few and far between, while the social rhetoric of left-wing parties often flirted with Euroscepticism. The French Socialist Party stressed a risk of 'social dumping' in the EU, and campaigned in favour of the adoption of trans-European minimum wages and the reduction of working hours across the EU, but along the lines of current French legislation. It appeared to be less concerned with the actual functioning of such measures than with the reaction of an electorate ready to sanction the policies of the right-wing government.

A common Eurosceptic argument

Critiques of the current direction of European integration are strengthened by the confusion postulated by the major political groups. Moreover, two strong tendencies fought for a predominant role in the social agenda of the 2004 campaign: on the one hand, the discourse of groups hostile to European integration, and on the other hand, that of groups firmly convinced of the need to revise and reform the current process. The first group comprised a rather heterogeneous ensemble of organisations drawing their main arguments from the incumbent social cost of European integration. They either favoured the status quo (i.e. the Swedish Junilistan) or a pure withdrawal from the EU (i.e. the British UKIP). Eurosceptic social arguments were even more vigorous in new member states where similar parties denounced the degradation of the social and economic situation following EU accession. This was, for example, the case of the socialist MLP in Malta, and the Czech communists of the KSČM, as well as several Polish parties. The second group was mainly found in Western Europe. Faced with the growing concerns of citizens about the renegotiation of their social benefits due to the deterioration of the market, these groups acted as promoters of a 'different Europe', characterised by the development of 'social justice'. Examples included the Spanish coalition IU-ICV-EUA or the Déi Lénk in Luxembourg, but it was sometimes difficult to know whether their arguments were disguised Euroscepticism or not. Indeed, altogether, utopian notions of a 'different Europe' were abundantly thrown on political agendas and debates, without it being clear whether they constituted real alternatives, or whether they represented a simple rejection of European integration. More generally, the debate on the European social dimension in the 2004 electoral campaign seemed above all linked to the EU's incapacity to impose itself in the media and public sphere, and to balance out the strong resistance of the national cultures, and the intensity of popular mistrust towards its social model. This was coupled with the failure of political leaders to present the

European project in a coherent and audible manner, and to confirm their willingness to protect and reinforce its democratic character.

Dominique Bellec

Bibliography

Gerstlé, J., Semetko, H. A., Schoenback, K. and Villa, M., 'L'européanisation défaillante des campagnes nationales', in G. Grunberg, P. Perrineau and C. Ysmal (eds), *Le vote des Quinze: Les élections européennes du 13 juin 1999*, Paris, Presses de Sciences Po, 2000, pp. 95–118.

Mink, G., 'European Integration and Social Mutations in Central Europe', *Foreign Policy*, 2, 2004: 373–86.

→ Campaign (Sociology of); European Elections (2004); Euroscepticism; Extreme Left; Extreme Right; Germany; Issues; Left; Nationalisation of European Elections; Second-Order Elections.

Sovereignism

The terms 'Euroscepticism' and 'sovereignism' are regularly referred to in the media and European public discourse to account for the ideology and the 'hard-line' Eurosceptic standpoint (as proposed by Taggart and Szczerbiak 2002) of various partisan formations (or embryonic formations), reaching from the right to the left, which find in the European elections an arena of political opportunity that they recurrently struggle to find at the national election level (Mair 2000). The expression 'sovereignism' first appeared in the early 1990s, above all in France but also in the United Kingdom where it is most commonly termed 'independence' (Preston 1994). However, this categorisation remains essentially dependent on the struggles between the political actors over the operational classification. Thus, during the 2004 European election, the National Front (FN) attempted to monopolise this political label across the French electoral stage by proclaiming itself to be the 'only sovereignist movement' at the time of their traditional Parisian march in commemoration of Joan of Arc. It goes to show that if the scientific apprehension surrounding this political fact is indeed still a sensitive issue today, the terms and ideology are both saturated in common sense. The notion of 'sovereignism' should thus be regarded not as an analytical concept but rather as a category of classification resulting from European political experience and is principally deployed by political actors whose mutual interest is to paradoxically denounce the construction of a political Community space (arising from the Maastricht and Amsterdam treaties which they had rejected) which on the other hand ensures their existence. Since 1994, in the context of an enlarged Europe, the geography of this nebulous political concept has changed and is only hesitantly debated.

Anatomy of a heterogeneous political family

The main borders of this political family can be discerned from the parliamentary groups in the European Parliament. During the 1994 European elections, the creation of a new political group in the European Parliament (symbolically entitled 'Europe of the Nations', EDN, with a 19-strong membership whose overall majority had been elected in France on the 'Majority for Other Europe' list led by James Goldsmith and Philippe de Villiers) is significant for a number of factors. Notably, it attests to a new political visibility surrounding political sovereignism, tinged with nationalism

(Benoit 1997), and has also reinforced debates which accompanied the controversial ratification of the Maastricht Treaty in several European countries (particularly in France, the United Kingdom or still more in Denmark where the first referendum failed in June 1992 and led to the creation of the 'June Movement' led by Jens-Peter Bonde, an MEP since 1979 once closely affiliated to the Danish communists and founder, in 1972, of the People's Movement Against the EC). During the following legislature (1999–2004), the numerous elected sovereignist representatives proceeded to divide themselves into two parliamentary groups based on a heterogeneous ideological profile: the 'Union for Europe of the Nations' (UEN, 21 members) and the 'Europe of Democracies and Differences' (EDD, 16 members). The UEN notably brings together the majority of French elected representatives from the 'Gathering for France' (RPF, Rassemblement pour la France, founded in November 1999 by Charles Pasqua and Philippe de Villiers prior to their separation), members from the Danish People's Party (PPD, Dansk Folkeparti) founded in October 1995, the elected Italian sovereignists from the National Alliance (Alleanza Nazionale, ex-MSI) and also the elected Irish officials from Fianna Fáil (FF). In regards to enlargement, this parliamentary group has also accommodated representatives from Poland, Latvia and Slovakia. The group 'Europe of Democracies and Differences' (EDD), chaired by J.-P. Bonde, seats him, and his fellow elected officials from his own political group (JuniBevægelsen), in addition to members from UKIP (United Kingdom Independence Party whose electoral symbol is none other than the Sterling Pound – £), dissenting elected representatives from the RPF (united under the banner 'Combats souverainistes'), as well as those of the 'hunting, fishing, nature, traditions' list (CPNT)

led by Jean Saint-Josse and last but not least the elected Calvinist representatives from the ultra conservative Staatkundig Gereformeerde Partij (SGP). Following the elections of 2004 June, the UEN totalled 27 members (statistics from 3 January 2005) including nine elected representatives from the National Alliance, seven from the Polish PiS party (Prawo i Sprawiedliwosc: Rights and Justice) whose electorate is however predominantly in support of European integration, and four Irish elected representatives (FF). This is not to mention the Lithuanian and Latvian elected representatives. Due to the electoral defeat of the sovereignist list led by Charles Pasqua (RPF), the group no longer comprises any French elected representatives. As for the 'Independence and Democracy' group (ID, 36 members as at 3 January 2005), the principal delegations are now composed of UKIP (10 elected representatives) and the clerical and ultra-traditionalist party of the League of Polish Families (Liga Polskich Rodzin, ten elected representatives). Also included are the elected representatives from the Umberto Bossi Northern League (four elected representatives), those from the Nils Lundgren's 'June List' created in Sweden in the aftermath of the 'no' to European single currency in 2003 (Junilistan, three elected representatives) – whose significant electoral outcome (14.4 per cent) attests the establishment of the sovereignism in Northern Europe – and the elected representatives of the Movement for France led by Philippe de Villiers (MPF, three elected representatives). Despite this outcome, the French sovereignist camp still suffered serious electoral setbacks (from 13 per cent in 1999 to less than 9 per cent of the votes in 2004). For the sake of thoroughness, it is also important to include reference to those MEPs not registered as sovereignists. This notably includes six Polish members of the movement Samoobrona (Self-defence) as well as the seven French members of the FN and the sovereignist opinions of other MEPs, particularly members of the EPP which is, of late, sympathetic towards Euroscepticism. Further consideration should also underline that these sovereignist movements participate in a vast network of political organisations which, since 1992, created an anti-Maastricht European alliance (The European Anti-Maastricht Alliance, TEAM), which aims at co-ordinating sovereignist campaigns at the European level.

A nationalist ideology 'against the Amsterdam machination'

This rough parliamentary geography is testament to the multifaceted character of these movements, classified by Hix and Lord under the inclusive label 'anti-Europeans' (Hix and Lord 1997: 45–9). Such a diversity of viewpoints can firstly be identified from the historical partisan dynamics from whence they proceed. From this line of approach, certain sovereignist movements were born from the spilt with governing pro-European parties (the Movement of the Citizens in 1992, the RPF in 1999), whilst others resulted from militant mobilisations amongst party executives during certain European referendums (the June Movement in Denmark and Sweden) or from parliamentary debates sparked by the ratification of European treaties (UKIP in 1993). Furthermore, others still represent a strategic and ideological evolution of the older political parties which, with the intensification of European construction, have adopted a more sovereignist attitude which can be seen in the example of the SGP founded in the Netherlands in 1918, but which since 1984 had chosen a new 'political formula' (as referred to by Mosca 1996)

asserting 'national independence in a Europe of co-operation' and validating its hostility regarding Community integration, perceived as a threat to national 'diversity' in Europe. Finally, others result from a series of organisational changes of 'right-wing radical populism' as analysed by Betz (2004), with the example of the Danish People's Party founded in 1995 following a split from Fremskridtspartiet (FP, Progress Party) and whose current programme is to fight 'any attempt which could endanger the sovereignty and constitutional freedoms of the Danish citizens'. In maintaining an ideological standpoint concerning diversity, whilst the UKIP has explicitly called for an exit strategy from the EU (during the last European elections, its populist slogan was: 'Say No' to the presence of the United Kingdom within the EU but also to the European Constitution, and to the 'unlimited' immigration from the EU), the majority of these movements opted for a protest, populist and even sometimes xenophobe spokesperson, with regard to European integration, intending to defend the 'Other Europe' project (to adopt the name of the list presented during the 1994 European elections, by Goldsmith and de Villiers) or the 'Europe without Union' project, to paraphrase the Danish MEP Bonde. As noted by Lacroix (2004), this 'national-sovereignism' shares, however, an assertion that the nation-state must remain the main, if not the only, place to exercise sovereignty. Renouncing Habermas's own post-national perspective, the demand for sovereignty is plural, comprising a range of arguments. The first component concerns morals, notably adopted by sovereignist organisations with religious foundations who interpret the EU as representing a dissolution of values on which they base their conservative struggle in support of 'sovereignty in its own circle', to use the expression formerly used by a Calvinist Dutchwoman recently restored by the SGP. Further arguments include economic issues (particularly pertinent for the rather anxious sovereignist movements in Northern Europe who see European integration as calling into question the welfare state model threatened by globalisation), monetarist issues (such as expressed by former party opposition to the single currency), identity issues (the resounding denunciation of the 'non-European' character of Turkey during the 2004 election campaign) and finally the oft-expressed political concerns. The central point of this anti-European ideology is the consideration of the nation-state as a political form, carrying political allegiances and legitimacy, and being insuperable. In other words, any prospect of dissociation between the democratic idea and the inherited history of a nation poses a threat to the political sovereignty and freedom of individuals. Within this approach, the prospect for a European citizenship based on residency, along with a post-national identity or 'constitutional patriotism' is unthinkable. According to sovereignist rhetoric, all this involves a 'historical misinterpretation'. Denouncing the artificial character of European integration, this discourse promotes, conversely, the depths of memberships and national loyalties based 'on a transmitted culture, a learned history, a jointly practised language' (the MPF electoral manifesto during the 1999 European elections) and even shows, for some observers, the celebration of an essentialist conception of the nation:

> The foundations, they are the nations. There is no will to be born European, there is a will to be nations together in Europe, to recognise each other, is to recognise the other in the fundamental fact of birth. To be born here and not elsewhere ... To exalt in the nation, is not to deny the universal but to refuse the disappearance of a work of reason imposed by history; an unquestionable figure of political duty, a tested form of public life in favour of a *maybe* without quality (General States of National Sovereignty, 19 October 1998).

In this reactionary version, containing rather strong Barrès-like accents, sovereignism also attests the will of its ideologists to naturalise a European history in the process of construction; a history in which it refuses to be recognised.

Yves Déloye

Bibliography

Benoit, B., *Social-Nationalism: an Anatomy of French Euroscepticism*, Aldershot, Ashgate, 1997.

Betz, Hans-Georg, *La droite populiste en Europe: Extrême ou démocrate?*, Paris, CEVIPOF-Autrement, 2004.

Hix, S. and Lord, C., *Political Parties in the European Union*, Basingstoke, Macmillan, 1997.

Lacroix, J., *L'Europe en procès. Quel patriotisme au-delà des nationalismes?*, Paris, Cerf, 2004.

Mair, P., 'The Limited Impact of Europe on National Party Systems', *West European Politics*, 23, 4, 2000, pp. 27–51.

Preston, P. W., *Europe, Democracy and the Dissolution of Britain: an Essay on the Issue of Europe in UK Public Discourse*, Aldershot, Dartmouth, 1994.

Taggart, P. and Szczerbiak, A., 'The Party Politics of Euroscepticism in EU Member and Candidate States', Sussex European Institute, Working Paper 51, Brighton, 2002 (http://www.sussex.ac.uk/Units, SEI/pdfs/wp51.pdf).

→ Citizen (EU); Cleavages; Denmark; European Elections (1979–1999); European Elections (2004); European Electoral Sociology; European Referendums; Euroscepticism; Extreme Right; France; Identity; Latvia; Left; Multi-Level Governance; Observers; Poland; Populism;

Right; Sweden; Symbolism; Turkey; United Kingdom.

Spain

The 2004 European elections in Spain were marked by the tragic attacks of 11 March, occurring just before the 14 March general elections. The change of government three days later, with the victory of the PSOE (Spanish Labour Socialist Party) over the PP (Popular Party) which had been in power until then, marked the political agenda of the European election on 13 June. Against all electoral predictions in the week preceding the 14 March elections, the PSOE gained the majority of votes with 42.6 per cent (8.4 per cent more than in 2000). The victory of PSOE could have been motivated by two factors: (1) increased electoral participation, which rose from 68.7 per cent in 2000 to 77.2 per cent in 2004; (2) the share of votes coming from other political forces. It is within this framework that the possible impact of the terrorist attack on the electorate must be considered.

Political context and public opinion

The European elections were the object of two opposed strategies to reconfirm the previous March results. The PSOE placed great importance on securing EP elections, so as to dissipate doubts spread by the PP, according to which the socialists had won by reason of an emotional vote. A European victory would thus be seen as confirming the election of José Luis Rodriguez Zapatero's government and consolidate the modification of the electoral cycle, starting with their victory at the municipal and regional elections in May 2003. A victory at European Parliament elections would have represented the third consecutive socialist victory. On the other hand, the PP's strategy was to try to turn European elections into a second round of the general elections. In fact, their victory would have proved that the March results were a mistake produced by the impact of the attacks, and that the PP, as suggested by polls, was supposed to have won such elections. It is in this context that EP elections took place, putting an end to the electoral cycle started in May 2003. Prior to this date, Spanish citizens had already participated in three different elections (municipal, regional and legislative). 2004 had been a year characterised by almost constant electoral campaigns and elections, and was meant to finally end in June. A post-electoral study by the Sociological Research Centre (CIS) on the 14 March elections destroyed the myth according to which the PP would have undoubtedly gained an important victory at legislative elections if the attack had not taken place. According to the CIS report, the PP was leading by a minor advantage when the campaign started. This advance was reduced to a virtually even match on the eve of 11 March. From 27 February onwards, a movement had started which was clearly in favour of PSOE.

Voting system and electoral campaign

On 13 June 34 592 318 electors were called to polling stations to elect 54 MEPs, ten less than in the European elections of 1999, in a single constituency and with a proportional electoral system based on the d'Hondt method. The loss of a certain number of deputies and the establishment of the single district led to the formation of coalitions, sparing many from being expelled from the

European electoral scene. With the exception of the PSOE, led by José Borrell (future President of the European Parliament) and of the PP, led by Jaime Mayor Oreja, all parties formed coalitions. Among the main ones were the following coalitions. Firstly, the IU-ICV-EUA formed by post-communists of the IU (United Left), Group IC (Initiative for Catalonia-Greens) and EuiA (United and Alternative Left) headed by Willy Meyer of the IU. Secondly, the coalition GalEusCa, acronym of 'Galicia, Euskadi and Catalonia', formed by the four nationalist parties, CiU (Catalonian Convergence and Union), the PNV (Basque Nationalist Party), the BNG (Galician Nationalist Bloc) and the PSM-EN (Socialist Party, Nationalist Mallorque-Entesa) for the Valencia community. At the head of the list was Ignassi Guardans of the CiU. Thirdly, the Nationalist coalition 'Europe of Peoples' integrating the ERC (the Catalonian Republican Left), the Basque Party *Eusko Alkartasuna* (EA), the Aragon Party Chunta Aragonesista (CHA), the Andecha Astur of the Asturies (AA), the Conceju Nacionaliegu Cantabrie (CNC) and the coalition ICLR(Citizen Initiative-Greens) of the La Rioja region. At the head of this list was Bernat Joan of the ERC.

Main parties' electoral manifestos

The PP's programme was centred on the fight against international terrorism, and the establishment of common rules for the storage of explosives, making robbery and other offences facilitating terrorist acts difficult. Secondly, it was concerned with the necessity of promoting and maintaining social and economic cohesion as one of the basic principles of European solidarity. The PP also promised to work from the European level to improve and modernise education and research, and to promote all necessary changes securing a system based on respect for the environment. Finally, the PP favoured a common foreign and security policy based on the reinforcement of Atlantic ties.

For its part, the PSOE started its declaration of intents by stressing what it considered the two most pressing objectives: to end the gridlock on European Constitution negotiations, and to withdraw Spanish troops from Iraq, allowing Europe to become an independent actor on the international scene. The socialists were in favour of replacing preventive war with preventive diplomacy. They also pleaded for co-operation with rather than subordination to the United States. Similarly, their programme emphasised the need for co-operation with Africa and the Middle East, the Euro-Mediterranean Association, dialogue with the Arab world and the development of relations with South America. Moreover, they promised to reinforce the European policy for Co-operation and Development, aiming to achieve 0.7 per cent of GDP. They also vowed to fight for the equality of women and against the violence between sexes, for 'quality' employment, and to centre their efforts to build a strong Europe based on a competitive economy. Lastly, they pleaded for the concession of a more important role for regions and municipalities.

Willy Meyer's IU-ICV-EUA coalition was based on the transformation of Europe to make it more 'social', ecologic, democratic, feminist, more united and engaged in the maintenance of peace. This coalition of left-wing parties favoured an autonomous EU free from the hegemony of the United States. It recommended the dismantlement of NATO and the withdrawal of foreign bases from European territory, as well as the elimination of all nuclear arms and weapons of mass destruction.

For the GalEusCa coalition, peoples and citizenship had to be at the centre of a European construction based on pluralism, diversity, and the respect and consolidation of the different cultures belonging to it. This coalition also acknowledged the existence of the 'nations' of Catalonia, Galicia and the Basque Country at the European Council, and favoured the presence of these autonomous communities in central government's delegation to European institutions. Its aim was the participation of different regions in the management and control of communitarian funds.

The aim of the so-called 'Europe of peoples' was to achieve higher levels of participation among populations and regions within the European Union. Its aim was autonomy. Its programme suggested recognition of all languages at the European level and asked for the regional control of all structural funds.

Analysis of electoral results

The electoral campaign was centred on the candidature of the socialist José Borrell and PP candidate Jaime Mayor Oreja with a quasi-exclusive left–right competition, without smaller parties troubling the debate of the two main ones. For the first time since 1993, televised debates between the two candidates were broadcast by private stations Tele 5 and Antena 3.

The electoral battle was centred on the Spanish national scene, focusing on issues such as terrorism and the withdrawal of Spanish troops from Iraq. Little was said about Europe and European integration. These elections were clearly dominated by domestic politics, with parties either wanting to reaffirm the March socialist victory or, in the case of the PP, write it off as the mere consequences of the terrorist attacks. The motto of the campaign of the PSOE, 'We come back to Europe' offered a break from the axis formed by the preceding government, which had placed international politics under the influence of Atlantic ties. In fact, the socialists were aiming for a return to 'Old Europe', based on the Paris–Berlin axis, rather than on the Washington–London axis.

The PSOE won the elections with 25 seats and 6 621 570 votes. The PP came second with 24 seats and 6 315 294 votes. The IU-ICV-EUA coalition gained two seats and 636 458 votes; GalEusCa won two seats and 790 051 votes, while the list 'Europe of Peoples' succeeded in securing one seat and 380 095 votes.

The strategy used by the PSOE and by the PP to portray European elections as a confirmation or a second round of legislative elections was confirmed by election results. The PSOE won the election for the third consecutive time, opening a new political cycle after eight years of the José Maria Aznar government. However, contrary to what pre-election surveys had predicted, the PP did not lose everything, and was separated by the PSOE by a very small margin. Finally, presenting 13 June as a 'revenge' for the 14 March elections led the PP to make significant progress compared to the general elections, dispelling the hypothesis of a sanction vote aiming at punishing the party after so many years in government. Meanwhile, this progress went hand in hand with minor improvements for the PSOE, whose electoral notoriety increased, serving as a vote of confidence in José Luis Rodriguez Zapatero's new government.

However, participation rates were the lowest in Spanish electoral history since the return to democracy. It is clear that voters still consider European elections as of secondary importance, thus leading to overall apathy and low participation. Moreover, levels of electoral participation in European elections may vary, depending on whether the polls are held separately, with no other type of election to galvanise it. For instance, when European elections were held on their own in 1999, participation rates reached 54.7 per cent, whereas in 2004, participation lowered to 45.9 per cent with nearly 32 points less than for the March general elections. Other important factors were the predominance of national issues in the electoral campaign, as well as the fatigue of Spanish citizens after a year of elections and campaigning coupled with a significant electoral trauma. Results aside, the main problem with the 2004 EP elections was the high percentage of abstainers, leading to very low electoral turnout. While this is a phenomenon present in most European countries, it left a bitter taste to the end of Spain's electoral tour.

Gabriel Colome

Bibliography

Alcantara, M. and Martinez, A. (eds), *Política y gobierno en España*, Valencia, Tirant lo Blanc, 2001.
Molas, I. and Bartomeus, O., *Estructura de la competencia política en España (1986–2000)*, Barcelona, ICPS, 2001.

→ Abstention; Campaign (Sociology of); Election Manifestos; Electoral Cycles; Electoral Strategy; European Elections (1979–1999); European Elections (2004); Federations of Political Parties; Forecast; Issues; Left; Mapping Europe: European Electoral Geography; Second-Order Elections; Social Europe.

Strasbourg

In 1949, the town of Strasbourg was selected as the host town for the Council of Europe, the first pan-European organisation of the post-war period in 1948. From a geographical perspective, the fact that the borders of Alsace straddle both Germany and Switzerland, in addition to its proximity to Luxembourg, contributes to its unique location, and so renders this region a crossroads from many points of view. Moreover, Strasbourg is also a particularly significant choice in terms of the lingering history of this city which was keenly fought-over and contested for a long time between Germany and France. Once the symbol of Franco-German rivalry, the town of Strasbourg has now become the symbol of a reconciliation which goes to the very heart of European integration. However, beyond this symbolic reflection, what could have induced parliamentary representatives from countries so recently locked into one of the most destructive wars in European history, to come to work together, particularly in such a town?

It is truly, at this point in time, that Strasbourg deserves its title of 'Capital of Europe'. As the seat of the Council of Europe, it also accommodates the European Court of Human Rights, in addition to 71 diplomatic representations and consulates, the European Parliament, the European Ombudsman, the Assembly of European Regions, Eurocorps' headquarters and even the Franco-German television channel Arte.

Whereas the seat of the ECSC institutions was established in Luxembourg, it was actually decided in 1952 that the parliamentary assembly would hold its plenary sessions in the Council of Europe's auditorium in Strasbourg, the only institution to possess the necessary facilities for such an event. Even if the assembly were to remain at Strasbourg, in 1958 it was decided that the seat of the new European Communities, the EEC and Euratom, would be temporarily fixed in Brussels. As the political commissions and groups developed the practice of meeting close to both the European Commission and Council of Ministers, the three locations of Brussels, Luxembourg and Strasbourg thus gradually became essential for the operational business of the European Parliament. Efforts to unite the European Parliament into one unique location never amounted to much because of divergent interests of the member states concerned. During the 1970s, whilst Luxembourg undertook the construction of an auditorium to accommodate assembly sessions as requested by the European Parliament, protests from France enabled the safeguarding of the status quo, as agreed in 1977. Following the introduction of elections by universal suffrage in 1979, the European MEPs insisted on the specification of a single location, feeling that that their duties were incompatible and constrained by this geographical ambiguity. However, the fact that Brussels was the only and logical choice of seat for the elected officials in the European Parliament fuelled both France's and Luxembourg's resolve to defend their respective towns as legitimate options for the work of the assembly, so resisting any attempt from the MEPs to assert any contrary facts.

The construction of the 'Caprice des Dieux'[1] building in Brussels in 1989 failed to prevent the definitive establishment of Strasbourg as the seat of the European Parliament during the Edinburgh Council in 1992. Despite representing a perennial source of conflict within the institution, the European Parliament seat in Strasbourg was further confirmed by the Treaty of Amsterdam. This agreement obligates the European Parliament to annually hold at least twelve sessions in Strasbourg, whilst also maintaining its Secretariat General in Luxembourg, and meetings of the commissions and political groups in Brussels. In 1999, Strasbourg completed the construction of the new European Parliament building (the IPE IV), which has a total surface area of 200 000 square metres, a height of 60m, equipped with a 1133 office tower, a 750-seat auditorium for the MEPs and a 750-seat visitor balcony, conference rooms for the commissions, groups and joint committees, a press room, restaurants and bars. In honour of the oldest member of the first European Parliament to be elected by universal suffrage, the IPE IV was named after 'Louise Weiss' as an impassioned homage to the founding-leaders of the European project. The building façades are entirely glazed, symbolising the transparency of European democracy and its openness to the outside, whilst the auditorium itself is an immense sphere visible from the outside of the building and without a single gap which represents the unity and sovereignty of parliamentary decision-making. From the cathedral axis in Strasbourg, the office tower leaves an impression of being unfinished, like Europe itself, in a perpetual process of construction. In a way, this new building can be interpreted as even representing the expression of the institutionalisation of the European Parliament in the European political and legal landscape.

The division of the European Parliament into three distinct places of work, however, confers on the institution a particular style that some precisely associate with the 'European' character of the Parliament. For example, the regular herding of institutional actors (elected members, assistants, civil servants) forms one of the specificities, as termed by Abélès, of the European 'tribe'. The activity which prevails during the Strasbourg plenary sessions constitutes yet another defining characteristic. It is this setting which represents a particular moment of institutional life. The entire group of elected officials are indeed reunited for a few days during which many meetings are arranged (political groups, national delegations, commissions, emergency resolution negotiations, etc.). Such a dense number of meetings happening together, essentially attracts attention from a range of individuals (journalists, lobbyists or visitors).

The plurality of work locations (in Strasbourg, Brussels and also in constituencies) undeniably constitutes a certain eccentricity attached to the European political profession and implies a particular and constraining division of political work: monthly sessions in Strasbourg, two weeks devoted to committee work in Brussels and one week with the political groups. If MEPs want to ensure at least a minimal presence in their respective constituencies, even the most dedicated MEPs must manage their diary very rigorously and be able to handle a restrictive and often demanding lifestyle.

The French MEPs, notably from the Alsace region, regularly mobilise themselves to lobby for the retention of Strasbourg as the seat of the European Parliament. Supported by the French government, they strongly oppose attempts from other MEPs to undermine the Alsace capital (similar to the decision to limit the plenary session week to four days). The defence of Strasbourg thus becomes a national cause. The consequences and symbolic and financial systems are of notable importance. Only by accommodating numerous students and tourists is the city able to persistently exercise the prestige related to its status as 'Capital of Europe' for which the European Parliament, more than any other institution, remains the emblem. The presence in Strasbourg of the hundreds of people who participate in each session additionally represents an extremely important economic advantage for the city and its surrounding region.

Willy Beauvallet
Sébastien Michon

Note

1. Oval industrial cheese equally famous in France for its shape as it is for its poor taste. Derogative connotation.

Bibliography

Abélès, Marc, *Everyday Life with the European Parliament*, Paris, Hatchet, 1992.

→ Brussels; Citizen (EU); European Parliament; Interest Groups; Luxembourg.

Sweden

In Sweden, since 1995, EP elections have seen an increase in non-voting that illustrates most of the electors' scepticism towards the EU. Another characteristic of Swedish EP elections is that these elections have functioned as a sanction of the social-democrat government in power, led since 1996 by Göran Persson. Until 2004, however, disaffection for voting had not generated changes in the party system.

In 1994, the average turnout in the EU countries was 56.7 per cent, whereas only 41.6 per cent of the Swedish voted in the first EP elections in 1995. The Swedish turnout in 1999 and 2004, respectively 38.8 per cent and 37.8 per cent, have been much lower than the average of the other EU countries (49.8 per cent in 1999 and 45.7 per cent in 2004). Among all elections, the turnout of the 2004 elections (37.8 per cent) was the lowest ever in Swedish political history, and the lowest among the 'old' EU members.

Voting system and division into constituencies

Voting in EP elections, which is not compulsory in Sweden, takes place at the national level on a proportional basis. Electors vote for a political party and, since the 1998 legislative elections, can also vote for a candidate. The distribution of seats occurs according to the modified St-Laguë method. To participate in the seat distribution, parties must win at least 4 per cent of the ballots. To be better positioned on the list, a candidate must win at least 5 per cent of the ballots obtained by his party. The candidate who receives the greatest number of votes takes the first position on the list, the second takes the second one, etc.

During European electoral campaigns, specifically European stakes usually have the edge on national ones. Since 1995, the year of Sweden's EU accession, the themes of European defence and Swedish neutrality, and the single currency and the future of the Swedish model of the welfare state, which are recurring themes in campaigns, have structured opinions and debates. In 2004, the debate focused on the draft directive on the services of the European Commission. This directive aims at encouraging the free movement of services according to the model of the free movement of persons and capital in the EU. According to the social-democrats, this directive could destroy the Swedish model.

Since 1995, the Swedish political elite has progressively become favourable to the EU, whereas public opinion remained more Eurosceptic. If electors had voted in favour of Sweden's EU membership during the 1994 referendum (52.3 per cent were favourable), they more obviously rejected (55.9 per cent were against it) Sweden's joining the monetary union during the September 2003 referendum.

Analysis of electoral results

The Swedish political system is divided in two blocs opposed on the question of Europe. On the left, the former communists of the Left Party (Vänsterpartiet, V) and the ecologists of the Green Party (Miljöpartiet de gröna, Mp) are clearly against the EU and still ask today for Sweden's withdrawal. The Social-Democrat Party (Socialdemokratiska arbetarepartiet, SAP) is more divided on the question, although the party leadership is favourable to a more thorough EU integration. On the right, all the parties were favourable to Sweden's EU accession during the 1994 referendum: the Christian Democrat Party (Kristdemokraterna, Kd), representing the conservative right, the Liberal Party (Folkpartiet Liberalerna, Fp) and the moderate conservatives of the Moderate Party (Moderata samlingspartiet, M). In 2003, the former Agrarian Party, the Centre Party (Centerpartiet, C) was the only one within the right to be opposed to the country's membership of monetary union. Table 1 presents the evolution of the results in EP elections.

Since 1995, EP elections have been a series of political defeats for the Social-Democrat Party (SAP). In the first EP elections in 1995, the Social-Democrats in power obtained their worst result since 1911, with a decrease of 17 points in relation to the 1994 legislative elections. The Greens and the left won seats in these elections. Four years later, the same pattern occurred. The SAP only won 26.1 per cent of the ballots, marking a decrease of 10 points in comparison to the 1998 legislative elections. In 1995 as in 1999, record abstention rates were registered, contributing to the bad results of the Social-Democrats. But it was not until the 2004 election that a party succeeded in challenging the monopoly of the seven great political groupings seated in the national parliament: the June List (Junilistan), which stands in favour of a 'slight' Euroscepticism, reflected the opinion of most of the Swedish by declaring itself in

Table 1 Results of the EP elections in Sweden, 1995–2004

	1995	1999	2004
SAP (ESP)	28.1 (7)	26.0 (6)	24.7 (5)
M (EPP-ED)	23.2 (5)	20.7 (5)	18.2 (4)
JL (IND/DEM)	–	–	14.4 (3)
V (EUL/NGL)	12.9 (3)	15.8 (3)	12.8 (2)
Fp (ELDR)	4.8 (1)	13.9 (3)	8.0 (2)
C (ELDR)	7.2 (2)	6.0 (1)	6.3 (1)
Mp (Greens)	9.5 (2)	9.5 (2)	5.9 (1)
Kd (EPP-ED)	7.6 (2)	7.6 (2)	5.7 (1)

Source: http://www.val.se

favour of the country's remaining in the EU without any new power transfers to the European institutions.

The Social-Democrat prominence has continued to decrease since Sweden's first participation in EP elections, the SAP going from seven MEPs in 1995 to five in 2004. However, Social-Democrats have always succeeded in maintaining their position of first Swedish party in EP elections, sharing about half of the mandates available with the moderates of the right since 1995 (54.5 per cent in 1995, 50 per cent in 1999 and 47.4 per cent in 2004). Compared to the 2002 legislative elections, the parties that managed to improve their results are the Left Party and the Green Party, both Eurosceptic, and the moderates, more Europhile. In contrast, the Social-Democrats, the People's Party and the Christian Democrats obtained lower results. If we compare legislative and EP elections since 1995, we notice that the Social-Democrats have systematically obtained better results in national elections, whereas the Greens and the left – both opposed to the EU and quick to capture the ballots of popular Euroscepticism – obtain their best results in European elections.

As for the mandates obtained by the political groups in the EP, the ESP and the EPP-ED conservatives obtained five seats each, the EDLR group and the IND/DEM three seats each, the EUL/NGL two seats, and the Greens one seat. Of the elected representatives 42.1 per cent (8/19) are MEPs renewing their position, 47.4 per cent (9/19) are women and 26.3 per cent (5/19) are former national MPs. Finally, 53.3 per cent of the Swedish electors are men, and the majority of non-voters are women.

At the local level, another winner of the 2004 EP elections is the extreme-right nationalist party Sverigedemokraterna (Sweden Democrats), which tripled its national result of 1.1 per cent of valid ballots, obtaining 3.4 per cent of the ballots in the province of Skåne, in the south of the country, and up to 6.2 per cent in the city of Landskron, where the turnout was however only 31.1 per cent. As Euroscepticism becomes institutionalised with the emergence of a Eurosceptic grouping, the number of Swedish MEPs decreased in 2004 from 21 to 19.

The June List

After the 2004 EP elections, in which 24 parties and 391 candidates confronted each other, the electoral objectives of Gorän Persson's Social-Democrat Party were to increase the 38.8 per cent turnout and improve the results (28.1 per cent) they obtained in the previous EP elections. Neither goal was achieved.

In September 2003, four days after Swedish Minister of Foreign Affairs Anna Lindh's murder, a majority of the Swedish had rejected by referendum the adoption of the euro, in spite of the efforts of the government and the Svenskt Näringsliv (Confederation of Swedish Enterprises) that had invested 500 million Swedish Crowns (55 million euros) to try to convince the public opinion of the advantages of the euro for Sweden. Following the Danish example, a populist June List, supported financially by several Swedish billionaires, ran in EP elections four months after it was created. Led by former members of the Social-Democrat Party, this movement illustrated a centre-right economic Euroscepticism. The main slogans of the June List campaign were 'No to EU Constitution' and 'Referendum on EU Constitution'. Its leaders say they are in favour of Sweden's remaining in the EU while calling for a reduced co-operation between the two. They are opposed to the new Constitution and Sweden's adoption of the euro, in conformity with the explicit title of Nils Lundgren's book (*Europe Yes, Euro No*).

The June List led, with a 1 300 000 Sweden Crown budget (€143 000), an intensive campaign that enabled it to channel the votes of Eurosceptics from the left and the right. This list had not been taken seriously when, on 11 February 2004, Nils Lundgren, former group chief economist at Nordbanken, and Lars Wohlin, former Director of the Swedish Central Bank, introduced it to the press. In public opinion, they were soon seen as the 'rebels', the representatives of the 'smalls' against Brussels' impersonal power. According to a survey of Swedish television, 23 per cent of the June List electors had previously voted for the Social-Democrats and 13 per cent

for the right. Nineteen per cent of the voters over 65 years old voted for the June List, whose three elected representatives, Nils Lundgren, Lars Wohlin and Hélène Goudin, a school teacher in Piteå, in Northern Sweden, are 62 years old on average. Thanks to this electoral success, the party will have its campaign expenses reimbursed by the Swedish government.

The Social-Democrat leaders, armed with the 39.8 per cent of the ballots that they obtained in the 2002 legislative elections, had considered that 35 per cent of the ballots would be 'fair'. Since they did not pass the 25 per cent mark, the party obtained in these elections the worst results ever.

EP elections in Sweden were dominated by the challenging of the Social-Democrat Party, its leader Prime Minister Göran Persson, and the euro. If Social-Democrats are still deeply divided on the European question, a large section of the electors seem to want to content themselves with a Europe of free trade. After the No vote to the euro in 2003, all the parties showed a stronger scepticism towards the EU. Like the 1999 EP elections, the 2004 ones were the opportunity for anti-European political forces to criticise the Swedish government's political line and vote against Europe. The winner of these elections is the June List that took the Social-Democrat's European political line as their target. Following the pattern of extreme-right Ny Demokrati (New Democracy) in 1991 and the Danish June List, within four months, a group of individuals firstly gathered around the September 2003 campaign against the euro adoption managed to create a new political party, obtain more than 14 per cent of the ballots and become the country's third party after the Social-Democrats and the moderate right, thus restructuring the Swedish political space. With the Left Party and the Greens, the June List strengthens a Eurosceptic bloc that now accounts for nearly 40 per cent of the Swedish voters, a genuine counter-power in the face of the national elites. Perhaps strengthened by a higher abstention rate amongst the left electors, the SAP's failure in the latest EP elections shows that Social-Democrat Prime Minister Göran Persson, who has been in power since 1996, has still not managed to reassure voters who distrust the EU.

Niilo Kauppi

Bibliography

Aylott, Nicholas and Magnus Blomberg, 'The European Parliament Election in Sweden, June 13 2004', 2004, available at http:// www.sussex.ac.uk/sei/documents/ epernbrefsweden.pdf.

Reif, Karl Heinz and Schmitt, Hermann, 'Nine Second-Order National Elections: a Conceptual Framework for the Analysis of European Elections Results', *European Journal of Political Research*, 8, 1980, pp. 3–44.

➜ Mapping Europe: European Electoral Geography.

Symbolism

'Democratic deficit', weakness of European identity, incantatory references to a 'European public space', calls for a supranational governance closer engaged with civil society in the management of public affairs . . . These recurring expressions in the debate about the European Union raise the issues of its legitimacy, of the articulation between the representation of the ideal political order internalised by citizens and the actual political order or, in other words, of the future of the symbolic dimension of politics in the context of European integration.

Political symbolism encompasses all organised systems of signs, overloaded with meanings, and functioning as a reactivation of cultural codes of behaviour. Symbolism is, in its nature, polysemic, thus allowing for diverse and changing interpretations. Therefore, it facilitates unity even where agreement does not prevail or, in other words, for the creation of the 'solidarity with consensus' according to Kertzer's phrase. Symbolism works at two levels: first, at the cognitive level by referring to meanings instilled by primary or secondary socialisation; second, at the emotional level through the mobilisation of positive or negative projections related to identification or rejection. Such projections structure an ordered vision of the world, a representation of time and space. The social functions of political symbolism consist in ensuring the dominance of the public authority on the stage, conveying schemes of perception of reality which attribute the control over events and organisation of social life to the office-holders. It is about putting forward the elites as such and highlighting their command. Thus, the system of government is able to demand allegiance from the citizens and to induce the latter to unite around it. However, political symbolism can also be a tool for protest against the established order through a counter-use, a deviation by the opposition or the production of alternative signs. Consequently, it is both material for and a means of competition and political dialogue, and, hence, a privileged tool for their analysis.

Political symbolism acts in a specific fashion according to the principles of justification which characterise each form of domination. In the modern democratic framework, universal suffrage remains the major source of legitimacy and the formal body for the allocation of power for which periodical consultation sets the pace of public life. Therefore, a significant part of the symbolic codes derives from the expression of the people's will through the polls. Since the introduction of direct universal suffrage in 1979, European elections have given rise to ad hoc symbolic codes, which were reinstated by the June 2004 elections without any major upheavals.

A European electoral ritual?

Symbols are classically classified into three categories. The first one is composed of all the symbols which relate to the liturgy, ceremonies, rituals and regulated behaviour. The electoral ritual constitutes the ideal means to frame the competition for power and thus to contain it. It imposes an authorised version of history through its related tales and favours the development of a common conscience amongst citizens by inviting them to simultaneously accomplish the same act. Nevertheless, European elections fail to generate this 'community of action' in that they do not have uniform schedules and procedures. In 2004, the voting process was stretched over four days, from 10 to 13 June, in the 25 member states of the Union. The heterogeneity of the ritual was highlighted by the controversy between the Commission and the Netherlands regarding the publication of the results. The provisions in the Act on European elections by universal suffrage of 20 September 1976, which regulate the issue, impose on member states an obligation to maintain the embargo on the results in their respective countries until the closing of the last polls in order not to influence votes. On the grounds of the need for transparency, the Dutch local authorities, with the support of their government, refused to keep the votes secret, thereby inciting protests from the Commission. Similar breaches of the embargo on the results by local authorities occurred in Germany, Denmark and Sweden but did not receive much attention as voting in these countries took place on the last day. Not only was the ritual not simultaneous, but it was also far from being perfectly regulated. The international media echoed the possibility that certain citizens could vote twice in two different countries with all the necessary legal documents. Finally, the ritual also created discriminations. A discourse denouncing the exclusive nature of European citizenship was fostered by frustrations expressed by non-European immigrant communities for not being able to participate in voting in their resident country whereas EU citizens from other member states residing in the host country for a much shorter time could.

As was the case in earlier elections, the 2004 European elections did not give the opportunity to enter a period specific to the electoral campaign suspending the usual constraints of the political game. Due to the lack of a majority rule and also to the possibility for an alternation at the European level, they did not achieve the traditional voting role of the 'ritual humiliation of the elites', as conceptualised by the anthropologists, which consists of the reinstatement of the conditional and delegated nature of democratic power through the short-term inversion of the relations of dominance by the obligation imposed on leaders to request approval from those who are governed. The highlights of the campaign were generally consigned to the now common appearance in national meetings of representatives from friendly parties from other member states or leaders of transnational federations. The staging of 'premieres' such as the creation of the Party of the European Left in Rome or the launch of the European centre party in Paris received more attention. Similarly, animated hearings of José Manuel Durão Barroso as applying president of the Commission before the European Parliament provided further dramatisation. However, these events did not manage to bring about a higher media coverage in comparison to the previous European elections. Where there were new practices, they either only related to specific national contexts, as was the case in Spain, where a head-to-head political debate between two candidates on television took place for the first time since 1993 when José Maria Aznar refused to participate in such a show, or occurred in an anecdotal manner, like the French Greens taking buses of voters to visit the European Parliament in Brussels before inviting them to a meeting or the Italian government sending text messages to all voters possessing mobile phones as an incentive to vote. The fact that European elections thus appear as a privileged forum for experiments providing new means of interaction between candidates and voters does not necessarily contribute to giving them more credit as a political act. Therefore, the time of the elections is not really in rupture with the normal time. In spite of the repetition of certain codified forms of behaviour, these have little political impact. Innovation remains negligible and not very cumulative. In this respect, the level of ritualisation is low.

Similarly, in European electoral competition, the authorised language, a major component of any ritual, remains embryonic. The language barrier in a Europe which now has 20 official languages, coupled with the voters' low level of knowledge regarding European issues, seem to be the main obstacles to the development of common rhetorical references. Although a specialised vocabulary for EU matters does exist, it does not constitute an area of meanings likely to provide materials (routinised metaphors, key words, slogans) for efficient public-oriented political speeches.

Even at the mere level of advertising through images, which is more instantaneous and less codified than symbolism, finding meanings that would be acceptable and efficient in all national contexts has proved to be difficult. Thus, in May 2004, in an advert by the European Parliament which was designed to create an incentive for citizens to vote by emphasising the importance of choice at all stages of life, a sequence showing a baby choosing between the mother's two breasts was censored in Great Britain and banned in Ireland, where the display of a breast was considered shocking yet did not spark any problems elsewhere. This example reflects the cultural limits of what can be said and what cannot, the changing borders of public and private spheres, and the links between politics and ethics which are specific to each country. Furthermore, although the criticism of the EU institutions is shared across Europe, its features remain influenced by the national context. For instance, the Scandinavian countries insist on the issues of transparency and conflicts of interests much more than other countries.

Objective readings of Europe

The second largest category of signs, after liturgy, encompasses all material symbols, which are necessarily intertwined with the electoral ritual. First, there are objects, which act as 'places of memory' where collective experience and mutual recognition slowly accumulate for members of a political community. The European Union now has a widely known symbol with the twelve star flag, although it does not create as much collective attachment as the national colours (Lager 1995; Hedetoft 1998; Shore 2000). The European stars are widely used on election posters and photographs. They are also sometimes the object of counter-uses or confronted by signs of assertion of national identity such as the silver sterling symbol put forward by the UKIP. Except for the twelve stars, the EU symbolic directory is empty. Although 'Strasbourg' and 'Brussels' are regularly used to refer to the European decision-making places, the European Union does not have monuments, such as the 'Elysée' or 'Westminster', which have acquired a representation value in the eyes of the general public. Prior to the elections, in March 2004, the Van Hulten report by the European Parliament Committee for the control of the budget, adopting the view that the Strasbourg Parliament should be abandoned, highlighted once again the problem of the lack of a fixed territorial basis for the assembly and the political inability of the latter to control the conditions under which it is staged vis-à-vis the member states.

In addition to objects, material symbols also relate to human incarnations of Europe. The role of the office-holders, beyond the people actually holding EU offices, will be addressed here. This role constitutes both a more or less codified element of the structure of rules concerning all rituals and a dynamic model of governmental behaviour and of the signs used in the latter. It is linked not only to the practical needs of the offices concerned but also to the ways in which the exercise of these offices are staged. The addition in the Parliament of 100 new MPs and the massive presence of representatives from new member states *de facto* imply the introduction of a degree of novelty in the task of the EU legislature, even though continuity is to some extent guaranteed by a higher rate of renewal of the incumbents' offices than during the previous elections. The Members of the European Parliament still do not have a unique status. Moreover, their competencies remain poorly understood and underestimated by citizens and the proportional nature of the elections does not favour individualisation of the stakes. Candidates to the European Parliament more often than not have a second-order political profile at the national level and they are not able to develop their reputation because of a limited media-covered campaign. Like any European election, the 2004 election witnessed candidates who tried to take advantage of their reputation in non-political backgrounds to get seats, with variable degrees of success, and the multiplication of lists from socio-professional categories, ideological, religious or cultural minorities and interest groups. The diversity of discourses thus emerging does not contribute towards a clarification of the professional identity of the European MEPs in the eyes of the public. Once in office, the newly elected MEPs have to gain a working knowledge of the complex mechanisms of the institution and get to grips with a high level of technical expertise in one or several fields of public action, which does not really entail a reinforcement of a general profile of politics able to fulfil the expectations of the media. These complex EU political games, together with the absence of bipolarisation and the intertwining of national and transnational partisan cleavages, constitute another obstacle to the affirmation of high-level personalities. This was observed in 2004, with the renewal of an agreement between the EPP and the ESP in order to organise the distribution of offices, and by the election of Josep Borrell, who is relatively unknown on the international stage, rather than Bronislaw Geremek, a historic symbol of the Polish resistance to communism, a representative of the new member states and a well-known intellectual. Therefore, the role of the MEPs remains structurally weak, and the deepening of its codification does not guarantee a better public recognition.

European elections increasingly influence the development of the role of the president of the Commission, since the latter has to obtain the investiture from the European Parliament and take into account its views throughout the mandate. Such a role is also little institutionalised, as underlined by the very unequal profiles and leaderships of the successive office-holders (Joana and Smith 2002; Drake 2000). Originally, José Manuel Durão Barroso had the disadvantage of coming from a small country which was not a founder of the European Communities, and mainly of appearing as a second choice candidate between the member states whilst managing to provoke a violent rejection from numerous left-wing political forces due to his liberal positions and pro American stances concerning the war in Iraq. He was criticised in relation to his expertise and European involvement during the hearings before the European Parliament. He managed to obtain a vote of confidence, but with a rather disappointing majority in comparison to the previous office-holders, and experienced serious difficulties when it came to the composition of his Commission. Within the new composition of the enlarged college of 25 members, with new prerogatives for the president but in competition with new institutional actors, Barroso's future personal status and capacity to embody Europe remain uncertain.

Immaterial symbols and referential Europe

The third category of symbols, the immaterial objects, comprises the idea-forces around which systems of beliefs, founding stories which play the role of myth of the origins, values which serve as poles of attraction or repulsion, are organised. All rituals mirror one or several 'hidden texts' which give them a meaning and are structured around each other to form a global approach to the world. The electoral ritual is grounded on the legitimising fiction of the people's sovereignty. Such a fiction was particularly undermined during the 2004 European elections, on the one hand by a turnout of under half of the electorate at the EU level and a quarter in the new member states, and on the other hand by the fact that the majorities in power at the national level were largely disowned. In addition to this repeated denial of the discourse justifying European integration in the name of the democratic participation of citizens, results appeared, for the first time with a real intensity, as a protest against Europe as a referent itself. The traditional criticisms of European integration were again voiced in more or less identical terms as the past versions of sovereignty discourses, declining in Denmark but flourishing in Sweden with the Junilistan movement, long-lasting in its logic in France with the Front National, in Belgium with the Vlaams Blok and in Italy with the Lombard League, emerging in Poland with the Catholic camp advocating a normative definition of European identity. However, in the United Kingdom, the complete and undisguised rejection of belonging to the European Union by the UKIP, which was successful in terms of votes, was unprecedented. Moreover, the increase of behaviour around 'constructive suspicion', which does not reject the EU but aims to profoundly reform it (Europa Transparant of Dutch Paul Van Buitenen, Hans-Peter Martin's movement in Austria) has become more widespread. Therefore, the formerly intangible dogma of union was rejected either in its entirety or in its practical details.

The debate around the referent Europe was expected before the elections, due, on the one hand, to the then current constitutional process which opened the redesigning of internal arrangements of the EU system and its principles of legitimacy and, on the other hand, the recent and future enlargements which revised new borders. Although the mythology attached to the notion of constitution, which notably made allusion to American history, could operate within the Convention for the Future of Europe, it had but limited influence during the campaign for the 2004 elections. Since the issue divided political forces and was seen as likely to frighten voters, it has been most frequently reported at a later date. The mode of future ratification of the Constitutional Draft Treaty was raised more often than its contents were. The controversy relating to the values set forth by the text remained limited. 'Social Europe' was not a structuring stake; the appropriateness of the reference to the Christian heritage of Europe in the preamble of the Constitution was only a significant electoral argument in Poland. With regard to enlargement, the integration of ten new member states was taken for granted and discussions only speculated as to the results. The candidacy of Turkey, announced as a major point of contention in the election, did not manage to secure the victory of strategies which directly focused on it, such as Philippe de Villiers' Mouvement pour la France. Since again there was no unanimity on the issue in all political forces, the topic was set aside. As usual, the European political debate aimed at the general public remained limited in the identity and normative aspects, values and identity having been considered as too dangerous, inefficient or inappropriate resources in an electoral perspective.

François Foret

Bibliography

Drake, H., *Jacques Delors: Perspectives on a European Leader*, London, Routledge, 2000.

Hedetoft, U. (ed.), *Political Symbols, Symbolic Politics: European Identities in Transformation*, Aldershot, Ashgate, 1998.

Joana, J. and Smith, A., *Les commissaires européens: Technocrates, diplomates ou politiques?*, Paris, Presses de Sciences Po, 2002.

Lager, C., *L'Europe en quête de ses symboles*, Berne, Peter Lang, 1995.

Shore, C., *Building Europe: the Cultural Politics of European Integration*, London, Routledge, 2000.

→ Act of 1976; Brussels; Campaign (Sociology of); Citizen (EU); Electoral Operations; European Electoral Act; European Parliament; European Public Sphere; Europeanisation (of National Political Life); Investiture of the Commission; Luxembourg; Members of the European Parliament (Legal and Political Status); Representation; Symbols and Practice of Elections; Turkey; Universal Suffrage.

Symbols and Practice of Elections

The analysis of the symbolic and practical conditions of European elections is a good indicator of the level of Europeanisation of electoral technologies used to select MEPs. Even if progress has recently been noted in this field, we are still faced with a contrasted electoral scenery – and even more so since the 2004 enlargement. The Treaty of Amsterdam, whose aim was to reform the EU before its enlargement towards Central and Eastern European countries, established a certain number of 'common principles to all member States' (in the cautious terms of Article 190 of the treaty introducing the European Communities) for the election of MEPs. They included a choice of list or transferable votes (the Irish model since 1922); a proportional system; possibilities of division into electoral constituencies which 'nevertheless must not globally breach the proportional character of the poll'; a minimal threshold for the attribution of seats which must 'not exceed 5 per cent of the expressed votes at the national level', etc. (Decisions of the Council of 25 June 2002 and of 23 September 2002 amending the Act leading to election of the MEPs under universal suffrage of 20 September 1976).

Despite this effort to move towards a 'uniform electoral procedure', already promised by the Treaty of Rome in 1957, the symbolic and practical modalities of the poll remain stamped by a 'truly national mark' (Jean-Louis Burban, *Le Monde*, 23 November 1978). Traditionally, a wide variety of electoral methods (mobile ballot box, postal vote, etc.) for European elections have been retained because member states have a tendency to utilise electoral rules and technologies used in national elections. There was, in common with previous European elections, an absence of conformity and of electoral unity during the European elections of 2004.

Yves Déloye

→ Ballot; Compulsory Voting; Electoral System; Electoral Operations; Electoral Technology; European Electoral Act; Polling Stations; Postal Voting; Symbolism; Territorial Organisation; Universal Suffrage.

Tenure

'Representatives are elected for a five-year period'. Limited to this concise formula contained in Article 3 of the Act on European Elections by direct universal suffrage of 20 September 1976, the length and regulation of the European mandate makes no reference to the indefinite re-eligibility of representatives. Inherent to the political systems of individual member states, this measure seemed obvious at the time of the introduction of direct universal suffrage. Nonetheless, the European Parliament comes across as a particularly unstable political assembly, characterised by frequent turnover and the short tensure of its elected members (Corbett et al. 2003). A recent census of MEPs at the end of the fifth legislature further underlines the lack of stability of the European Parliament's personnel.

Going back to the 53 per cent of exiting MEPs at the first Euro-25 elections of June 2004, the 'fifteen' have shown a tendency to reconfirm existing positions (Table 1). In fact, re-election rates at the start of the sixth legislature were 7 points higher than in 1999 (46.4 per cent), and over 10 points greater than in 1994 (42.7 per cent). After the elections of 1994 and 1999, marked by a high turnover of representatives, Europe witnessed the return of a global stability equivalent to the first elections of 1984 (56.7 per cent) and 1989 (50.2 per cent).

Such stabilisation is equally a factor in

Table 1 Evolution of re-election rates in the European Parliament (1984–2004)

	1984 (10)	1989 (12)	1994 (12)	1999 (15)	2004 (15)
Belgium	56.5	50	52	44	54.2
Denmark	68.8	50	37.5	50	42.9
Germany	72.7	51.9	46.5	69.7	66.7
France	43.6	33.3	35.6	31	44.9
Ireland	46.7	53.3	46.7	80	30.8
Italy	50	27.2	24.1	22.4	41
Luxembourg	50	16.7	83.3	16.7	50
Netherlands	56	50	48.4	41.9	59.3
United Kingdom	65.4	69.1	62.1	42.5	78.2
Grece	33.3	50	32	36	16.7
Spain		73.3	43.8	51.6	46.3
Portugal		64	32	40	41.7
Austria				71.4	72.2
Finland				56.3	57.1
Sweden				54.5	31.6
Total	*56.4*	*50.2*	*42.7*	*46.4*	*53*

the reduction of the number of rotations between two general elections. It conceals, nevertheless, a great diversity of situations characteristic to each national delegation. In 2004, while Germany and Austria re-elected nearly two-thirds of their representatives (66.7 and 72.7 per cent), and the UK more than three-quarters (78.2 per cent), Ireland and Sweden only re-elected one MEP out of three and Greece only one in four (16.7 per cent). This unequal repartition of re-election rates appears to be constant in time. The German and Anglo-Saxon delegations have benefited from a great stability since 1979, while France, Italy and Greece have replaced an average of more than 60 per cent of their representatives.

Such evolution of re-election rates tends to increase the duration of the political careers of representatives. After the readjustments that took place at the end of the fifth legislature, the number of MEPs having been re-elected at least once, and with a legislative experience of more than five years, reached 46.3 per cent (290 out of the 626 representatives up to 18 May 2004) (Nancy et al. 2004). While inferior to the re-election rates witnessed in national parliaments, such figures take on a different dimension when considering the number of 'brakes' and regulations limiting the formation of actual 'Euro careers' (youth of institutions, weakness of attributes and competencies, absence of uniform electoral procedures, list-based voting, national issues and the 'second-order' nature of EP elections, different degrees of party control over electoral campaigns, etc.).

Figures on the duration of MEP mandates or their political 'longevity' exist, and contribute to the consolidation of the role of the European Parliament within the institutional triangle. Amongst the 290 re-elected members, a real majority known as 'permanent' representatives (242) was

continuing its mandate without interruption, while a minority (48) known as 'intermittent' had been reappointed after a break. The average cumulative experience of 'permanent' MEPs reached 12 years, while those of the 'intermittent' ones 11.3. The majority of these re-elected parliamentarians had between five and ten years of legislative work experience behind them. However, levels of political tenure were higher amongst the 'permanents', with 35 MEPs having spent more than 15 years in Strasbourg, 15 of whom had occupied their position since the first EP election of 1975, reaching a total of 25 years of European legislative work. While more than half of them were EPP members, five were ESP representatives. The majority of them were German (9/15) or UK (3/15) representatives.

Such experiences were rare within the 'intermittent' camp, with only two representatives having between 22 and 25 cumulative years of EP mandate, and 11 with more than 15 years. Interestingly, these two MEPs had first been appointed before the introduction of direct universal suffrage (Astrid Lulling, Christian Democrat from Luxembourg first elected in 1965; and Colette Fresch, Liberal from Luxembourg as well, appointed since 1969). Amongst the others, five had been elected for the first time in 1979. The two most enduring figures have been the Italian non-registered Marco Pannella (21.5 years), and British Labour Gordon Adam (24.2 years). Partisan and geographical repartitions must be put into perspective, since the relative duration of political tenure is largely dependent on the date of accession of individual member states. The recent nature of many countries' EU membership also tends to encourage the re-election of members with continuous, albeit shorter experience. Nonetheless, the establishment of actual 'Euro careers' is well underway in Germany and in the

United Kingdom (Scarrow 1997), while its development is still embryonic in countries like France, Italy, the Netherlands and Belgium. The relative repartition amongst parties, of figures of political tenure, is determined by the political history of elections. Generally, it underlines the continuous efforts of the ESP socialists who accounted for more than half of the 'permanent' re-elected members, and very few 'intermittent' ones. The length of legislative experience appeared to be less important amongst the Christian Democrats and EPP conservatives, though it was longer and less continuous. After unaffiliated MEPs, the ENU Eurosceptics and the radical GUE/NGL left registered the highest share of re-elected members.

At the June 2004 elections, only seven 'permanents' and five 'intermittent' with more than 15 years of experience were re-elected. Among these figures who were pursuing solid European parliamentary careers were some of the Parliament's leading figures, such as the Christian Democrat President Ingo Friedrich, EPP President Hans-Gert Poettering, GUE/NGL President Francis Wurtz, or the German President of the Foreign Affairs Commission, Elmar Brok. Election after election, the non-codification of re-election procedures favoured the consolidation of real European political careers. It enabled the specialisation of certain figures within the role of MEP contributing, as in the United States, to the institutionalisation of this supranational parliamentary arena (Polsby 1968).

Guillaume Marrel
Renaud Payre

Bibliography

Corbett, R., Jacobs F. and Shackleton M., *The European Parliament*, Londen, Catermille, 2003 (5th edition).

Nancy, J., Wypych, J. and Piérot, R., *Chronique élections 2004: Données historiques*, Bruxelles, Parlement européen (Direction générale de l'information et des relations publiques), Direction de la communication, Division de la coordination centrale, 2004.

Polsby, N. W., 'The Institutionalization of the US House of Representatives', *American Political Science Review*, 62, 1, 1968, pp. 144–68.

Scarrow, S. E., 'Political Career Paths and the European Parliament', *Legislative Studies Quarterly*, 22, 2, 1997, pp. 253–63.

→ Act of 1976; Composition of the European Parliament; Eligibility; European Parliament; Incompatibility; Members of the European Parliament (Legal and Political Status); Parliamentary Mandate.

Territorial Organisation

The issue of territory occupies a significant place during European elections and thus far, the European Parliament is still composed of 'representatives of the people of the states' joined together in the EU rather than representatives of the people of the EU (Article 189 TEC). The global European level thus remains devoid of an election and remains 'decentralised' to some extent, although the idea of transnational lists has come a long way, and may result in a quota of MEPs elected within the framework of a single and large constituency (Article 7 of the Resolution of the European Parliament adopted in 1998). For European elections, the perennial question of territory, and thus the division of electoral constituencies, cuts across two levels. The first is formed by the national territory of each EU member state. It enables the allocation of the number of seats and the appointment of a proportion of MEPs, in accordance with 'common principles', particularly by the proportional electoral system, but according to appreciably different methods (Article 190 of the Amsterdam Treaty). The second level is infra-national, since certain states have chosen (and are now obliged, over a certain population) to organise their election within regional districts, varying in nature and size.

This fragmentation of the European space impacts the political representation of member states in the European Parliament and also the composition of political groups. The first consequence concerns the inequalities of representation brought about by the selected formula of allocation of seats across countries. Stemming from the idea that the number of elected representatives in each member state must ensure appropriate representation for the people of the states joined together in the EU, two principles have simultaneously been mobilised. The first principle is directed at the representation of citizens, since the number of seats allocated to each country is based on the size of the population, as of the time of its last census. The second is focused on the representation of the territories, insofar as each state, regardless of size, is guaranteed a minimum level of representation in the European Parliament (in 2004, five seats were allocated to Malta). The draft European Constitution fixes the threshold to six seats for the smallest states, but simultaneously specifies that in the future no country should account for more than 96 seats. With this territorial 'corrective measure', representation is thus conceived as being regressively proportional; in other words, it does not follow a strict rule of proportionality, based on the number of inhabitants. This absence of linearity has brought about very significant inequalities in representation: in 2004, one German MEP represented nearly 840 000 inhabi-

tants, whilst one Maltese MEP represented less than 80 000 inhabitants, a proportional variation in representation amounting to 1:10. In other words, from one member state to another, the weight of a vote varies significantly. The variation in the number of seats at stake also causes a change in the outcomes of the proportional formula. The district magnitude (the number of seats at stake in each constituency), constitutes an essential determinant of the proportionality of a system (Rae 1967; Taagepera and Shugart 1989). In countries with a smaller magnitude, the degree of proportionality is thus reduced, which can result in a significant modification of their results and consequently the composition of groups in the European Parliament (Costa 2000).

The question of dividing the constituencies also makes sense at the infra-national level. The Amsterdam Treaty introduced the opportunity for member states to determine territorial constituencies, provided that on the whole this does not undermine the proportional character of the vote or challenge the nature of the MEP mandate, who remains the representative of the state. This provision, optional, but nonetheless recommended for countries with over 20 million inhabitants, follows from the adoption of the 'principle of proximity', aimed at bringing European citizens closer to MEPs. In 2004, the overwhelming majority of countries gave priority to the national constituencies. Others opted for a division of their territory (Table 1).

Some countries maintained their former electoral boundaries, such as Belgium (four), Ireland (four) and the United Kingdom who, since the 1999 election, adopted the system of proportional voting within 12 districts (of which one, Northern Ireland, uses single transferable vote). However, France also

Table 1   Number of seats and practice of dividing electoral boundaries (constituencies) in the EU member states (2004)

Country	Number of MEPs	Number of constituencies	Number of inhabitants	Level of representation**
Germany	99	1	82 536 680	833 703
Austria	18	1	8 067 289	448 182
Belgium	24	4*	10 355 844	431 494
Cyrus	6	1	715 137	119 190
Denmark	14	1	5 383 507	384 536
Spain	54	1	40 409 330	748 921
Estonia	6	1	1 356 045	226 008
Finland	14	1	5 206 295	371 878
France	78	8	59 630 121	764 489
Greece	24	1	10 554 404	439 767
Hungary	24	1	10 142 362	422 598
Ireland	13	4	3 936 636	304 895
Italy	78	1	57 844 017	741 590
Latvia	9	1	2 331 480	259 053
Lithuania	13	1	3 462 553	266 350
Luxembourg	6	1	448 300	747 167
Malta	5	1	394 641	78 928
The Netherlands	27	1	16 192 572	599 725
Poland	54	13	38 218 531	707 751
Portugal	24	1	10 407 465	433 644
Czech Republic	24	1	10 203 269	425 136
United Kingdom	78	12	59 862 820	767 472
Slovakia	14	1	5 379 161	384 226
Slovenia	7	1	1 995 033	285 005
Sweden	19	1	8 940 788	470 568

* 3 unchanged electoral colleges.
** Overall across subdivisions if applicable. Read: 1 MEP per XXX XXX inhabitants.

abandoned its single national constituency in favour of eight large interregional districts, while Poland, the most populated new member, chose to organise its election within 14 constituencies. At the same time, Italy and Germany preferred to stick to a system mixing several geographical levels. Dividing the country into multiple constituencies is certainly more commonplace in the more populated countries, but this criterion does not explain everything as Belgium, with just over 10 million inhabitants, is divided into four districts, whilst Spain, with, like Poland, about 40 million prefers to retain its whole national territory as a single constituency.

The study of these various infranational divisions highlights three points of interest. The first concerns the nature of electoral constituencies. In Belgium, the borders of the electoral units reflect cultural as well as linguistic and historical foundations. Conversely, in France, Ireland, Poland and the

United Kingdom, constituencies have an almost self-standing electoral function insofar as they constitute 'ad hoc' districts, constructed by grouping pre-existing units. Their size, in purely numerical terms, must facilitate the relationship between the electorate and the MEPs whilst ensuring that the proportional character of the electoral formula is not undermined. The second point concerns the significant impact of magnitude, as previously mentioned. For example, in France, in 2004, in the French Centre Region, which comprises six seats, over 14 per cent of the votes cast was needed in order to secure one MEP. Yet this threshold was only 7 per cent in the French Ile-de-France constituency, where 14 seats were allocated. In the same vein, in the North-East of Great Britain, the only constituency to be allocated three MEP seats, over 17 per cent of the votes cast was required to capture a seat, yet across the rest of the country approximately 12 per cent of votes translated to more than nine seats. The third point relates to the part played by the constituencies in the transformation of votes into seats. In France, Ireland, Belgium and the United Kingdom, within each constituency, various political forces presented their list, and it is at this level that votes were counted and seats allocated. This unit thus constituted a decision-making space, and the smaller its size, the more the geographically concentrated political forces were favoured. Similarly, other countries limited the impact of geographical concentration and, consequently, the 'autonomous' capacity of the constituencies either by establishing, as in Italy, a national electoral quota (which allocates the number of seats in relation to the list, and will hence be distributed by constituency), or by imposing a threshold of votes to be secured across the whole country (5

per cent in Poland). Only parties meeting these conditions can participate 'locally' in the distribution of the seats. Finally, in Germany, the infra-national dimension is present through the opportunity offered to political parties to run either at the federal or Länder level; however, to secure seats, they are required in all circumstances to reach at least 5 per cent of the votes at the national level. These restrictions thus limit, even prohibit, any strictly 'local' involvement. These different situations serve to highlight the choice faced in fragmenting the electoral space, and the methods for doing it. These choices are not neutral operations but rather intrinsically related to preferences as to where power should be located, what the relations between voters and their representatives should be, and, ultimately, what the European Parliament should represent.

Annie Laurent

Bibliography

Costa, O., 'Quelles leçons pour le manque d'harmonisation des modes de scrutin aux élections européennes', in P. Delwit and J.-M. De Waele (eds), *Le mode de scrutin fait-il l'élection?*, Bruxelles, Editions de l'Université de Bruxelles, 2000.

Rae, D., *The Political Consequences of Electoral Law*, New Haven, Yale University Press, 1967.

Taagepera, R. and Shugart, M. S., *Seats and Votes: the Effects and Determinants of Electoral Systems*, New Haven, Yale University Press, 1989.

→ Electoral Behaviour; Electoral Strategy; Electoral Technology; European Constitution; European Elections (2004); European Parliament; France; Identity; Members of the European Parliament (Legal and Political Status); Multi-Level Governance; Representation; Symbols and Practice of Elections.

Treaty of Rome

(25 March 1957)

The two treaties signed in Rome on 25 March 1957 were drafted together and simultaneously ratified in each of the six participant states (France, Italy, the Federal Republic of Germany and the three Benelux countries), thus entering into force on 1 July 1958. One of these treaties established the European Atomic Energy Community (EAEC), also known as Euratom. The other treaty gave birth to the European Economic Community (EEC), usually referred to in the 1950s and 1960s as the Common Market, a name that only partially reflects the objectives set forth by the treaty. This latter treaty soon appeared to be the main foundation of European integration, and of such importance that it is now commonly referred to as the Treaty of Rome in the singular. Having been adopted for an unlimited period of time, this treaty has remained the basis of integration for half a century despite being subject to numerous revisions over time, notably by four important treaties between 1986 and 2001 (Single European Act, Maastricht Treaty, Amsterdam Treaty and Nice Treaty). It will reportedly disappear when the Constitutional Treaty, which was adopted by the European Council in 2004, enters into force following ratification in the 25 EU member states.

In order to understand the objectives of the Treaty of Rome, the environment in which it was drafted must be properly considered. The two agreements signed on 25 March 1957 were the result of what has been called the 'relaunching of 1955' which stemmed from the resounding failure of the EDC (European Defence Community) Treaty signed in 1952 and then rejected on 30 August 1954 by the French parliament, despite having already been ratified in four out of six member states. It begged the question as to whether this crisis was going to categorically block European integration, and thus unravel the progress made since the aftermath of the Second World War which was undoubtedly slow but was nevertheless marked by the great determination on the part of certain leaders. In order to overcome the failure, several convinced Europeans were keen to ensure an immediate relaunching of integration. Consequently, the European Coal and Steel Community (ECSC), which was considered to be a significant achievement, was established by the famous Schuman declaration of 9 May 1950. However, although all pro-Europeans agreed to narrow the scale of the project to focus on economic considerations, rather than on political and military issues which were deemed to be too sensitive – too much exposed to the reluctance of all those who wanted to preserve the requisites of national sovereignty – an important debate emerged as to the practical details of the relaunching, and, among others, on the institutional options.

Since spring 1955, several projects had come to life, predominantly within ECSC circles in Luxembourg and also within the diplomatic spheres in the Benelux states. When the ECSC Common Assembly advocated a resolution to support the extension of sectoral integration into the domains of transport and energy, Jean Monnet, the architect behind the Schuman plan and President of the ECSC High Authority, sought to endorse the creation of a new community in a highly symbolic sector, that of civil nuclear ('peaceful') power. In contrast, Johan Willem, the Dutch Foreign Minister, was eager to reintroduce general economic integration back onto the agenda, an issue he had been supporting since his Cabinet appointment in 1952. Being a close associate of both these different actors, Paul-Henri Spaak, the Belgian Foreign Minister and former president of both the consultative Assembly of the Council of Europe and also the European Movement, succeeded in drawing up a synthesis which pulled together the different initiatives, known as the 'Benelux memorandum'. Discussed by the foreign ministers of the six at the Messina conference in early June 1955, this text provided the basis for the negotiations which led to the Treaties of Rome.

At the institutional level, the aim was to define a system which would be sufficiently efficient in order to push European integration forward, yet not be too supranational in order to allay popular concerns and avoid inducing a new failure. The scope for action was thus relatively narrow and the negotiators had to adapt the four-party model of the ECSC. In place of the High Authority, an independent Commission has the sole right of initiative, but little decision-making power, which mainly lies in the hands of the Council (of Ministers). An Assembly – which was only named European Parliament in 1962 – is responsible for giving advice prior to the decision of the Council and exerting a political control over the Commission, but had, under the 1957 treaty provisions, no real legislative or budgetary competencies. A fourth institution, the Court of Justice, was established to guarantee compliance with the treaty in terms of its implementation and interpretation, whilst the Economic and Social Committee is a purely consultative body.

The Assembly is the weakest link in the decision-making chain, although it is mentioned in the Treaty of Rome as representing the 'peoples of the states brought together in the Community' (Article 137) and is referred to prior to the other institutions. It is composed of representatives chosen by the national parliaments, but is entitled 'to draw up a proposal for elections by direct universal suffrage in accordance with a uniform procedure in all member states or in accordance with principles common to all member states' (Article 138). From the outset, it could only pretend a weak democratic legitimacy, with limited powers of scrutiny over the Commission and with no accountability over the Council. It can ask written or oral questions (Article 140), discuss the annual report of the Commission (Article 143), and vote a motion of censure to force resignation of the college (Article 144).

The institutional framework is identical in both the Treaties of Rome. However, an annexed convention brings in some rationalisation and substance by providing that the Assembly and the Court of Justice will have jurisdiction for the three communities (EEC, EAEC, ECSC). It also reiterates that the Assembly may later be elected by direct universal suffrage, thus becoming distinct from the other coexisting European parliamentary Assemblies, notably the Assembly of the Council of Europe which also sits in Strasbourg, and the Assembly of the Western Europe Union based in Paris.

Marie-Thérèse Bitsch

Bibliography

Bitsch, M.-T., *Histoire de la construction européenne de 1945 à nos jours*, Bruxelles, Complexe, 2001 (2rd edition).
Gerbet, P., *La construction de l'Europe*, Paris, Imprimerie nationale, 1999.
Serra, E. (ed.), *La relance européenne et les traités de Rome*, Milan, Giuffrè, 1989.

→ European Parliament; Universal Suffrage.

Turkey

While the Laeken European Council (December 2001) hoped and prayed for a debate on the institutional future of Europe enlarged after 1 May 2004 to ten new members, it was the prospect of another enlargement that was not scheduled yet, that imposed itself in the June 2004 elections campaign.

The debates on Turkey's EU membership have sometimes veiled the strength of the relations between the EEC/EU and Turkey: the change of Turkish candidacy to the status of associate member (from 1959); an association agreement in which Article 28 defined a complete accession prospect (1963); EEC membership candidacy (1987) and the Council's refusal (February 1989, after the Commission's opinion) to start accession negotiations ('without questioning its eligibility for accession to the Community'); coming into force of a customs union, however deprived of freedom of movement for persons, services and capital (1996); finally, status of candidate to accession granted by the Helsinki European Council (December 1999). Eventually, accession negotiations between Turkey and the EU started on 3 October 2005.

This article tries to shed light on the way in which this issue is today posed in European debates particularly during pre- or post-electoral periods.

Turkey: the 'new European issue'

Turkey imposed itself on the agenda of debates on Europe from the end of 2002. At least three reasons explain this development. The first stems from the conclusions of the Copenhagen European Council on 12–13 December 2002. The Council had to simultaneously determine two dates: that of the accession of the ten CEEC candidates (1 May 2004); and that of the beginning of Turkey's accession negotiations (initially scheduled for 1 July 2005). However, the Council postponed to the end of 2004 the decision relating to this second date, conditional on whether Turkey meets (or does not) the Copenhagen criteria (defined in 1993) concerning civil, political and cultural rights. In the event of an affirmative reply, it was planned to open the negotiations 'without delay'. In the meantime, the process was changed. The report delivered by the European Commission to the Council on 6 October 2004 recommended the opening of negotiations, but accompanying them with new suspensive clauses in relation to previous enlargements and posing the prospect of a Turkish accession for 2015. Finally, the 17 December 2004 Council set the accession schedule.

The second reason concerns the 3 November 2002 Turkish legislative elections and the victory of the Justice and Development Party (AKP), stemming from the Islamic party Refah (forbidden in 1997) then Fazilet (forbidden in 2001) in an institutionally secular Turkey where Islam is sociologically prevailing. It is also part of the international law-and-order context after 11 September 2001, where Islam plays an important role in European public opinions, complicated by the 'fight against terrorism', the second Intifada and the war in Iraq. But it also suggested a 'role' for Turkey, led by a government that, to be in accordance with the Copenhagen criteria, undertook important reforms (abolition of death penalty, civil rights, some degrees of protection of minority languages, etc.). This political Islam is now promoted by the Erdogan government as a 'democratic Islam'. In this perspective, some consider Turkey as a 'bridge' between the West and the Middle East, after it played a role in the East–West relations during the Cold War (Turkey has been a member of the Council of Europe and NATO since 1951).

The third reason is related to the European institutional agenda and to the Convention's work (February 2002–July 2003). The debates over the Treaty establishing a Constitution for Europe quickly interfered with the Turkey issue, which also sits on the Convention. The Convention's President Valéry Giscard d'Estaing was one of the catalysts of the debate, stating on 7 November 2002 that 'Turkey is not a European country' and that its accession would generate 'the end of the European Union'. In doing so, the future of European integration and its institutional reform to 25 or 27 countries (Bulgaria and Romania in 2007 and even Croatia) focused on the impact of the accession of a 71-million-inhabitant country (the most inhabited after Germany), sociologically Muslim, and that has common borders with Iran, Iraq and Syria. Some have defended the alternative of a 'privileged partnership' like the French and German conservative parties (CDU/CSU and UMP), while a dispute was taking place over what room shall be given to the 'European religious heritage' in the Constitution.

Cleavages and stakes of the 'Turkish issue'

The June 2004 EP elections did not end these discussions. The prospect of the Council of 17 December 2004, followed by the Luxembourg meeting of 3 October 2005 continued to feed them as the prospect of potential national referendums on the matter doomed. The difficulty of 'mapping' the terms of the discussion can be explained by the fact that it affects as much European integration (institutions, identity and borders of Europe) as national debates (immigration and Islam) or in some cases, the historical weight (often 'reinvented') of the relations with the former Ottoman Empire (Hungary, Austria) or Turkey (Germany).

Some member states actively committed themselves in favour of Turkey's accession. This is particularly the case for the UK where its position is in accordance with the vision of a EU as a little politically integrated free exchange space. Ireland, and most of the new EU members shared this vision, except for Hungary due to historical antagonisms with the former Ottoman Empire. Sweden, Finland and Italy are also favourable to it. For Poland, Turkey's membership would lead the way for Belarus' and Ukraine's which Warsaw has long been defending. The German Chancellor Gerhard Schröder also defended Turkey's accession prospect while the German Grünen led a campaign in the EP elections in this direction. But their motive is different from the British one, the membership of Turkey being part, for them, of a stronger EU political integration.

Others opposed it, such as Austrian Chancellor Wolfgang Schussel who wanted to include in the June 2004 proposed report on his country's presidency some criticisms on the Turkish domestic situation. At the same time, the European campaign focused on the opposition of the Austrian majority party (ÖVP) to Turkey's membership, particularly from the idea of the supposedly 'irreconcilable' character between a 'Muslim country' and the EU.

In France, while the president had just reaffirmed that France was favourable to Turkey's membership, the majority party UMP made the decision, on 6 April 2004, to declare themselves opposed to it, particularly because they feared that the debate would be profitable to the nationalist and extreme- right parties. Actually, if the UDF European campaign focused over the opposition to 'non-European' Turkey's accession to the EU, this theme has largely been taken over by the pro-sovereignty MPF, the Front National and the MNR ('Europe, yes. Turkey, no!' list).

In the Netherlands, the Pim Fortuyn list (LPF) did the same as the Danish People's Party (DF) in Denmark, or the North League, a member of the Italian governmental coalition, despite the favourable position of the Italian government.

These cleavages do not necessarily coincide with the state of public opinion. While 76 per cent of Austrians declare themselves against Turkey's accession, 75 per cent of the French share the same opinion, 57 per cent in Germany, and nearly 50 per cent in Denmark. The Mediterranean countries stand out: the issue is not really controversial and nearly half of the Italians declare themselves in favour of the Turkish accession as do 54.6 per cent of the Spanish (*Libération*, 15 October 2004).

But these cleavages do not literally correspond to the ideological cleavages. In Denmark, the Social-Democrats, the main opposition party, took a stand against the prospect of Turkey's accession during the June 2004 European campaign to such a point that sometimes they shared arguments with the populist right of the Danish People's Party. The debate crosses the political parties, as the debate at the French parliament showed (without voting) on 19 October 2004. Therefore, the PS declared itself in favour of the accession prospect under three conditions (12 October 2004): Turkey's recognition of the Armenian genocide, solving of the Cyprus issue; and EU tax and social harmonisation. Some leaders have, however, stood out by declaring themselves against Turkey's accession. Among them, some were also against the European Constitution project (Laurent Fabius or Henri Emmanuelli) whereas others supported it (Robert Badinter). Finally, sometimes national cleavages resurface: among the European Grünen, the Austrian representatives expressed their reservation regarding Turkey in autumn 2004.

The 'Turkish issue' also belongs to the national and international dimensions. On the one hand, the transnational communities stemming from the Turkish immigration represent 3.7 million people in the EU who are mainly in Germany (about 2.5 million, among whom 600 000 are German), the Netherlands (270 000), Austria (200 000) and France (370 000). To these transnational communities, we can add Bulgaria's Turkish minority (800 000), a country whose EU membership is scheduled for 2007. One of the debate's axes is about the potential impact of Turkey's accession on such communities. In Germany, the dual nationality project had given way in 1999 to a petition campaign initiated by the CDU in the Hesse land, presented at that time as a campaign 'against the Turkish'. In October 2004, a similar initiative about Turkey's accession was considered by the CDU, but was then rejected. This is also closely akin to a 'geostrategic' conception: German Minister of Foreign Affairs Joshka Fischer, promoting a new trans-Atlantic partnership associated to the modernisation of the Middle East via Turkey's EU membership as a new kernel of European integration.

Arguments on Turkey focus in turn on the institutional dimension of European integration, the EU's political and strategic weight in the world, and Turkey's accession's economic and demographic impact. But, by becoming circular, these arguments end up cancelling one another out and preserving only one determining register: that of Europe's identity. Islam is an essential object (since it is essentialised) of these debates, a magnifying mirror of the identity ambiguities of an 'enlarged' European citizenship, in a context of suspicion towards Islam and Muslims, particularly reinforced after 11 September 2001.

Christophe Bertossi

➜ Mapping Europe: European Electoral Geography.

U

United Kingdom

Introduction

The home of 60 million inhabitants, the United Kingdom is the third most populated country (after Germany and France) of the enlarged European Union. While Winston Churchill was one of the key participants of The Hague conference of 1948, the United Kingdom originally chose to stay out of the ECSC when it was founded in 1950. Even though the UK's successive demands to join the EEC in the 1960s were regularly opposed by the French President de Gaulle, the United Kingdom eventually joined the Community in 1973. However, ever since this date, the relationship between the United Kingdom and 'Europe' has been tenuous and has often been described as strained and occasionally difficult to retain. For many, the United Kingdom remains the heart of Euroscepticism within the European Union, highlighted by incidents such as Margaret Thatcher's demand for a budget rebate in the 1980s. Similarly, the very fact that successive prime ministers have decided to keep their country out of the Schengen agreements and the single currency has undoubtedly made a strong impression on public perceptions of Britain's place in Europe. The country's media, by far the most violently Eurosceptic of the EU on a whole, have certainly also made a lasting impression.

Political context and public opinion

In the United Kingdom, the 2004 elections for the European Parliament were held in conjunction with a series of other local elections, including the London mayoral and the London assembly elections, and a series of local council elections. This series of elections also took place against the backdrop of a particularly difficult year for Prime Minister Tony Blair and his government. Widespread public dissatisfaction concerning the handling of the Iraq conflict, controversial policy decisions such as the introduction of much increased university tuition fees etc., left the government and its leader with their lowest recorded ratings in opinion polls since 1997. Three years into their second mandate and at least a year before the expected date of the next general election, it was therefore predicted by most political analysts that the Labour Party would fall victim to the 'mid-term' effect of the 2004 European elections.

At the same time, British public opinion concerning European integration was particularly negative as illustrated by recent Eurobarometer results. According to Eurobarometer 60 of autumn 2003, the United Kingdom and the Netherlands were the only two countries of the 15 member states of the EU in which fewer people felt attached (42 per cent) than not attached (56 per cent) to Europe. Similarly, 34 per cent of British citizens held a negative image of the EU (against 27 per cent holding a positive image), and unlike all the other member states, a greater proportion of the population (29 per cent) thought that their country's membership of the EU was a bad thing rather than a good one (28 per cent). Finally, at the end of 2003, the UK was also the only country in which more people distrusted the European Parliament and the European Commission (44 per cent each) than could place their trust in them (31 per cent and 26 per cent respectively). It should be noted, however, that similar ratings concerning the national parliament and national government proved yet more negative (27 per cent trust and 62 per cent distrust for Westminster, 24 per cent trust and 68 per cent distrust for the government).

In summary, the 2004 European Parliament elections in the United Kingdom took place within a particularly controversial context, highlighted by voters expressing defiance against the incumbent government and characterised by elements of strong Euroscepticism. The three-fold elections provided the opportunity and the possibility for voters to express their dissatisfaction not only towards the European Union institutions but also their own national government.

The parties and the campaign

The 2004 European election campaign was by and large a systematic reflection of the aforementioned governmental fragility, interjected with attempts by the various forces of the opposition to capitalise on their unpopularity.

In 2003, the main opposition party, the Conservatives, attempted to regain the hearts and minds of the British public and in doing so they decided to terminate the leadership of Ian Duncan Smith. In a designed effort to rejuvenate their tired and lacklustre party they placed their hopes of electoral success in the leadership of the charismatic Michael Howard. The 2004 elections were to be a significant indicator of whether their new strategy was likely to pay the dividends they hoped it would

bring. The party's campaign was geared towards a traditionally Eurosceptic core electorate, which often included vibrant attacks against the project of a new European Union Constitution and even against the prospect of ever joining the European single currency.

However, a more intense Eurosceptic and vehemently anti-government and anti-establishment campaign on their right from the United Kingdom Independence Party (UKIP), a movement solely dedicated to the promise to pull the country out of the European Union, confronted the Conservatives. The party's campaign, endorsed by a variety of popular entertainment celebrities such as Robert Kilroy-Silk (a former BBC presenter fired for anti-Islam comments) and actress Joan Collins lifted the party to an unprecedented level in pre-election polls. Even further to the right of the political spectrum, the openly xenophobic British National Party (BNP) made little effort to conceal their highly strategic agenda of primarily focusing on the local election campaign rather than the European one.

At the centre and left of the spectrum, this time, the Liberal-Democrats led a campaign that was faithful to their traditionally pro-European agenda and hoped to capture some moderate but dissatisfied former Labour voters. Similarly, the Green Party hoped to repeat the success they had in the 1989 European Parliament elections (14.9 per cent) and also to retain their existing number of representatives in Strasbourg.

The electoral system and constituencies

While British general elections are held under a plurality electoral system, Great Britain used a proportional representation system for the European Parliament elections (d'Hondt method). The country was divided into 11 large regions: Scotland, Wales, London, South-East,

South-West, Yorkshire and Humberside, Eastern, North-East, North-West, East Midlands and West Midlands. Northern Ireland uses a completely different election and electoral system more closely based on the Irish single transferable vote tradition. For the first time, in an effort to increase levels of turnout (see related article) four out of the eleven British regions used postal voting exclusively.

Turnout

Altogether, turnout for the 2004 European Parliament elections was raised to 38.2 per cent of the electorate, which is obviously a substantial increase when compared to the record low of 24 per cent in 1999. This spectacular improvement can be partly explained by the synchronisation of several elections, partly by the use of postal voting in a third of the regions, but also, to a certain extent, by the relative intensity of the campaign, and the absence of other elections since 2002.

Results

The results of the election in Great Britain and Northern Ireland are detailed in Tables 1 and 2 respectively. While European, local and London elections were all held at the same time, the results of the European elections were only known on the evening of 13 June, while the results of the sub-national races were known on the evening of the 10th. However, while the sub-national contest seemed to highlight a strong success for the Conservatives and the Liberal Democrats, the European Parliament election results proved to be a bitter disappointment for the Conservative Party.

Table 1 Results of the election in Great Britain

Party	% 2004	Change	Seats 2004	Change
Conservative	26.7	–9.0	27	–8
Labour	22.6	–5.4	19	–6
UKIP	16.1	+9.2	12	+10
Liberal Democrats	14.9	+2.3	12	+2
Green	6.3	–	2	–
BNP	4.9	+3.9	0	–
Respect (Centre Left)	1.5	+1.5	0	–
SNP	1.4	–1.3	2	–
Plaid Cymru	1.0	+0.9	1	–

Table 2 Results of the election in Northern Ireland

Candidate	Party	Election stage	Result stage 1	Change
Allister, J.	DUP	1	31.9	+3.6
De Brun, B.	Sinn Féin	1	26.3	+9.0
Nicholson, J.	UUP	3	16.6	–1.0
Morgan, M.	SDLP	Not Elected	15.9	–12.1

At the national level, and as in 1999, the Conservatives managed to retain their poll position. However, with a score of only 26.7 per cent of the vote, they lost no less than 9 percentage points since 1999 and even suffered their worst ever result in a national contest. It is undeniable that this result can be partly attributed to the fact that the UKIP held out for third place, obtaining 16.1 per cent of the votes, an increase of 9.2 points from 1999, although a number of other explanations must also be taken into account.

The Labour Party, which obtained the second place in the election with 22.6 per cent of the vote, lost 5.4 points from their 1999 performance. Although they resisted slightly better than the Conservatives to the Eurosceptic (UKIP) and pro-European (Liberal Democrats) challenges of the relatively smaller parties, the disappointing result was interpreted to be a serious warning to the incumbent government.

While most of the media attention was devoted to the high score of the UKIP, the Liberal Democrats progressed by 2.3 points to achieve 14.9 per cent of the vote and therefore retained their 12 representatives in Strasbourg. Similarly, the Greens built upon their 1999 performance with 6.3 per cent of the votes and two MEPs, confirming, together with the Liberal Democrats, that the pro-European side of the political spectrum resisted stubbornly to the progress of the UKIP, a party which seems to have tapped into a reservoir of ex-Conservative supporters.

Finally, one should not overlook the very strong performance of the BNP, an extreme-right movement, which obtained 4.9 per cent of the vote (+3.9 from 1999), their best performance in a national election so far. On the other hand, nationalist parties in Scotland (Scottish National Party) and Wales (Plaid Cymru) lost significant ground, declining by 7.5 and 12.2 percentage points respectively.

In Northern Ireland, the European election results confirmed the radicalisation of the electorate that had developed since the collapse of the Good Friday agreement. While the moderate Social-Democrat Labour Party (SDLP) and Ulster Unionist Party (UUP) had topped the 1999 election in which a member of the radical Protestant Democratic Unionist Party (DUP) had also been elected, the 2004 elections gave the two first seats to the representatives of the radical DUP and Sinn Féin, who respectively progressed by 3.6 and 9 points, while the UUP candidate was barely elected after losing 1 point from the party's 1999 performance. The SDLP, the traditional choice of the moderate Catholics, lost 12.1 points from their 1999 result and did not manage to return a representative to the European Parliament.

On a regional basis, the traditional electoral geography of British politics was largely respected, albeit with a decline of the Labour dominance: the Conservatives led the contest in six English regions, while Labour remained the strongest party in Scotland, Wales and three English regions, although they almost managed to bridge the gap with the Conservatives in London. The UKIP achieved its best score in the East Midlands, where they obtained 26.1 per cent of the votes, a mere 0.3 points behind the leading Conservatives. The BNP obtained major breakthroughs in Yorkshire and Humberside (8 per cent of the votes), the North-East, North-West, and the East and West Midlands, obtaining over 6 per cent of the vote in all of these regions. The Liberal Democrats continued to show a fairly even geographical spread, with a best result of 18.3 per cent of the votes in the South-West.

Political significance and conclusions

One of the main results of the British European election of 2004 is the relatively impressive increase in levels of turnout as compared to the appalling level of 24 per cent in June 1999. Just one or two years before the next general elections, this could confirm the importance of election cycles in explaining participation in second-order elections (see related article). It could also be partly attributed, however, to more technical reasons, such as the conjunction of up to three different elections and the use of generalised postal voting in 4 out of 12 constituencies. Indeed, with the exceptions of Northern Ireland (where 51.2 per cent of the people turned out to vote) and Wales (where it is in line with postal voting regions), turnout was higher in the four test regions than in all the other ones, with an average difference of about 5–6 points.

However, beside the relatively high scores of third parties such as the UKIP, the Liberal Democrats, or even to some extent the BNP, the results of the European election may seem to confirm the importance of the second-order election theory in understanding citizens' behaviour in such elections, it should also be noted that it was the main opposition party, the Conservatives, who suffered from the disaffection of voters for British traditional political forces rather than the Labour Party. Similarly, the two main national parties of Scotland and Wales also saw their share of the vote decline quite significantly in this election.

This may suggest that the main conclusion that can be drawn from the results of the 2004 European Parliament election, is not so much that it was a quintessentially second-order election, but more to the point there can be a hidden bonus for parties campaigning on European issues, whether positively (Liberal Democrats) or negatively (UKIP) as opposed to parties campaigning on general national issues. This result seems to confirm the scenarios that also took place in several other European democracies.

Michael Bruter
Sarah Harrison

Bibliography

Electoral Commission, *Public Opinion and the 2004 Elections: a Study of Attitudes Towards Elections for the European Parliament and London's Mayor and Assembly*, 2003 (web address: http://www.electoralcommission. org.uk/).

Lodge, J., *The 1999 Elections to the European Parliament*, Basingstoke, Palgrave Macmillan, 2001.

Mellows-Facer, A. et al., *European Parliament Elections 2004*, London, House of Commons Library, 2004.

→ Mapping Europe: European Electoral Geography.

Universal Suffrage

Ever since the start of European integration, the principle of direct universal suffrage to elect a European parliamentary assembly has been part of the official demands of the supporters of political unification. It is therefore the case that following the initiative of Frenchman Paul Reynaud, in May 1948, during the Hague Congress, a resolution was written and introduced accordingly. Regarded as being too extreme due to its federal inspirations, this proposal was rejected despite the prestigious support it generated. The final resolution adopted by the Congress settled on a call for the institution of a 'European assembly' to be made up of elected members of national parliaments, with the aim 'to examine the political and legal implications' of a future union or European federation.

Indeed it was this solution which inspired the architects of the Treaty of Paris signed on 18 April 1951 establishing the European Coal and Steel Community, in addition to the Treaties of Rome, signed on 25 March 1957, creating the European Economic Community (the EEC) and the European Atomic Energy Community (Euratom). However, it is acknowledged that with regards to the ECSC, Article 21 of this treaty is somewhat ambiguous in stipulating that the Assembly is formed of delegates who are called by national parliaments to represent them once a year or are elected by direct universal suffrage, according to the procedure established by each High Contracting Party. Following the end of the negotiations which led to the Treaties of Rome, the ECSC Common Assembly was subsequently transformed into a new expanded assembly and with jurisdiction over the three communities who took the initiative on 30 March 1962 to change its name to the 'European Parliament'. Its next election by direct universal suffrage was provided for in Article 138 of the EEC Treaty and in identical terms by Article 108 of the Euratom Treaty. These founding articles notably stipulate that the Assembly is formed of delegates who are called by national parliaments to represent them according to the procedure established by each member state. Paragraph 3 of the same articles, however, commits the Assembly to develop 'drafts' in order to allow the election by direct universal suffrage according to a uniform procedure in all the member states. The Council was charged to reach a unanimous decision, formulate the provisions and recommend them for adoption by the member states.

Since 22 October 1958, the political and institutional affairs committee of the European Parliamentary Assembly created within its framework a working group –

chaired by the Belgian socialist Fernand Dehousse – with the intention of drafting a convention relating to the organisation of the first European elections by direct universal suffrage. Adopted by the European Parliamentary Assembly on 17 May 1960, this nerve-racking project 'to directly bring people together for the construction of Europe' largely prefigured the provisions which would later be retained for the first European elections by direct universal suffrage (quinquennial legislature, rejection of imperative mandates, incompatibility, etc.). This text also provided that after a transitional period, the European Parliamentary Assembly would formulate 'provisions which would reduce according to a procedure as uniform as possible for the election of the representatives' (European Parliament 1969: 236–43). Particularly due to the stubborn hostility of General de Gaulle who complained that the fate of the people who composed the EEC would be subjected 'to laws which would vote in the foreign deputies' (extracted from the press conference on 15 May 1962), this first initiative robustly remains formally in effect but no longer enforced, despite the fact that this project was regularly revived as much within the European confines as within the national parliaments of the six member states (Herman and Hagger 1980: 17) with support from European movements (the Action Committee for the United States of Europe, Centre for European Federalist Action, Europa-Union Deutschland) which saw an increase in resolutions in support of this principle throughout the 1960s (European Parliament 1969: 337–42).

Following the first enlargement of the Community at the end of 1973, the political affairs committee of the European Parliament awarded the Dutch socialist Schelto Patijn the responsibility of drafting a new convention. However, it was due to the part played by the heads of states and governments of the nine and at the initiative of Valéry Giscard d'Estaing, the then President of the Republic, that the changes were reached. During the Paris Summit on 9–10 December 1974, these individuals declared 'that the objective laid down by the Treaty of election of the Assembly by universal suffrage should be carried out as quickly as possible'. Thus called upon, the European Parliament immediately reacted and undertook a vote, during its meeting on 14 January 1975 on the new draft convention as drafted by Patijn. However, due to the complexity of national procedures concerning the ratification of 'the Act concerning the election of representatives to the Parliament by universal suffrage', adopted on 20 September 1976 by the Foreign Ministers of the EEC (European Parliament 1977: 9–21), it took over two years to take effect. Originally established in 1978, the first election of the European Parliament by direct universal suffrage – ordained as 'the election of the century' by the Commission information service – finally took place on 7 and 10 June 1979, over 28 years after the signature of the Treaty of Paris.

As is so often the case in parliamentary history, the adoption of this principle is accompanied by many beliefs and prophecies (amongst an abundance of literature see Burban 1979; Marquand 1979: 67–86; Sasse et al. 1981: 21–7). For some observers, the election by direct universal suffrage of the Members of the European Parliament paves the way for an increase in powers of a Strasbourg institution which also serves to reinforce its independence and even supports the advent of a new democratic legitimacy in Europe, or even heralds the birth of 'the European man' as termed by Louise Weiss during the inauguration of the new Parliament in July 1979. For the critics (who are mainly encountered in France, or in Denmark where just under 54 per cent of the electorate voted in the direct election of the European Parliament or in the United Kingdom where strong opposition is met by the Labour Party), this election signals 'the abdication' (to borrow the terms used by Michel Debré whose Gaullist rhetoric is close to that of the PCF which, with the support of Jean-Paul Sartre, denounces a 'deception' favourably disposed towards a 'German-American Europe') of a national sovereignty threatened by a 'supranational Europe' which, through an election affecting nearly 180 million citizens, transcends the inherited frontiers of electoral history.

Yves Déloye

Bibliography

Burban, J.-L., *Le Parlement européen et son élection*, Bruxelles, Bruylant, 1979.

European Parliament (Commission politique), *Pour l'élection du Parlement européen au suffrage universel direct. Recueil de documents*, Luxembourg, Office des publications officielles des Communautés Européennes, 1969.

European Parliament (Secrétariat – Direction générale de la recherche et de la documentation), *Elections du Parlement européen au suffrage universel direct. Rapport, résolutions et débats du Parlement européen*, Luxembourg, Office des publications officielles des Communautés Européennes, 1977.

Herman, V. and Hagger, M., *The Legislation of Direct Election to the European Parliament*, Farnborough, Gower, 1980.

Marquand, D., *Parliament for Europe*, London, Jonathan Cape, 1979.

Sasse, C. et al., *The European Parliament: Towards a Uniform Procedure for Direct Elections*, Florence, European University Institute; Luxembourg, Office for Official Publications of the European Communities, 1981.

→ Act of 1976; European Parliament; European Parliamentary Assembly; Treaty of Rome.

V

Voters

The Maastricht Treaty (1992) has restructured European electorates, granting all citizens the right to vote in local and European elections in the EU country where they live (Magnette 1999). Political philosophers and lawyers were eager to find a new term defining this unusual step, referring to 'post-national democracy', 'multinational community', 'multi-layered citizenship', but few have considered the political aspects of this new reality. The Convention for the Future of Europe has defined EU citizenship in Article 17, stipulating that: 'a citizen of the European Union is any person bearing the nationality of a member state'. It is therefore time to ask what the function of voter actually entails in this context of EU citizenship

Prior to the Maastricht Treaty, there were only two categories of people when it came to voting rights: nationals and foreigners. Some member states – in particular Scandinavian countries – had granted the right to vote to all foreigners in certain local elections. However, with the Maastricht Treaty, three categories of people with different rights emerged in the same territory: country nationals; EU citizens enjoying rights specified by the Treaty (i.e. right to vote and eligibility in municipal and European elections); third country nationals who may or may not be granted the right to vote depending on their host country's individual legislation.[1] Does this mean that, as some complain, the notion of EU citizenship separates foreigners based on their nationality? In truth, it interposes a new form of citizenship, which includes certain categories of people to the potential detriment of others. However, it could be argued that *any* division of the public space aims to exclude in order to better include and define (Bertossi 2001; Déloye 2004). Therefore, the problem is not so much with the existence of these demarcations, indispensable to the existence of a political community, but with the criteria employed to define them. Nationality of a member state is the most important one. In fact, it has led the Commission to conclude that enjoying rights identical to those of the nationals of one's country of residence is an important aspect of integration (Proposal relating to the right of vote of EU citizens in all member states for local and European elections, COM (88) 371, 24 June 1988). Nevertheless, this choice has several practical consequences. The first is the inequality of access to EU citizenship rights, depending on the more or less inclusive rules of residence fixed by individual member states. Indeed, some countries require their voters to principally reside in the national territory (Finland, France), while others ask that they pledge that they have an intention to stay (Germany, Belgium, Greece, Spain, Portugal and Italy), another group barely asking would-be voters to register on the electoral rolls (Austria, Denmark, United Kingdom, Ireland, Netherlands and Sweden).

Moreover, the notion of residence is understood in various ways (Bertossi 2001). For instance, in the case of Luxembourg, it has been reduced from ten to five years since the law of 18 February 2003. Similarly, several countries limit the access to EP voting rights to their nationals if they live in another

EU country. This is the case for the United Kingdom, which reserves such access to civil servants, members of the military forces, and to nationals who have resided outside the country for at least five years. Austria, Denmark, Portugal and the Netherlands limit this right to only those of their citizens who reside within the EU. Sweden, Belgium, France, Spain, Greece and Italy guarantee this option to all their nationals, regardless of the country they live in. As for Ireland, voting rights are limited to EU citizens living within the national territory. Clearly, the condition of voters varies greatly depending on country, length of stay and nationality. Nevertheless, what can be said about the other right of voters, that of running as election candidates? It appears that not all countries acknowledge this eligibility. France is known (with the constitutional revision of 23 June 1992) for its 'external' application of the Treaty of Maastricht. In fact, European citizens cannot be elected as mayor, or deputy-mayor, so as to avoid their participation in Senate elections, a way to conservatively dissociate national sovereignty from European citizenship on the sensitive question of local elections. Also, rules regarding eligibility age vary significantly: 18 in Finland, Sweden, Denmark, Germany, Spain, Netherlands and Portugal, 19 in Austria, 21 in Belgium, Greece, Luxembourg and the United Kingdom, 23 in France, and 25 in Italy. Interestingly, it is almost as if some countries are still worried about the hypothetical 'social dangerousness' of their young citizens.

Another consequence of the attribution of European citizenship based on member state nationality is the continued inconsistencies, at the EU level, as to whether nationality is based on the right of the soil (*jus soli*) or the right of the blood (*jus sanguini*), notwithstanding the evolution of some nationality laws in the past few years (Weil and Hansen 1999).

For instance, two Turkish citizens settling respectively in Belgium and in Germany will qualify as voters in European elections at different times. The first one rapidly, acquiring Belgian nationality after seven years of residence and by mere declaration, the second one with great difficulty since his chances of acquiring German nationality are almost non-existent. What is more, the European Charter of Fundamental Rights, based on the 'indivisible and universal values of human dignity, of liberty, equality and solidarity' states that 'all citizens enjoy equal rights' (Article 20) and even forbids 'any discrimination based on nationality' (Articles 21–22) except for the 'specific provisions' of the treaties. These considerations give rise to an interesting question: if the nationality-citizenship link is essential, must it remain unique? Could the EU grant citizenship directly, regardless of member state nationality? While the hypothesis of a 'European nationality' is not being debated at this time, its idea is nevertheless worth considering. Such nationality could represent a reward for the integration of non-EU citizens, and their contribution to the development of the European project. At the same time, the notion of citizenship would be based on the willingness to participate in a community of destiny. After all, the statutes of the European People's Party (EPP) foresee the possibility of individual subscriptions (Article 6). If parties could potentially become citizens' associations directly open to EU residents, why would it be different when it comes to citizenship?

Olivier Ihl

Note

1. In the UK, Commonwealth citizens represent a fourth distinct category.

Bibliography

Bertossi, C., *Les frontières de la citoyenneté en Europe: Nationalité, résidence, appartenance*, Paris, L'Harmattan, 2001.

Déloye, Y., 'Le débat contemporain sur la citoyenneté au prisme de la construction européenne', *Etudes européennes revue en ligne du Centre d'Etudes Européennes de Strasbourg (CEES)*, no. 4, 2004 (http://www.etudes-europeennes.(fr).

Magnette, P., *La citoyenneté européenne*, Bruxelles, Editions de l'Université de Bruxelles, 1999.

Weil, P. and Hansen, R. (eds), *Nationalité et citoyenneté en Europe*, Paris, La Découverte, 1999.

➜ Citizen (EU); Electoral Register; Right to Vote.

Voting Within the European Parliament

The history of the European Parliament (EP) is one of continuous rationalisation of its operation, which authorises a multiplicity and increasing intensity of pressures which surround it. The cultural, political and social heterogeneity of this assembly continues to be accentuated, the elected representatives now originating from 25 states and almost 200 political parties. The material constraints related to the plurality of seats and the recourse to 20 working languages are unrelenting. The number of MEPs, which is now fixed at 732, reaches an unreasonable level, which impacts on the capacity of the assembly to deliberate and limits the ability of the political groups to combine their interests and to simplify the stakes. The European Parliament must also reach a compromise with an overcrowded agenda; during the 1999–2004 legislature, it adopted over 3000 texts, including more than 500 directives. It must also make the best of far-sighted treaties where, in a great number of cases, its silence can be understood as tacit approval; its powers thus depend on its capacity to give an opinion. And yet treaties also establish that, in budgetary and legislative fields, the assembly must declare a majority of its members (that is, 366 votes) and not that of the voters. Finally, MEPs must accept the consequences of a very strict conception regarding the 'personal and individual' character of the voting rights, excluding any possibility of delegation.

Faced with such constraints, MEPs have consistently adapted the rules of their assembly (the current version, adopted in July 2004, being the sixteenth) towards an increasingly larger rationalisation of its decision-making powers. The agenda of plenary sessions and voting procedures have become the subject of detailed attention. In order to facilitate the decision-making process, MEPs in particular brought about a division between deliberation and voting; after consideration of a certain number of items on the agenda, the elected representatives make a decision as a whole during the 'voting hour'. At each plenary session, these intensive voting meetings are held according to the same schedules, and selected so as to ensure a maximum turnout amongst MEPs. As a further safeguard, bells resound across all the Parliament's buildings ten minutes prior to the start of the vote and again at its opening, serving as a reminder. The convergence of MEPs towards an often sparse auditorium is one of the strong images – and inevitably unflattering – of decision-making at the European level.

During the monthly sessions in Strasbourg, the voting hours take place at midday on Tuesday, Wednesdays and Thursdays. On Tuesday, the MEPs decide on the examined reports the day before and in the morning, which generally only achieve simple majorities. The most important and longest voting meeting is held on Wednesday, whereby the legislative texts requiring consideration of the majority of members are voted on. This is usually attended by four-fifths of the elected representatives. A third voting hour takes place on Thursday, concerning less controversial texts. The afternoon is dedicated to debates on human rights; where still, the votes are gathered at the end of the debates. The 'mini-sessions', which take place approximately six times a year in Brussels, commence on Wednesday afternoon and finish around midday on Thursday; one hour of voting is held at the close of the session.

The MEPs vote by either a show of hands or an electronic vote (Corbett et al. 2003: 146). Electronic voting, which excludes any possibility of delegation, is used upon the initiative of the president or at the request of a political group, generally when a vote is tangential. Either a group or at least 37 MEPs can demand a vote by roll-call. The rule allows for a very heavy oral procedure. In practice, electronic voting with a personal recording of results is more preferential; the verbal voting process comprises a list of voters, listed by political group, which indicates the direction of each vote. The nominal vote is generally called by the leaders of the political groups who intend to demonstrate the intensity of their commitment on a case, to reinforce the discipline of voting amongst their members or to reveal internal divisions within another group. In comparison with the American Congress, this instrument is rarely used, to the regret of the lobbyists, who would wish to systematically control the position of the elected representatives, and the researchers, with the latter constituting an essential source of information (Hix et al. 2004). All appointments, whether being internal within the Parliament or external (President of the Commission, Members of the Court of Auditors, Ombudsman) are entitled to secret ballots; other votes can be requested by a fifth of the members of the Parliament, which is very rare.

Voting practices are codified and routinised exercises in the extreme, led by an unrestrained rhythm, of which observers fail to understand very much. The rule precisely establishes the way in which the texts are voted on, in order to limit the maximum number of votes (while returning 'packages' of null and void amendments) and to avoid delaying tactics. Additionally it supports 'compromise amendments' which originate from several political groups, the responsible committee or from the rapporteur. Finally, the chair of the meeting enjoys great freedom to modify the order of consideration of the amendments or to take a vote 'in block', in order to simplify the procedure. However, with regards to the budget or a highly controversial text, it is often the case that voting will last over two hours. In such a case, the MEPs complain about their fate as 'voting machines', called to decide hundreds of times according to interminable lists provided by their group or by visual instructions given by their superiors.

Rationalisation of voting procedures entails broader perverse effects. The voting hours support the hyper-specialisation and the absenteeism of elected representatives at plenary sittings, those able to reach a decision on the texts without attending the debates. It is thus commonplace to find that deliberations mobilise but a few MEPs and consist of the repetition of positions and arguments outlined in committee. The division between the debates and votes also gives the impression that deliberation of the European Parliament has little influence on the final decision. Even if the plenary debates often influence the settled positions within the groups, a smokescreen argument nonetheless emerges. The voting hour system also harms the 'mediatisation' of parliamentary activities, the delay in reaching a decision hence depriving the deliberation of a major part of its interest. Journalists, observers or lobbyists who follow a case must thus have patience to wait for the outcome of the vote – which is sometimes only reached the following day. It also happens that the agreement reached in committee and confirmed at a plenary sitting during the deliberations can be called into question when it comes to the time of the vote: it only takes these involved MEPs (rapporteurs, draftspersons, co-ordinators, topic specialists etc.) to convince their colleagues within their respective political groups. These incidents clarify the discrepancy which can exist between the members of the committee in charge of the case and the plenary assembly, the former being much more sensitive than their colleagues to certain problems or the arguments of the representatives with mobilised interests. The generalisation of the co-decision procedure has amplified this hiatus insofar as the first reading is notably followed by the specialists in the case, whilst the latter creates a broader mobilisation due to the need to amalgamate a superabundant majority.

In spite of its perverse effects, the European Parliament leaders prohibit any challenge of voting rationalisation. The suppression of voting hours would go back to prompting the presence of MEPs in the auditorium in a continuous way or at the close of each item on the agenda. The duration of the votes being unforeseeable (it can vary from a few seconds to over one hour in the event of a massive tabling of amendments, repeated requests for electronic or roll-call voting, or explanations of voting procedures or incidents), any return to the former situation would limit the possibility of scheduling work for the assembly. In addition, the large groups fear the randomised nature of results that ballots on the texts produce which do not require a qualified majority in a sparse auditorium; the history of the assembly shows that, in such a configuration, a small group of elected representatives or a national delegation can disproportionately influence the outcome of decisions. Finally, the group leaders appreciate voting hours because they facilitate 'whipping'. The rule's provisions which support compromise amendments and leave the meeting chair a certain degree of freedom over the organisation of voting, are defended for their contribution in going beyond partisan cleavages. Their questioning would allow 'small groups' or isolated MEPs to multiply delaying tactics and to block deliberations more easily, as was regularly observed during the early 1980s.

Olivier Costa

Bibliography

Corbett, R., Jacobs, F. and Shackleton, M., *The European Parliament*, London, Harper, 2003 (5th edition).
Hix, S., Raunio, T. and Scully, R., 'Fifty Years of Research on the European Parliament', *Journal of Common Market Studies*, 41, 2, 2004, pp. 191–202.

→ European Parliament; Members of the European Parliament (Legal and Political Status); Parliamentary Groups.

W

Women

(Female Representation at the European Parliament since 1979)

After the June 2004 European elections, the largest democratic Parliament in the world had 222 women among 732 representatives (30.3 per cent). Still far from parity, this result is largely superior to the average number of women elected in the national houses of the 25 member states (Table 1).

Nevertheless, while the number of women has risen constantly among MEPs, although irregularly, over the past 20 years (going from 16 per cent in 1979 to 30 per cent in 1999), it stagnated in 2004 (Table 2). Among the ten new member states, half of them have a female representation which draws the average towards the bottom: Latvia, the Czech Republic, Poland and above all Cyprus and Malta, these two small states having only men as MEPs.

The enlargement is not enough to explain the fall, since, in the previous Europe of the 15, the proportion of female MEPs was constant in two countries and fell back in four others (Finland, Germany, Denmark and Spain). In France it was feared that the move from the 'total' proportional system to the interregional one would be prejudicial to women, even if coupled with the compulsory alternated parity (law of 6 June 2000). In fact, the number of women among the French delegation – with a reduced number from 87 to 78 – slightly increased, even if the progression is less than in 1999.

As in the fifth legislature, the two most powerful political groups account for the largest number of female members: 79 out of 200 in the European Socialist Party (PSE) and 67 out of 268 in the European Popular and Democrat Party (PPE-DDE). Nevertheless, in proportion, the Greens/ALE are leaders of the most feminised groups (42.8 per cent) followed by the Union for the Europe of Nations (UEN, 41.4 per cent), followed by PSE (39.5 per cent), the Alliance of the Democrats and the Liberals for Europe (ADLE, 29.5 per cent) and the PPE-DE (25 per cent); and finally the European Unitarian Left (GUE-NGL) and the Independence and Democracy group (IND/DEM) with 11.9 per cent and 8.1 per cent of women respectively.

Historically, the ancestor of the European Parliament, whose representatives were appointed by national parliaments among their own members, was of a very masculine composition: the Common Assembly of the ECSC, then, from 1957, the European Communities Assembly, only consisted of 1.2 per cent of women in 1952, and 5.5 per cent in 1979. Since it has been elected by direct universal suffrage, the European Parliament has tried to prove itself open to women. Symbolically, it was twice presided over by a woman: Simone Veil (from 1979 to 1982), then Nicole Fontaine (from 1999 to 2001). The irony is that they were both French, when in France itself, no woman has ever chaired either the National Assembly or the Senate. In 2004, nearly 70 per cent of the countries sent to the Strasbourg Parliament a more female delegation than in their own national assembly. The difference, of some eight points on

Table 1   Elected women in the European Parliament and national parliaments in the 25 member states, in 2004 (in per cent)

Country	European Parliament (on 22/07/04)	National parliament (at last election)	Difference (in points of %)
Sweden	57.9	45.3	+ 12.6
Luxembourg	50.0	23.3	+ 26.7
The Netherlands	44.4	36.7	+ 7.7
France	43.5	12.3	+ 31.2
Slovenia	42.8	12.2	+ 30.6
Austria	38.8	33.9	+ 4.9
Ireland	38.5	13.3	+ 25.2
Lithuania	38.5	22.0	+ 16.5
Denmark	35.7	36.9	–1.2
Finland	35.7	37.5	–1.8
Slovakia	35.7	16.7	+ 19.0
Hungary	33.3	9.1	+ 24.2
Estonia	33.3	18.8	+ 14.5
Spain	33.3	36.0	–2.7
Germany	31.3	31.8	–0.5
Belgium	29.1	34.7	–5.6
Greece	29.1	13.0	+ 16.1
Portugal	25.0	21.3	+ 3.7
United Kingdom	24.3	19.7	+ 4.6
Latvia	22.2	21.0	+ 1.2
Czech Republic	20.8	17.0	+ 3.8
Italy	19.2	11.5	+ 7.7
Poland	12.9	20.4	–7.5
Cyprus	0	16.1	–16.1
Malta	0	9.2	–9.2
Average	*30.3*	*22.5*	*+ 7.8*

Source: Union inter-parliamentary and European Parliament.
Five of them show more than 40% of women in their delegation (two reach or go above 50%), Sweden being ahead, followed by Luxembourg, the Netherlands, France, then Slovenia.

average, is over 30 points in three countries, including France. Classified in fourth position for the MEPs' proportion (43.5 per cent), it reaches 18 per cent for the one elected at the National Assembly (12.3 per cent).

In this sense, France is an emblematic case which makes it possible to understand why the European Parliament works for women as a 'royal path', an alternative way, to enter politics. From the beginning, as a new arena, without a tradition of exclusion, it was seen by them as easier to access. In 1979, they did not have to compete with the 'outgoers' who make the investiture at the National Assembly so difficult. Moreover the Strasbourg Assembly was not so coveted by politicians. 'Perceived as a far away assembly, without any real power, the European Parliament was constantly used by the French political leaders as an

Table 2 Evolution of the number of elected women at the European Parliament per country, 1979–2004 (in %, beginning of the legislature)

Country	1979	1984	1989	1994	1999	2004	Evolution 1999–2004 (in %)
Germany	14.8	19.7	30.9	35.4	37.4	31.3	–16.3
Austria	–	–	–	–	38.1	38.8	+ 1.8
Belgium	8.3	16.7	16.7	32.0	28.0	29.1	+ 3.9
Denmark	31.2	37.5	37.5	43.8	37.5	35.7	–4.8
Spain	–	10.0	15.0	32.8	34.4	33.3	–3.1
Finland	–	–	–	–	43.7	35.7	–18.3
France	22.2	20.9	23.5	29.9	40.2	43.5	+ 8.2
Greece	–	8.3	4.2	16.0	16.0	29.1	+ 81.8
Ireland	13.3	13.3	6.7	26.7	33.3	38.5	+ 15.6
Italy	13.6	9.9	12.4	12.6	11.5	19.2	+ 66.9
Luxembourg	16.7	50.0	50.0	50.0	33.3	50.0	+ 50.1
The Netherlands	20.0	28.0	28.0	32.2	35.5	44.4	+ 25.0
Portugal	–	4.0	12.5	8.0	20.0	25.0	+ 25.0
United Kingdom	13.6	14.8	14.8	18.4	24.1	24.3	+ 0.8
Sweden	–	–	–	–	40.9	57.9	+ 41.5
Average	*16.3*	*17.7*	*19.3*	*25.9*	*30.2*	*30.3*	*+ 0.3*

Source: European Parliament.

elephant cemetery, the refuge for non-elected politicians at the national poll, or the nursery for young hopes sent there to stay . . . the shortest possible time' (Fontaine 2002: 16). From then onwards, in a less harsh electoral competition, women found better chances to run the election with success. A final reason particular to France (and the United Kingdom) is to be found in the differences of the poll mode: whereas the National Assembly is elected by the uninominal poll, the 'most difficult one' for women, European elections are on a proportional list system, more propitious – especially when 'integral' – to a 'negotiated' feminine presence with the political parties, as with the application of an alternated equity.

Although stronger in numbers at the Strasbourg Assembly, women have still not won, in proportion, the leadership positions. So, amongst the top MEPs, their under-representation is obvious, constituting less than 15 per cent of the super elite (42 persons) formed by the president and the vice-presidents of the European Parliament, the political group presidents, and the permanent commission presidents.

At the beginning of this sixth legislature, the election of the new bureau of the European Parliament, in July 2004, once more revealed the inequity of women when it comes to political power. They only hold two of 14 vice-presidencies, one of them being third in the hierarchy, the other one in the lowest rank. Only the quaestors postings have generously been awarded to them – they hold four out of five. As far as the powerful conference of presidents is concerned – that is the organ of political direction of the European Parliament composed of the Parliament president and group presidents – it is composed of six men and two women.

Although two women succeeded in taking their place among seven group presidents, they only co-chair minor groups (the Greens and the Union for the Nations of Europe). Last but not least, female MEPs are scarce at the powerful posts of the permanent commissions. In the conference of commission presidents, they are only four among the 16 members (25 per cent). Although there is one woman at the head of one of the two under-commissions (the one for Human Rights), women only chair three commissions out of 20, that is 15 per cent (the coveted one of Monetary and Economic Affairs, the Development Commission, and the Commission for Women's Rights and Sexual equality). Bearing in mind that in 1984 they occupied six commission presidencies out of 18 (33.3 per cent), a certain loss of female influence can be seen at the Strasbourg Assembly.

The ultimate mark of their subordination, the commission composition still bears the signs of a traditional division of political work between the sexes. The female MEPs are under-represented in the very 'regalian' Foreign Affairs (17.9 per cent) and Monetary and Economic Affairs (18.4 per cent). There are also sectors symbolically perceived as 'masculine': Constitutional Affairs (14.8 per cent), Fishing (18.2 per cent), Transport and Tourism (23.5 per cent), International Trade (24.2 per cent). In contrast, women are over-represented in the commissions reputed as being of 'feminine competence', starting with the Commission for Women's Rights which is nearly 95 per cent female.

If women still suffer a power deficit, with difficulties in overcoming the 'glass ceiling', their presence in number at the European Parliament – where they are the most assiduous of members – has contributed to the accelerated consciousness in the European Parliament of the political dimension of the equality between men and women. It is an important result when it sees its legislative power being affirmed and when half of the laws which are applied in the member states are of communitarian origin.

Mariette Sineau

Bibliography

Fontaine, N., *My Battles at the Presidency of the European Parliament*, Paris, Plon, 2002.

Freedman, J., 'Women in the European Parliament', *Parliamentary Affairs*, 55, 1, 2002, pp. 179–88.

Vallance, E. and Davies, E., *Women of Europe: Women MEPs and Equality Policy*, Cambridge, Cambridge University Press, 1986.

→ Composition of the European Parliament; European Parliament; European Parliamentary Assembly; Representation.

Y

Young People

(European Electoral Behaviour)

The question of young people's relation to politics is extremely sensitive for any political system. Work on political socialisation having showed the crucial importance of the first political socialisation in individuals' attitude formation, it is indeed important for the stability of a political system on a long-term basis that new generations inherit the values and standards that govern it to make them accept the political domination they will undergo as citizens. Like any system in search of legitimacy, the EU is endowed with policies and instruments of legitimacy of which some are intended in particular for young people. A certain number of programmes developed by the Commission (Erasmus then Socrates programmes for students, the 'Youth for Europe' programme for disadvantaged young persons) can be interpreted in this way. The attention paid to this specific population also appears in the decision to include in the sample of the opinion polls financed by the Commission – the Eurobarometers – the population aged 15 or more (and not 18 or more as is mostly the case). Furthermore, six Eurobarometers based entirely or partially on a 'Young people' sample were carried out.

At first sight, the attention paid by the EU to young people is mutual. From the 1960s, Inglehart noted that young people were more favourable to European integration than their elders. Forty years later, the same is true. The data collected after the 2004 EP elections by the European Commission thus show that 79 per cent of the European citizens aged from 18 to 24 regard the EU membership of their country as a good thing, against 70 per cent of the population as a whole. They also trust more European institutions (52 per cent of the 18/24s against 46 per cent of the total population). Young people are not, however, more Europhile than their fellow-citizens whatever the question is. Thus they do not declare themselves more attached to Europe than the elders, and feel only little more EU citizens (68 per cent against 66 per cent for all the population) according to the 2004 post-electoral poll data (Flash Eurobarometer 162, June 2004).

Such ambivalence in the young people's opinion towards EU integration seems more intelligible once one has accepted the fact that through the effect of age group another variable expresses itself, the diploma. Indeed, given equal qualification, young people do not declare themselves more in favour of European integration than the rest of the population. In other words, young people are more in favour of European integration only because they are better educated than older generations. Education is indeed a factor which predisposes to a certain trust in the existing institutions, whether they are national or European. This trust has, however, not found expression in a feeling of membership to Europe amongst young people, which tends to relativise the singularity of their attachment to European integration. In addition, if young Europeans are on average more favourable to the EU than their elders, national variations are noticeable. Thus, during the accession referendums in Austria, Finland and Sweden, young Finnish voted more in favour of European integration, whereas young Austrians and Swedish voted more against EU membership than other citizens. In total, young people's opinions towards European integration seem more ambivalent than they appear at first sight. A similar statement can be made as far as their electoral behaviour is concerned.

Young people's relative trust in European institutions might make them more likely to vote in EP elections than other citizens. We must say, however, that this is not the case. In 2004, 67 per cent of young people stated that they did not vote in the EP elections, compared with 54 per cent of all the 25 member states' electorate. More generally, a negative differential between young people's turnout and overall citizens' turnout can be seen whatever EP election is considered. The lowest young people's turnout must therefore be understood at least partly as a consequence of age. The European average reflects here again very strong national disparities. In 2004, 74 per cent of Italian young people said they voted, against 38 per cent in Germany, 40 per cent in France and 31 per cent in Austria. Above all, young people stand out by abstention records in Finland (23 per cent), Estonia (14 per cent) and Great Britain (12 per cent) (EUYOUPART enquiry, July 2004). In fact, it seems that young people's participation in EP elections reflects and amplifies the behaviour observed in the national electoral body as a whole. We thus find at the European level what we have already observed at the national level: young people offer through their political opinions and behaviours what Percheron called 'a magnifying mirror' of the whole population's trends.

The uncertainty regarding voting or not, or regarding selection among opposing candidates and lists, tends to develop and prolong itself, sometimes until polling day, among all the electorate, but is even more marked among young people. For instance, during the 2004 EP elections, 31 per cent of the 15/24s made up their minds on the last day, against 19 per cent of the registered electors. They are also less likely than the whole electorate to know what was the result of these elections in their country (57 per cent of the 18/24s against 60 per cent of all the population). However, young people are different from their elders in the reasons they give to justify their abstention. They emphasise more the fact that they were too busy to vote (22 per cent against 13 per cent of all the population) and that they had not been given enough information to make a choice during these elections (50 per cent against 19 per cent). They are much fewer in proportion to explain their choice due to factors more directly linked to the political situation in general and at the European level in particular. Thus, only 12 per cent of young people put forward their lack of trust and a dissatisfaction towards politics (against 22 per cent of all the population) and 5 per cent say they did not vote because voting has no consequence (against 9 per cent). Young people thus give priority to the personal factors rather than political factors to explain their abstention in EP elections.

Beyond turnout, young people's electoral behaviour is also marked by a greater volatility that leads them during EP elections to vote even more than the whole population either in favour of emerging political forces, such as the Junilistan lists in Sweden or Hans-Peter Martin in Austria, or of other smaller parties in the 2004 EP elections. In France, in 2004, young people voted more for the Green Party and the Front

National than citizens as a whole (16 per cent of the 25/34s voted for the Greens against 7.5 per cent and 22 per cent for the Front National against 10 per cent). There again, in the context of second-order elections where voting for small parties is particularly marked, young people's electoral behaviour does not seem distinctive compared to the behaviour of all the electorate, but appears rather as a 'magnifying mirror'.

Through their opinions and behaviours, young people seem then neither more attached to European integration than their elders, nor more disillusioned. Young people's electoral behaviour in EP elections reflects in broad outline what it is at the national level. The 'early years' political moratorium' as it is described by Muxel (2001) for France, also concerns the European issues, despite the relative greater attention young people pay to it. The study of young people's opinions and behaviour is particularly interesting as they reflect and magnify the attitudes of all the electorate, and they often appear to herald trends that may become generalised in the medium term, since young people are more sensitive to the effects of economic circumstances and periods than the rest of the population.

Céline Belot

Bibliography

Muxel, A., *L'éxperience politique des jeunes*, Paris, Presses de Sciences Po, 2001.

Conclusion: European Parliament Elections and the Emergence of a European Demos

Michael Bruter, Yves Déloye and Sarah Harrison

While looking at the question of the emergence of a mass European identity (Bruter 2005; Habermas 1992), a number of scholars have been confronted with the question of the existence or possible creation of a European *demos* and what it would signify (Smith 2005). *Demos* is a Greek word which literally means 'people', but, as in French and unlike in English, it is conceived as a singular concept. This apparently anodyne difference reveals a paradox that some authors have felt less than comfortable with. Does democracy – and European Parliament elections suggest that the European Union aims for some level of internal systemic democracy – require the pre-existence of a 'single', unified, conception of a people to represent?

On the basis of the findings of this *Encyclopaedia*, we argue that the way in which European elections take place suggests that the large amount of scientific debate regarding the supposed non-existence of a European *demos*, and the way in which it is supposed to imply the impossible emergence of a European identity and of European democracy is, in fact, unconvincing. It seems to be the product of a largely 'anglo-centric' controversy in that it is inspired by a linguistic oddity which contrasts with the relative lack of difference between the European and national *demos* contexts in a number of ways. Indeed, doctrinal arguments arose as to whether a naturally (but only in English) plural connotation of the European people would condemn the idea of a supposedly ideally singular European *demos* to be a sheer chimera.

The argument on the lack of a European demos

The arguments surrounding the abstract and absent category of a European *demos* is probably largely due to the methodological individualism of many political scientists who abandoned the quest for a European identity for decades, while holistic sociologists and historians were directing some deserved attention to it. Indeed, the non-*demos* model is largely based on sociological top-down conceptions of which – if any – objective criteria may create a sense of unified identity among the citizens of a given community. This theory may seem convincing *prima facie* in that a number of researchers have also considered the question of what – if anything – could constitute the essence of a European shared heritage (Wintle 1996; Smith 2005). It is largely understood that despite some overlapping common foundations, no clear historical tradition has ever comprehensively and exclusively bonded the European continent. The large Greek and Roman empires both failed to include the whole of Europe (even at the height of the Roman glory, Scotland and large segments of Scandinavia and Eastern Europe were excluded from the Roman area of influence), while encompassing large non-European areas of the Mediterranean. Similarly, modern religious and ideological revolutions, such as Judaism, Christendom and the Renaissance, also failed to conquer some parts of Europe (for example, the non-Christian parts of the Balkans, including Albania and Bosnia), while rapidly expanding to non-European territories (Bruter 2005). For these reasons, many supporters of the theory of the non-existence of a European *demos* have claimed that this overall absence of a fully shared European historical heritage was largely responsible for the impossible perspective of either a European identity or a European democracy.

Similarly, the same scholars point to the absence of other common references and tools of communication – the absence of a shared European language, of trans-European mass media and public sphere, and of a common European 'culture' and set of values. Indeed, in the European Union alone, 20 different European languages are regularly spoken, research on shared European values (Deth and Scarbrough 1995) shows limited convergence, and the plurality of European cultures is highlighted by the European Union itself, not least in its official motto: 'united in diversity'. As for the absence of a truly European public sphere, we can note that existing research (Gerstlé in this volume) has shown that even

European topics are most often approached from national angles. Similarly, attempts at unifying the European media scene have been both scarce and rather unsuccessful. Of it, most citizens probably only note the almost solely technical co-operation of Eurovision, more (in)famous for its odd song contest, an apparent symbol of the gap between European visions and real life culture, and the limited impact of Euronews and Arte, and the failure of the first trans-European newspaper, *The European*, in the 1990s.

Under these circumstances, should we conclude, like a large segment of the literature, that European Parliament elections are, indeed, bound for failure because they cannot rest on the edifice of a stable and unified European *demos*? And are we to conclude, as has often been the case, that the apparently low turnout in European Parliament elections, is indeed the 'obvious' proof that this *demos* is lacking? That the attempt at creating a true European democracy and a true European civic act is condemned to impotency because there is no such thing as a 'European people'?

European Parliament elections or the identity cry of a complaining demos

In many ways, this *Encyclopaedia* has helped to show that such is not the case. It should first be pointed out that many *demoi* have emerged without the pre-existence of a shared language (Switzerland, Belgium, China, Canada), a shared religion (Netherlands, Ireland), or a common 'culture', however defined. When it comes to nation-states, Gellner (1983) pointed out that nationalism precedes the nation, and indeed, in many cases, we know of nationalist traditions which only used the main claimed tenets of a national culture as an improbable pretext to justify the original political conceptions of their leaders (the first Irish nationalists were Protestant). Similarly, when it comes to Europe, some authors – such as Habermas (1992) and Bruter (2005) – have argued that the institutions themselves made possible the emergence of a European identity regardless of whether or not there is such a thing as an 'objective' Europeanness. For Habermas, this is the strength of constitutional patriotism, which may lead citizens to respect and show allegiance to their institutions. For Bruter, it constitutes the civic component of a European identity, whereby citizens, if only because of the very existence of political institutions, acknowledge the relevance of the European political system in determining their political condition, rights and duties as individual citizens.

In this sense, this *Encyclopaedia* has shown that despite utterly national elements – best evidenced by the second-order model – European elections, by their very existence, have progressively participated in the catharsis of a European consciousness. Rather than 'testing' any form of 'affection' or 'disaffection' of European citizens for their political system every five years, European elections have progressively acquired a momentum of their own, like a European metronome, which has finally started to beat more and more in rhythm. Indeed, in their article on a European electoral act, Déloye and Ihl illustrate the late but progressive emergence of European elections as a true form of European democracy, and introduce the possible change inaugurated by the 2004 elections. Similarly, Bruter shows that while support for European integration does not predict turnout in European Parliament elections, European identity, particularly conceived as a squared variable, does (Bruter 2004). Similarly, we have seen throughout this volume that the parties which take a clear stance on European issues, be it pro-European or Eurosceptic, tend to receive a clear electoral bonus. In this respect, Harrison's and Bruter's article on the United Kingdom, Lozach's on Germany, and Harrison's on the strategies of extreme-right and extreme-left parties tell four particularly meaningful stories.

Of course, a number of authors have shown that the national element is still – if only by design – largely present in European elections, even in 2004, but throughout this book, a number of contributors have also shown that at last, 'something' European is finally happening in European elections. Alongside the variety of electoral dates, technologies and rules, we have started to see the emergence of trans-European attitudes, from the quasi-universal mid-term phenomenon, to the progressively co-ordinated programmes of major political parties within each of the four main families across the European Union. But perhaps more importantly than anything else, the very similarity of the second-order election pattern throughout the EU, and also the wholly transnational complaints about the lack of focus of European Parliament election campaigns, shows a critical Europeanisation of the vote. Indeed, we have seen that in many cases, citizens now criticise European Parliament elections and institutions from 'within', thereby showing a paradoxical but profound sense of identity and appropriation.

Similarly, as mentioned in the introduction, for the first time in 2004, the definition of an explicitly clear link between the majority within the European Parliament and the presidency of the European Commission has given the only directly democratic institution within the European Union political system a truly visible democratic face. What is more, the affirmation by the Parliament of its democratic power in the context of the vetting of the first version of the proposed Barroso Commission has contributed for the first time to the fundamental valuation and responsibility of the European Parliament as the heart of the representativeness and accountability functions within the European polity. The argument of this book could therefore be that the European Parliament, as an institution, and European Parliament elections as a central democratic moment, have finally come out of the dark ages in 2004. Indeed, by proving that the choice of citizens finally mattered, they ceased to legitimise the perception that they might really be nothing more than a meagre sweet coating on a travesty of democracy, and thus possibly heralding instead the age of a true basis of accountability, representation and transparency in the functioning of the European political system.

All these changes really occurred *after* the 2004 elections. This means that if these breakthroughs really are to matter, it will only be visible in the 2009 elections and after. Then, perhaps, an increased sense of interest of citizens for 'their' European elections and 'their' European Union may lead us to confirm that a European people can really exert its collective political and democratic sovereignty without the need to pretend that a European *demos* is an artificially singular entity. Whether it rests on shared language, religion or culture would thereby be shown to be a relatively meaningless question when compared to the fundamental if unconscious emergence of a mass European civic identity.

So what do European Parliament elections tell us about the existence or otherwise of a European *demos*? Until 2004, they were perceived to have so little political impact, and were treated so secondarily by the various European parties and mass media that they were never allowed to be a catharsis of European democratic practice. Instead, they were largely instrumentalised by a multitude of political and social actors. In this sense, it is likely that the relatively low turnout in elections and the tone of the campaigns had no connection with the suspected 'problem' of a lack of a singular *demos*. Instead, the institutional changes that we have described have been accompanied by a new demand of the European public at the most paradoxical of times. Indeed, as the French electorate was getting ready to reject the draft Constitutional Treaty by a majority of 55 per cent, it expressed, more clearly than ever before, a profound desire for citizens to be democratically associated with the debate on the future of Europe rather than just presented with the sometimes obscure results of the compromises agreed by their leaders. Unlike largely nationally themed European election campaigns, the clearly European theme of the French referendum led to intense popular involvement in the political debate, and a truly high level of turnout. In fact, copies of the draft Constitutional Treaty and books commenting on it almost sold like a series of Agatha Christie bestsellers. Internet 'blogs' were overwhelmed by citizens' comments on what Europe should do, and what Europe should be. What is more, the reasons given by a majority of 'No' camp voters had to do with the weakness of European democratic procedures which they wanted reinforced and the absence of a social Europe, *not* a desire for 'less' European Union. Who – if not a *demos* – may ask for the right to discuss the goals, policies and democratic organisation of its political system?

On the basis of the insights of this *Encyclopaedia*, we therefore conclude that European Parliament elections, as of 2004, presented a contrasting picture. On the one hand, they were largely made national by the elites, be they the politicians who designed different electoral rules in each country, the parties, which chose to campaign on overwhelmingly national issues, or the media, which chose to take almost exclusively nation-centric perspectives when highlighting their take on the stakes of the election, by and large summarised as some dramatic 'test' for the governments in place. On the other hand, there is absolutely no evidence that this particular lack of interest for the 'European' in European elections is in any way shared or even echoed by the public.

In fact, some elements support the opposite thesis, that of a democratic demand by an emerging *demos*. The bonus given to parties which take a stance on European issues, the impact of European identity as a predictor of participation, and the clear difference made by a European – rather than national – campaign in the context of the 2005 referendum suggest, if anything, a true demand for a genuinely European democracy. The major institutional changes inaugurated in 2004 and this strong pressure from citizens may finally allow European Parliament elections in the future to become the real platform – instead of referendums and mass surveys – of an emerging democratic debate on Europe. In fact, 25 years after the first election of the European Parliament using direct universal suffrage, these combined changes may, in retrospect, have made the 2004 European Parliament elections the first viable embryo of a genuine European civic and democratic act.

Bibliography

Bruter, M., *Citizens of Europe? The Emergence of a Mass European Identity*, Basingstoke, Palgrave Macmillan, 2005.

Bruter, M., 'European Identity and the Vote in the 2004 European Parliament Elections', paper presented at the conference on European Parliament Elections, European Parliament, Strasbourg, 17–18 November 2004.

Deth, J. and Scarbrough, E., 'The Concept of Values', in Jan W. van Deth and Elinor Scarbrough (eds), *The Impact of Values*, Oxford, Oxford University Press, 1995.

Gellner, E., *Nations and Nationalism*, Ithaca, Cornell University Press, 1983.

Habermas, J., 'Citizenship and National Identity: Some Reflections on the Future of Europe', *Praxis International*, 12, 1, 1992, pp. 1–19.

Smith, A., 'Set in the Silver Sea: English National Identity and European Integration', paper presented at European Research Group Workshop on National Identity and Euroscepticism: a Comparison between France and the United Kingdom, 13 May 2005.

Wintle, M. (ed.), *Culture and Identity in Europe*, London, Avebury, 1996.

Index

Note: Entries in the index are referenced by page number but only refer to the first mention in each article. For example, an entry such as 'xiv' suggests that the whole article or chapter may be relevant and not only this page itself. Also note that categories such as 'elections', 'European elections' or 'European integration' are omitted from the index as they are covered throughout this *Encyclopaedia*.

abstention   xiv, 1, 262, 335, 349, 360, 388, 391, 396, 400, 405, 412, 442, 464, 502
   see also turnout
accession   *see* enlargement
advertising   8, 28, 31, 72, 114, 275, 304, 411, 469
age   10, 15, 36, 55, 103, 118, 143, 148, 232, 275, 277, 291, 299, 302, 341, 420, 422, 436, 493, 501
alignment   28, 43, 92, 99, 157, 345, 379, 402
allegiance   xiii, 12, 50, 205, 268, 392, 457, 467, 506
Amsterdam Treaty   22, 34, 41, 75, 102, 118, 132, 134, 148, 155, 173, 198, 221, 274, 288, 342, 348, 367, 427, 437, 454, 462, 472, 477, 480
Annan, Kofi   60
anthropology   ix, xiii, 68, 263, 468
Aristotle   41, 212
Australia   18, 20, 88, 117, 140
Austria   xx, 1, 10, 13, 29, 36, 45, 76, 80, 102, 110, 118, 138, 142, 148, 155, 161, 170, 174, 184, 198, 209, 214, 217, 226, 241, 253, 264, 274, 319, 350, 359, 381, 384, 392, 401, 409, 421, 423, 428, 431, 435, 471, 474, 478, 483, 492, 498, 502

ballot   1, 18, 19, 22, 29, 36, 62, 65, 101, 111, 117, 118, 134, 154, 176, 230, 237, 242, 250, 252, 257, 271, 302, 324, 334, 358, 362, 388, 400, 409, 411, 413, 442, 464, 495
ballot box   19, 20, 117, 154, 200, 243, 257, 291, 326, 359, 411, 413, 418, 473
Barroso, José Manuel   132, 289, 468, 507
behaviour   xiii, 1, 10, 13, 18, 28, 34, 60, 64, 74, 89, 115, 121, 152, 156, 178, 193, 197, 242, 263, 270, 277, 301, 333, 342, 353, 358, 374, 378, 379, 393, 398, 400, 404, 416, 421, 467, 489, 501

Belgium   xvii, xviii, 2, 7, 10, 19, 20, 21, 25, 29, 32, 37, 45, 58, 79, 93, 100, 102, 104, 106, 109, 115, 118, 135, 140, 142, 148, 154, 174, 180, 183, 214, 217, 241, 253, 264, 269, 276, 297, 309, 318, 328, 342, 358, 367, 381, 392, 400, 409, 411, 423, 431, 435, 436, 471, 474, 477, 492, 498, 505
blank vote   *see* blank and invalid vote
blank and invalid vote   15, 22, 358
border   xvi, 47, 100, 102, 120, 138, 142, 167, 254, 268, 293, 297, 351, 440, 461, 472, 478, 483
Briand   xiii
Brussels   8, 23, 25, 42, 49, 53, 61, 66, 70, 72, 82, 164, 173, 211, 246, 277, 294, 309, 328, 331, 363, 374, 461, 466, 469, 495
budget   26, 104, 162, 172, 180, 211, 224, 228, 283, 332, 341, 375, 376, 407, 412, 428, 451, 466, 470, 481, 485, 494
Bulgaria   xvii, 128, 139, 483
bureaucracy   14, 46, 51, 88, 104, 114, 131, 209, 254, 351

campaign   xiii, 5, 8, 9, 13, 24, 27, 31, 38, 42, 52, 61, 64, 71, 76, 85, 87, 90, 100, 102, 105, 116, 118, 121, 133, 138, 143, 147, 151, 160, 164, 178, 182, 189, 200, 209, 213, 218, 223, 224, 228, 231, 237, 245, 252, 257, 267, 270, 284, 285, 292, 296, 304, 310, 312, 324, 328, 333, 338, 347, 349, 353, 377, 379, 387, 389, 391, 394, 398, 402, 404, 411, 413, 427, 435, 440, 442, 445, 452, 456, 458, 464, 468, 475, 482, 486, 506
Canada   88, 505
candidate   10, 18, 20, 24, 27, 29, 37, 54, 62, 65, 71, 76, 85, 88, 90, 96, 101, 104, 105, 111, 115, 117, 121, 134, 147, 155, 176, 187, 226, 228, 232, 236, 240, 241, 245, 252, 257, 267, 272, 273, 275, 282, 287,

Printed in the United States
139015LV00002B/8/P

9 781403 994844